Designing, Deploying, and Evaluating Virtual and Augmented Reality in Education

Gokce Akcayir
University of Alberta, Canada

Carrie Demmans Epp
University of Alberta, Canada

IGI Global
PUBLISHER of TIMELY KNOWLEDGE

A volume in the Advances in Educational Technologies and Instructional Design (AETID) Book Series

Published in the United States of America by
IGI Global
Information Science Reference (an imprint of IGI Global)
701 E. Chocolate Avenue
Hershey PA, USA 17033
Tel: 717-533-8845
Fax: 717-533-8661
E-mail: cust@igi-global.com
Web site: http://www.igi-global.com

Library of Congress Cataloging-in-Publication Data

Names: Akcayir, Gokce, 1990- editor. | Demmans Epp, Carrie, 1969- editor.
Title: Designing, deploying, and evaluating virtual and augmented reality in education / Gokce Akcayir and Carrie Demmans Epp, editors.
Description: Hershey, PA : Information Science Reference, 2021. | Includes bibliographical references and index. | Summary: "This book examines the use of virtual and augmented reality in educational settings"-- Provided by publisher.
Identifiers: LCCN 2020006891 (print) | LCCN 2020006892 (ebook) | ISBN 9781799850434 (hardcover) | ISBN 9781799854890 (paperback) | ISBN 9781799850441 (ebook)
Subjects: LCSH: Virtual reality in education. | Augmented reality in education. | Instructional systems--Design.
Classification: LCC LB1044.87 .D478 2021 (print) | LCC LB1044.87 (ebook) | DDC 378.1/73468--dc23
LC record available at https://lccn.loc.gov/2020006891
LC ebook record available at https://lccn.loc.gov/2020006892

This book is published in the IGI Global book series Advances in Educational Technologies and Instructional Design (AE-TID) (ISSN: 2326-8905; eISSN: 2326-8913)

British Cataloguing in Publication Data
A Cataloguing in Publication record for this book is available from the British Library.

For electronic access to this publication, please contact: eresources@igi-global.com.

Table of Contents

Advances in Educational Technologies and Instructional Design (AETID) Book Series

Lawrence A. Tomei
Robert Morris University, USA

ISSN:2326-8905
EISSN:2326-8913

Mission

Education has undergone, and continues to undergo, immense changes in the way it is enacted and distributed to both child and adult learners. In modern education, the traditional classroom learning experience has evolved to include technological resources and to provide online classroom opportunities to students of all ages regardless of their geographical locations. From distance education, Massive-Open-Online-Courses (MOOCs), and electronic tablets in the classroom, technology is now an integral part of learning and is also affecting the way educators communicate information to students.

The **Advances in Educational Technologies & Instructional Design (AETID) Book Series** explores new research and theories for facilitating learning and improving educational performance utilizing technological processes and resources. The series examines technologies that can be integrated into K-12 classrooms to improve skills and learning abilities in all subjects including STEM education and language learning. Additionally, it studies the emergence of fully online classrooms for young and adult learners alike, and the communication and accountability challenges that can arise. Trending topics that are covered include adaptive learning, game-based learning, virtual school environments, and social media effects. School administrators, educators, academicians, researchers, and students will find this series to be an excellent resource for the effective design and implementation of learning technologies in their classes.

Coverage

- Digital Divide in Education
- K-12 Educational Technologies
- Classroom Response Systems
- Online Media in Classrooms
- Adaptive Learning
- Educational Telecommunications
- Virtual School Environments
- Game-Based Learning
- E-Learning
- Instructional Design

IGI Global is currently accepting manuscripts for publication within this series. To submit a proposal for a volume in this series, please contact our Acquisition Editors at Acquisitions@igi-global.com or visit: http://www.igi-global.com/publish/.

The Advances in Educational Technologies and Instructional Design (AETID) Book Series (ISSN 2326-8905) is published by IGI Global, 701 E. Chocolate Avenue, Hershey, PA 17033-1240, USA, www.igi-global.com. This series is composed of titles available for purchase individually; each title is edited to be contextually exclusive from any other title within the series. For pricing and ordering information please visit http://www.igi-global.com/book-series/advances-educational-technologies-instructional-design/73678. Postmaster: Send all address changes to above address.

Titles in this Series

For a list of additional titles in this series, please visit: www.igi-g

Assessment Tools for Mapping Learning Outcomes With Learning Object
G. R. Sinha (Myanmar Institute of Information Technology, Mandalay, Mya
Information Science Reference • © 2021 • 300pp • H/C (ISBN: 978179984

Building STEM Skills Through Environmental Education
Stephen T. Schroth (Towson University, USA) and Janese Daniels (Towson
Information Science Reference • © 2021 • 300pp • H/C (ISBN: 978179982

Redesigning Teaching, Leadership, and Indigenous Education in the 21st
Leesha Nicole Roberts (University of Trinidad and Tobago, Trinidad and Tc
Information Science Reference • © 2021 • 350pp • H/C (ISBN: 978179985

Advancing Online Course Design and Pedagogy for the 21st Century Lear
Daniel Chatham (Middlebury Institute of International Studies at Monterey,
Information Science Reference • © 2021 • 315pp • H/C (ISBN: 978179985

Socioscientific Issues-Based Instruction for Scientific Literacy Developme
Wardell A. Powell (Framingham State University, USA)
Information Science Reference • © 2021 • 359pp • H/C (ISBN: 978179984

Fostering Communication and Learning With Underutilized Technologies
Mohammed Banu Ali (Institute of Management, University of Bolton, UK) a
of Manchester, UK)
Information Science Reference • © 2021 • 270pp • H/C (ISBN: 978179984

Stagnancy Issues and Change Initiatives for Global Education in the Digit
Theresa Neimann (Oregon State University, USA) Jonathan J. Felix (RMIT
(University of Southern Mississippi, USA) and Elena Shliakhovchuk (Natior
Information Science Reference • © 2021 • 300pp • H/C (ISBN: 978179984

Simulation and Game-Based Learning in Emergency and Disaster Manag
Nicole K. Drumhiller (American Public University System, USA)
Information Science Reference • © 2021 • 300pp • H/C (ISBN: 978179984

IGI Global
PUBLISHER of TIMELY KNOWLEDGE

701 East Chocolate Avenue, Hershey, PA 17033
Tel: 717-533-8845 x100 • Fax: 717-533-86
E-Mail: cust@igi-global.com • www.igi-globa

Detailed Table of Contents

The continued development of mobile technologies has provided individuals the opportunity to work, learn, and play across a variety of contexts. The growth of these mobile devices has afforded an equivalent rise in popularity in augmented reality (AR) technologies. Though it has seen widespread adoption across a number of industries, AR has yet to see consistent integration in the realm of education. Several individuals and organizations have cited AR as being poised for mainstream educational adoption despite continued setbacks. The purpose of this chapter is to examine the claims surrounding AR for teaching and learning to understand what is being done and what is possible with the technology right now. This chapter provides a review of a variety of academic and non-academic sources towards the construction of a framework for AR for teaching and learning. Recommendations for research and practice are discussed.

Mixed reality (MR) applications are widely considered to be effective educational tools. However, the use of MR alone cannot ensure learning, and studies even suggest that the affordances of this technology could decrease the mental processes required for the acquisition of new knowledge. Like any other technological innovation, the educational possibilities of MR are closely related to the design of its contents. Despite this, there are no design recommendations for MR focused on learning. Educational psychology presents a range of empirically proven design guidelines for multimedia learning environments. This chapter reviews existing guidelines and categorizes them into principles related to the perception of information and the related essential information processing (design principles) and principles aiming at promoting generative learning (activating principles). These principles are translated to MR-learning environments.

This chapter focuses on applying design science research for virtual reality learning environment (VRLE) design processes. Six selected case studies are presented in the context of VRLEs. The case selections were analyzed in terms of their contributions to design knowledge. The objective of this book chapter is twofold: 1) for researchers, the design knowledge contributions of case studies are highlighted for future reference, and 2) for developers and practitioners, design principles are presented for the development of VRLEs. The final outcome of the present study is a conceptual model describing the current design knowledge in the field of VRLEs and identifying the research gaps that should be addressed in future research on the educational use of VR.

In recent years, teachers have started to integrate augmented reality (AR) technology as a potential learning tool into classroom activities. The main concern is the quality of the existing applications rather than brand-newness. Therefore, this chapter focuses on the components of a good educational AR application based on the experiences of teachers and to examine the current situation on the integration of AR to learning environments. Qualitative methodology was used in this study. The sample consisted of 24 teachers working in public schools in Turkey. The data were collected via semi-structured interviews and analyzed through the thematic analysis. The results showed that the components of a good AR application in education were gathered under four main themes: "analysis process," "design process," "teaching-learning process," and "evaluation components." Implications for the design and use of the AR applications in educational settings were also included in the study.

The affordances of computer-based virtual reality (VR) make it a natural fit for role-play. Although role-play has been commonly used in VR-based learning environments, the discussion of design details and guidelines is limited. In this chapter, the authors present a design case and aim to share their experiences of designing role-play in OpenSimulator-supported VR during a three-year design project for providing teaching training to graduate teaching assistants in STEM disciplines. The design of role-play bridges the technical and pedagogical affordances of VR. The authors discuss the design details from several aspects, including the formulation of role-play, types of role-play, and implementation. The authors also report the success and constraints in implementing role-play. With this design case, the authors intent on sharing the knowledge about the design and practice of VR-based role-play.

This study aims to examine students' knowledge of shapes as well as the views of the students and their teachers about the use of AR applications in teaching and learning geometry in second-grade mathematics lessons. A convergent parallel mixed methods research design was employed. The data collected for this study come from tests on the knowledge of shapes, as well as semi-structured interviews with students and their teachers and open-ended questionnaires. The participants of the study comprised three primary school second-grade teachers and the students from these teachers' classrooms. The quantitative data were analyzed via paired sample t-test, while the data derived from the qualitative sources were analyzed by using a content analysis method. The results show that the AR application in the second-grade mathematics lessons positively affected the students' knowledge of shapes. In addition, both students and their teachers considered AR technologies as a facilitator for learning geometrical shapes.

Chapter 12
Affordances and Pedagogical Implications of Augmented Reality (AR)-Integrated Language Learning 242
Babak Khoshnevisan, University of South Florida, USA
Sanghoon Park, University of South Florida, USA

Technologies have permeated the field of language education in recent decades. Language education has been informed by the technology-enhanced practices. Researchers have exhausted a variety of technologies and technological tools in the field of language education. Augmented reality (AR) is one of the emerging technologies that has been exploited in both education and language education. However, it is reported that educators' lack of knowledge and confidence in employing emerging technologies such as AR are limiting the use of these technologies in language education. To dive into the employed AR-related practices in language education, this chapter will (1) introduce the definition of AR, (2) discuss the underlying theories undergirding AR-integrated language learning, (3) present both the affordances and thorny issues accompanied with AR, and lastly, (4) share pedagogical implications of AR-integrated language learning to inform and usher the practices of language educators.

Chapter 13
Learning to Follow Directions in English Through a Virtual Reality Environment: An Eye Tracking Study and Evaluation of Usability 262
Jorge Bacca-Acosta, Fundación Universitaria Konrad Lorenz, Colombia
Julian Tejada, Federal University of Sergipe, Brazil
Carlos Ospino-Ibañez, Fundación Universitaria Konrad Lorenz, Colombia

Learning how to give and follow directions in English is one of the key topics in regular English as a Foreign Language (EFL) courses. However, this topic is commonly taught in the classroom with pencil and paper exercises. In this chapter, a scaffolded virtual reality (VR) environment for learning the topic of following directions in English is introduced. An eye tracking study was conducted to determine how students perceive the scaffolds for completing the learning task, and an evaluation of acceptance and usability was conducted to identify the students' perceptions. The results show that scaffolds in the form of text and images are both effective for increasing the students' learning performance. The gaze frequency is higher for the textual scaffold, but the duration of gaze fixations is lower for the scaffolds in the form of images. The acceptance and usability of the VR environment were found to be positive.

This study examines the role of virtual reality (VR) in the promotion of writing with greater complexity and lexical density. Using a combination of neuroimaging and traditional measures, the author characterizes differences in writing complexity and lexical density scores across four different pedagogical modalities: VR alone, VR followed by a textbook reading, textbook reading followed by VR, and textbook reading alone. Middle school students recruited from a rural middle school in the Mid-Atlantic Region of the United States responded to two prompts related to science content found in VR environments and a textbook. The authors hypothesized that exposure to a virtual environment prior to responding to the writing prompts would enhance both argumentative and summative writing products, when compared to participants who only had access to the textbook experiences. Participants who were exposed to the VR environment then had access to a textbook demonstrated significantly greater writing complexity and lexical density scores than those who had VR alone, or access to the text alone.

A description and psychometric validation is offered of the evaluation instrument COMPASS-Ar, conceived to check the level of competence achieved by future teachers—after participating in the ITINER-Ar Project (2018-19)—in the collaborative design of augmented didactic itineraries (ADIs) using augmented reality. This instrument—assessed by experts—consists of 30 items to measure the acquired didactic, digital, socio-collaborative, and creative competences involved in ADI development on the basis of an analytical rubric—created ad hoc and validated by means of the Delphi method—which specifies the requirements of each score through a (1-5) Likert-type scale. After evaluating a sample of 322 subjects, the assessment of reliability provided a Cronbach's alpha = .979. Construct validity was tested using factor analysis. Both the Kaiser-Meyer-Olkin test and Bartlett's sphericity test revealed that the instrument under study has a unidimensional nature. It can be concluded that this is a valid and reliable instrument.

Foreword

The term mixed reality was originally introduced by Paul Milgram and Fumio Kishino in 1994 in a paper entitled "Augmented Reality: A class of displays on the reality-virtuality continuum". It broadly defines any technology that blends real-world objects with digital representations. Augmented reality (AR) superimposes multimedia content such as images, texts, and/or sounds over a display of the actual environment using portable or head-mounted devices, whereas virtual reality (VR) provides immersive experiences where an artificial or virtual environment is rendered to simulate real environments. This taxonomy of displays define the opposite ends of the spectrum where certain aspects of an environment may be more or less augmented with informative and engaging digital content. The past decade has seen the rapid development of sensors and processing capability in many devices, enabling novel forms of user interactions. In other words, the boundaries of these opposite ends have shifted considerably in their applications. In turn, these technologies have become increasingly more common in the classroom, leading to more availability of high-quality curricular content and affordability of devices (Tacgin, 2020).

Research on the subject of how mixed reality technologies adapt to learner differences has been mostly limited by these factors. It is almost certain that applications involving personalization including intelligent recommendations, web search, adaptive interaction systems and user interfaces, as well as targeted advertising will become increasingly common in these emerging learning environments. Given the increased risk for cognitive load in immersive environments, there is a need for careful design of instruction to promote meaningful learning experiences to benefit from increased student engagement and presence (Makransky, Andreasen, Baceviciute, & Mayer, 2020; Makransky, Terkildsen, & Mayer, 2019). Challenges may also arise from socio-cultural differences, where some students might require further support to learn how to collaborate and teach one another in the context of learning while performing inquiries into complex topics (Dunleavy, Dede, & Mitchell, 2009). These issues represent a significant opportunity for educational researchers and calls on them to investigate further fundamental questions about learning and teaching with responsive immersive technologies through collaborations that span across different disciplines.

These chapters included in this IGI Global Reference Book entitled *Designing, Deploying, and Evaluating Virtual and Augmented Reality in Education* exemplify the pivotal role of virtual and augmented reality in contemporary educational research and practice. A key aspect of these emerging technologies is the role of affordances in shaping not only how users learn and behave, but also how they engage in the learning experience (see also Liu, Dede, Huang, & Richards, 2017). The issue of stages in the implementation of such technologies, including their design, deployment, and evaluation, has received considerable critical attention. In order to identify both opportunities and challenges to the dissemination of augmented and virtual reality technologies, different applications are examined towards a broad range of users, software and hardware, and educational settings.

The book summarizes these applications along four major themes: (1) theoretical frameworks and conceptual underpinnings of the affordances of virtual and augmented reality; (2) instructional approaches and considerations in the use of virtual and augmented reality to support learning and teaching; (3) case examples to promote learning and sophisticated understanding across domains and disciplines; and (4) methodological approaches to appraise the effectiveness of technology in attaining instructional goals. Since the focus is on the education applications of augmented and virtual reality, it is noteworthy to mention that several chapters incorporate or emphasize different elements from each theme. Of particular concern is the need for systematic approaches to theory-driven analysis of learning processes and outcomes to push the field forward. This volume provides new insights into these approaches and will contribute to a deeper understanding of best practices in the area.

Eric Poitras
Faculty of Computer Science, Dalhousie University, Canada
August 16th, 2020

REFERENCES

Dunleavy, M., Dede, C., & Mitchell, R. (2009). Affordances and limitations of immersive participatory augmented reality simulations for teaching and learning. *Journal of Science Education and Technology*, *18*(1), 7–22. doi:10.100710956-008-9119-1

Liu, D., Dede, C., Huang, R., & Richards, J. (Eds.). (2017). *Virtual, augmented, and mixed realities in education*. Springer. doi:10.1007/978-981-10-5490-7

Makransky, G., Andreasen, N. K., Baceviciute, S., & Mayer, R. M. (2020). Immersive Virtual Reality Increases Liking but Not Learning with a Science Simulation and Generative Learning Strategies Promote Learning in Immersive Virtual Reality. *Journal of Educational Psychology*. Advance online publication. doi:10.1037/edu0000473

Makransky, G., Terkildsen, T. S., & Mayer, R. E. (2019). Adding immersive virtual reality to a science lab simulation causes more presence but less learning. *Learning and Instruction*, *60*, 225–236. doi:10.1016/j.learninstruc.2017.12.007

Milgram, P., Takemura, H., Utsumi, A., & Kishino, F. (1995, December). Augmented reality: A class of displays on the reality-virtuality continuum. In *Telemanipulator and telepresence technologies* (Vol. 2351, pp. 282–292). International Society for Optics and Photonics. doi:10.1117/12.197321

Tacgin, Z. (2020). *Virtual and Augmented Reality: An Educational Handbook*. Cambridge Scholars Publishing.

Preface

Augmented reality (AR) and virtual reality (VR) have brought new opportunities. Our relatively limited experiences using these technologies in our everyday lives have allowed us to imagine and create new possibilities for interacting with the world. The most known and popular examples of AR include filters which were introduced by Snapchat and are now available on Instagram and other video and image software. These filters overlay virtual templates on what the camera captures, and thus enable users to change how something looks for aesthetic or social reasons as well as to disguise the things they would rather others not see. Another well-known AR example is the game Pokemon Go that has an estimated 603 million users around the world (Statista, 2020). In addition to these more ubiquitous applications, there are successful VR implementations. VR applications are widely used in museums so that people can visit the museum no matter where they are physically located. This widely used application of VR expanded following the temporary closure of many museums that was done in response to the COVID-19 pandemic (Unesco, 2020). In addition to improving access to museum exhibits, virtual museums enhance pre-existing experiences by presenting additional digital materials (Kersten, Tschirschwitz, & Deggim, 2017).

Excitement over the opportunities and affordances that these technologies offer has carried over into academic fields, with AR and VR's potential for supporting and expanding learning being a focus within education. Using AR and VR in education has been an active area of research over the last decade (Garzón & Acevedo, 2019) as the popularity of these approaches has increased along with the increased availability of more affordable VR solutions (e.g., Google Cardboard). The emergence of research in this area followed promising results seen in early research (e.g., Nakasugi & Yamauchi, 2002; White, Jay, Liarokapis, Kostakis, & Lister, 2001) and has contributed to excitement around the educational use of these technologies.

Coinciding with this excitement, a large body of research has investigated the effectiveness of specific applications of AR and VR in education. Over the last decade, these studies have revealed that VR and AR can support positive outcomes when used in educational settings (Akçayır & Akçayır, 2017; Garzón & Acevedo, 2019; Garzón, Kinshuk, Baldiris, Gutiérrez, & Pavón, 2020). Currently, we know these technologies can facilitate learning of various subjects. They can also be used to promote acquisition of diverse skills. However, this ability does not ensure positive learning outcomes in all cases, because the effectiveness of these applications depends on many factors that include application features (Guimarães, Alves, Durelli, Guimarães, & Dias, 2018) and pedagogical approaches (Garzón, et al., 2020). For this reason, the attributes of an application, implementation approaches, and specific characteristics of learning settings should be thoughtfully considered before using an AR/VR tool in the classroom.

In academic studies, we usually see AR/VR applications that are tailored for a specific learning setting in terms of content and learner age. This creates a gap in our knowledge of how AR/VR can be used in classroom settings because instructors can usually only access pre-existing AR/VR applications. Thus, they cannot modify the applications to suit their learners' needs. In such cases, the attributes of the application that is being considered should be questioned to determine the extent to which that application matches with the specific needs of the learner group. After an appropriate AR/VR application has been identified for the specific learning setting, implementation strategies should be designed carefully to support and facilitate student learning.

The implementation strategies used play a role in how effectively AR/VR supports learning. These strategies cover when to use the application, how long the application should be used, the environments in which learners will interact with the application, and how they will interact with the AR/VR application. One of the major determiners of which strategies are used are the pedagogical approaches instructors are familiar with and comfortable using. The selected pedagogy influences learning outcomes because it shapes and drives learner experience. When pedagogical approaches for using AR/VR in education are examined, it is seen that traditional and common pedagogical methods and strategies fall short of supporting and facilitating learning. This failure in the application of existing implementation strategies is due to the unique characteristics of AR and VR, the specific context of use, and the nature of content delivery (Geris & Özdener, 2020). This insufficiency can also be seen in a recent systematic review on VR in higher education; almost three quarters of the studies did not report an applied pedagogical approach (Radianti, Majchrzak, Fromm, & Wohlgenannt, 2020). Work on exploring and building new pedagogical approaches specific to the use of AR/VR in education is still in its infancy. There is a need for more research to provide empirically supported theoretical frameworks, methods, and strategies specific to the use of AR/VR in education (Akçayır & Akçayır, 2017; Cabero-Almenara, Fernández-Batanero, & Barroso-Osuna, 2019; Sommerauer & Müller, 2018). This kind of research can also contribute to establishing a common understanding of terms such as immersion and reality that have been used differently across the literature (Radianti et al., 2020).

This book contains chapters that explore various aspects of the use of AR/VR in education to help us better understand design, deployment, and evaluation processes. This way, the book will provide research-based insight that could contribute to the development of effective learning environments. Additionally, it will advance theoretical knowledge in this area by including chapters focused on the development of theoretical models and strategies.

The target audience of this book consists of teachers, instructors, researchers, technologists, curriculum designers, instructional designers, and industry leaders who are interested in educational technologies. Researchers can identify possible research problems and gaps in the literature. Teachers and instructors can find practical implications for using AR/VR in their classrooms. The insights provided about learning experience designs could benefit curriculum and instructional designers. Technologists, such as AR/VR application developers, can find implications for effective learning tool designs and features. We hope that the efforts put into this book by the authors, reviewers, editors, and many others will contribute to the growth and development of research on AR and VR in education.

INTRODUCTION TO THE CONTENT OF THE BOOK

Chapters submitted to this book situated their work with respect to both the theoretical and the practical considerations associated with using virtual and augmented reality in education. The 15 chapters of the book include review studies, theoretical discussions, and empirical research. The chapters focus on three areas that consider applicable theoretical and conceptual frameworks, discuss practical considerations, and report on case studies that investigate AR/VR use in specific learning domains. The varied work across these areas may advance research on AR/VR in education. We have organized the chapters starting from the ones with a potentially broad scope of application to those with a focus on specific integration contexts that target a learning domain or learner level. A brief description of each chapter follows.

Chapter 1: Learning in Virtual Environments – What About Paradigms and Metamodels? An Illustration Through Enaction and Trinologic

In this chapter, Mellet-d'Huart (2021) introduces a metamodel named Trinologic to contribute to addressing the aforementioned need for educational models for VR. The model aims to support and facilitate the design of virtual reality environments for learning. This model was founded on three concepts: actualization, potentialization and virtualization. The chapter also includes conceptual points for VR design within the context of the Trinologic metamodel. Additionally, why, when, and how to use VR to support learning processes are discussed.

Chapter 2: Building an Instructional Design Model for Immersive Virtual Reality Learning Environments

Chapter 2 also presents a model for educational VR environments to address the absence of learning design models for these environments. The proposed instructional design model by Tacgin and Dalgarno (2021) draws upon Dalgarno and Lee's (2010) affordance model and Tacgin's (2018) immersive virtual reality learning environment development stages for teaching concepts and procedures. Specific learning strategies and affordances related to immersive virtual reality learning environments are discussed with respect to the features of current immersive VR systems and technologies.

Chapter 3: Augmented Reality in Research and Practice – A Content Analysis of Claims in Education

The models presented for VR environments (Chapters 1 and 2) were followed with an examination of AR research and practice in education. This chapter, by Petrovich and Foster (2021), provides a review of a variety of academic and non-academic sources towards the construction of a framework for AR for teaching and learning. Through this review, the study examined claims surrounding augmented reality and its adoption as an educational tool. The results were presented in accordance with its overarching framing of (1) Technology, (2) Pedagogy, and (3) Content (TPC). The findings were discussed regarding best practices, learning outcomes, barriers to adoption, and general beliefs about teaching and learning with AR.

Chapter 4: Design Principles for Educational Mixed Reality – Adaptations of the Design Recommendations of Multimedia Learning

This chapter specifically focuses on the design aspect of educational mixed reality applications rather than providing a general view of using AR/VR for educational purposes. To provide design recommendations for mixed reality learning, Yepes-Serna, Wolf, Söbke, and Zander (2021) reviewed existing guidelines and created an overview of design heuristics for mixed reality that are based on the psychological foundations of learning processes. They categorized guidelines into design principles; strategies to support efficient information processing (e.g., essential, extraneous, and social cues) and activating principles; and recommendations to stimulate active and generative mental processes.

Chapter 5: Developing Design Knowledge and a Conceptual Model for Virtual Reality Learning Environments

Keeping the focus on the design aspect, Lähtevänoja, Holopainen, Vesisenaho, and Häkkinen (2021) present six case studies in the context of VR learning environments. Each case was examined with respect to its contribution to design knowledge. Based on these examinations, a conceptual model was presented to describe current design knowledge on the educational use of VR. Building upon vom Brocke, Winter, Hevner, and Maedche's (2020) model, the presented model has three components: (1) the problem space, (2) the solution space, and (3) the evaluation.

Chapter 6: What Makes an Educational Augmented Reality Application Good? Through the Eyes of Teachers, as Its Practitioners: Educational Augmented Reality Applications

Chapter 6 focuses on the teachers' perspectives and shares experiences of teachers' integration of AR into their teaching practices. With a qualitative approach, Fidan (2021) conducted interviews with 24 teachers who had previously integrated AR into their lessons. Based on these interviews, the components that are believed to have helped teachers identify good AR apps were presented under the following themes: "analysis process", "design process", "teaching-learning process", and "evaluation components". Implications and future research directions were provided based on the teachers' opinions and experiences.

Chapter 7: Role-Play in Virtual Reality – A Teaching Training Design Case Using OpenSimulator

Dai, Ke, Dai, Pachman, and Yuan (2021) explored a frequently used practice in VR applications, role-play, and presented a design case. They discussed role-play in VR contexts from the perspectives of the formulation of role-play, the types of role-play, and implementation. They argue that using contextualized prompts, incorporating domain-specific information as environmental prompts, and the multiple situational constraints that can be encountered during implementation all need to be considered when designing and using role-play in VR environments.

Chapter 8: Using Augmented and Virtual Reality to Improve Social, Vocational, and Academic Outcomes of Students With Disabilities

As the chapters start to focus on specific learning domains and learner groups, Chapter 8 explores AR and VR in special education. As AR and VR previously showed potential for helping to prepare individuals with disabilities to work more independently, Kellems, Yakubova, Morris, Wheatley, and

Chen (2021) examined the use of AR and VR in promoting the academic, social, and vocational skills of students with disabilities. Based on this examination, recommendations were made regarding instructional design for implementing AR/VR in special education contexts. Tools and applications for teachers and other practitioners also were shared, and future research directions for using AR/VR in special education were provided.

Chapter 9: Augmented Reality an Educational Resource for the Nursing Graduate

In this chapter on health science education, Soberanes-Martín (2021) proposes a mobile AR application, called the Urethral Catheter Application Technique (UCAT), to be used in nursing education. This application works through QR codes placed on dummies to teach catheterization techniques for both male and female patients. The chapter presents the development process of the UCAT application, and teachers' and students' perceptions of the quality of the augmented reality application.

Chapter 10: A Research Map to Leverage Augmented Reality in K12 Science Education

This chapter (Wu & Wen, 2021) presents a research map for designing inquiry based science education where AR has been integrated. With respect to this application context, a framework called Questioning, Investigating, Making, and Synthesising (QIMS) was proposed. This framework is built on Kolb's (1984) experiential learning cycle along with the authors' previous work on inquiry-based learning. It can provide insight on how AR-integrated activities can shape students' interests for learning and motivation, and how these activities can be integrated into academic curricula.

Chapter 11: The Use of Augmented Reality Applications in Second Grade Mathematics Course – Students' Knowledge of Shapes

In this chapter, Bozan, Akçay, and Karahan (2021) examine the use of AR in second-grade mathematics education. In addition to students' learning of shapes, the views of the students and their teachers were explored within schools that have varying socio-economic contexts. The study showed that AR was found to help students learn geometry concepts in all schools regardless of the socioeconomic context.

Chapter 12: Affordances and Pedagogical Implications of Augmented Reality (AR) Integrated Language Learning

Moving from mathematics education to language education, Khoshnevisan and Park (2021) discussed using AR in language learning. Their foci were affordances and issues related to AR use in language learning. Additionally, they provided pedagogical implications of AR-integrated language learning such as using AR within a game setting for higher motivation.

Chapter 13: Learning to Follow Directions in English Through a Virtual Reality Environment – An Eye Tracking Study and Evaluation of Usability

Continuing with language learning, this chapter (Bacca-Acosta, Tejada, & Ospino-Ibañez, 2021) introduces a scaffolded VR environment for learning the topic of following directions in English. The impact of scaffolding (text help and visual help) as well as the usability of the introduced VR environment were examined. This examination revealed that scaffolds in the form of text and images are both effective for increasing the students' learning performance, and VR learning tasks were perceived as interesting and motivating.

Chapter 14: Virtual Reality Simulations in Science Education – Learning Science by Writing

Lamb (2021) examined the role of VR in promoting middle school students' writing with greater complexity and lexical density. The study examined four conditions: VR alone, VR followed by a textbook reading, textbook reading followed by VR, and textbook reading alone. Among these conditions, participants who used the VR first and then used a textbook demonstrated significantly better writing performance in terms of writing complexity and lexical density.

Chapter 15: Compass-AR. Assessment of Teaching Competences Acquired With Augmented Itineraries Design-Based Learning Methodology

An evaluation instrument, COMPASS-AR, which was developed as part of the ITINER-AR Project, was presented in this chapter by Del-Moral, Villalustre, and Neira-Piñeiro (2021). The instrument was developed in an effort to improve infant and primary education teacher training. It aims to assess the level of competency of pre-service teachers participating in the collaborative design of augmented didactic itineraries using augmented reality. Verification of the instrument was presented and the future research directions of the ITINER-AR Project were shared.

CONCLUDING REMARKS

All chapters contribute to the work on AR/VR in education. Many of these contributions focused on research that explored using AR/VR for educational purposes. Others focused on the implications of using AR/VR in education or provided recommendations for practice. Some chapters contributed to both foci. As AR/VR technologies continue advancing, instructor use of these technologies to support learning is expected to diversify. This diversity of application will include features such as AR-based multi-user interactive environments and devices such as AR/VR glasses. Even though these technologies have been available for many years, they are not widely used in educational contexts yet. The reasons for this difference between research and practice mainly stem from the challenges instructors face when integrating AR/VR technologies. These challenges include limited access to an application with innovative features and a lack of funding for new devices. As the AR/VR technology industry continues to grow alongside research on AR/VR, more applications will be available to instructors and more learners will have access to devices that support AR/VR. This move towards learners having devices that enable these teaching and learning approaches is evident in the widespread use of smartphones.

Thanks to the efforts of the researchers, educators, and industry professionals who have been using AR/VR in education, it has been a steadily growing area. To keep this momentum and jointly direct the field, all of us need to keep exploring how AR and VR can best support learning and teaching. Creating and maintaining strong communication among the different classes of stakeholders is also needed to facilitate and accelerate the advancement of this area.

Gokce Akcayir
University of Alberta, Canada

Carrie Demmans Epp
University of Alberta, Canada

REFERENCES

Akçayır, M., & Akçayır, G. (2017). Advantages and challenges associated with augmented reality for education: A systematic review of the literature. *Educational Research Review*, *20*, 1–11. doi:10.1016/j.edurev.2016.11.002

Cabero-Almenara, J., Fernández-Batanero, J. M., & Barroso-Osuna, J. (2019). Adoption of augmented reality technology by university students. *Heliyon (London)*, *5*(5), e01597. doi:10.1016/j.heliyon.2019.e01597 PMID:31193247

Dalgarno, B., & Lee, M. J. (2010). What are the learning affordances of 3-D virtual environments? *British Journal of Educational Technology*, *41*(1), 10–32. doi:10.1111/j.1467-8535.2009.01038.x

Garzón, J., & Acevedo, J. (2019). Meta-analysis of the impact of Augmented Reality on students' learning gains. *Educational Research Review*, *27*, 244–260. doi:10.1016/j.edurev.2019.04.001

Garzón, J., Kinshuk, Baldiris, S., Gutiérrez, J., & Pavón, J. (2020). How do pedagogical approaches affect the impact of augmented reality on education? A meta-analysis and research synthesis. *Educational Research Review*, *31*, 100334. doi:10.1016/j.edurev.2020.100334

Geris, A., & Özdener, N. (2020). Design models for developing educational virtual reality environments: A systematic review. In G. Guazzaroni & A. S. Pillai (Eds.), *Virtual and Augmented Reality in Education, Art, and Museums* (pp. 1–22). IGI Global. doi:10.4018/978-1-7998-1796-3.ch001

Guimarães, M. P., Alves, B. C., Durelli, R. S., Guimarães, R. F. R., & Dias, D. C. (2018). An approach to developing learning objects with augmented reality content. In Lecture Notes in Computer Science: Vol. 10963. *Computational Science and Its Applications (ICCSA 2018)*. Springer. doi:10.1007/978-3-319-95171-3_59

Kersten, T. P., Tschirschwitz, F., & Deggim, S. (2017). Development of a virtual museum including a 4D presentation of building history in virtual reality. *The International Archives of the Photogrammetry, Remote Sensing and Spatial Information Sciences*, *42*(W3), 361–367. doi:10.5194/isprs-archives-XLII-2-W3-361-2017

Kolb, D. A. (1984). *Experiential learning: Experience as the source of learning and development.* Prentice-Hall.

Nakasugi, H., & Yamauchi, Y. (2002). Past viewer: Development of wearable learning system for history education. In *Proceedings of the International Conference on Computers in Education*. IEEE.10.1109/CIE.2002.1186223

Radianti, J., Majchrzak, T. A., Fromm, J., & Wohlgenannt, I. (2020). A systematic review of immersive virtual reality applications for higher education: Design elements, lessons learned, and research agenda. *Computers & Education*, *147*, 103778. doi:10.1016/j.compedu.2019.103778

Sommerauer, P., & Müller, O. (2018). Augmented reality for teaching and learning – A literature review on theoretical and empirical foundations. *Proceedings of European Conference on Information Systems (ECIS)*, 1–17. https://aisel.aisnet.org/ecis2018_rp/31

Statista. (2020). *Number of active users of Pokémon Go worldwide from 2016 to 2020*. Retrieved from https://www.statista.com/statistics/665640/pokemon-go-global-android-apple-users/

UNESCO. (2020). *Virtual Museums on Underwater Cultural Heritage respond to the Covid-19 crisis*. Retrieved from https://en.unesco.org/news/virtual-museums-underwater-cultural-heritage-respond-covid-19-crisis

vom Brocke, J., Winter, R., Hevner, A., & Maedche, A. (2020). Special Issue Editorial- Accumulation and evolution of design knowledge in design science research–A journey through time and space. *Journal of the Association for Information Systems*, *21*(3), 520–544. https://aisel.aisnet.org/jais/vol21/iss3/9

White, M., Jay, E., Liarokapis, F., Kostakis, C., & Lister, P. (2001). A virtual interactive teaching environment using XML and augmented reality. *International Journal of Electrical Engineering Education*, *38*(4), 316–329. doi:10.7227/IJEEE.38.4.5

Chapter 1
Learning in Virtual Environments:
What About Paradigms and Metamodels? An Illustration Through Enaction and Trinologic

Daniel Mellet-d'Huart
Independent Researcher, France

ABSTRACT

This chapter addresses the questions of why, when, and how to use virtual reality to support learning processes for human beings. It focuses therefore on what can and cannot be done in a real environment versus what can and cannot be done in a virtual environment, as well as on how using virtual reality can make some types of learning easier as long as certain conditions are fulfilled. These conditions include the shifting of some inner beliefs and the choice of an accurate paradigm. The paradigm of enaction will be presented as an example of an accurate paradigm for virtual reality. Some conceptual keys and landmarks for design will be proposed in the context of the Trinologic metamodel developed by the author. Such metamodels should facilitate the connection between human actions, learning, and the characteristics of the outer world, whether this world is real or virtual.

FOREWORD

This chapter addresses the topic of *learning in virtual environments* and *virtual environment for learning (VEL)*. It will therefore address the field of education, among other subjects. It will focus on how virtual reality can support and facilitate learning processes. Terms such as *virtual reality (VR)* or *virtual environment (VE)* will be used in a very generic way, encompassing the whole family of associated technologies such as *mixed reality*, *augmented reality*, *full-scale simulation*, *serious games* and so on.

The focus of this chapter will not be on the state of the art, nor on recent developments in the sector, nor on technologies, nor on pedagogy. It will focus on timeless issues that might be relevant for

DOI: 10.4018/978-1-7998-5043-4.ch001

the conception and the design of VEs for learning. Therefore, in order to think out of the box, it might challenge some of the reader's deep beliefs. Using a new media requires thinking that is consistent with the characteristics of this media. Transposition may work but could produce poor results. One cannot produce novelties with old ways of thinking. And switching from a real environment to a VE is quite a radical change as far as learning is concerned. It is important to recognize that although most of what can be done in real environments can also be done in VEs, certain things that can be done in real environments are not possible in virtual ones. It is therefore fundamental to emphasize the things that cannot be done in real environments but can be done in VEs. This is a key point in rethinking learning approaches using VEs.

Although pedagogical issues are crucial, they will not be addressed in this chapter either. As shown by Fowler (2015), there is an important need for pedagogy in the field of VELs. Radiantia et al. (2020) point out that a lack of explicit learning theories becomes evident through reviews of existing applications. They call for a theory on VR for educational applications and the clarification of ambiguity, and for a taxonomy of learning theories. Holopainen et al. (2020) claim that completely new pedagogical approaches, including objectives, contents, methods and assessments, are required for learning environments. As a minimum, it will be taken as a given that the use of virtual reality can be correlated to active and embodied pedagogies as *learning by doing* or *hands-on learning* as a basic approach and provide the learner with first-hand experiences (Martín-Gutiérrez, et al., 2017). Some other general rules will be found in the *Necessary Nine* (Johnson-Glenberg, 2019). Of course, some other educational issues could be considered, for example: How to handle and address errors? In what situations are feedback or corrections necessary and how should they be provided? How should theoretical content be provided? What is the exact place and role of educators, teachers and trainers when VEs are used? How can activities be articulated in virtual and in real environments? How are progress and learning to be assessed? Is an Intelligent Tutorial System necessary? Such questions will have to be discussed and answered elsewhere.

INTRODUCTION

Learning in a virtual environment presents certain specificities. This chapter will use different perspectives and viewpoints to present arguments showing how learning experiences might be renewed by using virtual reality thus making learning a much easier experience. The properties of the medium will be analyzed, considering whether they support learning processes or not. Regarding the design and the conception of a VEL, this chapter will emphasize the importance of choosing and/or making explicit the choice of a paradigm to guide the entire development of a project. Finally, it will explain and illustrate how an interdisciplinary metamodel can support and facilitate project development.

ISSUES AROUND VR AS A MEDIUM

How to built an efficient and supportive VEL is a question that has not yet been fully answered. This chapter will consider any situation that involves learning processes. It will focus on how to create a more varied and easier learning experience for the learner by means of virtual reality. Hands-on learning can already be provided in VEs and it might also be possible to teach abstract content hands-on in a VE.

Attention will be given to differentiating what can and cannot be done in a real environment versus what can and cannot be done in a VE.

What can be Done in Real Environments That Cannot be Done in Virtual Environments

Researchers who pioneered VR sought to reproduce reality in a totally artificial way, linking together the most advanced developments in computer sciences, computer graphics, robotics and other disciplines (Mazuryk & Gervautz, n.d.). Because this was their quest, they made various assumptions about what is a successful VE and the characteristics that make it effective. From these assumptions evolved the idea that a successful VE had to be *realistic*, *immersive* and provide the user with a feeling of *presence*. These concepts are still used and discussed today (Johnson-Glenberg, 2018) and clearer definitions are expected (Radiantia et al., 2020). This quest to reproduce reality encounters several limitations, firstly from a technological and economical point of view; that is, on the one hand the question of technological developments and the state of the art and on the other hand, economic contingencies, and specifically what the client is willing to pay for.

Secondly, there are limitations that are inherent in the properties of the medium and of the technologies that are used, taking into account both the properties of the real world and the anatomical and physiological properties of the user's body. These limitations include the following. (1) Firstly, gravitational limitations. Gravitational rules cannot be changed or transferred in VEs. Therefore, a virtual object can neither have weight nor support the weight of a user (*ex. A user cannot sit on a virtual seat within a VE*). (2) The nature of the technologies employed means that neither the computer program nor its devices can generate chemicals to simulate human senses such as smell and taste. At most, a specific device could spray some stored chemicals. (3) The user's perceptive capacities are limited by human physiology. It would be feasible to overcome some of these limitations by changing the scale of the perceptual stimuli or by attributing specific sensory modalities (Lenay et al., 2004) to elements or objects that cannot be perceived in the real world (*e.g. X-rays, reactivity, gas, movement of air, atoms...*). These principles could also support processes which would enable disabled people to improve their perception of the world (Tixier et al., 2013). (4) A fourth category of limitations is attributable to human factors. The chief limitations are the self-limitations of the human brain and especially the imagination and the creativity of the conceptors of VEs. Very often human beings forget to question what seems obvious to them and are impeded by false beliefs, for example, believing that something would be impossible without asking themselves: "*How could we make it possible?*" Sometimes, considering the state of the art also limits designers, both because of human reflexes of imitation and due to the false belief that what has not been done yet, has not been done because it would be impossible to do it. This situation is often born of false beliefs and insufficient digging for new solutions. Moreover, it is well known, and this is said without judgement, that researchers today are expected to be fast and to produce quickly tangible results. They, therefore, obviously lack the time to postpone the initial developments in order to deal properly with deeper issues that need to be addressed before development can begin. Failure to address these issues in time may lead to poor results caused by conformism and self-limitation.

What can be Done in Virtual Environments That Cannot be Done in Real Environments

The author has already developed some considerations about possible advantages of using VR to support learning situations (Mellet-d'Huart, 2009). Many things that cannot be done or perceived in real environments could be done or perceived in VEs. This means that almost everything can be shown or included in a VE, even things that cannot be perceived by human beings in the real world, or things that do not exist in the real world, or memories from the past, or imagination of the future… For instance, with regard to learning processes, hands-on trials can be organised in VEs with no risk and at almost no cost. The direct consequences of any action can be shown and perceived by the learner consecutively to the action, even if this would not be feasible in the real world. Abstract knowledge can be tried out in VEs as if it were concrete and perceivable... In fact, there are no limitations regarding the modification of the spatial and temporal properties of a VE.

FROM A MORE 'PHILOSOPHICAL' POINT OF VIEW

To address the objective of providing through VEs learning experiences that are easier than in real or traditional learning situations, it becomes necessary to consider some deeper and more philosophical issues. Of course this is not a matter of addressing fundamental philosophical questions, but simply of digging a little deeper behind the conscious intentions of the conceptors. To what extent did they consider the specificity of using VR? To what extent did they consider the suitability of the technology used for the learning theories to which they refer? To what extent did they consider the question of the paradigm? When they use terms like *virtual reality*, what do these words actually mean?

This chapter addresses questions, which are easily ignored when conceiving and developing a VEL. The answers might seem obvious, but they are not. The more deeply the participants consider these questions before starting a project, the greater is the likelihood of developing an efficient and innovative support for learning. These questions include the following: Is it possible to have a clear picture of what is called *reality*, both in the human mind and in matters related to the outer world? Is the chosen *paradigm* coherent with the choice of using a VE to support learning processes? Are there clear design engineering landmarks to support and facilitate the development of software and communication within a team coming from different disciplines and using different jargons? Are learning contents well defined and how are they split into learning objectives within the VE?

Testimonial

In 1998, the author had an insight while working for a vocational training organisation for adults. He ascertained that certain types of learning were particularly difficult to achieve through traditional teaching methods and in real environments. From this observation arose the following question: could VR facilitate learning? Could a more direct contact be established between the learner and what is to be learned? Could VEs support embodied experiences? At that time, applications of VR were rare and limited, so the author looked with great interest at how artists were approaching and using it. He was soon convinced that the major added value of VR for learning lay not in the reproduction of reality as it is perceived, but in developing VEs where learners could explore aspects of reality that they would not normally be able to perceive sensorially. This was a counterpole to the attitude of most researchers at that time, whose dominant belief was that VEs had to reproduce *'reality'* and to be *'realistic'*. Although those words were poorly defined, it seemed that a unanimous agreement about what constituted reality existed. What is *reality*? Is *reality* what human beings perceive? Do VEs have to be *realistic* irrespective of the learning content and objectives? Is the concept of *presence* interesting? If so, does presence depend upon the technical quality of VEs and their devices or do other factors intervene? Is *presence* the core condition that enables the user to behave in a VE as if he were evolving in a real environment? Can a VEL be autonomous and context-free?

What is Reality?

Can *reality* be defined, both in the human mind and with regard to the outer world? Is reality what human beings actually perceive? Is the experience of perception the same for everybody? If this were the case, everybody would agree on what is and what is not real. Over time, it has often been claimed that VEs have to be *realistic*. This was an important maxim for the pioneers of VR (Mazuryk & Gervautz, n.d.). To produce realistic visual sensations and to generate perceptive experience that imitates as closely as possible human experience in everyday life has been a challenge for the researcher in computer science for many years. Because the perspective here is different, this claim can be questioned. Firstly because *realism* is not a well-defined concept. Also because something that is difficult to learn in the real world might become easier to learn in an *unrealistic* virtual world where its properties could be changed and directly experienced. What cannot be perceived in the real world is generally taught as abstract content. Abstract content transformed into concrete content within a VE might be learned hands-on. This is precisely what VR can support: hands-on methods. To clarify his argument, the author will define how he differentiates *reality* from what he names *the Real*.

Reality

Because human beings live in a physical body and in a particular environment, their perceptions of the outer world depend on their physiology and on their position within their surroundings. With their perceptive body, human beings situate landmarks around them and from those landmarks, using the combination of their previous experiences and of the distinctions that they are used to applying to the outer world, they imagine something that they call *reality* which is just a production of their mind. Because it is a production of the mind, reality has, in fact, little to do with what the outer world really is. Because human beings share the same physiology, because they have many experiences in common and because they communicate together through words that are abstract and shared amongst a community, they might think that their way of perceiving the outer world is universal. But it is not. Reality is a reconstruction that occurs within each individual mind, and this reconstruction is always unique.

The Real

As it is important to name what could exist independently of the fact that it might or might not be perceived, the author names *the Real* what really exists whether or not human beings can conceptualise it, perceive it or approach it through an instrument. *The Real* is something that humans try to approach but will never reach, both because of their own biology and because they are part of it. However, through

VR and embodied explorations, new aspects of *The Real* could possibly be addressed and experienced in ways that they have never been experienced before. Often, these aspects cannot be accessed directly through the human body only because they are too big, too small or lie beyond the spectrum of human understanding.

The Concept of Presence, Learning Contexts and Human Factors

The concept of *presence* presupposes that the technical quality of the VE and the performances of the devices used to recreate appropriate sensations would constitute the core conditions enabling the user to feel the *presence* of the VE. Could *presence* alternatively be regarded as a subjective concept that can depend largely on the conditions of use and of the human environment in which learning occurs? From the first person: How do I feel present with regard to what I have to perform in the VE? *Presence* can also be regarded as a personal experience. The physiology of the human mind and its function of producing thoughts mean that, for a human being, being present to whatever is around them is not a permanent experience no matter what the characteristics of their environment. This is why most Oriental traditions have developed so many meditation techniques to slow down the mind. And slowing down one's mind is a way to increase one's ability to be present. Therefore, a user's quality of presence will mostly depend on internal factors such as intentions and involvement in the tasks they are about to complete within the VE. These qualities can be developed considerably by commitments that the learner makes before using the VE. Experience shows that a user can really be and feel present in a VE even if the technical quality of the VE is poor, as long as as it makes sense for them to use it.

Another assumption is that a VEL should be autonomous and context-free. Is this really possible? Human beings need to feel connected to other human beings if they are to develop their motivation to act and to learn. Hence any VEL necessarily exists within a context. This is why educational issues are so important. Another possible model is the *enactive* approach in biology (Varela, 1994), which assumes that a biological organism can only exist within a context and in interaction with its environment. These contexts invariably include human components. Learning motivations are profoundly linked to emotional and affective factors. The learning context should be set up in such a way that it contains human beings able to support the motivation of the learners. This also means that the sense of *presence* in this approach is context-dependent and could be modulated, enhanced or limited by human factors.

ABOUT PARADIGMS

Over time, scientific developments have increased through techniques of observation, through the isolation of studied objects in neutral environments and as a result of a logic of analysis and deconstruction. The sciences have reached the point where these practices are no longer so efficient and, in some areas of research, can even be counterproductive. The example of contemporary physics is particularly illustrative of this renewal of approaches. These new developments require new research paradigms. And, mainly because of the embodied experience of the learner but also because the proposed experiences might be so different from everyday life experiences, using a medium such as VR encourages an extensive renewal of approaches to learning. It is more efficient when attempting to renew an approach to consider which paradigm is the most appropriate.

Definition and Function of a Paradigm

Because human beings are part of the world in which they live they cannot observe this world in its entirety. Scientific knowledge born of observation will therefore always remain incomplete. Although the horizon of the unknown can move backwards as science and knowledge move forward, there will always be material for new discoveries and new learning. But, on the other hand, there will also always be residual ignorance. And human beings, especially researchers, cannot ignore this residual ignorance. They have to make statements about what these unknown territories are. In order to develop new knowledge, bases must be provided in which to ground the new knowledge. Because this grounding must be based on unknown elements, researchers have to proceed as if they knew what these unknown elements were. In this they are guided by their beliefs and speculations. This is precisely what a *scientific paradigm* is. A *paradigm* is a way of saying: *"That is what I consider to be true, out of all that is unknown. And I need to clarify what I believe because, depending on what I consider to be true or false, my research will be different in terms of what I postulate, the methodology I will use and the new knowledge that it might produce."* It can also be said that research hypothesis is a set of statements about which aspects of the unknown might become known through the research, while a paradigm is a set of beliefs about what is not addressed by the research and what will, for sure, remain unknown after the completion of the research. These paradigms will change over time as the horizon of the unknown moves backwards. This is why it is so important to be explicit about what the researchers consider to be true when they embark on their research. In other words, to explain what their paradigm is and also to continue in pursuit of new paradigms.

How to Choose a Paradigm Suitable for Learning in Virtual Environments?

"How to choose a paradigm that is coherent with the choice of using a VE to support learning processes?" In the fields of education and long-life learning, *constructivist* and *constructionist*, and more recently, *connectivist* paradigms have long been dominant in learning disciplines. When made explicit, they still are (Fowler, 2015). These paradigms have been very useful in bringing about a great deal of progress and in reaching a better understanding of learning processes. In this context, *cognition* has mainly been regarded as a black box that can be considered independently from the body in which it is taking place. But things are changing. In cognitive science the question has been posed: could a paradigm based on biology and on embodiment theory be more supportive for scientific discoveries (Stewart et al., 2011)? Moreover, with the advent of VR, constructivist and constructionist paradigms have reached their limits when connectivist may still be under exploration. In so far as VR incorporates the user's body by means of various devices, one has to consider that the learning process occurs through the body of the user. In order to take this into account, the paradigm underlying the development of a VEL has to say something about how human beings learn through their bodies.

The Paradigm of Enaction

Winn (2003) proposed that learning in artificial environments could be enhanced by paying more attention to embodiment, embeddedness and dynamic adaptation (Winn, 2002). This is why the author has decided to use the *paradigm of enaction*, which comes from cognitive biology (Maturana, 1980). There might be other appropriate paradigms of which the author of this chapter is unaware. The key aspect is that the paradigm should consider that the learning process occurs in a biological body, because it is through the body that a VE can be experienced. *"All components and aspects of human life are linked together and rooted in biological foundations. Therefore, we join Maturana and Varela (1980) when they approach cognitive biology through embodiment. In line with their claims, we consider that language has biological roots (Maturana et al., 1995) and encloses basic universal structures*." (Mellet-d'Huart, 2005)

WHEN AND HOW TO USE VIRTUAL REALITY TO SUPPORT LEARNING?

Generally speaking, it is interesting to use VR when something would be impossible, expensive, dangerous or counterproductive to realize in the material world (Bailenson, 2016). This can also be applied to learning applications. But some types of learning can be achieved very easily and efficiently in the real world. For these types of learning, VEs are not needed unless safety issues, economic considerations or questions of availability of training situations are involved. The focus should rather be oriented to situations where learning is difficult to achieve in a real situation (Mellet-d'Huart, 2009). Learning welding, at that time (2000-2005), was such a situation. Learning welding hands-on in the real world is difficult. The welding process involves high temperatures that generate a strong and blinding light. Because of this intense light, learners can see neither the process nor the effects of their own gestures on the process. They therefore receive no effective feedback, either on the quality of their gesture or on the quality of their welding. Quality analysis can only occur hours or days later when the piece is cut or x-rayed, by which time it is too late for the learners to make any correlation between the result they achieved and their own action. This is why a VEL was developed which respected most of the characteristics of the real situation but suppressed the blinding effects of the strong light. Moreover, the system provided the learners with immediate feedback on the quality of their welding (Da Dalto et al. 2007, 2008) (video CS WAVE Demonstration).

An important set of questions arose: can connections exist between the characteristics of the learning content and the characteristics that the VE should have in order to support and facilitate learning? Would it be possible to find a common typology that could be applied to both the learning processes and the characteristics of a VE? In an attempt to answer these questions, the author has developed Trinologic, a metamodel that could include such a typology. VEs are like universes, and what best defines a universe is its space-time characteristics.

Design Engineering Landmarks

With regard to the design of VEs for learning, the author will consider two main questions: (1) Can design engineering landmarks be found that would support and facilitate the description of the specifications for the VE and the learning processes, for the development of software and for communication within a team coming from different disciplines and using different jargons? (2) How can learning content be defined and split into learning objectives? Does VR make a difference? Must VELs be *'realistic'* in order to support learning, no matter what the content of the learning or the learning objectives? Might *'unrealistic'* VELs offer better support for learning than *'realistic'* VELs?

Trinologic: A Three-in-One Metamodel

In the context of VR, Durlach and Mavor (1995) encouraged the setting up of conceptual models based on cognitive sciences to support the design of applications dealing with games, education and training. Following their advice, the author has designed a metamodel to support and facilitate the design of VEs for learning. It is called Trinologic. Trinologic is based on the assumption that every human being simultaneously lives in three different space-times. It is organized around three core concepts, each of which specifies a particular space-time and defines its main characteristics. These concepts are: actualization, potentialization and virtualization (Mellet-d'Huart, 2006).

The *paradigm of enaction* is the basis of the *Trinologic metamodel*. Beyond its paradigm, the underlying assumption behind Trinologic is that everything exists simultaneously in three different space-time dimensions. *Trinologic* is organized as a threefold topology. First called a '*model of (en)action*' at the time of its creation, *Trinologic* was initially developed in order to support and facilitate the design of VEs for learning. The term *Trinologic* is a reference to the coexistence of three dimensions (*'trino' from the latin 'trinus', triple or threefold*) and its operation as a logical system ('*logic*'). It is a metamodel because it is dependent neither on the situation nor on the discipline that is used to approach it. It has been designed to facilitate analysis and understanding of human action, transdisciplinary communication and design of VEs… As a result, it can be used both to analyse learning activities and to characterize VEs.

These concepts can contribute to describing embodied human activity and to the analysis and the division of human learning activities into three categories. Because these concepts are connected with specific characteristics of space-times, they can also be used to define the main characteristics of a VE. Once these three concepts have been clearly understood, they can help build bridges between different disciplines and facilitate communication between experts or professionals whose backgrounds are in different disciplines. All the experts will thus know exactly how their own contribution to the project field should be oriented and characterised by knowing how each concept of Trinologic is applied within their own disciplines.

About Humans: Acting and Being

In their everyday lives human beings, through the use of language, are used to making distinctions (Varela, 1980). In this process of making distinctions, it might be difficult to consider that things that appear to be different at a conceptual level could exist and be true simultaneously. Considering the simultaneous coexistence of the human being in three different space-times might be perceived as a challenge by the mind, but if our intuitive experience can recall different qualities of memories, this might correspond to different experiences of time and space. Approaching Trinologic might seem counter-intuitive. Moreover, the materialistic culture we are living in encourages us to accord more value to what is tangible than to what is not. From this perspective, only one space-time dimension is perceived as tangible, that is to say, that which exists here and now. It will be referred to here as *actualization*.

As explained previously, Trinologic is organized around three core concepts: *actualization*; *virtualization* and *potentialization*. These three concepts are mainly defined in terms of their relationship with time and space. As an initial approach, they might be defined abstractly as follows: (1) *Actualization*: What exists here and now and is embodied in the present moment. (2) *Virtualization*: What exists in the past or in the future but has no existence right now, and exists anywhere in space but has no existence right here. (3) *Potentialization*: What exists in its own circular time where everything will be repeated continuously following the same processes and in the same order. Its space is curved. It always returns to any point on its trajectory, and always in the same order.

Actualization

Human beings are used to performing concrete actions in their environments. This they do in the present moment and in the place where they are. That is their only chance to act. There is no possibility of acting either in the past or in the future. In order to act in their environments, they use the parts of their bodies that are dedicated to action: the skeleton and the muscles, with the help of the heart. If performed accurately these actions will have an impact on the outer world, which will be modified in some way. To perform actions in the present moment, virtualization is necessary in order to anticipate, and potentialisation is necessary in order to mobilize the energy needed to perform the action.

Virtualization

Human beings also exist both in the past and in the future, anywhere and at any time, either nearby or far away. Therefore, they use their minds, which are mainly embodied in the brain. An important characteristic of the brain is that it has no direct contact with the outer world but is enclosed by the cranial bones. Although the brain carries out important tasks in terms of understanding what is happening in the outer world and preparing future actions, it is totally dependant upon the senses to *'know'* anything about the outside world. Maturana and Varela (1987) used the metaphor of the submarine which has no windows but only dials showing abstract variations on various indicators, which correspond to the senses. By interpreting these data, the brain develops an idea about what surrounds the body, and this idea becomes identified as reality. Thanks to its ability to integrate past experiences and to deduce how the outer world might be impacted by the action of the body, the brain can make simulations and choices about what will be actualized.

Potentialization

Human beings also exist through the internal organs of their bodies: the heart, the lungs, the digestive organs and the whole body as a physiological entity repeatedly perform the same processes. Each system has its own requirements and its own rhythm and constantly repeats the same cycles, although not exactly in the same way, because its permanent interaction with its environment causes it to modify its pace. This is also where emotions arise from inner physical sensations. These emotions are later taken over by the virtualisation system which gives them a name and interprets them. Basically, they are manifestations of living energy. The main purpose of potentialization is to provide energy to the whole body (*e.g. through oxygen and nutrients*) so that actualization and virtualization can exist.

In this approach, actions are considered to be embedded and embodied processes that involve actualization, virtualization and potentialization simultaneously. The term "*action*" encompasses both the outer and the inner processes that a human being engages when acting. In this approach, *doing nothing* is also regarded as realising an action. Only a dead body has the ability literally to do nothing, to perform no action. Therefore, a particular formalism is proposed in order to support action modeling. The *Trinologic model*, based on an enactive paradigm, is a global and systemic model. Theories supporting this model are derived from the neurophysiology of action (Berthoz, 1997, 2003), and cognitive biology

(Maturana and Varela, 1980). Because Trinologic supports the study of embodied action it is strongly connected to the theory of *enaction* (Varela et al., 1991; Varela, 1994).

Trinologic and its Correspondances in Physiology of Action

Trinologic is an enactive metamodel, supported by a conceptual framework. It is enactive in that it can only consider an object in its environment and its environment can be characterized by the same structure. The conceptual framework integrates generic operators. It is based on: (1) a dynamic cycle of action ; (2) a *Trinologic* structure; (3) three basic operators: *actualization*, *potentialization*, and *virtualization*. This framework constitutes a formal system that can be used dynamically and iteratively and can be organized on different levels. The Trinologic model supports a model of action and hence a model of learning. The Trinologic model is supported by neurophysiological theories. For Berthoz, *action* can be deconstructed into three different steps: (1) the anticipation of possible action and its foreseen consequences on the environment; (2) decision-making and the engagement of action; and (3) the execution of the chosen action in the human being's external environment (*the "real world"*).

The Anticipation of Possible Action - Virtualization

According to Berthoz, before acting in a particular context human beings explore different possible actions through mental simulation. In this way they anticipate the possible consequences of future actions. They therefore use models which have been developed over time through their experiences and learnings and which they also apply to new situations. These models result from the analysis and conceptualization of previous actions. They are used to support anticipation and to predict new situations. These processes minimize contextual elements and enhance structural and invariable elements. This approach is reflected in the concept of *virtualization*.

Decision-Making - Potentialization

Human beings have to preserve their existence as living beings, and so they have to control and evaluate both their internal and emotional states. Because their purpose is to sustain life and to ensure that the biological entity remains alive, they also have to look out for the risks that they might encounter in their environment. Their past experiences provide their frame of reference. Various levels of inner states can be distinguished, ranging from internal visceral states to high-level mental states. Decision-making involves evaluating the existing risks by scanning the environment and searching for significant details. Decision-making can be irrational and an accurate anticipation might be rejected simply due to an inner feeling of insecurity. This approach is reflected in the concept of *potentialization*.

Execution of an Action - Actualization

Executing an action involves engaging body movements. Its aim is often to induce intentional changes in the environment, to protect the body. Moving a biological body in an environment means dealing with inertia, gravity and equilibrium, as well as evaluating distances and the forces to be engaged. This process is based on imitation, experience and practice. So human beings develop internal and external markers as visual cues in order to organize their actions. This approach is reflected in the concept of *actualization*.

Trinologic and its Correspondances in Linguistics

It is interesting to note that Trinologic shares also structures found in linguistics, and more particularly in grammar. When verbs are conjugated, which is how they are organised in most languages, they are differentiated in a threefold system between first (*I/we*), second (*you/you*) and third person (*he/she/it/they*). These three persons can be connected to the three core concepts of Trinologic.

First Person - Actualization

The first person (*I/we*) is used to describe in words one's own deeds and feelings. The purpose of the first person is to execute appropriately targeted and anticipated actions in order to produce expected changes or effects in the environment. The first person commands actions in the environment external to the organism. It organizes body movements within space. It is therefore based on the development of sensory and motor skills. By observing and imitating, the individual can act autonomously, develop actions and make realizations. The first person is the "*doer*" or the actor, interacting with the environment here and now, which is where and when the body exists. The first person is connected with actualization. It is an active position which enables the action to become actual through the mobilization of the sensitive and effectrice surfaces required for their execution. The organism develops movements to achieve its goals. The first-person space-time is rooted in the present and the here and now. What occurs occurs now, within a temporal window for possible actions on the world. Space is condensed and circumscribed to here, within the spatial window for possible action on the world. Space-time is concentrated here in a particular context. The first person is that which actualizes its existence in the world through action. The generic operator of the first person is "*actualization* ".

The Second Person - Potentialization

The second person (*you singular and plural*) is used to address another person or other people, to make demands, to give orders… From an internal point of view, the second person has to do with decision-making and is focused on maintaining the equilibrium of the organism (Maturana, 1980; Maturana et al., 1995). Therefore, it is directly connected to emotional internal states and does not refer to rational considerations. It is connected to the desire for durability of any living organism. It focuses on internal states, survival issues, welfare and peer relationships. It supports the engagement that is necessary to execute the action. This is where emotioning (Maturana, 1980) occurs, based on inner states. In a certain way, the second person is timeless. It is rooted in natural and physiological cycles. The second person meshes emotions with space-time events. In this model, the process engaged by decision-making is identified as *potentialization*.

The Third Person - Virtualization

The third person (*he/she/it/they*) provides the possibility of describing in words the deeds of another person. It is the position of the observer who says what they perceive. By observing another person's actions, one can better understand how to act on and in the world. From an internal point of view, the third person supports anticipation and simulation of action and its expected or foreseen consequences. It deals with abstraction, causation, generalization and conceptualization. As neurophysiologists explain, one might unconsciously or consciously imitate other people. The third person refers to cognition, from acquiring causation to abstract reasoning. Its main process, therefore, is *virtualisation*. Time can be visited in different ways. If hierarchical and chronological it may support causation. Events can be located from past to future. But one can move and explore freely past and future. Past experiences are used as references to simulate new actions and to anticipate possible consequences of future actions. Space can be approached as an Euclidean space. It is flat and can be abstractly manipulated. We identify its main process as *virtualization*.

Trinologic Applied to a Virtual Environment for Learning

The Trinologic metamodel can be used as a typology to analyse and break down learning processes. As an illustration, we will consider the activity of a truck-driver (Mellet-d'Huart, 2004). The job analysis of a truck-driver might show that their activities are complex, composite, and of varied natures, including driving on the roads, preparing and planning journeys, or vigilance with regard to possible risks or incidents.

Preparation and Planning of Journeys - Virtualization

As far as learning processes are concerned, we will find here a large range of mental activities such as abstraction, mental simulation, anticipation, referring to knowledge, calculation, planning, evaluating… The truck driver will have to plan and organise their travel depending on the final destination. Some stops might have to be organized on the way. The driver might know that some parts of the roads will be closed for works and that there will be some detours. Most of this planning takes place prior to the departure of the vehicle and might be corrected or modified en route. In order to be realised, this activity requires that the person take a step back from what is happening here and now to make projections. This might necessitate jumping into different scales of space and of time. And of course, in this category we also find previously acquired knowledge about traffic laws and how to behave when driving.

These processes will impact on the real world only if they are followed by actions or only if they are actualized. By their very nature, virtualization processes remain unenacted. The reference of the mental activities may be found in the past, in the future or in both past and future. The only place where virtualization cannot occur is here and now. Virtualization is a process and, as such, requires time. In order for the process to take place it requires data acquired either from past experiences or from previously learned knowledge. Because the preparation takes place before the action, developing simulations of possible results implies making projections into the future. So if a VE is required to facilitate this kind of learning, it has to be unrealistic from a perceptual point of view. It is not meant for immediate realisation here and now. It might or might not be enacted. And if it is, this would be later and maybe somewhere else. The most important focus is generally not on how to perform the action physically but what impact it will have on the outer world. Therefore, its representation in a virtual world does not have to be realistic in terms of perception but will have to comply either with the inner beliefs of the person, or with their past experience or with their knowledge, and show how what might happen could be a consequence of such laws. In most cases, in VEs things or facts that normally cannot be perceived are rendered perceivable. Therefore, the representation will have to be congruent with predefined models in order to illustrate the consequences of a particular model when applied to an object or a particular situation. For this reason it must be possible to change scale and to move instantly anywhere and at any time.

Driving - Actualization

As far as learning processes are concerned, the focus is on realising a direct action in a particular environment. Direct action means that the focus is on the gesture and on the bodily capacities. Both the motivation and the anticipation of the action are addressed elsewhere. Actualization is about how bodily capacity and behavioural actions modify the outer world. Therefore, the world must be approached here and now as a three-dimensional and material entity. Bodily actions can only exist here and now. This is the reason why this kind of learning can in most cases be hands-on and occur in the real world. Nevertheless, if this is not possible, VEs can be used. These will have specific characteristics. The scale used for both spatial and temporal properties is 1:1. The archetypes of such VEs are full-scale simulators. In this case the structures of the VE must be almost identical to those of the real world. When we refer to structures we are not referring to details. The perceptual structures, therefore, should be realistic but do not need to include the appearance of the details of the scene. Regarding actualization, VEs do not have to be specific. They have to refer to a category of situations that may look alike. The truck driver, through actualization, will develop the ability to drive a real or a realistic truck in a real or realistic environment: various types of road, different traffic and weather circumstances, with the truck empty truck or fully charged, etc.

Being Safe on the Roads - Potentialization

As far as learning processes are concerned, we will mainly address here the question of decision-making on the spot. For the truck driver, we will consider how to face different kinds of risks. (1) The driver will face the kind of unexpected events that could occur on the roads. For instance, a ball might suddenly roll into the road, suggesting that some children have been playing with the ball and that those children are nearby. The danger is that they might run unexpectedly after the ball, into the road and right in front the truck. The truck driver will therefore have to slow down the vehicle in order to avoid an accident. (2) To avoid mechanical incidents or the risk of accidents, the truck driver will have to operate various mechanical controls on the vehicle on a regular basis. Such risks could include the explosion of a tyre or brake failure. He has to be prepared to react appropriately if this were to happen. (3) The truck driver also has to consider human factors, for example, fatigue after having been on the road for too long. The risk is of falling asleep. And he has to interact with other drivers, police officers, clients, etc.

If something unforeseen happens, how will the learner react and develop a set of appropriate responses? Most of the time such events occur sporadically and unexpectedly. This is a crucial aspect of any learning concerning security issues, incidents, accidents, breakdowns or conflicts… There must be particular focus on details. Here, very specific situations are considered. Details are usually indicators that something is not right, that something may be wrong or that a danger is looming. Regarding the general structures of a VE, the requirement here is great precision with respect to perceptual details. What was not important for actualisation is highly important for potentialization. Incidents, most of the time, have an open cycle of development. Unless this cycle is interrupted, all the phases of the incident will be developed. The VEL must include those models.

Acting in a Real World

Acting in a real world is always a complex activity composed of actualisation, potentialization and virtualization processes in constant interaction. These three components exist simultaneously. This is also true of most learning activities in that they are not deconstructed or simplified. Nevertheless, deconstruction presents many advantages in supporting and facilitating learning. Later on, the actions that have been deconstructed must be returned to a global action in order to be applied in the real world. The example of the truck driver illustrates this idea. Deconstruction enables easier focus on simple elements and aids rehearsal until some automatisms have been acquired. Because of their infinite plasticity, VEs are interesting supports for deconstructing learning activities. The Trinologic model is suitable both for simple actions and for deconstructing complex activities. It also supports the reverse movement from deconstruction to entirety.

The Dynamics of the Trinologic Model

The Trinologic model is a dynamic model. This means that the three components are in constant interaction and that none of those components could exist without the two others. It also means they all exist at the same time, linking the three space-times together although the nature and the properties of each space-time are different. In order to choose what to do next, the outcomes both of virtualization processes and of potentialization processes are important. Whereas the former anticipate what can be done next, the latter will decide which anticipation has to be engaged and/or inhibited depending on the amount of energy required and on the internal condition of the organism. The purpose of decision-making is to select the actualized outcome of the action. Decision-making is the purpose of potentialization.

ISSUES, CONCLUSION AND PERSPECTIVES

Over the last years, numerous VEs have been developed to support learning situations. Several papers (Freina, & Ott, n.d.; Hu-Au, & Lee, 2018; Kamińska, et al., 2019; Radiantia et al., 2020) have been dédicated to exploring existing applications and attempting to analyze or to typologise them. Unfortunately, most of these recent attempts have only produced interesting results by making differentiations following technical criteria, as mentioned by Fowler (2015) in the title of his paper "*Where is the pedagogy?*" He also claims that most of the learning applications that make their paradigm explicit are developed on a constructivist paradigm or on derivatives of the constructivist paradigm. As yet there has been no mention of the use of an enactive paradigm. For most applications, neither paradigms nor pedagogical choices are mentioned, as if only technical issues, immersion or other characteristics of VEs can influence learning outcomes. The absence of pedagogical information and the heterogeneity of those applications make it difficult to develop pedagogical comparisons. However, a single VEL could be a wonderful context in which to multiply experiments with different types of pedagogy, either embedded or articulated with the educational context of the learning situation. In this context of rare pedagogical approaches looking at VELs as specific objects, the research of William Winn (2002, 2003) remains a reference. Do researchers intend to wait for major players such as Microsoft (2019) to articulate pedagogical approaches with technical approaches?

In any case, using VR as a medium to support learning processes is not a neutral choice and, if we are to exploit its unique benefits, it cannot be approached using traditional methods. VR supports an embodied and embedded approach to acting and learning. The user can move and behave in a VE just as if they were in a real environment (Johnson-Glenberg, 2018) . The plasticity of the medium, enabling the creation of learning situations that could not previously have been be created, represents an unprecedented chance to renew pedagogical approaches. In order to bring about these learning situations, certain conditions must be respected: (1) Knowing the new possibilities offered by VR, as well as its limitations ; (2) Renewing the paradigms underlying the research in order to achieve coherence between design and medium ; (3) Sharing a metatool that encapsulates a methodology for analysing human learning processes with the same categories and that will also guide the choices involved in characterizing the VE.

This chapter has presented arguments to show how learning experiences can be renewed by using VR and how, as a result, learning could become a much easier experience. Various considerations have been taken into account: (1) references to some deeply-rooted clichés about VR which are generating unnecessary limitations in the minds of VEL designers. (2) the choice of a paradigm that is both coherent and supportive for the use of VEs to help with learning *(e.g. the enactive metamodel).* (3) to facilitate the conception and the design of VELs, the development of metamodels that can provide the various disciplines involved with a shared typology of analysis that would be a bridge between the deconstruction of learning and the design of an accurate VE *(e.g. the Trinologic approach).* Moreover, the actors coming from various disciplines need to have shared concepts and shared models in order to work together. Based on VR, a very plastic medium, a VEL can be manipulated in many ways in order to make learning easier, which cannot be done in a real environment. VR should therefore be a wonderful playground for pedagogues. Unfortunately, many of them are missing although they would be welcome to join. The field is complex and collective efforts are necessary.

REFERENCES

Bailenson, J. N. (2016). The trials and tribulations of narrative. *VR. MediaX.* Available at, https://vhil.stanford.edu/news/2016/the-trials-and-tribulations-of-narrative-in-vr-mediax/

Berthoz, A. (1997). *Le sens du mouvement.* Odile Jacob.

Berthoz, A. (2003). *La décision.* Odile Jacob.

Da Dalto, L., Steib, D., & Balet, O. (2008). CS WAVE: Learning welding motion in a virtual environment. *Proceedings of IIW Conference, 52,* 167-172.

Da Dalto, L., Steib, D., Mellet-d'Huart, D., & Balet, O. (2007). *CS WAVE: Virtual reality for welder's training.* Welding in the World.

Dede, C. (2009, January 02). Immersive interfaces for engagement and learning. *Science, 323*(5910), 66–69. doi:10.1126cience.1167311 PMID:19119219

Durlach, N., & Mavor, A. (Eds.). (1995). Virtual reality. scientific and technological challenges. Naval Training Systems Center.

Fowler, C. (2015). Virtual reality and learning: Where is the pedagogy? *British Journal of Educational Technology, 46*(2), 412-422.

Freina, L., & Ott, M. A. (n.d.). *Literature review on immersive virtual reality in education: state of the art and perspectives*. Available from, https://progesis.itd.cnr.it/download/eLSE%202015%20Freina%20Ott%20Paper.pdf

Holopainen, J., Lähtevänoja, A., Mattila, O., Södervik, I., Pöyry, E., & Parvinen, P. (2020). Exploring the learning outcomes with various technologies - Proposing design principles for virtual reality learning environments. In *Proceedings of the 53rd Hawaii International Conference on System Sciences, Hawaii (UH).* 10.24251/HICSS.2020.004

Hu-Au, E., & Lee, J. (2018). Virtual reality in education: A tool for learning in the experience age. *International Journal of Innovation in Education, 4*. Advance online publication. doi:10.1504/IJIIE.2017.10012691

Johnson-Glenberg, M. C. (2018). Immersive VR and education: Embodied design principles that include gesture and hand controls. *Frontiers in Robotics and AI, 5*, 81. doi:10.3389/frobt.2018.00081

Johnson-Glenberg, M. C. (2019). The necessary nine. In Learning in a Digital World. Perspective on Interactive Technologies for Formal and Informal Education, Springer Singapore.

Kamińska, D., Sapiński, T., Wiak, S., Tikk, T., Haamer, R. E., Avots, E., Helmi, A., Ozcinar, C., & Anbarjafari, G. (2019). Virtual reality and its applications in education: Survey. *Information, 10*(10), 318. doi:10.3390/info10100318

Lenay, C., Gapenne, O., Hanneton, S., Marque, C., & Genouëlle, C. (2004). Sensory substitution: limits and perspectives. In Touching for Knowing. John Benjamins Publishers. ff doi:10.1075/aicr.53.22lenff. ffhal-02434266f

Martín-Gutiérrez, J., Efrén Mora, C., Añorbe-Díaz, B., & González-Marrero, A. (2017). Virtual technologies trends in education. EURASIA J Math Sci and Tech, Ed, 13(2), 469-486.

Maturana, H., & Varela, F. (1980). *Autopoiesis and cognition: The realization of the living*. Reidel Publishing. doi:10.1007/978-94-009-8947-4

Maturana, H. R. (1980). Biology of cognition. In H. R. Maturana & F. J. Varela (Eds.), *Autopoiesis and Cognition: The Realization of the Living* (pp. 5–58). Reidel Publishing. doi:10.1007/978-94-009-8947-4_1

Maturana, H. R., Mpodozis, J., & Letelier, J. C. (1995). Brain language and the origin of human mental functions. *Biological Research, 28*, 15–26. www.informatik.umu.se/~rwhit/MatMpo&Let(1995).html PMID:8728817

Maturana, H. R., & Varela, F. J. (1987). *The tree of knowledge: The biological roots of human understanding*. New Science Library/Shambhala Publications.

Mazuryk, T., & Gervautz, M. (n.d.). *Virtual reality - history, applications, technology and future*. http://citeseerx.ist.psu.edu/viewdoc/summary?doi=10.1.1.42.7849

Mellet-d'Huart, D. (2004). *De l'intention à l'attention: contributions à une démarche de conception d'environnements virtuels pour apprendre à partir d'un modèle de l'(én)action* (Doctoral dissertation). Université du Maine, France.

Mellet-d'Huart, D. (2005). He/She-You-I formalism: a heuristic model of (en)action to make Decisions. *Modeling Natural Action Selection, Proceedings of an International Workshop Edinburgh.*

Mellet-d'Huart, D. (2006). A model of (en)action to approach embodiment: A cornerstone for the design of virtual environments for learning. *Virtual Reality (Waltham Cross), 10*(3-4), 253–269. doi:10.100710055-006-0038-2

Mellet-d'Huart, D. (2009). Virtual reality for training and lifelong learning - *Themes in Science and Technology Education, 2*(1).

Radiantia, J., Majchrzak, T. A., Frommb, J., & Wohlgenanntc, I. (2020). A systematic review of immersive virtual reality applications for higher education: Design elements, lessons learned, and research agenda. *Computers & Education, 147*(April), 103778. doi:10.1016/j.compedu.2019.103778

Stewart, J., Gapenne, O., & Di Paolo, E. (Eds.). (2011). *Enaction: Towards a new paradigm for cognitive science*. MIT Press.

Tixier, M., Lenay, C., Gapenne, O., & Aubert, D. (2013, February). From perceptual supplementation to the accessibility of digital spaces: The case of free exploration of city maps for blind persons. *IRBM, 34*(1), 64–68. doi:10.1016/j.irbm.2012.12.005

Varela, F. J. (1994). Autopoiesis and a biology of intentionality. In Autopoiesis and Perception. School of Electronic Engineering.

Varela, F. J., Thompson, E., & Rosch, E. (1991). *The embodied mind: Cognitive science and human experience*. MIT Press. doi:10.7551/mitpress/6730.001.0001

Winn, W. (2002). Learning in artificial environments: Embodiment embeddedness and dynamic adaptation. *Techniques Instruction Cognition and Learning., 1*, 2002.

Winn, W. (2003, November-December). Beyond constructivism: A return to Science-based research and practice. *Educational Technology, 43*(6), 5–14.

ADDITIONAL READING

Arango, F., Aziz, E., Esche, S. K., & Chassapis, C. (2008). A Review of Applications of Computer Games in Education and Training. In Proceedings of *38th Annual Frontiers in Education Conference*. Saratoga Springs, NY, 2008, pp. T4A-1-T4A-6. CS WAVE Demonstration. Available at, https://youtu.be/Q-bAwn5Z9yk

Jensen, L., & Konradsen, F. (2018). A review of the use of virtual reality head-mounted displays in education and training. *Education and Information Technologies, 23*(4), 1515–1529. doi:10.100710639-017-9676-0

Pellas, N., Fotaris, P., Kazanidis, I., & Wells, D. (2019). Augmenting the learning experience in primary and secondary school education: A systematic review of recent trends in augmented reality game-based learning. *Virtual Reality (Waltham Cross), 23*(4), 329–346. doi:10.100710055-018-0347-2

Phon, D. N. E., Ali, M. B., & Halim, N. D. A. (2014). Collaborative Augmented Reality in Education: A Review. In *International Conference on Teaching and Learning in Computing and Engineering*, Kuching, 2014, pp. 78-83, 10.1109/LaTiCE.2014.23

Radu, I. (2014). Augmented reality in education: A meta-review and cross-media analysis. *Personal and Ubiquitous Computing, 2014*(18), 1533–1543. doi:10.100700779-013-0747-y

Saleeb, N., & Dafoulas, G. (2010). Pedagogical immigration to 3D virtual worlds: A critical review of underlying themes and their concepts. In *International Conference on Information Society*, London, 2010, pp. 401-409, doi: 10.1109/i-Society16502.2010.6018737

Scott, E., Soria, A., & Campo, M. (2017). Adaptive 3D Virtual Learning Environments—A Review of the Literature. In IEEE Transactions on Learning Technologies, vol. 10, no. 3, pp. 262-276, 1 July-Sept. 2017, doi:10.1109/TLT.2016.2609910

KEY TERMS AND DEFINITIONS

Actualization: What exists and occurs here and now.

Cognition: The experience of living mirroring itself in past and future *(cf. Virtualization)*.

Learning: Linking present experiences to past and future through a reflective movement *(cf. Virtualization)*.

Potentialization: All that exists and occurs in a circular space-time and of which the objective is the perpetuation of the existence of an organization.

Real: All that exists, independently of whether or not it can be perceived or known by human beings. The Real supports actualization. It is the place where living and acting take place. The Real exists here and now, in the sphere of *actualization*.

Reality: How the outer world exists in the human mind. A production of the mind that exists independently of an actual experience of acting in the world. It is therefore a part of virtualization.

Trinologic: A metamodel that postulates the simultaneous existence of three different space-times in human beings and in their perception of the outer world. It is organized around *actualization*, *virtualization* and *potentialization*.

Virtual: That which has the characteristics of *virtualization*. Remark: When qualifying reality, which is already a virtualized approach to the outer world, this term indicates a reflective movement that objectifies elements of reality that already exist somewhere in the human mind.

Virtual Reality: An ensemble of program and devices interposed between an actual person and the Real in which they exist. When used, Virtual Reality is actualized by computer calculation and provides the user with a perceptual experience, here and now, of something that is not actual but virtualized.

Virtualization: What exists and occurs anywhere *(nearby or far away)* and at any time *(in the past or in the future)* except for here and now. That includes *learning* and *cognition*.

Chapter 2
Building an Instructional Design Model for Immersive Virtual Reality Learning Environments

Zeynep Tacgin
Marmara University, Turkey

Barney Dalgarno
University of Canberra, Australia

ABSTRACT

The recent increase in affordability of immersive virtual reality learning environments (IVRLEs) grows the interests of university, school, and industry training contexts. Due to their unique affordances, these environments have the potential to lead to a paradigm shift in learning experience design. The absence of learning design models, however, represents a significant challenge to the widespread and effective utilisation of this technology platform. Several researchers have proposed design models for virtual reality learning environments (VRLEs). The majority of these models don't explicitly consider the unique characteristics of Immersive environments. This research describes an instructional design model for IVRLEs, which draws upon Dalgarno and Lee's affordance model for VRLE and Tacgin's IVRLE development stages for teaching concepts and procedures. The specific learning strategies and affordances of IVRLEs are matched with the features of current IVR systems and technologies.

INTRODUCTION

The transformative potential of Virtual Reality (VR) technologies ensures that they continue to attract the attention of educational researchers. A growing number of educators in a wide range of fields seek to integrate VR technologies into their particular area. A substantial body of research supports the idea that the educational affordances of VR have the potential to enhance or potentially transform the learning experiences of students (Aebersold et al., 2018; Hu, Wu, & Shieh, 2016; Ke, Lee, & Xu, 2016). For the last five years, experience and visualisation based fields such as medicine, science, engineering,

DOI: 10.4018/978-1-7998-5043-4.ch002

mechanics, architecture, etc. have made substantial breakthroughs in integrating VR technologies into their learning environments (LEs).

The power of VR comes from providing opportunities to represent both tangible and intangible phenomenon with a high level of visual realism. The highly realistic portrayal of the environment has a direct relationship to the sense of presence and the feeling of immersion experienced by the user. As a consequence, immersive VR has the potential to cover users' perceptions like a cocoon (Tacgin, 2018) in the context of a wide range of different scenarios.

This capability of VR attracts schools, universities, students, teachers, and learners within the industry and the professions. Although the use of VR technologies to their full capacity can be expensive, and many educational organisations are not able to meet the growing demand. To solve these deficiencies, web companies like Google, YouTube, Facebook, etc. have developed and promoted plug-ins to support the integration of 360° video or 3D VR technology into their products. One of the most affordable solutions, for example, is Google Cardboard, which allows exploring 3D environments after attaching a mobile phone to the cardboard goggles. After Cardboard, several companies have created mobile phone-based HMDs. This cheaper method offers increased access to VR technologies; however, the opportunities for environmental interaction has limits within these virtual environments (VEs). The most affordable interactive solution is using joystick controllers like those offered by Samsung Gear, VR Box, and Oculus Go. Additional devices like Leap Motion can also be used for supporting interaction, but the integration of these supplementary devices to HMDs might be cumbersome for some users.

Aside from access to appropriate hardware, another challenge is the availability of proper learning content. Designing 3D models and building 3D environments can be an onerous process because of the required time, skills of the multidisciplinary specialist, and high costs. The game engines producers have released plug-ins for novice users (e.g. Vuforia). There are also free 3D models and authoring tools (e.g. InstaVR) for the creation of 360° videos. Many teachers, lecturers and academics can now create their interactive 360° videos and share these contents with anyone who has stereo 3D goggles and mobile phones. The availability of laser scanners has provided a mechanism to scan a real environment to build virtual 3D models without having to master sophisticated 3D modelling tools.

The easy to use content creation tools provide enormous potential for rapid growth in the development of relevant content to a wide range of educational fields. As the degree of realism of the representation and mechanisms for interaction continue to grow, the likelihood of science fiction scenarios (e.g. those portrayed by the film Matrix) becomes ever closer as does the probability that VR will become an essential learning tool for educational organisations.

The results of studies do not reach a consensus regarding the benefits or restrictions of using IVR to teach. Some of the research suggests that the integration of innovative VR technologies into the education could reduce learning time, provide permanent knowledge, support experiential learning to increase psychomotor skills, support motivation, etc. (Hussein & Nätterdal, 2015; Mujber, Szecsi, & Hashmi, 2004; Plante, Cage, Clements, & Stover, 2006; Reinhart & Patron, 2003). The rapid advancement in technology along with the growing body of research evidence suggests that the affordances of VR could have enormous potential to reshape instructional methods and educational systems. According to some comparative studies, IVR does not provide measurable advantages to the learners and, traditional learning techniques might offer better outcomes.

The reality perception of IVR users is shifted by virtual components thereby they can move around, interact with the objects or characters in the IVRLE like in real life (Mast, Kleinlogel, Tur, Bachmann, 2018; Tacgin, 2020b). This authenticity regarding the 3D and spatial representation of virtuality is the main distinguishing feature of IVR environments. The majority of instructional design models depends on cognitive learning theories and adapts the human brain perception using cognitive neuroscience methodologies to facilitate knowledge acquisition (Makransky, Terkildsen & Mayer, 2019). Even though the systematic shared components of instructional design models, the features of them change considering the used devices or environments (Ritz & Buss, 2016; Dalgarno & Lee, 2010, Tacgin, 2020b). That is why the unique information transfer structure of IVRLEs requires to apply new design dynamics for their instructional design processes. As seen in the study of Parong and Mayer (2018), Anderson, Konge and Soresen (2018) or Makransky, Terkildsen and Mayer (2019) applying conventional instructional design models to structure IVRLEs might not ensure that the unique affordances are utilised and consequently might not lead to improved learning outcomes. Although a range of functionalities and affordances of IVR technologies should able to be utilised in providing high fidelity simulated learning experiences. This study explains the fundamental terms regarding IVR to demonstrate the distinguishing features and design processes of IVRLEs. A comprehensive framework for designing IVRLEs was presented after analysing the current instructional models. This framework was applied to develop an IVRLE, myVOR, and the adapted features of the proposed model were introduced on the example of myVOR.

LITERATURE REVIEW

Virtual Reality

The concept of VR is in a state of flux (Sherman & Craig, 2018) because its definition and categories have been reshaped through developments in the enabling technologies. Nevertheless, VR can be defined as *a digital approximation of perceived reality but not reality itself (Ma & Choi, 2007).*

VR environments are represented using entirely computer-generated outputs (e.g. visual, aural, sensory feedback, etc.). VR can use either HMDs or computer screens to display a structured VE. Depending on the technology used, VR can be immersive or non-immersive. However, many people now use the term VR to refer only to immersive environments, that use an HMDs to render the VE (Aguinas, Henle, & Beaty Jr, 2001; Bamodu & Ye, 2013; Buttussi & Chittaro, 2018; Cohen et al., 2013; El Araby, 2002; Laura Ermi & Mäyrä, 2005; L Ermi & Mäyrä, 2011; Halarnkar, Shah, Shah, Shah, & Shah, 2012; Johnson, 2010; Liu, Dede, Huang, & Richards, 2017; Mahmoud, 2001; Muhanna, 2015).

A range variation of VR systems has been used for many years, particularly due to the increasingly understood value of simulations. The users of VR can experience high-risk conditions in a safe and controlled VEs. They can investigate either 2D or 3D VEs from different perspectives. VR environments not only present the duplication of real situations but also provide an opportunity to represent abstract or intangible environments (Aguinas et al., 2001; Alqahtani, Daghestani, & Ibrahim, 2017).

As well as the visual channel, VR environments can include multiple sensory channels (Osuagwu, Ihedigbo, & Ndigwe, 2015). Consequently, providing an authentic visual representation, real-time simulation, and interactions can allow VR environments to provide high fidelity user interfaces. Successful VR environments often use a high level of sensory fidelity for interaction (Bowman & McMahan, 2007) which usually involves the use of visual, audial and other stimuli. The *artificial environment generated by the VR system replaces the real one within the user's field of perception (Ma & Choi, 2007). Thereby, the brain's response is managed by sensory stimuli which make a user immersed in it.*

Immersive Virtual Reality

According to Dede (2009), the sense of "immersion in a digital experience involves the willing suspension of disbelief". "Total immersion" refers to the situation whereby the user is completely immersed in the VE and is removed from influences emanating from outside of the virtual world (VW). Psychological total immersion is provided via a sense of presence and is linked to high visual and interactive fidelity.

Presence refers to one's feeling of "being in there"(Riva et al., 2007). A user perceives the VE as real, by way of engaging with digital content that encapsulates a specific scenario and influences a user's perceptions of that scenario. Users of IVR can look around, walk around, and interact with the VW and its components (Azuma et al., 2001).

Immersion begins with physical, rather than mental (Sherman & Craig, 2018) because of the technological dependency of VR. The degree of immersion is related to the level of fidelity or, the level of perceived realism. The display technology, virtual scenario, and interaction types are essential components within high fidelity IVR environments.

HMDs are used as display systems and their quality influences the effectiveness of the virtual experience. HMDs usually are used alongside controllers or other additional interaction devices. In some environments, it is possible to interact using natural methods like gesture, gaze or voice control. Depending on the methods used, immersion might consist of sensory, challenge-based, imaginative, actual, symbolic/narrative and social components. The quality of the virtual scenario is another critical factor contributing to the degree of immersion that emphasises the significance of an environment's design.

Learning Affordances of IVR

In basic, IVRLEs provide similar advantages to the simulations. Authentic learning of some kinds of conceptual content in the physical world can be ineffective because of inherent limitations in accessing the environment where the theoretical content can be experienced. Accessing the actual environment might be hard due to factors like distance, time, price, scale, or security. Using IVRLEs can help to get rid of these restrictions of the physical environment such as experiencing the high-risk condition, demonstration of abstract concepts, self-evaluation of the practises, repetitive implementation of the situations and more.

First, the real environment might consist of high-risk or dangerous situations. Simulations and virtual LEs provide the opportunity to overcome these limitations and offer experiential learning where access to the real environment is not feasible (Bharathi & Tucker, 2015; Jen, 2007; Mills & Noyes, 1999; Ramasundaram, Grunwald, Mangeot, Comerford, & Bliss, 2005). Thus, individuals can learn new skills in a controlled environment (Osuagwu et al., 2015). For instance, the studies show that IVRLEs have been used to teach combat strategies in the military (Lele, 2013), surgical procedures to medical students (Papagiannakis et al., 2018; Buń, Górski & Turkowska 2018), hazard rules to the miners (Grabowski and Jankowski 2015) or moonwalk to the astronauts (Kong, Liu & An, 2018) though the learners can practise high-risk conditions in a safe environment. According to these studies, using IVRLE helps to reduce learning time and increase the motivation of learners.

Second, the 3D visualisation of abstract concepts is also possible using IVR. The demonstration helps the learners to understand phenomena and dynamic relationships. These users experience VEs from multi-perspectives. The students can observe human anatomy (Karambakhsh et al., 2019) or molecule structure (Taçgın, Uluçağ & Özüağ, 2016) in a 3D environment. The representation of both intangible context and complex systems in an IVRLE not only supports the imagination of learners but also increase the curiosity of students. Students are often motivated by the opportunity to explore an IVR and learn through realistic 3D experiences (Chuah, Chen, & Teh, 2011). According to Liou, Yang, Chen, and Tarng (2017), IVR can facilitate learners' knowledge construction process and reduce cognitive load. However, there is no consensus about the cognitive effects of IVRLEs. Depending on the design features of IVRLEs, this representation either might cause to the cognitive load (Makransky, Terkildsen & Mayer, 2019) or can help to reduce the cognitive burden (Hanson & Shelton, 2008).

The third affordance of IVRLEs comes from using computer systems. IVRLEs are capable of logging the data of users; therefore, computer-structured VWs allow users to reflect and evaluate their learning processes (Chuah et al., 2011). After implementing the learning scenario, the learners can review their actions and observe the correct practices of their incorrect implementations. The cognitive self-organisational skills of learners might become more robust as a result of reflecting upon the consequences of their learning experiences (Hanson & Shelton, 2008).

Lastly, in an interactive IVRLE, the learners become an active participant rather than being a passive audience. The users can reinforce their psychomotor skills after implementing a learning scenario via interacting the virtual content. The learners can experience the virtual scenario again and again until they become sure that they learnt. This repetitive implementation opportunity is a pearl for skill training for gaining expertise in several fields like medical (Herrmann-Werner et al., 2013). According to the design and scenario, IVR can provide discovery, inquiry and situated learning in a controlled and safe environment (Jen, 2007).

The majority of educational VR studies are focused on the cognitive and emotional effects of IVR (Chuah et al., 2011). However, IVR might be used to teach psychomotor skills, complex systems, and even attitudes. Due to the unique capabilities of IVR, selecting adequate technology and designing a LE is essential to maximise the learning benefits. Designing IVRLE draws upon the inter-relationship between the technological aptitudes and the psychological sense of presence.

IVR Environment Design

There are no well-accepted principles for designing 3D IVR. Several factors can reshape the specifications of LE, and the pathway of ID can refresh during development. Project management stages can be helpful in planning and coordinating this process (Tacgin, 2018).

After determining the learning goals of the IVR environment, selecting affordable devices is important (Pantelidis, 1997; Vergara, Rubio, & Lorenzo, 2017). The initial step should be choosing the adequate HMD, which can be a tethered (connected via a data cable to the computer), mobile phone-integrated or standalone. Oculus Rift or HTC Vive are examples of tethered HMD. Previous studies showed that cable and computer dependency of tethered HMDs might limit the experience of users (Taçgın, 2017) and these devices are only suitable for indoors (Santos et al., 2009). Mobile phone integrated HMDs (e.g. Cardboard, Merge) are cheaper; however, the limited interaction capabilities (Anthes, García-Hernández, Wiedemann, & Kranzlmüller, 2016) make them less attractive. Additionally, the high latency of mobile-based HMDs can cause cybersickness for some users. These HMDs might be more suitable for watching 360° videos. Standalone HMDs like Oculus Go, Oculus Quest or HTC Focus provide portable, all in one and high quality user experiences.

Each HMD has different technical features that affect the design of the IVR environment. In particular, the degree of freedom (DoF) (Coulter, Saland, Caudell, Goldsmith, & Alverson, 2007) and field of view

(FoV) are essential components in defining the user's visual and interactive experience. HMDs can either be 3DoF or 6DoF. 3DoF HMDs tracks only the head movement of the users, thus, IVR users remain at a stable location during their practices, and they can move around using controllers (Alhalabi, 2016). 6DoF HMDs track both head movement and overall position to allow walking into the virtual space via physical movement. IVR designers should consider DoF before designing an active user field in the VE. For 3DoF environments, only a particular area of the presented 3D environment can be actively observed by the users at one time. The angle of the environment that can be viewed will typically range from 30 to 110 degrees according to the HMDs FoV specifications.

The other essential step of IVR design is determining the interaction type. According to Ovtcharova and Vieira (1995), interaction types for the tasks to be undertaken within an IVR provide the semantic map for the VR prototype. Therefore, interaction should be considered in the early stages, along with the overall goal of the IVR application. Designers can use controllers, gesture recognition, gaze, audial control systems or more (Sherman & Craig, 2018) for the interaction. After determining the input method for interaction, designers can build icons, buttons and other content (Alger, 2015).

There are several nuances to design of a VE. Users' familiarity with icons and metaphors is essential for this selection (Sherman & Craig, 2018). VR systems include a combination of wholly structured virtual objects, environments and avatars to provide psychological immersion using high fidelity designs. 3D modelling and selection of texture are critical for the authenticity of IVR environments (Vergara et al., 2017). Proximity to reality affects the presence of users.

Buttons and other navigation items are not components of physical reality, and consequently, there is the potential for these interaction elements to take away from the visual realism and therefore, the sense of immersion. These components of IVR should be designed using transparent (or barely visible) components (Alger, 2015). IVR environments also need adequate audio to increase psychological immersion.

Users can see a particular part of the VR environment because of the FoV. The essential content of the application should be in this zone. Main virtual objects and interactive components should be within the FoV of users. Interactive virtual objects should be placed 0.5-1m from users for 3DoF HMD applications because users cannot see objects closer than this distance (Alger, 2015).

Each IVR environment has unique structural and visual features to design. Experiencing and evaluating the various IVR environments can help to stimulate the imagination of the designer to create better applications.

IVR Instructional Design

The integration of game components and emerging technologies (like IVR) into LEs has the potential to enhance the learning experience of learners (Kirkley & Kirkley, 2005; Kirkley, Tomblin, & Kirkley, 2005). Today, constructivist learning theories are accepted by many educators as the underpinning pedagogical approaches behind active learning opportunities. It also acknowledged that the provision of dynamic experiential learning environments presents design challenges.

A core purpose of ID is to achieve desired learning outcomes by designing learning components in the LE. ID models generally depend on cognitive learning principles and involve the selection of learning elements to facilitate the knowledge acquisition of learners. The LE should be designed after considering the individual differences of learners in terms of their prior experiences and learning preferences.

Existing VR ID models are usually structured for designing computer-based non-IVR because of the popularity and widespread usage of e-Learning. According to Goodwin, Wiltshire, and Fiore (2015) and Kirkley and Kirkley (2005) traditional ID models for designing 2D VWs are not always suitable to design and develop IVRLEs through the different dynamics of 3D IVRLEs.

Designing IVRLEs requires the application of innovative technologies and the flexibility to adapt the ID components. The direct implementation of traditional strategies and practices to the IVRLEs might pose a problem because it requires the combination of actional, symbolic, and sensory factors to create an immersive experience (Dede, 2009; Dede et al., 2017). Conventional ID models use cognitive learning strategies to identify the learning activities likely to lead to learning outcomes. Even though well-accepted strategies like the provision of feedback and the use of drill and practice activities can still be of value in IVR, there are some unique affordances within IVRLEs which lead to the need for different design approaches.

There are few studies which propose ID for 3D VRLEs. The majority of them investigate non-IVR rather than IVR. Additionally, several studies have suggested underpinning frameworks for understanding the unique opportunities or learning affordances provided by VRLEs. Experiential Modes model of Appelman (2005), the sample and parameters of Chuah et al. (2011), the model of Chen, Toh, and Fauzy (2004), the model of Goodwin et al. (2015), the design proposal of Hanson and Shelton (2008), the learning affordance model of Dalgarno and Lee (Dalgarno & Lee, 2010) and the model for sensory IVR (Tacgin, 2018) provide building blocks towards a design model for IVRLEs. This study uses the keystones of these models and applies them to create a useful and adaptable IVRLE design model.

Experiential Modes (EM)

EM is a kind of umbrella model to determine the essential components of IVRLEs. According to Appelman (2005), the creation of LEs focuses on what educators want to do, rather than the desired experiences of the learner. The increasing experiential features of dynamic IVRLEs presents a challenge for instructional designers. EM was developed to help identify the fundamental variables for consideration within the design of IVRLEs. EM provides a methodology to help designers to specify the components of a student-centred LE.

Even though EM was not empirically tested by Appelman, the offered framework of EM helps to create a bridge between the attributes of the LE and components of an IVRLE which can be perceived by the learner. Therefore, designers can select suitable techniques to translate their ideas for a LE into an IVRLE. Once EM is structured, the desired perceptions, related components and their features, adequate technology, methodology, and physical environment can be designated (Appelman, 2005) following the components presented in Table 1.

Table 1. The components of EM adapted from (Appelman, 2005)

	Learning environment attributes		Learners perceptions within the environment		
Features controlled by the designer	Virtuality	The degree of representation of persons, places, or things	Interaction	Communication or contact with a person or thing	***Physical environment-related***
	Physical structures & background	Infrastructures: hidden affordances or capabilities Superstructures: real or virtual definitions of space Background: smells, sound, & light	Sensory immersion	Engagement through visual, auditory, haptic, kinesthetic, & olfactory senses	
	Spatial boundaries	Real or virtual limitations of access or motion	Mobility	Freedom of motion to another place	
	Time boundaries	Limits of time imposed on activities	Apperception of time	The apperception of the flow of time	***Related to perceived and applied technology and methodologies***
	Individuals, objects, and events	Interaction with an existing person, environment, or object	Access to information	Options available for gathering information	
	Technologic features	Tools and processes available to use	User control / manipulation	The functionality and the features of the technologies	
	Density of context	The context of regular content from the initial level of learning	Perception of contents	Awareness of the scope of content	***Related to thought the idea of content***
	Tangibility	Lack of embodying concepts	Cognitive change	Understanding and perceiving new procedures, concepts, and principles	
	Reality	The degree of probability with a real person, area, object or process	Emotional changes	Building new attitudes and values of people, scope, space or objects	

According to Appelman, determination of the required components of the LE may takes hours, days or even weeks. Designers can use the EM model for selecting the macro elements of their LE, but ID focuses on the micro-decisions as well. Dexterity of designers will reshape and construct these micro-decisions.

The Model of Chen et al. (2004)

Chen et al. (2004) developed an ID model for VRLEs building on Mayer's multimedia principles grounded in cognitive load theory along with the constructivist paradigm. Their framework applied the stages of recursive, reflective design and development. The design, development, and evaluation stages of LE are used repetitively after a participatory nonlinear design process that takes account of the desired learning components. During this nonlinear process, a summative evaluation, packaging, diffusion, and adaptation stages are implemented to finalise the LE. Chen applied this framework within her research in which she used 3D and spatial representation in the computer-based VR to facilitate learning in complex cognitive applications. Moreover, a statistically significant difference was determined between experimental (VR) and control (non-VR) groups which supported the argument that 3D contexts helped the learners in reducing cognitive effort and achieving the desired learning outcomes (Chen, 2006).

The Sample and Parameters of Chuah et al. (2011)

Chuah et al. (2011) investigated the emotional effects of design and sustainable mentoring in VRLEs. They used the Kansei Engineering methodology to support the expressions, emotions, and feelings using particular design parameters. The Semantic Differential Scale was used within data collection. They derived an ID model based on the constructivist VRLE model of Chen, Toh, and Ismail (2005). They used design components to provide (1) coaching, (2) navigational aids, (3) modelling, (4) environment richness, (5) information resources, (6) narration, (7) problem representation, (8) objectives and, (9) multimedia design principles.

After implementing their computer-based VRLE, they determined a strong relationship between the design components and the emotional change of the participants. As presented in Figure 2, the environment richness was the most strongly linked component to emotions. This link supports the importance of high fidelity design of IVRLEs. The second most effective design component was coaching, and information resources, representation of the problem and multimedia design principles were also found to be significant. Finally, scenario fidelity and interaction within the IVRLE were also remarkable, along with learning components and instructions IVRLEs.

The Model of Goodwin et al. (2015)

Despite the lack of strategy and design principles, Goodwin et al. (2015) argue that VRLE can potentially optimise the learning outcomes of individuals. Their approach is based on cognitive science principles and builds on their investigation of the interaction between brain, body and the environment. According to their proposal, structuring a VRLE is essential to teach theoretical knowledge and psychomotor skills. They offered a 'Strategy of Structured Enactive Engagement in Learning (SEEL)'. The necessary steps of this strategy are: (1) Analyze / Determine Instructional Context, (2) Analyze / Identify Instructional Resources, (3) Establish / Revise the Learning Environment, (4) Implement/Guide Learning and (5) Analyze/Assess/Revise Learning Outcomes.

The Design Proposal of Hanson and Shelton (2008)

Hanson and Shelton (2008) proposed an ID model for IVRLEs grounded in design-based research methodology and building on the analysis and design phases of the ADDIE model.

In their model, determining the learning outcomes and adequate learning strategies are essential steps in determining the components of a VRLE. After deciding on these components, the features of the interface emerge seamlessly. They applied these stages to develop a discovery-based VRLE (Hanson &

Shelton, 2008); however, they did not implement their VRLE design model and evaluate its applicability to the development of effective VRLEs.

The Model of Dalgarno and Lee (2010)

Dalgarno and Lee (2010) presented a general model illustrating the unique characteristics and learning affordances of VRLEs. They aimed to reveal critical features of VRLEs and the connection of these essential features to specific categories of learning outcomes. Figure 1 introduces this model.

Figure 1. The affordance model for 3D virtual learning environments (Dalgarno & Lee, 2010)

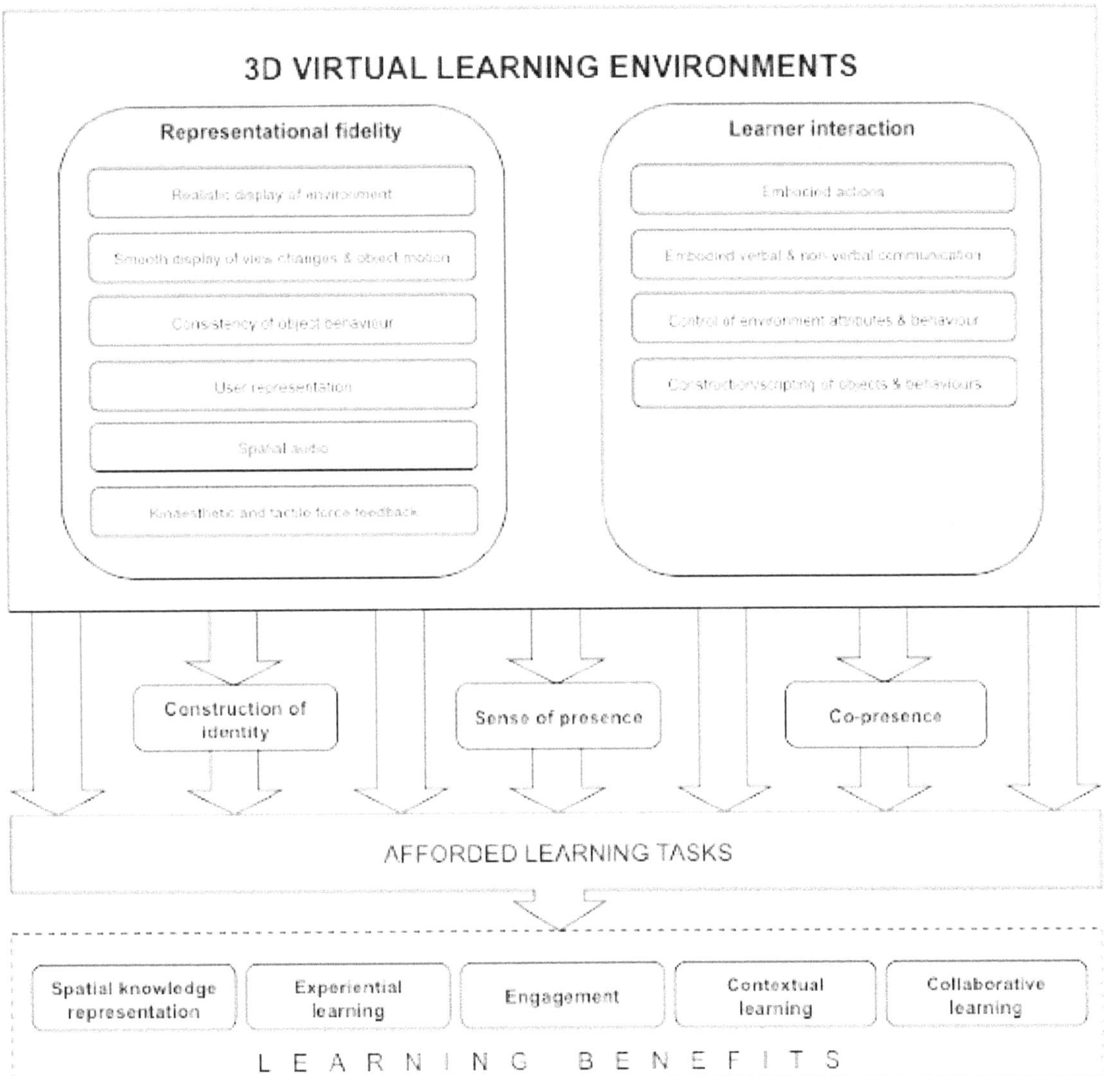

Even though this model was not tested empirically, it was derived following an extensive review of a large number of theoretical and empirical studies. Presence, interaction, and fidelity are offered as the critical components of 3D VRLEs. They also emphasised the importance of representation of spatial knowledge. According to their model, 3D VRLEs are particularly suitable for collaborative, experimental and contextual learning.

Sensory Immersive VR Simulation Development Model of Tacgin

Tacgin (2018); Taçgın (2017) designed, developed and evaluated an IVRLE to teach concepts and procedures. She organized the ID process using project management techniques. After generating the initial prototype of the IVRLE, she applied this environment on the target audience. She continued with cyclic design-development and evaluation phases to reach the final version of the IVRLE.

Figure 2. Sensory immersive VR simulation development model in procedural Learning (Tacgin,2018)

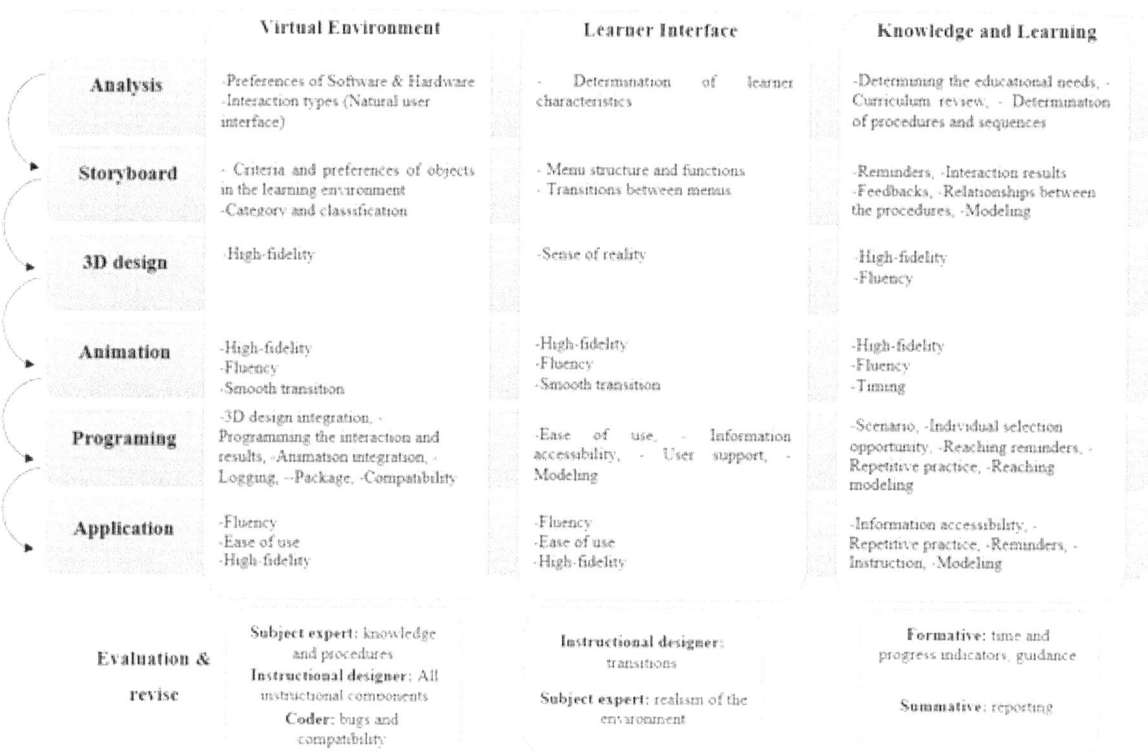

As seen in Figure 2, this model proposes that design be undertaken iteratively during development. After the project completed, the ID stages are illustrated as presented in Figure 2. According to this model, there are three essential components to design of an IVRLE: (1) virtual environment, (2) learner interface and (3) knowledge and learning. This model uses seven basic processes sequentially and iteratively during development. Each step includes distinct characteristics to support the teaching of concepts and procedures.

Table 2. Instructional design components in VR environments (Tacgin, 2018)

Features of the environment	Learning method	Key features
Discover	Discovery-based	Interactivity Navigation Instruction and guidance Monitoring Degree of immersion High fidelity Embodiment Recording Instant feedback Repeatability Context Design components Motivators Learning outcomes
Embodiment	Individual	
Experimentation	Experiential	
Questioning	Inquiry-based	
Problem-solving	Problem scenario	

Afforded Conditions to Use IVRLE

When should we use IVRLE to teach? The answer to this question should emerge as part of a needs analysis. IVR might be a useful tool to teach both knowledge and skills. Designers can develop IVRLEs to teach concepts, procedures, phenomenon or attitudes to the learners.

Considering the intuitive interactivity of IVR, teaching hands-on practices might be sufficient using IVRLE. IVRLEs are suitable to teach theoretical knowledge as well. The visualisation power of IVR facilitates to understand complex systems or intangible concepts. Both synchronous and repetitive representation of visuals, texts or audial impressions helps brains' dual coding process to facilitate the mental imagery and memorisation.

The high-fidelity presentation of visuals and scenarios is the keystone to teach different phenomenon and attitude. The trainers can experience circumstances and cases in the structured VW and become able to observe the alternative consequences of their actions that support situation learning.

IVR might support both individual and collaborative learning. Moving from the research and mentioned reasons IVRLE might be appropriately used to:

- Teach psychomotor skills,
- Teach sequential procedural knowledge and rules,
- Demonstrate the complex and intangible concepts and mechanisms,
- Support decision making of the learners providing alternative scenarios and using discovery learning,
- Regulate attitudes of learners using provided alternative scenarios,
- Apply experiential, problem based or inquiry learning,
- Learn high-risk situations into the low-risk LE,

The demographic abilities, cognitive styles and prior knowledge of the learners are also essential to determine an adequate learning strategy before designing IVRLE. Table 2 offers key features of IVRLEs for particular learning strategies.

Figure 3. Instructional Design Model for Immersive Virtual Reality Learning Environments

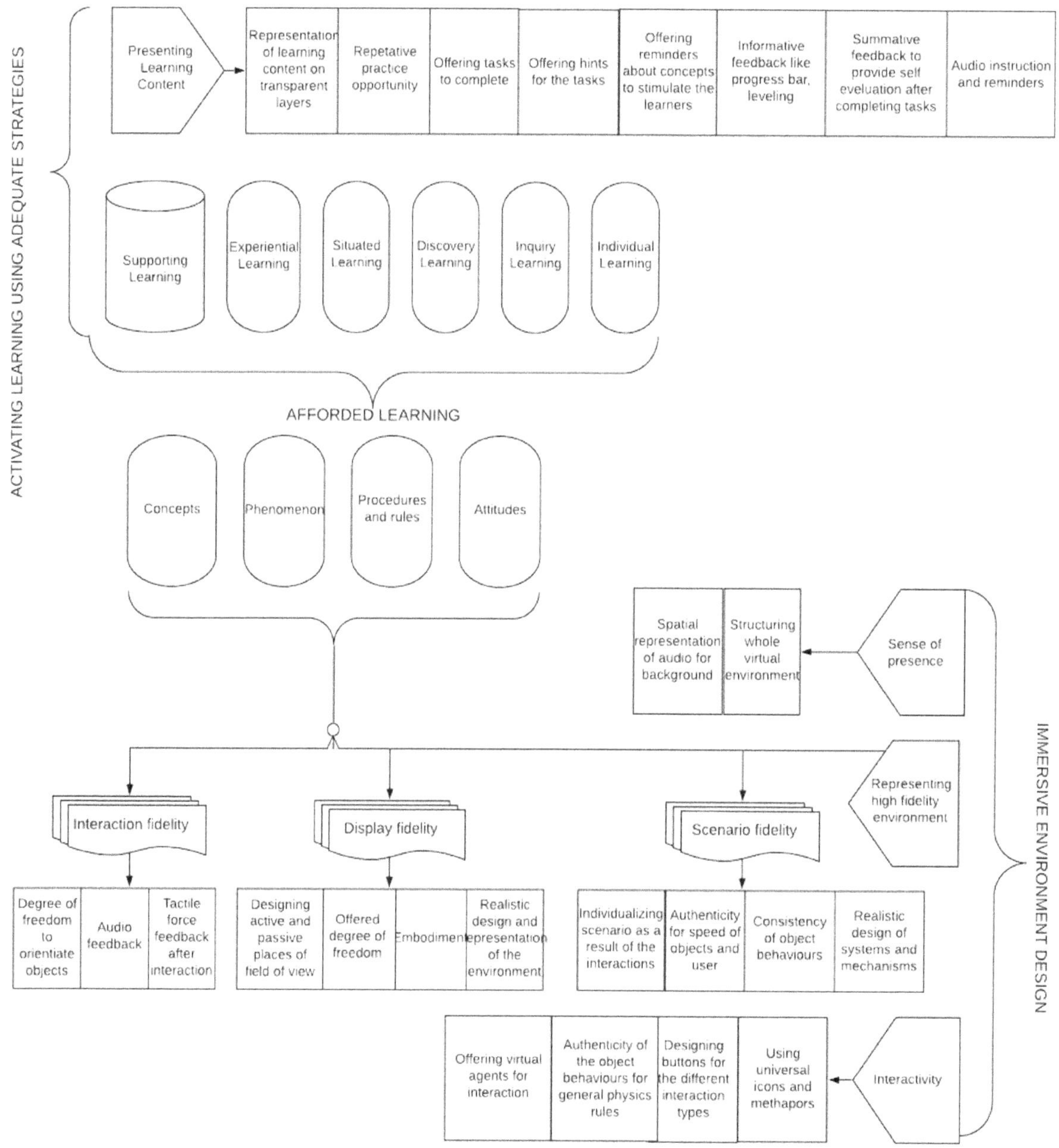

The research indicates that IVRLEs provide more effective learning outcomes for teenagers and adults rather than children, although there have been few studies to date concerning IVR usage by children. Well-designed IVRLEs should consist of high fidelity components to provide psychological presence; therefore, this environment can facilitate the learning process of both expert and novice learners.

THE PROPOSED MODEL

Under the light of mentioned above, Figure 3 presents a conceptual ID model for designing IVRLEs. This model was developed considering the nature and features of IVR environments after applying the stages of Tacgin (2018) model and characteristic components of Dalgarno and Lee (2010) model.

The conventional ID models use learning space sufficiently to present information to the learners. Computer-aided models can be used to represent the knowledge on-screen; therefore, arranging learning components and link them for interaction are significant for these traditional models. However, the dynamics of IVR environments are different, and knowledge representation on IVR should be more flexible than non-immersive ones. Users can interact with each virtual object realistically; for instance, they can interact with the door instead of an exit button to quit from the application. This authenticity is essential because these navigation panels or texts are not part of our physical reality and offering these components using transparent interfaces can contribute to a sense of immersion within an IVRLE.

In terms of providing immersion, authenticity is essential for giving a feeling of presence in IVR. That is why VW should reflect the duplication of reality wherever possible. If designers develop boxer application, they should use boxer gloves instead of controllers or sterile doctor gloves for medical training applications. Using this authentic representation is likely to have an effect on motivation, learning and feeling like `being in there`.

The expected authenticity of IVRLE can be provided via scenario, display and interaction fidelity. Each kind of fidelity is significant to support the sense of presence, but depending on the desired learning outcomes, their importance can vary. For example, interaction and represented real-life conditions might be essential for skill-based training. Scenario and responsive feedback might be sufficient to teach attitudes to the learners.

A particular ID model cannot be accepted as wholly accurate to apply, but the main structure can be modified to design LE. This study used the presented ID model to design and develop an IVRLE.

METHOD: APPLYING THE MODEL

The study described in this section drew upon the model above in the design of an IVRLE to teach surgical procedures to trainee nurses. The offered model in this study built upon the models of Dalgarno and Tacgin. The proposed model of Tacgin (2017) was structured using the essential components of Dalgarno's (2010) affordance model to develop a surgical training IVRLE to teach preoperative procedures and concepts to the nursing students.

The initial version of myVOR was empirically tested on 14 participants four times in a month, and myVOR was revised using the gathered data and feedbacks of the participants. The results of Tacgin's study demonstrated some particular deficiencies of the initial version of myVOR. Computer dependency and cables of tethered HMD caused usability issues for the participants. The display quality and the impact of physical factors like sunlight influenced the IVRLE experience of participants. Also, each of the participants required practice prior to learning via IVRLE and assumed a level of prior theoretical knowledge, they recommended enhancements to the IVRLE incorporating additional hints and instructions.

This study used the data of the previous design-based research to develop the second version of myVOR. The development story of myVOR was introduced by Tacgin (2019) stage by stage. The second version of myVOR was designed applying the steps of the proposed ID model, and one of the standalone high-quality HMD; Oculus Quest was used for this version. This study introduces myVOR 2.0 project and its features to explain the usage of the proposed model.

Through the use of design-based research, the study aimed to demonstrate the relationship between theory-design-implementation while embodying principles about teaching and learning (Cengizhan, 2007). Design-based research is intrinsically linked to, and its development nourished by, multiple designs and research methodologies. Researchers assume the functions of both designers and researchers, drawing on procedures and methods from both fields, in the form of a hybrid methodology (Wang & Hannafin, 2005).

The necessities of the design-based research process (Barab, 2006; Barab & Squire, 2004; Wang & Hannafin, 2005) have been ordered as (1) often conducted within a single setting over a long time, (2) iterative cycles of design, enactment, analysis, and redesign, (3) contextually dependent interventions, (4) document and connect outcomes with the development process and the authentic setting, (5) collaboration between practitioners and researchers and (6) lead to the development of knowledge that can be used in practice and can inform practitioners and other designers.

The Project

The Project Team and Process

The ideal core team to develop an IVRLE should include at least an instructional designer, a 3D model designer, and a coder. The subject expert/s should be part of this process, depending on the field and learning outcomes.

Two 3D designers, an instructional designer, a nurse, and a coder, developed the initial version of myVOR. The first version of myVOR was developed in eight months, and the 3D designers designed 224 surgical instruments and the other components of the virtual operating room. Also, some of the 3D models were used from the Unity Asset Store.

This version of myVOR was developed by an instructional designer in three months who designed, integrated and coded to adopt a new version to the Oculus Quest.

1st Step: Analysis of Practical Problems

This project aimed to develop an IVRLE to teach concepts to the learners. The experimental and discovery learning methods are used to teach the names of surgical instruments.

The results of the previous study (Taçgın, 2017) indicated a lack of theoretical knowledge of the 3rd-year nursing candidates about the surgical instruments. They were not familiar with the terms and the atmosphere of the operating room despite the taken lectures and internship because of the high-risk conditions. The results of the initial research showed that the students required hints and instructions to guide them during learning and repetitive implementation opportunities to reach the desired learning outcomes. High fidelity and realistic representation of the tools and the operating room were also essential to comprehend the differences between similar-looking surgical instruments. The following study Taçgın (2020) applied myVOR 1.0 to the 1st-year students to compare the perceived effectiveness of the LE. The results showed that the perceived effectiveness of myVOR 1.0 was somewhat dependent upon the prior knowledge of the learners.

These results reveal the significance of design regarding the learning needs of learners. In particular of myVOR, learners need better display quality to investigate the instrument detail. The learning outcomes should be offered clearly, and instructions should be easy to access. They also need a more ergonomic and standalone HMD to experience myVOR freely.

2nd Step: Development of the Solutions

The needs analysis within the project identified specific learning requirements. Repetitive experience, demonstration, a lack of practice into the field, the unique needs of adult learners, realistic representation of the spatial objects, concept training, familiarisation with the environment and high-risk conditions were contributing parameters to the design.

Considering today's technologies and the previous study of the researcher, IVRLE was supposed to be a possible solution. High fidelity design can be presented via a high-quality display. Besides, previous studies showed that cables of tethered HMDs could be barriers to learning. The HMD chosen for the project should be ergonomic, easy to use, and high resolution. It also should provide expanded interaction opportunities to users.

Regarding the requirement, Oculus Quest was selected as a standalone HMD. Designed virtual operating room and the surgical instruments were integrated using the Unity game engine.

Names and features of each interactive virtual object were assigned to provide concept training. The interaction was added to all of the small virtual objects in myVOR 2.0 including documents, notebook, clamps, retractors, etc. due to providing a flexible discovery learning environment to the students.

Navigation components were added to jump between scenes. Four main scenes were developed for this virtual operating room. First, the main scene was designed to teach surgical instruments and discover the operating room. Second, a virtual agent was used in the instruction scene to introduce the usage of controllers. Third, the videos were recorded within a real operating room with the support of an experienced surgical nurse, and these video recordings were added to help learners to comprehend how these instruments should be used in real-life situations. Lastly, the practice scene was designed to implement the stages, offered in the videos, and using the surgical instruments for preparing the operating room before the surgery.

Audio and haptic feedbacks were added for grab interaction; thus, when the user grabs an item into myVOR 2.0, the controllers vibrate, and the user hears an appropriate sound effect. Moreover, the progress bar was added to observe how many items had been discovered so far during myVOR 2.0 experience.

Lighting and textures of the virtual operating room were set to increase the fidelity and presence of the learners. Sterile hand representation and animation were used instead of the controllers to help contribute to a sense of presence.

3rd Step: Evaluating Research Solutions in Practice

Seven instructional designers –a male and six females – evaluated the usability of successive versions of myVOR 2.0 four times within a month. The age of participants varied from 30 to 65. The male participant had VR experience; however, only one female participant had VR experience before this project. The other five participants used an HMD for the first time.

Figure 4. The video selection screen of myVOR

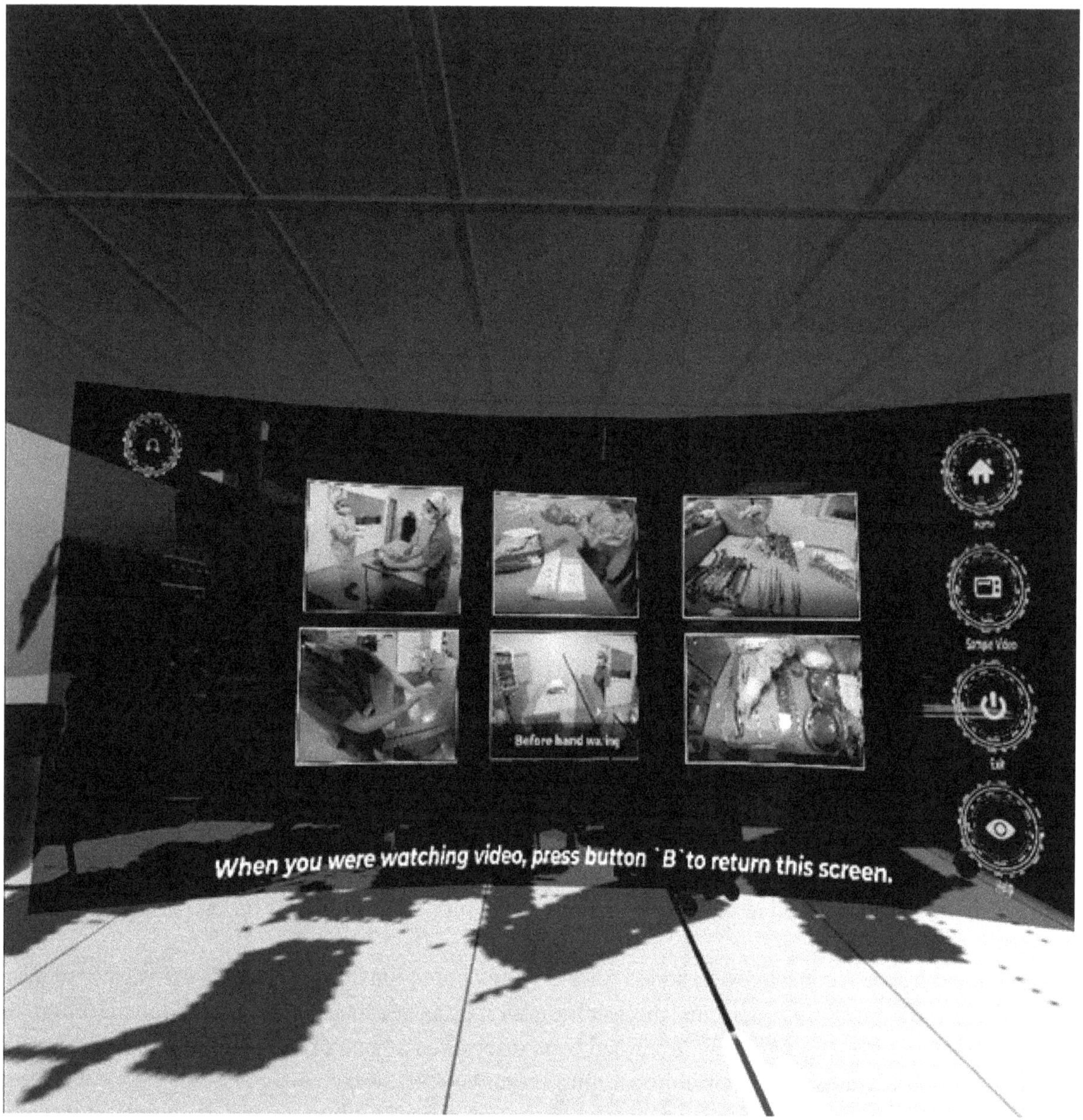

After each implementation, the researcher revised the interface and features of myVOR drawing on the feedback of the participants. A video camera was used to record each session during the application, and participants' verbal feedback was analysed using these recordings.

The first session was an adaptation process for the participants. They were surprised by the realistic design of the environment. They tried to learn the usage of controllers. Despite the 6DoF HMD, the participants were not able to physically walk around all the time because of the boundaries of physical space. The virtual operating room was larger than the real place. In this case, they used the left-hand scroll button to move around or right-hand scroll buttons to rotate the room. The moving speed with a scroll was arranged as 0.5 by the researcher. The participants suggested that this speed was too fast and might cause dizziness. Following the direction of a researcher, they discovered and walked around the operating room, grabbed the items, read their names and features, looked out of the window and located the surgical nurse in the VE, visited the other scenes, and watched videos. During the first session, it was determined that participants had trouble reading the menu items. Also, they felt dizziness when they were watching the video recordings. Videos were recorded as 2D and presented using `play far plane` option.

To explore whether the participant's initial reactions might have been influenced by the unfamiliarity or novelty of the IVRLE, no changes were made to the environment between the first and second sessions. It was thought that participant's reactions might have been influenced by the fact that this was the first VR experience for the majority of them. Therewithal, four of the participants evaluated the speed slower in the second session than the first session. The others claimed that they did not notice the difference for speed, but they also felt more comfortable than the first session. Also, five of the participants saw some of the virtual items for the first time, and they suggested that they might be newly added. Their problems reading menu items persisted, and they mentioned that the texts below the menu icons were not readable and seemed to be flickering. Their problems watching the video persisted for some of the videos. In the second session, the familiarity of the participant was higher, and they asked for tasks to do.

Before the third session, a new panel was added to present a set of intended learning outcomes of myVOR 2.0, the speed was decreased 0.5 to 0.4, and the bigger font size was used for the menu items. Except for one participant, none of them noticed the differences in speed. They liked to see learning outcomes but required more specific tasks. Furthermore, they were able to read the menu items, but they said that it was still flickering.

Texts of the menu had a bright turquoise colour. The researcher noticed that the reason for perceived flickering from a distance was the brightness of this colour. The brightness was reduced for the fourth session. The learning outcomes were reorganised, and a new scene was added to provide practice opportunity after learning. At the practice screen, an empty surgical container, basket, and two extra tables were offered to participants. Two hints were provided to set arrangements. They should replace the items after watching related videos. They were able to follow how many instruments they arranged using the progress bar. They can carry the tools one by one, or they can use the container to select the items as they wish and bring them cumulatively.

During the fourth session, it was observed that they wanted to complete their tasks, followed the instructions and hints and, spend much more time into myVOR.

4th Step: Reflecting Design Principles to Product

High fidelity: myVOR 2.0 was designed as a duplication of the real operating room. The monitors and the surgical instruments were created realistically, considering the serration, jaws, material, textures as presented in Figure 5. After the interaction, **motion and reflections** of these instruments were realistic thanks to the use of **gravity and kinematic** features. The users can move around freely, so mesh collider was assigned to all of the items into myVOR. **Curved and transparent panels** were used for supporting immersion.

Figure 5. The scenes and interfaces of myVOR

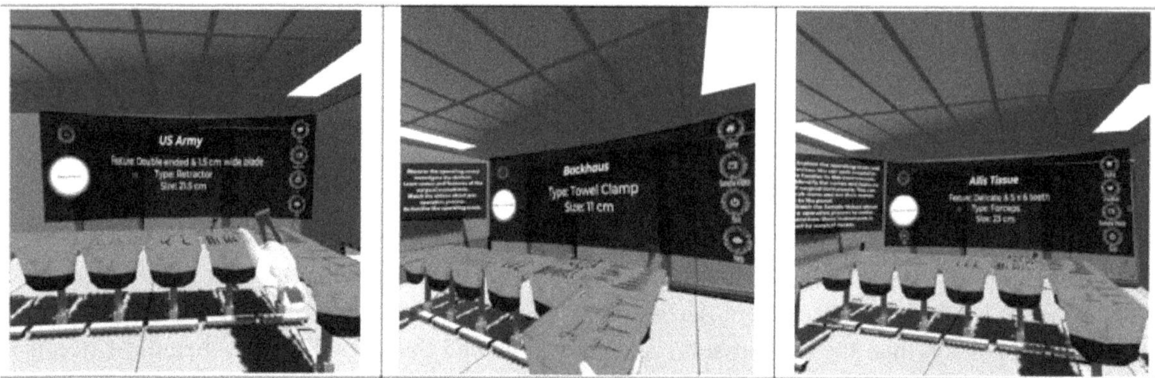

Session 1 and 2	Session 3	Session 4

Interaction: The users can interact with every small item into myVOR. They were able to use both of their hands. They can interact with the menu items or other navigation components from a **distance**. When they targeted to the related object from a distance, they can see the line from their hand to the item to focus it.

Feedback: The **haptic** feedback was offered via the vibration of controllers. The users heard two different picks up the **sound** for the metal items, and the papers. They can see the **name and the features** of the instruments at the panel screen synchronously. The **progress** bar was offered to follow how much percentage of myVOR was discovered or tools arranged.

Figure 6. Practice scenes of myVOR

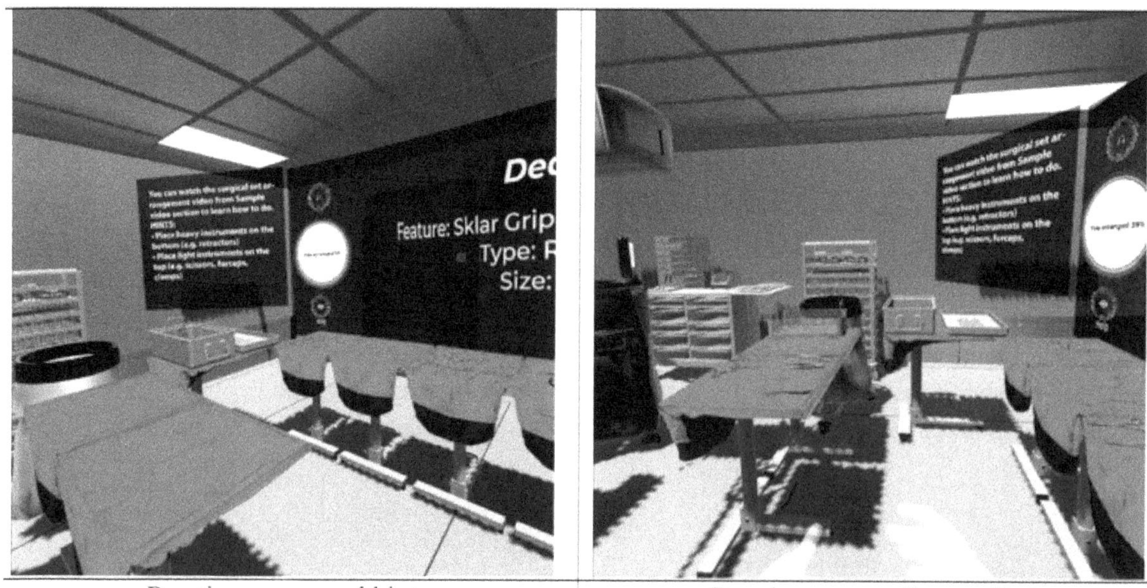

Practice screen and hints	Practice screen after applied

Practice: The practice scene (Figure 6) was added to provide an opportunity to apply the stages presented at the video scene. This scene aimed to facilitate the **knowledge acquisition** of the learners. **Tasks** and **hints** were offered into this screen.

Instruction: Three fundamental information was offered in the instruction scene to teach the **usage** of controllers. Also, **audio** information and **learning outcomes** were available for each stage. Vocalising videos provide multi-information channels for users.

Figure 7. The instruction screen and the virtual agent of myVOR

Virtual agent: As seen in Figure 7, a modelled surgical nurse was used as a virtual agent. During the application, she was typing behind the room, and the users can hear the typing sound from a 10-metre distance. Also, she presented the instruction of myVOR in the related scene.

Navigation: The universal **metaphors** were used for the **icons** of menu items. Each button was designed for standard and **hover** features. The menu items were arranged to be **accessible**.

Audio: Two different **sound effects** were used to grab action. The typing sound effect was added to perceive from 10 meters distance to the users, and the virtual surgical nurse was selected as a sound resource **(background sounds).** The other sound effect was used for activating hover features of menu items. Besides, audio information was added to every scene to provide learning outcomes, instruction and the purpose of the scenes. The researcher dubbed all of the videos. Even water sounds (e.g. sterile hand washing) or the real hospital background sounds were added to the videos to support immersion.

RECOMMENDATIONS AND CONCLUSION

There are numerous of IVR studies in the literature, but very few reports on a systematic design and development process. Those that have reported on systematic design processes have tended to propose models appropriate for non-IVRLE. These models don't take account of the unique affordances of IVRLEs. Additionally, those proposing design processes tend to be somewhat theoretical, and they propose models that haven't been testing in practice. It has been argued in this paper that the distinguishing features of IVR environments require a fresh view for designing IVRLEs. Accordingly, an ID model for creating IVRLEs has been proposed, and this model has been applied to the development of a sample IVRLE.

Using project management stages and scientific methods for ID can help designers to increase learning outcomes (Tacgin, 2018); thus, design-based research methodology can be a valuable pathway for designers. Offering an ID model after applying the stages of design-based research methodology requires long term research that consists of gathering and analysing qualitative and quantitative data.

Selecting learning strategies and techniques after a thorough needs analysis is an essential step before deciding to develop an IVRLE. The prior knowledge and age of the target audience are also important. Furthermore, the design features of IVRLEs are not only related to the learning subject and its requirements but also the functionalities of selected hardware might either restrict or expand the design opportunities of IVRLEs.

Equally critical is the choice of an instructional strategy to achieve the desired learning outcomes. The specifications of the target audience (Elmqaddem, 2019; Taçgın, 2020), along with the intended learning outcomes and instructional approach, will then guide the decision about the hardware and software components of the IVRLE. This stage also helps to determine the required expertise within the project team. Typically, IVRLE creation process requires instructional designers, graphical designers, subject experts, coders and even set designers, prop creators, and sound effects people skilled in hardware integration and probably an audio/video engineer because virtual objects need to be modelled and painted, sounds must be recorded, created, or algorithmically shaped, the physics simulations and the world must be programmed, the interface must be designed and programmed. Moreover, the physical hardware must be acquired, integrated, and installed in the venue (Sherman & Craig, 2018).

Designing 3D IVRLEs needs to draw upon both theoretical and practical knowledge, and represent them into the spatial virtual space. Before developing IVRLE, these features should be determined at the stage of design using the storyboard to create the prototype of an actual IVRLE (Tacgin, 2019). A storyboard can help to see interactions, feedbacks, learning components, relationships and other components of the IVRLE. The development should be initiated after having a consensus by team members about the storyboard.

Designing IVR has different dynamics than non-IVR. The main advantage of IVR is providing a powerful sense of presence using various design components to support immersion. The authenticity of IVRLE is essential to surrounding the perception of users, and it can be represented via a realistic scenario, display fidelity and interaction features. According to Makransky, Terkildsen, and Mayer (2019) just providing presence is not enough to achieve learning because in some cases IVR can cause cognitive overload on learners. The reason for these results might be related to the application of ID. According to Fowler (2015), the model of Dalgarno and Lee (2010) has missing pedagogical components to consider and he proposed an enhanced version of this model; however, that model has not yet been empirically evaluated.

Duplication of realistic visuals, interactions and consequences facilitate learning and scaffolding of learners. Using virtual agents and characters also have greater effects on the learners to reinforce their immersion and presence (Fox, Ahn, et al., 2015). According to research, in well-designed environments, learners will have more excellent retention of knowledge and understanding of the content and keep their attention longer in the LE (Parong & Mayer, 2018). Designing learning scenarios and offering individual cases in the IVRLE can also contribute to attitudinal outcomes. Experiencing different high-risk circumstances in safer IVRLE also helps to gain the required expertise for several fields. Provided high fidelity and authenticity of a LE can change according to the desired learning outcomes.

The literature has several significant studies which seek to find the ideal ID model for the development of IVRLEs. Each of these models presents different approaches and elements within the ID process. This study combined the theoretical background of the model of Dalgarno and Lee (2010) with the practical implementation and data of Tacgin (2018); (Taçgın, 2020)'s research considering the dynamics of today's IVR technologies.

It is not possible to articulate a single ID model that will be effective for every learning context. The nature of LE reshapes regarding the educational needs of the learners. Designing IVRLEs requires instructional designers to think outside the square and put aside preconceptions drawn from their previous knowledge about non-IVRs. They need to thoroughly understand the real-life situations on which the environment is based to consider the appropriate use of embodiment, immersive interactions, and physical environment characteristics. IVR environments can be designed as egocentric or exocentric. Still, the egocentric design is recommended (Angulo & de Velasco, 2014) in this research to put users to the centre of VE to provide the feeling of `being in there` and increase psychological immersion.

REFERENCES

Aebersold, M., Voepel-Lewis, T., Cherara, L., Weber, M., Khouri, C., Levine, R., & Tait, A. R. (2018). Interactive anatomy-augmented virtual simulation training. *Clinical Simulation in Nursing*, *15*, 34–41. doi:10.1016/j.ecns.2017.09.008 PMID:29861797

Aguinas, H., Henle, C. A., & Beaty, J. C. Jr. (2001). Virtual reality technology: A new tool for personnel selection. *International Journal of Selection and Assessment*, *9*(1-2), 70–83. doi:10.1111/1468-2389.00164

Alger, M. (2015). *Visual design methods for virtual reality*. Ravensbourne. http://aperturesciencellc.com/vr/VisualDesignMethodsforVR_MikeAlger.pdf

Alhalabi, W. (2016). Virtual reality systems enhance students' achievements in engineering education. *Behaviour & Information Technology*, *35*(11), 919–925. doi:10.1080/0144929X.2016.1212931

Alqahtani, A. S., Daghestani, L. F., & Ibrahim, L. F. (2017). Environments and System Types of Virtual Reality Technology in STEM: A Survey. *International Journal of Advanced Computer Science and Applications*, *8*(6).

Andersen, S. A. W., Konge, L., & Sørensen, M. S. (2018). The effect of distributed virtual reality simulation training on cognitive load during subsequent dissection training. *Medical Teacher*, *40*(7), 684–689. doi:10.1080/0142159X.2018.1465182 PMID:29730952

Angulo, A., & de Velasco, G. V. (2014). Immersive simulation of architectural spatial experiences. *Proceedings of the XVII Conference of the Iberoamerican Society of Digital Graphics (SIGraDi)*.

Anthes, C., García-Hernández, R. J., Wiedemann, M., & Kranzlmüller, D. (2016). *State of the art of virtual reality technology*. Paper presented at the 2016 IEEE Aerospace Conference. 10.1109/AERO.2016.7500674

Appelman, R. (2005). Designing experiential modes: A key focus for immersive learning environments. *TechTrends*, *49*(3), 64–74. doi:10.1007/BF02763648

Azuma, R., Baillot, Y., Behringer, R., Feiner, S., Julier, S., & MacIntyre, B. (2001). Recent advances in augmented reality. *IEEE Computer Graphics and Applications*, *21*(6), 34–47. doi:10.1109/38.963459

Bamodu, O., & Ye, X. M. (2013). *Virtual reality and virtual reality system components*, Paper presented at the Advanced Materials Research. 10.2991/icsem.2013.192

Barab, S. (2006). *Design-Based Research: A Methodological Toolkit for the Learning Scientist*. Cambridge University Press.

Barab, S., & Squire, K. (2004). Design-based research: Putting a stake in the ground. *Journal of the Learning Sciences*, *13*(1), 1–14. doi:10.120715327809jls1301_1

Bharathi, A. K. B. G., & Tucker, C. S. (2015). *Investigating the impact of interactive immersive virtual reality environments in enhancing task performance in online engineering design activities*, Paper presented at the ASME 2015 International Design Engineering Technical Conferences and Computers and Information in Engineering Conference. 10.1115/DETC2015-47388

Bowman, D. A., & McMahan, R. P. (2007). Virtual reality: How much immersion is enough? *Computer*, *40*(7), 36–43. doi:10.1109/MC.2007.257

Buń, P., Górski, F., & Turkowska, K. (2018). Virtual Reality Training Application of Medical Procedure. In *Smart Technology* (pp. 49–58). Springer. doi:10.1007/978-3-319-73323-4_6

Buttussi, F., & Chittaro, L. (2018). Effects of different types of virtual reality display on presence and learning in a safety training scenario. *IEEE Transactions on Visualization and Computer Graphics*, *24*(2), 1063–1076. doi:10.1109/TVCG.2017.2653117 PMID:28092563

Cengizhan, S. (2007). Proje temelli ve bilgisayar destekli öğretim tasarimlarinin; bağimli, bağimsiz ve iş birlikli öğrenme stillerine sahip öğrencilerin akademik başarilarina ve öğrenme kaliciliğina etkisi. *Türk Eğitim Bilimleri Dergisi*, *5*(3), 377–403.

Chen, C. J. (2006). The design, development and evaluation of a virtual reality based learning environment. *Australasian Journal of Educational Technology*, *22*(1), 39–63. doi:10.14742/ajet.1306

Chen, C. J., Toh, S. C., & Fauzy, W. M. (2004). The theoretical framework for designing desktop virtual reality-based learning environments. *Journal of Interactive Learning Research*, *15*(2), 147.

Chen, C. J., Toh, S. C., & Ismail, W. M. F. W. (2005). Are learning styles relevant to virtual reality? *Journal of Research on Technology in Education*, *38*(2), 123–141. doi:10.1080/15391523.2005.10782453

Chuah, K. M., Chen, C. J., & Teh, C.-S. (2011). Designing a desktop virtual reality-based learning environment with emotional consideration. *Research and Practice in Technology Enhanced Learning*, *6*(1), 25–42.

Cohen, A. R., Lohani, S., Manjila, S., Natsupakpong, S., Brown, N., & Cavusoglu, M. C. (2013). Virtual reality simulation: Basic concepts and use in endoscopic neurosurgery training. *Child's Nervous System*, *29*(8), 1235–1244. doi:10.100700381-013-2139-z PMID:23702736

Coulter, R., Saland, L., Caudell, T., Goldsmith, T. E., & Alverson, D. (2007). The effect of degree of immersion upon learning performance in virtual reality simulations for medical education. *InMedicine Meets Virtual Reality*, *15*, 155–160. PMID:17377256

Dalgarno, B., & Lee, M. J. (2010). What are the learning affordances of 3-D virtual environments? *British Journal of Educational Technology*, *41*(1), 10–32. doi:10.1111/j.1467-8535.2009.01038.x

El Araby, M. (2002). Possibilities and constraints of using virtual reality in urban design. *Proceedings of the 7Th International CORP Symposium.*

Elmqaddem, N. (2019). Augmented Reality and Virtual Reality in Education. Myth or Reality? *International Journal of Emerging Technologies in Learning*, *14*(03), 234–242. doi:10.3991/ijet.v14i03.9289

Ermi, L., & Mäyrä, F. (2005). Fundamental components of the gameplay experience: Analysing immersion, *Worlds in play. International Perspectives on Digital Games Research*, *37*(2), 37–53.

Ermi, L., & Mäyrä, F. (2011). Fundamental Components of the Gameplay Experience: Analysing Immersion In S. Günzel, M. Liebe & D. Mersch (Eds.), *DIGAREC Keynote-Lectures 2009/10* (pp. 88-115) Potsdam: University Press. http://pub.ub.uni-potsdam.de/volltexte/2011/4983

Fowler, C. (2015). Virtual reality and learning: Where is the pedagogy? *British Journal of Educational Technology*, *46*(2), 412–422. doi:10.1111/bjet.12135

Fox, J., Ahn, S. J., Janssen, J. H., Yeykelis, L., Segovia, K. Y., & Bailenson, J. N. (2015). Avatars versus agents: A meta-analysis quantifying the effect of agency on social influence. *Human-Computer Interaction*, *30*(5), 401–432. doi:10.1080/07370024.2014.921494

Goodwin, M. S., Wiltshire, T., & Fiore, S. M. (2015). *Applying research in the cognitive sciences to the design and delivery of instruction in virtual reality learning environments*, Paper presented at the International Conference on Virtual, Augmented and Mixed Reality. 10.1007/978-3-319-21067-4_29

Grabowski, A., & Jankowski, J. (2015). Virtual reality-based pilot training for underground coal miners. *Safety Science*, *72*, 310–314. doi:10.1016/j.ssci.2014.09.017

Halarnkar, P., Shah, S., Shah, H., Shah, H., & Shah, A. (2012). A review on virtual reality. *International Journal of Computer Science Issues*, *9*(6), 325.

Hanson, K., & Shelton, B. E. (2008). Design and Development of Virtual Reality: Analysis of Challenges Faced by Educators. *Journal of Educational Technology & Society*, *11*(1), 118–131.

Hu, R., Wu, Y. Y., & Shieh, C. J. (2016). Effects of Virtual Reality Integrated Creative Thinking Instruction on Students' Creative Thinking Abilities. *Eurasia Journal of Mathematics Science & Technology Education*, *12*(3), 477–486.

Hussein, M., & Nätterdal, C. (2015). *The benefits of virtual reality in education-A Comparision Study* [Bachelor of Science Thesis, University of Gothenburg, Göteborg]. https://gupea.ub.gu.se/bitstream/2077/39977/1/gupea_2077_39977_1.pdf

Jen, C. C. (2007). Formative research on the instructional design process of virtual reality based learning environments. *ICT: Providing choices for learners and learning Proceedings ASCILITE Singapore 2007*, 149-156.

Johnson, E. A. (2010). *A study of the effects of immersion on short-term spatial memory* [Master of Science, Purdue University, Indiana]. https://docs.lib.purdue.edu/cgi/viewcontent.cgi?article=1030&context=techmasters

Karambakhsh, A., Kamel, A., Sheng, B., Li, P., Yang, P., & Feng, D. D. (2019). Deep gesture interaction for augmented anatomy learning. *International Journal of Information Management*, *45*, 328–336. doi:10.1016/j.ijinfomgt.2018.03.004

Ke, F., Lee, S., & Xu, X. (2016). Teaching training in a mixed-reality integrated learning environment. *Computers in Human Behavior*, *62*, 212–220. doi:10.1016/j.chb.2016.03.094

Kirkley, S. E., & Kirkley, J. R. (2005). Creating next generation blended learning environments using mixed reality, video games and simulations. *TechTrends*, *49*(3), 42–53. doi:10.1007/BF02763646

Kirkley, S. E., Tomblin, S., & Kirkley, J. (2005). *Instructional design authoring support for the development of serious games and mixed reality training*, Paper presented at the Interservice/Industry Training, Simulation and Education Conference (I/ITSEC).

Kong, X., Liu, Y., & An, M. (2018, July). Study on the Quality of Experience Evaluation Metrics for Astronaut Virtual Training System. In *International Conference on Virtual, Augmented and Mixed Reality* (pp. 416-426). Springer. 10.1007/978-3-319-91581-4_31

Lele, A. (2013). Virtual reality and its military utility. *Journal of Ambient Intelligence and Humanized Computing*, *4*(1), 17–26. doi:10.100712652-011-0052-4

Liu, D., Dede, C., Huang, R., & Richards, J. (Eds.). (2017). *Virtual, Augmented, and Mixed Realities in Education*. Springer. doi:10.1007/978-981-10-5490-7

Ma, J. Y., & Choi, J. S. (2007). The Virtuality and Reality of Augmented Reality. *Journal of Multimedia*, *2*(1), 32–37. doi:10.4304/jmm.2.1.32-37

Mahmoud, A. H. (2001). Can Virtual Reality Simulation Techniques Reshape the Future of Environmental Simulations. *Online Planning Journal*. http://www.casa.ucl.ac.uk/planning/articles4/vrsim.htm

Makransky, G., Terkildsen, T. S., & Mayer, R. E. (2019). Adding immersive virtual reality to a science lab simulation causes more presence but less learning. *Learning and Instruction*, *60*, 225–236. doi:10.1016/j.learninstruc.2017.12.007

Mast, S. M., Kleinlogel, E. P., Tur, B., & Bachmann, M. (2018). The future of interpersonal skills development: Immersive virtual reality training with virtual humans. *Human Resource Development Quarterly*, *29*(2), 125–141. doi:10.1002/hrdq.21307

Mills, S., & Noyes, J. (1999). Virtual reality: An overview of user-related design issues revised paper for special issue on “Virtual reality: User Issues” in Interacting with Computers, May 1998. *Interacting with Computers*, *11*(4), 375–386. doi:10.1016/S0953-5438(98)00057-5

Muhanna, M. A. (2015). Virtual reality and the CAVE: Taxonomy, interaction challenges and research directions. *Journal of King Saud University-Computer and Information Sciences*, *27*(3), 344–361. doi:10.1016/j.jksuci.2014.03.023

Mujber, T. S., Szecsi, T., & Hashmi, M. S. (2004). Virtual reality applications in manufacturing process simulation. *Journal of Materials Processing Technology*, *155*, 1834–1838. doi:10.1016/j.jmatprotec.2004.04.401

Osuagwu, O., Ihedigbo, C., & Ndigwe, C. (2015). Integrating Virtual Reality (VR) into traditional instructional design. *West African Journal of Industrial and Academic Research*, *15*(1), 68–77.

Ovtcharova, J., & Vieira, A. (1995). Virtual prototyping through feature processing. In *Virtual Prototyping* (pp. 78–90). Springer. doi:10.1007/978-0-387-34904-6_7

Pantelidis, V. S. (1997). Virtual reality and engineering education. *Computer Applications in Engineering Education*, *5*(1), 3–12. doi:10.1002/(SICI)1099-0542(1997)5:1<3::AID-CAE1>3.0.CO;2-H

Papagiannakis, G., Trahanias, P., Kenanidis, E., & Tsiridis, E. (2018). Psychomotor surgical training in virtual reality. In *The Adult Hip-Master Case Series and Techniques* (pp. 827–830). Springer. doi:10.1007/978-3-319-64177-5_41

Parong, J., & Mayer, R. E. (2018). Learning science in immersive virtual reality. *Journal of Educational Psychology*, *110*(6), 785–797. doi:10.1037/edu0000241

Plante, T. G., Cage, C., Clements, S., & Stover, A. (2006). Psychological benefits of exercise paired with virtual reality: Outdoor exercise energizes whereas indoor virtual exercise relaxes. *International Journal of Stress Management*, *13*(1), 108–117. doi:10.1037/1072-5245.13.1.108

Ramasundaram, V., Grunwald, S., Mangeot, A., Comerford, N. B., & Bliss, C. (2005). Development of an environmental virtual field laboratory. *Computers & Education*, *45*(1), 21–34. doi:10.1016/j.compedu.2004.03.002

Reinhart, G., & Patron, C. (2003). Integrating augmented reality in the assembly domain-fundamentals, benefits and applications. *CIRP Annals*, *52*(1), 5–8. doi:10.1016/S0007-8506(07)60517-4

Ritz, L. T., & Buss, A. R. (2016). A framework for aligning instructional design strategies with affordances of CAVE immersive virtual reality systems. *TechTrends*, *60*(6), 549–556. doi:10.100711528-016-0085-9

Riva, G., Mantovani, F., Capideville, C. S., Preziosa, A., Morganti, F., Villani, D., Gaggioli, A., Botella, C., & Alcañiz, M. (2007). Affective interactions using virtual reality: The link between presence and emotions. *Cyberpsychology & Behavior*, *10*(1), 45–56. doi:10.1089/cpb.2006.9993 PMID:17305448

Santos, B. S., Dias, P., Pimentel, A., Baggerman, J. W., Ferreira, C., Silva, S., & Madeira, J. (2009). Head-mounted display versus desktop for 3D navigation in virtual reality: A user study. *Multimedia Tools and Applications*, *41*(1), 161–181. doi:10.100711042-008-0223-2

Sherman, W. R., & Craig, A. B. (2018). *Understanding virtual reality: Interface, application, and design*. Morgan Kaufmann, Elsevier.

Taçgın, Z. (2017). *Ameliyathanede kullanılan cerrahi setlerin öğretimine yönelik bir sanal gerçeklik simülasyonunun geliştirilmesi ve değerlendirilmesi* [Development and evaluation of a virtual reality simulation to teach surgical sets used in the operating room] (473100) [Thesis of Doctoral, Marmara University, İstanbul]. http://dspace.marmara.edu.tr/handle/11424/39092

Tacgin, Z. (2018). Proposing an Instructional Design Model With Designing and Developing Sensory Immersive VRLE to Teach Concepts And Procedures. In Academic Studies in Educational Science. Montenegro: IVPE.

Tacgin, Z. (2019). From storyboard to practice: My virtual operating room. *Fusion Journal,* (16), 36-49. https://search.informit.com.au/fullText;dn=032943111810950;res=IELLCC

Taçgın, Z. (2020a). The perceived effectiveness regarding Immersive Virtual Reality learning environments changes by the prior knowledge of learners. *Education and Information Technologies*, 1–19. doi:10.100710639-019-10088-0

Tacgin, Z. (2020b). *Virtual and Augmented Reality: An Educational Handbook*. Cambridge Scholar Press.

Taçgın, Z., Uluçay, N., & Özüağ, E. (2016). Designing and Developing an Augmented Reality Application: A Sample Of Chemistry Education. *Journal of Turkish Chemical Society: Chemical Education, 1*(1), 147–164. https://www.cambridgescholars.com/virtual-and-augmented-reality

Vergara, D., Rubio, M., & Lorenzo, M. (2017). On the design of virtual reality learning environments in engineering. *Multimodal Technologies and Interaction, 1*(2), 11. doi:10.3390/mti1020011

Wang, F., & Hannafin, M. J. (2005). Design-based research and technology-enhanced learning environments. *Educational Technology Research and Development, 53*(4), 5–23. doi:10.1007/BF02504682

ADDITIONAL READING

Alger, M. (2015). Visual design methods for virtual reality. *Ravensbourne.* http://aperturesciencellc.com/vr/VisualDesignMethodsforVR_MikeAlger. pdf

Concannon, B. J., Esmail, S., & Roduta Roberts, M. (2019). Head-Mounted Display Virtual Reality in Post-Secondary Education and Skill Training: A Systematic Review. In Frontiers in Education (Vol. 4, p. 80). Frontiers. doi:10.3389/feduc.2019.00080

Geris, A., & Özdener, N. (2020). Design Models for Developing Educational Virtual Reality Environments: A Systematic Review. In Virtual and Augmented Reality in Education, Art, and Museums (pp. 1-22). IGI Global. doi:10.4018/978-1-7998-1796-3.ch001

Radianti, J., Majchrzak, T. A., Fromm, J., & Wohlgenannt, I. (2020). A systematic review of immersive virtual reality applications for higher education: Design elements, lessons learned, and research agenda. *Computers & Education, 147*, 103778. doi:10.1016/j.compedu.2019.103778

Sonalkar, N., Mabogunje, A., Miller, M., Bailenson, J., & Leifer, L. (2020). Augmenting Learning of Design Teamwork Using Immersive Virtual Reality. In *Design Thinking Research* (pp. 67–76). Springer. doi:10.1007/978-3-030-28960-7_5

Tacgin, Z. (2020). *Virtual and Augmented Reality: An Educational Handbook*. Cambridge Scholars Publishing.

KEY TERMS AND DEFINITIONS

Experiential Learning: A learning method of teaching by doing.

Haptic: A technology which is used to provide sense of touch via additional hardware components in the virtual environment.

High Fidelity: Metaversity of virtual objects and environments.

Immersive Virtual Reality: A computer generated 3D environment which effects the reality perception of the users, whom awareness of physical reality differentiate regarding the the degree of immersion.

Standalone HMD: A new generation head mounted display technology that consists of all hardware components in a single device.

Virtual Reality: A computer generated 3D environment to simulate real or non-real conditions.

Chapter 3
Augmented Reality in Research and Practice:
A Content Analysis of Claims in Education

Mark Eugene Petrovich Jr.
https://orcid.org/0000-0002-6219-9241
Drexel University, USA

Aroutis N. Foster
Drexel University, USA

ABSTRACT

The continued development of mobile technologies has provided individuals the opportunity to work, learn, and play across a variety of contexts. The growth of these mobile devices has afforded an equivalent rise in popularity in augmented reality (AR) technologies. Though it has seen widespread adoption across a number of industries, AR has yet to see consistent integration in the realm of education. Several individuals and organizations have cited AR as being poised for mainstream educational adoption despite continued setbacks. The purpose of this chapter is to examine the claims surrounding AR for teaching and learning to understand what is being done and what is possible with the technology right now. This chapter provides a review of a variety of academic and non-academic sources towards the construction of a framework for AR for teaching and learning. Recommendations for research and practice are discussed.

INTRODUCTION

The ongoing development of digital media technologies has spurred constant debate regarding the purpose and nature of technology integration in schools (Cuban, 1986). The rise of mobile devices, including smartphones and tablets, has provided individuals with opportunities across education, work, and personal contexts. Advances in hardware and software, coupled with decreases in overall product cost, have provided access to these devices at an unprecedented rate. The Common Sense Media census reported that 91% of 8- to 18-year-olds polled have access to a smartphone in their home (Rideout &

DOI: 10.4018/978-1-7998-5043-4.ch003

Robb, 2019). Similarly, a Pew Research Center (Anderson, 2019) survey on mobile technology usage indicated that within the US 96% of respondents aged 18 or older owned their own mobile device. While mobile technologies continue their rise as an essential aspect of everyday life, individuals are granted greater access to the ability to work, learn, and play across a variety of contexts (Johnson et al., 2010). The growth of mobile devices has afforded an equivalent rise in popularity for several digital media technologies.

One such technology, augmented reality (AR), operates at the intersection of the virtual and the real. The proliferation of mobile technologies has led to widespread adoption of AR within a number of disciplines, including medicine (Eckert, Volmerg, & Friedrich, 2019), marketing and tourism (Dadwal & Hassan, 2016), and assembly training/maintenance (Webel, Bockholt, Engelke, Gavish, Olbrich, & Preusche, 2013). This technological-pedagogical revolution has been identified as being poised to profoundly transform education (Bower, Howe, McCredie, Robinson, & David, 2014). The 2010 Horizon Report (Johnson, Smith, Willis, Levine, & Haywood, 2010) suggested simple augmented reality as being two to three years from widespread adoption in the realm of education. This categorization included the adoption of well-established technologies that have become mainstream through the use of global cellular networks. In 2011, the Horizon Report reinforced its belief in augmented reality as it made its transition from a gimmick to a bonafide game-changer (Johnson, Smith, Willis, Levine, & Haywood, 2011). Despite increased interest, accessibility, and utility of AR experiences in education, the technology would disappear from the Horizon Report until 2016, when it was once again categorized as being two to three years from widespread adoption (Johnson, Becker, Cummins, Estrada, Freeman, & Hall, 2016). Without explanation, the 2018 Horizon Report cited AR as being four to five years from adoption. Though it was noted that the market for AR was growing exponentially and was expected to double within the next five years, the technology was somehow further from adoption than was predicted in previous years (Becker et al., 2018). Ultimately, the 2019 Horizon Report acknowledged the backwards progress of AR in terms of mainstream adoption (Alexander et al., 2019). Though the Horizon Report illustrates only one perspective on the current progress and future potentials of AR, it is far from the only source to claim the technology's readiness to adapt to the mainstream in education (Emiroğlu & Kurt, 2017; FitzGerald et al., 2013; Kroeker, 2010; Ong, 2010). Irrespective of the reasons for these setbacks, the experts in terms of AR are not confident the technology is prepared for mainstream adoption in education.

STATEMENT OF THE PROBLEM

Research has suggested a wide variety of potential learning outcomes from AR integration in educational contexts (Akçayır & Akçayır, 2017; Dunleavy, Dede, & Mitchell, 2009; Wu, Lee, Chang, & Liang, 2013). Though AR technologies have retained their popularity in educational research, they are seemingly no closer to widespread adoption than they were almost a decade prior. The current trajectory of research into AR for teaching and learning has yet to encourage and prepare researchers, instructors, and students for widespread adoption of this technology into the classroom and beyond. Existing studies often target the research (empirical and theoretical) literature produced in a purely academic context. Subsequently, there is a gap in terms of identifying the claims and findings from education in practice and in non-academic contexts. In order to gauge the possibilities and learning outcomes of these AR implementations for educational contexts, an evaluation of the current claims, applications, and affordances of AR must be undertaken across a variety of settings. The purpose of this study is to present an overview of various forms of literature including journal articles, online magazines, and print media in order to evaluate what is possible and what is being done right now as it relates to educational AR experiences. This study will focus on empirical and non-empirical research which elaborates on implementations across a variety of educational contexts. In order to address this purpose, the following research questions are posed:

RQ1: What are the claims surrounding augmented reality and its adoption as an educational tool?
RQ2: What themes and categorizations emerge from the claims surrounding augmented reality and its usage in educational contexts?

BACKGROUND

A Brief History of Augmented Reality

The successful implementation of an augmented, immersive, and accessible peripheral has long since been the subject of scholarly investigation. Vannevar Bush's (1945) As We May Think introduced his conceptualization of a head-mounted camera fashioned to a pair of ordinary glasses in an effort to make the wealth of human knowledge more accessible. The first occurrence of AR technologies appeared in the 1950s with the patent of cinematographer Morton Heilig's Sensorama (Matuk, 2016). The device was meant to create a physically immersive theater experience using stereoscopic images, body tilting, wind, and aromas which occurred throughout trigger points in a cinema experience. Over a decade later, Ivan Sutherland (1968) was experimenting with a stereoscopic display which projected 3D imagery directly to the wearers' field of view. The imagery displayed would change perspective based on the direction of the wearer's gaze. Sutherland's device was nicknamed "The Sword of Damocles" due to the imagery evoked by the pole that connected the display to the ceiling and its comparison to the parable by the same name. Though popularized as the first virtual reality (VR) headset, the view provided by the head-mounted display was not completely opaque (Sutherland, 1968). As a result, users were not completely cut-off from their surroundings as is expected within VR experiences. This transparency, coupled with the overlay of 3D graphics, is often cited as an early precursor to more traditional AR technologies. In 1985, the VIDEOPLACE lab introduced an early version of a human-machine interface (Krueger, Gionfriddo, & Hinrichsen, 1985). The lab utilized cameras and on-screen projections which enabled users to emit shadows that interacted with digital on-screen elements. Caudell and Mizell (1992) presented a prototype for position sensing and real-world registration which would enable a computer-generated image to be superimposed onto a real-world object. As a result of this research, Caudell coined the term augmented reality to refer to the compositing of digital images over the physical world. In what is sometimes heralded as the first "real" augmented reality system, Rosenberg (1993) presented a metaphor using Virtual Fixtures. By drawing comparison to drawing a straight line with the use of a ruler, Rosenberg discusses the reduced requirement in mental processing, increased speed in conducting the task, and increased accuracy in the outcome of the line drawing. The Virtual Fixtures system expanded on this metaphor by enabling the projection of sensory information over an individual's workspace. In one of earliest public appearances of AR technology, the NFL debuted Sportsvision in 1998 to project the yellow first-down marker on a live NFL broadcast (Taylor, 2015). For the first time, viewers could conclusively see when the football was moved past the first-down marker in real-time.

Though a variety of AR technologies were introduced across industrial, commercial, and consumer contexts since the NFL's launch of Sportsvision (e.g. NASA's X-38 navigation technology, open-source software AR toolkit, Google Glass, Microsoft HoloLens; Billinghurst, Kato, & Poupyrev, 2001; Dodevska, Mihić, & Manasijević, 2018; Lv, Feng, Li, & Feng, 2014; Yoshinaga, 2017), none of these technologies have become as pervasive as Pokemon GO. Pokemon GO, released in 2016, is an augmented reality mobile phone game that enables players to catch the eponymous Pokemon and gain rewards for physical activity. A growing body of research has examined Pokemon GO and its potential to encourage physical activity, as well as potential issues inherent in drawing attention to a mobile device in crowded cities or late at night (Althoff, White, & Horvitz, 2016; Howe, 2016; McCartney, 2016). During its rise to prominence, Pokemon GO has given equivalent attention to AR technologies broadly. With re-invigorated interest within the public sphere, augmented reality has since been poised to make the leap to mainstream adoption across a variety of contexts. Despite the increase in interest, there still exist several misunderstandings or mischaracterizations as to what constitutes an AR experience. While a variety of definitions exist, a select number of definitions have seen wide acceptance in the literature.

Defining and Characterizing Augmented Reality

Augmented reality refers to a wide range of technologies that integrate digital text, images, audio, and video onto a users' view of the physical world. Due to the ever-growing number of technologies integrating the digital and physical worlds, Milgram and Kishino (1994) presented a taxonomy of mixed reality. Their Reality-Virtuality (RV) Continuum is a means to connect completely real environments to completely virtual environments while describing the merging of real and virtual worlds as Mixed Reality (MR) in between. In offering an operational definition of AR, Milgram and Kishino (1994) state, "we take the term to refer to any case in which an otherwise real environment is augmented by means of virtual (computer graphics) objects" (p. 4). Despite the widespread use of the taxonomy in current research, the operational definition of AR is lacking in a means to separate it from other digital integration techniques such as film and digital compositing. Squire and Jan (2007) defined AR games as, "games played in the real world with the support of digital devices (PDAs, cellphones) that create a fictional layer on top of the real-world context" (p. 6). The 2010 Horizon Report defined AR as, "The concept of blending (augmenting) virtual data — information, rich media, and even live action — with what we see in the real world, for the purpose of enhancing the information we can perceive with our senses" (Johnson, Levine, Smith, & Stone, 2010, p. 21). Though these definitions acknowledge the usage of digital imagery superimposed over a physical space, they lack the specificity required to differentiate between virtual and other mixed-reality technologies.

As a result of this deficiency, the most widely accepted definition of AR characterizes it through the use of three unique aspects: 1) the combination of virtual and real objects, 2) the ability or opportunity to interact with these objects in real time, and 3) the accurate registration of three-dimensional real and virtual objects (Azuma, 1997). At the time, this definition was meant to expand AR acceptance beyond solely head-mounted display technologies while still maintaining the essential characteristics of the technology. For example, Azuma (1997) reasoned that films like Jurassic Park featured photorealistic 3D virtual objects blended with a physical environment, but it does not present an interactive medium. In presenting a succinct definition of AR, it can be understood as the overlaying of interactive digital elements onto the physical world in real time.

Augmented Reality in Education

The emergence of these immersive digital media experiences has afforded educators, learners, researchers, and practitioners the ability to approach education and training from a novel perspective. A growing body of research has examined AR experiences and their usage in educational contexts (Akçayır & Akçayır, 2017; Dalim, Kolivand, Kadhim, Sunar, & Billinghurst, 2017; Dunleavy, Dede, & Mitchell, 2009; Klopfer & Squire, 2008; Wu, Lee, Chang, & Liang, 2013). This research has presented insights surrounding the broader impact of AR in education, AR peripherals and applications, cognitive and non-cognitive learning outcomes of AR applications, and AR versus traditional applications in learning (Akçayır and Akçayır, 2017; Fotaris, Pellas, Kazanidis, & Smith, 2017; Radu, 2014).

As a result, AR technology has become akin to panacea as research has cited increased learning in the form of cognitive outcomes(e.g. critical thinking and reflection skills; Tscholl & Lindgren, 2014) and non-cognitive outcomes (i.e. presence, interest, and motivation; Guazzaroni, 2013; Sylaiou, Mania, Karoulis, & White, 2010) across a variety of contexts (e.g. early childhood to adult education, formal, informal; Bacca, Baldiris, Fabregat, & Kinshuk, 2019). In lieu of these claims, few studies have presented specific barriers to adoption for AR technologies which have the potential to contradict or disrupt these types of learning outcomes. Alkhattabi (2017) highlighted adoption barriers in schools based on teacher experience and proficiency. The study revealed that although a high percentage (80%) of the 200 survey respondents were excited about the possibility of AR integration in classrooms, issues such as lack of ICT infrastructure and teacher skills, high technology costs, and general resistance to change prevented AR from gaining ground in schools. Mundy, Hernandez, and Green (2019) argue that AR technologies require specific pedagogies which may impede on the amount of content which may be covered in traditional classrooms. In addition to these pedagogical concerns, research has often cited technological considerations beyond teacher skill and ICT support within schools. Rauschnabel, Rossmann, & tom Dieck (2017) cite data and user privacy concerns as a chief issue inherent with using AR technology. Similarly, several studies have presented technology or device failure, GPS errors, or lack of access to data connections as recurring issues (Dunleavy, Dede, & Mitchell, 2009; Wu, Lee, Chang, & Liang, 2013). It is evident that the claims surrounding AR's usefulness as an educational tool are mixed between benefits and drawbacks. Subsequently, there remains a lack of preparation in how to best utilize the strengths and minimize the weaknesses of AR technologies across educational contexts. In order to address this gap, further investigation is required to understand what is being said and what is possible with educational AR.

THEORETICAL FRAMEWORK

Despite the claimed advantages and disadvantages of AR, the integration of AR technologies into widespread educational contexts continues to elude mainstream adoption. It has been demonstrated that teaching is a complex activity which relies on the interplay of several types of knowledge (Mishra & Koehler, 2006). As such, it is insufficient to consider the effects of introducing technology to various contexts without also considering the pedagogical approach and desired content focus. Based on Shulman's (1986) seminal work regarding pedagogical content knowledge, the unique interplay and blending of content and pedagogy for instructional purposes, the technological pedagogical content knowledge (TPCK) framework describes the type of knowledge required by instructors for effective pedagogical practice within technology-enhanced learning environments (Mishra & Koehler, 2006). Within the framework, technology knowledge (TK) is knowledge concerning both standard (e.g. books and chalkboards) and advanced technologies (i.e. the Internet and smartboards); pedagogical knowledge (PK) is knowledge concerning the practices or methods of teaching and learning; and content knowledge (CK) is knowledge of the subject matter that is to be learned or taught (Mishra & Koehler, 2006). TPCK illustrates that in order to effectively integrate technology into their teaching practice, teachers are required to do more than understand the available tools; they also need to consider the techniques, skills, and knowledge requisite to apply these approaches to various contexts.

However, the conceptual frames of technology, pedagogy, and content need not be limited to the types of knowledge required by teachers to successfully operate in a digital world. Technology, pedagogy, and content (TPC) can be utilized to build lesson plans (e.g. What is the content to be learned? What is the pedagogical approach to be utilized? What technology can facilitate the process?) or assess existing teaching and learning practices across a variety of contexts. In evaluating this approach to TPC, it should also be understood that there remains a unique interplay between the elements of technology, pedagogy, and content. For example, in understanding the type of content to be learned within an informal setting, there may exist no clear link to formal disciplines such as physics or mathematics. From this perspective, technology may act not only as a tool to facilitate understanding, but also as the content itself in the form of technological literacy or information and communication technology competencies. Foster, Mishra, and Koehler (2011) have argued for the use of TPC as a mechanism to assess the quality of game-based learning environments. They claim that well-designed games integrate all three elements of TPCK, or technology, pedagogy, and content. Similarly, in this study, TPC provides a lens through which AR experiences can be examined within educational contexts. The framing of an educational experience based on the use of TPC enables an evaluation of specific features for facilitating learning outcomes. In addressing the claims of AR technology for teaching and learning, TPC will guide the considerations and coding scheme that forms the basis for evaluating the past, present, and future of educational augmented reality.

METHODOLOGY

It is imperative to examine the ongoing claims of AR for teaching and learning in order to identify which are substantial and which are based on conjecture and/or guesswork. This analysis is vital in illustrating what is possible with AR in educational contexts in the present while also providing insight for educators, teachers, designers, and students in understanding best practices and possibilities. Therefore, the purpose of this study is to present a review of AR literature across a variety of educational contexts which will elaborate on what is being said and done concerning educational AR.

Data Collection

In accomplishing this task, this study provides a comprehensive survey of claims for teaching and learning with augmented reality. The survey utilized a wide variety of sources including academic publications (journal articles, book chapters, and conference proceedings), books, online magazines, websites, and social media (e.g. twitter). This systematic search strategy is summarized in Figure 1. For all searches (e.g. databases, search engine, twitter), the following keyword combination was utilized: ((augmented reality) AND (education)). Additionally, all searches were automatically filtered by language ("English") and publication date (2000 to 2019) with the exception of Twitter which dates to 2006.

Two databases were identified for the initial search: ERIC (https://eric.ed.gov/) and ScienceDirect (https://www.sciencedirect.com/). ERIC was chosen as an access point targeting educational research and resources, while ScienceDirect was selected for its large selection of multidisciplinary subject-matter with applicability to AR (e.g. social sciences, computer science, STEM). Articles identified in these databases were required to contain the above search terms in the title, keyword, or abstract section(s) to be included for analysis. A similar search was conducted through the Google search engine. The web search was conducted as a means to identify online publications, corporate websites, and consumer blogs or websites which discuss the use of AR in educational contexts. Following the entry of the search terms, the top ten results were collected in December 2019. An identical search was completed for every year from 2000 until 2019 by creating a custom search range (Jan 1, 20XX – Dec 31, 20XX). In identifying tweets from Twitter, an identical search strategy to the web search was implemented. While the tweets in subsequent years grew too numerous to be included in this survey in their entirety, the search was narrowed through Twitter's "Top" filter. "Top" tweets are ranked based on relevance to keywords and their popularity measured through likes, retweets, and replies. The top ten tweets for each year (2006-2019) that included AR and education were selected for inclusion in this survey. This search strategy identified a total of 863 resources. Following the collection of these resources, all sources were vetted by the inclusion and exclusion criteria described in the next section.

Inclusion and Exclusion Criteria

Results included in this study were required to be: a) focused on the research, implementation, development, or discussion of AR technologies in educational contexts; b) presented in journal articles, conference proceedings, books, book chapters, online magazines, newspapers, websites, and/or tweets; c) empirical or non-empirical; d) published between the years of 2000 and 2019; and e) published in English. Resources were excluded if they did not meet the aforementioned criteria or if they were: a) presented in the format of a dissertation or thesis; b) discussed "mixed-reality" as opposed to explicitly targeting AR; and c) misinterpreted or confused virtual reality technologies with AR technologies. Ultimately, resources were also excluded if they f) were not available after contacting the original author/publisher. The data collection strategy described here is not meant to be an exhaustive listing of AR in education, but instead it serves as a diverse collection of varied perspectives that enables the analysis and interpretation of claims from a variety of sources. Following the application of the inclusion and exclusion criteria, a total of 719 resources were included for data analysis.

Figure 1. Flow chart demonstrating data collection strategy across all sources

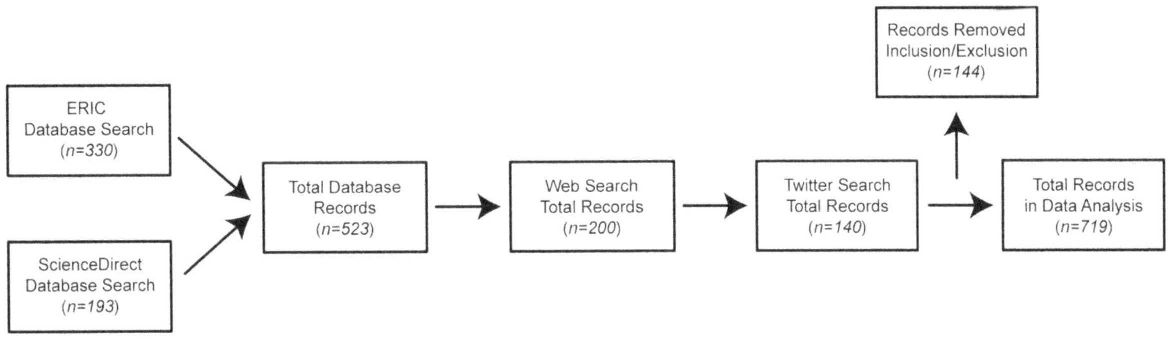

Data Analysis

The collected sources were analyzed for best practices, learning outcomes, barriers to adoption, and general beliefs about research, implementation, teaching, and learning with AR. Using this approach, over 400 claims were identified from these sources and were written verbatim or paraphrased for further data analysis.

In order to best analyze the data, a qualitative content analysis was utilized. Krippendorf (2004) defines content analysis as, "a research technique for making replicable and valid inferences from texts (or other meaningful matter) to the contexts of their use" (p. 18). Content analysis describes a family of analytic approaches, both quantitative and qualitative in nature, which provide an interpretive and systematic approach to textual analysis (Berg, 2001, Catanzaro, 1988). Qualitative content analysis seeks to present data in words and themes to enable interpretation of results (Bengtsson, 2016). Specifically, this study implemented a latent analysis to discover the underlying meaning of the claims surrounding AR in educational contexts (Berg, 2001, Catanzaro, 1988; Cho & Lee, 2014). To identify the meaning of the claims of AR, a dual inductive-deductive analysis was utilized. Qualitative content analysis is unique in its flexibility to utilize inductive, deductive, or a combination of both analyses in developing themes (Elo & Kyngäs, 2008). Using this inductive-deductive approach, a coding scheme was developed.

Beginning with the inductive coding process, resources were first decontextualized into meaningful units or codes (Downe-Wamboldt, 1992). Codes were then subjected to a process of recontextualization as a result of a constant comparison to the original data. For each resource, codes were compared to the original text to ensure that all claims which addressed the research questions were identified and extracted. Subsequently, a categorization process was utilized to condense the overall codes into overarching categories while maintaining the meaning of the coded unit (Graneheim & Lundman, 2004). Finally, a deductive coding process was used to ascribe the developed categories to the thematic headings of Technology, Pedagogy, and Content (TPC).

Following the completion of the coding scheme, the first author (master coder) coded all claims resulting from the compiled resources. After principal coding, an external researcher (reliability coder) coded a random subsample of approximately 20% of all claims. Inter-rater agreement using Cohen's kappa (k=0.78) fell between the range of 0.61 – 0.80, which illustrates substantial agreement (Cohen, 1960; Landis & Koch, 1977). The remaining sections of this chapter will describe the categorized claims and their sub-categories in order to make recommendations on future directions for AR technologies in education.

RESULTS

Stemming from the coding process described above, the framework for the claims of AR resulted in three emergent themes: 1) Technology, 2) Pedagogy, and 3) Content. A clear distinction arose between the three overall themes, as both technology and pedagogy were comprised of a sole category, though the content theme contained six sub-categories: cognitive, affective, design, motivational, social, and psychomotor outcomes. As a result of some claims with negative valence regarding AR outcomes in education, several categories include potential drawbacks or disadvantages to integrating this technology into the realm of education. The valence (positive/negative) of these claims are a direct result of opportunities and/or barriers as presented by the surveyed resources. While a summary of the claims for augmented reality can be viewed in Figure 2, this figure presents a non-exhaustive list of every possible claim. Overall themes (TPC) and sub-categories are presented in full, while selected claims which best exemplify the themes are presented and discussed in their relevant sections. The following sections will discuss the overarching themes and the sub-categories that comprise them in greater detail.

Technology

Within the broad theme of technology, claims for AR in education were focused on positive and negative aspects of technology integration. While some of these claims were targeted at AR specifically, there were also claims which could be generalized to include a wide variety of learning technologies. General claims revolved around standard technical problems (camera usage, Internet availability, GPS limitations, device brightness/resolution) for mobile devices, file size limitations, and ergonomic issues. The claim which occurred most frequently in this category involved discussion of the cost of AR technology. Specifically, early discussions stated that, due to limitations such as battery life, computational power, cameras, and tracking sensors, an AR-enabled device would cost upwards of $100,000 (Chen, 2009). The Tech Expo (2011) also likened AR to home desktop computers or console gaming systems by claiming that interaction occurs on a screen with QR-codes/markers acting as controllers. Their preferred solution, AR Goggles or a head-worn display, was believed to be prohibitively expensive to be a solution for schools in the short term. As technology progressed, the opinion on AR's fiscal viability began to shift. AR quickly made the transition from wholly inaccessible to all but the wealthiest consumer to a low-cost and widely accessible tool. Some went as far as to suggest that AR could reduce business and research laboratory costs by replacing staff with autonomous processes (Ferrer-Torregrosa, Torralba, Jimenez, García, & Barcia, 2015). When examining barriers to AR adoption, research indicated that students found the technology very easy to use and likened it to the experience of playing a game (Di Serio, Ibáñez, & Kloos, 2013). In addition to ease of use, AR was lauded as being a more effective way to enable learners to access content (Bloxham, 2013). Though technological claims on AR trended positively when approaching the present day, the technology was not without its critics.

Figure 2. Claims of augmented reality framework stemming from the extant literature

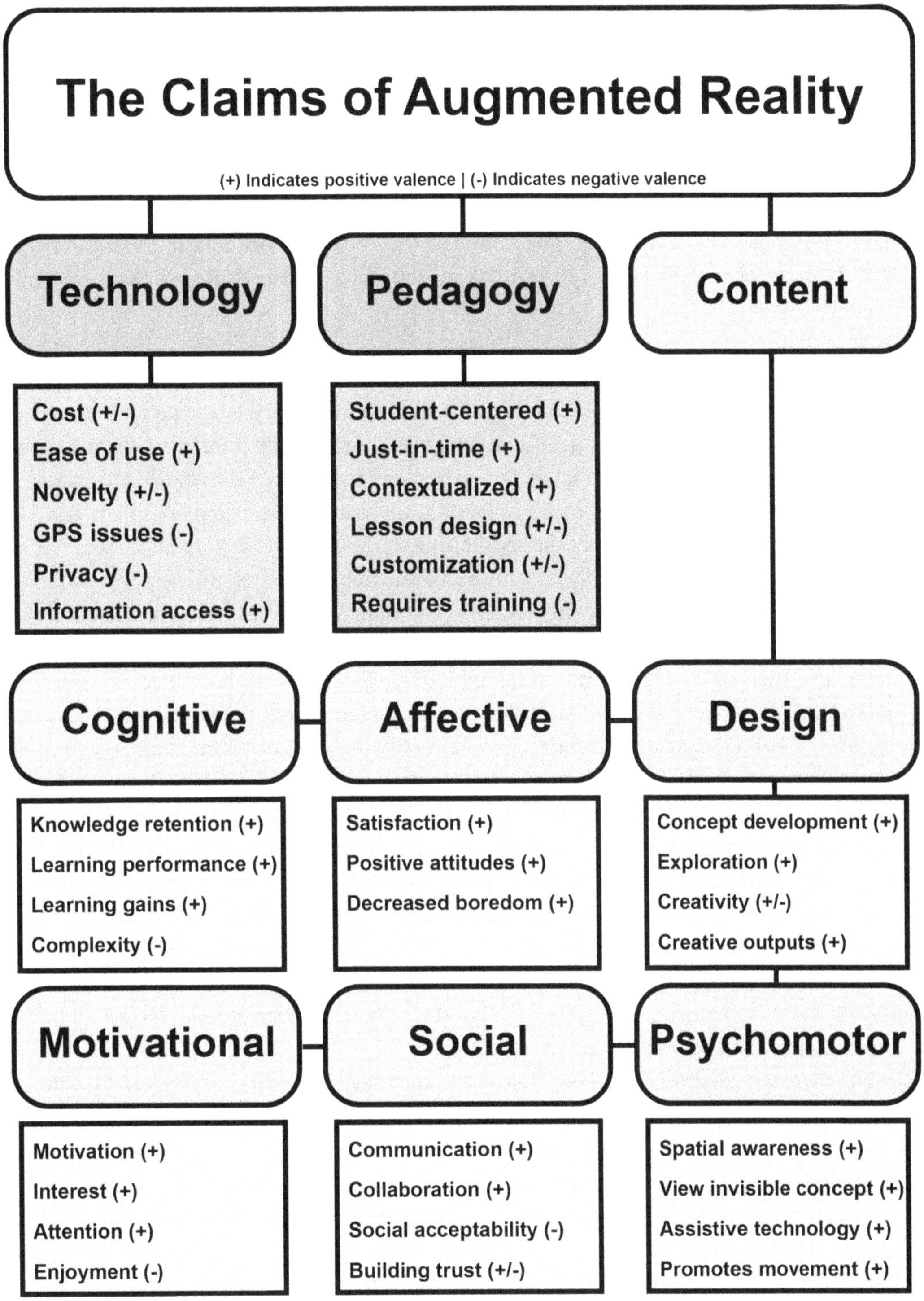

Folkestad & O'shea (2011) called into question how much of students' engagement was due to the benefits of using AR and how much was based on the novelty of a mobile handheld device for educational purposes. Perhaps most significant were the discussions on information overload, intrusive technology, and privacy concerns. Bonsor and Chandler (2018) liken the potential information overload of everyday AR usage to the "CrackBerry" phenomenon and Internet addiction. They believe that an overreliance on AR could mean that people may begin to miss out on what is happening in front of them in the real world. Through the progression of image-recognition software, AR toolkits have been able to more easily facilitate access to information using marker and marker-less systems. As a result, concerns have been raised regarding the potential of AR technologies to provide facial recognition with access to linked information from online profiles (e.g. Facebook, Twitter, etc.). These privacy concerns are relatively common since the inception of the technology, though they became particularly salient during the introduction and testing of Google Glass (Arthur, 2013; Rauschnabel, He, & Ro, 2018).

Pedagogy

Claims organized under the pedagogy theme broadly refer to the ability to create and utilize effective teaching and learning practices. Some specific claims focus on individual learning theories and/or approaches, while others examine AR's effect on the instructor's role in an AR-enhanced learning environment. AR was almost universally championed as facilitating a situated learning approach which emphasizes learning within authentic contexts (Harley, Poitras, Jarrell, Duffy, & Lajoie, 2016). AR's ability to provide in-situ overlays and supplementary information enables learners to interpret and synthesize information at their own pace. Subsequently, claims also identified AR as being proficient in enabling the delivery of just-in-time feedback (Immerman, 2019). This approach allows students to become active learners within the interactive environment as facilitated by AR interventions. Several claims supported AR as a tool to facilitate student-teacher and student-student interactions. Zarraonandia, Aedo, Díaz, and Montero Montes (2014) designed a presentation system utilizing a head-mounted display for presenters to increase communication and feedback between lecturer and listener. The system was said to provide continuous, private, and immediate feedback to aid lecturers in adapting content and their pace of explanation while improving the overall flow of presentation. While these face-to-face interactions were most prevalent, there were also cases of research investigating AR's potential to improve interactions in distance and/or online education as well (Vafa, Sappington, & Coombs-Richardson, 2018). In addition to distance and asynchronous learning, others saw potential in AR's ability to bridge the gap between formal and informal learning environments (Koutromanos & Avraamidou, 2014). Salmi, Thuneberg, and Vainikainen (2016) identified AR as being a good tool for a variety of learners which bridged the gap between learning contexts in an effective way.

Conversely, there were a few discussions that illustrated that instructors are not readily able to create and guide AR interventions for their specific teaching needs. Though some of these claims highlight technological and design related issues, they are discussed here in terms of pedagogy as limiting an instructor's educational approach during instruction. From this perspective, several limitations inhibit an instructor's potential use of AR technologies across contexts. Mota, Ruiz-Rube, Dodero, and Arnedillo-Sánchez (2018) detail the need for technological and content experts to create lasting and effective AR interventions. Though drag-and-drop interfaces have facilitated instructors in "code free" solutions, the creation of assets and interactive elements continue to limit instructors' possibilities in creating new content modules. Even if an instructor is skilled in the usage of computer graphics, the time investment is such that a secondary instructor would be required for proper implementation within a course structure (Tzima, Styliaras, & Bassounas, 2019). In addition to this limitation due to time, even more claims have been cited regarding a lack of training for educators using this technology and negative attitudes or resistance to adoption of AR (Bower, Howe, McCredie, Robinson, & Grover, 2014; Dunleavy & Dede, 2014; Scrivner, Madewell, Buckley, & Perez, 2016). Williams (2018) believed that only the most open-minded and innovative instructors are prepared to apply AR applications in education. Finally, there were some claims which highlighted an inherent bias when attempting to integrate AR into formal classrooms. If schools did not have the resources to provide mobile devices for all students, a Bring Your Own Device (BYOD) approach disadvantaged students that could not afford or did not have present access to a mobile device or tablet (Holz, 2018). Though the introduction of low-cost devices and software have narrowed this gap, the lack of access to the required technology has relegated AR to an immersive side activity as opposed to something that can be reliably implemented as a continuous tool within a curriculum.

Content

While some resources attempted to target content-specific outcomes (e.g. STEM; Fourtane, 2019), most claims examined were made in relation to education broadly and as such could be applicable across a variety of subject areas. As a result, the content component of this framework has been adapted to focus on the specific learning outcomes associated with using AR in educational contexts. Specifically, six sub-categories of learning outcomes were identified: a) cognitive; b) affective; c) design; d) motivational; e) social; and f) psychomotor. Also evident in this analysis were more skeptical outlooks on AR's contribution across disciplines: "Experts 5 years ago: 'Augmented reality will transform education, healthcare, construction, commerce...' Experts Today: Pokemon!!!'" (Levie, 2016). Such resources suggested that AR may have failed to live up to its expectation as a practical tool and was instead best suited for use in entertainment. Similarly, PBS Wisconsin Education (2009) shared a claim against "over-hyping" AR for fear that it would become diluted and meaningless before the world had the opportunity to explore its myriad of benefits. While these types of claims were in the minority, they should not be discounted given the rise to prominence of such game-based AR experiences such as Ingress and Pokemon GO. In the following sections, each sub-category will be introduced, defined, and discussed with exemplars.

Cognitive Outcomes

The cognitive outcomes sub-category focused specifically on changes involved in a learner's conscious intellectual effort. While these outcomes were characterized in a number of ways, they traditionally refer to knowledge retention and recall. Erbas and Demirer (2019) investigated the effects of AR activities on students' academic achievement within a biology course, however, no significant difference was found between study and control group academic achievement scores. Despite these findings, a myriad of studies championed AR for its promotion of reflective learning, knowledge retention, academic achievement, and knowledge acquisition (Achuthan, Francis, & Diwakar, 2017; Gün & Atasoy, 2017; Pérez-López & Contero, 2013). Salmi, Thuneberg, and Vainikainen (2016) investigated the cognitive aspects related to AR within informal learning contexts. Their results indicated that AR technologies were beneficial to the cognitive gains of students who otherwise belong to the lowest achieving school group. Additionally, students who were already performing at a high level were provided an increased challenge and higher quality in terms of learning outcomes. Though there appears to be growing support for positive cognitive achievements when using AR technologies, other studies have found difficulty in achieving these types of outcomes. Dunleavy, Dede, and Mitchell (2009) found that AR created an immersive environment that was too complex for many students. The technology, coupled with the task of recognizing and interpreting new content, could be too much for some learners. Though support exists for AR in terms of decreasing learners' cognitive load (Küçük, Kapakin, & Göktaş, 2016), there remains an argument that indicates these types of environment can contribute to quite the opposite (Baumeister et al., 2017).

Affective Outcomes

The affective outcomes sub-category focuses on learner feelings, emotions, and attitudes towards the usage of AR technology itself and/or curricula supported by AR technology broadly. Despite its potential, this sub-category was relatively small in relation to cognitive outcomes discussed above. This category also remains unique as the claims within are distinctly positive, with no cited exemplars discussing a negative affective reaction to AR technology use for teaching and learning. The most prevalent claims in terms of affective outcomes cited increased satisfaction (Che Hashim, Abd Majid, Arshad, & Khalid Obeidy, 2018). A study consisting of 77 7th grade students revealed that students were satisfied with their use of AR applications, found the delivery method interesting and easy to use, and would like to utilize the technology again in the future (Karagozlu, Kosarenko, Efimova, & Zubov, 2019). Similar claims characterized these affective outcomes as increased in positives attitudes and/or outlooks (Wojciechowski & Cellary, 2013). Harley, Poitras, Jarrell, Duffy, and Lajoie (2016) sought to investigate the role that positive emotions play in supporting cognitive outcomes in AR-enabled learning environments. In total, 31 undergraduate students' emotions and learning outcomes were compared prior to and just after an AR guided historical tour. Their results indicated an increase in not only cognitive outcomes, but also an increase in positive emotions such as overall enjoyment of the experience as well as a decrease in boredom when using AR. The results of this study illustrate the interplay of learning outcomes across the cognitive and affective sub-categories.

Design Outcomes

The third sub-category of learning outcomes is centered around the topics of design thinking, creativity, and innovation. Broadly, claims in these categories stated that AR technologies aided learners in concept development, encouraged exploration, and increased their capacity for innovation. One claim suggested that AR's ability to alter a physical environment with digital augmentations in a nearly infinite number of ways provides the necessary nurturing of creativity and imagination for a variety of learners (Roylance, 2017). Wei, Weng, Liu, and Wang (2015) presented a pilot study which utilized a teaching scheme that integrated AR into a creative design course. Results of the study suggest that the AR-enhanced teaching scheme helped students to experience the complete creative design process, enhances the teaching of creative design, encourages student creativity, and improves the creativity of student outputs. Similarly, Yilmaz and Goktas (2017) introduced a study on the effects of an AR-enhanced intervention on students' narrative skill and overall level of creativity. The study divided 100 fifth-grade students between control (non-AR intervention) and experimental (AR-enhanced intervention) groups. Results revealed statistically significant increase in narrative skills and creativity in storytelling. Similar to the results from the affective outcomes of AR usage, the design outcomes were relatively limited in terms of negative outcomes. There was a single claim documented which claimed AR had the potential to hinder creativity, though this stemmed from a potential poor student interaction with the technology (or a technological outcome).

Motivational Outcomes

The fourth sub-category of learning outcomes focuses on the claims for why and how individuals may re-engage with content following the use of AR for teaching and learning. Broadly, these claims involve motivation as well as some of its sub-constructs (attention, engagement, interest) as well as anticipation. Additionally, this category includes learner perceived and realized levels of enjoyment as they relate to future potential to re-engage with an educational experience. Cheng (2017) describes a quantitative study examining 153 students' motivation when engaged with an AR book reading activity. Results indicated that, in general, student motivation to learn was high during the intervention's usage of an AR book. Additionally, motivational factors such as attention and confidence mediated students' behavioral intention to learn. These factors were only statistically significant when students intended to re-engage in future AR-enabled learning opportunities. While this and other similar claims focused on re-engaging with the specific AR technology, many claims of motivation revolved around student interests and motivation to engage with a specific content area, such as STEM (Hsu, Lin, & Yang, 2017). Similarly, Khan, Johnston, and Ophoff (2019) presented a study focused on academic achievement in a biology course. The study cited that 78 participants completed an AR-enabled learning activity centered around human anatomy. Following a pre-post assessment, results indicated that overall student motivation had increased after completion of the intervention. More specifically, the attention, satisfaction, and confidence factors of motivation showed a statistically significant increase from pre-test to post-test. Others have suggested that AR may not only be a tool for motivation within the classroom, but also to augment the student experience on campus. This claim stems from the ability for colleges and universities to market and promote themselves, while also communicating with students in an accessible new medium (Roylance, 2017).

Social Outcomes

The fifth learning outcomes sub-category examines claims regarding social outcomes of utilizing AR for teaching and learning. Overall, these claims focus on the fostering of communication (student-student and student-teacher), collaboration, and building trust. Though not a direct negative of AR usage, some claims highlighted the idea that this technology promotes user autonomy. While this contradicts the social aspects displayed here, this could be considered a negative outcome of certain AR-enhanced interventions and was included here as such. The largest groups of claims in this sub-category involved general discussion of communication and collaboration as facilitated by an AR-enabled intervention (Lukosch, Billinghurst, Alem, & Kiyokawa, 2015). A web search for Pokemon GO revealed a myriad of quotes and discussions about players being drawn to social aspects of the game. One group of players stated:

You'll just run into people and spark up conversations immediately. We met this one guy who drove up from San Jose to collect Pokémon in the park, and he had more knowledge about this game than anyone else we've met so far. We called him the Guru (Wingfield & Isaac, 2016).

Miller and colleagues (2019) illustrated several outcomes in a study of 218 college students. For example, the group found that individuals are socially inhibited on challenging tasks by intelligent avatars being in their field of view akin to how individuals struggle on challenging tasks when being observed. They also found that an individual wearing AR goggles feel less socially connected when talking to an individual not wearing AR goggles (Ouellette, 2019). Like Pokemon GO, Google Glass left its own mark on the broad usage of AR technologies. Developers and early adopters claimed to feel like "social pariah" when wearing the technology (Gibbs, 2014). Though the use of a mobile phone is much more widely accepted than the Google Glass, still more AR adopters have claimed feeling awkward or outside the realm of social acceptability when holding up their phone during conversations or when walking around (Hurley, 2017).

Psychomotor Outcomes

The sixth sub-category for learning outcomes involves learning as demonstrated through physical skills such as movement and coordination. Additional perceptions are characterized in this category including claims around spatial recognition, depth perception, and the senses. Hurley (2017) indicates that the spatial-contextual awareness afforded by AR technologies enables users to explore their surroundings and provides feedback relevant to their time and place. The same author claimed that AR could become a real-time visual assistive technology. In building on this supposition, he surmised that AR would eventually move towards the integration of hearable components that would enable AR devices to provide real-time audio translation as well (Hurley, 2017). Other claims were more general in citing increased in spatial ability or reasoning (Lin, Chen, & Chang, 2015). Ultimately, one of the most interesting psychomotor aspects of AR-enabled environments is the visualization of invisible or abstract concepts. Yoon and Wang (2014) conducted a study with 70 students between fifth and seventh grade. One of the most discussed aspects of AR in the post-intervention interviews were the visualization of invisible phenomenon enabled by AR. In this case, the authors captured student interactions with magnets and provided feedback on the magnetic pull back to them in real-time.

THE CLAIMS OF AUGMENTED REALITY: ADVANTAGES AND DISADVANTAGES

The overarching benefit of this survey and subsequent analysis of the claims of AR is that it provides a systematic approach to discussing this developing technology as well as the benefits and drawbacks imposed through its use in teaching and learning experiences. Through a discussion of the encompassing themes and sub-categories, the positive and negative affordances for teaching and learning with AR technologies were made explicit. In addition, the broad examination of claims for AR usage provided perspective on which claims were supported by empirical research, and which were unsubstantiated or reasoned conjecture based on assumption or anecdotal evidence. Despite the number of claims here, it is evident that there is currently a lack of knowledge in the realm of teaching and learning with augmented reality technologies. Specifically, two key issues were identified as it relates to the claims of AR for teaching and learning: (a) the research (empirical or theoretical) support underlying these claims; and (b) recognition of the interplay between overall themes and sub-categories.

Empirical and Theoretical Support for Claims

In recent years, an increasing number of publications have emerged providing systematic reviews on AR within educational contexts broadly, as well as in targeted settings such as primary and secondary education (Akçayır & Akçayır, 2017; Bacca, Baldiris, Fabregat, & Graf, 2014; Garzón, Pavón, & Baldiris, 2019; Pellas, Fotaris, Kazanidis, & Wells, 2019). In their review, Garzón, Pavón, and Baldiris (2019) claim a wide variety in terms of the topics, target groups, academic levels, and more could indicate that AR technologies have achieved a level of maturity that has enabled them to take root in educational settings. Despite these claims, systematic reviews target the research (empirical and theoretical) literature produced in an academic context. These reviews intentionally target studies of emerging research and interventions that have yet to reach mainstream adoption. As a result, these systematic reviews miss the claims and findings from contextualized interventions and existing curricula that may seek to integrate AR technologies into education. Additionally, none of the research studies identified in this survey were longitudinal in nature. As a result, it is difficult to assess the performance or potential of sustained AR adoption. The characteristics of these claims signify that it is still premature to suggest AR is prepared for mainstream adoption. Continued analysis and more in-depth examinations of the use and outcomes of AR technologies is required. Chatzopoulos, Bermejo, Huang, and Hui (2017) conducted a survey of AR that includes commentary on hardware, software, research, training, and entertainment usage. Their study casts a wide net to analyze academic and non-academic publications concerning educational AR. Additional studies of this nature, a combination of literature across academic and non-academic sources, are imperative in assessing the readiness of AR for mainstream adoption.

Figure 3. Intersections of technology, pedagogy, and content in the claims of augmented reality

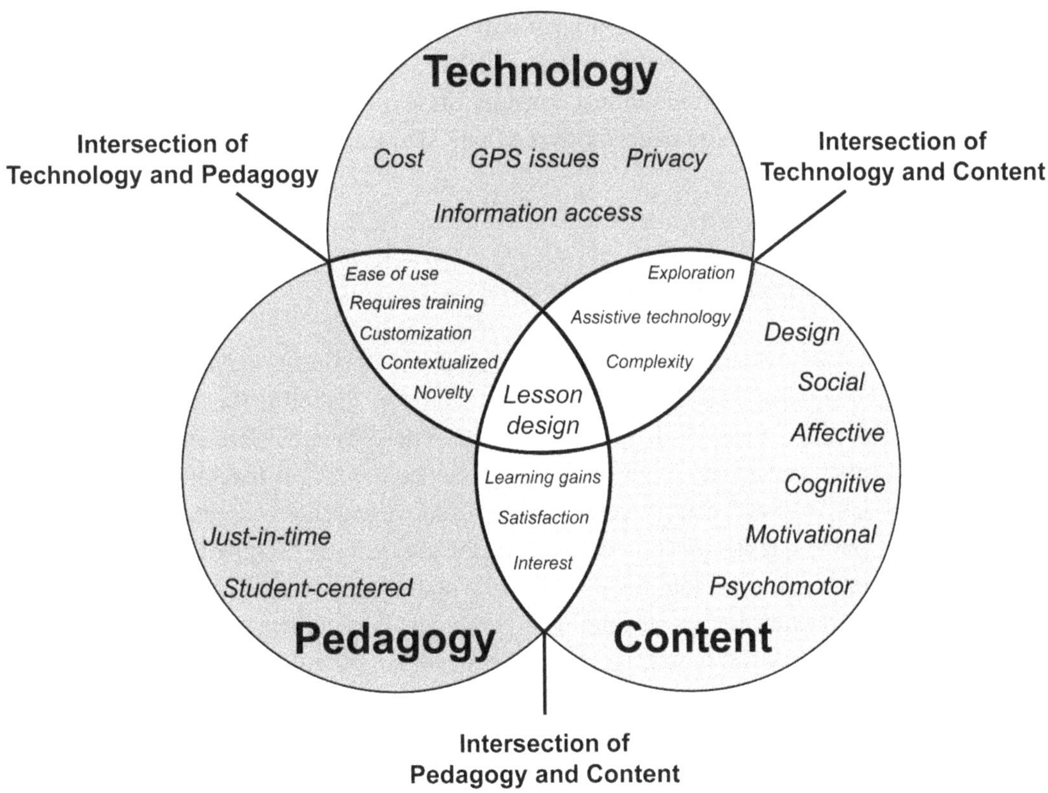

Interplay Between Themes and Categories

Following the identification of themes and sub-categories within this survey, it became evident that there were inherent similarities across the categories of technology, pedagogy, and content. Mota, Ruiz-Rube, Dodero, and Arnedillo-Sánchez (2018) highlighted the need for technological experts to be able to integrate AR into the classroom. In addition, more numerous claims suggested that teachers needed additional training to prepare for AR adoption. Though these claims were situated within the pedagogy theme, they have repercussions in terms of technology in addition to shaping how instructors conduct their teaching with AR and similar educational technologies. As a result, this survey illustrates the unique interplay of technology, pedagogy, and content when attempting to integrate educational technology into one's instruction (Mishra & Koehler, 2006). Figure 3 provides insight into the intersections of Technology and Pedagogy (TP), Pedagogy and Content (PC), and Technology and Content (TC) as they relate to AR in education. Crews (2018) exemplified the intersection of these claims in his discussion of how teachers might use AR in their instruction: a) AR reduces time and effort in setting up activities and allow teachers to break through the noise to engage students (P); b) AR allows the testing of students' understanding and helps facilitate interest (C); and c) aids teachers, even those who aren't tech-savvy, in facilitating the exploration of contextualized worlds (T). This discussion surrounding lesson plans with AR, specifically how teachers can use AR experiences in their own practice, necessitates the consideration of technological, pedagogical, and content-related factors. In order to take advantage of this relationship between themes, instructors, teachers, designers, and researchers must consider: What content is meant to be learned? What pedagogical approach will be used? What technology should be utilized? AR technologies, as discussed previously, are not panacea despite some of the claims identified within this chapter. Stakeholders in AR adoption must consider these questions when designing applications, curricula, and their supports as there is currently no "one size fits all" solution in augmented reality implementation and outcome.

CONCLUSION AND IMPLICATIONS

This chapter presented a survey of the extant literature on AR within educational context. Both academic (journal articles, book chapters, conference proceedings) and non-academic (books, online magazines, websites, social media) sources were utilized in this search. These sources were analyzed for best practices, learning outcomes, barriers to adoption, and general beliefs about teaching and learning with AR. Using this approach, over 400 claims were identified and were written verbatim or paraphrased for further data analysis. Using qualitative content analysis, the claims were assigned to various categories. These categories were then grouped into further umbrella codes, or themes. The completed framework was comprised of three overall themes (technology, pedagogy, and content), while the content theme was divided into six sub-categories (cognitive, affective, design, motivational, social, and psychomotor outcomes).

Based on the findings presented here, there are several key implications of the survey within this chapter. The first implication revolves around teachers' and instructors' usage of the framework to identify potential learning outcomes for their lessons or curricula. These learning outcomes could be linked to classroom objectives to aid instructors' decision on whether to try and implement an AR intervention in their classroom. For policymakers, this framework may aid in providing perspective on the potential value added by AR, in addition to other educational technologies, given proper supports and training to instructors and students. While it is not currently expected that AR becomes a pervasive classroom tool, this chapter seeks to highlight AR's potential as a supplemental technology with high potential and minimal risk.

Another set of implications from this survey involves the development of guidelines for future research in the area of AR for teaching and learning. The claims here, both academic and non-academic, should be empirically verified utilizing a variety of research designs and assessments. Specifically, there was a lack of observed longitudinal studies which utilized AR in their design. Claims regarding the mainstream adoption of AR in education cannot be verified until it is confirmed that AR can be an effective teaching tool in the long term. Furthermore, the claims in this chapter cannot be used as empirical findings, but instead as a guide to direct future research. Predominantly this is because the claims stem from a variety of sources which are potentially unsubstantiated, but also because the literature on AR in education is constantly shifting and evolving. This should be an opportunity to assess, verify, and scrutinize the claims within this chapter and utilize them as a basis for future research studies. From this perspective, the framework seeks an immediate impact on those seeking to research and utilize educational AR, while also providing direction for future adoption by highlighting issues of importance and those which have yet to be investigated thoroughly.

When considering barriers to adoption, the appearance of privacy concerns within AR cannot be understated. Rauschnabel (2019) summarized several empirical articles regarding AR and privacy concerns. In particular, he noted that users are aware of the privacy risks of such a technology, but it does not prevent their usage of it because: a) users feel a level of control over AR devices; b) they don't feel their personal life is worth hiding; c) the consequences seem abstract and may only be relevant in the future; and d) users accept living in a world in which privacy doesn't exist. While these findings may be sufficient for justification of commercial use, and as evidenced by this study's discussion of AR claims, privacy is an ongoing concern in the realm AR and education. Fineman (2018) presents several concerns including physical security, identity and access, privacy, and data security. In terms of large-scale integration in K-12 contexts and beyond, these barriers present significant hurdles in both short and long-term AR adoption. As AR continues to become more ubiquitous, privacy concerns are poised to become a daunting obstacle in the field of education.

The final implication for this study involves the integration of technology, pedagogy, and content. Designing, integrating, and teaching with technology is a difficult task for even the most experienced of instructors. Until there are considerations for the integration of these three domains, it is unlikely that there will be considerable progress in creating feasible interventions that can be adopted at a large scale. Successful integration of AR technologies, as with all educational technology, requires the creation and maintenance of the dynamic interplay between the TPC constructs. These considerations should be highlighted in the design, development, and integration of AR interventions by designers, instructors, teachers, and researchers to provide the most effective outcomes for students and all learners alike.

REFERENCES

Achuthan, K., Francis, S. P., & Diwakar, S. (2017). Augmented reflective learning and knowledge retention perceived among students in classrooms involving virtual laboratories. *Education and Information Technologies*, *22*(6), 2825–2855. doi:10.100710639-017-9626-x

Agrawal, A. J. (2018, February 15). *3 reasons augmented reality hasn't achieved widespread adoption*. Thenextweb. https://thenextweb.com/contributors/2018/02/16/3-reasons-augmented-reality-hasnt-achieved-widespread-adoption/

Akçayır, M., & Akçayır, G. (2017). Advantages and challenges associated with augmented reality for education: A systematic review of the literature. *Educational Research Review*, *20*, 1–11. doi:10.1016/j.edurev.2016.11.002

Alexander, B., Ashford-Rowe, K., Barajas-Murphy, N., Dobbin, G., Knott, J., McCormack, M., Pomerantz, J., Seilhammer, R., & Weber, N. (2019). *EDUCAUSE Horizon report: 2019 higher education edition*. EDUCAUSE.

Alkhattabi, M. (2017). Augmented reality as E-learning tool in primary schools' education: Barriers to teachers' adoption. *International Journal of Emerging Technologies in Learning*, *12*(02), 91–100. doi:10.3991/ijet.v12i02.6158

Althoff, T., White, R. W., & Horvitz, E. (2016). Influence of Pokémon Go on physical activity: Study and implications. *Journal of Medical Internet Research*, *18*(12), e315. doi:10.2196/jmir.6759 PMID:27923778

Anderson, M. (2019). *Mobile Technology and Home Broadband 2019*. Pew Research Center.

Arthur, C. (2013). *Google Glass: is it a threat to our privacy?* The Guardian. https://www.theguardian.com/technology/2013/mar/06/google-glass-threat-to-our-privacy

Ayers, J. W., Leas, E. C., Dredze, M., Allem, J. P., Grabowski, J. G., & Hill, L. (2016). Pokémon GO—A new distraction for drivers and pedestrians. *JAMA Internal Medicine*, *176*(12), 1865–1866. doi:10.1001/jamainternmed.2016.6274 PMID:27635638

Bacca, J., Baldiris, S., & Fabregat, R., & Kinshuk. (2019). Framework for designing motivational augmented reality applications in vocational education and training. *Australasian Journal of Educational Technology*, *35*(3).

Bacca, J., Baldiris, S., Fabregat, R., & Graf, S. (2014). Augmented reality trends in education: A systematic review of research and applications. *Journal of Educational Technology & Society*, *17*(4), 133–149.

Baumeister, J., Ssin, S. Y., ElSayed, N. A., Dorrian, J., Webb, D. P., Walsh, J. A., Simon, T. M., Irlitti, A., Smith, R. T., Kohler, M., & Thomas, B. H. (2017). Cognitive cost of using augmented reality displays. *IEEE Transactions on Visualization and Computer Graphics*, *23*(11), 2378–2388. doi:10.1109/TVCG.2017.2735098 PMID:28809700

Becker, S. A., Brown, M., Dahlstrom, E., Davis, A., DePaul, K., Diaz, V., & Pomerantz, J. (2018). *NMC horizon report: 2018 higher education edition*. EDUCAUSE.

Bengtsson, M. (2016). How to plan and perform a qualitative study using content analysis. *NursingPlus Open*, *2*, 8–14. doi:10.1016/j.npls.2016.01.001

Berg, B. L. (2001). *Qualitative research methods for the social sciences*. Pearson.

Billinghurst, M., Kato, H., & Poupyrev, I. (2001). The magicbook-moving seamlessly between reality and virtuality. *IEEE Computer Graphics and Applications*, *21*(3), 6–8.

Bloxham, J. (2013). *Augmented reality in education: teaching tool or passing trend?* The Guardian. https://www.theguardian.com/higher-education-network/blog/2013/feb/11/augmented-reality-teaching-tool-trend

Bonsor, K., & Chandler, N. (2018). *How Augmented Reality Works*. Howstuffworks. https://computer.howstuffworks.com/augmented-reality.htm

Bower, M., Howe, C., McCredie, N., Robinson, A., & Grover, D. (2014). Augmented Reality in education–cases, places and potentials. *Educational Media International*, *51*(1), 1–15. doi:10.1080/09523987.2014.889400

Braun, V., & Clarke, V. (2006). Using thematic analysis in psychology. *Qualitative Research in Psychology*, *3*(2), 77–101. doi:10.1191/1478088706qp063oa

Bush, V. (1945). As we may think. *Atlantic Monthly*, *176*(1), 101–108.

Catanzaro, M. (1988). Using qualitative analytical techniques. *Nursing research. Theory into Practice*, 437–456.

Caudell, T. P., & Mizell, D. W. (1992, January). Augmented reality: An application of heads-up display technology to manual manufacturing processes. In *Proceedings of the Twenty-Fifth Hawaii International Conference on System Sciences* (Vol. 2, pp. 659-669). 10.1109/HICSS.1992.183317

Chatzopoulos, D., Bermejo, C., Huang, Z., & Hui, P. (2017). Mobile augmented reality survey: From where we are to where we go. *IEEE Access: Practical Innovations, Open Solutions*, *5*, 6917–6950. doi:10.1109/ACCESS.2017.2698164

Che Hashim, N., Abd Majid, N. A., Arshad, H., & Khalid Obeidy, W. (2018). User Satisfaction for an Augmented Reality Application to Support Productive Vocabulary Using Speech Recognition. *Advances in Multimedia*, *2018*, 2018. doi:10.1155/2018/9753979

Chen, B. X. (2009). *If you're not seeing data, you're not seeing*. Wired Magazine. https://www.wired.com/2009/08/augmented-reality/

Cheng, K. H. (2017). Reading an augmented reality book: An exploration of learners' cognitive load, motivation, and attitudes. *Australasian Journal of Educational Technology*, *33*(4).

Cho, J. Y., & Lee, E. H. (2014). Reducing confusion about grounded theory and qualitative content analysis: Similarities and differences. *Qualitative Report*, *19*(32), 1.

Cohen, J. (1960). A coefficient of agreement for nominal scales. *Educational and Psychological Measurement*, *20*(1), 37–46. doi:10.1177/001316446002000104

Crews, J. (2018). *Five ways teachers can use—and create—augmented reality experiences*. EdSurge. https://www.edsurge.com/news/2018-01-22-five-ways-teachers-can-use-and-create-augmented-reality-experiences

Cuban, L. (1986). *Teachers and machines: The classroom use of technology since 1920*. Teachers College Press.

Dadwal, S. S., & Hassan, A. (2016). The augmented reality marketing: A merger of marketing and technology in tourism. In Mobile Computing and Wireless Networks: Concepts, Methodologies, Tools, and Applications (pp. 63-80). IGI Global. doi:10.4018/978-1-4666-8751-6.ch004

Dalim, C. S. C., Kolivand, H., Kadhim, H., Sunar, M. S., & Billinghurst, M. (2017). Factors influencing the acceptance of augmented reality in education: A review of the literature. *Journal of Computational Science*, *13*(11), 581–589. doi:10.3844/jcssp.2017.581.589

Di Serio, Á., Ibáñez, M. B., & Kloos, C. D. (2013). Impact of an augmented reality system on students' motivation for a visual art course. *Computers & Education*, *68*, 586–596. doi:10.1016/j.compedu.2012.03.002

Dodevska, Z. A., Mihić, M. M., & Manasijević, S. (2018). The role of augmented reality in defensive activities. In *Proceedings of the 8th International Scientific Conference on Defensive Technologies OTEH* (pp. 590-593). Academic Press.

Downe-Wamboldt, B. (1992). Content analysis: Method, applications, and issues. *Health Care for Women International*, *13*(3), 313–321. doi:10.1080/07399339209516006 PMID:1399871

Dunleavy, M., & Dede, C. (2014). Augmented reality teaching and learning. In J. Spector, M. Merrill, J. Elen, & M. Bishop (Eds.), *Handbook of research on educational communications and technology* (pp. 735–745). Springer. doi:10.1007/978-1-4614-3185-5_59

Dunleavy, M., Dede, C., & Mitchell, R. (2009). Affordances and limitations of immersive participatory augmented reality simulations for teaching and learning. *Journal of Science Education and Technology*, *18*(1), 7–22. doi:10.100710956-008-9119-1

Eckert, M., Volmerg, J. S., & Friedrich, C. M. (2019). Augmented reality in medicine: Systematic and bibliographic review. *JMIR mHealth and uHealth*, *7*(4), e10967. doi:10.2196/10967 PMID:31025950

Elo, S., & Kyngäs, H. (2008). The qualitative content analysis process. *Journal of Advanced Nursing*, *62*(1), 107–115. doi:10.1111/j.1365-2648.2007.04569.x PMID:18352969

Emiroğlu, B. G., & Kurt, A. A. (2017). Use of augmented reality in mobile devices for educational purposes. In G. Kurubacak & H. Altinpulluk (Eds.), *Mobile Technologies and Augmented Reality in Open Education* (pp. 95–117). doi:10.4018/978-1-5225-2110-5.ch005

Erbas, C., & Demirer, V. (2019). The effects of augmented reality on students' academic achievement and motivation in a biology course. *Journal of Computer Assisted Learning*, *35*(3), 450–458. doi:10.1111/jcal.12350

Ferrer-Torregrosa, J., Torralba, J., Jimenez, M. A., García, S., & Barcia, J. M. (2015). ARBOOK: Development and assessment of a tool based on augmented reality for anatomy. *Journal of Science Education and Technology*, *24*(1), 119–124. doi:10.100710956-014-9526-4

Fineman, B. (2018). *Securing your reality: Addressing security and privacy in virtual and augmented reality applications*. EDUCAUSE Review. https://er.educause.edu/articles/2018/5/securing-your-reality-addressing-security-and-privacy-in-virtual-and-augmented-reality-applications

FitzGerald, E., Ferguson, R., Adams, A., Gaved, M., Mor, Y., & Thomas, R. (2013). Augmented reality and mobile learning: The state of the art. *International Journal of Mobile and Blended Learning*, *5*(4), 43–58. doi:10.4018/ijmbl.2013100103

Folkestad, J., & O'shea, P. (2011). An analysis of engagement in a combination indoor/outdoor augmented reality educational game. *Journal of Science Education and Technology*, *7*(1), 30–37.

Foster, A., Mishra, P., & Koehler, M. (2011). Digital game analysis: Using the Technological Pedagogical Content Knowledge framework to determine the affordances of a game for learning. In *Learning to Play: Exploring the Future of Education with Video Games*. Peter Lang Publications.

Fotaris, P., Pellas, N., Kazanidis, I., & Smith, P. (2017). *A systematic review of augmented reality game-based applications in primary education*. Academic Conferences International Limited.

Fourtane, S. (2019). *Augmented reality: The future of education*. Interesting Engineering. https://interestingengineering.com/augmented-reality-the-future-of-education

Garzón, J., Pavón, J., & Baldiris, S. (2019). Systematic review and meta-analysis of augmented reality in educational settings. *Virtual Reality (Waltham Cross)*, *23*(4), 447–459. doi:10.100710055-019-00379-9

Gibbs, S. (2014). *Google Glass review: useful – but overpriced and socially awkward*. The Guardian. https://www.theguardian.com/technology/2014/dec/03/google-glass-review-curiously-useful-overpriced-socially-awkward

Graneheim, U. H., & Lundman, B. (2004). Qualitative content analysis in nursing research: Concepts, procedures and measures to achieve trustworthiness. *Nurse Education Today*, *24*(2), 105–112. doi:10.1016/j.nedt.2003.10.001 PMID:14769454

Guazzaroni, G. (2013). Emotional mapping of the archaeologist game. *Computers in Human Behavior*, *29*(2), 335–344. doi:10.1016/j.chb.2012.06.008

Gün, E. T., & Atasoy, B. (2017). The effects of augmented reality on elementary school students' spatial ability and academic achievement. *Egitim Ve Bilim*, *42*(191).

Harley, J. M., Poitras, E. G., Jarrell, A., Duffy, M. C., & Lajoie, S. P. (2016). Comparing virtual and location-based augmented reality mobile learning: Emotions and learning outcomes. *Educational Technology Research and Development*, *64*(3), 359–388. doi:10.100711423-015-9420-7

Holz, S. (2018). *Education and Augmented Reality - Really?* Neo Blog. https://blog.neolms.com/education-augmented-reality-really/

Howe, K. B., Suharlim, C., Ueda, P., Howe, D., Kawachi, I., & Rimm, E. B. (2016). Gotta catch'em all! Pokémon GO and physical activity among young adults: Difference in differences study. *BMJ (Clinical Research Ed.)*, 355. doi:10.1136/bmj.i6270 PMID:27965211

Hsieh, H. F., & Shannon, S. E. (2005). Three approaches to qualitative content analysis. *Qualitative Health Research*, *15*(9), 1277–1288. doi:10.1177/1049732305276687 PMID:16204405

Hsu, Y. S., Lin, Y. H., & Yang, B. (2017). Impact of augmented reality lessons on students' STEM interest. *Research and Practice in Technology Enhanced Learning*, *12*(1), 2. doi:10.118641039-016-0039-z PMID:30613251

Hurley, D. (2017). *The future of language learning: Augmented reality vs virtual reality*. Pearson. https://www.pearsoned.com/future-language-learning-augmented-reality-vs-virtual-reality-pearson-blog/

Immerman, D. (2019). *Just-in-time: The revolutionary new way to learn.* PTC. https://www.ptc.com/en/product-lifecycle-report/just-in-time-revolutionary-new-way-to-learn

Johnson, L., Becker, S. A., Cummins, M., Estrada, V., Freeman, A., & Hall, C. (2016). *NMC horizon report: 2016 higher education edition*. The New Media Consortium.

Johnson, L., Levine, A., Smith, R., & Stone, S. (2010). *The 2010 horizon report*. The New Media Consortium.

Johnson, L., Smith, R., Willis, H., Levine, A., & Haywood, K. (2011). *NMC horizon report* (2011 edition). The New Media Consortium.

Karagozlu, D., Kosarenko, N. N., Efimova, O. V., & Zubov, V. V. (2019). Identifying students' attitudes regarding augmented reality applications in science classes. *International Journal of Emerging Technologies in Learning*, *14*(22), 45–55. doi:10.3991/ijet.v14i22.11750

Khan, T., Johnston, K., & Ophoff, J. (2019). The impact of an augmented reality application on learning motivation of students. *Advances in Human-Computer Interaction*, *2019*, 2019. doi:10.1155/2019/7208494

Klopfer, E., & Squire, K. (2008). Environmental Detectives—The development of an augmented reality platform for environmental simulations. *Educational Technology Research and Development*, *56*(2), 203–228. doi:10.100711423-007-9037-6

Koutromanos, G., & Avraamidou, L. (2014). The use of mobile games in formal and informal learning environments: A review of the literature. *Educational Media International*, *51*(1), 49–65. doi:10.1080/09523987.2014.889409

Krippendorff, K. (2004). *Content analysis: An introduction to its methodology* (2nd ed.). Sage.

Kroeker, K. L. (2010). Mainstreaming augmented reality. *Communications of the ACM*, *53*(7), 19–21. doi:10.1145/1785414.1785422

Krueger, M. W., Gionfriddo, T., & Hinrichsen, K. (1985, April). VIDEOPLACE—an artificial reality. In *Proceedings of the SIGCHI Conference on Human Factors in Computing Systems* (pp. 35-40). Academic Press.

Küçük, S., Kapakin, S., & Göktaş, Y. (2016). Learning anatomy via mobile augmented reality: Effects on achievement and cognitive load. *Anatomical Sciences Education*, *9*(5), 411–421. doi:10.1002/ase.1603 PMID:26950521

Laine, T. (2018). Mobile educational augmented reality games: A systematic literature review and two case studies. *Computers*, *7*(1), 19. doi:10.3390/computers7010019

Landis, J. R., & Koch, G. G. (1977). The measurement of observer agreement for categorical data. *Biometrics*, *33*(1), 159–174. doi:10.2307/2529310 PMID:843571

Levie, A. [levie]. (2016, July 10). *Experts 5 years ago: "Augmented reality will transform education, healthcare, construction, commerce..." Experts today:"Pokemon!!!"*[Tweet]. Twitter. https://twitter.com/levie/status/752197211602038784

Lin, H. C. K., Chen, M. C., & Chang, C. K. (2015). Assessing the effectiveness of learning solid geometry by using an augmented reality-assisted learning system. *Interactive Learning Environments*, *23*(6), 799–810. doi:10.1080/10494820.2013.817435

Lukosch, S., Billinghurst, M., Alem, L., & Kiyokawa, K. (2015). Collaboration in augmented reality. *Computer Supported Cooperative Work*, *24*(6), 515–525. doi:10.100710606-015-9239-0

Lv, Z., Feng, L., Li, H., & Feng, S. (2014). Hand-free motion interaction on google glass. In SIGGRAPH Asia 2014 Mobile Graphics and Interactive Applications (pp. 1-1). doi:10.1145/2669062.2669066

Matuk, C. (2016). The learning affordances of augmented reality for museum exhibits on human health. *Museums & Social Issues*, *11*(1), 73–87. doi:10.1080/15596893.2016.1142815

McCartney, M. (2016). Margaret McCartney: game on for Pokémon GO. *BMJ: British Medical Journal (Online), 354.*

Milgram, P., & Kishino, F. (1994). A taxonomy of mixed reality visual displays. *IEICE Transactions on Information and Systems*, *77*(12), 1321–1329.

Miller, M. R., Jun, H., Herrera, F., Villa, J. Y., Welch, G., & Bailenson, J. N. (2019). Social interaction in augmented reality. *PLoS One*, *14*(5), e0216290. doi:10.1371/journal.pone.0216290 PMID:31086381

Mishra, P., & Koehler, M. J. (2006). Technological pedagogical content knowledge: A framework for teacher knowledge. *Teachers College Record*, *108*(6), 1017–1054. doi:10.1111/j.1467-9620.2006.00684.x

Mota, J. M., Ruiz-Rube, I., Dodero, J. M., & Arnedillo-Sánchez, I. (2018). Augmented reality mobile app development for all. *Computers & Electrical Engineering*, *65*, 250–260. doi:10.1016/j.compeleceng.2017.08.025

Mundy, M. A., Hernandez, J., & Green, M. (2019). Perceptions of the effects of augmented reality in the classroom. *Journal of Instructional Pedagogies*, 22.

Ong, A. (2010). Contextualized interdisciplinary learning in mainstream schools using augmented reality-based technology: A dream or reality? *Educational Technology*, 23–27.

Ouellette, J. (2019). *Augmented reality changes how people interact and communicate, study finds.* Arstechnica. https://arstechnica.com/science/2019/05/augmented-reality-changes-how-people-interact-and-communicate-study-finds/

PBS Wisconsin Education. [PBSWisconsinEdu]. (2009, August 12). *What is the potential of augmented reality in education? Check out the video on Layar...* http://bit.ly/uEg5C [Tweet]. Twitter. https://twitter.com/PBSWisconsinEdu/status/3267430045

Pellas, N., Fotaris, P., Kazanidis, I., & Wells, D. (2019). Augmenting the learning experience in primary and secondary school education: A systematic review of recent trends in augmented reality game-based learning. *Virtual Reality (Waltham Cross)*, *23*(4), 329–346. doi:10.100710055-018-0347-2

Pérez-López, D., & Contero, M. (2013). Delivering educational multimedia contents through an augmented reality application: A case study on its impact on knowledge acquisition and retention. *Turkish Online Journal of Educational Technology-TOJET*, *12*(4), 19–28.

Radu, I. (2014). Augmented reality in education: A meta-review and cross-media analysis. *Personal and Ubiquitous Computing*, *18*(6), 1533–1543. doi:10.100700779-013-0747-y

Rauschnabel, P. (2019). *Study: Augmented reality and privacy concerns*. Philipp Rauschnabel. http://www.philipprauschnabel.com/2019/02/research-on-augmented-reality-privacy/

Rauschnabel, P. A., He, J., & Ro, Y. K. (2018). Antecedents to the adoption of augmented reality smart glasses: A closer look at privacy risks. *Journal of Business Research*, *92*, 374–384. doi:10.1016/j.jbusres.2018.08.008

Rauschnabel, P. A., Rossmann, A., & tom Dieck, M. C. (2017). An adoption framework for mobile augmented reality games: The case of Pokémon Go. *Computers in Human Behavior*, *76*, 276–286. doi:10.1016/j.chb.2017.07.030

Rideout, V., & Robb, M. B. (2019). *The Common Sense census: Media use by tweens and teens, 2019*. Common Sense Media.

Rosenberg, L. B. (1993, September). Virtual fixtures: Perceptual tools for telerobotic manipulation. In *Proceedings of IEEE virtual reality annual international symposium* (pp. 76-82). IEEE. 10.1109/VRAIS.1993.380795

Roylance, W. (2017). *Augmented reality: A holistic approach to creativity*. Diplomatic Courier. https://www.diplomaticourier.com/posts/augmented-reality-holistic-approach-creativity

Salmi, H., Thuneberg, H., & Vainikainen, M. (2016). Making the invisible observable by augmented reality in informal science education context. *International Journal of Science Education. Part B*, *7*(3), 253–268.

Scrivner, O., Madewell, J., Buckley, C., & Perez, N. (2016, December). Augmented reality digital technologies (ARDT) for foreign language teaching and learning. In 2016 future technologies conference (FTC) (pp. 395-398). IEEE.

Shulman, L. S. (1986). Those who understand: Knowledge growth in teaching. *Educational Researcher*, *15*(2), 4–14. doi:10.3102/0013189X015002004

Squire, K. D., & Jan, M. (2007). Mad City Mystery: Developing scientific argumentation skills with a place-based augmented reality game on handheld computers. *Journal of Science Education and Technology*, *16*(1), 5–29. doi:10.100710956-006-9037-z

Sutherland, I. E. (1968, December). A head-mounted three-dimensional display. In *Proceedings of the December 9-11, 1968, Fall Joint Computer Conference, Part I* (pp. 757-764). Academic Press.

Sylaiou, S., Mania, K., Karoulis, A., & White, M. (2010). Exploring the relationship between presence and enjoyment in a virtual museum. *International Journal of Human-Computer Studies*, *68*(5), 243–253. doi:10.1016/j.ijhcs.2009.11.002

Taylor, T. (2015, January 29). *Behind the NFL's yellow 1st down line, and what's next for sports TV.* Sports Illustrated. https://www.si.com/edge/2015/01/29/behind-nfl-yellow-first-down-line-sportsvision-technology

The Tech Expo. [TheTechExpo]. (2011, April 30). *The rise of augmented reality in #education* http://ow.ly/4Keq8 #AR *#augmentedreality*[Tweet]. Twitter. https://twitter.com/TheTechExpo/status/64262215791943680

Tscholl, M., & Lindgren, R. (2014). Empowering digital interactions with real world conversation. *TechTrends*, *58*(1), 56–63. doi:10.100711528-013-0721-6

Tzima, S., Styliaras, G., & Bassounas, A. (2019). Augmented reality applications in education: Teachers point of view. *Education in Science*, *9*(2), 99. doi:10.3390/educsci9020099

Vafa, S., Sappington, K., & Coombs-Richardson, R. (2018). Using augmented reality to increase interaction in online courses. *International Journal of Educational Technology and Learning*, *3*(2), 65–68. doi:10.20448/2003.32.65.68

Vaismoradi, M., Turunen, H., & Bondas, T. (2013). Content analysis and thematic analysis: Implications for conducting a qualitative descriptive study. *Nursing & Health Sciences*, *15*(3), 398–405. doi:10.1111/nhs.12048 PMID:23480423

Webel, S., Bockholt, U., Engelke, T., Gavish, N., Olbrich, M., & Preusche, C. (2013). An augmented reality training platform for assembly and maintenance skills. *Robotics and Autonomous Systems*, *61*(4), 398–403. doi:10.1016/j.robot.2012.09.013

Wei, X., Weng, D., Liu, Y., & Wang, Y. (2015). Teaching based on augmented reality for a technical creative design course. *Computers & Education*, *81*, 221–234. doi:10.1016/j.compedu.2014.10.017

Williams, A. S. [AdamScottWillia]. (2018, November 10). *A great look at the pro's & cons of AR in the classroom! #eci833 #education #edtech Augmented reality in education* [Tweet]. Twitter. https://twitter.com/AdamScottWillia/status/1061138121096654848

Wingfield, N., & Isaac, M. (2016). *Pokémon Go brings augmented reality to a mass audience*. The New York Times. https://www.nytimes.com/2016/07/12/technology/pokemon-go-brings-augmented-reality-to-a-mass-audience.html

Wojciechowski, R., & Cellary, W. (2013). Evaluation of learners' attitude toward learning in ARIES augmented reality environments. *Computers & Education*, *68*, 570–585. doi:10.1016/j.compedu.2013.02.014

Wu, H. K., Lee, S. W. Y., Chang, H. Y., & Liang, J. C. (2013). Current status, opportunities and challenges of augmented reality in education. *Computers & Education*, *62*, 41–49. doi:10.1016/j.compedu.2012.10.024

Yilmaz, R. M., & Goktas, Y. (2017). Using augmented reality technology in storytelling activities: Examining elementary students' narrative skill and creativity. *Virtual Reality (Waltham Cross)*, *21*(2), 75–89. doi:10.100710055-016-0300-1

Yoon, S. A., & Wang, J. (2014). Making the invisible visible in science museums through augmented reality devices. *TechTrends*, *58*(1), 49–55. doi:10.100711528-013-0720-7

Yoshinaga, T. (2017). Introduction to next-generation AR devices: Overview and case study of Microsoft HoloLens and Google Tango. *Journal of the Visualization Society of Japan*.

Zarraonandia, T., Aedo, I., Díaz, P., & Montero Montes, A. (2014). Augmented presentations: Supporting the communication in presentations by means of augmented reality. *International Journal of Human-Computer Interaction*, *30*(10), 829–838. doi:10.1080/10447318.2014.927283

Zünd, F., Ryffel, M., Magnenat, S., Marra, A., Nitti, M., Kapadia, M., Noris, G., Mitchell, K., Gross, M., & Sumner, R. W. (2015). Augmented creativity: Bridging the real and virtual worlds to enhance creative play. In SIGGRAPH Asia 2015 Mobile Graphics and Interactive Applications (pp. 1-7). Academic Press.

ADDITIONAL READING

Altinpulluk, H. (2019). Determining the trends of using augmented reality in education between 2006-2016. *Education and Information Technologies*, *24*(2), 1089–1114. doi:10.100710639-018-9806-3

Ferdig, R. E. (2006). Assessing technologies for teaching and learning: Understanding the importance of technological pedagogical content knowledge. *British Journal of Educational Technology*, *37*(5), 749–760. doi:10.1111/j.1467-8535.2006.00559.x

Foster, A., Mishra, P., & Koehler, M. (2011). Digital game analysis: Using the Technological Pedagogical Content Knowledge framework to determine the affordances of a game for learning. In *Learning to Play: Exploring the Future of Education with Video Games*. Peter Lang Publications.

Foster, A., Shah, M., Barany, A., Petrovich, M. E., Cellitti, J., Duka, M., Swiecki, Z., Siebart-Evenstone, A., Kinley, H., Quigley, P., & Shaffer, D. W. (2018, June). Virtual Learning Environments for Promoting Self Transformation: Iterative Design and Implementation of Philadelphia Land Science. In *International Conference on Immersive Learning* (pp. 3-22). Springer, Cham. 10.1007/978-3-319-93596-6_1

Foster, A. N., & Mishra, P. (2009). Games, Claims, Genres, and Learning. In R. Ferdig (Ed.), *Handbook of Research on Effective Electronic Gaming in Education* (pp. 33–50). IGI Global. doi:10.4018/978-1-59904-808-6.ch002

Hsu, C. Y., Tsai, M. J., Chang, Y. H., & Liang, J. C. (2017). Surveying in-service teachers' beliefs about game-based learning and perceptions of technological pedagogical and content knowledge of games. *Journal of Educational Technology & Society*, *20*(1), 134–143.

Katz-Buonincontro, J., & Foster, A. (2012). Examining students' cultural identity and player styles through avatar drawings in a game-based classroom. In *Assessment in Game-Based Learning* (pp. 335–353). Springer. doi:10.1007/978-1-4614-3546-4_17

Kaya, O. S., & Bicen, H. (2019). Study of augmented reality applications use in education and its effect on the academic performance. *International Journal of Distance Education Technologies*, *17*(3), 25–36. doi:10.4018/IJDET.2019070102

O'Shea, P. M. (2011). Augmented reality in education: Current trends. *International Journal of Gaming and Computer-Mediated Simulations*, *3*(1).

KEY TERMS AND DEFINITIONS

Affective Outcomes: A sub-category of learning outcomes that focuses on the moods, feelings, or attitudes that result from an educational experience.

Affordances: Features of an object, interface, or application that indicate what can be done or accomplished by using the object.

Augmented Reality (AR): The overlaying of interactive digital elements onto the physical world in real time.

Claims of AR: An assertion concerning augmented reality which focuses on the best practices, learning outcomes, barriers to adoption, and general beliefs about teaching and learning with AR.

Pedagogical Outcomes: A set of outcomes which are concerned with the ways in which teachers design, integrate, and implement effective teaching practice into their instruction.

Psychomotor Outcomes: A sub-category of learning outcomes that focuses on physical movement, sensory input, and spatial perception.

Technological Outcomes: A set of outcomes which are concerned with technological possibilities, advantages, and disadvantages when utilizing technology within one's instruction.

Technological Pedagogical Content Knowledge (TPACK): A framework to describe the type of knowledge most worth knowing for instructors attempting to integrate educational technologies into their instruction.

Chapter 4
Design Principles for Educational Mixed Reality?
Adaptions of the Design Recommendations of Multimedia Learning

Vanesa Yepes-Serna
Bauhaus-Universität Weimar, Germany

Mario Wolf
https://orcid.org/0000-0002-0972-1117
Bauhaus-Universität Weimar, Germany

Heinrich Söbke
https://orcid.org/0000-0002-0105-3126
Bauhaus-Universität Weimar, Germany

Steffi Zander
University of Applied Sciences Magdeburg-Stendal, Germany

ABSTRACT

Mixed reality (MR) applications are widely considered to be effective educational tools. However, the use of MR alone cannot ensure learning, and studies even suggest that the affordances of this technology could decrease the mental processes required for the acquisition of new knowledge. Like any other technological innovation, the educational possibilities of MR are closely related to the design of its contents. Despite this, there are no design recommendations for MR focused on learning. Educational psychology presents a range of empirically proven design guidelines for multimedia learning environments. This chapter reviews existing guidelines and categorizes them into principles related to the perception of information and the related essential information processing (design principles) and principles aiming at promoting generative learning (activating principles). These principles are translated to MR-learning environments.

DOI: 10.4018/978-1-7998-5043-4.ch004

INTRODUCTION

Mixed reality (MR) has become a fast-developing field of application and research (Dörner et al., 2019; Schmalstieg & Höllerer, 2016), and MR technologies are increasingly used as educational tools. Describing the merging of the real world and virtual elements with the idea to create new and immersive environments, the most applied scheme to understand the range of technologies combined by MR is the "reality–virtuality continuum" (Milgram et al., 1994). The continuous spectrum of this scheme connects the two poles of reality to virtual reality. The area in between the two extremes is defined as MR. Through this range, MR comprises all possible variations of technologies such as augmented reality (AR) and virtual reality (VR) combining real and virtual objects. Moreover, compared to other media, MR has some distinctive characteristics such as immersion and spatiality. Based on the reality–virtuality continuum, this chapter does not refer to one particular technology of MR. Instead, MR refers to a wide spectrum of technologies between the two poles.

The opportunities of MR-based learning environments have been explored in many research reviews (Akçayır & Akçayır, 2017; Chen et al., 2017; Freina & Ott, 2015; Garzón & Acevedo, 2019; Merchant et al., 2014; Radu, 2014; Sommerauer & Müller, 2018). The reviews reveal that advantages of MR for learning are seen in the highly realistic presentation of information that otherwise is not accessible, for instance, when visualizing potentially dangerous situations (e.g., flight simulations and machines in areas with chemicals). Moreover, MR allows presenting relevant augmented and realistic information side by side. This integration of information sources allows for information processing while learning. Further, specifically spatial information can be presented highly realistically. This might be especially helpful for learners with less prior knowledge and less spatial abilities, as such learner prerequisites might be compensated by MR. MR learning environments also allow for new kinds of direct interactions with the learning content, which might support the processing of information and the integration of new knowledge in preexisting mental models of the learners, due to realistic manipulations which increase embodied experiences. Last but not least, MR environments are expected to generate a feeling of high immersion in the learning environment, which increases the motivation to engage oneself in learning. All these advantages are combined with the challenge of orienting and processing highly complex environments. Nevertheless, empirical studies reveal mixed results for learning and motivation in MR environments. At this, it is of high interest to generate empirically proven guidelines for the creation of MR for learning. Besides the question of support of human information processing, such guidelines and design recommendations should explicitly take into account the affordances of generative learning processes.

A good instance showing the necessity to take higher learning processes into account in the development and design of educational MR technologies are navigation systems: While navigation systems support spatial information processing, their affordances do not promote the acquisition of spatial knowledge since they are designed to anticipate mental processes and not to foster the acquisition of knowledge (Adler, 2001; Münzer et al., 2012). The anticipation of mental processes by media is also called *supplantation* and is critically reflected in terms of its potentials to foster a deeper understanding of digital materials (Höffler & Leutner, 2007; Salomon, 2012; Schnotz & Bannert, 2003).

An essential part of MR technologies in general and its usage in learning environments in particular is the design of the user interface (UI). UIs are composed of the interactions, the input devices, and the sensory stimuli, that support human–machine interaction. When different sensory stimuli are generated simultaneously, interfaces are known as multimodal. In the past years, guidelines for the general design for UIs for MR-based tools have been published (LaViola et al., 2017; Pangilinan et al., 2019). However, not all the features required for a regular UI are adequate for successful learning processes and up to date. There is little discussion on how to associate the existing UI heuristics and good practices with the current learning principles of multimodal learning. Further, the design for multimedia applications for learning purposes is already well covered by guidelines, the effectiveness of which has been empirically validated (Mayer, 2009). Although MR applications seem to have an advantage over other interventions (Garzón & Acevedo, 2019), there are no such guidelines for MR applications. Hence there is a need for specific standards for the development of educational MR user interfaces (Zender et al., 2018). Thus, the motivation of the present chapter is to analyze current design principles for media-supported learning and to evaluate the transferability for these principles to educational applications in MR. Consequently, this segment is a preliminary attempt to solve the research gap in heuristics for user interfaces of MR-based applications intended to support learning.

METHODOLOGY

The study was based on the assumption that MR learning environments should especially fulfill design guidelines, which address the human cognitive architecture, characteristics of human learning, and motivation processes. With the aim to create an overview of design heuristics for MR that are based on the psychological foundations of learning processes, the focus of the study lied on finding design recommendations for the perception as well for the deeper processing of digitally presented information. The methodological approach comprised three steps.

First, a literature review was conducted to gain a comprehensive overview of the fundamentals of design in the field of digital learning technologies. The analysis focused on theoretical and normative approaches as well as empirical findings referring to applications of various fields of multimedia learning, such as simulations, location-based apps, or quizzes.

In a second step, several interdisciplinary workshops were conducted aiming to identify and cluster design principles for MR applications. Therefore, the meaning of the findings of the literature review referring to the design of multimedia learning in general was discussed, and its potential role for MR learning applications was assessed. Through this deliberative process relevant design principles were identified, which were clustered on different levels of learning processes. Here, the perception of information and the deeper processing of information in working memory appeared as prominent. Both lines of processing were seen to be crucial to learn complex information. While the first is often addressed in interface design, the latter is part of design principles that focus on the acquisition of more complex knowledge, such as the acquisition of mental models. The workshops were attended by scientists of various disciplines, such as psychology and instructional and interface design, as well as civil engineering and urban planning.

As a result of the workshops, two approaches are used to categorize the presented design principles: On the one hand, the heuristics that make it possible to perceive and process information efficiently. In particular, such recommendations aiming at tailoring UI design for the human cognitive architecture (*design principles*); and on the other hand, the guidelines aiming at fostering generative learning—the active and effortful, motivated acquisition of new knowledge (*activating principles*). Those approaches rely on the cognitive load theory (Sweller et al., 2011) and the cognitive theory of multimedia learning (Mayer, 2009).

Third, the identified design principles from learning with multimedia were transferred to examples of MR learning environments in order to demonstrate its applicability. The selection of the presented applications followed an exemplary approach. The aim was to find for each identified design principle at least one case study.

In the process of transferring the design principles to MR examples, it is essential to highlight that those design principles are originally aligned with two-dimensional images. Characteristics of MR are not considered, as systematic studies on design principles for MR are less common due to the novelty of the technology. However, as these design principles are based on fundamental psychological parameters of human information processing and cognitive architecture, we suggest that they may also be applicable to MR environments. Since this study might mark one of the beginnings in the field of MR design principles, the findings should be part of recommendations for future research.

An essential part of the design guidelines addresses designers and developers. Yet, the design guidelines may also be helpful for stakeholders in the education context, such as decision-makers, teachers, and students.

LEARNING MODELS

Psychological models of learning with media are well suited to inform designers of educational learning contents (e.g., desktop, MR, VR, and AR-based) on how to tailor the design of such materials to the cognitive and motivational-affective system of human information processing. Basic characteristics of human information processing and the corresponding design principles for educational media are incorporated in the *cognitive-affective theory of multimedia learning* by Moreno (*CATML*; 2007). This model is based on Mayer's widely known *cognitive theory of multimedia learning* (*CTML*; Mayer & Moreno, 2003; Mayer, 2009) as well as on *cognitive load theory* by Sweller et al. (*CLT*, 2011).

All of those models are grounded on the same basic psychological assumptions:

Limited Capacity Assumption

Information processing consists of perceptual and selective attentional processes in sensory memory, organizing processes of information in the working memory, and the storage of information in the long-term memory. Thereby, a critical limitation of the amount of information to be processed at the same time is known as the *working memory*. Based on Miller (1956) and Baddeley (1992), all models assume a limited capacity regarding the amount and the time for organizing information in the working memory before the integration of the new information into the structures of the long-term memory. When learning with media, we are exposed to different kinds of information representations. (e.g., text and pictures). The amount of such representations is even increased in MR as multimodal information is presented, and multiple interactions are allowed. This increases orientation processing and also the amount of to be processed information. Perceiving, selecting, organizing, and integrating these multiple representations requires the limited resources of the working memory. This is considered to impose cognitive load on the limited resources (Mayer & Fiorella, 2014; Sweller et al., 2011). For this reason, it is of importance to tailor instruction of MR learning environments to the characteristics of the working memory. Tailored instructional materials allow economic and resource-respective processing, resulting in a deep understanding of the contents and information storage in the long-term memory.

Dual-Channel Assumption

Based on Paivio (1990), the *dual-channel assumption* states that different cognitive systems are involved in the processing of verbal-auditive and pictorial-visual information and that information from those different modalities is represented semantically and also by their specific sensory characteristics (visual and verbal-auditive) long term memory. The basic assumption that different sensory input is processed in different cognitive subsystems is reflected in CATML, CTML, and CLT. This assumption builds the idea for the design recommendation to present pictorial information together with auditory-verbal information to avoid a split of attention when multiple information sources have to be processed in an only-visual manner (cf. the split-attention effect and modality principle; Sweller et al., 2011; Mayer, 2014). As MR integrates multimodal information, such assumptions and the related empirically proven design principles built a solid basis and should be amplified in the future.

Active Processing Assumption

Humans have to actively engage in the processing of information in order to develop a coherent mental model of multiple representations, meaning that learners have to select incoming information actively, to organize this information in the working memory and to integrate it with preexisting schemata in the long-term memory (Fiorella & Mayer, 2016). A good MR-learning environment should support not only the selection of information (perception processes) but also learning strategies that support the organization and integration of information and to generate one's own mental model of the content.

Related to this, the effects of motivational-affective factors render the core of the CATLM, which extends the strictly cognitive approach of the CTML. The CATLM posits that the design of multimedia materials should seek to increase situational interest, motivation, and positive affect by arguing that the resulting engagement can lead users to spend more time interacting with the learning materials fostering consequent beneficial effects on comprehension. Beside this, Moreno (2007) moreover incorporates tactile, olfactory, and other sensory input to the CTLM model. When talking about educational MR, design should be considered—specifically those sensory, tactile, and embodied interactions with learning materials, and their role for intrinsically motivated learning should be proven empirically. This leads to a fourth basic psychological assumption, which, might be integrated into the theoretical background of the CTML and CATLM: the role of the body in cognition—embodiment.

A Fourth Assumption, Embodied Cognition

The latter argument substantiates that the basic psychological assumptions by Mayer (2014) described above might be amplified by a fourth assumption, embodiment, when talking about the design of educational MR. Various studies suggest that embodied interactions and gestures are involved in learning processes and may support learning (e.g., Chu & Kita, 2011; Goldin-Meadow et al., 2009; Macken & Ginns, 2014), and that movement influences cognition (Castro-Alonso et al., 2019). Thus, embodiment should be considered as an additional dimension when designing educational user interfaces for MR, as MR applications allow direct interactions via 2D- and 3D-gestures and movements—embodied interactions—with the respective educational content. Nevertheless, not all movements can be related to the acquisition of robust mental models, and the design of environmental settings should encourage learners to link their gestures with specific concepts or reasoning processes represented by particular movements.

A range of researchers proposes guidelines for embodiment fostering learning (DeSutter & Stieff, 2017; Lindgren & Johnson-Glenberg, 2013; Mayer, 2014; Wilson, 2002).

Based on the described models, Mayer (2014) subdivided the design principles for educational media into three categories: principles to manage essential processing, principles to manage extraneous processing, and principles based on social cues. These categories are integrated and referred in this chapter as design principles, which include all principles that help to process the complexity of information, e.g., segmenting and pre-training. We also present a second group, activating principles, that unifies principles supporting perception, selection, and organization of information in the working memory, e.g., coherence, signaling, and spatial and temporal contiguity. This compilation of activating principles also includes principles based on social cues, covering foundations that are more focused on the stimulation of motivational and affective factors during information processing, e.g., personalization, voice, image, and embodiment. The following sections describe these principles and explain their application to the design of educational MR, along with examples from research and development.

DESIGN PRINCIPLES: AIMING AT EFFICIENT INFORMATION PROCESSING

An essential objective of the design of user interfaces is to facilitate the collection and processing of information. In the following, principles that facilitate information acquisition and processing are presented and discussed with reference to MR.

Multimedia Principle

The simultaneous textual and visual representation supports learning processes. Numerous empirical studies support that knowledge acquisition is more effective when images (static or dynamic) and words are presented together rather than with the usage of texts alone (Mayer & Moreno, 2003; for an overview, see Mayer, 2014). However, the usage of images should always align with the learning goals (Clark & Mayer, 2016). Furthermore, visuals and text need to be attuned/coordinated to create meaning for the learner, and images should be added only when they support and complement the learning topic (see Coherence Principle for MR examples).

Modality Principle

Presenting information via audio rather than on-screen text can improve learning. Especially when describing images or contents, the use of the auditive channel can result in a significant learning gain when compared with the presentation of written information (Mayer, 2009). The use of images along with auditory information enhances learning processes to a higher degree than visual-pictorial information combined with visual- textual information. Thus the integration of spoken text into an MR learning tool is considered to decrease the cognitive load in comparison to visual text in MR (Makransky et al., 2019). This principle is seen to be inherently supported by AR and, therefore, considered as a core element of MR user interfaces (Sommerauer & Müller, 2014). Furthermore, it is seen as a remedy to the split attention effect (Dixon et al., 2018). Overall, the integration of auditory information should systematically be explored when designing MR learning tools. However, the effectiveness depends on the length of the textual information and on the pre-knowledge of learners (Sweller et al., 2011).

Coherence Principle

Extraneous or non-related words, pictures, and sounds should be excluded from an interface aimed at learning. This approach is particularly relevant in MR user interfaces where only the essential information should be displayed in order to avoid that learners use their limited process capacity on extraneous material instead of focusing on the learning goal (Mayer & Moreno, 2003). In their public Egyptian Oracle Project, Gillam & Jacobson (2015) aimed to represent an ancient Egyptian temple with educational purposes. Since the learning goal of this project is to instruct in a typical religious or public ceremony during the late Egyptian period, the authors propose a graphic depiction that is a symbolic representation of a cult in Egypt instead of a realistic portrayal. In order to do so, the virtual environment includes a minimum of architectural features required to be a representative example of a temple of the mentioned historical period, knowingly reducing factual features that can interfere with the learning objective. As an illustrative application of the coherence principle, in this project, realistic details were excluded intentionally to provide users clear instructional targets such as the universal features from this kind of temples by avoiding technical aspects related to the architecture of each historical period.

Another relevant application of the coherence principle is the driving simulator by the Teen Driver Safety Research team at Children's Hospital of Philadelphia. As described by Jacobson (2017), the learning goal of the simulator is to teach teenagers how to drive. Therefore, the research team decided to work with low-resolution images instead of highly realistic ones in order to direct student's attention to important aspects related to safe driving.

Signaling Principle

To promote learning, interfaces should highlight the organization and relevance of the materials by using clues and signals. The *signaling principle* states that a multimedia message can be learned more deeply when the hierarchy of the contents is highlighted by clues (Mayer, 2014). Extraneous cognitive processes are reduced when these cues help to direct the attention of the user to the most relevant parts of the material (Richter et al., 2016). In MR environments, signaling techniques can support attentional processes (e.g., selection of relevant information) addressing educational challenges such as frustration and high dropout rates. This was the case in the project *P.I.A.N.O.* by Ulm University in Germany and the Carnegie Mellon University in the US (Rogers et al., 2014). In *P.I.A.N.O.*, music notation is projected onto a regular piano to facilitate correct fingering creating an augmented piano by means of a short-throw projector. The signaling principle techniques are distinctly applied in the three different modes offered by the system helping to reduce the mental effort related to the task with specific annotations: a *listen mode* that helps to visualize rhythm and melody only; a *practice mode* that shows the note visualization only when the correct key is pressed; and a *play mode* without visualizations that measures the accuracy of the performance.

Contiguity Principle

The *contiguity principle* states that corresponding words and pictures should be presented near to each other in time and space to support learning and to reduce the imposed load on the limited capacity of working memory. The advantage of presenting corresponding information and images together is a reduced need to search for the adequate integration of different sources and therefore allowing the user to redirect these cognitive resources to understand the material (Mayer, 2009). In MR interfaces, augmentations should appear at a short distance in space and time from its corresponding object. A practical application of this principle appears in the project *AuCity* (Söbke et al., 2018). *AugView* (Augview Limited, 2016), the commercial application facilitated for civil engineering education, highlights otherwise invisible configurations by superimposing technical infrastructure, such as water pipes and sewers directly on the street where these structures are located based on a geographical information system (GIS; see Figure 1).

Figure 1. AR app AugView illustrating water pipes (left: screenshot, right: application scenario (Authors)

As an example on another scale, a toolkit designed for for mechanical engineer students seeks to develop the ability to create and read orthographic and axonometric projections by increasing the spatial ability of the users (Martín-Gutiérrez et al., 2010). In order to reach the goal, the augmented book is part of a course with different stages showing students tridimensional versions that complement the training activities directly on an exercise sheet.

Segmenting Principle

Short learning units that learners can repeat on demand facilitate learning. The *segmenting principle* is especially relevant when contents incorporate a high level of complexity or the learner is not familiar with the topic (Clark & Mayer, 2016). In digital scenarios, such as e-learning contents, this principle can be applied by segmentation of the contents in units or chapters that allow users to control their own progress. Correspondingly, in MR environments, this method is also available together with more opportunities presenting information in segments by the use of different layers, perspectives, and interaction metaphors.

An interesting example of a technique that allows students to manage the stream of information and progress at their own pace is the aircraft engine disassembly simulation by Xie et al. (2019). In this case, the engine simulation is part of a procedure comprised of three sections of increasing difficulty, as aforementioned, namely Introduction, Tutorial, and Practice. Furthermore, different points of view are used to present a general impression of the engine, in the following stage, users can interact and disassemble the mechanism according to a specific sequence that can be adapted to different levels of difficulty.

Personalization Principle

Studies have shown that the use of conversational or personal style when addressing the learner can increase knowledge retention (Reichelt et al., 2014). In digital environments, this notion works together with what is known as the *voice principle*, indicating that a human voice, rather than an artificial or machine one is considered beneficial to the learning process (Clark & Mayer, 2016). In MR educational environments, personalization should also be extended to pedagogical agents, where these kinds of characters address students in a natural and personal style while using a human-like voice, since it has been demonstrated that students engage more in understanding contents when these learning environments are perceived as a dialog with a peer (Mayer, 2014). The use of conversational style should be addressed by including personal and individualized interactions with tutors and pedagogical agents. Nevertheless, the content needs to be adapted to personal requirements.

The VR application *Virtual Orator* highlights the core of personalization style in an exposure therapy training for public speaking anxiety (Takac et al., 2019). In addition to incorporate audiences with adjustable responses ranging from encouraging to negative, the environment also includes characters that can address personalized questions and comments to the trainee. The performance of the speaker is also evaluated by its personal interactions with the virtual audience, namely, quality of eye contact and the number of views to presentation slides.

Embodiment Design Principles for Learning

The incorporation of movements has been proven beneficial to learning (see Learning Models). However, not all movements can be related to successful learning, and MR educational environments should promote the association of related gestures with its particular concept or reasoning process. In their study from 2017, DeSutter & Stieff proposed three principles that could support meaningful learning throughout embodiment, stating that these kinds of environments need to: (a) include scaffolds to promote the progressive introduction to gestures and its relationship with the learning objective, (b) leverage movements to simulate high-fidelity spatial operations that would otherwise be imagined by the learner, and (c) link innovative tools, such as visualizations or other simulations, to embodied actions through interface elements and input devices.

As a practical example of the application of these principles, the researchers developed an embodied interface for organic chemistry training. When using this application, students can move to the left or the right, and a molecule shifts accordingly, representing how the object would appear when seen in a macroscopic scale. A second example is the VR application *Rotate it!*, aiming to train spatial abilities with the focus on mental rotation in particular (see Figure 2). Interactions with the objects are possible via direct interaction by grabbing an object and moving it around in three dimensions. By using virtual hands and rotation gestures to perform the rotation tasks, spatial abilities are fostered, especially for low-spatial-abilities learners. This is possible by the application of the embodiment principle (Zander et al., 2020).

Figure 2. VR application to perform spatial ability tasks by the use of direct interactions with the tridimensional figures (Authors)

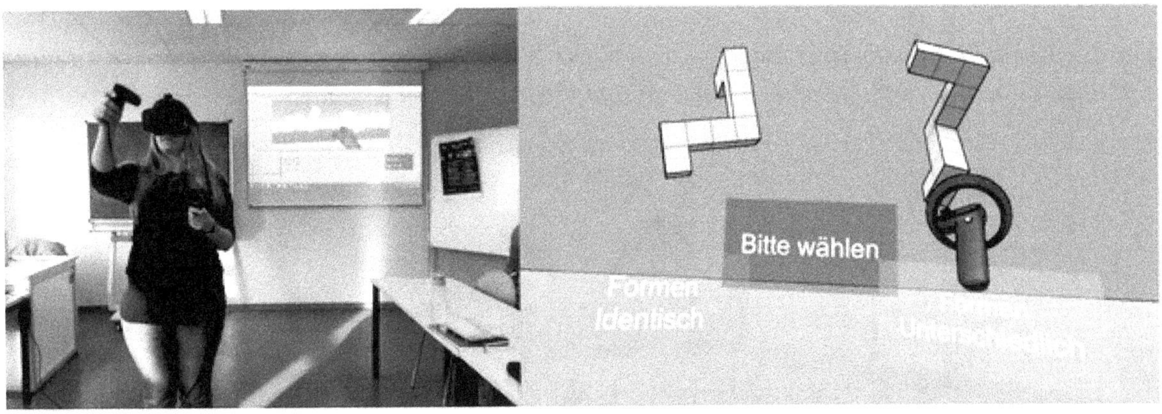

ACTIVATING PRINCIPLES: STIMULATING MENTAL PROCESSES

In the following part, those principles are described and applied to the use of educational MR, which supports the active processing of information. It was shown above that Mayer's principles, on the one hand, were shown to enable information processing by addressing the basic characteristics of the human cognitive architecture. On the other hand, in the basic assumptions of CTML and CATLM, it is stated that learning is the active processing of information. Various authors argue that besides the facilitation of information processing by the application of design principles, instructional designers should also apply principles that encourage active information processing (Mayer, 2009; Sweller et al., 2003). As an example, Bjork & Bjork (2011) refer to the implementation of *desirable difficulties,* arguing that learning tasks that deliberately require higher mental effort increases long-term learning outcomes. Based on these various principles that are known to stimulate the required mental processes applicable to MR, the following is a discussion of central empirically proven activating principles from the areas of the CTML and CATLM.

Generative Drawing

Generative drawing involves the creation of sketches of newly acquired subject matter leading to an increased mental effort beneficial to learning. The process of actively generating an external model of what was learned is seen to support learning by an active process what reconstructing the complex structures of the learning content (Leutner & Schmeck, 2014; Fiorella & Mayer, 2016). In MR, this principle can be applied in the location-based augmented reality for civil engineers, introduced in Figure 3). Söbke et al. (2018) describe the principle being applied in an instructional setting in the curriculum of civil engineering. Students were asked to draw sewer networks in the application, using their knowledge acquired about the relevant variables (e.g., depth, inclination, and angles of the underground) that influence how to design and plan sewer networks. This led to a deeper examination of the learning content.

A second example is the VR *Rotate it!* application. Its backend here allows users to integrate their own spatial objects and thereby create their own mental rotation tasks. A study seeks to investigate whether learners' development of rotation tasks for VR and its digitalization in a simple software fosters mental rotation (see Figure 3).

Figure 3. Learners creating their own tasks by the use of generative drawing for its subsequent digitalization and use in a VR application for mental rotation task solving (Authors)

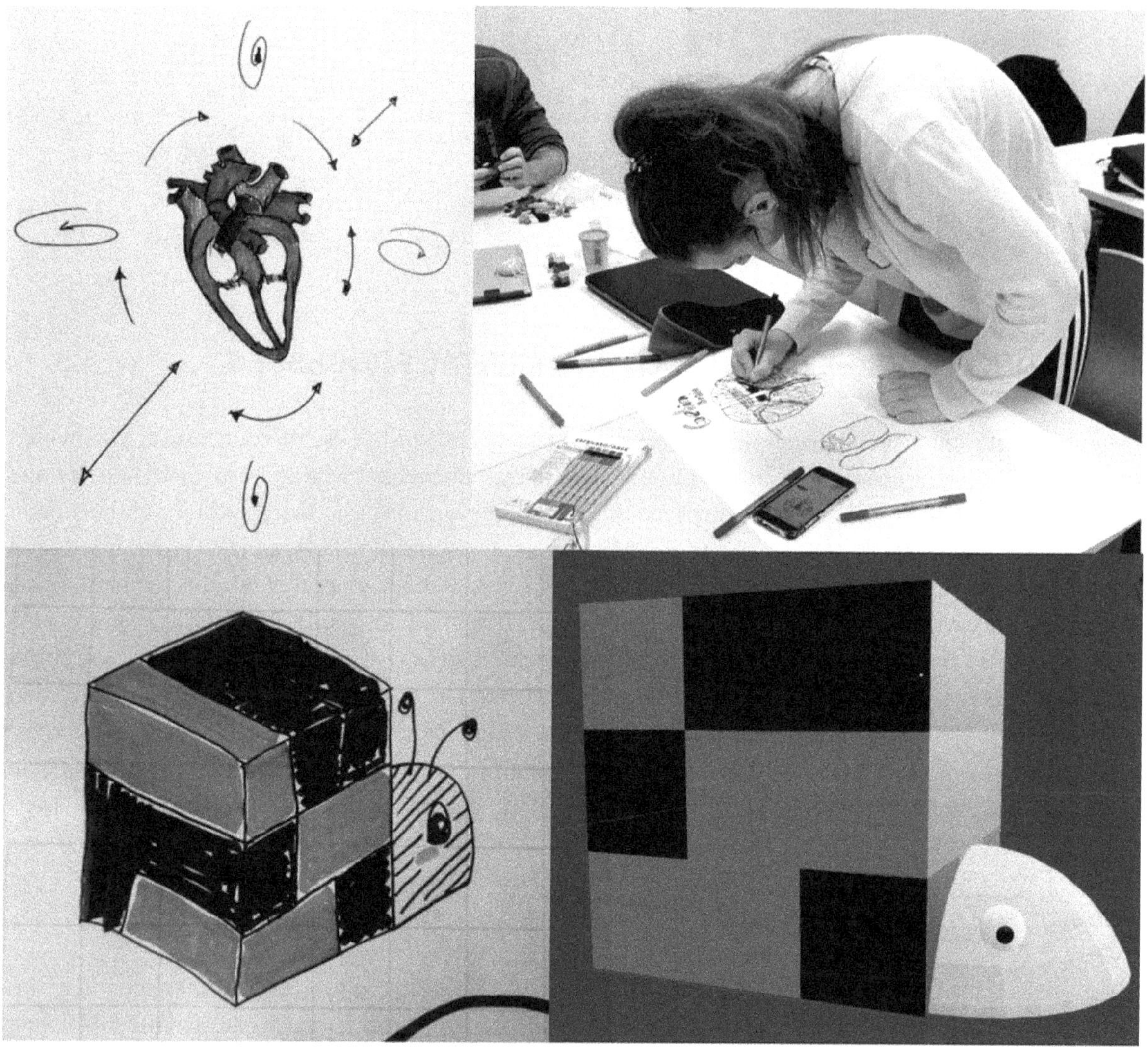

In *Rainwater Management*, which is developed in a collaboration of civil engineers, psychologists, and computer scientists, it is possible to create one's own learning scenario via an authoring tool. The tool allows for the manipulation of core factors when planning cities in regard to rainwater management, such as the amount of rain, ground inclination, and ground texture (see Figure 4). A study seeks to analyze the conditions and effects of self-generation of such complex scenarios.

Figure 4. Rainwater Management virtual reality simulation for civil engineering educational purposes (Authors)

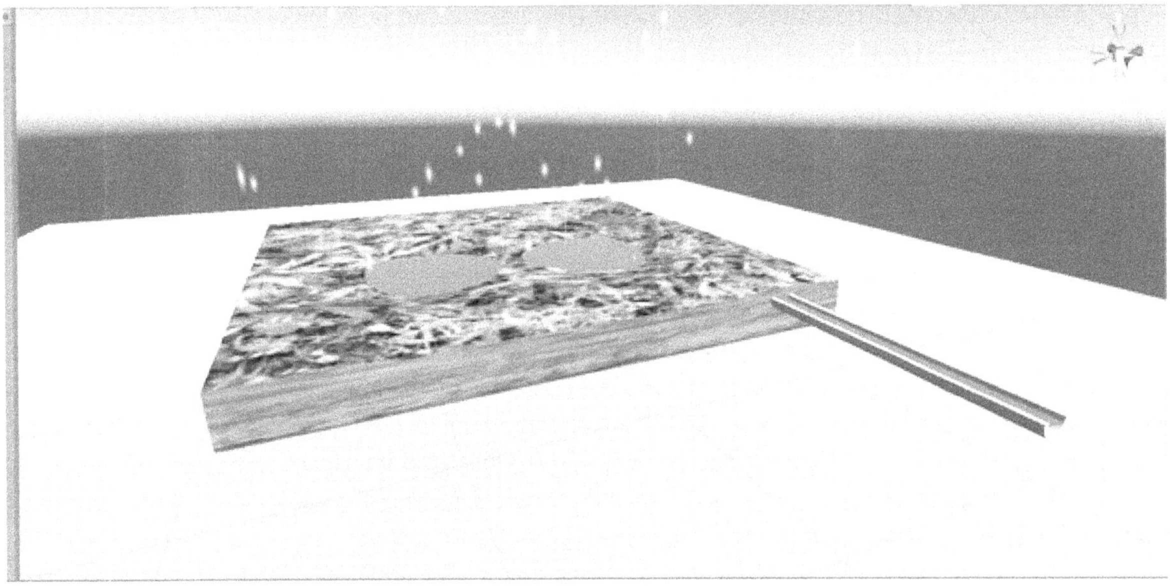

Self-Explanation

Self-explanation is when learners explain to themselves what they have just learned. Here too, increased mental effort can be activating and beneficial to learning (Roy & Chi, 2005; Mayer, 2014). In the example of *AugView* presenting sewer networks, students were instructed to explain their drawings and thoughts to each other (Söbke et al., 2018). This can be seen as an example of how this principle can easily be applied in small groups. A further implementation option is to integrate prompts in the MR that ask the learner for an explanation of the information or model learned (Mayer & Fiorella, 2014). This is closely connected to the metacognitive strategies principle, in which learners are prompted to reflect on their learning processes (e.g., current status, planning, the effectiveness of applied strategies, and quality of the result). Depending on the instruction goal, this can also be applied in MR when the active execution of self-regulated learning strategies should be fostered (Hung et al., 2014).

Coherence Formation in Multiple Representations

Coherence formation in multiple representations allows learners to actively search and reflect about coherences between text and image information. This process is regarded as conducive to learning and activation (Seufert, 2003). An interesting illustration of the application of this principle can be seen in the research of Müller-Plath and her collegues (2019) where a 3D navigation simulator of a sailboat was used to understand the acquisition of orientation and wayfinding abilities by sailors at the Baltic coast. As part of the study and in order to evaluate the quality of the cognitive map acquired by the participants, the simulator users were encouraged to produce hand drawings of the route after learning the course by using a classical navigation paper chart (i.e., paper map) and a GPS assisted navigator or electronic charting system (ECS). The results of this series of experiments showed that drawings are clear indicators of the quality of the students' mental models and that the use of digital tools could be harmful to learning when their digital representations are not accompanied by the use of further depictions, such as drawing or paper-based contents, to promote the reflection on the associations between different representations.

Gamification

Suits defines a *game* as "the voluntary attempt to overcome unnecessary obstacles" (Suits, 2005). The game-related activity of playing is carried out voluntarily for its own sake; it is intrinsically motivated (Ryan & Deci, 2000). Malone draws on the approach of intrinsically motivated learning scenarios (Malone, 1981) and establishes heuristics for the design of "enjoyable user interfaces" (Malone, 1982). Similarly, the approach of serious games is to exploit the entertainment that games provide to support additional purposes, such as learning (Ratan & Ritterfeld, 2009). *Gamification*, i.e., the use of game elements in real-world contexts (Deterding et al., 2011), also exploits the motivation generated by game elements to "engage users" (Zichermann, 2011). In the following, games and gamification are uniformly referred to by the term *game elements*. The purpose of designing user interfaces using game elements is, therefore, to prompt users to engage in activities that promote mental processes, which are considered to be beneficial for knowledge acquisition. The framing as a game allows to cause the users to perform activities that are on the one hand conducive to learning, and on the other hand, would not be performed with the same frequency without the motivation emanating from game elements and thus would have less impact on learning. A great variety of MR-based learning activities using game elements are known in the literature (Alrehaili, 2019; Eleftheria et al., 2013; Hammady et al., 2016; Villagrasa et al., 2014).

A distinction may be drawn between encouraging entire learning activities and encouraging partial activities. Palmas et al. (2019) describe the use of game elements to support a complete MR-based learning activity: Supported by game elements, the efficiency of an MR-based tutorial for assembling drum sets is increased. An example of encouraging partial activities is the study by Zander et al. (2020), introducing a rotation restriction called a *powerbar* as a playful constraint of software-supported mental rotation tasks. The playful constraint of the powerbar actually led to a reduction of physical rotational movements while fostering mental rotations. In summary, the use of game elements in user interfaces for MR may be used to induce the user to perform learning activities that would not be performed as often, with the same intensity or not at all without game elements. The use of game elements may be supported by different constructive measures including software frameworks (e.g., Hensen et al., 2019), modeling frameworks (e.g., Bucchiarone et al., 2019), conceptual frameworks (e.g., Arnab et al., 2015; Söbke et al., 2017), and strategies for gamifying the usage context of applications (e.g., Söbke, 2019).

Collaboration Principle

Various learning theories, such as situated learning (Lave & Wenger, 1991), emphasize the importance of learning collaboratively in groups, because it leads to engagement and communication and thus facilitates learning (Rogoff, 1998). Dillenbourg defines *collaborative learning* as a "situation in which two or more people learn or attempt to learn something together" and describes the foundations of collaborative learning (Dillenbourg, 1999).

The cooperation of several people in a group can have various effects beneficial to learning. For example, diverse knowledge of various group members may be brought together to form common knowledge, which becomes available to all group members in the end. Furthermore, collaboration within the group is more activating if group members are aware that the achievement of others depends on their activities. Group members are therefore usually more motivated to pursue such activities. Furthermore, self-determination theory identifies social relatedness, along with competence and autonomy, as being one of the basic human needs whose fulfillment is conducive to increasing intrinsic motivation (Ryan & Deci, 2017). Here, the collaboration principle also fits the motivational-affective parts of the CATLM.

Two different functions of MR tools supporting collaboration can be distinguished as follows.

Communication Support

A variety of MR tools support indirectly learning by improving communication, e.g., MR glasses that allow a common perspective of all participants (Kulik et al., 2011), multi-window techniques that support different perspectives (e.g., ego perspective and bird's eye view) of the collaborators (Gugenheimer et al., 2017; Kunert et al., 2019) and thus allow asymmetric interactions (Bortolaso et al., 2019). In remote maintenance, MR tools serve as a communication medium between different persons who are not in the same physical location and who need to solve tasks collaboratively (Mourtzis et al., 2017). Communication casually promotes learning, although information relevant to learning is not presented in the MR tool independently but is transmitted as part of the communication. Further, learning is usually not the primary goal of the remote maintenance scenario, although targeted use for learning activities is feasible (Alexander et al., 2017). Commercial software packages known as *social VR* are available that support communication via virtual spaces (McVeigh-Schultz et al., 2019).

Educational Medium

MR tools may be used as a collaborative learning medium, i.e., the MR learning tools provide the information to be learned collaboratively. The collaboration of the learners may be stimulated by organizational guidelines. Examples are AR-guided digital scavenger hunts, where users must reach points of interest to gain on-site experience (Söbke et al., 2019). Digital scavenger hunts can be conducted individually, but putting together groups (here, three persons, each taking a different role) might result in a more efficient learning process. The approach to foster collaboration by assigning roles to the group members may also be supported by characteristics of the MR tool employed itself. For example, the tool may provide multiple perspectives (Bortolaso et al., 2019; Gugenheimer et al., 2017). However, an MR tool providing multiple perspectives might become more complex and thus more costly. A simple variant of providing several perspectives that can be realized on an organizational level is the coupling of MR glasses with an external screen: the interactions of the user wearing MR glasses can then be observed in the virtual world by other users, who can also advise on possible interactions and provide information to the user wearing MR glasses. The approach described is especially helpful for MR environments that are not multi-user enabled. Detailed guidelines for organizational measures (such as an investigation of the optimal group size; Melero et al., 2015) are still almost unavailable and will have to be adopted from established learning tools.

In summary, communication support is a fundamental design feature of MR learning tools. Furthermore, the established interaction approaches for collaborative learning environments (e.g., Dillenbourg, 1999) should be considered for their applicability. Building on this foundation, specific features of MR learning tools, such as the capability of combining different perspectives, may be exploited if required. However, these features tend to require considerable technical efforts and innovative approaches, most of which have not yet reached market maturity. The fostering of collaborative learning through organizational measures such as the assignment of roles is considered to be a remedy to high technical efforts.

DISCUSSION

The present chapter provides design guidelines for MR-based learning tools. Based on research from the field of multimedia learning, current recommendations to design multimedia learning interfaces are compiled and discussed according to their application to educational MR.

The guidelines have been categorized into design principles, strategies to support efficient information processing (e.g., essential, extraneous, and social cues) and activating principles, recommendations to stimulate active and generative mental processes. In summary, this chapter provides a comprehensive compilation of design guidelines for MR user interfaces focused on learning and therefore provides a helpful guide for the development and evaluation of MR for educational applications. However, it needs to be pointed out that the design guidelines should be understood as an over-arching framework for the development and evaluation of MR applications. Therefore, in order to apply these guidelines to specific MR applications it is required to consider each application's technological features as well as its functional context.

Furthermore, this chapter shows that educational MR is still in its beginnings regarding its application and empirical examination of the relevant multimedia principles. From the perspective of educational psychology, there are three main fields of research needed when applying multimedia principles to the opportunities that are presented in MR-learning environments: First, the presentation formats addressed by Mayer (2014) and Moreno (2007) have to be proven and updated by the amplified presentation and interaction formats in augmented and virtual reality. Second, regarding this, approaches on embodied cognition should especially be taken into account in the theoretical background of these models. Systematic research on design recommendations for embodied educational MR is still missing and deserves more attention. Finally, alongside this, learner prerequisites are still missing in the empirical studies on the design of MR, although from multimedia research, it is well known that spatial abilities, pre-knowledge, motivation, emotions, and interest affect the outcomes when learning with different kinds of media designs. Especially for pre-knowledge, a range of studies exists, showing that the respective multimedia design principles are mainly efficient for learners of medium or low pre-knowledge (Sweller et al., 2003), also for working memory (Wiley et al., 2014) and spatial abilities (Höffler, 2010) such effects were empirically proven.

Although the presented design principles are mostly addressed to designers and developers, also other stakeholder groups can benefit from the identified principles. For example, when it comes to the didactic design of the educational context in which the application is to be used, the remarks on collaboration may be of help for teachers. Also, with gamification elements outside the application, interactions between users and applications might be controlled. The design guidelines may also be helpful when assessing the quality of MR applications in educational contexts, e.g., for teachers or decision-makers deciding whether to use or buy an application. Further, the following design guidelines may be helpful for other stakeholders, such as students, when analyzing user interfaces and the underlying design intentions. While the boundaries to access MR applications are continuously declining, and its benefits to learning are analyzed increasingly, the authors understand the revealed findings as a relevant and opportunely stepping-stone to improve the design of MR applications and foster its integration in learning contexts.

CONCLUSION

Despite the efforts to include a wide range of aspects in the study, this chapter makes no claim to completeness. Possible extensions include the alignment with existing frameworks, as given, for example, by Quintana et al. (2004) or the incorporation of well-known general challenges of UI design, as discussed, for example, by Soloway et al. (1994). However, to the best of our knowledge, the present compilation is one of the first theoretical attempts to provide an overview of design principles that can be understood as a guideline for the development of educational MR environments. The presented principles are not only collected but also clustered regarding their purpose in the learning process. This study could be a starting point to define and investigate heuristics more focused on specific characteristics of MR, such as immersion, spatiality, and embodied interactions.

As implications of our findings, we understand that there is a need to precisely analyze how activating learning principles could be included in user interface design for MR learning environments. Further research should also focus on the question of how activating design principles have to be implemented in learning environments based on MR technologies in order to generate effective educational MR applications.

REFERENCES

Adler, J. L. (2001). Investigating the learning effects of route guidance and traffic advisories on route choice behavior. *Transportation Research Part C, Emerging Technologies*, *9*(1), 1–14. doi:10.1016/S0968-090X(00)00002-4

Akçayır, M., & Akçayır, G. (2017). Advantages and challenges associated with augmented reality for education: A systematic review of the literature. *Educational Research Review*, *20*, 1–17. doi:10.1016/j.edurev.2016.11.002

Alexander, T., Ripkens, A., Westhoven, M., Kleiber, M., & Pfendler, C. (2017). Virtual tele-cooperation: Applying AR and VR for cooperative tele-maintenance and advanced distance learning. In T. Andre (Ed.), *Advances in human factors in training, education, and learning sciences* (pp. 234–244). Springer International Publishing.

Alrehaili, E. A., & Osman, H. A. (2019). A virtual reality role-playing serious game for experiential learning. *Interactive Learning Environments*, 1–14. Advance online publication. doi:10.1080/10494820.2019.1703008

Arnab, S., Lim, T., Carvalho, M. B., Bellotti, F., de Freitas, S., Louchart, S., Suttie, N., Berta, R., & De Gloria, A. (2015). Mapping learning and game mechanics for serious games analysis. *British Journal of Educational Technology*, *46*(2), 391–411. doi:10.1111/bjet.12113

Augview Limited. (2016). *Augview | Augmented Reality Mobile GIS*. Author.

Baddeley, A. (1992). Working memory. *Science*, *255*(5044), 556–559. doi:10.1126cience.1736359 PMID:1736359

Bjork, E. L., & Bjork, R. A. (2011). Making things hard on yourself, but in a good way: Creating desirable difficulties to enhance learning. In M. A. Gernsbacher, R. W. Pew, L. M. Hough, & J. R. Pomerantz (Eds.), *Psychology and the Real World: Essays Illustrating Fundamental Contributions to Society* (pp. 59–68). Worth Publishers.

Bortolaso, C., Bourdiol, J., & Graham, T. C. N. (2019). Enhancing communication and awareness in asymmetric games. *Joint International Conference on Entertainment Computing and Serious Games*, (pp. 250–262). Springer. 10.1007/978-3-030-34644-7_20

Bucchiarone, A., Cicchetti, A., & Marconi, A. (2019). GDF: A gamification design framework powered by model-driven engineering. *Proceedings of the 2019 ACM/IEEE 22nd International Conference on Model Driven Engineering Languages and Systems Companion, MODELS-C 2019*, 753–758. 10.1109/MODELS-C.2019.00117

Castro-Alonso, J. C., Paas, F., & Ginns, P. (2019). Embodied cognition, science education, and visuospatial processing. In J. C. Castro-Alonso (Ed.), *Visuospatial processing for education in health and natural sciences* (pp. 175–205). Springer. doi:10.1007/978-3-030-20969-8_7

Chen, P., Liu, X., Cheng, W., & Huang, R. (2017). A review of using augmented reality in education from 2011 to 2016. In E. Popescu, Kinshuk, M. K. Khribi, R. Huang, M. Jemni, N.-S. Chen, & D. G. Sampson (Eds.), Innovations in smart learning (pp. 13–19). doi:10.1007/978-981-10-2419-1

Chu, M., & Kita, S. (2011). The nature of gestures' beneficial role in spatial problem solving. *Journal of Experimental Psychology. General*, *140*(1), 102–116. doi:10.1037/a0021790 PMID:21299319

Clark, R. C., & Mayer, R. E. (2016). *E-learning and the science of instruction: Proven guidelines for consumers and designers of multimedia learning*. John Wiley & Sons. doi:10.1002/9781119239086

DeSutter, D., & Stieff, M. (2017). Teaching students to think spatially through embodied actions: Design principles for learning environments in science, technology, engineering, and mathematics. *Cognitive Research: Principles and Implications*, *2*(1), 22. doi:10.118641235-016-0039-y PMID:28386586

Deterding, S., Dixon, D., Khaled, R., & Nacke, L. (2011). From game design elements to gamefulness: Defining gamification. *Proceedings of the 15th International Academic MindTrek Conference: Envisioning Future Media Environments*, 9–15. http://dl.acm.org/citation.cfm?id=2181040

Dillenbourg, P. (1999). What do you mean by collaborative learning? In P. Dillenbourg (Ed.), Collaborative-learning: Cognitive and computational approaches (pp. 1–19). Academic Press.

Dixon, D., Terton, U., & Greenaway, R. (2018). Reducing the split-attention effect in assembly based instruction by merging physical parts with holograms in mixed reality. *CSEDU 2018: Proceedings of the 10th International Conference on Computer Supported Education*, Vol. 1*: CSEDU*, 235–244. 10.5220/0006691202350244

Dörner, R., Broll, W., Grimm, P., & Jung, B. (2019). *Virtual und augmented reality (VR/AR): Grundlagen und Methoden der Virtuellen und Augmentierten Realität* (2nd ed.). Springer Vieweg. doi:10.1007/978-3-662-58861-1

Eleftheria, C. A., Charikleia, P., Iason, C. G., Athanasios, T., & Dimitrios, T. (2013). An innovative augmented reality educational platform using gamification to enhance lifelong learning and cultural education. *IISA, 1–5*. Advance online publication. doi:10.1109/IISA.2013.6623724

Fiorella, L., & Mayer, R. E. (2016). Eight ways to promote generative learning. *Educational Psychology Review*, *28*(4), 717–741. doi:10.100710648-015-9348-9

Freina, L., & Ott, M. (2015). A literature review on immersive virtual reality in education: State of the art and perspectives. *The Role of Internet in Education – Change and Transformation*, (April), 199–205. doi:10.12753/2066-026X-13-131

Garzón, J., & Acevedo, J. (2019). Meta-analysis of the impact of Augmented Reality on students' learning gains. *Educational Research Review*, *27*(April), 244–260. doi:10.1016/j.edurev.2019.04.001

Gillam, R., & Jacobson, J. (2015). *The Egyptian Oracle Project: Ancient ceremony in augmented reality*. Bloomsbury Publishing.

Goldin-Meadow, S., Cook, S. W., & Mitchell, Z. A. (2009). Gesturing gives children new ideas about math. *Psychological Science*, *20*(3), 267–272. doi:10.1111/j.1467-9280.2009.02297.x PMID:19222810

Gugenheimer, J., Stemasov, E., Frommel, J., & Rukzio, E. (2017). ShareVR: Enabling co-located experiences for virtual reality between HMD and non-HMD users. *Proceedings of the 2017 CHI Conference on Human Factors in Computing Systems*, 4021–4033. 10.1145/3025453.3025683

Hammady, R., Ma, M., & Temple, N. (2016). Augmented reality and gamification in heritage museums. In T. Marsh, M. Ma, M. F. Oliveira, J. Baalsrud Hauge, & S. Göbel (Eds.), *Serious Games: Second Joint International Conference, JCSG 2016* (pp. 181–187). Springer International Publishing. 10.1007/978-3-319-45841-0_17

Hensen, B., Koren, I., & Klamma, R. (2019). Gamification support for learning in spatial computing environments. *Journal of Universal Computer Science*, *25*(12), 1644–1665.

Höffler, T. N. (2010). Spatial ability: Its influence on learning with visualizations—A meta-analytic review. *Educational Psychology Review*, *22*(3), 245–269. doi:10.100710648-010-9126-7

Höffler, T. N., & Leutner, D. (2007). Instructional animation versus static pictures: A meta-analysis. *Learning and Instruction*, *17*(6), 722–738. doi:10.1016/j.learninstruc.2007.09.013

Hung, I.-C., Yang, X.-J., Fang, W.-C., Hwang, G.-J., & Chen, N.-S. (2014). A context-aware video prompt approach to improving students' in-field reflection levels. *Computers & Education*, *70*, 80–91. doi:10.1016/j.compedu.2013.08.007

Jacobson, J. (2017). Authenticity in immersive design for education. In D. Liu, C. Dede, R. Huang, & J. Richards (Eds.), *Virtual, Augmented, and Mixed Realities in Education* (pp. 35–54). Springer. doi:10.1007/978-981-10-5490-7_3

Kulik, A., Kunert, A., Beck, S., Reichel, R., Blach, R., Zink, A., & Fröhlich, B. (2011). C1x6: A stereoscopic six-user display for co-located collaboration in shared virtual environments. *ACM Transactions on Graphics, 30*(6), 188. doi:10.1145/2070781.2024222

Kunert, A., Weissker, T., Froehlich, B., & Kulik, A. (2019). Multi-window 3D interaction for collaborative virtual reality. *IEEE Transactions on Visualization and Computer Graphics*, *1*. Advance online publication. doi:10.1109/TVCG.2019.2914677 PMID:31059449

Lave, J., & Wenger, E. (1991). *Situated learning: Legitimate peripheral participation*. Cambridge University Press. doi:10.1017/CBO9780511815355

LaViola, J. J. Jr, Kruijff, E., McMahan, R. P., Bowman, D. A., & Poupyrev, I. (2017). *3D user interfaces: Theory and practice*. Addison-Wesley.

Leutner, D., & Schmeck, A. (2014). The generative drawing principle in multimedia learning. In R. Mayer (Ed.), *The Cambridge handbook of multimedia learning* (pp. 433–448). Cambridge University Press., doi:10.1017/CBO9781139547369.022

Lindgren, R., & Johnson-Glenberg, M. (2013). Emboldened by embodiment: Six precepts for research on embodied learning and mixed reality. *Educational Researcher*, *42*(8), 445–452. doi:10.3102/0013189X13511661

Macken, L., & Ginns, P. (2014). Pointing and tracing gestures may enhance anatomy and physiology learning. *Medical Teacher*, *36*(7), 596–601. doi:10.3109/0142159X.2014.899684 PMID:24787529

Makransky, G., Terkildsen, T. S., & Mayer, R. E. (2019). Adding immersive virtual reality to a science lab simulation causes more presence but less learning. *Learning and Instruction*, *60*, 225–236. doi:10.1016/j.learninstruc.2017.12.007

Malone, T. W. (1981). Toward a theory of intrinsically motivating instruction. *Cognitive Science*, *5*(4), 333–369. doi:10.120715516709cog0504_2

Malone, T. W. (1982). Heuristics for designing enjoyable user interfaces: Lessons from computer games. *Proceedings of the 1982 Conference on Human Factors in Computing Systems*, 63–68. 10.1145/800049.801756

Martín-Gutiérrez, J., Luís Saorín, J., Contero, M., Alcañiz, M., Pérez-López, D. C., & Ortega, M. (2010). Design and validation of an augmented book for spatial abilities development in engineering students. *Computers & Graphics*, *34*(1), 77–91. doi:10.1016/j.cag.2009.11.003

Mayer, R. E. (2009). *Multimedia learning* (2nd ed.). Cambridge University Press. doi:10.1017/CBO9780511811678

Mayer, R. E. (2014). Principles based on social cues in multimedia learning: Personalization, voice, image, and embodiment principles. In R. Mayer (Ed.), The Cambridge handbook of multimedia learning (16, pp. 345–370). Cambridge University Press.

Mayer, R. E., & Fiorella, L. (2014). 12 principles for reducing extraneous processing in multimedia learning: Coherence, signaling, redundancy, spatial contiguity, and temporal contiguity principles. In R. Mayer (Ed.), *The Cambridge handbook of multimedia learning* (p. 279). Cambridge University Press. doi:10.1017/CBO9781139547369.015

Mayer, R. E., & Moreno, R. (2003). Nine ways to reduce cognitive load in multimedia learning. *Journal of Educational Psychology*, *38*(1), 43–52. doi:10.1207/S15326985EP3801_6

McVeigh-Schultz, J., Kolesnichenko, A., & Isbister, K. (2019). Shaping pro-social interaction in VR an emerging design framework. *Proceedings of the Conference on Human Factors in Computing Systems*, 1–12. 10.1145/3290605.3300794

Melero, J., Hernández-Leo, D., & Manatunga, K. (2015). Group-based mobile learning: Do group size and sharing mobile devices matter? *Computers in Human Behavior*, *44*, 377–385. doi:10.1016/j.chb.2014.11.078

Merchant, Z., Goetz, E. T., Cifuentes, L., Keeney-Kennicutt, W., & Davis, T. J. (2014). Effectiveness of virtual reality-based instruction on students' learning outcomes in K–12 and higher education: A meta-analysis. *Computers & Education*, *70*, 29–40. doi:10.1016/j.compedu.2013.07.033

Milgram, P., Takemura, H., Utsumi, A., & Fumio, K. (1994). A class of displays on the reality-virtuality continuum. *SPIE Proceedings Volume 2351: Telemanipulator and Telepresence Technologies*, 282–292.

Miller, G. A. (1956). The magical number seven, plus or minus two: Some limits on our capacity for processing information. *Psychological Review*, *63*(2), 81–97. doi:10.1037/h0043158 PMID:13310704

Moreno, R. (2007). Optimising learning from animations by minimising cognitive load: Cognitive and affective consequences of signalling and segmentation methods. *Applied Cognitive Psychology: The Official Journal of the Society for Applied Research in Memory and Cognition*, *21*(6), 765–781. doi:10.1002/acp.1348

Mourtzis, D., Zogopoulos, V., & Vlachou, E. (2017). Augmented reality application to support remote maintenance as a service in the robotics industry. *Procedia CIRP*, *63*, 46–51. doi:10.1016/j.procir.2017.03.154

Müller-Plath, G. (2019). How does digital navigation on sailboats affect spatial abilities at sea? *TransNav. International Journal on Marine Navigation and Safety of Sea Transportation*, *13*(2).

Münzer, S., Zimmer, H. D., & Baus, J. (2012). Navigation assistance: A trade-off between wayfinding support and configural learning support. *Journal of Experimental Psychology. Applied*, *18*(1), 18–37. doi:10.1037/a0026553 PMID:22141461

Paivio, A. (1990). *Mental representations: A dual coding approach* (Vol. 9). Oxford University Press. doi:10.1093/acprof:oso/9780195066661.001.0001

Palmas, F., Labode, D., Plecher, D. A., & Klinker, G. (2019). Comparison of a gamified and non-gamified virtual reality training assembly task. *Proceedings of the 11th International Conference on Virtual Worlds and Games for Serious Applications (VS-Games)*, 1–8. 10.1109/VS-Games.2019.8864583

Pangilinan, E., Lukas, S., & Mohan, V. (Eds.). (2019). *Creating augmented and virtual realities: Theory and practice for next-generation spatial computing*. O'Reilly Media, Inc.

Quintana, C., Reiser, B. J., Davis, E. A., Krajcik, J., Fretz, E., Duncan, R. G., Kyza, E., Edelson, D., & Soloway, E. (2004). A scaffolding design framework for software to support science inquiry. *Journal of the Learning Sciences*, *13*(3), 337–386. doi:10.120715327809jls1303_4

Radu, I. (2014). Augmented reality in education: A meta-review and cross-media analysis. *Personal and Ubiquitous Computing*, *18*(6), 1533–1543. doi:10.100700779-013-0747-y

Ratan, R., & Ritterfeld, U. (2009). Classifying serious games. In U. Ritterfeld, M. Cody, & P. Vorderer (Eds.), *Serious games: Mechanisms and effects* (pp. 10–22). Routledge.

Reichelt, M., Kämmerer, F., Niegemann, H. M., & Zander, S. (2014). Talk to me personally: Personalization of language style in computer-based learning. *Computers in Human Behavior*, *35*, 199–210. doi:10.1016/j.chb.2014.03.005

Richter, J., Scheiter, K., & Eitel, A. (2016). Signaling text-picture relations in multimedia learning: A comprehensive meta-analysis. *Educational Research Review*, *17*, 19–36. doi:10.1016/j.edurev.2015.12.003

Rogers, K., Röhlig, A., Weing, M., Gugenheimer, J., Könings, B., & Klepsch, M., … Weber, M. (2014). Piano: Faster piano learning with interactive projection. *Proceedings of the Ninth ACM International Conference on Interactive Tabletops and Surfaces*, 149–158.

Rogoff, B. (1998). *Cognition as a collaborative process. In* Handbook of Child Psychology (Vol. 2). John Wiley & Sons.

Roy, M., & Chi, M. T. H. (2005). The self-explanation principle in multimedia learning. In R. Mayer (Ed.), *The Cambridge handbook of multimedia learning* (pp. 271–286). doi:10.1017/CBO9780511816819.018

Ryan, R. M., & Deci, E. (2000). Intrinsic and extrinsic motivations: Classic definitions and new directions. *Contemporary Educational Psychology*, *25*(1), 54–67. doi:10.1006/ceps.1999.1020 PMID:10620381

Ryan, R. M., & Deci, E. L. (2017). *Self-determination theory: Basic psychological needs in motivation, development, and wellness*. Guilford Publications. doi:10.1521/978.14625/28806

Salomon, G. (2012). *Interaction of media, cognition, and learning: An exploration of how symbolic forms cultivate mental skills and affect knowledge acquisition*. Routledge. doi:10.4324/9780203052945

Schmalstieg, D., & Höllerer, T. (2016). *Augmented reality: Principles and practice*. Addison-Wesley Professional.

Schnotz, W., & Bannert, M. (2003). Construction and interference in learning from multiple representation. *Learning and Instruction*, *13*(2), 141–156. doi:10.1016/S0959-4752(02)00017-8

Seufert, T. (2003). Supporting coherence formation in learning from multiple representations. *Learning and Instruction*, *13*(2), 227–237. doi:10.1016/S0959-4752(02)00022-1

Söbke, H. (2019). A case study of deep gamification in higher engineering education. In M. Gentile, M. Allegra, & H. Söbke (Hrsg.), *Proceedings of the Games and Learning Alliance, 7th International Conference*. 10.1007/978-3-030-11548-7_35

Söbke, H., Baalsrud Hauge, J., & Stefan, I. A. (2017). Prime example ingress: Reframing the pervasive game design framework (PGDF). *International Journal of Serious Games*, *4*(2), 39–58. doi:10.17083/ijsg.v4i2.182

Söbke, H., Baalsrud Hauge, J., Stefan, I. A., & Stefan, A. (2019). Using a location-based AR game in environmental engineering. In E. van der Spek, S. Göbel, E. Y.-L. Do, E. Clua, & J. Baalsrud Hauge (Eds.), *Entertainment Computing and Serious Games: Joint International Conference on Entertainment Computing and Serious Games* (pp. 7–10). 10.1007/978-3-030-34644-7_47

Söbke, H., Zander, S., & Londong, J. (2018). Augmented Reality als Lernmedium: Potenziale und Implikationen. *Innteract, 3*. Advance online publication. doi:10.14464/awic.v3i0.282

Soloway, E., Guzdial, M., & Hay, K. E. (1994). Learner-centered design: The challenge for HCI in the 21st century. *Interaction, 1*(2), 36–48. doi:10.1145/174809.174813

Sommerauer, P., & Müller, O. (2014). Augmented reality in informal learning environments: A field experiment in a mathematics exhibition. *Computers & Education, 79*, 59–68. doi:10.1016/j.compedu.2014.07.013

Sommerauer, P., & Müller, O. (2018). Augmented reality for teaching and learning: A literature review on theoretical and empirical foundations. *26th European Conference on Information Systems: Beyond Digitization: Facets of Socio-Technical Change.*

Suits, B. (2005). *The Grasshopper: Games, life and utopia.* Broadview Press Ltd.

Sweller, J., Ayres, P., & Kalyuga, S. (2011). *Cognitive load theory.* doi:10.1007/978-1-4419-8126-4

Sweller, J., Ayres, P. L., Kalyuga, S., & Chandler, P. (2003). The expertise reversal effect. *Educational Psychologist*, 23–31. doi:10.1207/S15326985EP3801_4

Takac, M., Collett, J., Blom, K. J., Conduit, R., Rehm, I., & De Foe, A. (2019). Public speaking anxiety decreases within repeated virtual reality training sessions. *PLoS One, 14*(5), e0216288. doi:10.1371/journal.pone.0216288 PMID:31150399

Villagrasa, S., Fonseca, D., & Durán, J. (2014). Teaching case: Applying gamification techniques and virtual reality for learning building engineering 3D arts. *Proceedings of the Second International Conference on Technological Ecosystems for Enhancing Multiculturality*, 171–177. 10.1145/2669711.2669896

Wiley, J., Sanchez, C. A., & Jaeger, A. J. (2014). The individual differences in working memory capacity principle in multimedia learning. In R. E. Mayer (Ed.), *Cambridge handbooks in psychology. The Cambridge handbook of multimedia learning* (pp. 598–619). Cambridge University Press., doi:10.1017/CBO9781139547369.029

Wilson, M. (2002). Six views of embodied cognition. *Psychonomic Bulletin & Review, 9*(4), 625–636. doi:10.3758/BF03196322 PMID:12613670

Xie, Y., Zhang, Y., & Cai, Y. (2019). Virtual reality engine disassembly simulation with natural hand-based interaction. In Y. Cai, W. van Joolingen & Z. Walker (Eds.), VR, Simulations and Serious Games for Education (pp. 121–128). Springer. doi:10.1007/978-981-13-2844-2_11

Zander, S., Montag, M., Wetzel, S., & Bertel, S. (2020). A gender issue? How touch-based interactions with dynamic spatial objects support performance and motivation of secondary school students. *Computers & Education, 143*, 103677. doi:10.1016/j.compedu.2019.103677

Zender, R., Weise, M., von der Heyde, M., & Söbke, H. (2018). Lehren und Lernen mit VR und AR: Was wird erwartet? Was funktioniert? In D. Schiffner (Ed.), *DeLFI Workshops 2018 Proceedings der Pre-Conference-Workshops der 16. E-Learning Fachtagung Informatik co-located with 16th e-Learning Conference of the German Computer Society (DeLFI 2018).* Academic Press.

Zichermann, G. (2011). *A long engagement and a shotgun wedding: Why engagement is the power metric of the decade.* Presentation at Gamification Summit, San Francisco. http://goo.gl/jlaO0

ADDITIONAL READING

Bacca, J., Baldiris, S., & Fabregat, R., & Kinshuk. (2019). Framework for designing motivational augmented reality applications in vocational education and training. *Australasian Journal of Educational Technology*, *35*(3), 102–117.

Dirin, A., & Laine, T. H. (2018). User experience in mobile augmented reality: Emotions, challenges, opportunities and best practices. *Computers*, *7*(2), 33. Advance online publication. doi:10.3390/computers7020033

Kerr, J., & Lawson, G. (2020). Augmented reality in design education: Landscape architecture studies as AR experience. *International Journal of Art & Design Education*, *39*(1), 6–21. doi:10.1111/jade.12227

Koren, I., Hensen, B., & Klamma, R. (2018). Co-design of gamified mixed reality applications. *2018 IEEE International Symposium on Mixed and Augmented Reality Adjunct (ISMAR-Adjunct)*, 315–317. IEEE. 10.1109/ISMAR-Adjunct.2018.00094

Krüger, J. M., Buchholz, A., & Bodemer, D. (2019). Augmented reality in education: Three unique characteristics from a user's perspective. *ICCE 2019: Proceedings of the 27th International Conference on Computers in Education, 1*(December), 412–422.

Ladwig, P., & Geiger, C. (2019). A literature review on collaboration in mixed reality. In M. E. Auer & R. Langmann (Eds.), *Smart industry & smart education* (pp. 591–600). Springer International Publishing. doi:10.1007/978-3-319-95678-7_65

Li, J., Spek, E. D. d., Feijs, L., Wang, F., & Hu, J. (2017). Augmented reality games for learning: A literature review. In N. Streitz & P. Markopoulos (Eds.), *Distributed, ambient and pervasive interactions* (pp. 612–626). Springer International Publishing. doi:10.1007/978-3-319-58697-7_46

Peters, D. (2013). *Interface design for learning: Design strategies for learning experiences*. New Riders.

Pirker, J., Lesjak, I., Kopf, J., Kainz, A., & Dini, A. (2020). Immersive learning in Real VR. In M. Magnor & A. Sorkine-Hornung (Eds.), *Real VR: Immersive Digital Reality: How to Import the Real World into Head-Mounted Immersive Displays* (pp. 321–336)., doi:10.1007/978-3-030-41816-8_14

Prit Kaur, D., Mantri, A., & Horan, B. (2019). Design implications for adaptive augmented reality based interactive learning environment for improved concept comprehension in engineering paradigms. *Interactive Learning Environments*, 1–19. doi:10.1080/10494820.2019.1674885

Schafer, D., & Kaufman, D. (2018). *Augmenting Reality with Intelligent Interfaces. Artificial Intelligence: Emerging Trends and Applications, 221*. IntechOpen., doi:10.5772/intechopen.75751

Zhang, Y., & Zhao, Q. (2017). Interactive augmented reality to support education. In N. Lee (Ed.), *Encyclopedia of computer graphics and games* (pp. 1–8)., doi:10.1007/978-3-319-08234-9_82-1

KEY TERMS AND DEFINITIONS

Activating Principle: Guidelines aiming at fostering generative learning, the active and effortful, motivated acquisition of new knowledge. Recommendations to stimulate active and generative mental processes.

Augmented Reality (AR): The superimposition of computer-generated information on a user's sensory channels, mainly visual and auditory channels, generating a composite view of the real world.

Design Principle: A group of recommendations, rules, or heuristics that intend to provide information for design development. In the specific case of this chapter, the authors discuss specific directions for the development of learning digital environments in MR.

Generative Learning: This theory is based on the assumption that the human brain constructs its own perceptions about problems, scenarios, and experiences, suggesting that new ideas must be integrated with a preexisting mental schema. This schema may consist of personal experiences previously acquired knowledge and learner cognition. The process of establishing relationships between stimuli and the stored information is called *generation*.

Mixed Reality (MR): Mixed Reality is the overarching term for a variety of technologies on a continuous spectrum between the two poles of reality and virtuality. Well-known variants of MR technology are virtual reality (VR) and augmented reality (AR). Compared to other media, MR has some distinctive characteristics such as immersion and spatiality.

User Interface (UI): The means by which the user of a digital device such as a computer, interact with it, including software and input devices. UIs are composed of the interactions, the input devices, and the sensory stimuli, that support human-machine interaction. These stimuli can be visual, auditive, haptic, or olfactory. Currently, visual stimuli are prevalent in what is known as the *graphical user interface* (GUI).

Virtual Reality (VR): Simulation of an interactive computer-generated image or environment by the use of technical equipment such as helmets or glasses with incorporated screens and gloves integrating sensors.

Chapter 5
Developing Design Knowledge and a Conceptual Model for Virtual Reality Learning Environments

Antti Lähtevänoja
University of Jyväskylä, Finland

Jani Holopainen
University of Helsinki, Finland

Mikko Vesisenaho
https://orcid.org/0000-0003-1160-139X
University of Jyväskylä, Finland

Päivi Häkkinen
https://orcid.org/0000-0001-6616-9114
University of Jyväskylä, Finland

ABSTRACT

This chapter focuses on applying design science research for virtual reality learning environment (VRLE) design processes. Six selected case studies are presented in the context of VRLEs. The case selections were analyzed in terms of their contributions to design knowledge. The objective of this book chapter is twofold: 1) for researchers, the design knowledge contributions of case studies are highlighted for future reference, and 2) for developers and practitioners, design principles are presented for the development of VRLEs. The final outcome of the present study is a conceptual model describing the current design knowledge in the field of VRLEs and identifying the research gaps that should be addressed in future research on the educational use of VR.

INTRODUCTION

DOI: 10.4018/978-1-7998-5043-4.ch005

The use of information and communications technology (ICT) is increasing in various educational institutions as well as in workplace learning settings. However, in order to effectively use ICT in educational settings, information about learning outcomes in a variety of technology-enhanced learning environments, as well as the design of its usage as part of the entire learning path, need to be known. The types of ICT used in educational contexts include computers, tablets, mobile phones, augmented reality (AR), virtual reality (VR), and robots.

This article presents the development of design knowledge and a conceptual model for virtual reality learning environments (VRLEs). Following Gregor and Hevner (2013), the article aims to help researchers to understand the design knowledge contributions of their studies regarding VRLEs and position them better. Furthermore, for the practical development of VRLEs, the aim of the article is to make visible and point out which kinds of design knowledge should be taken into consideration when designing VRLEs. Based on the findings of Radianti et al. (2020), it would be beneficial to share the best practices across different subjects in the field of VRLE research. In furtherance of that purpose, six case studies presenting different levels of design knowledge from specific subjects, limited to more abstract and mature knowledge, are introduced. The case study selection was drawn from a systematic literature review in the field of VRLEs (Lähtevänoja et al., forthcoming). The focus of the case study selection is on various design knowledge contributions and differentiated design knowledge following Gregor and Hevner (2013) and vom Brocke et al. (2019). Although the analyzed case studies did not directly conduct design science research methodologies, they provide design knowledge and understanding for further research and development, which are summarized in a conceptual model of VRLEs at the end of the article. The application of the conceptual model among practitioners and in future research is also discussed.

BACKGROUND

Virtual Reality and Virtual Reality Learning Environments

VR can be defined as an artificial, computer-generated digital environment in which users can interact with the environment (Milgram & Kishino, 1994). In VR the real-world physical boundaries (e.g. gravity) can be exceeded. Furthermore, VR can enable activities and interactions which may be dangerous, expensive or even impossible in real world (Tatli & Ayas, 2011). In addition to games and entertainment, virtual reality can be used in educational settings. VRLEs can be viewed with many technologies (e.g., head-mounted displays [HMDs] and desktop monitors). In this study, "VRLE" is used to mean an HMD-based VRLE.

However, while VRLEs have potential in educational settings, active learning in VR is not gained automatically. For example, it is dependent on various dimensions with multiple factors, such as the successful integration of VR into broader pedagogical and social scenarios of the classroom (Gouveia et al., 2017). In addition, more research on the learning outcomes of VRLEs is needed to justify the acquisition of the technology to educational institutions (Holopainen et al., 2020; Vesisenaho et al, 2019). Based on a systematic literature review regarding the use of VRLEs in higher education (Radianti et al., 2020), only a few articles address how VRLEs can be adapted to the teaching curriculum. While there are an increasing number of studies addressing these issues, the research field lacks coherent frameworks combining existing knowledge on VRLEs and guiding future research (Sandoval, 2014; Walsh et al.,

2002). In this article, we address this challenge by developing a conceptual model for designing VRLEs both to aid in the practical development and the research of VRLEs.

The potential use cases for VRLEs in educational settings include conducting field tests in science, technology, engineering, and mathematics (STEM) subjects that could be hazardous in real life (Bennett et al., 2019; Lynch & Ghergulescu, 2017); conducting safety training simulations that could be expensive in real life (Andersen et al., 2020; Buttusi et al., 2017; Jung et al., 2018); and visualizing three-dimensional (3D) models from different angles, which could be difficult using only two-dimensional (2D) monitors (Doak et al., 2020; Zinchenko et al., 2020). In addition, using VRLEs in learning has been found to increase learning motivation and engagement (Buttusi et al., 2017; Olmos-Raya, 2018; Stepan et al., 2017). Furthermore, VRLEs have been found to help students concentrate (Olmos-Raya et al., 2018) and to improve learning outcomes (Alhalabi, 2016; Krokos et al., 2019; Kwon et al., 2019).

In terms of learning outcomes, existing studies in the field of VRLEs have focused on learning whether HMD-based VR is more effective in learning than other technologies, such as cave automatic virtual environments (CAVEs) or desktop-based VR (e.g., Alhalabi, 2016; An et al., 2016; Bertrand, 2017; Chen et al., 2019). While some studies found that VRLEs were more effective than other technologies (CAVE, desktop-based VR) (Agrawal et al., 2018; Alhalabi, 2016; Sportillo et al., 2018), most of the studies have not found a difference between VRLEs and desktop-based VR or CAVE (An et al., 2018; Bertrand, 2017; Elbert et al., 2018). Some studies found that the CAVE system (Chen et al., 2019) or desktop VR (Makransky et al., 2017) had significantly better learning outcomes than the VRLE group.

While understanding learning outcomes in VRLEs is important, data on the practicalities of the use of VRLEs in educational contexts is needed in order to comprehend the educational impact of VRLEs. For example, it would be beneficial to study at what point in the learning path (e.g., a university course) VRLEs should be used with other technologies and learning methods to enhance learning. Although VR makes it possible to conduct learning methods that cannot be carried out in ordinary educational settings, it is not likely that it will be an appropriate substitute for all of the more conventional assignments and methods (Sathe et al., 2017).

As the studies conducted in the field mostly focus on a single technological or design detail, those studies provide fairly limited design knowledge. The studies were conducted in only a few contexts, concentrating on limited research settings, such as one learning topic or the differences between two technologies in one lesson (e.g., between desktop VR and head-mounted-display VR). One way to obtain more design knowledge is to conduct research using design science research (DSR) methodologies. By defining the design theories of VR technology, study results can be interpreted more accurately with implications for practitioners, such as designers and developers (Walsh et al., 2002). By using these methodologies, we can also obtain a wider perspective on the issue under study (Hevner et al., 2004). Some studies in the field of VRLEs have already applied DSR methodologies (Cochrane et al., 2017; Cowling et al., 2018; Holopainen et al., 2020; van Wyk et al., 2014). Most studies on VRLEs are not design studies, but the analysis of those studies using DSR methods and frameworks can reveal some novel design knowledge and understanding (vom Brocke et al., 2019).

Design Science Research and Design Knowledge

Design science in general is widely accepted within the learning sciences community (Sandoval, 2014). Design science-based methodologies used in the learning sciences include design-based research (DBR, or its synonym, development research), which has been long used in the educational field. It focuses on solving complex, real-world problems critical to education (Cotton, 2008). However, according to Sandoval (2014), confusion remains about the use of design research as a methodology in the educational field. In the present study, design science research approaches originating from information systems science are applied to obtain a multidisciplinary perspective on the topic.

Information systems (IS) are implemented to improve the effectiveness and efficiency of an organization (Hevner et al., 2004). Indeed, IS research is used to "further develop knowledge that aids in the productive application of information technology to human organizations and their management" (Hevner et al., 2004; *Information Systems Research*, 2002, inside front cover). Design theories from information systems research can develop internally consistent links between the basic theory and design for application and testing in certain contexts such as using VRLEs in educational contexts (Walsh et al., 2002).

Design Science Research

DSR has been a significant part of IS since the birth of the field. Vom Brocke et al. (2019) have provided a simple definition of DSR: "The goal of DSR is to generate knowledge on how to build innovative solutions to important problems effectively" (vom Brocke et al., 2019, p. 5). In IS, DSR contributes especially to the construction of a range of socio-technical artifacts such as the implementation of VRLEs in educational institutions (Gregor & Hevner, 2013). In DSR, an artifact contains knowledge. Methods, constructs, models, and design theories are all examples of artifacts in DSR (Gregor, 2002; March & Smith, 1995). Artifacts that are based on information systems are not static. They evolve as the technology develops and new methods to use the technology are found (Gregor, 2002). As stated by March and Smith (1995), the performance of an artifact is also related to the environment in which the artifact operates. This is particularly challenging in educational institutions as many factors contribute to learning outcomes, such as learning motivation and available learning resources including learning materials. Artifacts must be representations that support reuse and replication by future research projects (vom Brocke et al., 2019). Examples of these representations are technological rules explaining which technology should be used to achieve a certain effect. Artifacts contain different levels of design knowledge and have a different contribution type (e.g. a technological rule or design theory) (Gregor & Hevner, 2013).

Design Knowledge Model

In the design knowledge model of Gregor and Hevner (2013), design knowledge is categorized into three levels based on their contribution type: 1) situated implementation of design artifact; 2) nascent design theory–knowledge as operational principles/architecture; and 3) well-developed design theory about embedded phenomena (Figure 1).

The first level represents a "situated implementation of design artifact" providing specific, limited, and less mature design knowledge. This situated implementation of an artifact can be, for instance, a software product or an implemented process. In the context of VRLEs, artifact implementations can be, for example, the effect of a VRLE as a technology on a single direct learning outcome (e.g., memory retention or skill transfer) or a single indirect learning outcome (such as motivation or engagement). In the first level, the developed artifact's improvement over an existing artifact is evaluated (Gregor & Hevner, 2013).

The second level represents "nascent design theory–knowledge as operational principles/architecture." This level provides more abstract, complete, and mature design knowledge with artifacts, including constructs, methods, models, design principles, and technological rules. They generalize the understanding of why and how the artifacts satisfy the goals of the problem space (vom Brocke et al., 2019). In the context of VRLEs, second-level studies can, for example, apply the knowledge gained in the first level. For instance, if it is found in a first-level study that VR enhances motivation, at the second level, researchers can study the circumstances in which VR works well. Second-level knowledge usually provides a deeper understanding of the surrounding phenomena (e.g., by providing longitudinal data or comparing different technologies and their separate or parallel use). While in first-level studies a newly developed artifact is compared with an existing one, in a second-level study, two or more new artifacts are developed and compared with each other (and possibly to an existing one, as in the first-level study).

At the third level, which is "well-developed design theory about embedded phenomena," abstract, complete, and mature design knowledge is conceptualized, and the artifacts represent mid-range and/or grand design theories. Following Gregor (2006), different types of theories in IS can be classified into a taxonomy. In the taxonomy, there are five types of theories in information systems: theory for analyzing ("what is"), theory for explaining ("how and why something happened"), theory for predicting ("what will be"), theory for explaining and predicting ("what is," "how," "why," and "what will be"), and theory for design and action (design theory). Different types of theories produce different kinds of knowledge, and the types are interrelated (Gregor, 2002; Gregor, 2006.) While the third-level-of-design-knowledge model (Gregor & Hevner, 2013, Figure 1) contains mainly design theories, the lower levels constitute mainly design principles (how to design) or instantiations (what to design). In the context of VRLEs, third-level artifact can be a design theory explaining how to use the VRLE as a part of a certain learning path (e.g. university course).

According to Gregor and Hevner (2013), design theories contain prescriptive knowledge (providing prescriptions for design and action), while the other types of theories in the taxonomy contain descriptive

Figure 1. Design science research contribution types. Adapted from Gregor and Hevner 2013

Maturity of Design Knowledge	Contribution Types	Example Artifacts
More complete and mature knowledge	Level 3: Well-developed design theory	Design theories
⇕	Level 2: Nascent design theory. Design knowledge as operational principles.	Design principles, methods, models, technological rules
More limited and less mature knowledge	Level 1: Situated implementation of artifact	Instantations– software products or implemented processes

knowledge. Descriptive theories are needed in a situation in which nothing or very little is known about the phenomenon in question (Fawcett & Downs, 1986, p. 4, according to Gregor, 2002). Prescriptive knowledge is further explained by Aken (2004, p. 227) this way: "If you want to achieve Y in situation

Z, then perform action X." Design theories containing prescriptive knowledge can be applied to the field and tested. Broader and more mature design knowledge then generates more generalizable design theories (Gregor & Hevner, 2013).

Components of Design Knowledge

Vom Brocke et al. (2019) presented a model of the components of design knowledge for a specific DSR project. The design knowledge for a specific DSR projects consist of three larger components: 1) the problem space, 2) the solution space, and 3) the evaluation (Figure 2).

Following vom Brocke et al. (2019), in order to create differentiated design knowledge and understanding, one must consider the context (of the study), the goodness criteria (i.e., the objectives of the study), the representation (of the artifact), and the process of the study (how the artifact was developed). In the problem space, this means defining the context domain, stakeholders, time, and space as well as goodness criteria related to the technology, information, interaction, and society in order to deepen the understanding of the problem space and use those criteria as objectives for evaluating the solution. DSR projects are meant to solve problems in a defined application domain (vom Brocke et al., 2019). It is, therefore, essential to fully understand the problem as well as its positioning in the problem space. As vom Brocke stressed, discovering the problem and learning about the relevant space, as well as the scope and size of the problem, are important for every DSR project. In the context of VRLEs, problem spaces can include, for example, the educational institution and its stakeholders (students, teachers, administration) and the curriculum used in the educational institution.

Figure 2. Components of the design knowledge for a specific project. Adapted from vom Brocke et al. (2019)

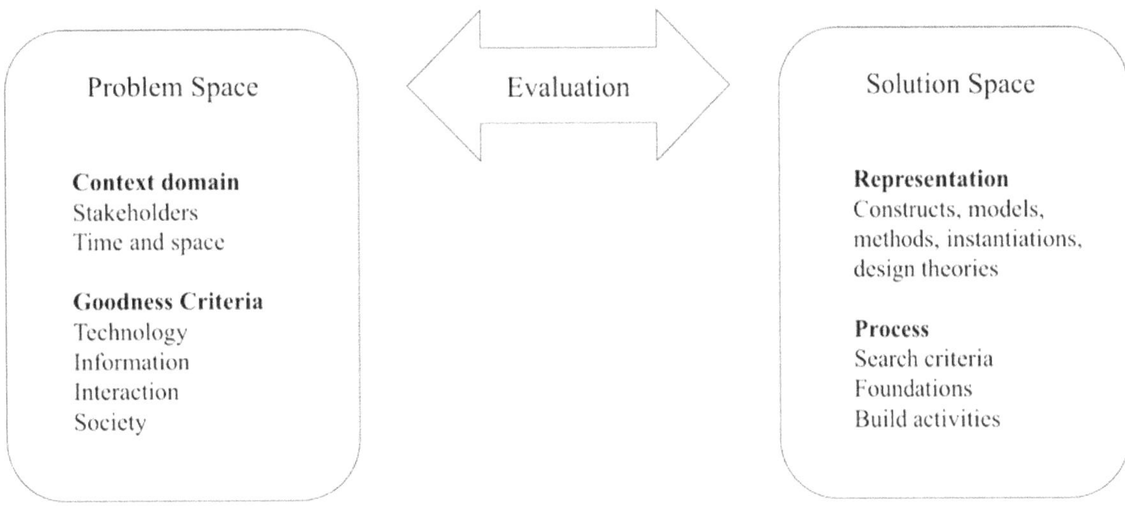

Following vom Brocke et al. (2019), when a project is positioned in the problem space, the situational context and research goals of the project are established. This is important for future research: According to vom Brocke et al. (2019), the effective reuse of design knowledge is predicated on how well the problem space projects onto the new research project in question. In practice, this means how well the new research context and goals of the grounding projects in the knowledge base align with the new research project.

It is important to remember, especially in the context of developing technology such as VRLEs, that a relevant problem may not be as relevant tomorrow (vom Brocke et al., 2019). VR technology develops very rapidly, and while the development solves some problems and challenges, it can also create new ones. The problem space, as well as the solution space, is in constant change. In addition, as vom Brocke et al. stressed, any practical design solution has socio-technical aspects when describing the goodness criteria. This means that in order to achieve a satisfactory solution, several categories of technology need to be combined (e.g., usability, accessibility, performance). Those categories (and included requirements) will then be used as acceptance criteria for the solution. Some specific socio-technical aspects regarding the use of VRLEs in educational institutions include, for example, the teacher training needed to use the technology.

In the solution space, detailed definitions are needed on the representation of the solution, including constructs, models, methods, instantiations, and design theories. Detailed definitions are needed as well on the processes involved devising the solution, including search criteria, foundations, and built activities. According to the definition, the design knowledge essentially links the problem and the solution space (Venable, 2006). The successful evaluation and validation of the design knowledge requires well-defined real problems as well as an understanding of the antecedents and dynamics of the visible problems. Similarly, the solution space requires understanding the capabilities and restrictions of suggested solutions and related technologies.

The solution space of the model includes both the representation (results such as developed artifacts) and process (design processes that include the built activities to create, assess, and refine the artifacts of the DSR in iterative building-evaluation cycles). These built activities contain a search process to identify the best design candidates in the solution space. In practice, this can mean suggesting future research avenues or combining previous research to form better solution designs (vom Brocke et al., 2019). However, a trade-off can exist between the projectability and fit of the design knowledge; often, a good fit of the design knowledge implies a greater limitation to a specific context (vom Brocke et al., 2019). For example, if the knowledge is developed within the context and domain of primary school students, the knowledge probably cannot be transferred to the context of adult or work-life education. In this space, it is important to make clear which artifacts were developed (e.g., constructs, models, instantiations, design theories), how the artifacts were developed, and which underlying theories were used to build the artifacts. The developed artifact determines the design knowledge level of the study, thus connecting the models of Gregor and Hevner (2013) and vom Brocke et al. (2019).

Some of these socio-technical aspects can be thought of as antecedents. In educational settings, various antecedents to the use of ICT exist, such as teachers' attitudes toward the use of ICT (Barak et al., 2007; Berger et al., 2019) and their educational beliefs (e.g., constructivism) (Hermans et al., 2008). Those antecedents belong to the "problem space" portion of the model (Figure 2). However, they are rarely considered in the existing studies. In addition, some restrictions apply to the problem space of vom Brocke's model. In the context of VRLE use in educational settings, restrictions include the high cost of VR equipment and environments (Farra et al., 2019) and teachers' lack of skills in using ICT in educational settings (Forkosh-Baruch et al., 2019).

In the evaluation phase, evidence on the extent to which a solution solves a problem using the chosen, specific evaluation method is provided (vom Brocke et al., 2019). In the context of VRLEs, that can mean, for example, testing how well students remember when using a VR-assisted memorization technique application (i.e., how well the developed solution meets the goodness criteria). In the evaluation phase, it is essential to assess whether the artifacts and design process were credible so that the outcomes of the study can be explained with confidence.

METHOD FOR ANALYZING THE CASE STUDIES

For the case study analysis, the following method was used. First, the case studies were selected from a literature review (n=43) on VRLEs and learning outcomes (Lähtevänoja et al., unpublished). While all of the studies in the literature review could be analyzed within the framework, the focus of the present study is mainly to present our analysis framework and conceptual method. To achieve this, easy-to-comprehend examples were selected. Therefore, six studies with simple and coherent structures were selected to be analyzed further. Case studies 1-4 (Agrawal et al., 2018; Holopainen et al., 2020; Krokos et al., 2019; Papachristos et al., 2017) were selected to portray the second-level design knowledge of Gregor and Hevner (2013) with varying developed artifacts (e.g., technological rules). Case studies 5-6 (Cheng et al., 2015; Teranishi et al., 2018) were selected to portray the first-level design knowledge of Gregor and Hevner (2013) and to demonstrate which details differentiate first-level design knowledge from second-level knowledge. After the case study selection, the studies were positioned onto the framework of vom Brocke et al. (2019) and the design knowledge model of Gregor and Hevner (2013), which was presented earlier in more detail.

In the following discussion, we describe the model from vom Brocke et al. (2019) that was modified for the field of VRLEs (Figure 3). In order to position our study within the model of vom Brocke et al. (2019), the following questions were used to evaluate the three components of design knowledge (vom Brocke et al., 2019), problem space, solution space, and evaluation: 1) Problem space: What is the study context? 2) Problem space: How was the problem positioned in the problem space? 3) Problem space: What were the measured outcomes and why were they measured? 4) Solution space: What were the artifacts developed? How were the artifacts built and on what facts were they based? 5) Evaluation: Is the problem-solution fit credible? (Is the problem valid? How well do the measured outcomes address the problem? How well do the measured outcomes define the artifact? How well do the measured outcomes define the artifact design process?)

Regarding the first point — "What is the study context?" — information is needed about the key problem domain and key stakeholders in the problem space who will affect and be affected by the design solution (vom Brocke et al., 2019). The context also includes information about the participants in the study (e.g., primary school students, university students), the age of the participants, the domain (e.g., school, work-life), and the learning topic (e.g., motor skills, remembering). If relevant, the time and space (e.g., geographical details, for instance, whether the school in question is a rural or an urban school) can also be reported. The second point — "How was the problem positioned in the problem space?" — involves questions regarding the problem cloud: How was the problem scoped and sized within the problem space? The third point — "What were the measured outcomes and why were they measured?"

— includes information about the goodness criteria. Goodness criteria essentially guide the development of evaluation methods in order to assess the solution developed (vom Brocke et al., 2019). In practice, goodness criteria include the measured outcomes and the reasons those outcomes were measured. Vom Brocke et al. (2019) further stressed that the entire projectability (the effective reuse of the developed design knowledge) will be predicated on how well the new research context and goals align with the context and goals of the grounding projects from the knowledge base (vom Brocke et al., 2019). In that space, it is important to report what the measured outcomes were, why they were measured, and how the measurement was done in practice (e.g., by interviewing or by using questionnaires). On the solution side of the model, point 4 (What were the artifacts developed, how were the artifacts built, and on what facts were they based?) assesses the artifacts developed by the study in question. As stated earlier, artifacts can be constructs, models, software instantiations, or design theories. In this step, it is important to report what artifacts were developed and which study results they were based on. Point 5 in the evaluation phase includes several questions aimed at assessing the measurement and evaluation phase of the study, as well as the design of the study, to find out whether the study outcomes can be explained with confidence. In addition, they assess whether the developed artifacts are credible and whether the results of the study are generalizable.

Figure 3. Modified model from vom Brocke et al. (2019) in the context of VRLEs, which will be used as a basis for the case study analysis

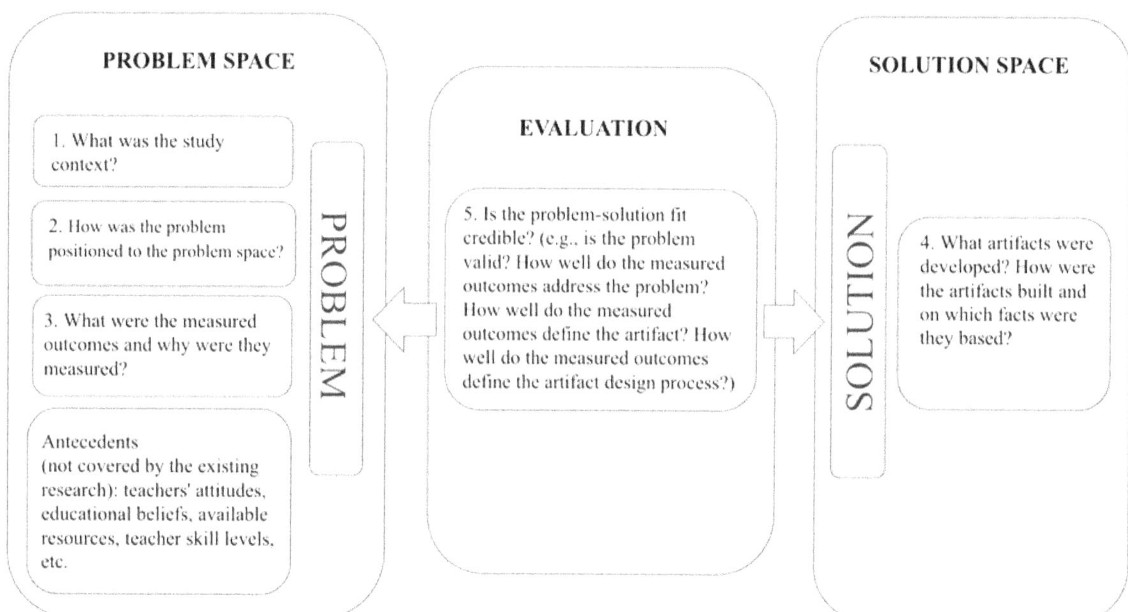

CASE STUDIES

In the following discussion, six case studies already conducted in the field are presented to portray the current design knowledge related to VRLEs. The selection criteria are based on the studies' contributions to design knowledge in terms of differentiated design knowledge and understanding (Gregor & Hevner, 2013; vom Brocke et al., 2019), which is also the analytical framework and how the case studies are presented.

Case Study 1: Immersive VR Improves Spatial Recall

Krokos et al. (2019) studied whether a classical memorization technology, a memory palace, implemented in an HMD VR environment would lead to better recall than using the same memory palace application with a desktop-based VR. In the memory palace technique, items (e.g., words) are placed onto a mental model of an environment. The idea is to aid the recollection of items by using environmental attributes and spatial mapping.

Problem space. The context of the study was to recall human faces using a memory palace among university students (n=40). Males were over-represented in the study population (75%). The problem position focused on developing better tools to help people to memorize things and recall information. The scope of the study was to develop a universal tool (not tied to any age group/context) for memorizing and recalling things. The study aimed to broaden the research and the problem cloud in the field by comparing two different technologies: VRLE and desktop VR.

The measurements used in the study were a memory recall test and subjective confidence rating, which were used to measure the recall efficiency and confidence of the participants. After seeing faces, participants were shown only numbers instead of the faces. Subsequently, they needed to connect the right number and face. During the study, all participants experienced both technologies, two different virtual environments with two different sets of faces (within-subjects design).

Solution space. The results of the study indicate that the task performance in the HMD VR condition was better than in the desktop VR condition. Participants also made fewer errors and were slightly more confident in the HMD VR condition. More interestingly, when participants changed from the HMD VR condition to the desktop VR condition, their performance deteriorated, and when they changed from the desktop VR condition to the HMD VR condition, their performance improved. In conclusion, HMD-based VR was found to support better recall of information than desktop VR.

The study provides different kinds of artifacts. First, it provides a technological rule (In order to have X, you need to use Y [Aken, 2004].): In order to have better recall with memory palace (X), use immersive VR over desktop-based VR (Y). Second, this knowledge can also be used as a design principle when designing new memorization and recall tools or virtual reality-based learning environments. The study also contributes to the existing knowledge on how spatial mnemonics works across different technologies.

As the study provides technological rules and design principles as artifacts (vom Brocke et al., 2019), the design knowledge in the study is second-level design knowledge (Gregor & Hevner, 2013, Figure 1). One possible way to deepen the knowledge would be to propose content-specific design principles such as how to make an efficient virtual memory palace. From the perspective of practical use, one possible future research avenue would be to study how to use this memory palace method as part of a longer learning path (e.g., as part of a university course).

Evaluation. Because of the within-subjects design and the fairly large number of participants (n=40), the results of the study are generalizable. However, the overrepresentation of males can limit the generalization. It seems that the artifact is fit for the problem space as the proposed solution solves the problem (to improve the recall of faces). However, as the study is one of the first on memory palaces and immersive VR, more data is needed to know whether the measure used addressed the problem well. It is worth noting that another study with a different approach comparing the effects of HMD VR and desktop VR on memory palaces did not find statistically significant differences between the groups (Huttner et al., 2017).

Case Study 2: No Difference in Learning Outcomes Found Between Low-Cost and High-End VR Headsets

Papachristos et al. (2017) studied whether there are differences between the effects of expensive and low-cost VR headsets on learning outcomes and user experience (e.g., satisfaction and workload). In the context of VRLEs, it is important to consider and study low-cost equipment as educational institutions usually do not have a great deal of money to spend on equipment (e.g., VR glasses).

Problem space. The context of the study was learning planets among undergraduate university students (n=30). Females were overrepresented in the study population (87%). The problem positioning for the study focused on whether a low-cost VR headset could be used to achieve the same learning outcomes and user experience ratings as an expensive one. While the expensive headset was a high-end VR headset connected to a computer (Oculus Rift DK2), the low-cost headset was a plastic version of the Google Cardboard VR headset, using smartphone as display. The study was scoped to the pedagogical use of VR but not to any particular age group.

The measurements used in the study consisted of measuring perceived spatial presence, usability, workload, simulator sickness, and satisfaction with post-test questionnaires and learning outcomes with pre- and post-test knowledge tests.

Solution space. The study did not find any differences between the low-cost and expensive VR equipment in the studied variables. Therefore, it seems that low-cost VR equipment could work well in terms of learning. The results regarding educational institutions are interesting: If the low-cost VR headset provides learning outcomes and satisfaction levels that are as good as the high-end headset in certain types of learning tasks, educational institutions could save a great deal of money.

The knowledge presented in this study is second-level design knowledge (Gregor & Hevner, 2013, Figure 1), providing technological rules regarding the choice of VR technology (vom Brocke et al., 2019). The developed knowledge could be deepened further by studying, for example, whether there are any differences between the low-cost and high-end VR headsets in other types of learning tasks (e.g., motor skills, conceptual learning, interactive tasks). In addition, the comparison between the two types (low-cost and high-end) could be studied in a longer course (e.g., a university course) to investigate the effects in a longitudinal research setting.

Evaluation. The study provided data on both the performance of the application and the user experience aspect of the application and technology. The overrepresentation of females can limit the generalization of the study results. It seems that the problem-solution fit is good as the proposed artifact solves the problem. (Low-cost VR glasses work as well as the expensive ones; therefore, schools can save money by buying the low-cost glasses.) As this is one of the first studies that has compared low-cost and expensive VR glasses, it is difficult to tell whether the measured outcomes address the problem well. In addition, comparisons such as this should be repeated in the future as both the low-cost and expensive glasses improve to see if there continue to be no differences between them.

Case Study 3: VR Driving Simulator Improves Young Drivers' Latent Hazard Anticipation and Mitigation Skills

Agrawal et al. (2018) studied car driving skills with VR among young drivers. They wanted to know if VR could be used to improve young drivers' latent hazard anticipation and mitigation skills. They compared three different groups: HMD-based VR, desktop-based VR, and a desktop-based placebo-group.

Problem space. The context of the study was the learning of driving skills among young drivers (15-18 years old) (n=36) who already had a driver's license. Males were slightly over-represented in the study population (64%). The problem positioning focused on improving young drivers' driving skills with simulators. The problem cloud was built on top of previous research and known issues in the driving skills of young drivers (e.g., latent hazard anticipation).

The study included two measurements, hazard anticipation and hazard mitigation, which were measured using eye-tracking, in-game analytics, and post-test driving simulator evaluations.

Solution space. The VR group had significantly better results. Drivers in the VR group showed a significantly greater proportion of latent hazard anticipation than the other groups. The VR group was also found to mitigate potential threats better. Therefore, it seems that a VR-based driving simulator could bring improved learning outcomes. The study provides knowledge on technological rules as artifacts: the VR-based driving simulator worked better than the desktop-based driving simulator for training latent hazard anticipation and mitigation skills. Therefore, the knowledge presented by this study is second-level design knowledge (Gregor & Hevner, 2013, Figure 1). Future research avenues to deepen the knowledge include studying the VR environment used more closely (e.g., which components of the VR driving simulator work best). Future research could also focus on studying with which combinations (theory class, VR driving simulator, and real driving) students achieve the best learning outcomes.

Evaluation. The study presents a finding about the performance of the technologies used but not from the user experience point-of-view. The small study population could affect the generalizability of the results. The problem-solution fit seems to be good as the proposed artifact (VRLE) seems to work best in the study context. More research on the topic is needed to learn how well the measured outcomes address the problem.

Case Study 4: Immersive VR Works Best With Higher Levels of Bloom's Taxonomy

Holopainen et al. (2020) studied learning outcomes with three different technologies: 2D video, 3D video, and immersive VR. The study investigated whether there were differences between the effects of these technologies on learning outcomes on different levels of Bloom's Taxonomy.

Problem space. The context of the study was learning to sew jeans fabric (n=96). Females were slightly overrepresented in the study population (63%). The ages of the participants were mixed: less than 18 years old (under 3%), 19-24 years old (42%), 25-34 years old (41%), and more than 35 years old (13%). The problem positioning focused on studying whether there are differences between the technologies on learning outcomes, especially on higher levels of Bloom's Taxonomy. The study also aimed to investigate the affordances of both HMD-based VR and desktop-based VR.

The measurements of the study consisted of learning outcomes (understanding, remembering, and ability to apply, pre-and post-test) and perceived affordances for each technology (post-test questionnaire).

Solution space. Regarding the learning outcomes, the results indicated that there were no statistically significant differences between the technologies (2D video, 3D video, and immersive VR) in understanding and remembering in Bloom's Taxonomy. However, regarding the ability to apply, the VR group achieved the highest rate of correct answers. There was a statistically significant difference between VR and 2D videos in the ability to apply but no significant difference between VR and 3D videos.

From the results of the study, Holopainen et al. (2020) provided some design principles and technological rules for making VRLEs. Therefore, the knowledge presented by the study belongs to the second level of the design knowledge model (Gregor & Hevner, 2013, Figure 1). The first design principle is that VRLEs should be used in the higher levels of Bloom's Taxonomy (e.g., the ability to apply). This result was in line with the previous research conducted on the topic (Kwon et al., 2019; Parmar et al., 2016), which also indicates that VRLEs work better in the higher levels of Bloom's Taxonomy. These can be thought of as technological rules: In order to have X, you need to use Y (Aken, 2004). In other words, to learn higher levels of Bloom's Taxonomy, use VRLE as a learning tool. The following statement can be transferred to empirical generalization, which can later be tested with further research: "The use of VRLEs leads to higher learning outcomes in higher levels of Bloom's Taxonomy."

Regarding the affordances of the technologies, Holopainen et al. (2020) identified several principles, which explained the differences of VR compared with the other two technologies. These principles can be used as design principles for making effective VRLEs. The principles include immersion (the immersive effect of VRLEs), challenging learning environments (VRLEs provide enough challenge for learning, including tasks), and engagement with and motivation toward the content and technology. On the basis of this study, it can be concluded that while designing both the virtual learning environment and the practical use of it in educational settings, it is important to choose a technology that aligns with the learning objectives (Holopainen et al., 2020).

Evaluation. The proposed solution (VRLE) was valid as it improved the learning outcomes, but the problem-solution fit of the proposed solution was not good as 3D video worked just as well in learning higher levels of Bloom's Taxonomy. More research is needed to know whether there is a difference on learning outcomes between the 3D video and VRLEs. Future research avenues for deepening the knowledge of this study include the use of VRLEs as part of a longer learning path (e.g., a university course). All levels of Bloom's Taxonomy could also be studied as the current study included only three levels. Furthermore, more longitudinal research is needed to discover whether the learning outcomes change over time.

Case Study 5: Immersive VR Improves Learning in Construction of Self-Built Computers

Teranishi et al. (2018) studied whether immersive VR improves learning outcomes in the construction of self-built PCs (installation process and naming the parts).

Problem space. The context of the study was learning PC assembly among university students (n=6) who had never assembled a PC before. The problem positioning focused on studying whether immersive VR improves learning the construction of self-built PCs. The challenge is that the number of PCs in the assembly exercise at the university was small due to budget constraints and the learning takes time because there are not enough computers for everyone. It was suggested that VRLEs could help to solve these problems.

Regarding the measurements of the study, both the learning outcomes (pre- and post-test) and usability of the system (including the application and the hardware, using questionnaires) were measured.

Solution space. Regarding the learning outcomes, the study results show that there was a significant improvement regarding the test questions about installation but not regarding the test questions about naming the parts. Regarding the usability, the scores for usefulness, favorability, ease of operation, and understandability exceeded the medium point (over 3 on a scale of 1 to 5), while responsiveness to the application and readability did not exceed the medium point.

The knowledge presented in this study belongs to the first level of the design knowledge model, providing situated implementation of the artifact (software products). The design knowledge does not reach the second level as there are no comparison groups. (It cannot be said whether desktop VR or other methods work just as well as immersive VR in this case.) However, the knowledge presented in the study aids future research by giving a preliminary indication that immersive VR can be used as a learning tool in learning tasks related to constructing self-built PCs.

Evaluation. As the proposed solution improved the learning outcomes, the solution can be stated as valid. However, the study sample was small. In addition, the fit of the solution was not good as there was no comparison group using some other technology or no technology at all. For example, a 3D video might have worked just as well. More research on the topic is needed to learn whether the problem could be solved with VRLEs or with some other technology or method. Future research to deepen the knowledge should involve bigger samples and include comparison group(s) in the research setting. In addition, it would be beneficial to study the retention of the learning outcomes (e.g., by including delayed measurements).

Case Study 6: Immersive VR Enhances Social Understanding and Social Skills for Children With Autism Spectrum Disorders

Cheng et al. (2015) studied whether a VRLE can improve the social understanding and skills of children who have autism spectrum disorders (ASDs).

Problem space. The context of the study was improving social understanding and social skills (10-13 years old) in children with ASDs and social impairments (n=3). All of the studied children were boys. The problem positioning focused on evaluating a VRLE system for enhancing the social understanding and social skills of children with ASDs. It was built on previous research, which studied desktop-VR-based systems for training social skills.

The study measurements consisted of measuring the change in the participants' behavior in social skills and social understanding once per week over the course of a 6-week period. The measurements were taken by observing the behavior of the children using two scales: a social events card and a social behaviors scale.

Solution space. Regarding the learning outcomes, the social skills and social understanding were improved in all participants. In addition, teachers reported that the VR system was helpful by providing visual stimuli and other assistance for the children to develop their social understanding and skills.

The knowledge presented by this study belongs to the first level of the design knowledge model, providing a situated implementation of the artifact (software products). The study provides knowledge about the usability of the VRLE for the purpose of teaching social skills and understanding. The design knowledge does not reach the second level as there were no comparison groups. However, the knowledge presented in the study aids future research by giving a preliminary indication that immersive VR can be used as a tool for learning social understanding and social skills.

Evaluation. The proposed solution seems to be valid for the problem as social understanding and social skills were improved. The measurements used provide good information about changes in social understanding and social skills, but the small study population limits the generalizability of the results.

The fit of the solution is unknown as there was no comparison group who used some other technology or did not use any technology. More research on the topic is needed to learn whether the measures used addressed the problem well.

Future research avenues to deepen the knowledge include the inclusion of comparison group(s) in the research setting. The system could also be tested among children with other disabilities. Furthermore, it would be beneficial to study the retention of the learning outcomes (e.g., by including delayed measurements).

FINDINGS AND DISCUSSION: PRESENTING THE CONCEPTUAL MODEL

The main goal of this study was twofold: First, the aim was to provide help for researchers to understand and position the knowledge contributions of studies regarding VRLEs. The second aim was to make the design knowledge that should be considered when designing VRLEs visible. To do this, six case studies were selected, presented, and analyzed. While first- and second-level design knowledge are well presented in the field, third-level design knowledge is scarce. On the basis of the case studies, some future research avenues were proposed in order to deepen design knowledge on VRLEs. In this section, ways to deepen the current knowledge into third-level design knowledge are also discussed. Ultimately, as our conceptual model, we propose two models (see Figures 4 and 5) based on the models introduced by Gregor and Hevner (2013) and vom Brocke et al. (2019).

Design knowledge from all levels is important (see Figure 4). The first-level studies (cases 5 and 6) build the base for the higher design knowledge levels, and they guide future research toward the right path. Although first-level design knowledge brings new knowledge about what contributes to learning outcomes in VR, it does not consider a wider framework around the phenomenon of learning in VR. For example, it does not take other technologies (e.g., desktop VR) into consideration by comparing them. However, it provides valuable design knowledge for higher design knowledge levels. It can be said that the higher knowledge level studies continue on from the first-level design knowledge studies.

At the second level, the research would delve deeper into the learning topic (cases 1-4). Here, the focus is more on the design of the learning topic, keeping in mind the results from the first level (what kind of controller or narration worked). Furthermore, the developed application from the first level can also be compared with other technologies that can be used for studying the topic. Comparisons may also reveal pros and cons of these technologies and guide researchers in designing parallel and complementary use cases.

At the third level, VRLEs can be thought of as part of the entire learning path, and studies could investigate which parts of the learning path should be done in VR and which using other learning methods (with or without ICT). Again, this third level is built from the results of the first- and second-level design knowledge. Some practical examples of the three design knowledge levels for VRLE research, based on Gregor and Hevner (2013), are illustrated in Figure 4. This model introduces every knowledge level as having both a solution objective and design.

Figure 4. Examples of three design knowledge levels for VRLEs, based on Gregor and Hevner (2013)

First-level design knowledge (e.g., case studies 5 and 6) Solution objective: Learning outcomes of VR Design: What are the learning outcomes of a specific learning topic/method/technology?
Second-level design knowledge (e.g., case studies 1-4) Solution objective: Design principles for building VRLEs Design: How should the VRLEs be designed to be effective for certain types of learning or certain topics (e.g., memory retention, skill transfer, learning safety procedures)? How should tasks be designed and introduced in the VRLE? How do VRLEs compare with other technologies?
Third-level design knowledge (n/a) Solution objective: Building design theories Design: How should VRLEs be used as part of the learning path and with other learning technologies? Prescriptive knowledge, combining the results from the lower design knowledge levels.

No studies on VRLEs were found during the case study selection to have third-level design knowledge. One possible reason for this is the immaturity of the field: Head-mounted-display-based VR came widely to consumer markets as late as 2015. In addition, the field as a whole is still widely undeveloped: The devices are still very expensive for educational institutions. This prevents wider usage of the devices, and thus studying the phenomena takes effort. The question remains: Is it even possible to have design theories about VRLEs at this point? As stated by Gregor and Hevner (2013), design theories require some maturity from the field in general. Theory building, especially in the case of high-level design theories, is an exhaustive process, requiring knowledge building and complete understanding of the theory in terms of when it works and why (Gregor & Hevner, 2013). Essentially, to reach the design theory stage, a great deal of empirical testing and combining of previous studies needs to be done. Furthermore, future studies in the field should be constructed so that they provide complementary design knowledge to the field.

In Figure 5, the knowledge based on the selected case studies is summarized based on the framework by vom Brocke et al. (2019). In the following, this knowledge is explained in detail with some evaluation of the possible future research avenues to fill the gaps. In the solution space, knowledge presented by the case studies is categorized according to the knowledge type and level based on the design knowledge model of Gregor and Hevner (2013). While the case selections were based on a systematic literature review in the field of VRLEs (Lähtevänoja, forthcoming) representing a broad spectrum of design knowledge, it is important to note that the case selections are not exhaustive.

Figure 5. Design knowledge from the case studies, based on the model of vom Brocke et al. (2019)

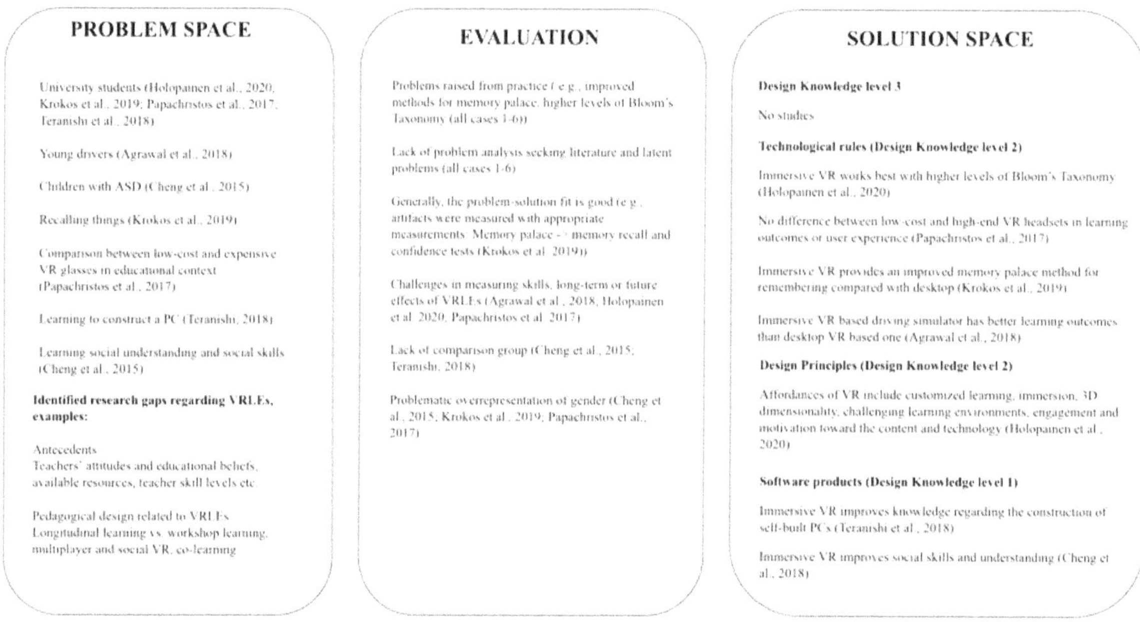

From Figure 5, we can see that much of the research has concentrated on university students. This could be due to the ease of recruiting students from a researcher's campus to take part in research. Future research should focus more on different age groups in order to contribute more to design knowledge. For example, it would be beneficial to know if the result of Papachristos et al. (2017) (the low-cost VR headset does not differ significantly from the high-end VR headset in learning outcomes and user experience) works with younger populations as well. In addition, while the result of Holopainen et al. (2020) showed that immersive VR worked best with the higher levels of Bloom's Taxonomy, there is a need for more data on whether this holds true with different education levels and different learning topics.

It is understandable that, for a new field such as VRLEs, the first studies are quite general and the problem cloud is not yet visible in its entirety, as can also be concluded from the systematic literature review by Radianti et al. (2020), who found that the current studies regarding VRLEs focus mainly on usability. The first studies were based on existing theories and frameworks. When more data is gathered and a suitable framework(s) is found to be used in the field, latent problems can be found and solution development can begin. In practice, this requires design theories, which do not yet exist in the field. At the beginning, the problems and challenges seem to be clear, but they are not necessarily latent problems.

The solution-problem fit was generally good in the case studies. For example, artifacts were measured with appropriate measurements, such as in Krokos et al. (2019), who measured memory recall with memory recall and confidence tests. However, there were also challenges in measuring learning. For example, information on the long-term effects of VRLEs is scarce at this point (Agrawal et al., 2018; Holopainen et al., 2020). Delayed measurements of learning outcomes are suggested for future research. In addition, the comparison between low-cost and expensive VR headsets should be repeated when the technology develops to investigate whether the effects persist (Papachristos et al., 2017).

Regarding study settings and design knowledge, the lack of comparison groups can be problematic as it is not known whether some other technology would have worked better to solve the problems (Cheng et al., 2015; Teranishi et al., 2018). Future research is, therefore, encouraged to broaden the current studies by adding different technologies (such as 3D videos and desktop VR) as comparison groups. In addition, the overrepresentation of gender could have influenced the reliability of the data (Cheng et al., 2015; Krokos et al., 2019; Papachristos et al., 2017).

In addition, as learning can also happen in social contexts and groups, it would be beneficial to study learning outcomes with multiplayer and social VR either in immersive VR or with some participants using desktop VR and some using immersive VR. In addition, several antecedents affecting the educational context, such as teachers' attitudes and educational beliefs, teachers' skill levels, and available educational resources, are among the current research gaps. However, certain challenges exist in studying the phenomena. For example, when studying learning motivation with VRLEs, the technology itself can affect motivation levels and distort the possible motivational effect of the VRLE content studied. One way to overcome this challenge is to use a longitudinal research approach.

CONCLUSION

When conducting research on the topic of VRLEs, it is important to communicate the design knowledge openly. In this chapter, we have suggested a conceptual model modified from the models of Gregor and Hevner (2013) and vom Brocke et al. (2019) as a base. The proposed models (Figures 4 and 5) can aid both the research and practical development of VRLEs by providing information on the study results and research gaps to gather design knowledge and understanding as well as to guide future research. To sum up, in order to position a study on the model of vom Brocke et al. (2019) and report its results, the following questions can be used: 1) Problem space: What is the study context? 2) Problem space: How was the problem positioned in the problem space? 3) Problem space: What were the measured outcomes and why were they measured? 4) Solution space: What were the artifacts developed? How were the artifacts built and on what facts were they based? 5) Evaluation: Is the problem-solution fit credible? (Is the problem valid? How well do the measured outcomes address the problem? How well do the measured outcomes define the artifact? How well do the measured outcomes define the artifact design process?)

In practice, the conceptual model (Figure 5) can be filled by answering these questions. In addition, with every point of the model, it is important to consider the gaps in the research and future research avenues that should be pursued to extend the design knowledge (Gregor & Hevner, 2013). Furthermore, it is important to further assess the outcomes of the study and discuss how to improve the credibility of the outcomes in future research.

The present study also has certain limitations, which could be used to guide future research. The case study selection (see, for example, Volkoff et al., 2013) was done by using a systematic literature review in the field of VRLEs as a base (Lähtevänoja, forthcoming), but the review in question only included studies that had measured learning outcomes. Therefore, future research should conduct a wider literature review that takes the field into wider consideration, such as the pedagogical choices and didactics embedded in the VRLEs.

The fields of VR and VRLEs are developing at a rapid pace. New affordable standalone VR headsets such as Oculus Quest (Oculus, 2020), which does not require a powerful PC, make the use of VR environments available to a wider public. In addition, new cloud-based rendering techniques (e.g., Pixel

Streaming (Unreal Engine, 2020)), will enable low-end VR headsets to be run in high resolution through the Internet in the future. These developments make it important to continue to investigate both the learning outcomes of VRLEs and the wider phenomenon of VRLE-aided learning.

REFERENCES

Agrawal, R., Knodler, M., Fisher, D. L., & Samuel, S. (2018). Virtual reality headset training: Can it be used to improve young drivers' latent hazard anticipation and mitigation skills. *Transportation Research Record: Journal of the Transportation Research Board*, *2672*(33), 20–30. doi:10.1177/0361198118758311

Aken, J. E. V. (2004). Management research based on the paradigm of the design sciences: The quest for field-tested and grounded technological rules. *Journal of Management Studies*, *41*(2), 219–246. doi:10.1111/j.1467-6486.2004.00430.x

Alhalabi, W. (2016). Virtual reality systems enhance students' achievements in engineering education. *Behaviour & Information Technology*, *35*(11), 919–925. doi:10.1080/0144929X.2016.1212931

An, B., Matteo, F., Epstein, M., & Brown, D. (2018). Comparing the performance of an immersive virtual reality and traditional desktop cultural game. In *Proceedings of the 2nd International Conference on Computer-Human Interaction Research and Applications* (Vol. 1). CHIRA. 10.5220/0006922800540061

Andersen, K., Gaab, S. J., Sattarvand, J., & Harris, F. C. Jr. (2020). METS VR: Mining evacuation training simulator in virtual reality for underground mines. *Proceedings of the 17th International Conference on Information Technology: New Generations (ITNG 2020).*

Barak, M. (2007). Transition from traditional to ICT-enhanced learning environments in undergraduate chemistry courses. *Computers & Education*, *48*(1), 30–43. doi:10.1016/j.compedu.2004.11.004

Bennett, J. A., & Saunders, C. P. (2019). A virtual tour of the cell: Impact of virtual reality on student learning and engagement in the STEM classroom. *Journal of Microbiology & Biology Education*, *20*(2). Advance online publication. doi:10.1128/jmbe.v20i2.1658 PMID:31388392

Berger, P., & Wolling, J. (2019). They need more than technology-equipped schools: Teachers' practice of fostering students' digital protective skills. *Media and Communication*, *7*(2), 137–147. doi:10.17645/mac.v7i2.1902

Bertrand, J., Bhargava, A., Madathil, K. C., Gramopadhye, A., & Babu, S. V. (2017a). The effects of presentation method and simulation fidelity on psychomotor education in a bimanual metrology training simulation. In *2017 IEEE Symposium on 3D User Interfaces, 3DUI 2017 — Proceedings* (pp. 59-68). 10.1109/3DUI.2017.7893318

Bhargava, A., Bertrand, J. W., Gramopadhye, A. K., Madathil, K. C., & Babu, S. V. (2018). Evaluating multiple levels of an interaction fidelity continuum on performance and learning in near-field training simulations. *IEEE Transactions on Visualization and Computer Graphics*, *24*(4), 1418–1427. doi:10.1109/TVCG.2018.2794639 PMID:29543160

Buttussi, F., & Chittaro, L. (2017). Effects of different types of virtual reality display on presence and learning in a safety training scenario. *IEEE Transactions on Visualization and Computer Graphics*, *24*(2), 1063–1076. doi:10.1109/TVCG.2017.2653117 PMID:28092563

Chan, J. C., Leung, H., Tang, J. K., & Komura, T. (2010). A virtual reality dance training system using motion capture technology. *IEEE Transactions on Learning Technologies*, *4*(2), 187–195. doi:10.1109/TLT.2010.27

Chen, X., Chen, Z., Li, Y., He, T., Hou, J., Liu, S., & He, Y. (2019). ImmerTai: Immersive motion learning in VR environments. *Journal of Visual Communication and Image Representation*, *58*, 416–427. doi:10.1016/j.jvcir.2018.11.039

Cheng, Y., Huang, C.-L., & Yang, C.-S. (2015). Using a 3D immersive virtual environment system to enhance social understanding and social skills for children with autism spectrum disorders. *Focus on Autism and Other Developmental Disabilities*, *30*(4), 222–236. doi:10.1177/1088357615583473

Cochrane, T. D., Cook, S., Aiello, S., Christie, D., Sinfield, D., Steagall, M., & Aguayo, C. (2017). A DBR framework for designing mobile virtual reality learning environments. *Australasian Journal of Educational Technology*, *33*(6), 54–68. doi:10.14742/ajet.3613

Cotton, W. (2008). Supporting the use of learning objects in the K-12 environment: A design-based research project. *Emerging Technologies Conference 2008.*

Cowling, M., & Birt, J. (2018). Pedagogy before technology: A design-based research approach to enhancing skills development in paramedic science using mixed reality. *Information*, *9*(2), 29–44. doi:10.3390/info9020029

Dalgarno, B., & Lee, M. J. (2010). What are the learning affordances of 3-D virtual environments? *British Journal of Educational Technology*, *41*(1), 10–32. doi:10.1111/j.1467-8535.2009.01038.x

Doak, D. G., Denyer, G. S., Gerrard, J. A., Mackay, J. P., & Allison, J. R. (2020). Peppy: A virtual reality environment for exploring the principles of polypeptide structure. *Protein Science*, *29*(1), 157–168. doi:10.1002/pro.3752 PMID:31622516

Downs, F. S., & Fawcett, J. (1986). The relationship of theory and research. McGraw-Hill/Appleton & Lange.

Farra, S. L., Gneuhs, M., Hodgson, E., Kawosa, B., Miller, E. T., Simon, A., ... Hausfeld, J. (2019). Comparative cost of virtual reality training and live exercises for training hospital workers for evacuation. *CIN: Computers, Informatics. Nursing*, *37*(9), 446–454. PMID:31166203

Forkosh-Baruch, A., & Avidov-Ungar, O. (2019). ICT implementation in colleges of education: A framework for teacher educators. *Journal of Information Technology Education*, *18*, 207–229. doi:10.28945/4312

Gouveia, C., Cook, C., Snyder, A., & Payne, S. (2017). "Nice to have" to "Can't do without": Aligning simulations and VR with current needs in the K-12 classroom. In B. K. Smith, M. Borge, E. Mercier, & K. Y. Lim (Eds.), *Making a difference: Prioritizing equity and access in CSCL, 12th International Conference on Computer Supported Collaborative Learning (CSCL) 2017, Volume 2* (pp. 723-724). Philadelphia, PA: International Society of the Learning Sciences.

Gregor, S. (2002). Design theory in information systems. *AJIS. Australasian Journal of Information Systems*, *10*(1), 14–22.

Gregor, S., & Hevner, A. R. (2013). Positioning and presenting design science research for maximum impact. *Management Information Systems Quarterly*, *37*(2), 337–355. doi:10.25300/MISQ/2013/37.2.01

Haj-Bolouri, A., Bernhardsson, L., Bernhardsson, P., & Svensson, L. (2016). An information systems design theory for adaptable e-learning. In *Proceedings of the 2016 49th Hawaii International Conference on System Sciences (HICSS)* (pp. 4414-4423). IEEE. 10.1109/HICSS.2016.550

Hermans, R., Tondeur, J., van Braak, J., & Valcke, M. (2008). The impact of primary school teachers' educational beliefs on the classroom use of computers. *Computers & Education*, *51*(4), 1499–1509. doi:10.1016/j.compedu.2008.02.001

Hevner, A. R., March, S. T., Park, J., & Ram, S. (2004). Design science in information systems research. *Management Information Systems Quarterly*, *28*(1), 75–105. doi:10.2307/25148625

Holopainen, J., Lähtevänoja, A., Mattila, O., Södervik, I., Pöyry, E., & Parvinen, P. (2020). Exploring the learning outcomes with various Technologies—Proposing design principles for virtual reality learning environments. *Proceedings of the 53rd Hawaii International Conference on System Sciences*, 12-21. 10.24251/HICSS.2020.004

Huttner, J., & Susanne, R. (2017). An immersive memory palace: Supporting the method of loci with virtual reality. *Proceedings of the 23th Americas Conference on Information Systems*, 1-10.

Jung, J., & Ahn, Y. J. (2018). Effects of interface on procedural skill transfer in virtual training: Lifeboat launching operation study. *Computer Animation and Virtual Worlds*, *29*(3-4), e1812. doi:10.1002/cav.1812

Krokos, E., Plaisant, C., & Varshney, A. (2019). Virtual memory palaces: Immersion aids recall. *Virtual Reality (Waltham Cross)*, *23*(1), 1–15. doi:10.100710055-018-0346-3

Kwon, C. (2019). Verification of the possibility and effectiveness of experiential learning using HMD-based immersive VR technologies. *Virtual Reality (Waltham Cross)*, *23*(1), 101–118. doi:10.100710055-018-0364-1

Lähtevänoja, A., Häkkinen, P., Vasalampi, K., Vesisenaho, M., & Holopainen, J. Learning outcomes in VR: Literature review. Manuscript in preparation.

Lynch, T., & Ghergulescu, I. (2017). Review of virtual labs as the emerging technologies for teaching stem subjects. In *INTED2017 Proceedings of the 11th International Technology, Education and Development Conference* (pp. 6082-6091). 10.21125/inted.2017.1422

March, S. T., & Smith, G. F. (1995). Design and natural science research on information technology. *Decision Support Systems*, *15*(4), 251–266. doi:10.1016/0167-9236(94)00041-2

Milgram, P., & Kishino, F. (1994). A taxonomy of mixed reality visual displays. *IEICE Transactions on Information and Systems*, *77*(12), 1321–1329.

Naik, G., Chitre, C., Bhalla, M., & Rajan, J. (2020). Impact of use of technology on student learning outcomes: Evidence from a large-scale experiment in India. *World Development, 127*, 104736. doi:10.1016/j.worlddev.2019.104736

Oculus. (2020, April 10). *Oculus Quest homepage*. https://www.oculus.com/quest

Olmos-Raya, E., Ferreira-Cavalcanti, J., Contero, M., Castellanos-Baena, M. C., Chicci-Giglioli, I. A., & Alcañiz, M. (2018). Mobile virtual reality as an educational platform: A pilot study on the impact of immersion and positive emotion induction in the learning process. *Eurasia Journal of Mathematics, Science and Technology Education, 14*(6), 2045–2057.

Papachristos, N. M., Vrellis, I., & Mikropoulos, T. A. (2017). A comparison between oculus rift and a low-cost smartphone VR headset: Immersive user experience and learning. In *Proceedings of the IEEE 17th International Conference on Advanced Learning Technologies, ICALT 2017* (pp. 477-481). 10.1109/ICALT.2017.145

Parmar, D., Bertrand, J., Babu, S. V., Madathil, K., Zelaya, M., Wang, T., Wagner, J., Gramopadhye, A. K., & Frady, K. (2016). A comparative evaluation of viewing metaphors on psychophysical skills education in an interactive virtual environment. *Virtual Reality (Waltham Cross), 20*(3), 141–157. doi:10.100710055-016-0287-7

Radianti, J., Majchrzak, T. A., Fromm, J., & Wohlgenannt, I. (2020). A systematic review of immersive virtual reality applications for higher education: Design elements, lessons learned, and research agenda. *Computers & Education, 147*, 103778. doi:10.1016/j.compedu.2019.103778

Sandoval, W. (2014). Conjecture mapping: An approach to systematic educational design research. *Journal of the Learning Sciences, 23*(1), 18–36. doi:10.1080/10508406.2013.778204

Sathe, V., Gupta, P., Kaushik, K., Bhat, S., & Deshpande, S. (2017). Virtual reality websites (VR WEB). In *Proceedings of the 2017 International Conference of Electronics, Communication and Aerospace Technology (ICECA)* (Vol. 1, pp. 647-652). IEEE. 10.1109/ICECA.2017.8203619

Stepan, K., Zeiger, J., Hanchuk, S., Del Signore, A., Shrivastava, R., Govindaraj, S., & Iloreta, A. (2017). Immersive virtual reality as a teaching tool for neuroanatomy. *International Forum of Allergy & Rhinology, 7*(10), 1006–1013. doi:10.1002/alr.21986 PMID:28719062

Tatli, Z., & Ayas, A. (2011). Development process of virtual chemistry laboratory. In *International computer & instructional technologies symposium*. Fırat University.

Teranishi, S., & Yamagishi, Y. (2018). Educational effects of a virtual reality simulation system for constructing self-built PCs. *Journal of Educational Multimedia and Hypermedia, 27*(3), 411–423.

Unreal Engine. (2020, April 10). *Pixel Streaming*. https://docs.unrealengine.com/en-US/Platforms/PixelStreaming/index.html

van Wyk, E., & De Villiers, M. R. (2014). Applying design-based research for developing virtual reality training in the South African mining industry. In *Proceedings of the Southern African Institute for Computer Scientist and Information Technologists Annual Conference 2014 on SAICSIT 2014 Empowered by Technology* (pp. 70-81). 10.1145/2664591.2664627

Venable, J. (2006.) The role of theory and theorising in design science research. In *Proceedings of the 1st International Conference on Design Science in Information Systems and Technology (DESRIST 2006)* (pp. 1-18). Academic Press.

Volkoff, O., & Strong, D. M. (2013). Critical realism and affordances: Theorizing IT-associated organizational change processes. *Management Information Systems Quarterly*, *37*(3), 819–834. doi:10.25300/MISQ/2013/37.3.07

vom Brocke, J., Winter, R., Hevner, A., & Maedche, A. (2019). Accumulation and evolution of design knowledge in design science research–A journey through time and space. *Journal of the Association for Information Systems*.

Zinchenko, Y. P., Khoroshikh, P. P., Sergievich, A. A., Smirnov, A. S., Tumyalis, A. V., Kovalev, A. I., Gutnikov, S. A., & Golokhvast, K. S. (2020). Virtual reality is more efficient in learning human heart anatomy especially for subjects with low baseline knowledge. *New Ideas in Psychology*, *59*, 100786. doi:10.1016/j.newideapsych.2020.100786

ADDITIONAL READING

Freina, L., Bottino, R., & Tavella, M. (2016). From e-learning to VR-learning: An example of learning in an immersive virtual world. *Journal of e-Learning and Knowledge Society, 12*(2), 102-113.

Freina, L., & Ott, M. (2015). A literature review on immersive virtual reality in education: State of the art and perspectives. In *Proceedings of the International Scientific Conference eLearning and Software for Education* (Vol. 1, p. 133).

Gregor, S., & Hevner, A. R. (2013). Positioning and presenting design science research for maximum impact. *Management Information Systems Quarterly*, *37*(2), 337–355. doi:10.25300/MISQ/2013/37.2.01

Mann, S., Furness, T., Yuan, Y., Iorio, J., & Wang, Z. (2018). All reality: Virtual, augmented, mixed (x), mediated (x, y), and multimediated reality. *arXiv*. arXiv preprint. arXiv:1804.08386.

Noroozi, O., Weinberger, A., Biemans, H. J., Mulder, M., & Chizari, M. (2012). Argumentation-based computer supported collaborative learning (ABCSCL): A synthesis of 15 years of research. *Educational Research Review*, *7*(2), 79–106. doi:10.1016/j.edurev.2011.11.006

Peffers, K., Tuunanen, T., Rothenberger, M. A., & Chatterjee, S. (2007). A design science research methodology for information systems research. *Journal of Management Information Systems*, *24*(3), 45–77. doi:10.2753/MIS0742-1222240302

van Wyk, E., & De Villiers, M. R. (2014). Applying design-based research for developing virtual reality training in the South African mining industry. In *Proceedings of the Southern African Institute for Computer Scientist and Information Technologists Annual Conference 2014 on SAICSIT 2014 Empowered by Technology* (pp. 70-81). 10.1145/2664591.2664627

Vesisenaho, M., Juntunen, M., Häkkinen, P., Pöysä-Tarhonen, J., Miakush, I., Fagerlund, J., & Parviainen, T. (2019). Virtual reality in education: Focus on the role of emotions and physiological reactivity. *Journal of Virtual Worlds Research*, *12*(1), 1–15. doi:10.4101/jvwr.v12i1.7329

vom Brocke, J., Winter, R., Hevner, A., & Maedche, A. (2019). Accumulation and evolution of design knowledge in design science research–A journey through time and space. *Journal of the Association for Information Systems*.

Walsh, K. R., & Pawlowski, S. D. (2002). Virtual reality: A technology in need of IS research. *Communications of the Association for Information Systems*, *8*(1), 296–313. doi:10.17705/1CAIS.00820

KEY TERMS AND DEFINITIONS

Design Knowledge: Knowledge presented by the developed artifacts. Examples of knowledge include constructs, methods, models, design principles and technological rules.

Design Principle: Practical knowledge, focusing on the principles on developing something.

Design Science Research: A research methodology that focuses on solving problems by developing artifacts.

Design Theory: The most mature design knowledge, includes prescriptive knowledge, providing prescriptions for action and design.

Technological Rule: A rule for using a specific technology (i.e., in order to achieve X, you have to use Y).

Virtual Reality: A computer-generated virtual world.

Virtual Reality Learning Environments (VRLEs): Computer-generated virtual worlds whose main purposes are educational.

Chapter 6
What Makes an Educational Augmented Reality Application Good?
Through the Eyes of Teachers, as Its Practitioners

Mustafa Fidan
Bartin University, Turkey

ABSTRACT

In recent years, teachers have started to integrate augmented reality (AR) technology as a potential learning tool into classroom activities. The main concern is the quality of the existing applications rather than brand-newness. Therefore, this chapter focuses on the components of a good educational AR application based on the experiences of teachers and to examine the current situation on the integration of AR to learning environments. Qualitative methodology was used in this study. The sample consisted of 24 teachers working in public schools in Turkey. The data were collected via semi-structured interviews and analyzed through the thematic analysis. The results showed that the components of a good AR application in education were gathered under four main themes: "analysis process," "design process," "teaching-learning process," and "evaluation components." Implications for the design and use of the AR applications in educational settings were also included in the study.

INTRODUCTION

Augmented reality (AR) is an interactive environment where the virtual objects (video, animation, 3D, etc.) are superimposed on the real-world settings. As an innovative technology based on the human-computer interaction (Wang, Ong & Nee, 2016), it has a visualization structure combining the computer-based information with the physical environment (Martin-Gutierrez et al., 2015). Azuma (1997) asserts that the AR enables the detection of virtual objects on the real world as a derivation of virtual reality (VR).

DOI: 10.4018/978-1-7998-5043-4.ch006

Hence, it supports the existing reality by offering three main features (Azuma, 1997): (i) the combination of virtual and real objects (ii) real-time interaction, and (iii) 3D referencing.

The virtual contents of AR applications (apps) are created using various image, graph or video processing techniques. Thus, the real world setting becomes more functional by means of virtual objects (Siltanen, 2012). The main tools used for AR are displays, input and tracking devices, and computers (Carmigniani & Furth, 2011). Besides the mobile devices (smart phones, PDAs, tablets, etc.), head mounted displays and spatial images (holograms, optical elements, radio-frequency, etc.) are used as display devices, and specially designed gloves or wireless wristbands are used as input devices. On the other hand, GPS, digital camera, and wireless and optical sensors are used as tracking devices (Carmigniani et al., 2011; Johnson et al., 2010; Koutromanos, Sofos & Avraamidou, 2015). Kounavis et al. (2012) stated that the AR apps required the components such as mobile device, camera, high-performance processor, large-capacity RAM, and wireless network. Similarly, from a hardware perspective, Craig (2013) emphasized that the AR apps consisted of the basic components such as sensors (cameras, GPS, gyroscope sensors, etc.), processor units (computer, tablet, etc.), and displays (screens of computers, mobile devices etc.).

According to Azuma et al. (2011), the AR technology is the result of the visualization of the virtual objects along with the real world in the same space; however, it is not limited to the sense of sight. This technology has a structure that appeals to the primary senses such as touching, smelling, and hearing, and also has the feature of perceiving and recognizing the gestures and facial expressions. Johnson et al. (2010) summarized the technologies used in the AR systems as follows: (i) GPS technology in which the real world location is integrated, (ii) "image diagnostic software" in which the virtual objects are integrated by recognizing the marker, (iii) "speech and voice systems" that enable voice recognition and playing the related sounds, (iv) "internet access" that enables the content storing and sharing by using social media and Web 2.0 technologies, and (v) "intuitive interfaces" that provide a natural interaction with the touchscreen, gyroscope, and haptic input technologies.

It has become increasingly important to use the AR technology in the field of education as well as the sectors such as advertising, marketing, architecture, amusement, defense, travel, and health. Accordingly, it has become a potential technology affecting the teaching-learning process. The AR technology, one of the developing technologies for the educational settings, has aroused intense interest among researchers recently. In the 2020 EDUCAUSE Horizon Report, it was predicted that the AR/VR (referred to as extended reality that embraces both technologies) technology would be widely used for the teaching-learning process and the educational technologies would follow a trend in line with this technology (Brown et al., 2020). In this context, AR is among emerging technologies for the educational environments. AR provides a learning environment adaptable to the real life environment, ensuring flexibility in learning (Barsom, Graafland & Schijven, 2016). In addition, the AR apps differ from the traditional teaching technologies in terms of providing realistic visuals, effective and friendly interfaces, and interactive contents (Wang, Anne & Ropp, 2016).

AR technology has drawn attention especially in the educational environments in concretizing the abstract concepts and simplifying the complex situations. In addition, it increases the students' motivation for lessons and attracts their attention by making lessons more enjoyable (Singhal, Bagga, Goyal & Saxena, 2012). In education, it is mostly used in teaching the inaccessible and invisible objects and phenomena and in applying different options involving dangerous situations. It also contributes to the development of students' both cognitive characteristics such as course achievement and affective characteristics such as attitude and motivation (Akçayır & Akçayır, 2017). Specifically, AR is an immersive environment for learning in different fields such as mathematics (Kaufmann & Dünser, 2007), science

(Fidan & Tuncel, 2019), language (Küçük, Yılmaz & Göktaş, 2014), and medicine (Liu, Jenkins, Sanderson, Fabian & Russell, 2010). The research results have showed that the AR apps generally contribute to the development of the cognitive attitudes such as course achievement of students and the affective features such as motivation (Akçayır & Akçayır, 2017; Fidan & Tuncel, 2019; Garzon & Acevedo, 2019). Moreover, it has been asserted that AR is a potential technology for ensuring permanence in learning, engaging students in lessons and making lessons more enjoyable, and providing them immersive and more realistic experiences (Fidan & Tuncel, 2019).

Despite its educational benefits, it has several technical limitations such as marker recognition, sensor sensitivity, and visual quality. Rabbi and Ullah (2013) have asserted that AR poses challenges in terms of performance, interaction, and visualization. Other drawbacks are the excessive cognitive load in sophisticated tasks and the high costs of wearable devices. Several studies have shown that AR can cause some ophthalmic and cervical disorders, especially at early grades (Akçayır & Akçayır, 2017; Fidan & Tuncel, 2019).

Poorly-designed AR apps make the learning difficult and reduce the students' interest. These apps can attract the students' attention as appealing innovations at first, but later on they may lose their attractiveness and effectiveness if not designed in a planned and systematic way. These negative situations affecting the learning process reveal the need for setting certain standards for the design of AR apps. Besides attracting the attention of the researchers in the field of education recently, the AR technology has begun to be integrated into the classroom activities as a potential tool. Therefore, the quality of the apps is of utmost concern for the researchers and professionals in the field of education.

On the other hand, although many studies have been conducted on the use of AR technology in education, there are very few studies providing a guideline for the instructional designers, educators and scholars who question the quality of AR apps. In case the AR environments are carefully designed based on the human-computer interaction allowing the users to have experiences, they contribute to the students' easier and permanent learning, especially in the educational context. In addition, the characteristics of educational materials have been specified by many researchers not in detail but in general terms.

However, there is a need to set more specific criteria and standards for the characteristics of the materials and to direct the design process accordingly. For example, Azuma (1997) customized the characteristics of AR apps as real and virtual combination, real-time interaction, and three-dimensional recording. Craig (2013) stated that the concepts of interaction and content play a key role in the design of AR apps. In addition to the functionality of AR apps, the User Interface (UI) and User Experience (UX) should also be prioritized. As a matter of fact, a poorly designed AR technology not including certain features can only have a weak effect on learning. Other important issues to be taken in to account in designing the AR apps are cognitive load, tracking methods, virtual contents, wearable devices, display, gamified story, haptic interface, and immersion (Akçayır & Akçayır, 2017; Cheng & Tsai, 2013; Ibanez & Delgado-Kloos, 2018). In order to reduce the effect of these limitations and ensure an effective learning in AR environments, it is important to reveal the unique characteristics of AR and to set specific standards for the instructional designers. Moreover, there is a lack of research on the AR design in education. Hence, the present study may contribute to the educational literature in terms of specifying the components of a good educational AR app in detail based on the teachers' opinions and, in this regard, differs from other technical studies.

In light of the above information, the purpose of this study was to reveal the components of a good educational AR application based on the experiences of teachers and to examine the current situation on the integration of this technology into the learning environments.

METHODOLOGY

The study was designed as a case study, one of the qualitative research methodologies, to reveal the teachers' opinions on the AR apps in education. Case study is a research methodology that examines in-depth a particular phenomenon, action or situation within the context of current life (Yin, 1994). The case can be any person, institution, environment or event.

Participants

The sample consisted of 24 volunteer teachers from different fields serving in the public schools in Turkey. They were selected using the criterion sampling method, one of the purposeful sampling techniques. The two criteria used for selecting the participants were as follows: (i) to have basic information on AR, and (ii) to have used the AR apps in the classroom. An interview form including both open- and closed-ended questions (demographic variables, acceptance or rejection to participate in the study, experience of using AR) was created using Google Forms in accordance with the purpose of the study. Some examples from the questions were as follows: "Would you like to participate in this study? Can you define AR technology? How does it differ from virtual reality? Have you ever integrated AR into your lessons? If so, give details." Firstly, this form was sent to 74 teachers and 33 of them provided a feedback. After their responses were evaluated, 24 participants were found to be eligible for this study. In addition, these teachers had used the apps at least once in teaching certain subjects till then. In other words, as the practitioners of curriculum, they had the competences to integrate the AR applications into the teaching-learning environment. Of them, 14 (58.3%) were females and 10 (41.7%) were males (aged from 25 to 46, $M = 35.8$, $SD = 2.27$). 11 participants had a master's degree. 6 participants had carried out a scientific study (dissertation, article, etc.) on the use of AR technology in education. The majority of them had used the apps designed by others by installing on their mobile devices from Google Play or Apple Store. The few of them had designed the marker-based AR apps by using the platforms such as Aurasma, HP Reveal. Table 1 shows the distribution of the teachers by their fields and the sample AR apps used in each field.

Table 1. Distribution of participants and the sample AR apps used in each field

Field	School	n	SampleAR apps
Science	Secondary	8	FenAR, Anatomy 4D, Elements 4D, Spacecraft, Animal 4D, Augment, Layar, Star Walk, Uzay 4D, Vücudumuz 4D, AR Flashcards, Plickers.
Maths	Secondary	3	Arloon Geometry, Magic Books, 3D Geometry Book.
Physics	High	2	FenAR, Aurasma.
Geometry	High	2	Augment, Arloon Geometry, Cleverbooks AR Geometry, GeoGebra Augmented Reality.
ICT	Secondary	2	Aurasma.
ELT	Secondary	2	HP Reveal, Magic book, Plickers, Magic Cards, Google Translate.
Social Sciences	Secondary	1	AR Bilim Kartları, Ataturk 4D, Anıtkabir AG, Magic Books AR, Plickers.
Chemistry	Secondary	1	Elements 4D, Aurasma.
Visual Arts	High	1	Quiver, Layar, Aurasma, Google Arts & Culture.
Biology	High	1	Anatomy 4D, Our Body 4D, LearnAR.
Early childhood	Pre-school	1	Quiver, Animals 4D, AR Flashcards, Zoo AR, Kral Sakir AR.
Total		24	

ICT: Information and Communication Technologies, ELT: English Language Teaching

Data Collection and Analysis

The data were collected via the semi-structured interviews. This technique, a part of the qualitative research, helps to gather information from different individuals on the same subject, event or phenomenon. An interview form was prepared, consisting of the following five open-ended questions: (i) What are the missing aspects of the AR apps that you use/examine in the lessons? (ii) What features do you think a good AR application should have? (iii) What difficulties did the students encounter while using the AR applications in the lessons? (iv) What are your suggestions for the educational AR design? (v) Which features of AR apps are challenging/attractive for the students? Furthermore, the probe questions ("How?", "Why?", "Give details.", "How could it be better?", "What do you recommend?", "Which application?", "Can you give an example?", etc.) were used to get detailed opinions of the participants. Moreover, this form included a demographics section providing the information such as gender, field, school type, graduation level, and the competence in AR. The opinions of two academicians specialized in the field of curriculum and instruction and an academician specialized in the field of educational technology were taken on the relevance of interview questions. Based on their feedback, the interview form was revised and finalized. A pilot study was conducted with the participation of five teachers (independently of the current study sample) for the comprehensibility of the open-ended questions. Prior to the interviews, each participant was informed about the purpose of study and they gave consent for this research. Afterwards, a time plan was made for the interviews. While six of the interviews were conducted face to face, the rest were conducted online via Skype or WhatsApp. The interviews lasted for 55 minutes on average (Min=45 min, Max=70 min) and each of them was recorded with the permission of the participant. The interviews were conducted in Turkish in the fall semester of 2018-2019 academic year. After the data analysis phase, the data was translated into English.

The thematic analysis method -identifying, analyzing, and reposting patterns in the qualitative data (Braun & Clark, 2006)- has been prevalently used for the data analysis. This analysis involves the conceptual clustering of similar data and themes by means of a qualitative research. Its stages are as follows: familiarizing with the data, coding, searching for themes, reviewing themes, naming themes, and reporting (Braun & Clark, 2006). Before the data analysis, each participant was given a code (T1, T2, T3, etc.) to ensure the privacy, and the data were transferred to the word processor (MS Word) software. The raw data was confirmed by the participants. The direct quotations from the teachers' opinions were used in the presentation of the findings. The validity and reliability issues were considered within the framework of qualitative paradigm. To ensure the internal and external validity, the following strategies were pursued: (i) systematically reporting the procedures of study in detail, (ii) avoiding the personal and biased comments, (iii) using purposeful sampling, and (iv) confirming the data by the participants.

In order to ensure the reliability, first of all, three researchers coded the data independently and then the percentage of the agreement (consensus) between these researchers was calculated using Miles and Huberman's (1994) formula. This value was found to be .91. The consistency percentages above .70 are considered as reliable (Miles & Huberman, 1994). Lastly, the coders also met on Skype to discuss and resolve the conflicts and finalized the codes and themes. In the findings section, the frequencies of codes were reported by digitizing. Yıldırım and Şimşek (2016) stated that the digitization of the qualitative data enhances the reliability.

FINDINGS

The results of the thematic analysis carried out based on the teachers' opinions and suggestions showed that the components of a good AR app in education were gathered under four themes: "analysis process", "design process", "teaching-learning process", and "evaluation components". It is clear that these themes emphasize the components of the instructional design. The themes reveal a picture based on the limitations and shortcomings of the existing AR applications or platforms. Analysis Process

The theme "analysis process" refers to the aspects regarding the needs analysis to be carried out prior to the design phase of the AR apps. In this regard, the teachers stated that their cost was very high; they were not prepared in line with the objectives and contents of the curriculum; and the physical, hardware and technological infrastructure in the schools was insufficient for the AR apps. Table 2 shows the codes of the theme "analysis process" and their frequencies.

Table 2. The codes of the theme "analysis process" and their frequencies

Codes	f
Affordability (Time, money, labor, reachability)	19
Content convenience (Complicated and abstract subjects, unreachable objects, relational concepts or events, dangerous or risky situations, repeatable subjects, spatial concepts)	15
Infrastructure convenience (Internet, display devices, minimum device requirements, speed)	15
Target audience convenience (Age, gender, grade, physical and cognitive developmental features)	10
Consensus	6
Equality of opportunity	3
Consistency with the course objectives	3

As seen in the Table 2, the teachers mostly highlighted the affordability, content, infrastructure, and target-audience relevance of the AR apps. For instance, T3 stated, *"Most of the existing apps do not address the crucial points of the subjects. I didn't like most of them. There are also practical ones. In addition, students do not focus on the main idea of the material. They see it only as a game or as a coloring activity..."* She complained about the scarcity of the AR apps on some specific subjects in science education. Although there are more apps in science course than other fields, the teachers have difficulties in integrating the applications into their courses. The reason is that the apps in the science course are designed for general subjects rather than the objectives of the course. She also expressed, *"For example, an app should be able to make the relationship between heat and temperature comprehensible. Students should be able to analyze the relationship between mass and weight well. There are many relational concepts in the field of science. I can say that it is the most important field where students have most of the misconceptions..."* It can be said that the apps are generally superficial and simple for the science course. Hence, it seems important that they need to activate the high-level cognitive skills of learners.

Similarly, T5 stated, *"AR apps offer us the events that we will not be able to experience in real life in a more realistic way... For example, if they enable us to experience the physical events, planets, and the events in space, it would be a great experience... If we, the subject matter teachers, are surveyed before the apps are designed, the subjects that we lack materials will be directly identified."* T6 also emphasized the professional designs and affordability issues. He said, *"These apps are a little different from the common video apps or multimedia apps. They should be designed more professionally. But for this, of course, money is needed. The Ministry of Education should allocate an extra budget for this. Interesting and difficult subjects should be analyzed and, accordingly, a plan should be made for the AR apps. In my opinion, although the apps are interesting for the secondary school level, the activities might be diversified by considering the subject contents."*

In the light of the above opinions, it can be said that a comprehensive needs analysis should be carried out on the contents and objectives of the course before designing an AR app. It is important to take the teachers' opinions as practitioners of curriculum. Reflecting this situation, T9 stated, *"In my opinion, the opinions of the currently working teachers should be taken and the apps should be improved based in line with the needs. The needs should be determined based on a common decision rather than what a single teacher wants. There is a subject called 'genetic' in biology and students have difficulty in understanding the topic of DNA. If our opinions are taken and it is focused directly on these critical subjects, more positive results will be obtained."* Moreover, she mentioned about the lack of infrastructure, *"Our infrastructure is not much suitable for these apps. There is no high-speed internet connection available for students to use uninterruptedly in the classroom. The internet provided by the Ministry of Education is too restrictive for access to many sites. The apps compatible with the EBA network will be more efficient..."*

Table 3. The codes of the theme "design process" and their frequencies

Codes	f	Codes	f
3D/4D model-based	17	Holographic	4
AR design platform	15	Accessibility	3
Application warehouse	10	Synchronicity	3
Multimedia contents	8	Haptic	3
Interactive	8	Holistic	2
Integrative	7	Adaptable	2
Language support	7	Hybrid tracking techniques	2
Ease of use	7	Systematic and hierarchic	2
Smart display devices	6	Compatible with devices	2
Health and safety	5	Help/guide elements	2
Zoom in/out	5	Recognition of markers	2
Ergonomic	4	Updateable	2
Wearable devices	4	Flexibility	2
Mobile-supported	4	Durability	1
User-friendly interface	4	Openness	1
Well-structured storyboards	4	Original	1
Cognitive load	4	Artificial intelligence supported	1
Emotional factors	4	Controllability	1

T9 put emphasis on the lack of apps in compliance with the objectives of lesson and the grade level, the expensiveness of apps, and the demanding endeavor required by the design. He stated, *"Science course should be suitable for objectives... Science is like an ocean, a wide range of subjects are available in it. The apps aren't being prepared in accordance with the course objectives. The app developers mostly seem to have identified a topic and developed an application on it. But you cannot use it in class in the fullest sense. The apps look as if they are going to be used in elective courses... Of course, the budget is also very important. It is not easy to prepare these apps. You need to know certain programming languages; you need to know graphic design. It requires a lot of efforts. Because of useful apps, they are all paid apps. Not only the teachers and students but also the schools do not have enough equipment."*

Table 4. The codes of the sub-themes of the theme "teaching-learning process" and the frequencies of the codes

Structural Convenience	f	Pedagogical Convenience	f
Interesting	16	Game based	7
Realistic	16	Entertainment based	6
Entertaining	13	Real life based	6
Funny	10	Collaborative learning based	4
Concretization	9	Experiment based	4
Informative	5	Problem based	3
Simple and sophisticated	3	Inquiry based	3
Focusable	2	Individualized learning based	2
Immersive	1	Practical activity based	2
Striking	1	Student centered	2
Comprehensibility	1	Discussion based	2
Incentive	1	Self-directed	2
Motivating	1	Technology based	1
		Extracurricular learning based	1
		Deep learning based	1
		Story based	1

Design Process

The theme "design process" refers to the technical and educational considerations in designing the AR apps. Table 3 shows the codes of this theme and their frequencies.

As seen in the Table 3, most of the teachers emphasized that the AR apps should be three-dimensional. For instance, T16 stated, *"The apps should be three-dimensional; thus, students can analyze the content more easily and realistically..."* Three dimensional modelling increases the perception of reality and provides an opportunity to examine the model from different angles. She said the following statements for the effects of AR on learning: *"It gives an opportunity to examine every point of the content in detail. The AR apps that work with special glasses and cardboards also attract the students' attention..."* This theme emphasizes the substantial components before the integration of AR with the application.

Some teachers emphasized that there is a need for a data warehouse that can be easily accessed by the AR apps related to the course. For instance, T8 stated, *"I see that the apps are too isolated. In fact, it would be better if there were a joint program that combined all of them. Such an application or platform should be in a way that we can download and use these apps easily from the application list arranged by subject. Otherwise, it is difficult to find the apps in this way.* Similarly, T21 mentioned, *"There must be an application pool arranged by topic... It is very difficult to find the apps on Google Play or the internet... It would be very useful if we had Google glasses for AR apps and we could use them in lessons... Especially, apps should be interactive; users may be directed with buttons or systems sensitive to motion or sound and thus interaction can be increased..."* In addition to the AR warehouse, she drew attention to the feature of interaction which is considered important for the effectiveness of learning and engagement.

Most of the teachers wanted to design their own AR apps via useful platforms. T13 stated, *"Unfortunately, there are few sites, programs or apps where we can design these apps. The useful ones always work to a certain extent. The applications such as "HP Reveal" and "Augment" are not fully efficient... Wearable technologies can be great for educational environments, our country -Turkey- is unfortunately late to adapt to the innovations in educational technologies..."* T9 also focused on the lack of language support by saying, *"The apps do not have language support. Most of them are in English, they are mostly understandable but it takes time to sort them out. There should be apps in Turkish because especially in lower classes it can be difficult for the children to understand the content in apps..."*. The apps designed in different languages can be difficult for learners. Hence, these apps can cause them to lose motivation and waste time. Along with the technical features of AR, some teachers also focused on the cognitive and emotional factors about its design. For instance, T3 stated, *"The colors and visuals should be suitable for students or not be exaggerated. Because students may have excessive cognitive load..."*. Accordingly, the design principles and elements are also considered important for the educational AR apps.

The participants underlined the marker-based AR apps. For instance, T3 mentioned that the students have to hold their mobile devices on the specially designed markers in the science course. It would be more realistic if the virtual objects appeared by holding the device on the real objects. Especially, it is difficult to use the marker-based apps in the pre-school education. Hence, few teachers focused on the interactive apps using several features such as holograph, haptic technology, etc.

Teaching-Learning Process

The theme "teaching-learning process" refers to the pedagogical use of AR apps in the classroom and their structural features. In this context, the codes formed based on the teachers' opinions were grouped under two sub-themes as "structural convenience" and "pedagogical convenience". Table 4 shows the codes of the sub-themes of the theme "teaching-learning process" and the frequencies of these codes.

As seen in the Table 4, the teachers emphasized on the interesting, realistic, entertaining, funny, and concretizing aspects of the apps in terms of the structural convenience. This theme includes the characteristics of the educational AR apps and the features activating students affectively. For instance, T6 stated, *"AR apps should attract the students' interest and not seem boring to them. Because the students need to focus on the subjects in the lessons... If we do not engage them in activities, they get bored in the lesson immediately. The new generation is more prone to technology and it attracts their attention during the lesson."* Similarly, T20 mentioned, *"I believe that the scenes we see in science fiction movies will come true in the future. Even, teachers will teach lessons in schools in this way. With holograms, they will present everything they desire in a more realistic and interesting way in the classroom. In our country, this technology has just begun to develop..."* According to these statements, the perception of reality and interaction can reach different dimensions. T21 also stated, *"In apps, there may be funny and sympathetic characters to whom students can feel themselves close. Even when experiencing an AR app in the classroom, it attracts the attention of students and they like it... It is possible for them to learn better with all the technologies that will connect with the real life... The most important feature of the apps is to be designed in an attractive and realistic way that students can learn the concepts about the lesson permanently without getting bored."* It can be said that the educational AR apps that motivate and energize the learners are more effective for learning than others. This is an essential design element for most teaching materials.

Table 5. The codes of the theme "evaluation components" and their frequencies

Codes	f
Gamification	7
Reinforcement of learning	6
Scanning-based evaluation	6
Visualizing the question	1
Reflection on similar situations	1
Jigsaw activities	1
Contest	1
Discovery-based evaluation	1
Question-answer based evaluation	1
True-wrong based evaluation	1
Interactive questions	1
Motion-sensitive answers	1
Task-completion	1
Application-based evaluation	1
Matching based evaluation	1

In addition, considering the pedagogical convenience, they underlined that there should be more apps based on game, entertainment, and real-life. This theme is related to the integration of AR with the teaching methods or approaches. For instance, T5 seems to have focused on the game-based AR apps with the following statements: *"Connecting the AR apps with real life can at least save us from getting lost in a completely virtual world... Applications can be developed in the form of games. Remember how quickly once "Pokémon Go" game spread among young people. Therefore, well-designed educational AR games can attract the students' attention. I also think these apps will be fun..."* T14 detailed the combination of AR with pedagogic methods and stated, *"In the lesson, I showed an application called FenAR. It was supported by problem scenarios and was very effective. In fact, it first attracted the attention of students, visualized the problems, and helped the students understand the relational elements better... Besides, such apps may be very useful in visualizing some experiments that we cannot carry out in laboratories due to the hazards or the inadequacy of materials..."* T20 put emphasis on the experiment-based AR apps in the science course. She stated, *"This technology has just begun to develop... Maybe, students will be able to conduct experiments in these environments and we will be able to enter wherever we want. Perhaps it will be a revolution for the medical field. In particular, students will do the activities and practices through AR apps..."* T6 also mentioned, *"If there are activities they can do in groups and if there is a tablet computer running the application in each group, it will be fine... These apps are great for both individual and collaborative learning..."* It can be said that AR supports the collaborative learning along with individual activities in the class. With respect to the theme "teaching-learning", it is important to combine AR with the pedagogical methods rather than just using it as a medium for learning environments.

Evaluation Components

The theme "evaluation components" refers to the activities designed for evaluating the students' learning through AR apps. Table 5 shows the codes of this theme and their frequencies.

As seen in the Table 5, the teachers emphasized that the apps should include gamification and reinforcement elements in terms of evaluation. Some teachers highlighted the importance of gamification and entertainment in the AR apps designed for evaluation. For instance, T6 stated, *"They should be especially prepared for evaluation. They should teach while entertaining. For example, an application that gives students awards, medals, and points by playing games may be created. Children love these kinds of game activities. Even point ranking can be included in the app and the students can see their own rank. They may feel as if they were in a game, like a maze puzzle. They can reach the award step by step through the AR App."* T10 also mentioned, *"There should be evaluation activities in the apps. Therefore, the apps should be repetitive and reinforcing. Questions can be internalized better through these apps. There must be interactive and more fun questions."*

In accordance with the affordability principles, T13 focused on the AR app as an evaluation tool in education. She stated, *"There is an application called Plickers. It is a really useful and practical application for both lower grades and high school students. It shows us 'who did what' using the multiple test logic by scanning the papers of the students in the class via augmented reality technology. A more fun AR application of this type can be developed. With these apps, they can solve questions and understand the subjects better."* On the other hand, T2 emphasized on the gesture-based AR apps for evaluation. She stated, *"While preparing evaluation activities, direct motion-sensitive apps can be developed. For example, after the question appears, we should be directed within the application via movements, gestures, and mimics. This can be time-saving. For example, a task can be assigned to the student and s/he tries to complete this task by means of the application. Such practices can be very useful to summarize topics at the end of the lesson. It can even be given to students as homework."* In the light of these statements, some teachers underlined that the AR apps have the evaluation features. T11 focused on the platforms where teachers can create their own AR apps. He stated, *"Thanks to some platforms, students learn the subjects better by gaming. AR can be used as an evaluation tool... It helps to reinforce learning of students."* Contrary to this, another teacher (T8) highlighted that some of them are paid and use the videos, graphics as virtual content, not the 3D models or moving pictures.

DISCUSSION AND CONCLUSION

In this study, the components of AR apps used in the educational environments were examined and, accordingly, it was attempted to identify the features that should be looked for in the design of the AR apps. The results showed that the AR apps used in the classroom -though appealing to the students' interest at first- were unpractical and had many shortcomings in terms of design and content. The components of the AR integration into education were determined considering the challenges and the teachers' suggestions.

According to the teachers' opinions, the components of a good educational AR app were clustered under four main themes: "analysis process", "design process", "teaching-learning process", and "evaluation components". The theme "analysis process" refers to the needs analysis and planning elements before the design of the apps. In this theme, the teachers emphasized that the AR apps should be economical and they should be designed in accordance with the course content and objectives and the infrastructure of the school. Also, they stated that the apps were not directly related to the course outcomes and content. At this point, it is clear that a good needs analysis should be made before proceeding to the design phase of the apps. The reason for this is that most of the participants had integrated the apps (not supporting the students' native language) created by others into the learning environments. They have difficulties in designing their own AR apps. Hence, the majority of teachers focused on the limitations of the existing apps and the need for modifying them.

The studies on this field have highlighted the contribution of the educational AR apps especially in teaching the abstract and complicated subjects, carrying out dangerous experiments, and reaching physically inaccessible objects (Argaw, Haile, Ayalew, & Kuma, 2017; Yoon, Anderson, Lin, & Elinich, 2017). The theme "design process" refers to the technical and instructional principles to be followed during the design of the AR apps. In this context, the teachers underlined that the apps should be three-dimensional, interactive, and integrable. Similarly, Azuma (1997) drew attention to the concepts of "3D registration of virtual objects" and "interaction" in the design of AR apps. Some researchers have stated that the two-dimensional contents can be used in apps as virtual objects (Liou et al., 2017; Turan, Meral & Şahin, 2018). It is noteworthy that, when the majority of studies on the educational AR apps was reviewed, it was seen that these apps were designed three-dimensionally and had a positive effect on the variables such as course achievement, attitude, and motivation (Cai et al., 2017; Fidan & Tuncel, 2019, Ibanez et al., 2020; Wu, Hwang, Yang & Chen, 2018). Fidan and Tuncel (2019) stated that the three-dimensional models of the AR apps give the opportunity to examine the content from different perspectives by making it more realistic and thus increase the permanence in learning.

In the current study, most of the participants also pointed out that the apps were considerably difficult to design and required a certain expertise. They emphasized that there should be a ready-made platform for them to design the AR apps and integrate the three-dimensional models into the content. In this regard, it is seen that there are significant limitations as well as the positive aspects of the existing educational AR apps. The most important of these limitations is their high cost and the insufficiency of the apps designed in line with the course contents and the student level. As a matter of fact, these elements are essential to the general teaching principles rather than being the unique characteristics of the AR technology. In addition, the design process of these apps is challenging, laborious, and costly. Moreover, there is a limited number of apps that the teachers can integrate into their lessons, and those on the market were mostly developed in different languages. Therefore, considering the other limitations, especially unaffordability, the necessity of integrated platforms for the educational AR design for teachers comes to the forefront. Although it is known in the related literature that there are Web 2.0 tools such as Layar, Augment, HP Reveal for designing these apps, these platforms either offer their users limited services in terms of content or charge certain fees for the components (Fidan & Debbağ, 2019). Anatomy 4D, The Brain AR, Spacecratf 4D, AR Flashcards, Science AR, Zooburst, etc. are among the other educationally designed popular apps (Kiryakova, Angelova & Yordanova, 2018). However, these apps have some limitations in that they offer an inadequate language support and are not directly related to course objectives. In addition, few teachers drew attention to the important issues such as accessibility (individuals with disabilities, etc.), health, and safety problems. Similar to this finding, some researchers pointed out that the marker-based AR apps caused back, neck, and arm pains, especially among the younger students (Fidan & Tuncel, 2019; Yilmaz & Batdi, 2016). Stearns, Findlater, and Froehlich

(2018) also stated that the accessibility issues for AR design were a crucial element neglected by the instructional designers.

The theme "teaching-learning process" refers to the integration of the AR apps into the learning environment. The teachers emphasized that the apps should have certain structural qualities such as being interesting, realistic, entertaining, funny, immersive, simple, and comprehensive. On the other hand, they asserted that the apps should include the elements that are based on games, learning with fun, real life, and collaborative learning. The previous meta-analysis studies in the literature have shown that the integration of immersive technologies such as AR into the educational environments positively affects the students' cognitive and affective characteristics (Garzon & Acevedo, 2019; Ozdemir, Sahin, Arcagok, & Demir, 2018; Tekedere & Göker, 2016). Similarly, Dunser et al. (2004) underlined the following design principles of AR: affordance, reducing cognitive overhead, low physical effort, learnability, user satisfaction, flexibility in use, responsiveness and feedback, and error tolerance. Finally, as for the theme "evaluation components", they emphasized that the AR apps should also include the elements such as gamification, competition, reinforcement of learning, and the visualization of the questions for the evaluation of learning. Especially all forms of AR, including games, have two common features: immersion and flow (Molnar & Szuts, 2019). In fact, these elements can inherently be described as the basic elements of the AR experience. The reason why the teachers focus on these elements in the present study is that the AR technology is in its infancy in Turkey, and the applications do not fully reflect the characteristics of AR. Similarly, Dunleavy (2014) put forward three design principles for the AR-based learning: (i) enable and then challenge, (ii) drive by gamified story, and (iii) see the unseen.

Fidan and Tuncel (2018) emphasized that the AR technology has its own characteristics and there should be certain standards especially in the apps developed for learning purposes. However, the basic design criteria for the AR apps and the cognitive theory principles for the multimedia learning should also be taken into consideration. Indeed, a good and systematic design of the AR apps can be an important determinant in the effectiveness of learning (Dunleavy, Dede & Mitchell, 2009; Wu, Hwang, Yang & Chen, 2018).

IMPLICATIONS, LIMITATIONS, AND FUTURE RESEARCH DIRECTIONS

The points and features put forward in this study for the educational AR design and its integration into the learning environments provide a guideline especially for the instructional designers and educational technologists. It is also considered to be a guide for those who will study AR. As a matter of fact, although some standards are similar in the development of learning materials used in education, each material has its own structure, and therefore, the instructional design should be shaped accordingly. In this regard, the studies on the quality of AR design are still in incubation period in the educational context. There is a need for more research to create well-designed and effective apps. As a result of this study, the teachers provided insights into the design and implementation processes of the educational AR apps.

Specifically, a detailed needs analysis should be made in accordance with the relevant discipline, and the design and instructional principles should be combined with the characteristics of AR technology. The abstract subjects (theorems, formulas, etc.) in physics, the three-dimensional objects in geometry, the inaccessible or invisible objects in astronomy, some dangerous experiments in science, and the subjects related to medicine and health are compatible with the structure of AR. On the other hand, the AR apps can be combined with the methods such as game-based learning, fun-based learning, cooperative learning, and real-life-based learning due to its structural convenience. At this stage, one of the important elements is the immersive nature of AR that enables the learners to interact in practice with the virtual objects in the real world and have stunning experiences.

The education ministries of countries can offer AR design environments to teachers. For example, the FATIH (Movement of Enhancing Opportunities and Improving Technology) Project has been carried out by the Ministry of National Education (MoNE) in Turkey to provide equal opportunities in education. The Educational Information Network (EIN) contributes to the content dimension of this project by offering a rich social learning environment to the teachers and students. In this context, an advanced AR design platform can be developed and integrated into this environment. In addition, a data warehouse can be created for the educational three-dimensional models. Indeed, such environments support the principle of affordability in teaching. Based on the findings of the current study and similar studies, a comprehensive guideline can be prepared for the educators and instructional designers to use in these environments.

As with any study, this study has also several limitations. First, the sample of the research consisted of only the teachers working at the time of study, and the data were collected from a small sample. Therefore, in future studies, the sample can be extended to include the students, prospective teachers, and instructional designers in order to specify the quality standards in more detail. However, the fact that the sample of this study consisted of the teachers who experienced the AR apps (installed via Google Play or Apple store) directly in their classroom environments enabled the practice-based interpretation of the findings; and this was one of the strengths of this study. Second, this study was designed using a qualitative methodology and therefore was limited to the interviews with the teachers. In future studies, the instruments can be developed for evaluating the AR apps, and the quantitative and qualitative approaches can be used together to increase the effectiveness of studies.

It is true that in the future, the environments like AR, where the users' interaction with the real world changes, will be one of the technological trends and add immersive experiences to the educational environments as well as other fields. As a matter of fact, the developments in the fields of artificial intelligence and human-computer interaction are harbingers of this. In addition, it can be envisaged that these technologies will prepare the ground for the formation of the AR environments and the emergence of different features. Therefore, in future studies, it is worth questioning the quality of educational AR designs (as AR matures) and determining the striking points for the effectiveness of learning and the evaluation of teaching-learning activities.

REFERENCES

Akçayır, M., & Akçayır, G. (2017). Advantages and challenges associated with augmented for education: A systematic review of the literature. *Educational Research Review*, *20*, 1–11. doi:10.1016/j.edurev.2016.11.002

Argaw, A. S., Haile, B. B., Ayalew, B. T., & Kuma, S. G. (2017). The effect of problem based learning (PBL) instruction on students' motivation and problem solving skills of physics. *Eurasia Journal of Mathematics. Science and Technology Education*, *13*(3), 857–871. doi:10.12973/eurasia.2017.00647a

Azuma, R. T. (1997). A survey of augmented reality. *Presence (Cambridge, Mass.)*, *6*(4), 355–385. doi:10.1162/pres.1997.6.4.355

Azuma, R. T., Baillot, Y., Behringer, R., Feiner, S. K., Julier, S., Mac, B., & Intyre, B. (2001). Recent advances in augmented reality. *IEEE Computer Graphics and Applications*, *21*(6), 34–47. doi:10.1109/38.963459

Braun, V., & Clarke, V. (2006). Using thematic analysis in psychology. *Qualitative Research in Psychology*, *3*(2), 77–101. doi:10.1191/1478088706qp063oa

Brown. (2020). *2020 EDUCAUSE Horizon report (Teaching and learning edition)*. EDUCAUSE.

Cai, S., Chiang, F.-K., Sun, Y., Lin, C., & Lee, J. J. (2017). Applications of augmented reality-based natural interactive learning in magnetic field instruction. *Interactive Learning Environments*, *25*(6), 778–791. doi:10.1080/10494820.2016.1181094

Carmigniani, J., & Furht, B. (2011). Augmented reality: An overview. In B. Furht (Ed.), *Handbook of augmented reality* (pp. 3–46). Springer. doi:10.1007/978-1-4614-0064-6_1

Carmigniani, J., Furht, B., Anisetti, M., Ceravolo, P., Damiani, E., & Ivkovic, M. (2011). Augmented reality technologies, systems and applications. *Multimedia Tools*, *51*(1), 341–377. doi:10.100711042-010-0660-6

Cheng, K.-H., & Tsai, C.-C. (2013). Affordances of augmented reality in science learning: Suggestions for future research. *Journal of Science Education and Technology*, *22*(4), 449–462. doi:10.100710956-012-9405-9

Craig, A. B. (2013). *Understanding augmented reality: Concepts and applications*. Morgan Kaufmann.

Dunleavy, M. (2014). Design principles for augmented reality learning. *TechTrends*, *58*(1), 28–34. doi:10.100711528-013-0717-2

Dunleavy, M., Dede, C., & Mitchell, R. (2009). Affordances and limitations of immersive participatory augmented reality simulations for teaching and learning. *Journal of Science Education and Technology*, *18*(1), 7–22. doi:10.100710956-008-9119-1

Fidan, M., & Debbağ, M. (2019). Artırılmış ve sanal gerçeklik araçları. In 101 Araçla Web 2.0 (pp. 497-559). Ankara: Pegem Akademi Yayıncılık.

Fidan, M., & Tuncel, M. (2019). Integrating augmented reality into problem based learning: The effects on learning achievement and attitude in physics education. *Computers & Education*, *142*, 103635. Advance online publication. doi:10.1016/j.compedu.2019.103635

Garzon, J., & Acevedo, J. (2019). Meta-analysis of the impact of augmented reality on students' learning gains. *Educational Research Review*, *27*, 244–260. doi:10.1016/j.edurev.2019.04.001

Ibanez, M. B., & Delgado-Kloos, C. (2018). Augmented reality for STEM learning: A systematic review. *Computers & Education*, *123*, 109–123. doi:10.1016/j.compedu.2018.05.002

Ibanez, M. B., Portillo, A. U., Cabada, R. Z., & Barron, M. L. (2020). Impact of augmented reality technology on academic achievement and motivation of students from public and private Mexican schools. A case study in a middle-school geometry course. *Computers & Education*, *145*, 103734. Advance online publication. doi:10.1016/j.compedu.2019.103734

Johnson, L., Smith, R., Levine, A., & Haywood, K. (2010). *The 2010 Horizon report*. The New Media Consortium.

Johnson, L. F., Levine, A., Smith, R. S., & Haywood, K. (2010). Key emerging technologies for post-secondary education. *Education Digest*, *76*(2), 34–38.

Kaufmann, H., & Dünser, A. (2007). Summary of usability evaluations of an educational augmented reality application. In R. Shumaker (Ed.), *Proceedings of the 2nd international conference on Virtual reality* (pp. 660-669). Berlin: Springer. 10.1007/978-3-540-73335-5_71

Kiryakova, G., Angelova, N., & Yordanova, L. (2018). The potential of augmented reality to transform education into smart education. *TEM Journal*, *7*(3), 556–565.

Kounavis, C. D., Kasimati, A. E., Zamani, E. D., & Giaglis, G. M. (2012). Enhancing the tourism experience through mobile augmented reality: Challenges and prospects. *International Journal of Engineering Business Management*, *4*(10), 1–6.

Koutromanos, G., Sofos, A., & Avraamidou, L. (2015). The use of augmented reality games in education: A review of the literature. *Educational Media International*, *52*(4), 253–271. doi:10.1080/09523987.2015.1125988

Küçük, S., Yılmaz, R., & Göktaş, Y. (2014). İngilizce öğreniminde artırılmış gerçeklik: Öğrencilerin başarı, tutum ve bilişsel yük düzeyleri. *Eğitim ve Bilim*, *39*(176), 393–404.

Liang, S. (2016). Design principles of augmented reality focusing on the ageing population. In *Proceedings of the 30th International BCS Human Computer Interaction Conference: Fusion!* BCS Learning & Development Ltd. 10.14236/ewic/HCI2016.2

Liou, H.-H., Yang, S. J. H., Chen, S. Y., & Tarng, W. (2017). The influences of the 2D image-based augmented reality and virtual reality on student learning. *Journal of Educational Technology & Society*, *20*(3), 110–121.

Liu, D., Jenkins, S. A., Sanderson, P. M., Fabian, P., & Russell, W. J. (2010). Monitoring with head-mounted displays in general anesthesia: A clinical evaluation in the operating room. *Society for Technology in Anesthesia*, *110*(4), 1032–1038. PMID:20357147

Martín-Gutiérrez, J., Fabiani, P., Benesova, W., Meneses, M. D., & Mora, C. E. (2015). Augmented reality to promote collaborative and autonomous learning in higher education. *Computers in Human Behavior*, *51*, 752–761. doi:10.1016/j.chb.2014.11.093

Miles, M. B., & Huberman, A. M. (1994). *Qualitative data analysis: An expanded sourcebook* (2nd ed.). SAGE Publications.

Molnar, G., & Szuts, Z. (2019). Augmented reality, games, art: Imersion and flow. In V. Geroimenko (Ed.), *Augmented reality games I: Understanding the Pokémon GO phenomenon*. Springer International Publishing., doi:10.1007/978-3-030-15616-9_5

Ozdemir, M., Sahin, Ç., Arcagok, S., & Demir, M. K. (2018). The effect of augmented reality applications in the learning process: A meta-analysis study. *Eurasian Journal of Educational Research*, *74*, 165–186. doi:10.14689/ejer.2018.74.9

Rabbi, I., & Ullah, S. (2013). A survey on augmented reality challenges and tracking. *Acta Graphica, 24*(1-2), 29–46.

Siltanen, S. (2012). Theory and applications of marker-based augmented reality. *VTT Science, 3*. Retrieved from http://www.vtt.fi/inf/pdf/science/2012/S3.pdf

Singhal, S., Bagga, S., Goyal, P., & Saxena, V. (2012). Augmented chemistry: Interactive education system. *International Journal of Computers and Applications*, *49*(15), 1–5. doi:10.5120/7700-1041

Tekedere, H., & Göker, H. (2016). Examining the effectiveness of augmented reality applications in education: A meta-analysis. *International Journal of Environmental and Science Education*, *11*(16), 9469–9481.

Turan, Z., Meral, E., & Sahin, I. F. (2018). The impact of mobile augmented reality in geography education: Achievements, cognitive loads and views of university students. *Journal of Geography in Higher Education*, *42*(3), 427–441. doi:10.1080/03098265.2018.1455174

Wang, X., Ong, S., & Nee, A. (2016). A comprehensive survey of augmented reality assembly research. *Advances in Manufacturing*, *4*(1), 1–22. doi:10.100740436-015-0131-4

Wang, Y., Anne, A., & Ropp, T. (2016). Applying the technology acceptance model to understand aviation students' perceptions toward augmented reality maintenance training instruction. *International Journal of Aviation, Aeronautics, and Aerospace*, *3*(4), 1–13. doi:10.15394/ijaaa.2016.1144

Wu, P.-H., Hwang, G.-J., Yang, M.-L., & Chen, C.-H. (2018). Impacts of integrating the repertory grid into an augmented reality-based learning design on students' learning achievements, cognitive load and degree of satisfaction. *Interactive Learning Environments*, *26*(2), 221–234. doi:10.1080/10494820.2017.1294608

Yıldırım, A., & Şimşek, H. (2016). *Sosyal bilimlerde nitel araştırma yöntemleri (10. baskı)*. Seçkin Yayıncılık.

Yilmaz, Z. A., & Batdi, V. (2016). A meta-analytic and thematic comparative analysis of the ıntegration of augmented reality applications into education. *Education in Science*, *41*(188), 273–289.

Yin, R. K. (1994). *Case study research design and methods* (2nd ed.). Sage Publications.

Yoon, S., Anderson, E., Lin, J., & Elinich, K. (2017). How augmented reality enables conceptual understanding of challenging science content. *Journal of Educational Technology & Society*, *20*(1), 156–168.

ADDITIONAL READING

Antonioli, M., Blake, C., & Sparks, K. (2014). Augmented reality applications in education. *The Journal of Technology Studies*, *40*(1/2), 96–107.

Arici, F., Yildirim, P., Caliklar, Ş., & Yilmaz, R. M. (2019). Research trends in the use of augmented reality in science education: Content and bibliometric mapping analysis. *Computers & Education*, *142*, 103647. doi:10.1016/j.compedu.2019.103647

Bacca, J., Baldiris, S., Fabregat, R., & Graf, S. (2014). Augmented reality trends in education: A systematic review of research and applications. *Journal of Educational Technology & Society*, *17*(4), 133–149.

Boz, M. S. (2019). *Eğitimde artırılmış gerçeklik uygulamalarının değerlendirilmesi.* Yenilik ve Eğitim Teknolojileri Genel Müdürlüğü: Ankara. Retrieved from http://yegitek.meb.gov.tr/meb_iys_dosyalar/2020_03/26132150_egitimdeartirilmisgerceklikuygulamalarinindegerlendirilmesi.pdf

Fidan, M., & Tuncel, M. (2018). Augmented reality in education research (2012-2017): A content analysis. *Cypriot Journal of Educational Sciences*, *13*(4), 577–589. doi:10.18844/cjes.v13i4.3487

Hsiao, K.-F., Chen, N.-S., & Huang, S.-Y. (2012). Learning while exercising for science education in augmented reality among adolescents. *Interactive Learning Environments*, *20*(4), 331–349. doi:10.1080/10494820.2010.486682

Hsu, T.-C. (2017). Learning English with augmented reality: Do learning styles matter? *Computers & Education*, *106*, 137–149. doi:10.1016/j.compedu.2016.12.007

Laine, T. H. (2018). Educational mobile augmented reality games: A systematic literature review and two case studies. *Computers*, *7*(19), 1–28. doi:10.3390/computers7010019

Vidal, E. C. E. Jr, Ty, J. F., Caluya, N. R., & Rodrigo, M. M. T. (2019). MAGIS: Mobile augmented-reality games for instructional support. *Interactive Learning Environments*, *27*(7), 895–907. doi:10.1080/10494820.2018.1504305

Walker, Z., McMahon, D., Rosenblatt, K., & Arner, T. (2017). Beyond Pokémon: Augmented reality is a universal design for learning tool. *SAGE Open*, *7*(4), 1–8. doi:10.1177/2158244017737815

KEY TERMS AND DEFINITIONS

3D Modelling: It is called the mathematical expression of an object in 3 dimensions with all its surfaces.

AR Design: It is a systematic process for creating augmented reality applications.

AR Design Platform: It is a web-based environment where a user can easily design a augmented reality application.

Augmented Reality: This immersive technology combines the virtual objects with real environment to enhance reality sense.

Game-Based Learning: It is a form of learning using computer games in education environments.

Instruction Principles: They are main cornerstones that guide the realization of the goals of education, planning, implementation, and evaluation of teaching-learning activities.

Quality of AR Design: It is defined as the standards for augmented reality application design in increasing the effectiveness of learning.

Wearable Technology: It has smart electronic or computer technologies representing accessories and clothes that can be worn easily on the human body.

Chapter 7
Role-Play in Virtual Reality:
A Teaching Training Design Case Using OpenSimulator

Zhaihuan Dai
Florida State University, USA

Fengfeng Ke
Florida State University, USA

Chih-Pu Dai
https://orcid.org/0000-0003-0977-0039
Florida State University, USA

Mariya Pachman
https://orcid.org/0000-0001-9140-5502
Florida State University, USA

Xin Yuan
Florida State University, USA

ABSTRACT

The affordances of computer-based virtual reality (VR) make it a natural fit for role-play. Although role-play has been commonly used in VR-based learning environments, the discussion of design details and guidelines is limited. In this chapter, the authors present a design case and aim to share their experiences of designing role-play in OpenSimulator-supported VR during a three-year design project for providing teaching training to graduate teaching assistants in STEM disciplines. The design of role-play bridges the technical and pedagogical affordances of VR. The authors discuss the design details from several aspects, including the formulation of role-play, types of role-play, and implementation. The authors also report the success and constraints in implementing role-play. With this design case, the authors intent on sharing the knowledge about the design and practice of VR-based role-play.

DOI: 10.4018/978-1-7998-5043-4.ch007

INTRODUCTION

Role-play describes the type of activity where learners take actions either as themselves or someone else to handle situations that are replications of real life (Mørch et al., 2015; Nestel & Tierney, 2007). In role-play, learners take on a specific identity and try to act, behave, and interact with other roles to fulfill the social expectations of this new identity in a simulated situation (Peng, 2008; Huang & Yeh, 2016). In this sense, role-play is also referred to as *simulation*, and researchers often use these two terms interchangeably to describe instructional activities of the same nature (e.g., Dalgarno, Gregory, Knox, & Reiners, 2016). As a pedagogical technique, role-play is used for skill acquisition, skill maintenance, and knowledge enhancement (Maier, 2002). The application of role-play is popular in many domains, including education, health care, business, military training, and so forth.

A promising platform that supports role-play is computer-based virtual reality (VR). Computer-based VR (hereafter VR) defines a computer-generated display that enables its users to develop a sense of being present in a simulated environment other than the actual physical environment they are in and to interact with that environment (Schroeder, 2008). VR is widely applied in education to encourage active participation while serving for teaching, learning, and training purposes (Dalgarno & Lee, 2010; Fowler, 2015; Taçgin, 2020). The immersive and interactive features make VR a natural fit for implementing role-play activities (Jamaludin, San Chee, & Ho, 2009). Many studies have integrated VR-based role-play as the instructional activity to provide teaching training and yielded positive findings (e.g., Cheong, 2010; Dalgarno et al., 2016). Yet, the details about designing such activities are lacking.

Graduate teaching assistants (GTAs) are extensively involved in undergraduate education in STEM disciplines as they take on essential teaching responsibilities, such as leading lectures, laboratories, and recitations, and frequently interact with undergraduate students (Bitting, Teasdale, & Ryker, 2017). However, GTAs often face the challenges caused by the lack of teaching preparation and training (Mark et al., 2012; Luft, Kurdziel, Roehrig, & Turner, 2004). To address the needs of pedagogical and professional preparation, we designed and developed a Mixed-reality Integrated Learning Environment (*MILE*) project to provide teaching training for STEM GTAs. In this design case (Boling, 2010), we report our experience of designing role-play in VR, which is central to the training project. We discuss the design of a variety types of role-play, and the success and constraints during implementation. The chapter will shed light on the design and practice of role-play in VR.

Theoretical Foundation of Role-Play

The core learning theory underpinning role-play is experiential learning theory (Kolb, 1984). According to Kolb (1984), learning is "the process whereby knowledge is created through the transformation of experience" (p. 38). The learning experience should involve learning events that engage learners actively rather than passively (Clark, Threeton, & Ewing, 2010). Kolb's (1984) experiential learning theory asserts that learning should be recognized as a process where knowledge is continuously obtained from the experiences of the learner.

To be specific, experiential learning theory suggests that complete learning experience should lead learners to go through a cycle with four learning modes (Kolb & Fry, 1975). Concrete experience and abstract conceptualization are two modes where learners can grasp experience. Reflective observation and active experimentation are stages for transforming experience. Such a learning process should be considered as a continuous cycle, and learners can begin at any one of the four modes (Kolb & Fry, 1975).

Role-Play in Educational VR

Educational applications of VR afford technological enhancements to role-play. VR supports remote access for learners to participate in role-play and to simulate roles in scenarios replicating the authentic contexts where the skills being taught are expected to be applied (e.g., Cheong, 2010; Dalgarno et al., 2016; Lane & Rollnick, 2007). The knowledge and skills acquired in the contexts that closely resemble the real-world are more likely to be transferred (Dede, 2009). Meanwhile, accessing VR remotely can be a remedy for logistical constraints faced by many institutions. For example, some universities have incorporated teacher training in VR as part of the curriculum to accommodate the limited resources for providing teaching practicum opportunities for pre-service teachers (O'Connor, 2009).

Using VR to host role-play contributes to the construction of the role, or the identity, that a learner is assigned to play (Fowler, 2015; Slater, 2017). The representational fidelity and interactive capabilities of VR allow learners to control features and behaviors while experiencing visual realism in the context (Dalgarno et al., 2016; Dalgarno & Lee, 2010). To take the control, learners perform embodied actions, including view control, navigation control, and 3D object manipulation (Dalgarno & Lee, 2010). Such an embodiment is crucial to forming and depicting an identity (Dickey, 2002). Moreover, learners are represented as avatars in VR (Warburton, 2009). With the realistic appearance of avatars, learners can participate more actively and engage more deeply in the identification of designated roles (Dalgarno et al., 2016; Jamaludin et al., 2009; Peng, 2008), and practice the skills associated with the role. For example, VR role-play is known to improve future teachers' understanding of diverse learners and inclusion (Mirliss, 2014), to give participants an insight on characteristics of a good teacher (Badilla Quintana, Vera Sagredo & Lytras, 2017), to change pre-service teachers' preconceived notions regarding their students and the needs of their students (Muir, Allen, Rayner, & Cleland, 2013).

VR-based role-play fosters learners' self-efficacy (e.g., Cheong, 2010; Jamaludin et al., 2009). Bandura (1997) states that the most significant source of self-efficacy is mastery experience and that successful mastery experience will increase self-efficacy. Role-play in a VR that duplicates the real world provides learners with enactive mastery experience where the target knowledge and skills can be practiced through acting out the allocated roles. If the experience is well designed, learners are more likely to have successful mastery experience during enactive role-play, and hence, their self-efficacy is more likely to be enhanced. However, the design of role-play learning experience in VR is scarcely discussed by researchers.

In the current literature, role-play is frequently used in educational VR applications (e.g., Aebersold, Tschannen, & Bathish, 2012; Badilla Quintana, et al., 2017; Cheong, 2010; Dalgarno et al., 2016; Jaeger, 2009; Jamaludin et al., 2009; Mirliss, 2014). Nonetheless, the design details were rarely revealed. A few researchers have taken initiatives to investigate the design of role-play. For example, Dalgarno et al. (2016) examined the use of role-play in VR for teaching practice. They introduced the design of the virtual settings and briefly discussed the purposes of role-play. However, their focuses on evaluating the usability of role-play activities were based on questionnaire responses. Jaeger (2009) described a theoretical framework for assessing the possibilities of implementing different types of educational activities in VR. Yet, the study examined role-play as a holistic activity, rather than analyzing how the specifics of role-play design contribute to a learning experience. Jambi, Gardner, and Callaghan (2019) introduced a data-driven, computational pedagogical framework for generating role-play activities in virtual environments. They also reported an evaluative experiment where role-play activities generated by the framework were applied, of which the results included learning effectiveness and model validation.

Although the framework provided insights on multiple levels of role-play generalization, the specifics of role-play formulation and implementation were not discussed. In this chapter, we document a design case (Boling, 2010) of designing role-play for a VR-based teacher training project (*MILE*). We aim to contribute to scholarship in VR-based learning by sharing and reflecting on our design and implementation experiences.

METHODOLOGY

What Is A Design Case?

A design case contains "descriptions of a real artifact or experience that has been intentionally designed" (Boling, 2010, p.2). The value of design cases is that the design of an artifact is descriptively examined to serve as a precedent and as a function of knowledge construction (Boling, 2010; Howard, Boling, Rowland, & Smith, 2012). The design case method has been recognized and employed by scholars to share design knowledge in fields such as VR-based learning (e.g., Roman & Racek, 2019). In this design case, our discussion of VR-based role-play design experience incorporates the following aspects: the description of instructional context, the highlights of the design that are of anticipated interest to other designers, the design processes, the experience of the design as it is enacted or used, as well as the reflection on any salient aspect of the design or process determined by the designers.

Instructional Context

GTAs form a unique group of instructors who play a vital role in undergraduate education (Luft et al., 2004). GTAs are commonly used in higher education institutes for teaching or assisting in teaching undergraduate-level courses (Park, 2011). In STEM disciplines, GTAs are often assigned to lead laboratories, recitation classes, or to be the primary instructors for a large percentage of lower-division courses (Luft et al., 2004). In their instructional roles, GTAs are expected to be experts not only in the subject matter but also in the pedagogical knowledge and skills. GTAs' teaching effectiveness directly affects the quality of undergraduate education in many institutions (Bitting et al., 2017). GTAs' are also prospective faculty members whose teaching preparation often comes from their experience as teaching assistants (Rushin et al., 1997). There has been an increasing concern about the pedagogical support and professional development opportunities afforded to GTAs (DeChenne, Enochs, & Needham, 2012).

The specific context of the design case we present in this chapter is situated in a land-grant university in the United States. To address the needs of quality GTA training in some STEM departments (e.g., Chemistry, Physics, Computer Science, and Mathematics) at the university, an interdisciplinary design team comprised of researcher from the Department of Instructional Systems and Learning Technologies and the Department of Computer Science collaboratively designed and developed the VR-supported, simulation-based, teacher training project. The goal of the project was to provide the GTAs with teaching practice opportunities during role-play and participatory simulation.

The Design of the Project

Software

We have been using the computer-based VR that was built in OpenSimulator to develop multiple simulated virtual campuses. OpenSimulator (2017) is a free, open-source multi-user 3D application server that can be installed on any computer with Windows, Mac, and Linux systems to create 3D virtual environments. OpenSimulator gives its users complete control of the server; therefore, it supports high levels of flexibility without the cost of licensing. It not only allows the use of the built-in building and programming tools to create 3D content but also supports the importation of assets (e.g., terrains, 3D content, animations, and audio) created by third-party software. The imported assets can be further modified using built-in tools. The programming tools implement Linden Scripting Language (LSL) and OpenSimulator Scripting Language (OSSL). Therefore, OpenSimulator embraces creative design while permitting designers to explore ways to push the boundaries of the functionalities of VR authoring toolkits.

To access the virtual environment created using OpenSimulator, we used an open-source third-party client viewer Firestorm Viewer (2019). The viewer is installed on the computers used by the design and development team, the facilitators, and the GTA participants. We created two types of user accounts and granted different levels of authority. The design and development team used accounts that have full editing privileges. The facilitators and GTAs were able to interact with 3D content in the virtual environments but needed to request permission before they could edit the virtual environment.

Design Cycle

This design case situates in a three-year teaching training project for STEM GTAs, *MILE*. The project follows an iterative design cycle (as shown in Figure 1). This design cycle also reflects that of designing role-play, as role-play composes the core training activity. The first year was contributed to conceptualization, as well as early design and development. We consulted experts in pedagogy and STEM subjects, including Chemistry, Physics, Mathematics, and Computer Science, and observed teaching in a variety of contexts, including lecture, laboratory, recitation, and office hour. These actions helped us identify the essential teaching competencies, the typical instructional activities, and the typical student behaviors in the various teaching contexts. Incorporating such information and the affordances of OpenSimulator-supported VR, we designed a variety of role-play (see Table 1). Further, we selected different types of role-play and intermingled them to form a series of teaching scenarios, which composed the units of teaching training (Ke, Pachman & Dai, 2020). The role-play design and integration are the primary focus of this design case and discussed with details in later sections.

The next steps were designing, developing, and testing. At the end of the first year, we prototyped one scenario for each of the four teaching contexts. We also started internal usability testing among the design and development team members regarding functionalities. The second year involved major design and development, as well as early-stage implementation. All scenarios were prototyped and tested during this year. In addition to internal usability testing, we invited GTAs from the four academic disciplines to conduct usability testing concerning training content and activities, as well as user experience. Both types of usability testing were conducted in multiple rounds. With the feedback collected from these testing, we refined the design and updated the prototyped scenarios. The polished scenarios, which were tested and refined multiple times, were delivered to the academic departments to implement the teaching training for their GTAs as we entered the third year of the project. The effectiveness of the training was examined by comparing the pre- and post-assessment on knowledge about teaching and teaching self-efficacy. Additionally, we screen-recorded the training sessions and analyzed the recordings to understand the GTAs' performance during training and to reflect on the design, with the intent to inform design improvement for future implementation.

Figure 1. Iterative design process

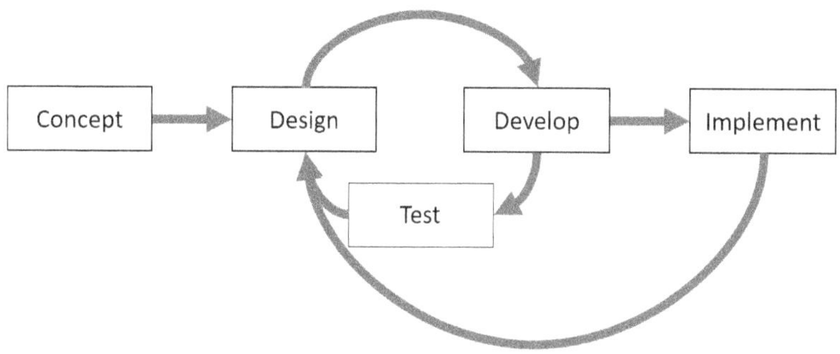

Participants and Data Collection

This design case uses the qualitative data collected during the design, development, and early implementation stages, as the project continues with the implementation cycles at this time. During the design and development stages, 16 GTAs volunteered to participate in usability testing. Data were collected at these stages from multiple sources: screen and webcam recording during the test sessions, onsite observation, interviews with the GTAs, and documentation of design changes and the design team meetings where the decisions were made. During the early implementation stage, 75 GTAs participated in the training either in small groups or as individuals based on the arrangements of their academic department. These participants were from representative departments that we purposefully selected from STEM disciplines, (i.e., Chemistry, Physics, Mathematics, and Computer Science) to provide rich information for teaching training in computer-based VR. We describe details of the collaboration with these departments in the Project Implementation section. Data collected during this period included screen and webcam recording of the training session, onsite observing, and post-training interviewing. Table 1 presents a summary of participant information.

Table 1. Information about participants

Participation	Department			
	Chemistry	Physics	Computer Science	Mathematics
Design & Development	3	5	5	3
Early Implementation	42*	7	19	7

Note: * indicates group participation

Project Implementation

Implementation of *MILE* is versatile and adaptive to department needs and arrangements. One department integrated this project as part of their week-long mandatory teaching training for new GTAs before the semester started. The time and location were restricted because of the overall training schedule. Therefore, the GTAs in this department participated in the VR-based teaching training in groups of about ten people using the same computer lab, where Firestorm Viewer was installed on each computer. The GTAs were provided with account information for entering the virtual environment and a headset with a microphone for speaking. They completed teaching training with this project within one morning, about four hours.

The other three departments allowed their GTAs to complete the training during the semester and complete the training at their own pace. One of these departments included *MILE* as mandatory teaching training for new GTAs, while the other two departments introduced *MILE* as an optional professional development opportunity. During training, some GTAs in these departments used their personal computers and access from their preferred locations while others chose to come to our research lab. We sent detailed instructions about Firestorm Viewer installation to the GTAs who used their personal computers.

Simulated Teaching Scenarios

With the information collected during the design conceptualization stage, we decided to include four instructional contexts in the training, namely lecture, recitation, office hour, and laboratory. The essential instructional activities and typical student behaviors that typically occur in these teaching contexts were also identified at this stage. Based on this information, we designed and developed five types of teaching scenarios, including teaching adaptively, teaching problem-solving, explaining for better understanding, office hour, and laboratory (in chemistry and physics). Each type of scenario includes multiple domain-generic sections that focus on the general teaching competencies needed by GTAs and multiple domain-specific sections that are tailored to academic discipline. GTAs can practice teaching a topic of their choice in domain-generic sections. In domain-specific sections, the topics to be taught are predetermined based on suggestions from subject matter experts. Additionally, each section has a unique location on the virtual campus, such as large or small virtual classrooms, virtual GTA offices, and labs.

We also developed an orientation scenario named training arena. This scenario is comprised of introductory activities to prepare the GTAs to become familiar with the essential functionalities of Firestorm Viewer (e.g., avatar navigation control and interaction with 3D objects) and with the training tasks in major teaching scenarios. The training arena is a flexible preparation step that can be tailored based on the GTAs' needs and prior experience.

The Design of Role-Play

The design of role-play was central to *MILE*. Our primary design concern was effectively triggering embodied actions to help GTAs construct their identity as an instructor and acquire the desired teaching competencies while role-playing in VR. To achieve this goal, we adopted Fowler 's (2015) framework for learning in VR. Fowler's model extended the technical affordances of 3D virtual learning environments identified by Dalgarno and Lee's (2010) model and embraced more emphasis on the pedagogy and design. The design of role-play in *MILE* explored ways to bridge both the technical and pedagogical affordances of VR.

The pedagogical input in Fowler's model is derived from the framework by Mayes and Fowler (1999), which presents three fundamental stages to form a learning experience. First, at the conceptualization stage, different representations of information are provided to learners. This stage is where learners acquire new knowledge and skills and receive feedback. This stage can be associated with conceptual immersion. Second, to enhance comprehension, the learners should perform some actions to apply new knowledge. This construction stage requires learner interactivities and immerse learners in the learning tasks. Third, the dialogue stage engages learners in interaction and discussion about emerged understanding, which contributes to social immersion. Fowler (2015) explicitly pointed out the use of role-play and the involvement of facilitative roles at this stage.

Fowler (2015) asserted that after merging with the technological features of VR, the three stages become concrete design practices. Conceptual immersion can be depicted by a space designed to integrate the new concepts and the representations of information. In this space, learners can interact with each other and exchange viewpoints related to the concepts and information. In *MILE*, the various teaching scenarios constitute spaces of this kind for introducing the knowledge and skills related to the desired teaching competencies. Task immersion involves higher levels of realism and manipulation during a VR learning experience. This can be exemplified by the execution of role-play and is characterized by experiential learning (Kolb, 1984). Social immersion is directly shown in VR, as this kind of virtual learning environment has been recognized by its multi-user features.

In the sections below, we discuss the experience of designing role-play in OpenSimulator-supported VR for *MILE*. Our design attempted to merge both pedagogical and technical affordances in role-play, and thus focused on three aspects: formulation of role-play, types of role-play, and implementation options.

Formulation of Role-Play

In general, role-play consists of four elements. The first element is the characters. The role-play in *MILE* involved two kinds of characters: 1) the avatars, which are the default representations of VR users and can be lively controlled by the users; and 2) the non-player characters (NPCs), which look the same as avatars in their appearances but are pre-programmed to perform specific actions when corresponding events are triggered or when a facilitator send corresponding commands. During training, the GTAs controlled their avatars to play an instructional role (e.g., lab instructor, lecturer) or a student role (e.g., an undergraduate student who attends the class) in cases of group training. The NPCs, on the other hand, were only used to play the student roles and were programmed to perform typical student behaviors. Illustration of both types of characters can be found in Figure 2, where the character wearing a white lab coat is a GTA-controlled avatar, and other characters are NPCs.

The second element is the activities. The activities constitute the essential instructional activities in the various simulated teaching scenarios. Activities are composed of content and events that can trigger the characters to perform participatory actions. The content describes the information presented to the GTAs, which can be domain-generic (e.g., pedagogical approaches) or domain-specific (e.g., homework items and solutions in a specific domain area). The events are circumstances that are designed to replicate the core classroom activities that we have identified and to stimulating the learning and practice of target teaching competencies. The events are executed through triggering the student characters (NPCs or role-played by the GTAs), objects, or both. An example event is that NPC students raise hands to ask questions while a GTA is lecturing. The content and events sketch the flow of activity and need to be planned based on the target teaching competencies and the academic domain. When the content and/or events are present, the GTAs are expected to take participatory actions (i.e., learner actions) that are feasible in OpenSimulator-supported VR and resemble teaching behaviors. These learner actions and examples are presented in Table 2.

Table 2. Learner actions

Learner Action	Description	Examples
Interacting with objects	Clicking or manipulating the objects in virtual environments.	Using media boards that access online simulations, online interactive whiteboards, and online concept map tools; clicking to pick a role card from a dispenser; clicking 3D information objects that distribute scaffolds or prompts.
Interacting with NPCs/facilitators/peers	Verbal communication with the NPCs, the facilitators, or GTAs peers in public chatting channel (i.e., nearby chat) or private chatting channel (i.e., instant message)	Sending text messages in nearby chatting; sending text messages in IM to a peer; using voice chatting
Presentation	Giving an oral presentation during the lecture	Presenting on a topic; explaining concepts
Demonstration	Exhibiting and modeling problem-solving or lab experiment procedures	Writing problem-solving steps on media boards that accessing online interactive whiteboards; Manipulating 3D objects that simulate lab equipment
Debriefing, reflection	Reviewing and reflecting on teaching practice and training experience	Answering reflective questions displayed in dialogue boxes; discussing with peers, facilitators, or both
Critique	Informal evaluation of the performance of the instructor roles, usually during debriefing moments	Criticizing the instructor's strategies of handling a classroom situation and discussing better solutions
Reading written information	Reading text-based information presented on media boards, notecards, or other objects	Reading activity instructions and role cards
Watching instructional videos	Watching instructional videos through media boards	Watching an orientation video on a media board when entering VR for the first time

The other two elements incorporated in the role-play in *MILE* are training aids and facilitators. We use training aids and facilitators to provide guidance to GTAs during the learning experience so that learning is more likely to happen (Kirschner, Sweller, & Clark, 2006; Mayer, 2004). Training aids are designed to scaffold the learning of pedagogical knowledge and skills and to support the completion of teaching tasks. Training aids are programmed to be displayed in the default dialogue boxes and to pop up when triggered. Such dialogue boxes can present plain text and clickable buttons. An example of a training aid can be found at the top right corner of Figure 2. In general, the initial training aids are triggered along with the event, such as a student asking for visual representations, and provide related pedagogical knowledge. Then, additional teaching aids may be triggered based on the GTAs reactions to the event. For example, in the event of a student asking for visual representations, if the GTA ignores the request, a training aid will be triggered to remind the GTAs to respond to the student. If the GTA intends to respond but demonstrate hesitation or difficulty in providing visuals, or directly requesting assistance, the training aids with different types of visuals will be triggered and sent to the GTA. If the GTA provides an intended visual representation, we assume the GTA has mastered this competency, and no additional training aids will be triggered unless the GTA requests additional information. Lastly, facilitators are trained to assist the overall training procedures and facilitated role-play activities based on established protocols. The facilitators use avatars and enter the virtual environment together with the GTA trainees. Ideally, the facilitators should be an expert in both pedagogy knowledge and in the subject matter, such as GTA supervisors, faculty who mentor GTAs, and experienced GTAs.

Figure 2. Screen capture of role-play in an office hour scenario

Types of Role-Play

Two major categories of role-play were incorporated in our project: object prompted role-play and agent prompted role-play. The general mechanism is when the designated objects or agents are triggered, they will send out contextualized cues, or prompts, to stimulate learners' reactions. The objects can be either information objects or environmental objects. Information objects, such as notecards and media boards, display information about pedagogy, subject matter, or activity instructions. Environment objects are 3D objects that are embedded in the virtual environment as a natural part of the background setting, such as chemistry lab equipment and instruments. Taking the chemistry lab scenario as an example, a fire emergency (as an animated object) and would give a visual stimulus to GTAs, prompting the GTAs who have been assigned as lab instructors to take actions to handle the emergency. Activities in object prompted role-play are planned and programmed into the associated objects. This kind of role-play can be activated in one of the two conditions—when a facilitator sends out the corresponding command or when the learners interact with the object (e.g., click on the object).

Agent prompted role-play describes the role-play activated or initiated by an agent. The agent can be a character in the role-play (i.e., an NPC or an avatar controlled by a GTA) or a facilitator. NPC prompted role-play functions in a similar way as object prompted role-play, in that the NPC actions are planned and programmed during the design phase and then performed when the facilitator sends out the corresponding commands. NPC actions replicate typical student classroom behaviors, for instance, raising questions and requesting additional learning materials. Such actions also integrate target teaching competencies being trained, such as using different representations or examples to explain a concept. Meanwhile, the facilitator can puppeteer the NPCs to carry out spontaneous interaction with the GTAs in instructional roles.

Peer prompted role-play assigns both instructional roles and student roles to the GTAs. Playing student roles allows the GTAs to put themselves in the shoes of the students that they may teach in the future. It also stimulates the GTAs to reflect on the implementation of a given pedagogical approach from a student's perspective (Hume, 2012). Peer prompted role-play may occur spontaneously but can also be planned by providing role cards. A role card describes the characteristics of either an instructional role or a student role. It also outlines what activities and actions are expected to be performed by the role and under what condition. We created a role card dispenser to store and to randomly distribute the role cards, in the form of notecard objects. When a person "touches," or clicks, the dispenser, the role card is allocated to the person. Figure 3 is an example of a student role card.

Figure 3. Role card example: a notecard describing a student role

The facilitator prompted role play is initiated by the facilitator and is usually supplementary. This kind of role-play has emerged from the cycles of testing, refining, and implementing. Our original design of object or agent prompted role-play involved using prompts to trigger activities that aim at specific teaching competencies. While such mechanisms functioned well during the usability testing and training for individual GTAs, some of the planned activities were not carried out, especially during peer prompted role-play. In this case, the facilitator would encourage or directly instruct the GTAs to play their roles.

Object prompted and agent prompted role-play are not mutually exclusive. Instead, they are intertwined to provide a cohesive learning experience that naturally simulates real-world practice. For example, in the fire emergency event in the Chemistry lab, an animated object simulates the outbreak of a fire while an NPC student asks the lab instructor, "There is a fire! Can you help me?" The selection of types of role-play to be integrated into each teaching scenario depends on variables such as the core teaching competencies needed for an instructional context, the number of learners, as well as the actions that learners may enact during role-play. Table 3 illustrates the learner actions that have been integrated into each role-play type.

Table 3. Types of role-play and supported learning actions

Learner Action	**Types of Role-play**				
	Object Prompted Role-play		**Agent Prompted Role-play**		
	Information object prompted	**Environment object prompted**	**NPC prompted**	***Peer prompted**	**Facilitator prompted**
Interacting with objects	√	√	√	√	√
Interacting with NPCs			√		
Interacting with facilitator	√	√	√	√	√
Interacting with peer				√	
Presentation	√	√	√	√	√
Demonstration	√	√	√	√	√
Debriefing and Reflection	√	√	√	√	√
Critique				√	
Reading written instruction	√	√	√	√	√
Watching instructional videos	√	√	√	√	√

Note:* indicates the activity is only available for group role-play
√ *indicates learner actions that can be integrated*

Implementation Options of Role-Play

The implementation of role-play in *MILE* is scalable because of the way it is formulated and varied in types. By triggering different objects and agents, role-play can be easily altered to train different numbers of GTAs and for a varied duration. As a result, the teaching training can be tailored to meet the diverse needs and practical conditions of the participating departments. Specifically, *MILE* was implemented in two ways: individual training and group training.

The training for individual GTAs adapted object prompted and NPC agent prompted role-play. When trained individually, the GTAs played the instructional roles and interacted with the NPC students during teaching practice. NPC-prompted role-play formed the major activities. In group training, the GTAs were randomly assigned to groups and stayed in the same group for the whole training. The GTAs were able to play either instructional roles or student roles, as the roles were drawn every time when a group starts a new teaching scenario. Therefore, notecard prompted role-play and peer prompted role-play formed the major activities while other types of role-play supplemented. Moreover, every time when a group began a new scenario, the GTAs were required to draw a new role card. With these arrangements, we intended to ensure that the GTAs have opportunities to act in different roles and to practice on all target teaching competencies if activities assigned to each role were not fully executed. When implemented for group training, reflection questions were integrated into the role cards. Debriefing and critiquing moments led by the facilitators were anchored at the end of each teaching scenario for all GTAs to discuss, reflect, and collaboratively discover the best practice of handling the events that they have just experienced during the scenario.

Role-Play Example

To illustrate our design, we present an example design matrix (Figure 4) with activities of role-play in the scenario *Explaining for better understanding*. The design matrix demonstrates the formulation of role-play for individual-based implementation. When adopting to group implementation, role cards will be created by describing the activities expected to be performed by, in this example, the two student roles. The role cards will also specify the timing to perform these activities.

Figure 4. Design matrix of role-play example

Timing		Start of the scenario	During GTA's lecturing	After GTA presented visuals	After GTA presented visuals	After GTA presented an example case	After GTA explained the example case
Target Teaching Competency		Explain a concept	Explain with alternative representations of the same information	Explain with alternative representations of the same information	Explain using examples or cases	Explain using examples or cases	
Character	**Character Name**	All NPC student	NPC student 1 John Smith	NPC student 1 John Smith NPC student 5 Michael Brown	NPC student 5 Michael Brown	NA	NA
	Action	Sitting (default gesture)	Raise hand and say (in text)	Say (in text)	Say (in text)	NA	NA
	Scripts	NA	*Excuse me. I don't understand this concept. it is too complex. Can you visualize it somehow?*	John: *Okay. I think I'm clear now.* Michael: *Well. I'm still lost. How are the different parts connected?*	Michael: *I see. Thank you.*	NA	NA
Object	**Type of object**	Dialogue box	Dialogue box	Dialogue box	Messaging (public channel)	Dialogue box	Dialogue box
	Purpose	Activity instruction	Training aid	Training aid	Announcement	Training aids	Debriefing
	Content	*You are going to give a lecture on a complex concept. Press Start to begin.*	*Visualizing the interrelations or the structures of a complex concept may help student understanding. You might want to try creating a create a concept map or a flow chart.*	*You could explain the subcomponents or parts of the concept and how they are connected to each other and to the main concept. Then, when parts are explained you could proceed with explaining the whole concept in all its complexity.*	*Now, it's the time to present your prepared example or case.*	*Do not forget to link your example or case to the concept.*	*Your lecture has come to the end. Reviewing what you have practiced, can you write down some approaches to explain a concept for better understanding?* <Space for text input>
Expected Learner Actions		1. Presentation 2. Interacting with objects and NPCs 3. Reading written instructions	1. Presentation 2. Interacting with objects and NPCs 3. Reading written instructions	1. Presentation 2. Interacting with objects and NPCs 3. Reading written instructions	1. Presentation 2. Interacting with objects and NPCs 3. Reading written instructions	1. Presentation 2. Interacting with objects and NPCs 3. Reading written instructions	NA
Facilitation conditions		Condition 1: If the GTA starts presentation, move on to the next event Condition 2: If the GTA does not start presentation, send a reminder: *Please start your lecture*	Condition 1: If the GTA provides visuals properly, continue to the next event Condition 2: If the GTA cannot provide visuals, send notecard *Visualization Examples* Condition 3: If the GTA ignores the request, send a reminder: *Your student is waiting for your help. Please respond to the student's request.*	Condition 1: If the GTA explains properly, continue to the next event Condition 2: If the GTA cannot address the student's needs, send notecard *Using Visuals* Condition 3: If the GTA ignores the request, send a reminder: *Your student is waiting for your help. Please respond to the student's request.*	Condition 1: If the GTA presents an example, continue to the next event Condition 2: If the GTA does not present an example, send a reminder: *Please try to give students an example or case that help them understand the concept*	Condition 1: If the GTA connects the example to the concept, continue to the next event Condition 2: If the GTA does not connects the example to the concept, send a reminder: *Please try to connect your example or case to the concept.*	NA

DESIGN CASE FINDINGS

Multiple salient themes of role-play design and the associated learning processes within the different types of role-play strategies have emerged from the qualitative data collected during this design case. These themes reflect the success or constrained role-play implementation experience.

Contextualized Prompts Stimulated Enactment of Core Actions

The contextualized prompts delivered by objects and agents were critical stimuli of the actions that embodied the target teaching competencies being trained. For instance, at the beginning of individual-based training sessions, the GTAs arrived at a virtual classroom and received a knowledge object (i.e., notecards) that prompted them to teach a topic to the students, which are NPCs. The GTAs would naturally start teaching in a way that they were familiar or comfortable with. This way of teaching may or may not demonstrate the target teaching competencies, such as using visual representations to help explain concepts and to accommodate the needs of students who learn better with visuals. If the GTAs did not use visual representations in their teaching, an NPC student would raise the hand and ask, for example, "It's really hard for me to understand how these concepts are related or different. Could you draw a concept map?" Then the GTAs would respond, or at least attempt to respond, to the student request by creating a concept map on the interactive web whiteboard in the virtual classroom. The same situation applied to group role-play, where this prompt was integrated into the description of a student role.

It was also commonly observed that the GTAs who role-played as the instructors took a teacher's tone when lecturing and interacting with the students. For example, when explaining a concept that the students needed help with, some GTAs would check on student comprehension by asking questions like, "Are you clear about this part now, (student name)?" When seeing the students (role-played by peers) randomly walking in the lab, the instructor GTAs tried to take classroom management actions, "Okay, everyone, we are about to start. Please take a seat."

Notably, the group role-play demonstrated dynamics. Based on the given prompts in their role cards, some GTAs creatively extended their roles. They asked follow-up questions after delivering the original prompts designed for their roles. They also supplemented other student roles by joining the conversation between those students and the instructors. For example, in an office hour scenario, a GTA in a student role was prompted to ask the instructor to explain how to solve a given practice problem. After the instructor (role-played by another GTA) explained the problem solution, the GTA followed by asking, "Okay, I got it, but I don't understand why are we doing this? How does this relate to my real life?" These questions not only prompted the instructor to think and respond but also led to a debriefing moment with the whole group to critique the way the instructor GTA handled these questions and to discuss how these questions can be handled better.

Facilitation was Essential to Learning and Role-Play Execution

In addition to the prompts delivered by the objects and virtual agents, the facilitation provided to learners by the training aids and by the facilitators served as powerful triggers that stimulated learning and role-play. Using the visual representation activity discussed earlier as an example. After the student requested for visuals, a training aid introducing commonly used types of visuals and additional resources for reference would pop up for the GTA instructor. In the circumstances where the GTA instructor ignored the student's request, another training aid would be delivered to remind the GTA to respond to the student. Some GTAs expressed difficulty in providing or using appropriate visuals to enhance their explanation of the concepts. They would ask the student to wait (e.g., "Well, let me think about it"), or hold on their response, and turned to the facilitator for help (e.g., "I'm not sure how to use visuals to present the concept"). The facilitator would send additional training aids related to visual representation or explain this information to the GTAs, who then were able to use some form of visuals to help the student.

The importance of facilitation was evident in the group training sessions. This design case involved group training sessions with four groups of 10 or 11 GTAs. We found that a limited number of GTAs in each group actively played their roles. Often, these active roles were the instructional roles and a few student roles. Some GTAs seemed to prefer observing the activities—they followed the instructor GTAs from scenario to scenario, they followed activity instructions to pick up a role card and opened them for reading. Still, they would never act out their roles. In this situation, the facilitator would remind and encourage participation or trigger objects and NPCs to prompt the role-play so that GTAs in the instructional role could enact teaching practice. If the GTAs who drew an instructional role but did not act, the facilitator had to instruct the group to repeat the step of picking up role cards, or to ask for volunteers to find other GTAs to play the instructional roles so that the activities can continue.

Domain-Specific Information Enhanced Learner Engagement

Although the teaching competencies being trained can be applied across disciplines, the GTAs became more engaged in the activities when domain-specific information presented during role-play, especially during group role-play. When domain-specific examples were used during the teaching practice, we observed active participation from more GTAs than when domain-generic examples were used. For instance, in the Chemistry department's group role-play in the teaching problem-solving scenario, a GTA instructor wrote down some chemical equations and asked the students to balance the equations by giving the coefficients of the molecules. All the student roles started actively interacting with the instructors and discussing possible solutions. Three GTAs in the same group, who had been quiet during the previous discussion on resolving ethical dilemmas in academics, were now eager to participate and to discuss possible solutions with the instructors and peers.

Situational Constraints

Some situational constraints appeared during implementation, which restrained role-play from achieving the optimal teaching training results. In individual training sessions, NPCs were extensively used to play the role of students and to prompt GTAs to act as an instructor. However, the VR toolkit has innate limitations in its auditory functions in the current VR platform. As a result, the NPCs mainly delivered prompting messages as text chat messages rather than in audio messages (i.e., voice chatting). Although the text-based prompts were functional in stimulating the intended teaching practice actions (e.g., answering questions, accommodating students' diverse needs), we found some GTAs concentrated only on communicating with the NPC students in typing. The view of their avatars became fixed on one part of the environment, and hence they missed other visual cues, such as other NPC students' animated behaviors. This could lead to a reduced degree of fidelity during role-play for these GTAs, even though they were immersed in the concepts and tasks for teaching training.

On the other hand, GTAs sometimes omitted the text-based NPC prompts due to the lack of audio signaling, given that the GTAs were well informed about this kind of prompting. Such a situation was often observed when the GTAs were new to the role-play in VR or when they were engaged in teaching activity. A typical case was, a GTA was lecturing on a topic while writing on a virtual whiteboard to help explain or as a demonstration, when an NPC said (in a text message), "Excuse me, I have a question." The GTA was focusing on talking and writing and hence would miss the text message. We tried to amend the situation by accompanying the words with animated gestures, such as raising a hand, which resolved the issue sometimes. Other times, the facilitator had to remind the GTA about the student message.

In the group training context, although group dynamics brought about some creative role-play, the success of role-play depended heavily on the GTAs' willingness to participate. We tried to accommodate and amend the situation by having the facilitator encourage participation or trigger the prompts. Therefore, most GTAs participated at least at some point and played their role to varied extend. A few GTAs, however, did not actively participate during the whole training. When reviewing the screen recordings, we found these GTAs were observing their peers' role-play. Although observation could still be a beneficial learning experience, the low level of involvement reduced the intensity of the training. The constraint of group role-play during the early implementation of *MILE* was also related to the time limitation and group size. Such factors reduced the opportunities for GTAs to role-play an instructor. The GTAs who did not draw an instructional role from the role card dispenser and who chose not to hold an instructional role hence lost the opportunities for enactive mastery experience.

CONCLUSIONS AND FUTURE PLAN

In this design case, we provided a critical review of our experience of designing and implementing different types of VR-based role-play for a teacher training project *MILE*. The design of role-play incorporated the pedagogical and technical affordances of VR learning environments discussed in Fowler's (2015) model. By doing so, we aimed to create a meaningful learning experience that supports the GTAs to learn and practice the core competencies needed for teaching in their disciplines. We also intended to help construct the GTAs' identity as college instructors. The role-play is categorized as object prompted or agent prompted, which can be combined and integrated to create teaching scenarios that resemble teaching experience in the diverse real-world contexts.

Multiple themes emerged during our implementation of role-play when the *MILE* was delivered to four participating academic disciplines. First, using contextualized prompts in role-play stimulates GTAs' enactment of actions embodying target teaching competencies. Second, both internal and external facilitation is critical for learning and execution of role-play in the virtual world. Third, incorporating domain-specific information as the environmental prompts in role-play could enhance learner engagement. Lastly, multiple situational constraints encountered during the implementation should be considered when designing and using VR-based role-play.

Based on these findings, our future plan is to continue enhancing the mechanisms of role-play in VR and to find ways to tackle the situational constraints. We will continuously dedicate our efforts to several areas. To support learning and provide effective learning guidance, we have been exploring different scaffolding strategies that are viable in an OpenSimulaor-supported VR, such as using the dialogue boxes to present question prompts as metacognitive and cognitive scaffolding. To further increase the level of fidelity, we intend to enhance the design of NPCs by integrating more student models representing varied types of learner and demonstrating different levels of interactivity (e.g., Ke, et al., 2020). We have also been exploring ways to enable and enhancing audio messaging and chatting. For example, brief auditory phrases such as "Wow! That's great!" "Aha," and "Alright" can be used together with NPCs' text-based prompts to draw the GTAs' attention. Such brief messages would not overload the bandwidth but would help to mitigate the existing auditory constraints of the environment (Lecon & Herkersdorf, 2014). To enhance implementation, we are exploring approaches to make the role-play more adaptable to diverse training needs and practical conditions. Particularly, to reduce the situational constraints of group-based training, we will explore potential ways to afford opportunities for every group member to lead at least one teaching scenario in an instructional role. As research has suggested, the level of GTA's involvement can drastically change after having a chance to play an instructor's role (e.g., Ke, et al., 2019). Lastly, the design of role-play can be further evaluated and validated using measures that have been employed in similar design-based studies (e.g., Schild et al., 2018) to examine learning experience design and usability. Such information could enlighten the exploration of adaptive implementation approaches.

ACKNOWLEDGMENT

The research reported in this chapter is funded by the National Science Foundation [grant number 1632965]. Any opinions, findings, and conclusions or recommendations expressed in these materials are those of the author(s) and do not necessarily reflect the views of the National Science Foundation.

REFERENCES

Aebersold, M., Tschannen, D., & Bathish, M. (2012). Innovative Simulation Strategies in Education. *Nursing Research and Practice*, *2012*, 1–7. doi:10.1155/2012/765212 PMID:22550573

Badilla Quintana, M. G., Vera Sagredo, A., & Lytras, M. D. (2017). Pre-service teachers' skills and perceptions about the use of virtual learning environments to improve teaching and learning. *Behaviour & Information Technology*, *36*(6), 575–588. doi:10.1080/0144929X.2016.1266388

Bandura, A. (1997). The anatomy of stages of change. *American Journal of Health Promotion*, *12*(1), 8–10. doi:10.4278/0890-1171-12.1.8 PMID:10170438

Bitting, K. S., Teasdale, R., & Ryker, K. (2017). Applying the geoscience education research strength of evidence pyramid: Developing a rubric to characterize existing geoscience teaching assistant training studies. *Journal of Geoscience Education*, *65*(4), 519–530. doi:10.5408/16-228.1

Boling, E. (2010). The need for design cases: Disseminating design knowledge. *International Journal of Designs for Learning*, *1*(1), 1–8.

Cheong, D. (2010). The effects of practice teaching sessions in second life on the change in pre-service teachers' teaching efficacy. *Computers & Education*, *55*(2), 868–880. doi:10.1016/j.compedu.2010.03.018

Clark, R. W., Threeton, M. D., & Ewing, J. C. (2010). The Potential of Experiential Learning Models and Practices in Career and Technical Education and Career and Technical Teacher Education. *Journal of Career and Technical Education*, *25*(2), 46–62. doi:10.21061/jcte.v25i2.479

Dalgarno, B., Gregory, S., Reiners, T., & Knox, V. (2016). Practising teaching using virtual classroom role plays. *The Australian Journal of Teacher Education*, *41*(1), 126–154. doi:10.14221/ajte.2016v41n1.8

Dalgarno, B., & Lee, M. J. (2010). What are the learning affordances of 3-D virtual environments? *British Journal of Educational Technology*, *41*(1), 10–32. doi:10.1111/j.1467-8535.2009.01038.x

DeChenne, S. E., Enochs, L. G., & Needham, M. (2012). Science, Technology, Engineering, and Mathematics Graduate Teaching Assistants Teaching Self-Efficacy. *The Journal of Scholarship of Teaching and Learning*, *12*(4), 102–123.

Dickey, M. D. (2002). 3D virtual worlds: an emerging technology for traditional and distance learning. Proceedings of Ohio Learning Network.

Firestorm Viewer. (2019). *Firestorm* (Version 6.0.2). The Phoenix Firestorm Project, Inc. Retrieved March 30, 2020 from https://www.firestormviewer.org/

Fowler, C. (2015). Virtual reality and learning: Where is the pedagogy? *British Journal of Educational Technology*, *46*(2), 412–422. doi:10.1111/bjet.12135

Huang, L. Y., & Yeh, Y. C. (2016). Mediated enactive experience versus perceived mastery experience: An enhancing mechanism versus a mediator of character attachment and internal political efficacy in serious games. *Computers in Human Behavior*, *55*, 1085–1096. doi:10.1016/j.chb.2015.10.029

Hume, A. C. (2012). Primary connections: Simulating the classroom in initial teacher education. *Research in Science Education*, *42*(3), 551–565. doi:10.100711165-011-9210-0

Jaeger, B. (2009, June). What educational activities fit virtual worlds: Towards a theoretical evaluation framework. In *2009 3rd IEEE International Conference on Digital Ecosystems and Technologies* (pp. 715-720). IEEE.

Jamaludin, A., San Chee, Y., & Ho, C. M. L. (2009). Fostering argumentative knowledge construction through enactive role play in Second Life. *Computers & Education*, *53*(2), 317–329. doi:10.1016/j.compedu.2009.02.009

Jambi, E., Gardner, M., & Callaghan, V. (2019, June). A Generalized Pedagogical Framework for Creating Mixed-Mode Role-Play in Multi-User Virtual Environments. In *International Conference on Immersive Learning* (pp. 158-171). Springer. 10.1007/978-3-030-23089-0_12

Ke, F., Dai, Z., Dai, C. P., Pachman, M., Chaulagain, R. S., & Yuan, X. (2020). Designing Virtual Agents for Simulation-Based Learning in Virtual Reality. In R. Zheng (Ed.), *Cognitive and Affective Perspectives on Immersive Technology in Education* (pp. 151–170). IGI Global. doi:10.4018/978-1-7998-3250-8.ch008

Ke, F., Pachman, M., & Dai, Z. (2020). Investigating educational affordances of virtual reality for simulation-based teaching training with graduate teaching assistants. *Journal of Computing in Higher Education*, •••, 1–21. doi:10.100712528-020-09249-9

Ke, F., Yuan, X., Pachman, M., Dai, Z., Naglieri, R., & Xu, X. (2019). *Perspective Taking in Participatory Simulation-based Collaborative Learning*. Academic Press.

Kirschner, P., Sweller, J., & Clark, R. E. (2006). Why unguided learning does not work: An analysis of the failure of discovery learning, problem-based learning, experiential learning and inquiry-based learning. *Educational Psychologist*, *41*(2), 75–86. doi:10.120715326985ep4102_1

Kolb, B. (1984). Functions of the frontal cortex of the rat: A comparative review. *Brain Research. Brain Research Reviews*, *8*(1), 65–98. doi:10.1016/0165-0173(84)90018-3 PMID:6440660

Kolb, D. A., & Fry, R. (1975). Toward an applied theory of experiential learning. In C. Cooper (Ed.), *Theories of group process*. Wiley.

Lane, C., & Rollnick, S. (2007). The use of simulated patients and role-play in communication skills training: A review of the literature to August 2005. *Patient Education and Counseling*, *67*(1), 13–20. doi:10.1016/j.pec.2007.02.011 PMID:17493780

Lecon, C., & Herkersdorf, M. (2014, August). Virtual Blended Learning virtual 3D worlds and their integration in teaching scenarios. In *2014 9th International Conference on Computer Science & Education* (pp. 153-158). IEEE.

Luft, J. A., Kurdziel, J. P., Roehrig, G. H., & Turner, J. (2004). Growing a garden without water: Graduate teaching assistants in introductory science laboratories at a doctoral/research university. *Journal of Research in Science Teaching*, *41*(3), 211–233. doi:10.1002/tea.20004

Maier, H. W. (2002). Role playing: structures and educational objectives. *The International Child and Youth Care Network, 36.*

Mark, K. P., Thadani, D. R., Calonge, D. S., Pun, C. F., & Chiu, P. P. (2011, October). In-service Teaching Assistant Training (InsTAT) for engineering and computer science graduate students in Hong Kong: A blended-learning approach. In 2011 Frontiers in Education Conference (FIE) (pp. F2E-1). IEEE.

Mayer, R. E. (2004). Should there be a three-strikes rule against pure discovery learning? *The American Psychologist*, *59*(1), 14–19. doi:10.1037/0003-066X.59.1.14 PMID:14736316

Mayes, J. T., & Fowler, C. J. (1999). Learning technology and usability: A framework for understanding courseware. *Interacting with Computers*, *11*(5), 485–497. doi:10.1016/S0953-5438(98)00065-4

Mirliss, D. (2014). Preparing future teachers: Taking the Perspective of Diverse Learners through Virtual World Role-Play. *International Journal of Gaming and Computer-Mediated Simulations*, *6*(2), 15–29. doi:10.4018/ijgcms.2014040102

Mørch, A. I., Hartley, M. D., & Caruso, V. (2015, July). Teaching interpersonal problem solving skills using roleplay in a 3D virtual world for special education: A case study in Second Life. In *2015 IEEE 15th International Conference on Advanced Learning Technologies* (pp. 464-468). IEEE.

Muir, T., Allen, J. M., Rayner, C. S., & Cleland, B. (2013). Preparing pre-service teachers for classroom practice in a virtual world: A pilot study using Second Life. *Journal of Interactive Media in Education*, *1*(3), 3. doi:10.5334/2013-03

Nestel, D., & Tierney, T. (2007). Role-play for medical students learning about communication: Guidelines for maximising benefits. *BMC Medical Education*, *7*(1), 3. doi:10.1186/1472-6920-7-3 PMID:17335561

O'Connor, E. A. (2009). Instructional and design elements that support effective use of virtual worlds: What graduate student work reveals about Second Life. *Journal of Educational Technology Systems*, *38*(2), 213–234. doi:10.2190/ET.38.2.j

OpenSimulator. (2017). *OpenSim* (Version 0.9.0.0). Retrieved March 30, 2020 from http://opensimulator.org/

Park, C. (2004). The graduate teaching assistant (GTA): Lessons from North American experience. *Teaching in Higher Education*, *9*(3), 349–361. doi:10.1080/1356251042000216660

Peng, W. (2008). The mediational role of identification in the relationship between experience mode and self-efficacy: Enactive role-play versus passive observation. *Cyberpsychology & Behavior*, *11*(6), 649–652. doi:10.1089/cpb.2007.0229 PMID:18954275

Rushin, J. W., De Saix, J., Lumsden, A., Streubel, D. P., Summers, G., & Bernson, C. (1997). Graduate Teaching Assistant Training: A Basis for Improvement of College Biology Teaching & Faculty Development? *The American Biology Teacher*, *59*(2), 86–90. doi:10.2307/4450255

Schild, J., Lerner, D., Misztal, S., & Luiz, T. (2018, May). EPICSAVE—Enhancing vocational training for paramedics with multi-user virtual reality. In *2018 IEEE 6th International Conference on Serious Games and Applications for Health (SeGAH)* (pp. 1-8). IEEE.

Schroeder, R. (2008). Defining Virtual Worlds and Virtual Environments. *Journal of Virtual Worlds Research*, *1*(1), 1–3. doi:10.4101/jvwr.v1i1.294

Slater, M. (2017). Implicit learning through embodiment in immersive virtual reality. In D. Liu, C. Dede, R. Huang, & J. Richards (Eds.), *Virtual, Augmented, and Mixed Realities in Education* (pp. 19–33). Springer. doi:10.1007/978-981-10-5490-7_2

Taçgın, Z. (2020). The perceived effectiveness regarding Immersive Virtual Reality learning environments changes by the prior knowledge of learners. *Education and Information Technologies*, •••, 1–19.

ADDITIONAL READING

Alexander, A. L., Brunyé, T., Sidman, J., & Weil, S. A. (2005). From gaming to training: A review of studies on fidelity, immersion, presence, and buy-in and their effects on transfer in pc-based simulations and games. *DARWARS Training Impact Group*, *5*, 1–14.

Bulu, S. T. (2012). Place presence, social presence, co-presence, and satisfaction in virtual worlds. *Computers & Education*, *58*(1), 154–161. doi:10.1016/j.compedu.2011.08.024

Burdea, G. C., & Coiffet, P. (2003). *Virtual reality technology*. John Wiley & Sons. doi:10.1162/105474603322955950

Dede, C. (2009). Immersive interfaces for engagement and learning. *Science*, *323*(5910), 66–69. doi:10.1126cience.1167311 PMID:19119219

Hew, K. F., & Cheung, W. S. (2010). Use of three-dimensional (3-D) immersive virtual worlds in K-12 and higher education settings: A review of the research. *British Journal of Educational Technology*, *41*(1), 33–55. doi:10.1111/j.1467-8535.2008.00900.x

Ke, F., Lee, S., & Xu, X. (2016). Teaching training in a mixed-reality integrated learning environment. *Computers in Human Behavior*, *62*, 212–220. doi:10.1016/j.chb.2016.03.094

Ma, T., Brown, I., Kulm, G., Davis, T. J., Lewis, C. W., & Allen, G. D. (2016). Constructing and role-playing student Avatars in a simulation of teaching algebra for diverse learners. *Urban Education*, *51*(5), 534–555. doi:10.1177/0042085914542658

Norman, G., Dore, K., & Grierson, L. (2012). The minimal relationship between simulation fidelity and transfer of learning. *Medical Education*, *46*(7), 636–647. doi:10.1111/j.1365-2923.2012.04243.x PMID:22616789

KEY TERMS AND DEFINITIONS

Avatar: The graphical representation of a user or a character in a virtual environment.

Experiential Learning: The process of learning through direct experience and reflecting on the experience to gain knowledge and skills.

Pedagogical Affordances: The pedagogical properties of an instructional environment or tool that enables certain kinds of learning to occur.

Prompt: A cue given to someone or an act of cueing someone to trigger another action or event to occur.

Role-Play: Act or behave in an identify either as oneself or someone else in given situations that replicating real life scenarios, for example as a technique of training.

Teaching Competencies: The knowledge, skills, and values that a teacher must possess to achieve successful practice of teaching.

Technical Affordances: The technological properties of an instructional environment or tool that enables certain kinds of learning to occur.

Virtual Reality: A computer-generated artificial environment that is displayed to users in such a way that user can be interacted with the seemingly real environment and develop a sense of being there.

Chapter 8
Using Augmented and Virtual Reality to Improve Social, Vocational, and Academic Outcomes of Students With Autism and Other Developmental Disabilities

Ryan O. Kellems
Brigham Young University, USA

Gulnoza Yakubova
University of Maryland, USA

Jared R. Morris
Brigham Young University, USA

Alex Wheatley
Brigham Young University, USA

Briella Baer Chen
University of Maryland, USA

ABSTRACT

Some individuals with disabilities are unable to work independently and often require additional instruction to complete basic tasks. To prepare students with disabilities for life after school, practitioners need to help them learn the skills necessary to live a happy, productive, and fulfilling life. Two technologies showing promise for such learning are augmented reality (AR) and virtual reality (VR) applications. This chapter will discuss how AR and VR can successfully be used to teach academic, social, and vocational skills to students with disabilities, including research that has been conducted to date. Additionally, guidance is provided for teachers seeking to use AR and VR in classroom and community learning environments. The chapter will conclude with directions for further research and future applications of AR and VR with students with disabilities.

DOI: 10.4018/978-1-7998-5043-4.ch008

INTRODUCTION

Many students with disabilities need specialized instruction in order to access the general education curriculum. Progress may be achieved in general education or special classroom settings by intensifying instruction or using specially designed interventions. Traditional interventions have involved changing the intensity of instruction (e.g., frequency of teaching a skill), changing the modality of instruction (e.g., explicit instruction, applied behavior analysis, small group versus large group), and changing the environment (e.g., resource/support classroom, authentic experiences in the community). As technology has increased in sophistication and access, new directions are developing in how traditional interventions are used.

Wong and colleagues (2015) identified many interventions currently used in schools as evidenced-based practices, among them "technology-aided instruction and intervention." Technology is not only becoming more common in schools, but is also proving successful in helping students with disabilities gain valuable skills. Students with disabilities have progressed in academic skills (e.g., Burton, Anderson, Prater, & Dyches, 2013), social skills (e.g., Macpherson, Charlop, & Miltenberger, 2015; Tetreault & Lerman, 2010), and vocational skills (e.g., Aldi, Crigler, Kates-McElrath, Long, Smith, Rehak, & Wilkinson, 2016; English, Gounden, Dagher, Chan, Furlonger, Anderson, & Moore, 2017) through incorporating various forms of technology in school and community-based learning environments.

This chapter begins by highlighting the history of technology use in interventions for students with disabilities, from the introduction of video modeling to current and future practices of virtual reality (VR) and augmented reality (AR). The focus then moves to implications for practitioners and suggestions for research, concluding with the vision of the authors for VR and AR use in the advancement of special education services. The objectives of this chapter are to (a) orient readers to VR and AR use within special education contexts, (b) provide guidance to practitioners on how to use VR and AR to support special education students, and (c) offer direction in furthering research and practice.

BACKGROUND

Current advances in technology have made innovative interventions available that in the past were either too expensive or simply not possible. Some of these interventions are well suited for students with disabilities. Two of these technologies that build upon the research-based strategy of video-based instruction are AR and VR as means of delivering video-based instruction.

Video-based interventions can be traced back to Bandura's (1978) social learning theory, which demonstrated how using video models of aggression could shape human behavior. Since Bandura's work, researchers and practitioners have explored video modeling applications across domains, including social and play skills, vocational skills and tasks, and academic learning.

Social skills were a logical first step for individuals with autism spectrum disorder (ASD) and other intellectual and developmental disabilities (IDD), since deficits in social communication and understanding are identifying characteristics. Video modeling has been used to teach students to initiate conversations (Nikopoulos & Keenan, 2004) and to maintain social skills. Focus on vocational skills followed. Researchers used video modeling to teach adults how to entertain customers in a retail establishment (Allen, Wallace, Renes, Bowen, & Burke, 2010). Kellems and Morningstar (2012) demonstrated how video modeling could be used to teach a variety of vocational skills to young adults with autism in authentic learning environments. Most recently, academic skills have been examined. Hart and Whalon (2012) were able to increase academic responding for a student with autism and intellectual disability. Other researchers have used video models to teach mathematics and handwriting (Kellems et al., 2016).

Video modeling has been effective for individuals with ASD and IDD due to prevalent deficits of these disabilities that video modeling can improve or remedy: restricted focus, inclination for visual stimuli, and discomfort for face-to-face interaction (Corbett & Abdullah, 2005). Video modeling engages individuals with ASD and IDD through the use of technology, a relevant and high interest means that narrows the field of attention. Video modeling also offers repetition in presentation and practice that does not require face-to-face interaction, thereby making the learning environment more comfortable and suited to skill level.

Video models have become more realistic and immersive over the last ten years. Advances in technology gives students opportunities to explore the pyramids, learn how to wield a lightsaber, learn about artists, or catch fictional creatures. Educators have become more familiar with technology integration over the years; however, they might not be fully aware of the advances in AR or VR or how to integrate these advanced video-based instructional tools into curricula or training modules.

Augmented Reality

AR technology bridges physical and digital worlds, providing digital information about the physical environment through videos, pictures, and other forms of media on mobile devices. AR has been shown to be effective as an assistive or instructional technology for helping students with disabilities to increase their independence and enhance their learning opportunities (Kellems, Cacciatore, & Osborne, 2019). Table 1 provides a summary of research that has been conducted related to AR and VR in individuals with disabilities. Recent studies have shown AR to be effective in preparing students to be college and career ready with improved social, academic, and vocational skills (Garzón, Pavón, & Baldiris, 2019). Researchers have shown that AR can improve focus on nonverbal social cues for children with autism spectrum disorders (Escobedo, Tentori, Quintana, Favela, & Garcia-Rosas, 2014). Chen and colleagues (2015) used AR to improve facial emotion recognition in children with autism. Other researchers have used AR to effectively teach mathematics skills to students with ASD and other disabilities (Cihak et al., 2016; Kellems et al., 2020; Kellems et al., 2019). McMahon, Cihak, Wright, and Bell (2016) successfully used AR to increase science vocabulary word acquisition in college students with intellectual disability and autism.

Researchers have also explored different ways of delivering AR-based instruction. Kelley, Rivera and Kellems (2016) found the model-lead test method effective for teaching college aged individuals with intellectual disabilities how to operate Google Glasses. Researchers have also started to explore other ways to deliver AR-based interventions via mobile technologies (Kellems et al., 2019). Many researchers are also seeking to add to the existing body of research by replicating previous studies with different age and disability demographics, as well as identifying new skills in which AR interventions can be successful.

Virtual Reality

VR is a technology platform that offers safe structured environments in which students with disabilities can learn and practice various skills repeatedly in simulated settings (Strickland, 1996; Wallace et al., 2010). VR-based intervention has shown effects similar to AR in students with disabilities, ranging from elementary school children (Cheng et al., 2015; Didehbahni et al., 2016; Ke & Lee, 2016) to adolescents and adults (Kandalaft, Didehbani, Krawczyk, Allen, & Chapman, 2013; Newbutt et al., 2016; Smith et al., 2014; Wallace, Parsons, & Bailey, 2017; Yang et al., 2017), with improvements in skill acquisition. Students with various disabilities have benefited from VR: For instance, students who are hard of hearing or deaf may benefit from VR programs offering closed captioning or sign language (Zirzow, 2015).

However, the majority of the studies have focused on students with ASD and IDD. VR has been an effective intervention for individuals with ASD, increasing social interaction and communication performance (Ke & Im, 2013), social cognition (Didehbani, Allen, Kandalaft, Krawczyk, & Chapman, 2016), job interviewing skills (Smith et al., 2014), and community safety skills (Josman, Ben-Chaim, Friedrich, & Weiss, 2008). Children with ASD ages 10-13 improved non-verbal communication, social initiation, and social cognition skills (Cheng et al., 2015). Studies with 7-16-year-old children (Didehbahni et al., 2016) and young adults with ASD (Kandalaft et al., 2013, Yang et al., 2017) also found that VR-based training could be successful in improving emotion recognition and theory of mind. Participants with ASD were observed to engage in behaviors within VR environments that reflected real-life behaviors (Parsons, Mitchell, & Leonard, 2004); they were eager to engage in meaningful interpretation of virtual scenes and discussions of how these scenes reflected appropriate real-life social responses (Parsons, Leonard, & Mitchell, 2006). Following a VR-based intervention, participants improved their ability to interpret facial expressions and perceive emotional content of cartoons and non-literal stories (Silver & Oakes, 2001) and to engage in socially appropriate judgments and reasoning in novel situations (Mitchell, Parsons, & Leonard, 2007). Walker, Vasquez, and Wienke (2016) showed that virtual environments can increase job interview skills in young adults with IDD.

VR has evolved over the years in both affordability and practicality, from desktop-based VR systems that cost $100,000 in the 1990's, to web-platform VR systems in the early 2000's, then VR systems with a laptop connected to a mobile phone costing a few hundred dollars. Accordingly, research on VR-based interventions in teaching children with ASD and IDD has increased in scope (Lorenzo et al., 2019; Newbutt et al., 2016; Strickland, McAllister, Coles, & Osborne, 2007). A recent systematic review of VR-based interventions found them moderately effective in teaching students with ASD and IDD (Mesa-Gresa, Gil-Gómez, Lozano-Quilis, & Gil-Gómez, 2018). According to Mesa-Gresa et al., a majority of VR studies have focused on teaching social skills (e.g., play, social interaction, interview skills) followed by emotion recognition. This is not surprising considering that the defining characteristic of ASD is challenges with social skills. The next most frequently targeted skills in a VR environment have been daily living skills, defined broadly (e.g., purchasing and driving, along with fire, street, and weather safety). Research has documented the effects of various types of VR from the 90's to current times as the technology has evolved and the advances in VR have followed. Early studies created a virtual environment which students accessed on the monitor of a desktop computer and navigated either by selecting their virtual avatar or entering the number that corresponded to their name. More recent studies have used immersive VR, either custom programmed by researchers using a specialized software or delivered in a spherical video-based VR intervention accessed with or without a headset.

Researchers and therapists foresee AR and VR becoming more affordable and accessible to teachers, parents, and students in the coming years. As this trend climbs, more districts should be able to adopt this technology, and more universities may partner with school districts to train new teachers on interventions this technology can support. Several teacher education programs around the country are using simulation training of teacher candidates with virtual avatars in a non-immersive format. As VR is becoming more user friendly (e.g., the new wirelessly operated, ergonomic, user-friendly Oculus Go headset), options for training teacher candidates in immersive VR environments are likely to gain further attention.

VR offers many advantages for teachers to provide instruction targeted to students' learning needs in a safe structured environment. As noted, VR can be particularly useful in teaching social skills to students with ASD and IDD, which has been the focus of the majority of studies. These studies have provided evidence of VR learning effectiveness and likelihood of generalization to authentic environments (Lorenzo, Pomares, & Lledo, 2013; Lorenzo et al., 2019; Mesa-Gresa et al., 2018). Via VR-based interventions, students with ASD from elementary grades to young adulthood have improved in a variety of social skills: for example, social interaction, social communication, emotion recognition, eye gaze, nonverbal gestural communication. These interventions involved custom-made virtual scenarios and virtual games with avatars. For example, Kandalaft and colleagues (2013) created a social skills training scenario in a Second-Life platform simulating office building, school setting, park in the community, and coffee shop to teach social skills, social functioning, and social cognition to young adults with ASD (18-26-year-olds). Following 10 sessions of intervention across five weeks, these young adults significantly improved their social skills and tended to maintain and generalize them at a 6-month follow-up. Similarly, Ke and Im (2013) used custom-made virtual environments created in a Second-Life platform to teach children ages 9-10 with ASD particular skills in social interaction and communication: recognizing body gestures and facial expressions as well as initiating, responding, and maintaining social interactions at a school cafeteria, playground, and birthday party. Following the VR-based intervention all children improved their ability to respond to and maintain social interactions, and most of the children improved the skill of initiating social interactions. Informal feedback from parents suggested the children transferred the skills to everyday social situations. In another study (Yuan & Ip, 2018), elementary school children with ASD significantly improved a range of social skills—including emotion expression and regulation, social interaction, reciprocity, adaptation, and affective expression—following an immersive VR environment for which they wore VR headsets. Other studies examining the use of VR-based interventions using either the Second-Life platform or immersive VR wearing headsets to teach social skills to children and young adults with ASD and IDD have found similar improvement (e.g., Cheng, Huang, & Yang, 2015; Didehbani et al., 2016; Ke & Lee, 2016).

VR can be effectively used in teaching a variety of independent living skills across home and community settings. For instance, as part of community-based instruction students can learn and practice numerous community skills, such as purchasing items, ordering food at a restaurant, or crossing streets, in a VR environment first and then practice generalization of skills in real settings by making a community trip (Cromby, Standen, Newman, & Tasker, 1996; Josman et al., 2008). Teaching children safety skills in a VR environment may reduce the potential hazards involved in teaching safety in real environments (Josman et al., 2008; Self, Scudder, Weheba, & Crumrine, 2007). For example, students can practice crossing the street safely or learn safety related to natural disasters such as fire or hazardous weather in a safe environment and have multiple opportunities to practice until mastery. This enables teachers to accommodate the needs of many learners without needing a one-to-one adult to student ratio.

When learning purchasing skills through VR, students viewed the intervention on a desktop computer, walked through the virtual environment using a joystick, and selected items using a mouse (Cromby et al., 1996). In this study 19 students with severe ID, ages 14-19, were assigned to either a control group that used VR to explore environments other than a supermarket and a treatment group that used the virtual supermarket to locate items from the shopping list and use the checkout lane. Students who received VR intervention generalized skills to a real supermarket: They moved through the store and located shopping list items more efficiently and accurately than students in the control group (Cromby et al., 1996). In a study that used low-tech VR accessed on a computer, children with ASD were randomly assigned either to a low-tech VR condition or to a visual strategies condition consisting of social stories, visual schedules, picture cards, role-play, and comic strip conversations to learn fire and tornado safety. Children in both groups learned the skills, though those using VR learned safety skills faster (Self et al., 2007).

A few studies have documented the effects of a VR-based intervention to teach transportation, mobility, and leisure skills to students with ASD. Adolescents and young adults with ASD exhibited better driving skills and executive functioning ability following a VR-based driving intervention than participants who received the traditional driver training program (Cox et al., 2017; Wade et al., 2016). When learning street-crossing skills in a VR intervention, all six participating children with mild-to-moderate ASD learned how to safely cross the street in a virtual environment, and three of them generalized these skills to a real street (Josman et al., 2008). Similarly, three children with mild to moderate ASD successfully learned street-crossing skills via an immersive, spherical based VR training that involved a 360-degree video recording of a real street and modeling of crossing the street (Dixon, Miyake, Nohelty, Novack, & Granpeesheh, 2019). Following the intervention all children were able to safely cross a street in the community.

Fitness can improve for some individuals with VR-based interventions. Using a VR-based fitness program that required participants to play games and engage in a range of physical activities, adults with moderate IDD improved their walk/run distance and total heart beat index (Lotan, Yalon-Chamovitz, & Weiss, 2009). But when using a VR-based program with game-like exercises, adults with severe IDD showed significant reduction in heart rate compared to the control group and the intervention did not improve their physical fitness (Lotan, Yalon-Chamovitz, & Weiss, 2010).

VR has many advantages in teaching vocational skills to prepare students for employment, including interview and interpersonal skills taught in a VR platform (Kandalaft et al., 2013; Smith et al., 2014). In a randomized controlled trial, adults ages 18-31 with ASD participated in VR training which included practicing an interview with a virtual avatar and didactic instruction (Smith et al., 2014). Following this intervention, the adults with ASD significantly improved in their job interview skills, gained confidence in their interview skills, and perceived the intervention to be user friendly. In a follow-up study, Smith and colleagues (2015) found that adults who had received the VR job interview training were 7.82 times more likely to accept a competitive position than adults who received traditional job interview training. Thus, training individuals with ASD and developmental disabilities in a VR environment may lead to better vocational outcomes. When teaching job interview skills to adults with IDD in a mixed reality laboratory consisting of a physical space with simulated people and subsequent live coaching sessions, adults with IDD improved job interview skills—improvement which generalized to interviews outside the virtual environment (Walker et al., 2016). While studies tended to use VR-based interventions related to broad social skills for teaching interview preparation, the potential of VR for teaching more complex technical skills affecting a person's job performance needs to be explored.

While research on VR-based interventions has been effective with a variety of non-academic skills, research using VR on academic skills is almost non-existent. However, for teaching academic skills to students with ASD and other developmental disabilities, VR could provide more authentic means of explaining content in certain subjects: For example, students could take a virtual trip to cultural heritage sites they have read about in a textbook, or they could learn body organs or natural phenomena in a science class. Study of the effects of VR on learning in general show that VR tends to be more effective than traditional computer-based instruction in helping neurotypical adults recall information (Krokos,

Plaisant, & Varshney, 2018). A study showed promising results in using a virtual environment to teach mathematics: number identification, number comparisons, numerical sequences, even and odd number concepts, and the four arithmetic operations. Elementary school children with dyscalculia interacted with the avatar in a virtual environment to play games and solve engaging challenges in a virtual city and forest. Following two hours per week of instruction for five weeks, children in the intervention group performed better than children in the traditional instruction group (Castro, Bissaco, Panccioni, Rodrigues, & Domingues, 2014).

TOOLS AND INSTRUCTIONAL DESIGN

Many tools exist to create VR content. Most of these tools are designed to create games for the purposes of recreational entertainment, though they can create serious educational games as well. Some tools are more expensive than others. Similarly, some tools require a higher level of expertise to create content.

AR tools such as HP Reveal allow teachers to create engaging lessons incorporating AR. VR headsets, laptop computers, tablets, and phones can also be used for incorporating AR and VR into instruction. IOS and android devices now have the ability to use AR in various apps, thus making it easier for teachers to use AR in classrooms.

Specialized cameras, such as those that allow for 360-degree recording, allow educators and other professionals to record environments that students can explore in the classroom. Recordings can be made of job sites or college campuses that will allow students to prepare for these experiences in the safety of their classroom. Websites such as NearPod.com provide similar experiences for exploring historical cities.

A few recommendations are important to consider when designing the integration of these tools into school curricula or vocational training programs. First, AR/VR lessons and activities should include skills that can be generalized to other contexts. Too narrow of a focus would cause for an increase in amount of lessons needed, thereby increasing the time demands to create engaging lessons. Second, a UDL framework could allow AR/VR to be used by more students and cut down on costs (i.e., procuring devices and software in bulk may yield a better discount on price per unit than buying devices just for select students with disabilities). A UDL framework could also make it easier for teachers to incorporate AR/VR in curricula or training programs as their environment would be arranged to handle such accommodations versus a stricter environment found in traditional frameworks. Finally, budget concerns need to be addressed. It would be wise for school and vocational programs to consider software programs and games that have greater longevity. It would be helpful to choose devices from companies that have good warranties and a track record of producing devices that receive frequent firmware updates for a long stretch of time.

APPLICATIONS FOR TEACHERS AND OTHER PRACTITIONERS

Teachers can use AR and VR in UDL contexts, allowing them the flexibility to provide individual feedback to one student while others are engaged in their own learning activity. AR and VR environments also allow students to work at their own pace in an environment that has been altered to provide a perceived safer, less socially demanding experience. Following are a few examples how this AR and VR technology can be utilized in school applications.

Teachers can use AR or VR to teach skills when traditional methods have not worked or do not provide a safe environment for the student learn. For example, students with ASD or ADHD may have trouble attending to in vivo presentation of material. Virtual learning can change the social and attentional demands for these students, giving them different ways to engage and connect with the content without changing the physical environment. In cases where it might be dangerous or labor intensive to practice in authentic environments (e.g., driving, crossing the street, cooking), AR/VR can allow for repeated practice without endangering students or creating periodic expenses.

Teachers may also choose to use AR/VR technologies in a push-in model of special education services. The push-in model involves educating students with disabilities in the general education classroom with their peers rather than pulling them out for resource or support classes. The push-in model may or may not use a co-teaching method, where a general education and special education teacher are in the same class together sharing duties of teaching the material to all students, regardless of disability status. Using AR/VR in this context allows teachers greater flexibility to move around the room and help a wider range of students. Students with IDD can receive the specialized instruction they need without changing environments and without monopolizing teacher time.

Another application for teachers is the ability to explore or incorporate student special interest areas that may not be possible with traditional teaching tools. For example, while books can provide information on the great pyramids of Egypt, they don't provide the immersive environment of exploring the pyramids from first-person perspective. Nor can books allow a student to excavate dinosaur fossils like can be done using AR/VR. In this way, AR/VR allows teachers to engage and provide alternate means of representation of content to students with IDD who are less likely to participate in traditional modes of learning.

AR/VR may have applications to how related services are delivered to students with IDD. Speech therapists and school psychologists may choose to use AR/VR with students when they have large caseloads spread across multiple schools. This could cut down on travel time to and from schools and classroom/office locations. It could also allow for services to be delivered timely in moments of crisis. For students who might be difficult to engage or participate in speech therapy or counseling, speech therapists and school psychologists could use AR/VR to change social and environmental demands, thereby increasing engagement and participation in services and increase the probability of IEP goal achievement.

FUTURE RESEARCH DIRECTIONS

Anticipating future development requires determining effectiveness of AR and VR as interventions for a wider range of academic, social, daily living, and vocational skills. Contexts or environments for AR and VR use also need further exploration (e.g., general education classroom, special education classroom, varied class size). Social validity of using these types of interventions in various school settings and among different stakeholders (e.g., school administration, teachers, parents) would also be required. Furthermore, the types of VR platforms and programs must be examined to determine the effects, practicality, and social validity of the interventions.

Research using VR- and AR-based interventions in the instruction of students with ASD and IDD varies in the types and areas of instruction addressed. The majority of research on VR interventions to date has focused on social skills instruction, with very few studies examining the application of VR in a few other instruction areas: academic, vocational, safety, communication, daily living, and physical activity. To use the technology to its fullest potential and achieve optimal student learning outcomes, research is necessary in these areas.

In teaching daily living skills for home and community, the potential of AR for enhancing students' independence across settings is considerable. For instance, students may safely cross a street while receiving AR instruction on their mobile phone, use the AR navigation map to get to a desired destination, or use the AR tape to get necessary measurements within their home. These benefits are evident in the increasing number of studies that have used AR to teach daily living and community safety skills to students with ASD and IDD due to the AR versatility (e.g., Bridges, Robinson, Stewart, Kwon, & Mutua, 2019; McMahon, Cihak, & Wright, 2015). Future research needs to examine effects of AR in teaching multi-step and complex tasks for home and community settings.

Moreover, training students in community skills in VR and generalizing those skills to authentic settings should be further examined. The comparative effects of AR and VR over traditional support strategies—regular video modeling, video prompting—need to be examined.

The potential of VR to train students in a secure environment, avoiding experiences that might jeopardize their safety, is critical. The authors were able to locate only one study that taught driving skills in VR (Wade et al., 2016) and very few studies that targeted safety skills (e.g., Josman et al., 2008; Self et al., 2007). Teaching complex daily living skills in home and community environments to students who need different levels of support via VR could be of interest to future research.

When teaching vocational skills to students with ASD and IDD, studies have tended to focus on job interview skills via VR (Kandalaft et al., 2013; Smith et al., 2014). But the potential of both VR and AR for improving employment outcomes of students with disabilities cannot be ignored. In order to improve transition to post-school life including work place outcomes, teaching multi-step, complex job skills using the strengths of AR and VR needs to be the focus of future research efforts. Studies should also examine the cases when AR is most effective and practical and those when VR would be preferred. Technology can be used as a temporary assistive device or a permanent support strategy. In some situations, wearing a VR headset might not be practical and AR would be indicated: for example, practicing to cross a street in a real setting to help with generalization or use as a permanent support strategy. Thus, comparison studies are necessary to match strategy to context.

Generalization of skills from VR to real life is another area of interest for future research. Studies examining the use of VR in teaching community, daily living, and social-communication skills should also examine the generalization of skills to authentic settings. As generalization of skills tends to be a challenge for students with ASD and IDD, generalization across settings, people, and various contexts of use can be important.

Although studies examining the use of AR in providing academic instruction are emerging, the authors could not locate studies reporting the application and effects of VR in providing academic instruction for students with ASD and IDD. Given the potential of AR and VR for teaching a broad array of skills to students with disabilities and considering the paucity of research on this topic, future research efforts are recommended to focus on the effects of VR in teaching academic skills across content areas, such as mathematics, science, literacy, and social studies. To use the technology in the most beneficial ways to enhance instruction and learning requires study of the effects, feasibility, and practicality of AR and VR in foundational academic and complex academic skills across grade levels and diverse learning characteristics of students with ASD and IDD.

The learning characteristics of students with ASD and IDD tended to be different in studies examining the use of AR and VR. The majority of studies examining the effects of AR focused on students with

ASD and IDD whose IQ was below average, while the majority of VR studies involved students with ASD whose IQ was average or above. Specifically, a large body of research has examined the effects of VR in teaching students with ASD who had average/above-average IQ with moderate support needs, and were included in general education classrooms for most of the school day (e.g., Ke & Im, 2013; Mesa-Gresa et al., 2018; Stichter, Laffey, Galyen, & Herzog, 2013; Yuan & Ip, 2018). A limited number of studies examined the effects of VR in teaching students with ASD who had intensive support needs, typically including limited/non-verbal communication skills and moderate to severe IDD (e.g., Lotan et al., 2009, 2010; Mesa-Gresa et al., 2018).

The type of VR used in studies varied: Some studies built virtual world scenarios using Second-Life platform (e.g., Didehbani et al., 2016; Kandalaft et al., 2013; Ke & Im, 2013) in which a student interacts with an avatar on a computer, some developed VR programs using various types of software other than Second-Life (Cox et al., 2017; Smith et al., 2014), and some used a spherical video-based VR, in which a participant accessed the intervention via a VR headset (Dixon et al., 2019). These studies provided various levels of immersion in a VR program. To determine what works best for what type of students in what contexts, future research must examine the effectiveness and practicality of different types of VR platforms. Such research would provide more accurate insight and better concerted effort into designing and providing VR instruction to students with various learning needs in a range of contexts.

Along with types of VR platforms, levels of immersion provided in VR should receive further attention. A recent review of studies that used VR in teaching social skills to individuals with ASD found that the level of immersion in VR (e.g., desktop-based/2D VR or 3D VR using a VR headset) impacted the success of the outcome. A high level of immersion in VR was more likely to lead to a positive outcome and to generalization into real life (Miller & Bugnariu, 2016). Therefore, research must continue to document effects, practicality, and feasibility of using immersive VR over traditional methods of instruction in teaching academic, daily living, and vocational skills to students having a diverse range of learning characteristics.

CONCLUSION

Advances in technology have made AR and VR increasingly accessible, creating opportunities for educational applications of AR and VR technology. This technology has provided support to individuals with disabilities, increasing their access to educational content and supporting their abilities to perform academic skills.

Practitioners preparing students with disabilities ultimately want to improve their short-term and long-term overall quality of life. To help prepare individuals with disabilities to work more independently, AR and VR have shown significant potential for teaching academic, behavioral, social, and vocational skills. With widely applicable and adaptable approaches, both AR and VR can be applied by teachers anywhere from classroom settings to community-based learning. This chapter demonstrates that AR and VR technology have great potential to improve the learning outcomes for individuals with disabilities.

ACKNOWLEDGMENT

This research received no specific grant from any funding agency in the public, commercial, or not-for-profit sectors.

REFERENCES

Aldi, C., Crigler, A., Kates-McElrath, K., Long, B., Smith, H., Rehak, K., & Wilkinson, L. (2016). Examining the effects of video modeling and prompts to teach activities of daily living skills. *Behavior Analysis in Practice*, *9*(4), 384–388. doi:10.100740617-016-0127-y PMID:27920969

Allen, K. D., Wallace, D. P., Renes, D., Bowen, S. L., & Burke, R. V. (2010). Use of video modeling to teach vocational skills to adolescents and young adults with autism spectrum disorders. *Education & Treatment of Children*, *33*(3), 339–349. doi:10.1353/etc.0.0101

Bandura, A. (1978). Social learning theory of aggression. *Journal of Communication*, *28*(3), 12–29. doi:10.1111/j.1460-2466.1978.tb01621.x PMID:690254

Bellini, S., & Akullian, J. (2007). A meta-analysis of video modeling and video self-modeling interventions for children and adolescents with autism spectrum disorders. *Exceptional Children*, *73*(3), 264–287. doi:10.1177/001440290707300301

Bridges, S. A., Robinson, O. P., Stewart, E. W., Kwon, D., & Mutua, K. (2019). Augmented reality: Teaching daily living skills to adults with intellectual disabilities. *Journal of Special Education Technology*. Advance online publication. doi:10.1177/0162643419836411

Burton, C. E., Anderson, D. H., Prater, M. A., & Dyches, T. T. (2013). Video self-modeling on an iPad to teach functional math skills to adolescents with autism and intellectual disability. *Focus on Autism and Other Developmental Disabilities*, *28*(2), 67–77. doi:10.1177/1088357613478829

Castro, M. V., Bissaco, M. A. S., Panccioni, B. M., Rodrigues, S. C. M., & Domingues, A. M. (2014). Effect of a virtual environment on the development of mathematical skills in children with dyscalculia. *PLoS One*, *9*(7), e103354. doi:10.1371/journal.pone.0103354 PMID:25068511

Chen, C. H., Lee, I. J., & Lin, L. Y. (2015). Augmented reality-based self-facial modeling to promote the emotional expression and social skills of adolescents with autism spectrum disorders. *Research in Developmental Disabilities*, *36*, 396–403. doi:10.1016/j.ridd.2014.10.015 PMID:25462499

Cheng, Y., Huang, C. L., & Yang, C. S. (2015). Using a 3D immersive virtual environment system to enhance social understanding and social skills for children with autism spectrum disorders. *Focus on Autism and Other Developmental Disabilities*, *30*(4), 222–236. doi:10.1177/1088357615583473

Cihak, D. F., Moore, E. J., Wright, R. E., McMahon, D. D., Gibbons, M. M., & Smith, C. (2016). Evaluating augmented reality to complete a chain task for elementary students with autism. *Journal of Special Education Technology*, *31*(2), 99–108. doi:10.1177/0162643416651724

Corbett, B. A., & Abdullah, M. (2005). Video modeling: Why does it work for children with autism? *Journal of Early and Intensive Behavior Intervention: JEIBI*, *2*(1), 2–8. doi:10.1037/h0100294

Cox, D. J., Brown, T., Ross, V., Moncrief, M., Schmitt, R., Gaffney, G., & Reeve, R. (2017). Can youth with autism spectrum disorder use virtual reality driving simulation training to evaluate and improve driving performance? An exploratory study. *Journal of Autism and Developmental Disorders*, *47*(8), 2544–2555. doi:10.100710803-017-3164-7 PMID:28540452

Cromby, J., Standen, P., Newman, J., & Tasker, H. (1996). Successful transfer to the real world of skills practiced in a virtual environment by student with severe learning disabilities. In P. M. Sharkey (Ed.), *Proceedings of the 1st European Conference on Disability, Virtual Reality and Associated Technologies* (pp. 305–313). Reading, UK: University of Reading.

Didehbani, N., Allen, T., Kandalaft, M., Krawczyk, D., & Chapman, S. (2016). Virtual reality social cognition training for children with high functioning autism. *Computers in Human Behavior*, *62*, 703–711. doi:10.1016/j.chb.2016.04.033

Dixon, D. R., Miyake, C. J., Nohelty, K., Novack, M. N., & Granpeesheh, D. (2019). Evaluation of an immersive virtual reality safety training used to teach pedestrian skills to children with autism spectrum disorder. *Behavior Analysis in Practice*. Advance online publication. doi:10.100740617-019-00401-1

English, D. L., Gounden, S., Dagher, R. E., Chan, S. F., Furlonger, B. E., Anderson, A., & Moore, D. W. (2017). Effects of video modeling with video feedback on vocational skills of adults with autism spectrum disorder. *Developmental Neurorehabilitation*, *20*(8), 511–524. doi:10.1080/17518423.2017.1282051 PMID:28632464

Escobedo, L., Tentori, M., Quintana, E., Favela, J., & Garcia-Rosas, D. (2014). Using augmented reality to help children with autism stay focused. *IEEE Pervasive Computing*, *13*(1), 38–46. doi:10.1109/MPRV.2014.19

Garzón, J., Pavón, J., & Baldiris, S. (2019). Systematic review and meta-analysis of augmented reality in educational settings. *Virtual Reality (Waltham Cross)*, *23*(4), 447–459. Advance online publication. doi:10.100710055-019-00379-9

Hart, J. E., & Whalon, K. J. (2012). Using video self-modeling via iPads to increase academic responding of an adolescent with autism spectrum disorder and intellectual disability. *Education and Training in Autism and Developmental Disabilities*, 438–446.

Josman, N., Ben-Chaim, H. M., Friedrich, S., & Weiss, P. L. (2008). Effectiveness of virtual reality for teaching street-crossing skills to children and adolescents with autism. *International Journal on Disability and Human Development: IJDHD*, *7*(1), 49–56. doi:10.1515/IJDHD.2008.7.1.49

Kandalaft, M. R., Didehbani, N., Krawczyk, D. C., Allen, T. T., & Chapman, S. B. (2013). Virtual reality social cognition training for young adults with high-functioning autism. *Journal of Autism and Developmental Disorders*, *43*(1), 34–44. doi:10.100710803-012-1544-6 PMID:22570145

Ke, F., & Im, T. (2013). Virtual-reality-based social interaction training for children with high-functioning autism. *The Journal of Educational Research*, *106*(6), 441–461. doi:10.1080/00220671.2013.832999

Ke, F., & Lee, S. (2016). Virtual reality based collaborative design by children with high-functioning autism: Design-based flexibility, identity, and norm construction. *Interactive Learning Environments*, *24*(7), 1511–1533. doi:10.1080/10494820.2015.1040421

Kellems, R. O., Cacciatore, G., & Osborne, K. (2019). Using an augmented reality–based teaching strategy to teach mathematics to secondary students with disabilities. *Career Development and Transition for Exceptional Individuals*, *42*(4), 253–258. doi:10.1177/2165143418822800

Kellems, R. O., Eichelberger, C., Cacciatore, G., Jensen, M., Frazier, B., Simons, K., & Zaru, M. (2020). Using video-based instruction via augmented reality to teach mathematics to middle school students with learning disabilities. *Journal of Learning Disabilities*.

Kellems, R. O., Frandsen, K., Hansen, B., Gabrielsen, T., Clarke, B., Simons, K., & Clements, K. (2016). Teaching multi-step math skills to adults with disabilities via video prompting. *Research in Developmental Disabilities*, *58*, 31–44. doi:10.1016/j.ridd.2016.08.013 PubMed

Kellems, R. O., & Morningstar, M. E. (2012). Using video modeling delivered through iPods to teach vocational tasks to young adults with autism spectrum disorders. *Career Development and Transition for Exceptional Individuals*, *35*(3), 155–167. doi:10.1177/2165143412443082

Kelley, K. R., Rivera, C. J., & Kellems, R. O. (2016). Effects of direct systematic instruction on Google glass orientation with individuals with intellectual disability. *Journal of Special Education Technology*, *31*(4), 207–216. doi:10.1177/0162643416673913

Krokos, E., Plaisant, C., & Varshney, A. (2018). Virtual memory palaces: Immersion aids recall. *Virtual Reality (Waltham Cross)*. Advance online publication. doi:10.100710055-018-0346-3

Lorenzo, G., Lledó, A., Arráez-Vera, G., & Lorenzo-Lledó, A. (2019). The application of immersive virtual reality for students with ASD: A review between 1990–2017. *Education and Information Technologies*, *24*(1), 127–151. doi:10.100710639-018-9766-7

Lorenzo, G., Pomares, J., & Lledó, A. (2013). Inclusion of immersive virtual learning environments and visual control systems to support the learning of students with Asperger syndrome. *Computers & Education*, *62*, 88–101. doi:10.1016/j.compedu.2012.10.028

Lotan, M., Yalon-Chamovitz, S., & Weiss, P. L. (2009). Improving physical fitness of individuals with intellectual and developmental disability through a virtual reality intervention program. *Research in Developmental Disabilities*, *30*(2), 229–239. doi:10.1016/j.ridd.2008.03.005 PMID:18479889

Lotan, M., Yalon-Chamovitz, S., & Weiss, P. L. (2010). Virtual reality as means to improve physical fitness of individuals at a severe level of intellectual and developmental disability. *Research in Developmental Disabilities*, *31*(4), 869–874. doi:10.1016/j.ridd.2010.01.010 PMID:20346616

Macpherson, K., Charlop, M. H., & Miltenberger, C. A. (2015). Using portable video modeling technology to increase the compliment behaviors of children with autism during athletic group play. *Journal of Autism and Developmental Disorders*, *45*(12), 3836–3845. doi:10.100710803-014-2072-3 PMID:24573335

McMahon, D., Cihak, D., & Wright, R. (2015). Augmented reality as a navigation tool to employment opportunities for postsecondary education students with intellectual disabilities and autism. *Journal of Research on Technology in Education*, *47*(3), 157–172. doi:10.1080/15391523.2015.1047698

McMahon, D. D., Cihak, D. F., Wright, R. E., & Bell, S. M. (2016). Augmented reality for teaching science vocabulary to postsecondary education students with intellectual disabilities and autism. *Journal of Research on Technology in Education*, *48*(1), 38–56. doi:10.1080/15391523.2015.1103149

Mesa-Gresa, P., Gil-Gómez, H., Lozano-Quilis, J.-A., & Gil-Gómez, J.-A. (2018). Effectiveness of virtual reality for children and adolescents with autism spectrum disorder: An evidence-based systematic review. *Sensors (Basel)*, *18*(8), 2486. doi:10.339018082486 PMID:30071588

Miller, H. L., & Bugnariu, N. L. (2016). Level of immersion in virtual environments impacts the ability to assess and teach social skills in autism spectrum disorder. *Cyberpsychology, Behavior, and Social Networking*, *19*(4), 246–256. doi:10.1089/cyber.2014.0682 PMID:26919157

Mitchell, P., Parsons, S., & Leonard, A. (2007). Using virtual environments for teaching social understanding to 6 adolescents with autistic spectrum disorders. *Journal of Autism and Developmental Disorders*, *37*(3), 589–600. doi:10.100710803-006-0189-8 PMID:16900403

Newbutt, N., Sung, C., Kuo, H., & Leahy, M. J. (2016). The potential of virtual reality technologies to support people with an autism condition: A case study of acceptance, presence and negative effects. *Annual Review of Cybertherapy and Telemedicine*, *14*, 149–154.

Nikopoulos, C. K., & Keenan, M. (2004). Effects of video modeling on social initiations by children with autism. *Journal of Applied Behavior Analysis*, *37*(1), 93–96. doi:10.1901/jaba.2004.37-93 PMID:15154221

Parsons, S., Leonard, A., & Mitchell, P. (2006). Virtual environments for social skills training: Comments from two adolescents with autistic spectrum disorder. *Computers & Education*, *47*(2), 186–206. doi:10.1016/j.compedu.2004.10.003

Parsons, S., Mitchell, P., & Leonard, A. (2004). The use and understanding of virtual environments by adolescents with autistic spectrum disorders. *Journal of Autism and Developmental Disorders*, *34*(4), 449–466. doi:10.1023/B:JADD.0000037421.98517.8d PMID:15449520

Self, T., Scudder, R. R., Weheba, G., & Crumrine, D. (2007). A virtual approach to teaching safety skills to children with autism spectrum disorder. *Topics in Language Disorders*, *27*(3), 242–253. doi:10.1097/01.TLD.0000285358.33545.79

Silver, M., & Oakes, P. (2001). Evaluation of a new computer intervention to teach people with autism or Asperger syndrome to recognize and predict emotions in others. *Autism*, *5*(3), 299–316. doi:10.1177/1362361301005003007 PMID:11708589

Smith, M. J., Fleming, M. F., Wright, M. A., Losh, M., Humm, L. B., Olsen, D., & Bell, M. D. (2015). Brief report: Vocational outcomes for young adults with autism spectrum disorders at six months after virtual reality job interview training. *Journal of Autism and Developmental Disorders*, *45*(10), 3364–3369. doi:10.100710803-015-2470-1 PMID:25986176

Smith, M. J., Ginger, E. J., Wright, K., Wright, M. A., Taylor, J. L., Humm, L. B., Olsen, D. E., Bell, M. D., & Fleming, M. F. (2014). Virtual reality job interview training in adults with autism spectrum disorder. *Journal of Autism and Developmental Disorders*, *44*(10), 2450–2463. doi:10.100710803-014-2113-y PMID:24803366

Stichter, J. P., Laffey, J., Galyen, K., & Herzog, M. (2013). iSocial: Delivering the social competence intervention for adolescents (SCI-A) in a 3D virtual learning environment for youth with high functioning autism. *Journal of Autism and Developmental Disorders*, *44*(2), 417–430. doi:10.100710803-013-1881-0 PMID:23812663

Strickland, D. C., McAllister, D., Coles, C. D., & Osborne, S. (2007). An evolution of virtual reality training designs for children with autism and fetal alcohol spectrum disorders. *Topics in Language Disorders*, *27*(3), 226–241. doi:10.1097/01.TLD.0000285357.95426.72 PMID:20072702

Tetreault, A. S., & Lerman, D. C. (2010). Teaching social skills to children with autism using point-of-view video modeling. *Education & Treatment of Children*, *33*(3), 395–419. doi:10.1353/etc.0.0105

Wade, J., Zhang, L., Bian, D., Fan, J., Swanson, A., Weitlauf, A., Sarkar, M., Warren, Z., & Sarkar, N. (2016). A gaze-contingent adaptive virtual reality driving environment for intervention in individuals with autism spectrum disorders. *ACM Transactions on Interactive Intelligent Systems*, *6*(1), 1–23. doi:10.1145/2892636

Walker, Z., Vasquez, E., & Wienke, W. (2016). The impact of simulated interviews for individuals with intellectual disability. *Journal of Educational Technology & Society*, *19*(1), 76–88.

Wallace, S., Parsons, S., & Bailey, A. (2017). Self-reported sense of presence and responses to social stimuli by adolescents with autism spectrum disorder in a collaborative virtual reality environment. *Journal of Intellectual & Developmental Disability*, *42*(2), 131–141. doi:10.3109/13668250.2016.1234032

Wallace, S., Parsons, S., Westbury, A., White, K., White, K., & Bailey, A. (2010). Sense of presence and atypical social judgments in immersive virtual environments: Responses of adolescents with Autism Spectrum Disorders. *Autism*, *14*(3), 199–213. doi:10.1177/1362361310363283 PMID:20484000

Wong, C., Odom, S. L., Hume, K. A., Cox, A. W., Fettig, A., Kucharczyk, S., Brock, M. E., Plavnick, J. B., Fleury, V. P., & Schultz, T. R. (2015). Evidence-based practices for children, youth, and young adults with autism spectrum disorder: A comprehensive review. *Journal of Autism and Developmental Disorders*, *45*(7), 1951–1966. doi:10.100710803-014-2351-z PMID:25578338

Yang, Y. D., Allen, T., Abdullahi, S. M., Pelphrey, K. A., Volkmar, F. R., & Chapman, S. B. (2017). Brain responses to biological motion predict treatment outcome in young adults with autism receiving virtual reality social cognition training: Preliminary findings. *Behaviour Research and Therapy*, *93*, 55–66. doi:10.1016/j.brat.2017.03.014 PMID:28384509

Yuan, S. N. V., & Ip, H. H. S. (2018). Using virtual reality to train emotional and social skills in children with autism spectrum disorder. *London Journal of Primary Care*, *10*(4), 110–112. doi:10.1080/17571472.2018.1483000 PMID:30083244

Zirzow, N. K. (2015). Signing avatars: Using virtual reality to support students with hearing loss. *Rural Special Education Quarterly*, *34*(3), 33–36. doi:10.1177/875687051503400307

ADDITIONAL READING

Bellini, S., & Akullian, J. (2007). A meta-analysis of video modeling and video self-modeling interventions for children and adolescents with autism spectrum disorders. *Exceptional Children, 73*(3), 264–287. doi:10.1177/001440290707300301

Bridges, S. A., Robinson, O. P., Stewart, E. W., Kwon, D., & Mutua, K. (2019). Augmented reality: Teaching daily living skills to adults with intellectual disabilities. *Journal of Special Education Technology*. Advance online publication. doi:10.1177/0162643419836411

Kellems, R. O., Cacciatore, G., & Osborne, K. (2019). Using an Augmented Reality–Based Teaching Strategy to Teach Mathematics to Secondary Students With Disabilities. *Career Development and Transition for Exceptional Individuals, 42*(4), 2165143418822800. doi:10.1177/2165143418822800

Kellems, R. O., Eichelberger, C., Cacciatore, G., Jensen, M., Frazier, B., Simons, K., & Zaru, M. (2020). Using Video-Based Instruction via Augmented Reality to Teach Mathematics to Middle School Students With Learning Disabilities. *Journal of Learning Disabilities, 53*(4), 0022219420906452. doi:10.1177/0022219420906452 PMID:32065040

Newbutt, N., Sung, C., Kuo, H., & Leahy, M. J. (2016). The potential of virtual reality technologies to support people with an autism condition: A case study of acceptance, presence and negative effects. *Annual Review of Cybertherapy and Telemedicine, 14*, 149–154.

Parsons, S., Leonard, A., & Mitchell, P. (2006). Virtual environments for social skills training: Comments from two adolescents with autistic spectrum disorder. *Computers & Education, 47*(2), 186–206. doi:10.1016/j.compedu.2004.10.003

Yuan, S. N. V., & Ip, H. H. S. (2018). Using virtual reality to train emotional and social skills in children with autism spectrum disorder. *London Journal of Primary Care, 10*(4), 110–112. doi:10.1080/17571472.2018.1483000 PMID:30083244

KEY TERMS AND DEFINITIONS

Autism Spectrum Disorder: Autism spectrum disorder (ASD) is a developmental disorder that affects communication and behavior. Although autism can be diagnosed at any age, it is said to be a "developmental disorder" because symptoms generally appear in the first two years of life.

Generalization: When a skill that was taught to an individual under one subset of conditions is then used by that individual in other applicable conditions independent of further explicit instruction.

Intellectual and Developmental Disabilities: A group of conditions that become present in the developmental stages of human physiology. The conditions are considered life-long impairments and adversely impact one or more major life functions. Examples include Autism Spectrum Disorder, Specific Learning Disability, and Intellectual Disability.

Intervention: A specific practice found in specialized instruction that targets one skill. Stages of the practice include collecting data on skill proficiency before, during, and after implementation. Checklists of implementation and data collection are followed.

Social Validity: Whether a practice is viewed as appropriate in cultural environments and accepted by stakeholders as being feasible and worth the time and effort to implement and tolerate.

Specialized Instruction: A mode of service delivery of core academic content that only includes a subset of students who have not been able to acquire skills taught by traditional methods to the entire student body.

Universal Design for Learning: A framework of instruction that targets multiple ways to optimize student engagement, representation of content, and expression of content knowledge all in the same learning environment.

Video Modeling: An evidence-based practice that involves filming a skill that can be viewed later by a learner in order to practice and acquire the targeted skill.

APPENDIX

Table 1. Summary of AR and VR studies with individuals with disabilities as participants.

Study	Technology	Platform	Content Area	Type of Learner	Major Findings
SOCIAL SKILLS					
Chen, Lee, & Lin, 2015	AR	AR-based self-facial modeling	Facial emotion recognition	Children with ASD ages 10-13 with average IQ	Each participant increased and maintained their understanding of facial expressions
Cheng, Huang, & Yang, 2015	VR	Immersive 3D environment via VR headset	Non-verbal communication, social initiation, social cognition	Children ages 10-13 with ASD	Each participant improved and maintained social skills after being introduced to the VR program
Didehbani, Allen, Kandalaft, Krawczyk, & Chapman, 2016	VR	Virtual world, Second Life™, displayed via monitor	Emotion recognition, social attribution, executive functioning	Children ages 7-16 with ASD and average IQ	Participants demonstrated improvements across the measured social skills
Kandalaft, Didehbani, Krawczyk, Allen, & Chapman, 2013	VR	Virtual world, Second Life™, displayed via monitor	Emotion recognition, theory of mind, conversational skills	Young adults ages 18-26 with ASD and average IQ	Participants showed increases in emotion recognition and theory of mind, which was maintained in real life social and occupational situations
Ke & Im, 2013	VR	Virtual world, Second Life™, displayed via monitor	Recognition of body gestures and facial expressions, and initiating, responding to, and maintaining social interaction	Children ages 9-10 with Asperger syndrome	Participants showed increased performance across the measured social skills
Ke & Lee, 2016	VR	3D virtual environment displayed via monitor	Flexibility, identity expression, norm construction	Children ages 8-11 with ASD and average IQ	Each participant demonstrated improvement across the measured social skills
Mitchell, Parsons, & Leonard, 2007	VR	3D virtual environment displayed via monitor	Socially appropriate judgements and reasoning	Adolescents ages 14-15 with ASD	Participants demonstrated improvements in social judgments and reasoning across two virtual settings
Stichter, Laffey, Galyen, & Herzog, 2013	VR	3D virtual learning environment displayed via monitor	Perspective-taking, recognition of facial expressions, executive functioning, parent and teacher reports of social skills	Adolescents ages 11-14 with ASD and average IQ	Participants showed improved social skills in terms of increased scores on parent reports, and on certain aspects of executive functioning such as cognitive flexibility and generativity
Yuan & Ip, 2018	VR	Four-sided cave automatic virtual environment (CAVE)	Emotion expression and regulation, social interaction	Elementary school aged children with ASD and average IQ	Children who used VR showed greater improvement in emotion expression and regulation, and social interaction and adaption
DAILY LIVING SKILLS					
Bridges, Robinson, Stewart, Kwon, & Mutua, 2019	AR	AR-based video modeling	Making the bed, ironing, setting an alarm	Adults ages 19-36 with moderate to severe IDD	Each participant increased their ability to independently complete their daily living task with the AR
Cihak et al., 2016	AR	AR-based video modeling	Brushing teeth	Children with ASD ages 6-7 with limited verbal communication	Each student learned to independently brush their teeth, and maintained the skill over time
Cromby, Standen, Newman, & Tasker, 1996	VR	Virtual environment displayed via monitor	Grocery shopping	Adolescents ages 14-19 with severe ID	Participants who practiced grocery shopping in VR were faster and more accurate than those who did not
McMahon, Cihak, & Wright, 2015	AR	Location-based AR mobile app	Using a map/following directions	Adults ages 20-24 with ASD and ID	Each participant successfully used the AR to find correct locations, which was more effective than paper maps and Google maps
SAFETY SKILLS					
Cox et al., 2017	VR	Virtual driving simulator	Driving	Adolescents and young adults ages 15-25 with ASD and average IQ	Participants showed improved driving skills and related executive functioning skills after using the VR training
Dixon, Miyake, Nohelty, Novack, & Granpeesheh, 2019	VR	Immersive 360 video via VR headset	Crossing the street	Children ages 4-10 with ASD	All participants were able to learn to safely cross the street in both the VR and real-world environments
Josman, Ben-Chaim, Friedrich, & Weiss, 2008	VR	3D virtual environment displayed via monitor	Crossing the street	Children ages 8-16 with ASD	All students showed improvement in the virtual environment, and half showed improvement in a real-life environment
Self, Scudder, Weheba, & Crumrine, 2007	VR	Virtual environment displayed via monitor and scent palate	Fire and tornado safety	Children ages 6-12 with ASD	Children who used VR learned the safety skills more quickly than those who didn't use VR, and showed some transfer of skills to the real-world environment
Wade et al., 2016	VR	Virtual driving simulator	Driving	Adolescents ages 13-18 with ASD	Participants showed decreased time to trial completion and fewer driving errors after training with the VR driving simulator

continued on following page

Table 1. Continued

Study	Technology	Platform	Content Area	Type of Learner	Major Findings
EMPLOYMENT SKILLS					
Smith et al., 2014	VR	VR training simulation, displayed via monitor	Job interview skills	Adults ages 18-31 with ASD	Participants who used the VR job training showed greater improvement during real life interviews and reported more confidence
Walker, Vasquez, & Wienke, 2016	MR	TLE TeachLivE™ MR lab using physical space and virtual people	Job interview skills	Young adults ages 18-22 with ID	Each participant showed improved interview skills and maintained and generalized the skills to a real-life environment
ACADEMIC SKILLS					
Castro, de, Bissaco, Panccioni, Rodrigues, & Domingues, 2014	VR	3D virtual environment displayed via monitor	Mathematics skills	Children ages 7-10 with dyscalculia	Participants who used the VR showed improvement in their math skills, whereas those who did not use VR did not
Kellems et al., 2019	AR	AR accessed via mobile app	Mathematics skills	Young adults ages 13-14 with LD	Each participant showed an increase in mathematical skills taught via AR
Kellems et al., 2020	AR	AR accessed via mobile app	Mathematics skills	Adults ages 21-24 with ID	Each participant showed an increase in all mathematics skills taught
McMahon, Cihak, Wright, & Bell, 2016	AR	AR-based flashcards displayed via mobile app	Science vocabulary	Adults ages 19-25 with ASD and ID	Each student showed increases in their ability to define and label the science vocabulary words using the AR
FITNESS					
Lotan, Yalon-Chamovitz, & Weiss, 2009	VR	Virtual game simulations displayed via wall projection	Distance of walk/run, total heart beat index, energy expenditure index	Adults ages 34-60 with moderate IDD	Participants who used VR showed improvements in total heart beat index and the distance they could walk/run
Lotan, Yalon-Chamovitz, & Weiss, 2010	VR	Virtual game simulations displayed via monitor	Heart rate at rest	Adults ages 25-58 with severe IDD	Participants who used the VR showed greater reductions in their heart rate at rest than those who did not use the VR
BEHAVIORAL SKILLS					
Escobedo, Tentori, Quintana, Favela, & Garcia-Rosas, 2014	AR	Object identification via AR mobile app	Attention/on-task behavior, positive emotion	Nonverbal children with ASD	Using the AR mobile app during therapy sessions helped increase participants' attention and positive emotions

* Note, AR = augmented reality, VR = virtual reality, MR = mixed reality, ASD = autism spectrum disorder, ID = intellectual disability, IDD = intellectual and developmental disabilities

Chapter 9
Augmented Reality:
An Educational Resource for the Nursing Graduate

Anabelem Soberanes-Martín
https://orcid.org/0000-0002-1101-8279
Universidad Autónoma del Estado de México, Mexico

ABSTRACT

Augmented reality is on the rise in education. This case study focuses on its incursion in the training of health professionals. The author has chosen this focus to address situations that the students do not do in the classroom because of the complexity or lack of laboratories. Thus, the author proposes to develop a mobile application with augmented reality. In the first phase, the proposal includes aspects of the technique of urethral probes, including videos and animations. The proposal also includes markers on mannequin present the information of the process for application with mannequins and patients. The results of the application are that the author identified that the augment reality enrich the process of learning for the valuation by the students and teachers. It showed that the virtual contents contribute to the education of the students of the infirmary.

INTRODUCTION

Universities should prepare to use emerging technologies by promoting new skills as a strategic element in achieving academic success for students. Some of these technologies include augmented reality (AR) and virtual reality (VR). This chapter focuses on augmented reality, which Martínez, Martínez and Navarro (2018) define as the visual combination of real and virtual elements that interact with each other. These elements usually are supported by the camera on a mobile device. According to Martins et al. (2019), this type of technology uses various channels and supports the benefit the creation of suitable environments for different learning styles. This technology favors a higher capacity for perception, abstract reasoning, and spatial reasoning.

DOI: 10.4018/978-1-7998-5043-4.ch009

Likewise, Arteaga and Pino (2018) point out that augmented reality introduces this technology use into various areas of education, which allows for the development of innate skills in the formation of the individual during his or her educational life process. Cabero-Almenara, Vázquez-Cano, and López-Meneses (2018) confirm these positions, expressing, "Augmented reality can help to increase the value of other technologies in the formative and practical aspect of the development of professional and academic skills of university students (p. 29)".

The area of health is no exception incorporated this technology, and there are various studies on augmented reality applied in nursing. Among these studies is the research of Wüller et al. (2019), which detected various case studies that make use of technology to support their tasks as well as their processes that they adopted. Some of the issues addressed are remote monitoring of temperature and heart rate, teaching anatomy, observing students during the process of medication to patients and wound care, and determining the devices (such as the clock, glasses, or the smartphone) that were tested in each study.

This chapter presents the proposal of a mobile application with augmented reality called Urethral Catheter Application Technique (UCAT), which incorporates technology in the teaching-learning process in one of the essential processes for nursing students, the urethral catheterization technique. This chapter addresses the use of augmented reality in higher education and the rationale for the process model used for its development. This model allows to researchers to identify the phases, to design a mobile application, and to recognize the role of each of the participants in the teaching-learning process (teacher-technology-student) in each phase. The objective of writing this chapter was to develop a mobile application with elements of augmented reality that address the technique of female and male urethral catheterization in human patients and dummies.

BACKGROUND

Education

Constantly updating devices leads to a more significant user-interface relationship and allows more people to have access to technologies that increase and enrich professional, academic, and daily life (Badilla & Sandoval, 2015). The Tecnológico de Monterrey (2017) indicates, "The best practices respond to a pedagogical approach oriented towards active learning (learning by doing) since it is the students who decide how to combine the increased information" (p. 13). Cabero, Barroso, and Llorente (2019) express that students show high levels of satisfaction when they participate in augmented reality experiences, regardless of the level of studies or curricular content they are dealing with; also, students find their use in different educational contexts interesting as a resource that promotes creativity, imagination, and curiosity of the person, in addition to building new knowledge and interacting directly with the virtual what contribute their learning (Cabero-Almenara, Vázquez-Cano & López-Meneses, 2018).

Some authors (Villalustre & Del Moral, 2018; León, Duque, & Escobar, 2018) point out that the experience in university training classrooms has been an innovative and motivating practice and serves as support to enhance teachers' roles. León, Duque, and Escobar (2018) mention that students are capable of developing skills based on discovery, research, and construction of knowledge in a dynamic, creative, and reflexive way using augmented reality. This is confirmed by Cabero-Almenara, Vázquez-Cano, & López-Meneses (2018), who express that the didactic experience of applying augmented reality with university students awakens real interest among students. Furthermore, it promotes motivation and collaborative and interactive training scenarios, and it helps create more open and creative education.

On the other hand, Cubillo et al. (2014) consider augmented reality as a tool at the service of education. As a technology with its characteristics, the mere visualization of virtual resources leaves the learning experience incomplete. Therefore, it is necessary to contextualize and for the teacher to directly or indirectly support the process to obtain a quality educational experience. Augmented reality also comes to replace the experience of field visits as it can do in the device itself (Harley et al., 2016).

Prendes (2015) identified six types of significant applications of augmented reality in education: (1) discovery-based learning, (2) professional skill development, (3) augmented reality educational games, (4) 3D object modeling, (5) AR books, and (6) instructional materials. Also, Jauregui (2016), who works in the field of training of health professionals, notes researchers have found different applications that make use of augmented reality. These applications are grouped in the following categories: (i) basic training, (ii) specific training, and (iii) information applications. Considering all classifications, the proposal focuses on the development of professional skills and contributes to specific training.

Alvarez-Marin et al. (2017) present some of the students' positive feedback on augmented reality technology, which allows them to visualize the entire problem. Another positive comment was that this technology brings the student closer to a proper visual understanding of the problem presented since the traditional way in which these exercises were performed has aspects that cannot easily be visualized. Therefore, the application with augmented reality seeks to "[...] have a positive impact on the students' ability to solve exercises on the subject, taking into consideration the opportunity they have to visualize elements that support their development and reasoning capacity" (Alvarez- Marin et al., 2017, p. 41).

However, one should consider what Mata-López and Tobón (2019) have said about the technological challenges of teachers: 1) prepare and maintain a team of competent technological teachers; 2) plan and organize processes to define projects; 3) systematically identify the requirements for the integration of educational technology; 4) redefine and refine the roles of teachers; and 5) manage resources in addition to providing maintenance and support (p. 5).

Similarly, Baroudi & Rodjan (2019) express that there are constraints, such as limited resources in Information and Communication Technology (ICT) and laboratories and that teachers are not trained in ICT. Similarly, León, Risco, and Alarcón (2014) indicate, "[...] the institutional infrastructure implemented leads to the success of the purpose, as long as an environment generated that is conducive to students acquiring the cognitive, attitudinal, procedural, and social skills that help them integrate into their structures" (p. 141).

Despite the benefits that augmented reality offers in teaching, one cannot lose sight of the fact that technology itself does not produce changes, but one must first reflect on whether it should be used (Martínez & Fernández, 2018). Various authors, such as Martins et al. (2019), point out several disadvantages, indicating that the excessive growth of information on the Internet has generated problems in finding quality teaching resources. Cabero-Almenara, Vázquez-Cano, and López-Meneses (2018, p. 32) point out that for adequate implementation, there are a series of disadvantages. Some are financial investment requirements that guarantee the access to technology in classrooms and training centers, to have specific training to manipulate the technology, and to propose training activities. Likewise, the use of augmented reality is associated with an increase in human distance that dehumanizes the teaching-learning processes. Finally, many of the systems are not adept to the different needs that students may have in the classroom.

Maquilón, Mirete, and Avilés (2017) point out that applying an innovative resource usually entails a specific training effort. If it is also an emerging technology that is still under development, this factor may cause the teacher to not consider augmented reality as a plausible resource. The idea that advanced computer knowledge or tedious training in applied technologies is necessary to use of augmented reality may also be a reason for rejecting augmented reality. However, there are technologies that teachers can learn quickly. For example, the use of augmented reality has some easy learning modes. However, the incorporation of augmented reality, which is presented below in the training of health specialists, has more benefits than damages.

Augmented Reality in Nursing

Augmented reality has a high potential for educational environments, mainly because it favors the learning and evaluation of knowledge by achieving a different contact with its object of study. This potential is an advantage for nursing students can use technology in their academic training. In this case, the technology allows one to link the nursing with virtual or augmented reality. This results in a scenario very similar to reality by simulating the abilities of mannequins. The mannequins have organs or complete parts of the human body that allow students to acquire manual abilities, to recognize the structure of the organs, and to learn to use different equipment. Virtual reality is used for complex skills training. This type of training can be done in a group or individually so that the student learns the basic rules that govern team activity.

Some authors realize that the experience of incorporating augmented reality in the area of health. Zhu, Hadadgar, Masiello, and Zary (2014) reviewed 25 articles on augmented reality interaction medicine. The areas of application were research, education, and technology. Among the topics that were detected are injection, laparoscopy, endotracheal intubation, forensic medicine, tissues, and cardiology. The objectives of the research were the development of learning systems, the validation of these systems, and improvement of learning. The stakeholders are mainly medical workers, students, residents, to mention a few. Furthermore, the primary devices used were computers, tablets, and smartphones. The research identified that 50% of users employed computer equipment for augmented reality, 68% used cameras and scoreboard devices, and 56% generated prototypes with augmented reality. Surgeries were identified as the main topic by 64% of users, and the same percentage of users applied traditional teaching techniques with some support of augmented reality. Additionally, 96% of users indicated that the augmented reality helps in the education process because it is practical, it reduces failures, it improves performance, it accelerates the learning process, and it provides new experiences.

Liao, Inomata, Sakuma, and Dohi (2010) presented a technological tool in support of medicine when performing neurological, cardiovascular, and oncological operations. The combination of hardware and software enhances surgical procedures. The researchers obtained different points that they processed to generate a three-dimensional image in detail. They used a screen the doctor who can see the organ with a minimum percentage of difference regarding the human vision. During the surgery, the application generates the process graphic models of the human or animal body to support a vision of internal elements that the human does not have; the system contemplates two computers one to perform and another to show the modeling. Additionally, a screen that shows the information is mounted on a robotic arm for its operation. This is a different way to incorporate the augmented reality because it does not need glasses or mobile phones in its implementation. Additionally, it allows more people to observe the same three-dimensional model.

Furthermore, Rahn and Kjaergaard (2014) reported that there are several advantages of working with augmented reality in the teaching and learning anatomy and physiology. Their experiment showed how the use of augmented reality appears to have the potential to facilitate student learning and increase their level of understanding of the subject. Students also identify the possibility of use for their future education. Another study by Pugoy et al. (2016), in which they determined the feasibility of prototypes with augmented reality in the teaching of nursing, seeks to generate dynamic content without requiring a profound degree in the technologies if the application to developed is user-friendly. Friendly and interactive are factors allow one to follow their development. The case studies taken to the classroom are essential to learning as long as the student understands the situation and analyzes the environment where the events occur in order to take action according to the event in question.

In the market, there are different technological options for developing mobile applications with augmented reality (Wikitude, Vuforia, and CraftAR), each with its own advantages as well as disadvantages. However, the education sector is inclined towards free use resources to allow the generation of content quickly for recognition in the market. Moreover, Rochlen, Levine, and Tait (2017) reported that augmented reality technology on internal anatomy was usefully supported by 92.5% of the participants, while over 80% felt that augmented reality technology promoted learning and should be incorporated into medical training.

As the authors discussed, the support of technology allows the teachers to transfer real situations to the classrooms, allowing the student to expand their vision of the area of health. However, to achieve the desired impact, the incorporated augmented reality one should consider the educational and technological aspects. In order for an augmented reality application to develop, software engineering is required. This is made up of a series of steps. The authors describe the process model used to develop the UCAT below.

Development Methodology

Cruz, Soberanes, Martínez, and Juárez (2012) used the process model to develop Interactive Computer Learning Environments. The authors used this model to develop applications. Additionally, the authors used this model because it considers documentation technology and education. Also, it has well-defined actions of the participants in its development of educational resources. As a process model, it indicates the activity of each of its phases and the product to be obtained.

The model proposes five actors: Content Expert, Teacher, Instructional Designer, Programmer, and Graphic Designer. The functions specify the description of the competences and skills as well as the number of persons required from each of them. One should note that the model is not restrictive in terms of different people for each role; however, it is highly recommended that each role is performed by different people to enrich the final product with their experience.

The Process Model is composed of six stages:

Stage 1 - Selection of the Topic: Researchers identify a particular topic based on the concept that a teacher prioritizes this topic as fundamental. Additionally, the teacher relies on content experts to determine the level of depth of this topic and to foster students' understanding of this topic. The information of this stage is integrated by the following: a) instrument of specifications of the topic; b) the diagnostic evaluation made at the beginning of the course; and c) graphics card of the topic to be covered.

Stage 2 - Instructional Design: This process is followed to obtain the preliminary didactic script established. In this process of analysis and development, the content expert, the teacher, and the instructional designer participate. The information of this stage is composed of: a) Instrument of the didactic script. b) Graphics card of the topic to be covered. c) The preliminary instrument of the didactic script.

Stage 3 - Characterization and Specification of the Requirements of the Environment: Characterization of elements necessary and specification of the conditions of the application. The requirements of the academic activity have been established. Additionally, the diverse functional and adaptable scenarios are outlined in the support software using the instructional designer and the "Mobile Reference" team. The information of this stage includes: a) preliminary instrument of the didactic script; and b) documentation of specification of functional requirements of the support software.

Stage 4 - Development of the software associated with the environment: This step includes the development of the software associated with the environment, the methodology of design, the implantation, and the implementation established. The programmer and graphic designer participate in this step, which includes: a) functional requirements specification document of the support software; and b) a functional prototype of the software for UCAT.

Stage 5 - Adequacy and Refinement of the Teaching Script: The teachers carry out the review and pilot test, in which the elements that require adaptation are identified with the participation of the content experts and the instructional designer. The information of this stage is considered by: a) functional prototype of the software for UCAT; b) finished didactic script; and. c) functional software.

Stage 6 - Evaluation of the Environment in Terms of Product Completeness: Once the teacher has tested the UCAT in the classroom, the team of development carries out an evaluation that involves the content experts, the teacher, and the programmer. The researchers measure instruments used to quantify technological, pedagogical, content-related, and aesthetic elements. The information of this stage is contemplated by a) finished didactic script; b) functional software; c) a document for evaluation of completeness; d) didactic scripts; and e) UCAT software.

The process is iterative. Once researchers complete all the stages, it is possible to return to the stage that researchers consider requiring more detail or refinement. Likewise, at the end of the process, researchers perform a continuous improvement analysis to detect areas of opportunity and improvement in the process to refine the practices learned and adopted during the process.

MAIN FOCUS OF THE CHAPTER

Issues, Controversies, Problems

Augmented reality makes use of mobile devices. In a study by Lagunes-Domínguez et al. (2017), the authors identified that more than 98% of students have the technological resources for mobile learning. Also, 92.65% of participants accepted the incorporation of mobile devices into the classroom.

However, like any technology, it has benefits and some limitations. Among the benefits of augmented reality in education is "capturing the attention of the target group by motivating them to participate more actively in the traditional classroom experiences, as well as those that are done entirely at a distance." (Bernal & Ballesteros-Ricaurte, 2017, p. 9). Cheng (2017) alludes to augmented reality while noting that its use encourages positive attitudes towards learning. Some research (Díaz-Campos, 2016; Prendes, 2015) points out that augmented reality is a technology that can help to improve the teaching-learning process. Likewise, augmented reality achieves greater access to information, and it generates innovative frameworks of activity, such as certain virtual groups, rewarding interactions, and new scales of values (Fombona, Pascual-Sevillano, & González-Videgaray, 2017).

Various authors have used the term e-health to refer to the application of ICT to the field of health. A health professional should develop adequate ICT competencies, for which appropriate strategies should be designed to allow higher education institutions to be sure that students have acquired the competences. The five competencies that the authors indicate are: (i) efficient use of ICT, (ii) access to information and communication, (iii) information and knowledge management, (iv) knowledge generation, and (v) knowledge dissemination (Humanante-Ramos, et al., 2018). The choice of this research problem is due to the perception of some difficulties that higher education universities have in integrating ICT in nursing as an indispensable means and resource for teaching and learning.

As expressed by Castaño-Calle and González (2019), in university students' environments, the community needs to make augmented and virtual reality more widely known as a technique and methodology that is applicable to the educational context. It is also necessary to develop actions that allow familiarization with augmented and virtual reality in the socio-educational field. Technologies are resources and means that can make teaching a process that is more conducive to learning that the technologies cannot see as an end in itself.

In order to achieve this, researchers need to identify how the augmented reality is going to implement. In order to do so, it is necessary to consider learning strategies, which are understood as: "[...] processes that lead to decision making -conscious and intentional-; they also lead to the selection of knowledge -whether conceptual, procedural and/or attitudinal- [...]" (León, Risco & Alarcón, 2014, p. 129).

Moreover, Montes de Oca and Machado (2011) define the teaching strategy as the sequence of actions that, "[...] taking into account all the components of the process, guide the selection of the most appropriate teaching methods and resources for the direction of learning, taking into account the conditions in which it takes place, the diversity of students, contents, and processes to achieve the proposed educational goals" (p. 483). A determining factor for proper learning and optimal academic development is the use of learning strategies (Visbal-Cadavid, Mendoza-Mendoza & Díaz, 2017, p. 73).

Finally, Pugoy et al. (2016) state that existing augmented reality initiatives in nursing originated in developed countries. Although it is a relatively new and expensive technology, augmented authors can use reality with budgetary and technological limitations. In this case, it is a public institution in a marginal area in a developing country with the limitations mentioned. Hence, the importance of developing an educational resource considering the educational issues and the technology to be used, the educational level to which it is directed, including the description of the functions of each of the actors involved in the teaching-learning process (teacher-technology-student).

This study examines: (i) the need for an augmented reality application; (ii) the development of an augmented reality application that contributes to the correct process of the urethral probe application technique (male and female); and (iii) teachers' and students' perceptions of the quality of the augmented reality application.

METHODS

The investigation is divided into four stages:

Stage 1: The authors established the study participants, they selected the aspects to include in the application (the types of augmented resources identified include: text, audio, 3D object, graphic, or video), they developed and selected the instruments to use to determine the benefit of the use of AR, and they determined the perceptions or opinions of teachers and students about the application of augmented reality.

The authors used random sampling to select individuals to participate in the study. The population of students in the Bachelor of Nursing degree program was 878 students. Among these students, 279 were in the third semester of the basic nursing course. The authors used this number as the population to calculate the sample size with 95% confidence and a 5% margin of error to obtain the size of 234 students (183 females and 51 males). A total of 12 teachers from the academy in the curricular area of the Bachelor of Nursing degree program participated (the author applied the same parameters of confidence level and margin of error). Three were males, and nine were females.

The authors applied three instruments: (i) The authors designed an evaluation instrument to assess what the subject requires of urethral catheters. This consisted of 10 closed reagents, called a diagnostic test (pre-test). The authors applied the same questionnaire, called a post-test, after interacting with UCAT; The authors analyzed the differences between the pre-test and post-test using Statistical Package for the Social Sciences (SPSS) version 20; (ii) Martinez and Fernandez's (2018) instrument is composed of 23 items on augmented reality objects. The authors adapted it to 15 questions on UCAT. The device is presented in Likert scale of 1 (totally disagree) to 4 (totally agree); and (iii) The heading for mobile educational applications proposed by Cebrian (2018) is composed of five items (100%): design represent to 10%, usability corresponds to 10%, processing speed agree to 20%, quality equivalent to 30%, and usability corresponds to 30%, each with four answers in the Likert scale.

Stage 2: This stage consisted of the development of the application with increasing reality, using the process model of Cruz et al. (2012). Below, the authors describe what they did in each phase:

1. Selection of the Theme: The authors identified the particular theme based on the concept that teachers prioritize as fundamental to determine the level of depth of the educational resource and to promote students' understanding. The application focused on students of the subject of basic nursing I. Based on phase 1 of the process model, the authors determined the categories that were considered in the application, specifying the content of each one.

2. Instructional Design: The authors followed the process to obtain a preliminary didactic script. The content experts and the instructional designer participated in the analysis and development process. The information on this stage included the didactic script and the graphic card of the topic to be covered.

3. Characterization and Specification of Requirements: The requirements of the academic activity were established. Additionally, the various functional and adaptable scenarios in the support software outlined by the instructional designer and the "Mobile Reference". The authors integrated the information from this stage into the functional requirements specification document of the support software.

4. Development of the Software Associated with the Environment: The design, implementation and deployment methodology were established with the participation of the UX designer and the 3D modeler. The information from this stage was integrated into the functional requirements specification document of the support software. Furthermore, the functional prototype of the software for the UCAT application was generated.

5. Adaptation and Refinement of the Teaching Script: The authors carried out the review and pilot test, in which the elements that require adaptation were identified. The content experts and the instructional designer participated in this stage. The information in this stage included the following: a) functional prototype of UCAT, b) finished didactic script, and c) functional software.

6. Evaluation of the Environment: The authors completed the evaluation in terms of product completeness. Once UCAT has been tested in the classroom, an evaluation was carried out with the participation of content experts and the designer. Measurement instruments were used to quantify technological, pedagogical, content, and aesthetic elements.

Six actors participated in the elaboration: UX Designer, 3D Modeler, Instructional Designer, and two teachers who are experts in the content of the subject in question. The actors produced two user's guides, which include instructions for the teacher and students on the use of the application. In the guide, the actors describe different aspects, ranging from the objectives pursued, the location of the application for downloading, and recommendations for the use of the resource.

Stage 3: This stage includes the incorporation of the application in the classroom. This stage begins by installing UCAT, applying the Pre-test, continuing with the teacher intervention, and using the application. The teacher applied the exercise of the subject, the post-test (see Figure 1), and the surveys on the teachers' and students' opinions of the application. The process of data analysis continued to finish with the presentation of results.

Figure 1. Process for UCAT incorporation

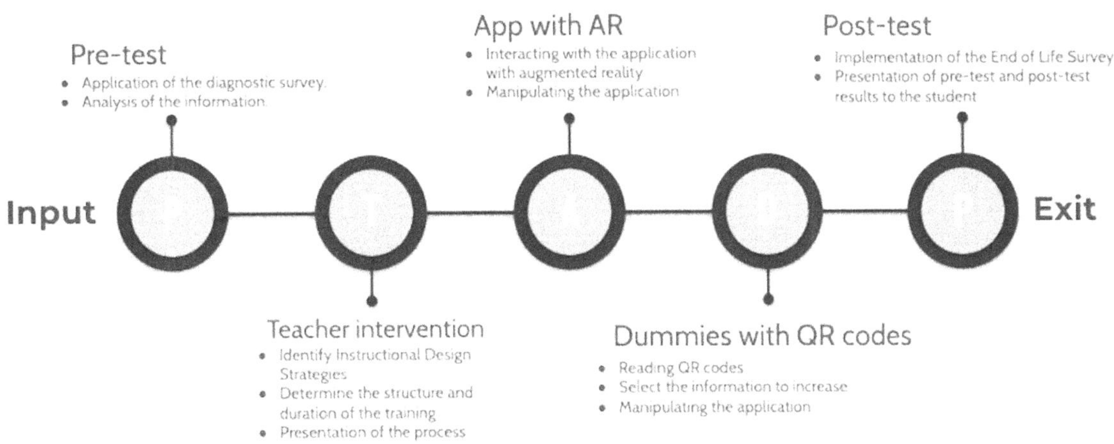

Stage 4: This stage includes using the augmented reality application.

Description of UCAT

The intervention of the use of UCAT application of aspects of the female and male urethral catheter technique, in which is required to download and run the home screen (see Figure 2), indicating the name of the material developed.

Figure 2. UCAT initial interface

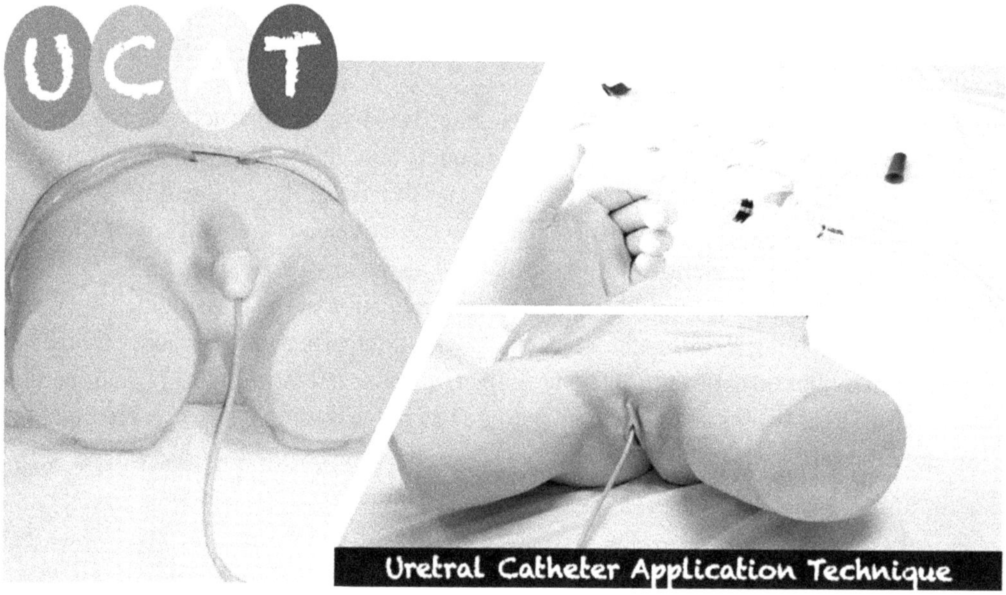

After the initial screen, a menu is presented that includes five aspects: 1) the basic concepts, 2) catheterization technique, 3) male urethral catheterization, 4) female urethral catheterization, and 5) additional information (see Figure 3).

Figure 3. Main menu interface

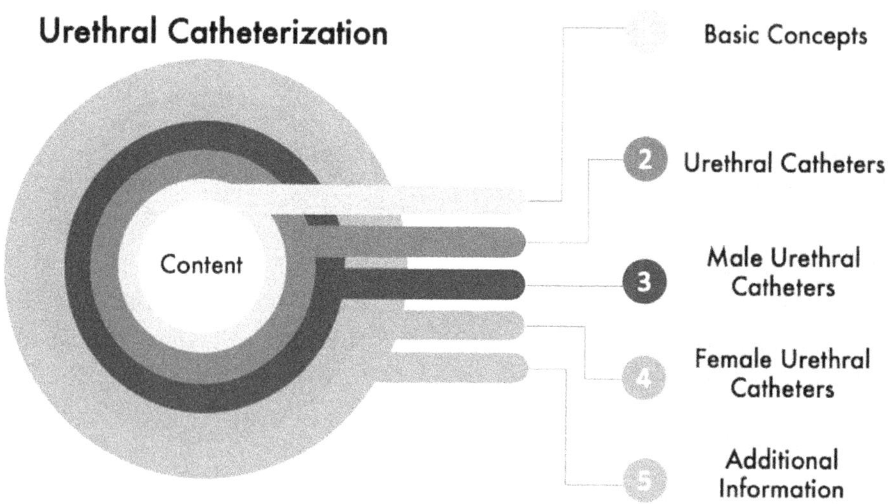

QR Codes Placed on the Dummies

QR codes were placed on the mannequins, which are read through the UCAT application, depending on the gender of each dummy, an interface is presented. Figure 4 shows the menu where the user selects the way to present the process with a dummy or a patient, and Figure 5 shows the options for a female dummy or a female patient.

Figure 4. Male catheterization menu

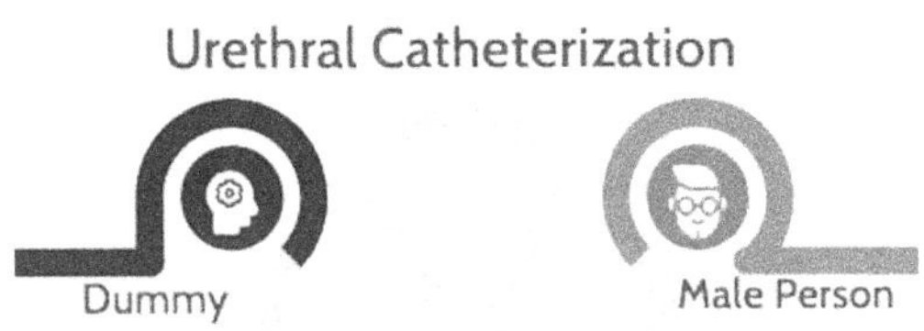

Figure 5. Female catheterization menu

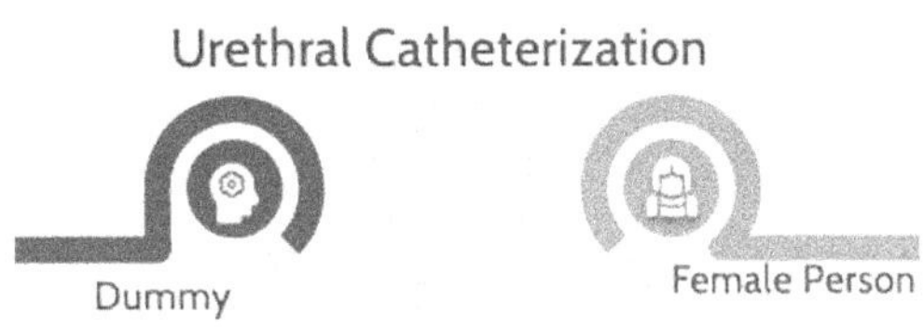

RESULTS

The results of the three instruments applied during the incorporation of the proposed. application.

Tests on the Topic Urethral Catheters

This instrument includes 10 closed questions on the topic of urethral catheters. In the pre-test, 41% of the students were correct, 54.7% were incorrect, and 4.3% did not answer. In the post-test (after using UCAT), 97.9% answered correctly, 1.7% answered incorrectly, and 0.4% did not answer. Figure 6 presents a comparative graph of the students' averages by test.

Figure 6. Pre-test and post-test comparison chart

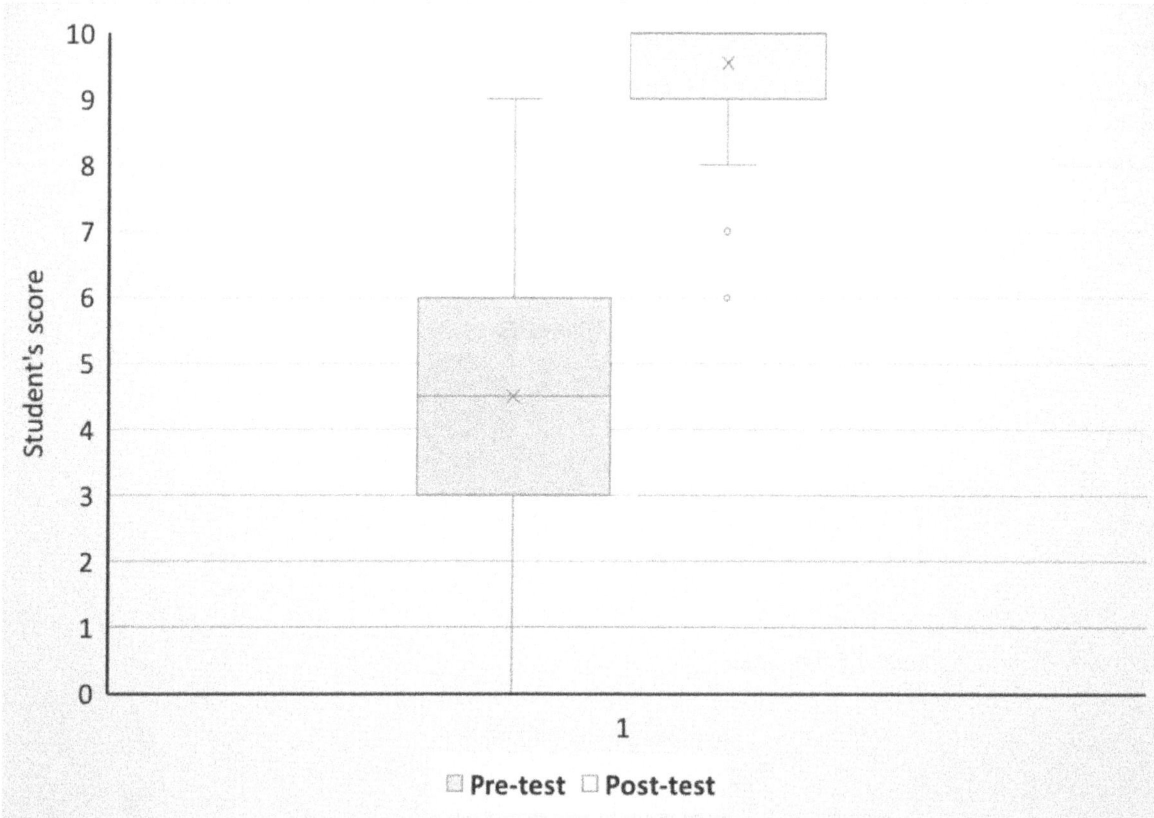

Table 1. T-test for two-sample dependent averages

	Pre-test	*Post-test*
Mean	4.50	9.50
Standard deviation	1.52	0.75
Pearson's correlation coefficient	0.09	
Statistician t	-47.23	
The critical value of t (one queue)	2.34	
The critical value of t (two queues)	2.60	

Table 2. F test for two-sample variances

	Pre-test	*Post-test*
Mean	4.5	9.55
Variance	2.31	0.57
F	4.08	
The critical value for F (one queue)	1.24	

Table 3. UCAT opinion survey

		Totally agree 4 %	3 %	2 %	Totally disagree 1 %
1	Find augmented reality useful in learning	16.00	84.00	0	0
2	Augmented reality allows us to acquire knowledge more quickly	40.80	56.20	3.00	0
3	Agree that the use of augmented reality is simple and clear	50.40	48.60	1.00	0
4	Find augmented reality easy to use	59.50	39.40	1.10	0
5	Agree that learning with the use of augmented reality has been easy	30.30	69.70	0	0
6	Consider the use of augmented reality for learning a good idea	52.00	45.00	3.00	0
7	Agree that learning is more enjoyable with augmented reality	38.00	62.00	0	0
8	Agree that using augmented reality for learning is fun	29.10	70.90	0	0
9	Like to use augmented reality as a tool for the study of university students	33.00	64.00	3.00	0
10	Agree that teachers help use augmented reality in learning	23.40	62.60	14.00	0
11	Have the resources to use augmented reality in learning	93.20	6.20	0	0
12	Know to manipulate augmented reality in learning	89.90	10.10	0	0
13	Feel insecure when using augmented reality applications	0	13.40	17.00	69.60
14	Intend to use the applications in training	28.70	62.20	6.00	0
15	Recommend the use of applications for learning	18.90	79.00	2.10	0

The authors used the t-test to calculate for dependent samples between pre-test and post-test, in table 1 was presented of results statistical.

The calculated (statistical) t-value is outside the critical t values for a two-tailed curve (-2.597 to 2.597). Thus, the authors reject the null hypothesis, implying that the μPre-test ≠ μPost-test with a p=0.01 does not have much significance since the difference between the mean of pre-test and post-test is very high (see Figure 6). As the authors wanted to know is how they got in and how they got out after using UCAT, they tested F concerning the deviations (Table 2).

The calculated (statistical) value of f is outside the critical values of F test of the curve (1.241). Thus, the authors reject the null hypothesis, which implies that σ́Pre-test ≠ σ́Post-test with a significance level of 0.01 (p=0.01).

Students' Opinions About UCAT

The student opinion survey, analyzed aspects such as usefulness in their learning, the speed of acquiring knowledge, the ease of use of augmented reality, if learning is more interesting with the use of the application, if the use of augmented reality for learning is fun for them, and if they like to use it as a tool for university study. Also, questions asked about having the necessary resources to use augmented reality. Table 3 shows the 15 aspects and the percentages of each of the options (1=totally disagree, 2=disagree, 3=agree, and 4=totally agree).

Some of the results to be highlighted are that students identify benefic the use of augmented reality.

Student and Teacher Opinions About UCAT's Quality

The augmented reality application quality rubric consists of five aspects: (i) design, (ii) usability, (iii) processing speed, (iv) quality, and (v) usability. Each aspect has four answers on the Likert scale, the 1st is 100%, the 2nd 75%, the 3rd 50% and the 4th 25%. Table 4 shows the results obtained by teachers and students.

Table 4. Comparison of results under the heading of application quality

	% Teachers	% Students
1. Design		
It has a modern and innovative design that is beautiful to the public for whom it was designed.	93.0	92.7
It has a good design that stands out from other apps of its style.	7.0	7.3
2. Manageability		
It is easy to use and intuitive – perfect for the target audience.	94.0	98.0
Easy to use, although it could present doubts if it is not used in the appropriate educational period.	4.0	2.0
Although useful, it is difficult to use. Specific skills are needed to use it and to understand it.	2.0	0
3. Processing speed		
The screen changes, and the processes, in general, are fast. The user does not have to wait for operations to be updated.	96.0	100.0
It has a good processing speed, although sometimes it takes a little longer than desired for its screen changes and processes.	4.0	0
4. Quality		
The student enjoys an unbeatable educational quality, including. having correct language, being didactic, and being instructive.	94.0	98.0
Quality, although it has certain didactic and educational shortcomings.	6.0	2.0
5. Usefulness		
Its use can be more than recommended in the classroom to complement students' learning, and, in turn, it can complement the teacher's explanations.	98.0	99.0
Its use brings specific knowledge to the student and helps the teacher in his or her explanations but does not complement it.	2.0	1.0

Regarding the results of the teachers, the authors observed that the teachers considered the UCAT to have a modern and innovative design, which is attractive for the public for whom it was designed. Furthermore, the teachers indicated that it is intuitive and easy to use, and it is perfect for the public for whom it is intended in terms of processing speed. The teachers expressed that the screen changes and the processes, in general, are fast. Regarding the quality, the teachers pointed out that it is unbeatable, educationally speaking. Specifically, it has functional language, it is didactic, and it is instructive. Finally, regarding the usefulness, the teachers expressed that its use of augmented reality can be more than recommended in the classroom to complement learning.

. The students considered the UCAT to have a modern and innovative design that is beautiful for those who are using the application. In terms of usability, the students indicated that it is easy to use, intuitive, and perfect for those for whom it intended. Regarding the speed of the process, all of the students expressed that the screen changes and the processes, in general, are fast. Concerning the quality, the students enjoy an unbeatable educational quality because it contains functional language, it is didactic, and it is instructive. Regarding the usefulness, the students expressed that the use of the application can be more than recommended in the classroom to complement the learning. At the same time, it complements the explanations of the teacher.

The authors observed no significant differences when comparing the values expressed by teachers and students. Globally, the authors obtained averages of 97.8% and 96.1%, respectively, compared with the values assigned by the heading, which is presented in Figure 7.

Figure 7. Comparative chart of the rubric, teachers, and students

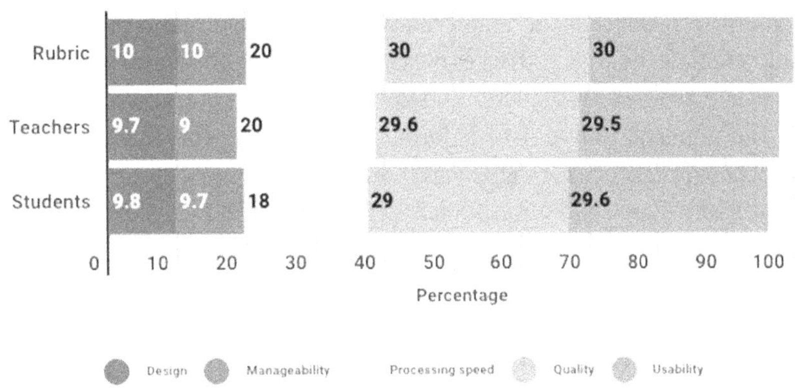

UCAT allows students to explore the topic of urethral catheters, which causes them problems when applying the technique. Thus, the application gradually allows them to explore the topic until the student can apply it in a real way to the patient by taking advantage of their interest in digital resources and the tendency to follow a learning rhythm. The percentages obtained from the questionnaires show that students and teachers accept the application as it enriches the learning process. Although it was possible to determine a notable improvement among the results of the questionnaires on the subject, it could not assure that a relationship exists between the motivation of the students and the performance they achieved. Some of the advantages of the UCAT are that after installation, students can practice anywhere, and anytime, they can check the process of catheters. And the teacher can review the results of the pre-test and the teacher adapt the activities of learning.

Likewise, the post-test serves as feedback to teachers and students to check if they attained knowledge on the subject of the subject and to be able to perform in real practice with the patient.

DISCUSSION

The percentages obtained from the questionnaires show that the application was accepted by students and teachers as support the learning process. Teachers and students identified that the virtual contents contribute to training nursing students. This is supported by Castillo et al. (2016b), who stated, "[...] use ICT to acquire or strengthen knowledge through the interaction of multimedia applications, such as videos, images, animations, and text; making the acquisition of knowledge more active [...]" (p. 96). Similarly, Martinez and Fernandez (2018) expressed considering AR as a technology that improves learning in higher education contexts. However, the teacher should always check if the application obtains the skills required by students to be able to perform later with patients.

Furthermore, they consider the ease of learning when using the UCAT, as well as its functioning, confirming that they consider augmented reality attractive for their learning. University students also like to use augmented reality as a study tool. Another issue was to ratify what was reported by Lagunes-Domínguez et al. (2017) on the percentage of students who have the necessary resources to use augmented reality in their learning.

The authors recognize that in addition to the disciplinary knowledge acquired through the use of the AR application, it promotes other aspects in the students, as indicated by several authors (Martínez & Fernández, 2018; Blas et al., 2019). For example, it promotes motivation, curiosity, and creativity, enhancing the acquisition of skills necessary for future professional careers. What the researchers can determine is the approval of the didactic materials with augmented reality by the teachers. However, as Cupitra-García and Duque-Bedoya (2018) express, "[...] these technological developments bring the challenge for the teacher to conceive didactic uses of mobile devices to improve the teaching-learning process" (p. 252). The important thing is to incorporate them without falling into excesses and to remember that they are a support tool for the teacher. Similarly, should consider limitations, such as the technological infrastructure of the institution, which sometimes limits the instructional design of teachers and the collaborative work considered in learning with the use of technology.

FUTURE RESEARCH DIRECTIONS

The UCAT application modifies aspects following the observations made by teachers and students in the field test. For the next semester, the authors will use a control group to compare the impact of the use of the mobile application with AR in the urethral catheterization process. Additionally, the authors will design and validate the instruments that will make it possible to determine the meaningful existence between performance, motivation, and quality of the educational resource developed. Also, the actors of the model of the process should modify other aspects of the application to strengthen the handling of the technique in question. The student should take this into account when interacting with humans, for example, when dealing with muscle tension, having to talk to a patient, having the patient move away, being afraid, and dealing with different body shapes.

CONCLUSION

The use of augmented reality contributes to student learning. This study confirms that the use of augmented reality contributes to student learning. If the authors start from the position of the application serving to improve the performance of students, they are valuable as a starting point to encourage processes and review with students that lead them to achieve the necessary skills. In this sense, the authors recommend didactic activities using technology designed to foster meaningful learning. Also, the authors observed that students had confidence in using the application identified because they answered that they do not feel insecure when using the UCAT. This position was confirmed because they express their intention to use the applications in their training.

The application allows the students to explore the urethral catheterization technique, which confuses the students when applying the technique first in mannequins and later in human patients. Thus, the application gradually allows the students to explore the subject until it can be mastered by taking advantage of their interest in digital resources and the tendency to follow a learning pace. Although the application allows exercising the technique, it is missing information on how the student would react in real situations. The authors can identify that the incorporation of the UCAT is a more active form of learning. In addition to allowing the creation of direct links between the classroom and real life, the researchers also identify that it does not cause confusion or misinterpretation of content and does not become a distraction that hinders the learning process.

Although it was possible to determine a notable student improvement among the results of the test (pre-test and post-test) on the subject, the results could not assure that there was a relationship between student motivation and the performance they achieved. Moreover, the UCAT strengthens the students' knowledge about the urethral catheterization and prepares them to apply the technique in the clinical fields later. The students must perform this technique after accrediting the theoretical subject. The UCAT experience with nursing students provides elements to identify what can be incorporated into other subjects and even other sciences that present similar problems in the teaching-learning process. In other words, the use of technological resources should be promoted by encouraging learning with augmented reality.

ACKNOWLEDGMENT

This research received no specific grant from any funding agency in the public, commercial, or not-for-profit sectors.

To all participants in the research, the actors in the development of the UCAT, especially students and teachers, for supporting the work with the application.

REFERENCES

Alvarez-Marin, A., Castillo-Vergara, M., Pizarro-Guerrero, J., & Espinoza-Vera, E. (2017). Augmented Reality as a Support to the Formation of Industrial Engineers. *Formación Universitaria, 10*(2), 31–42. doi:10.4067/S0718-50062017000200005

Arteaga, I. G., & Pino, C. W. (2018). *Augmented reality in educational settings. Atlante: Education and Development Notebooks*. Retrieved from https://www.eumed.net/rev/atlante/2018/09/realidad-aumentada-educativos.html

Badilla, M., & Sandoval, A. M. (2015). Augmented reality as technology applied to higher education: A developing experience. *Innovaciones educativas, 17*(23), 41-49.

Baroudi, S., & Rodjan, M. (2019). Behind the scenes: Teachers' perspectives on factors affecting the implementation of inquiry-based science instruction. *Research in Science & Technological Education*, 1–22. doi:10.1080/02635143.2019.1651259

Bernal, L., & Ballesteros-Ricaurte, J. (2017). Methodology for the construction of virtual learning objects supported in augmented reality. *Sophia, 13*(1), 4–12. doi:10.18634ophiaj.13v.1i.209

Blas, D., Vázquez-Cano, E., Morales, M. B., & López, E. (2019). Use of augmented reality apps in University classrooms. *Campus Virtuales, 8*(1), 37-48. (www.revistacampusvirtuales.es)

Cabero, J., Barroso, J., & Llorente, C. (2019). Augmented reality in university education. REDU. *Revista de Docencia Universitaria, 17*(1), 105–118. doi:10.4995/redu.2019.11256

Cabero-Almenara, J., Vázquez-Cano, E., & López-Meneses, E. (2018). Use of Augmented Reality Technology as a Didactic Resource in University Teaching. *Formación Universitaria, 11*(1), 25–34. doi:10.4067/S0718-50062018000100025

Castaño-Calle, R., & González, F. (2019). Augmented and virtual reality: appraisals, perceptions and attitudes of university students and their application in the educational framework. *Instituto Politécnico de Braganca,* 1-19.

Castillo, J. L., Martínez, M., Soberanes, A., & Sánchez, J. M. (2016a). Definition of learning styles in university students according to neurolinguistic programming. *Docencia e Investigación Educativa, 2*(3), 25–34.

Castillo, J. L., Soberanes, A., Peña, A., & Martínez, M. (2016b). The industrial designer's learning process in the field of packaging. *Pistas Educativas, 122*(CITEC 2016), 86-99.

Cebrián, D. (2018). *Heading for Educational Mobile Applications*. Retrieved from https://corubric.com/index.php?r=public-rubric%2Fview&id=491

Cheng, K. H. (2017). Reading an augmented reality book: An exploration of learner's cognitive load, motivation and attitudes. *Australasian Journal of Educational Technology, 33*(4), 53–69.

Cruz, R., Soberanes, A., Martínez, M., & Juárez, C. (2012). Modeling the process of developing Computer Interactive Learning Environments (CILE): An aid to instructional design. In R. Juárez, H. Jadwiga, G. Ibargüengoitia, & A. Cárdenas (Eds.), *Tendencias en investigación e innovación en ingeniería de software: Un enfoque práctico* (1st ed., pp. 95–100). Universidad Autónoma de Baja California.

Cubillo, J., Martín, S., Castro, M., & Colmenar, A. (2014). Autonomous digital resources through augmented reality. *RIED. Revista Iberoamericana de Educación a Distancia, 17*(2), 241-274. https://www.redalyc.org/articulo.oa?id=3314/331431248012

Cupitra-García, A., & Duque-Bedoya, E. (2018). Augmented teachers in the context of augmented reality: A reflection on its pedagogical use. *El Ágora USB, 18*(1), 245–255. doi:10.21500/16578031.3178

Díaz-Campos, B. (2016). Augmented reality in education. *Revista Entorno*, (61), 47-53.

Fombona, J., Pascual-Sevillano, M. A., & González-Videgaray, M. C. (2017). M-learning y realidad aumentada: Revisión de literatura científica en el repositorio WoS. *Comunicar, 25*(52), 63–72. doi:10.3916/C52-2017-06

Harley, J., Poitras, E., Jarrell, A., Duffy, M., & Lajoie, S. (2016). Comparing virtual and location-based augmented reality mobile learning: Emotions and learning outcomes. *Educational Technology Research and Development, 64*(3), 359–388. doi:10.100711423-015-9420-7

Humanante-Ramos, P. (2018). *The ICT competences of students entering university: An experience in the Faculty of Health Sciences of a Latin American university*. Educ Med. doi:10.1016/j.edumed.2018.02.002

Lagunes-Domínguez, A., Torres-Gastelú, C. A., Angulo-Armenta, J., & Martínez-Olea, M. Á. (2017). Exploration toward mobile learning in university students. *Formación Universitaria, 10*(1), 101–108. doi:10.4067/S0718-50062017000100011

León, A. P., Risco, E., & Alarcón, C. (2014). Learning strategies in higher education in a curricular competence model. *Revista de la Educación Superior, 4*(172), 123–144.

León, F., Duque, E., & Escobar, P. (2018). Strategies for formulating quality questions mediated by augmented reality to strengthen scientific thinking. *Revista Mexicana de Investigación Educativa, 23*(78), 791–815.

Liao, H., Inomata, T., Sakuma, I., & Dohi, T. (2010). 3-D augmented reality for MRI-guided surgery using integral videography autostereoscopic image overlay. *IEEE Transactions on Biomedical Engineering, 57*(6), 1476–1486. doi:10.1109/TBME.2010.2040278 PMID:20172791

Maquilón, J. J., Mirete, A. B., & Avilés, M. (2017). Augmented Reality (AR). Resources and proposals for educational innovation. *Revista Electrónica Interuniversitaria de Formación del Profesorado, 20*(2), 183–203. doi:10.6018/reifop/20.2.290971

Martínez, A., Martínez, J., & Navarro, F. (2018). *Virtual reality and augmented reality. Application development*. Ra-Ma.

Martínez, S., & Fernández, B. (2018, July). Objects of augmented reality: perceptions of pedagogy student. *Píxel-Bit. Revista de Medios y Educación*, (53), 207-220. doi:10.12795/pixelbit.2018.i53.14

Martins, A., Fracchia, C. C., Allan, C., Parra, S., Baeza, N., Celeste, C., . . . Laurent, R. (2019). Development of computer tools and their applications in the educational field. In *XXI Workshop de Investigadores en Ciencias de la Computación* (WICC 2019). Universidad Nacional de San Juan.

Mata-López, W., & Tobón, S. (2019). Analysis of factors associated to the enrollment and demand of computing-related careers. *Social Sciences*, *8*(1), 1. doi:10.3390ocsci8010001

Montes de Oca, N., & Machado, E. (2011). Teaching strategies and teaching-learning methods within Higher Education. *Humanidades Médicas*, *11*, 475–488.

Prendes, C. (2015). Augmented reality and education: Analysis of practical experiences. *Píxel-Bit. Revista de Medios y Educación*, *46*, 187–203.

Pugoy, R. A. D., Ramos, R. C., Figueroa, R. B., Rivera, M. H. C., Siritarungsri, B., Cheevakasemsook, A., Noimuenwai, P., & Kaewsarn, P. (2016). Augmented reality in nursing education: addressing the limitations of developing a learning material for nurses in the Philippines and Thailand. *Int J Open Distance e-Learning*. *2*(1), 11–24.

Rahn, A., & Kjaergaard, H. W. (2014). Augmented reality as a visualizing facilitator in nursing education. *Proceedings of the INTED*. 6560–8.

Rochlen, L. R., Levine, R., & Tait, A. R. (2017). First-person point-of-view-augmented reality for central line insertion training: A usability and feasibility study. *Simulation in Healthcare*, *12*(1), 57–62. doi:10.1097/SIH.0000000000000185 PMID:27930431

Tecnológico de Monterrey. (2017). *Edu trends. Augmented Reality and Virtual Reality*, Monterrey: Tecnológico de Monterrey. Retrieved from https://observatorio.tec.mx/edu-trends-realidad-virtual-y-realidad-aumentada

Villalustre, L., & Del Moral, M. (2018). Geolocation and Augmented Reality for Ubiquitous Learning in Initial Teacher Education. @tic. *Revista d'innovació educativa*, (21), 40-48.

Visbal-Cadavid, D., Mendoza-Mendoza, A., & Díaz, S. (2017). Learning strategies in higher education. *Sophia*, *13*(2), 70–81. http://www.redalyc.org/pdf/4137/413751844008.pdf

Wüller, H., Behrens, J., Garthaus, M., Marquard, S., & Remmers, H. (2019). A scoping review of augmented reality in nursing. *BMC Nursing*, *18*(1), 19. doi:10.118612912-019-0342-2 PMID:31123428

Zhu, E., Hadadgar, A., Masiello, I., & Zary, N. (2014). Augmented reality in healthcare education: An integrative review. *Journal of Life and Environmental Sciences*, *2*, e469. doi:10.7717/peerj.469 PMID:25071992

ADDITIONAL READING

Almenara, J. C., Villacé, I. D. L. H., & Bolado, J. S. (2018). *Augmented reality as an educational tool*. Ediciones Paraninfo.

Bajgoric, N., & Moon, Y. B. (2017). Business model for digital economy era: A framework based on the Churchman's theory of design integrity. *International Journal of Business and Systems Research*, *11*(3), 284–308. doi:10.1504/IJBSR.2017.085466

Castillo, J. L., Soberanes, A., Martínez, R., & Peña, A. (2016). Augmented reality as a tool in the learning process in the field of packaging and packaging of the industrial designer. *Pistas Educativas*, *122*, 87–99.

Chen, C., Ho, C., & Lin, J. (2015). The development of an augmented reality game-based learning environment. *Procedia: Social and Behavioral Sciences*, *174*, 216–220. doi:10.1016/j.sbspro.2015.01.649

González, L. (2017). Methodology for instructional design in the b-learning modality from Educational Communication. *Razón y palabra,* 21(3). 32-50.

Saalem, M., Mohamed, A., Gazala, Y., & Rajbunisa, A. (2019). Augmented reality-based education for the improvement of sustainable learning ability in OMAN educational system. *International Advanced Trends in Computer Science and Engineering*, *8*(12), 110–115.

Soberanes, A., Cruz, R., & Martínez, M. (2015). Interactive mobile computing teaching environments. In R. Cruz, G. López, & A. Pacheco (Eds.), *Emerging Technologies in education* (pp. 111–122). Pearson Education.

Sokołowicz, M. E. (2019). Student cities or cities of graduates? The case of Lodz and its students declared preferences. *Population Space and Place*, *25*(2), e2177. doi:10.1002/psp.2177

Warren, S., Sauser, B., & Nowicki, D. (2019). A bibliographic and visual exploration of the historic impact of soft systems methodology on academic research and theory. *Systems*, *7*(10), 1–15.

KEY TERMS AND DEFINITIONS

Catheterization Urethral: A technique that consists of inserting a catheter through the urethra into the urinary bladder.

Educational Resource: Material that can use in a teaching and learning situation.

Educational Technology: Information and communication technology incorporated into education to help improve activities in teaching and learning processes.

Mobile Learning: It is a branch of Information and Communication Technologies in education to make it more affordable through technological means.

Nursing: A person dedicated to the care of the sick.

Software Engineering: Set of methods, techniques, and tools for the development of computer programs (software).

Urethra: The conduit through which urine expelled from the bladder to the outside.

Urethral Catheter Application Technique (UCAT): Augmented reality application to practice the urethral catheterization process.

Chapter 10
A Research Map to Leverage Augmented Reality in K12 Science Education

Longkai Wu
National Institution of Education, Nanyang Technological University, Singapore

Yun Wen
National Institution of Education, Nanyang Technological University, Singapore

ABSTRACT

This chapter presents a research map of designing an AR-integrated science trail for an inquiry-based curriculum for K12 science learning. Despite the potential advantages of using AR in education and its suitability for supporting science learning through simulation activities, AR's concrete uses are relatively not as well understood as that of other technologies. Prior studies have shown the value of inquiry-based learning complemented by computer technology in a scenario-based learning environment. To appropriate the potential of AR in education, this chapter aims at summarizing pedagogical affordances of AR in science education and exemplifying an AR-integrated science trail design. A comprehensive research map of designing an AR-enhanced science trail by integrating inquiry-based learning is elucidated in this chapter to provide insights for the design of AR-integrated subject learning and out-of-classroom learning.

INTRODUCTION

Augmented Reality (AR) technologies have been featured for their enormous potentials in learning and are recognized as one of key emergent technologies for education (Johnson, Levine, Smith & Haywood, 2010). AR offers tremendous possibilities for students in facilitating sensory immersion, navigation and manipulation, and have been reported to promote positive emotions while learning, enhance collaborative learning, and create more efficient and better learning outcomes (Cheng & Tsai, 2013; Wen, 2018; Wu, Lee, Chang, & Liang, 2013). As AR has the capability of integrating digital information into real-

DOI: 10.4018/978-1-7998-5043-4.ch010

life scenarios, AR-enhanced inquiry lessons could engage learners in an immersive context to enhance scientific investigations where students can collect data outside classrooms, interact with an avatar, or communicate face-to-face with peers in a more authentic setting (e.g., Dunleavy, Dede, & Mitchell 2009). Despite the potential advantages of using AR in education and its suitability for supporting science learning through simulation activities, AR's concrete uses are relatively not as well understood as that of other technologies (Joseph & Uther, 2009). It has been recognised that AR is not designed for instructive pedagogies involving drill and practice techniques (Dunleavy, 2014), but we are only starting to understand how effective instructional or pedagogical designs for this emerging technology can be proposed. Existing review papers (e.g., Akçayır & Akçayır, 2017; Wen & Looi, 2019) on the topic have pointed out that more attention should be paid to exploring how to enhance the interaction between learners and the contextual information through pedagogical content design. As research in AR develops further, it will be important to ascertain what design approaches can optimise the distinct affordances of AR, and how one can mitigate its limitations and ultimately leverage its uses across the curriculum.

The potential of leveraging AR affordances to inquiry-based learning, particularly in science education, has been increasingly emphasized (e.g., Dunleavy et al., 2009; Nielsen, Brandt, & Swensen, 2016; Hsiao, Chang, Lin, & Wang, 2016). However, how to deploy the inquiry instructional technique and what scaffolding mechanisms can help to engage students in scientific inquiry activities should be further investigated (Ibáñez & Delgado-Kloos, 2018). Prior studies have shown that inquiry-based learning complemented by computer technology in a scenario-based learning environment can successfully increase learning motivation (Shih, Chuang, & Hwang, 2010; Soloway & Wallace, 1997). These inquiry-based learning tactics are student-centric exploration activities where teachers are facilitators, utilising structured techniques that prepare and encourage learners to problem-solve and learn proactively (Hwang, Wu, Zhuang, & Huang, 2013; Soloway & Wallace, 1997). When learners attain the techniques for problem-solving, they are better able to utilise the material to form a hypothesis or to propose answers to the problem (Looi, 1998). On this basis, we hypothesise that AR-based inquiry scenarios could be an effective innovative learning strategy in covering an extensive variety of domains– from observations and interactions to accessing actual scientific instruments or conducting more realistic experiments (Chiang, Yang & Hwang, 2014). We take the perspective that effective learning strategies supplemented with appropriate computer technology can greatly enhance learning motivation (Chu, Hwang, & Tsai, 2010; Jonassen, 1999; Hwang, Tsai, Chu, Kinshuk, & Chen, 2012; Jonassen et al., 1998). We argue that AR-based inquiry could be a point of entry into the transformation of classrooms into Splitter's (1991) communities of inquiry that preserve the "dimensions of inquiry and wonderment" at the forefront of the learner's daily learning activities (p.98).

In this chapter, we present a research map of designing an AR-integrated science trail for an inquiry-based curriculum for K12 science learning. The design is grounded with the situated learning theory which postulates that all learning occurs within a given context and the learning that happens is the outcome of the interaction and contact between the people, places, objects, process and culture within and related to the given situation (Brown, Collins, & Duguid, 1989). The purpose of the chapter is to exemplifying an AR-integrated science trail design to appropriate the potential of AR in science education.

LITERATURE REVIEW

Affordances of AR in Learning

The media characteristics of AR, in particular sensory immersion, navigation and manipulation, have shown to stimulate positive emotions in people while learning, and help produce efficient and better learning outcomes (Cheng & Tsai, 2013; Wu et al., 2013). In educational contexts, information is typically presented with visual, auditory, and sometimes tactile representations. Paper-based textbooks convey static visual content, such as text and diagrams. In contrast, AR offers the option of presenting content in a variety of other forms: static images become animations, 2D representations become 3D objects, text becomes sound, and non-interactive content becomes interactive. AR systems can assist students in visualising abstract science concepts or unobservable phenomena that are impossible to see and provide opportunities to manipulate and learn in 3D perspectives. For example, Matsutomo et al. (2012) use AR for presenting virtual magnetic fields on physical magnets and Tarng and Ou (2012) animate the life cycle of a virtual butterfly on a real plant. The medium of AR can thus present educational content through depictions of lifelike 3D objects and body-based representations, reaching learners through novel modalities and potentially facilitating deeper learning.

According to the findings of Radu's meta-review about AR in education, in "spatial domains — such as geometrical shapes, chemical structures, mechanical machinery, astronomy configurations, or spatial configuration of human organs research generally indicates that students learn better when using AR than when using either printed media or using desktop software" (2014, p.1535). For instance, in a series of studies, Vincenzi et al. (2003) describe how students learned the components of an aircraft turbine engine, using either by AR, videos, or textbooks, and it is revealed that with AR-learning, students exhibited better short-term memory and long-term memory. In Sin & Zaman's research (2010), students studied the characteristics of the solar system using either an AR or with textbooks, and the findings reveal that students using the AR system showed greater learning improvement than students using the textbook. This finding is also congruent with an analysis of students' learning in the subject of human anatomy by Nischelwitzer et al. (2007).

In addition to presenting learning content in novel ways, AR helps learners to experience and observe virtual components as part of their present environment by superimposing digital displays over real-life locations (Johnson, Adams, Estrada, & Freeman, 2014). Consequently, the augmentations help learners discover parts of the world and its phenomena in more tangible means than might otherwise be possible (Yoon & Wang, 2014), and encourage scientific inquiry in making observations, raising questions, collaborating with peers, and examining and analysing data (e.g., Dunleavy et al., 2009; Rosenbaum, Klopfer, & Pernç 2007; Squire & Klopfer, 2007).

Potentials of Integrating AR with Inquiry-Based Learning

Constructivists assert that individuals acquire knowledge from a direct understanding of the world, through a route of knowledge creation that occurs when learners are intellectually engaged in ''personally meaningful tasks'' (DeLay, 1996). Following this theory, engagement with the world is pertinent for the learning process and since user interaction is one of the principal features of AR, it offers an effective prospect of providing highly interactive experiences. As put forth by Chang et al. (2010), apart from reality, the most applicable method to produce a perspective based on authentic learning activities may be through the use of AR. Besides a good level of realism and interactivity, AR can provide life-like situated learning experiences that link experience to theory (Liestol, 2011).

Nielsen, Brandt & Swensen (2016) proposed the importance of incorporating features highlighted in inquiry-based science education into the AR activities. As science is a discipline where inquiry is central to the curriculum, an initial stimulus material (ISM) is important to raise curiosity in students, to give them enough room for their inquiries (Phillips, 2001). Students could learn to examine the ISM, in the form of a photo, video, presentation, or an activity, and then generate their own questions (Burnham, 2017). AR could be an engaging tool for ISM, and when combined with pedagogical inquiry activities could be an effective way of promoting students' understanding of science content (Chang, Wu & Hsu, 2013).

In the study by Chiang et al (2014), the authors concluded that inquiry learning with AR was more effective than conventional inquiry-based mobile learning approach. As Chiang and team (2014) explained, the students learnt effectively from the scenarios that offered real-world situations with accompanying learning resources in a unified and systematic way. This offers an edge over other conventional non-AR inquiry approaches, where learning materials and the topics of investigation are presented separately and asynchronously. In other inquiry approaches, students had to carry out observations, then organise their learning material separately. Therefore, with AR, students could receive information seamlessly. In the study, the students had explained that virtual learning resources integrated in the AR scenarios helped them to focus on their investigations as they did not need to spend time linking the supplementary materials to their real-world investigations. They were also found that it was helpful to access learning resources and learning tasks instantaneously, regardless of their whereabouts, therefore it was useful when they tried to understand the tasks and investigations. They explained that AR can connect real-world investigations with digital learning material with immediacy, and there is no lag time in learning. This is currently not a feature in other mediums such as videos. This is in line with the spatial and temporal continuity principles of the multimedia design theory by Mayer and Moreno (2003), in that learning with AR, with its depiction of actual scenarios, alongside with resources (pictures, content, videos) can help improve students' learning performance.

While considering inquiry learning with technology, one too has to consider the structure in which the lessons will be implemented. Instead of approaching inquiry as purely discovery on one's own, Mayer (2004) has found that there should be guidance, structure and objectives stated in the inquiry-based activities. Educators contend that AR integrated learning activities are promising in scaffolding students in inquiry (Cheng & Tsai, 2013; Kyza & Georgiou, 2018; Efstathiou, Kyza, & Georgiou, 2018). The scaffolding ability of AR tools is effective for students to acquire accurate knowledge during periods of exploration and inquiry (Yoon, Anderson, Lin & Elinich, 2017) and allows for the possibility of developing a narrative that promotes inquiry-based learning that is not easily supported in a typical classroom environment (Squire & Jan, 2007)

In scaffolding inquiry-based learning, AR activities can be used as a checkpoint that students must successfully complete before they are given their next task (Hou, 2012; Hwang et al., 2012). The technology can be applied as a tool for assessing and evaluating student learning and understanding (Salmi, Kaasinen, & Kallunki, 2012). In the process of exploring scientific theories in real-life settings, students acquire accurate knowledge of these concepts through inquiry and collaboration (Yoon et al, 2016).

THEORETICAL FRAMEWORK

Experiential Learning

David Kolb's (1984) experiential learning cycle (Fig.1) offers "the foundation for an approach to education and learning as a lifelong process" (Zuber-Skerritt 1992). As its name suggests, this theory affirms the significance of experiential activities. Experiential learning is in contrast with teacher-centred didactic instruction as it highlights independent judgment, critical thinking, and personal experience. Through a learning process, students translate the experience gained through the learning activity into their lives, thus transforming their attitudes and prompting further reflection.

Figure 1. Experiential learning cycle (Kolb, 1984)

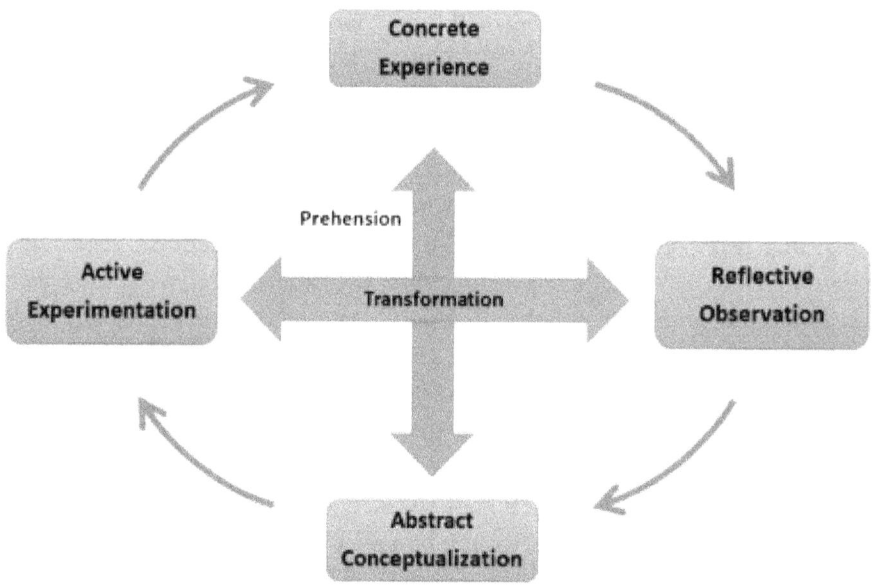

The vertical axis signifies knowledge gains, or the prehension dimension, by which knowledge can be gained through Concrete Experience or by Comprehension (the Abstract Conceptualisation), or by a combination of both. The horizontal axis signifies the elements of knowledge transformation or knowledge construction. Knowledge construction can be attained via Intention (the Reflective Observation), or via Extension (Active Experimentation).

According to Kolb, learning requires that learners first should obtain knowledge, followed by a phase of construction to complete the learning process. This construction is a transformation of knowledge gains into a mental model. Kolb argued that the optimal learning would pass through a cycle of the Concrete Experience, Reflective Observation, Abstract Conceptualisation, and Active Experimentation. Thus, an ideal learning situation occurs when learners have sufficient balance of these four stages during their learning experience.

Kolb's theory takes on a more holistic approach and emphasises how experiences, including cognition, environmental factors and emotions influence the learning process. Because AR environments integrate simulated information combined with the actual real-world environment and context in which they are located, students learn by modelling specific aspects of real-world complex systems, investigate by manipulating parameters and observing outcomes in a mediated authentic experience.

A Framework for Science Trail Leveraged with AR Technologies

We articulate a framework for science trail leveraged with AR technologies: Questioning, Investigating, Making and Synthesising (QIMS). This framework (Fig. 2) is built on Kolb's (1984) experiential learning cycle, as well as our previous work in inquiry-based learning with an emphasis on the role of questioning in inquiry. Using the affordances of AR technologies, students will be further empowered in a QIMS inquiry cycle in both virtual and real contexts, broadening and deepening their Concrete Experience, Reflective Observation, Abstract Conceptualisation, and Active Experimentation (Kolb, 2014).

Figure 2: QIMS Inquiry Framework

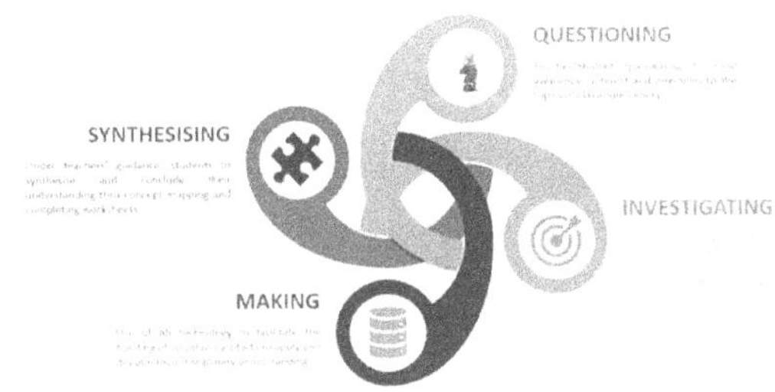

With reference to Kolb's cycle with comprehension and transformation dimensions, students will learn in AR environment to address our proposed staged QIMS framework (Figure 2). (1) Questioning: Students will be guided to raise possible guiding questions in a topic (e.g. climate change) ; (2) Investigating: Students will have a concrete experience of the phenomenon and effects (of climate change) in AR simulations and reflection on that experience; (3) Making: Students will apply the formation of abstract concepts (analysis) and generalisations (conclusions) which are then used to test hypotheses in making their own simulations, resulting in new experiences and inquiries; (4) Synthesising: Students will conclude their findings to summarize knowledge to capture both comprehension and transformation dimensions. Thus, the QIMS framework echoes well to the experiential learning theory that emphasises the correlation between concrete experience and learning.

In the classroom practice, formal learning often diverges from authentic activity, or 'the ordinary practices of the culture' (Brown et al., 1989, p. 34). We argue that an AR-mediated science trail is optimal for integrating a formal-like instruction in an informal context – and can provide an excellent prospect for increasing pupils' interest and motivation towards learning science (Vainikainen, Salmi, & Thuneberg, 2015). As an assistive tool for learning, AR presents an opportunity where it leverages the unique blending of real and virtual worlds to produce new educational opportunities.

For instance, students can take roles as botanists or plant investigators. With the AR as a mediating technological tool, students study the life cycles of plants instantly (which may otherwise not be always available, due to the ephemeral nature of natural phenomenon). Students will identify the plants, ascertain what sorts of conditions are optimal for the plant to grow, what conditions would impede a healthy growth of the plants. As part of the AR activity, they will collect virtual tools needed for the plant to grow well. Students can learn about how plants grow by experimenting with the various conditions to make the plant grow to a healthy size (amount of sun, water, carbon dioxide, fertiliser, types of soil). The activity will be anchored on their inquiries. By highlighting social negotiation as a vital aspect of the learning experience, this enhances self-directed and active learning opportunities in the classroom environment, and with the addition of AR technology will engage all learners in the classroom (Keneman, 2016). In this way, AR opens up possibilities of questioning possibilities, provides students different avenues of making sense of their learning, and thus encourages students to take on a more active role in their learning.

The scholastic lens of QIMS can also help researchers to investigate how AR can afford the different activities in the four stages. The construct Questioning includes: (1) observations by the teachers and researchers of students' engagement in questioning during the AR activities, and (2) questionnaire items about the students' self-perception of their engagement in questioning. The construct Investigating includes: (1) observations by the teachers and researchers of students' engagement in investigating during the AR activities, and (2) questionnaire items about the students' self-perception of their engagement in investigating. The construct Making includes: (1) assessment of quality of the artefacts created by the students in various sessions of the AR activities and (2) questionnaire items about the students' self-perception of the quality of their artefacts. The construct Synthesizing includes: (1) the oral presentation of the students with AR artifacts, and (2) questionnaire items about the students' self-perception of their synthesising.

A ROAD MAP FOR IMPLEMENTATION

As AR technologies are new to most schools, teachers may encounter new challenges while integrating it in classrooms and facilitating learning processes where students are challenged by technology-rich and authentic learning tasks. To make effective use of the technology, teacher's mode of working must become heavily reflective, explorative and experimental (Laurillard, 2012; Persico & Donatella, 2015). We propose a teacher professional development model (Table 1), adapted from the Turn-around Technology Integration Pedagogy Planning (TTIPP) model by Roblyer and Hughes (2019) as a road map to help with instructional problems in integrating such technology in classrooms. The TTIPP model is adopted as it provides a general approach to identifying and addressing challenges involved in integrating technology into teaching. Additionally, the importance of teacher-research collaboration (Song & Looi, 2012) and the participatory design approach among teachers (Laurillard, 2012) have been acknowledged in teachers' professional development. Teachers and researchers, teachers and teachers are advised to work together to accomplish the process of innovation and integration.

Table 1. Teachers' Professional Development to Implement AR adapted to TTIPP model

Phases	Steps	Main tasks
PHASE 1	Step 1: Identifying needs	In the first phase, to plan and analyse one's needs and environment accordingly. The instructor can start by identifying their 'Problems in practice', what they are trying to teach, how and what needs will be met by adding a technological component. This model is helpful as it takes into account the user's needs and not resorting to applying technology just for technology's sake.
	Step 2: Planning of resources	Step two is meant to assess the level of technological resources of needed for the integration. This includes knowing how comfortable the teacher is applying a certain technology and what is possible with the school resources. Teaching training might be given and the researchers will work together with the teachers to ensure a smooth integration.
	Step 3: Approach of integration	The final step of the first phase comprises establishing the possibilities of the technology. For instance, if the integration involves a directed strategy or a constructivist approach. With a directed strategy, one has to determine how technology can deliver information accurately and efficiently. With a constructivist approach, one has to determine how the technology can be integrated to help students develop skills and discover answers for themselves.
PHASE 2	Step 4: Design of an integration framework	Phase two deals with the design of an integration framework. In Step four, participants determine a concrete set of learning objectives, with measurable outcomes and a means of assessing student work. Participants also decide how they can structure the design with the framework for classroom inquiry (QIMS) leveraged with AR technologies.
	Step 5: Designing integration strategies	Step five is meant for designing integration strategies. How best can the technology be integrated and system for the lesson flow. Lesson packages can be designed to manage the flow of a smooth lesson delivery.
	Step 6: Implementation of the lesson	In step six, one prepares the instructional environment to implement the lesson. This includes perhaps a trial lesson to determine how to run the lesson, rules for using the technology, any possible issues. One can decide on possible back-up plans in case the technology does not run as planned.
PHASE 3	Step 7: Review of the implementation	Phase three is intended for 'Post instruction analysis and revisions.' This final phase is mainly a review, where the team reflects on the implementation and if changes are needed. It is here that the team should review if the objectives from step four were achieved and how students reacted to the use of the technology. The team also reflects on how enhancements could be made in future iterations.
	Step 8: Sharing & Review	In step eight, one implements their revisions based on the reflections and data gathered from the initial implementations. The final step involves sharing sessions of outcomes with peers and other clusters. By sharing lessons, one can gather feedback from other educators.

The following exemplifies how AR interactivity and student inquiries might be incorporated onto an AR platform, together with our QIMS inquiry framework (Table 2).

The following is a concreate example of a possible lesson scenario with a special AR platform: a "Garden Detective" AR trail that is designed with TaleBlazer software, an augmented reality (AR) software platform developed by the MIT Scheller Teacher Education Program (STEP) lab. The use of AR app encourages the development of inquiry processes and provides experiential learning based on real-world objects. The app plays the role of a learning facilitator and virtual guide across multiple locations in the school, which would not be possible with a single teacher.

1. Students are divided into small teams and introduced to the "Garden Detective" trail.
2. The app presents each team with the first set of clues. Based on the clues given, the students need to identify, search and go to the location of the correct plant in the eco-garden or school compound.
3. When the app detects that the team has arrived at the plant's location, the team is presented with a question or a puzzle in the AR app. With the correct solution, the team collects more educational information about the plant in the form of text, images or video, which can be used to solve later puzzles in the game.
4. The team progresses to the next stage of the detective trail and the next set of clues is given. Levels are shuffled so that teams will not be searching for the same plant at the same time.

Table 2. Examples of how AR and student enquires might be incorporated together

	Questioning	Investigating	Making	Synthesising
Example A: Human anatomy	• How does a liver work? • What is the function of the liver?	• Using AR, look inside a body to investigate organs and how they function individually and together.	• Make model (AR/non-AR) of the human body: as a blood cell passes through veins/arteries/the heart.	• Potential interactions: what happens if the liver is reduced to half the size? • What happens if the amount of red blood cells is increased by 10%?
Example B: Socio-scientific issues	• Why do some areas in Singapore flood? • How can we prevent them?	• Show with AR, the dramatic consequences of climate change on known central locations/places.	• Build AR or model constructions for renewable energy. • Story: energy crisis, where the mission is to solve it by finding renewable energy sources.	• Potential interactions: How can you describe the relationship between human activity and climate change?
Example C: Photosynthesis	• What do you understand by photosynthesis?	• Use AR to incorporate layers of information about a leaf, such as the cross-section through a leaf cell and the many different components	• Draw/Depict parts of a leaf- the lower/upper epidermis, stoma, wax cuticle, spongy mesophyll, and explain the function of these components.	• Potential interactions: How do you describe the relationship between the various components of the leaf?

DISCUSSION AND CONCLUSION

The intention of the research map proposed in this chapter is to utilise AR technology to enhance the effectiveness of experiential learning by building a learning system that can access richer learning information in a livelier authentic environment. Traditional learning environments are often inadequate, especially when learning contexts are limited and somewhat artificial. As such, learning activities and resources become divorced from their meaning in real life situations (Herrington, Reeves, & Oliver, 2010). Educators advocating authentic learning argue for the creation of more meaningful learning situations that require learning contexts used that reflect the real world, one in which corresponding skills and competencies will be deployed. As such, students could benefit from the integration of presentation of text and corresponding illustrations in a cohesive manner, rather than in a separate mode. Prior studies have also shown the value of inquiry-based learning complemented by computer technology in a scenario-based learning environment (e.g., Shih et al., 2010; Soloway & Wallace, 1997). Additionally, in inquiry-based learning, students are meant to work around a purposefully structured problem and assuming an active role in uncovering the solutions (Song & Wen, 2017). It calls for a consideration of multiple perspectives in the learning process and working towards finding solutions.

AR opens up more possibilities to create these problem scenarios which may be ordinarily limited, especially in the teaching of natural phenomenon. With AR, information on a particular topic can be made available and updated easily, without having to re-print existing display panels. AR allows for active, manipulatable representations, which is an effective way to enhance inquiry-based learning (Edelson, Gordon & Pea, 1999). It can provide direct access to information and can effectively aid teachers in diagnosing and correcting errors instantly (Edelson et al., 1999). AR supports such a learning environment, in which sensory experiences, interactivity and guiding functions of AR technologies can improve students' learning satisfaction and enable them to structure and apply their knowledge (Dalgarno & Lee, 2010; Dunleavy et al., 2009, Bower, 2008; Kye & Kim, 2008; Chiang et al., 2014).

The research map proposed in this paper is likely to shed light on whether and how AR-integrated activities can shape students' interests for learning and motivation, and this will ultimately inform how the academic curriculum can be appropriated and enacted in future. The scholastic lens of QIMS (Questioning, Investigating, Making and Synthesizing) conceptual framework can be applied to create a discussion with the extant research literature on how AR might potentially benefit students in learning, and how the various aspects of questioning, investigating, making, and synthesising could be improved in the AR activities for the students. Using the AR technologies, students will be empowered in a QIMS inquiry cycle in both virtual and real contexts, broadening and deepening their Concrete Experience, Reflective Observation, Abstract Conceptualisation, and Active Experimentation. Based on the research map, the studies in the near future will concentrate on how AR-based inquiry activities can be learning staged in an authentic context. The proposed research map will be an entry point into a well-designed holistic AR-enabled learning environment with active, joyful and meaningful discoveries in K12 science learning.

REFERENCES

Akçayır, M., & Akçayır, G. (2017). Advantages and challenges associated with augmented reality for education: A Systematic review of the literature. *Educational Research Review*, *20*, 1–11. doi:10.1016/j.edurev.2016.11.002

Bower, M. (2008). Affordance analysis - matching learning tasks with learning technologies. *Educational Media International*, *45*(1), 3–15. doi:10.1080/09523980701847115

Brown, J. S., Collins, A., & Duguid, P. (1989). Situated cognition and the culture of learning. *Educational Researcher*, *18*(1), 32–42. doi:10.3102/0013189X018001032

Burnham, S. (2007). Getting Year 7 to set their own questions about the Islamic Empire, 600-1600. *Teaching History*, *128*(September), 11–16.

Chang, C. W., Lee, J. H., Wang, C. Y., & Chen, G. D. (2010). Improving the authentic learning experience by integrating robots into the mixed-reality environment. *Computers & Education*, *55*(4), 1572–1578. doi:10.1016/j.compedu.2010.06.023

Chang, H. Y., Wu, H. K., & Hsu, Y. S. (2013). Integrating a mobile augmented reality activity to contextualize student learning of a socioscientific issue. *British Journal of Educational Technology*, *44*(3), 95–99. doi:10.1111/j.1467-8535.2012.01379.x

Cheng, K. H., & Tsai, C. C. (2013). Affordances of augmented reality in science learning: Suggestions for future research. *Journal of Science Education and Technology*, *22*(4), 449–462. doi:10.100710956-012-9405-9

Chiang, T. H. C., Yang, S. J., & Hwang, G. J. (2014). An augmented reality-based mobile learning system to improve students' learning achievements and motivations in natural science inquiry activities. *Journal of Educational Technology & Society*, *17*(4), 352–365.

Chu, H. C., Hwang, G. J., & Tsai, C. C. (2010). A knowledge engineering approach to developing mind-tools for context-aware ubiquitous learning. *Computers & Education*, *54*(1), 289–297. doi:10.1016/j.compedu.2009.08.023

Dalgarno, B., & Lee, M. J. W. (2010). What are the learning affordances of 3D virtual environments? *British Journal of Educational Technology*, *41*(1), 10–32. doi:10.1111/j.1467-8535.2009.01038.x

DeLay, R. (1996). Forming knowledge: Constructivist learning and experiential education. *Journal of Experiential Education*, *19*(2), 76–81. doi:10.1177/105382599601900204

Dunleavy, M. (2014). Design principles for augmented reality learning. *TechTrends*, *58*(1), 28–34. doi:10.100711528-013-0717-2

Dunleavy, M., & Dede, C. (2014). Augmented Reality Teaching and Learning. In J. Spector, M. Merrill, J. Elen, & M. Bishop (Eds.), *Handbook of Research on Educational Communications and Technology*. Springer. doi:10.1007/978-1-4614-3185-5_59

Dunleavy, M., Dede, C., & Mitchell, R. (2009). Affordances and limitations of immersive participatory augmented reality simulations for teaching and learning. *Journal of Science Education and Technology*, *18*(1), 7–22. doi:10.100710956-008-9119-1

Edelson, D. C., Gordon, D. N., & Pea, R. D. (1999). Addressing the challenge of inquiry-based learning. *Journal of the Learning Sciences*, *8*, 392–450. doi:10.120715327809jls0803&4_3

Efstathiou, I., Kyza, E. A., & Georgiou, Y. (2018). An inquiry-based augmented reality mobile learning approach to fostering primary school students' historical reasoning in non-formal settings. *Interactive Learning Environments*, *26*(1), 22–41. doi:10.1080/10494820.2016.1276076

Herrington, J., Reeves, S. C., & Oliver, R. (2010). *A Practical Guide to Authentic e-learning*. Routledge.

Hou, H. T. (2012). Analyzing the learning process of an online role-playing discussion activity. *Journal of Educational Technology & Society*, *15*(1), 211–222.

Hsiao, H. S., Chang, C. S., Lin, C. Y., & Wang, Y. Z. (2016). Weather observers: A manipulative augmented reality system for weather simulations at home, in the classroom, and at a museum. *Interactive Learning Environments*, *24*(1), 205–223. doi:10.1080/10494820.2013.834829

Hwang, G. J., Tsai, C. C., Chu, H. C., Kinshuk, K., & Chen, C.-Y. (2012). A context-aware ubiquitous learning approach to conducting scientific inquiry activities in a science park. *Australasian Journal of Educational Technology*, *28*(5), 931–947. doi:10.14742/ajet.825

Hwang, G. J., Wu, P. H., Zhuang, Y. Y., & Huang, Y. M. (2013). Effects of the inquiry-based mobile learning model on the cognitive load and learning achievement of students. *Interactive Learning Environments*, *21*(4), 338–354. doi:10.1080/10494820.2011.575789

Ibáñez, M. B., & Delgado-Kloos, C. (2018). Augmented reality for STEM learning: A systematic review. *Computers & Education*, *123*(May), 109–123. doi:10.1016/j.compedu.2018.05.002

Johnson, L., Adams, S., Estrada, V., & Freeman, A. (2014). *NMC Horizon Report: 2014*. The New Media Consortium.

Johnson, L. F., Levine, A., Smith, R. S., & Haywood, K. (2010). Key emerging technologies for elementary and secondary education. *Education Digest*, *76*(1), 36–40.

Jonassen, D. H. (1999). *Computers as mindtools for schools, engaging critical thinking*. Prentice-Hall.

Jonassen, D. H., Carr, C., & Yueh, H. P. (1998). Computers as mindtools for engaging learners in critical thinking. *TechTrends*, *43*(2), 24–32. doi:10.1007/BF02818172

Joseph, S. R., & Uther, M. (2009). Mobile devices for language learning: Multimedia approaches. *Research and Practice in Technology Enhanced Learning*, *4*(01), 7–32. doi:10.1142/S179320680900060X

Keneman, M. (2016). Empowering the foreign language learner through critical literacies development. *Journal of Language and Literacy Education*, *12*(2), 84–99.

Kirkley, S. E., & Kirkley, J. R. (2005). Creating next generation blended learning environments using mixed reality, video games and simulations. *TechTrends*, *49*(3), 42–53. doi:10.1007/BF02763646

Kolb, D. A. (1984). *Experiential learning: Experience as the source of learning and development*. Prentice-Hall.

Kye, B., & Kim, Y. (2008). Investigation of the relationships between media characteristics, presence, flow, and learning effects in augmented reality based learning augmented reality. *International Journal for Education Media and Technology*, *2*(1), 4–14.

Kyza, E. A., & Georgiou, Y. (2018). Scaffolding augmented reality inquiry learning: The design and investigation of the TraceReaders location-based, augmented reality platform. *Interactive Learning Environments*, 1–15.

Laurillard, D. (2012). *Teaching as a design science: building pedagogical patterns for learning and technology*. Routledge.

Liestol, G. (2011). *Learning through situated simulations: exploring mobile augmented reality*. ECAR.

Looi, C. K. (1998). Interactive learning environments for promoting inquiry learning. *Journal of Educational Technology Systems*, *27*(1), 3–22. doi:10.2190/L4Q4-8QMM-QPJ3-B5LJ

Martín-Gutiérrez, J., Fabiani, P., Benesova, W., Meneses, M. D., & Mora, C. E. (2015). Augmented reality to promote collaborative and autonomous learning in higher education. *Computers in Human Behavior*, *51*, 752–761. doi:10.1016/j.chb.2014.11.093

Matsutomo, S., Miyauchi, T., Noguchi, S., & Yamashita, H. (2012). Real-time visualization system of magnetic field utilizing augmented reality technology for education. *IEEE Transactions on Magnetics*, *48*(2), 531–534. doi:10.1109/TMAG.2011.2174208

Mayer, R. (2004). Should there be a three-strikes rule against pure discovery learning? The case for guided methods of instruction. *The American Psychologist*, *59*(1), 14–19. doi:10.1037/0003-066X.59.1.14 PMID:14736316

Mayer, R. E., & Moreno, R. (2003). Nine ways to reduce cognitive load in multimedia learning. *Educational Psychologist*, *38*(1), 43–52. doi:10.1207/S15326985EP3801_6

Nielsen, B. L., Brandt, H. & Swensen, H. (2016). Augmented Reality in science education–affordances for student learning. *Nordic Studies in Science Education, 12*(2), 157–174.

Nischelwitzer, A., Lenz, F. J., Searle, G., & Holzinger, A. (2007). Some aspects of the development of low-cost augmented reality learning environments as examples for future interfaces in technology enhanced learning. In *International Conference on Universal Access in Human-Computer Interaction* (pp. 728–737). Springer. 10.1007/978-3-540-73283-9_79

O'Shea, P., Dede, C., & Cherian, M. (2011). The results of formatively evaluating an augmented reality curriculum based on modified design principles. *International Journal of Gaming and Computer-Mediated Simulations*, *3*(2), 57–66. doi:10.4018/jgcms.2011040104

Persico, D., & Pozzi, F. (2015). Informing learning design with learning analytics to improve teacher inquiry. *British Journal of Educational Technology*, *46*(2), 230–248. doi:10.1111/bjet.12207

Phillips, R. (2001). Making history curious: Using initial stimulus material to promote enquiry, thinking and literacy. *Teaching History*, *105*, 19–24.

Radu, I. (2014). Augmented reality in education: A meta-review and cross-media analysis. *Personal and Ubiquitous Computing*, *18*(6), 1533–1543. doi:10.100700779-013-0747-y

Roblyer, M. D., & Hughes, J. E. (2019). *Integrating educational technology into teaching: Transforming learning across disciplines* (8th ed.). Pearson.

Rosenbaum, E., Klopfer, E., & Perry, J. (2007). On location learning: Authentic applied science with networked augmented realities. *Journal of Science Education and Technology*, *16*(1), 31–45. doi:10.100710956-006-9036-0

Salmi, H., Kaasinen, A., & Kallunki, V. (2012). Toward an open learning environment via segmented reality (AR): Visualizing the invisible in science centres and schools for teacher education. *Social and Behavioral Sciences*, *45*, 284–295.

Shih, J. L., Chuang, C. W., & Hwang, G. J. (2010). An inquiry-based mobile learning approach to enhancing social science learning effectiveness. *Journal of Educational Technology & Society*, *13*(4), 50–62.

Sin, A. K., & Zaman, H. B. (2010). Live Solar System (LSS): Evaluation of an Augmented Reality book-based educational tool. In *International Symposium in Information Technology* (Vol. 1, pp. 1–6). IEEE. 10.1109/ITSIM.2010.5561320

Soloway, E., & Wallace, R. (1997). Does the internet support student inquiry? *Don't ask. Communications of the ACM*, *40*(5), 11–16. doi:10.1145/253769.253771

Song, Y., & Looi, C. K. (2012). Linking teacher beliefs, practices and student inquiry-based learning in a CSCL environment: A tale of two teachers. *International Journal of Computer-Supported Collaborative Learning*, *7*(1), 129–159. doi:10.100711412-011-9133-9

Song, Y., & Wen, Y. (2018). Integrating various apps on BYOD (Bring Your Own Device) into seamless inquiry-based learning to enhance primary students' science learning. *Journal of Science Education and Technology*, *27*(2), 165–176. doi:10.100710956-017-9715-z

Splitter, L. J. (1991). Critical thinking: What, why, when and how. *Educational Philosophy and Theory*, *23*(1), 89–109. doi:10.1111/j.1469-5812.1991.tb00178.x

Squire, K., & Klopfer, E. (2007). Augmented reality simulations on handheld computers. *Journal of the Learning Sciences*, *16*(3), 371–413. doi:10.1080/10508400701413435

Tan, J., & Gopinathan, S. (2000). Education reform in Singapore: Towards greater creativity and innovation? *National Institute for Research Advancement (NIRA). RE:view*, *7*(3), 5–10.

Tan, K. (2001). Assessment for learning in Singapore: Unpacking its meanings and identifying some areas for improvement. *Educational Research for Policy and Practice, 10*(2), 91–103. doi:10.100710671-010-9096-z

Tarng, W., & Ou, K. L. (2012). A study of campus butterfly ecology learning system based on augmented reality and mobile learning. In *Proceedings of IEEE International Conference on Wireless, Mobile and Ubiquitous Technology in Education* (pp. 62–66). 10.1109/WMUTE.2012.17

Vainikainen, M.-P., Salmi, H., & Thuneberg, H. (2015). Situational interest and learning in a Science Centre Mathematics Exhibition. *Journal of Science Communication, 14*(4), 1–19.

Vincenzi, D. A., Valimont, B., Macchiarella, N., Opalenik, C., Gangadharan, S. N., & Majoros, A. E. (2003). The effectiveness of cognitive elaboration using augmented reality as a training and learning paradigm. *Proceedings of the Human Factors and Ergonomics Society Annual Meeting, 47*(19), 2054–2058. doi:10.1177/154193120304701909

Wen, Y. (2018). Chinese character composition game with the augment paper. *Journal of Educational Technology & Society, 21*(3), 132–145.

Wen, Y. (2019). An Augmented Paper Game with Socio-Cognitive Support. *IEEE Transactions on Learning Technologies*. Advance online publication. doi:10.1109/TLT.2019.2924216

Wen, Y., & Looi, C. K. (2019). Review of augmented reality in education: Situated learning with digital and non-digital resources. In *Learning on a Digital World: Perspective on Interactive Technologies for Formal and Informal Education* (pp. 179–193). Springer. doi:10.1007/978-981-13-8265-9_9

Wu, H.-K., Lee, S. W.-Y., Chang, H.-Y., & Liang, J.-C. (2013). Current status, opportunities and challenges of augmented reality in education. *Computers & Education, 62*, 41–49. doi:10.1016/j.compedu.2012.10.024

Yoon, S., Anderson, E., Koehler-Yom, J., Evans, C., Park, M., Sheldon, J., Schoenfeld, I., Wendel, D., Scheintaub, H., & Klopfer, E. (2016). Teaching about complex systems is not simple matter: Building effective professional development for computer-supported complex systems instruction. *Instructional Science, 45*(1), 99–121. doi:10.100711251-016-9388-7

Yoon, S., Anderson, E., Lin, J., & Elinich, K. (2017). How augmented reality enables conceptual understanding of challenging science content. *Journal of Educational Technology & Society, 20*(1), 156–168.

Yoon, S. A., & Wang, J. (2014). Making the invisible visible in science museums through augmented reality devices. *TechTrends, 58*(1), 49–55. doi:10.100711528-013-0720-7

Zuber-Skerritt, O. (1992). *Professional Development in Higher Education: A Theoretical Framework for Action Research*. UK Kogan Page.

ADDITIONAL READING

Akçayır, M., & Akçayır, G. (2017). Advantages and challenges associated with augmented reality for education: A Systematic review of the literature. *Educational Research Review*, *20*, 1–11. doi:10.1016/j.edurev.2016.11.002

Chiang, T. H. C., Yang, S. J., & Hwang, G. J. (2014). An augmented reality-based mobile learning system to improve students' learning achievements and motivations in natural science inquiry activities. *Journal of Educational Technology & Society*, *17*(4), 352–365.

Edelson, D. C., Gordon, D. N., & Pea, R. D. (1999). Addressing the challenge of inquiry-based learning. *Journal of the Learning Sciences*, *8*, 392–450. doi:10.120715327809jls0803&4_3

Kolb, D. A. (1984). *Experiential learning: Experience as the source of learning and development*. Prentice-Hall.

Mayer, R. E., & Moreno, R. (2003). Nine ways to reduce cognitive load in multimedia learning. *Educational Psychologist*, *38*(1), 43–52. doi:10.1207/S15326985EP3801_6

Squire, K., & Klopfer, E. (2007). Augmented reality simulations on handheld computers. *Journal of the Learning Sciences*, *16*(3), 371–413. doi:10.1080/10508400701413435

Wen, Y., & Looi, C. K. (2019). Review of augmented reality in education: Situated learning with digital and non-digital resources. In K. K. Bhagat & ... (Eds.), *Learning on a Digital World: Perspective on Interactive Technologies for Formal and Informal Education* (pp. 179–193). Springer. doi:10.1007/978-981-13-8265-9_9

Wu, H.-K., Lee, S. W.-Y., Chang, H.-Y., & Liang, J.-C. (2013). Current status, opportunities and challenges of augmented reality in education. *Computers & Education*, *62*, 41–49. doi:10.1016/j.compedu.2012.10.024

Yoon, S., Anderson, E., Lin, J., & Elinich, K. (2017). How augmented reality enables conceptual understanding of challenging science content. *Journal of Educational Technology & Society*, *20*(1), 156–168.

KEY TERMS AND DEFINITIONS

AR-Enhanced Inquiry: Engages learners in an immersive context to enhance scientific investigations where students can collect data outside classroom, interact with an avatar, or communicate face-to-face with peers in a more authentic setting.

Experiential Learning Cycle: Offers the foundation for an approach to education and learning as a lifelong process where students translate the experience gained through the learning activity into their lives, thus transforming their attitudes and prompting further reflection.

Inquiry-Based Learning Tactics: Student-centric exploration activities where teachers are facilitators, utilising structured techniques that prepare and encourage learners to problem-solve and learn proactively.

Professional Development Model: A road map to help with instructional problems in integrating such technology in classrooms.

QIMS Framework: The framework that is built on Kolb's experiential learning cycle and consists of four iterative stages: questioning, investigating, making, and synthesising.

Situated Learning Theory: Postulates that all learning occurs within a given context and the learning that happens is the outcome of the interaction and contact between the people, places, objects, process and culture within and related to the given situation.

Turn-Around Technology Integration Pedagogy Planning (TTIPP) Model: Provides a general approach to identifying and addressing challenges involved in integrating technology into teaching.

Chapter 11
The Use of Augmented Reality Applications in Second Grade Mathematics Course:
Students' Knowledge of Shapes

Mehmet Arif Bozan
https://orcid.org/0000-0003-3554-4828
Istanbul Aydin University, Turkey

Ahmet Oguz Akcay
Eskisehir Osmangazi University, Turkey

Engin Karahan
Eskisehir Osmangazi University, Turkey

ABSTRACT

This study aims to examine students' knowledge of shapes as well as the views of the students and their teachers about the use of AR applications in teaching and learning geometry in second-grade mathematics lessons. A convergent parallel mixed methods research design was employed. The data collected for this study come from tests on the knowledge of shapes, as well as semi-structured interviews with students and their teachers and open-ended questionnaires. The participants of the study comprised three primary school second-grade teachers and the students from these teachers' classrooms. The quantitative data were analyzed via paired sample t-test, while the data derived from the qualitative sources were analyzed by using a content analysis method. The results show that the AR application in the second-grade mathematics lessons positively affected the students' knowledge of shapes. In addition, both students and their teachers considered AR technologies as a facilitator for learning geometrical shapes.

DOI: 10.4018/978-1-7998-5043-4.ch011

INTRODUCTION

Technology has developed rapidly, affecting not only daily lives but also classrooms in the 21st century. Technology has potential in education, and especially in mathematics, which requires the use of innovative learning tools. The National Council of Teachers of Mathematics (NCTM) (2008) stated:

With guidance from effective mathematics teachers, students at different levels can use these tools to support and extend mathematical reasoning and sense making, gain access to mathematical content and problem-solving contexts, and enhance computational fluency. In a well-articulated mathematics program, students can use these tools for computation, construction, and representation as they explore problems. The use of technology also contributes to mathematical reflection, problem identification, and decision-making (p. 1).

There are many technological tools that are integrated into K-12 education to help students obtain rich and meaningful instruction. Among them are augmented reality (AR) applications, which have gained popularity in both academic and industrial circles in recent years. Before discussing AR, however, it is helpful to give information about extended reality (XR) and the virtuality continuum. XR has changed the manner in which individuals experience physical and virtual conditions. "Extended Reality (XR) encompasses a wide range of technologies along a continuum with real environments at one end and fully immersive virtual environments at the other" (Pomerantz, 2019, p. 138). XR is an emerging umbrella term that includes representative forms such as AR, mixed reality (MR), and virtual reality (VR). Milgram and Kishino (1994) presented the term "virtuality continuum" to explain the concepts related to real and virtual environments. The world in which the user interacts can be placed on a continuum depending on the amount of computer production. There is a real environment at one end of this continuum and a virtual environment at the other. As the continuum progresses from left to right, the amount of virtual images increases and the connection with reality weakens. Milgram and Kishino (1994) also stated that AR is related to MR, and AR has started to be used in the literature.

AR can be defined as a technological tool that covers the real world with some parts of a virtual world (Azuma, Baillot, Behringer, Feiner, Julier, & MacIntyre, 2001). Azuma (1997) defined AR as technology where virtual objects blend with the real world, while real and virtual objects interact with each other. AR allows the user to see the real world with virtual objects added or combined into it (Azuma, 1997; Milgram & Kishino, 1994). Azuma (1997) identified three characteristics of AR as follows: 1) it combines the real and the virtual; 2) it is interactive in real time; and 3) it registers in three dimensions (p. 356). AR has been applied in many fields, such as the military, industry, the private sector, medicine, advertising, and marketing applications, and now it has also begun to be used in education. AR applications are used in various educational disciplines, including sciences, social sciences, history, and mathematics (Carmigniani & Furht, 2011).

AR technology has a significant impact on teaching as it combines the teaching materials of the real and virtual worlds and allows teachers or students to control these materials. Using AR, students can have rich experiences and can extend their learning. In addition, given the growing interest and investment in AR by technology companies, students studying with these technologies will benefit from entrepreneurship in their future professional careers (NMC Horizon, 2016). Researchers have described five directions of AR in educational environments (Yuen, Yaoyuneyong, & Johnson, 2011):

- Discovery-based Learning
- Objects Modeling
- AR Books
- Skills Training
- AR Gaming

AR applications enable students to take a different perspective, which increases their affinity for text-based course material. Pictures, text, sounds, 3D objects, or 2D and 3D animations are common in the AR applications used in education (Wang et al., 2013). In this context, well-designed practices targeting the course objectives ensure the active participation of students and the permanence of knowledge gains (Küçük, Yılmaz, & Göktaş, 2014). AR technology enables the development of materials with virtual objects to be placed in the real world where abstract content and terms are embodied, allowing different learning styles and providing a student-centered perspective in a flexible and fun learning process (Özarslan, 2013). It is considered especially important to embody abstract concepts with AR applications. Yin, Song, Tabata, Ogata & Hwang (2013) stated that AR is quite effective in embodying abstract concepts. Kerawalla et al. (2006) stated that AR applications were successful in attracting students' interest to the lesson, and they were also effective in teaching the subjects by providing 3D images of subjects or objects from different angles that are difficult to cognitively grasp. Radu (2014) noted multiple learning benefits of AR, including: 1) increased content understanding, 2) long-term memory retention, 3) improved physical task performance, 4) improved collaboration, and 5) increased student motivation. In addition, Diegmann, Schmidt-Kraepelin, Eynden & Basten (2015) categorized the benefits of AR in educational environments within six categories:

1. State of Mind
    a. Increased Motivation.
    b. Increased Attention.
    c. Increased Concentration.
    d. Increased Satisfaction.
2. Teaching Concepts
    a. Increased Student-centered Learning.
    b. Improved Collaborative Learning.
3. Presentation
    a. Increased Details.
    b. Increased Information Accessibility.
    c. Increased Interactivity.
4. Learning Type
    a. Improved Learning Curve.
    b. Increased Creativity.
5. Content Understanding
    a. Improved Development of Spatial Abilities.
    b. Improved Memory.
6. Reduced Costs

With the AR applications that are being developed, students will be able to see materials they cannot access in the classroom environment in three dimensions (Billinghurst, 2002). AR applications, which were previously used in larger devices, have been used in mobile phones with this developing technology. In this way, it is easier for these applications to be introduced to classroom environments. AR has been used in the creation of the enriched educational environments needed to provide real learning experiences, where multiple senses can be actively used together with AR applications (Lai & Hsu, 2011). In this way, it benefits learners by combining skills and knowledge in a permanent way with the world in which they live. In addition to these benefits, AR encourages students to use their imagination and creativity (Klopfer & Yoon, 2004). Essentially, AR is student-centered, constructive, participatory, collaborative, interactive, cognitively rich, creative, challenging, problem-solving-oriented, meaningful, attractive, fun, and motivating (Dunleavy, Dede, & Mitchell, 2009; Kerawalla, Luckin, Selijefot, & Woolard, 2006). It is stated that AR applications also have positive effects on students' social relationships (Gopalan, Zulkifli, & Bakar, 2016). Somyürek (2014) stated that the use of AR in the field of education can:

- Add a third dimension to books.
- Train students in tasks that require cognitive and psychomotor skills.
- Provide three-dimensional displays in the field of science (physics, chemistry, biology) to show the relationships between concepts.
- Assist in museum education.
- Demonstrate concepts and spatial relationships in mathematics and geometry.
- Help to visualize concepts in geography education.
- Assist in health education.
- Assist in engineering education.

Kaufmann and Schmalstieg (2003) examined the effects of AR applications on students in mathematics and geometry courses. According to their findings, AR applications facilitate learning in geometry and mathematics courses, and they reached the conclusion that students developed stronger spatial skills. However, there are some difficulties in the use of AR applications for teaching and learning. A lack of materials and teachers' limited knowledge of how to use AR are among the main challenges. Durak and Karaoğlan Yılmaz (2019) highlighted that a lack of Internet access and lack of materials are the biggest problems for AR implementation.

BACKGROUND

Augmented Reality in Math Education

A large number of students consider mathematics to be a challenging subject because it consists of abstract concepts. Thus, the integration of AR applications into mathematics lessons can be considered as an alternative tool to embody abstract concepts. Sayımer and Küçüksaraç (2015) stated that the use of AR applications makes lessons and subjects more fun and attractive, and students' interest remains focused on the subject for a longer time. The NCTM (2014) stated that technology must be an essential tool in the classroom for meaningful mathematical learning. "Technology includes interactive whiteboards and a wide range of handheld, tablet, laptop, and desktop-based devices that can be used to help students make sense of mathematics, engage in mathematical reasoning, and communicate mathematically" (NCTM, 2014, p. 78). Visual materials are often used in mathematics education, especially to teach geometry concepts. Technological devices such as computers, mobile phones, and tablets are among the materials used in geometry teaching because they attract students' attention.

In particular, AR has the potential to be used in mathematics education because of the nature of the discipline. Estapa and Nadolny (2015) stated that "mathematics instruction is a natural fit for AR with benefits in manipulation, visualization, and authentic contexts" (p. 40). In courses on geographical landforms, for example, students cannot see each landform live or in three-dimensional geometric shapes. Hence, several studies suggested using AR applications in mathematics education. For example, Kaufmann and Schmalstieg (2003) developed a 3D AR application, Construct3D, for math and geometry thinking to observe the development of students' spatial skills. In this study, the researchers gave small cards containing barcodes of geometric shapes to students. The study concluded that the AR application provided a rich learning experience for learners and increased the students' understanding of three-dimensional geometry by making spatial relationships and complex three-dimensional structures visible. In addition to direct integration, AR applications were also implemented in a game format. For example, Dunleavy, Dede & Mitchell (2009) developed an AR game for middle and high school students, Alien Contact, to teach mathematics, language arts, and scientific literacy. The game allows students to solve problems and puzzles. The results showed that AR increased students' motivation and understanding of mathematics and their development of literacy skills.

Di Serio, Ibáñez, and Kloos (2013) found that the use of AR applications has positive impacts on students' attention, confidence, and interests. In another study investigating the relationship between the academic process, motivation, and participation of university students, Fonseca et al. (2013) conducted an experimental study, and concluded that the use of AR increased the motivation of the students and that AR is a good system for visualizing simple models, but less useful for visualizing detailed ones. The researchers also found that AR motivated students; increased their graphic abilities, spatial skills, academic performances, and levels of interest; and made students more active while providing significant spatial improvements.

Textbooks were another medium in which the AR technologies were integrated. For example, Gutierrez et al. (2010) designed an image-based AR book called AR-Dehaes. Using a webcam, 3D virtual models can be displayed on the screen by adding them to the image, and students can view 3D objects from all angles. As a result of that study, it was found that the use of AR developed the students' spatial skills. In addition, the study showed that students had a positive attitude towards AR-assisted education.

In the research results discussed here, AR-assisted teaching improved students' spatial skills, made students more active during the application, kept their interest in the course high, and increased their motivation. Students and teachers found it easy to use AR technology and were satisfied with the teaching.

Augmented Reality in Geometry Education

The subject of geometry involves the properties of geometric objects and shapes and their relations with each other. To make abstract concepts in geometry understandable for students, students should encounter the abstractions in geometry with the real objects in their daily lives (NCTM, 2000). In addition to finding geometric shapes in nature, Toptaş (2008) recommended that the analysis of geometric structures such as edges and angles on real objects and manipulatives should be used during geometry teaching. Geometry is an important part of the mathematics curriculum at every grade level, and the content of geometric shapes is one of the core subjects in the elementary mathematics curriculum. The goal of geometry education is to assist individuals in the process of establishing relations in their own world and realizing that their reasoning power should be the basic principle (Toptaş, 2008).

Clements (2004) stated that geometry instruction is taught to students in a very limited way. For example, students are able to recognize circles, but they experience problems in sorting squares (Clements, Swaminathan, Hannibal, & Sarama, 1999). In addition, identifying rectangles and triangles is difficult for most students (Clements, 2004). The importance of geometric concepts and features, and the relationships between them, should be paramount for those who teach geometry. However, geometric shapes cannot be taught effectively on worksheets; students should be allowed to embody geometric concepts by using concrete materials or computer software during the teaching process to recognize mathematical relationships more quickly. The NCTM (2000) emphasizes that in the context of supporting students' spatial skills, the geometry learning process should include various visual tools and methods. Clements (1998) stated that young children effectively learn about geometric shapes when manipulatives, drawings, and computers are integrated into the classroom and students engage with them.

Thornton et al. (2012) suggested that utilizing AR in the teaching and learning environment could increase students' spatial and visual abilities. In addition, other studies (e.g., Hartman & Bertoline, 2005; Kaufmann & Schmalstieg, 2003; Martín-Gutierrez, Trujillo, & Acosta-Gonzalez, 2013) found that the use of AR applications improved students' spatial abilities. Spatial skills have been linked to students' success in many fields, including mathematics, science, and astronomy. Spatial ability is one of the most significant cognitive features in learning geometry, and learning activities that are designed based on spatial visualization could improve geometric learning (Christou et al., 2007).

Examining the effects of AR applications on spatial abilities and academic achievements of students in a mathematics course, Gün (2014) conducted an experimental study with pre-test, post-test, and control groups with sixth-grade students. While the experimental group worked on geometry lessons with AR applications for 4 weeks, the control group worked with 2D drawings drawn on the blackboard. As a result of the study, it was determined that there was no significant difference between the control group and the post-test scores in terms of the students' spatial abilities and academic achievements.

Similarly, Gecü-Parmaksız (2017) conducted an experimental study to investigate the difference between the use of AR applications and physical manipulatives in teaching geometric shapes at the preschool level. AR applications were used for the teaching of geometric shapes in the experimental group and similar activities were carried out with physical objects in the control group. The results showed that AR applications had a positive effect on preschool students' spatial skills. However, there was no significant difference found in the classification of the circle shape between the groups.

When the studies in the literature are examined, the number of studies using AR applications in the field of education is quite high, and the number of studies in the field of AR technology has increased in recent years. However, studies on AR in mathematics and geometry teaching are limited. AR applications are less studied in the fields of elementary education because samples are not easily accessible, and the development of usable AR applications is not easy for these sample groups (Kara, 2018). However, the use of materials and/or technology at the elementary level allows students to better understand abstract concepts at a concrete thinking level, and AR applications are an important tool to teach such subjects concretely to primary school students.

MAIN FOCUS OF THE CHAPTER

Technology has become increasingly important in solving the problems experienced in classrooms. Geometry, a sub-branch of mathematics, also challenges primary school students with the abstractness of the concepts and topics. In a report published by the NCTM (2000), it was stated that three-dimensional shapes are important in teaching geometry and that teachers should encourage students to use their spatial skills. It was also stated that all of our senses should be used in geometry teaching (Royal Society, 2001). Piaget (1971) explained that in order to understand mathematical concepts, students need concrete materials with many experiences (as cited in Byoung, 2001). However, this takes place with two-dimensional shapes in teaching materials such as geometric bodies, boards, and textbooks in traditional education and especially in rural education. That prevents or complicates students' visualization in three dimensions (Accascina & Rogora, 2006). These difficulties and inadequate teaching methods have had important consequences. In light of all this information, it is seen that new teaching methods should be tried in the field of mathematics and applications that facilitate teaching should also be tried. That is why the field of mathematics was chosen as the focus of this study. In addition, another point that makes this research important is that it was carried out in three different locations, namely in a city center, a district, and a village. In this regard, it can be said that another aim of this research is to investigate the usability and effects of technology in different situations.

In summary, the aim of this study is to examine students' knowledge of shapes, as well as the views of the students and their teachers about the use of AR applications in teaching and learning geometry in a second-grade mathematics course. It is important to carry out research focusing on the opinions of students and teachers in the process of AR applications, especially in elementary school settings. Also, because the study sites are schools in different regions of the country, both geographically and socio-economically, this work provides information about the use of AR technologies in diverse settings. The following research questions drove this study:

1. How does second-grade students' knowledge of shapes develop through the use of AR applications in mathematics courses?
2. How does second-grade students' learning of shapes change in schools with different contextual factors?

RESEARCH METHODS

A convergent parallel mixed methods research design was employed. This particular research design was intended to compare and contrast statistical results with qualitative data for corroboration and validation, thus triangulating the quantitative and qualitative methods (Creswell & Plano Clark, 2010). In addition, the findings derived from three public schools in regions that are geographically and socioeconomically different were compared and contrasted in order to explore the contextual factors affecting the participating students' learning processes.

In the quantitative portion, a one-group pre-test/post-test design was used. "A one-group pretest-posttest design is a quasi-experimental research design in which the same dependent variable is measured in one group of participants before (pretest) and after (posttest) a treatment is administered" (Privitera & Ahlgrim-Delzell, 2019, p. 337). The qualitative portion of the study was conducted as a case study.

The case study method was selected in order to explore the phenomena (the participants' views on AR applications and their learning of shapes) within the context (the schools located in different regions) in which they occurred and from the perspectives of the participants (the teachers and their students) involved in the phenomena (Gall, Borg, & Gall, 1996). In order to explore contextual patterns and differences, a multiple case study design was chosen. Using multiple cases strengthens the findings by comparing and contrasting the patterns, thus increasing the robustness of the results (Yin, 1994).

Data Collection Tools

For in-depth investigations, data must be gathered from a variety of different sources. Thus, the data collected for this study come from tests on the knowledge of shapes, as well as semi-structured interviews with students and their teachers and open-ended questionnaires.

The test of the knowledge of shapes measures the students' knowledge of geometric shapes via photographs of historical scenes. The students were expected to find triangular prisms, cylinders, triangles, and rectangular shapes from these images. One of the goals of applying this test, according to the Turkish Ministry of National Education (2018) and the mathematics curriculum, is to help students associate the learning of geometric objects with everyday life and different civilizations while noticing geometric objects in works of art.

During the test development phase, the researchers decided the pictures and/or photographs used in the test questions. The relevance of the pictures and photos were taken into consideration, as well as the students' capacity. Then, the pictures and photographs used in the test were decided as follows: Egyptian pyramids, Stonehenge, Ephesus, the paintings of Kent Paulette and Gray Artus. After the test was designed, the opinions of experts were taken. The test was applied as a pre- and post-test in order to explore the changes in the participating students' knowledge and awareness of shapes through the instructional intervention.

The qualitative data in this study were obtained from semi-structured interviews and open-ended questionnaires. The semi-structured interview protocols for teachers and students focused on their views on the use of AR applications in mathematics courses. The interviews helped the researchers obtain in-depth knowledge about the participants' views on AR integration, as well as how these views had been formed through their experiences in teaching and learning. The interviews were conducted with both teachers and students after the instructional intervention. The interviews with the teachers took about 45 minutes, whereas each student interview was about 15 minutes long.

Research Context and Participants

This study examined the process and outcomes of the use of AR applications in teaching geometry in second-grade mathematics courses in the context of three different primary schools. For this purpose, the standards related to geometric shapes were first determined in the second-grade mathematics curriculum. The concepts addressed in the curriculum were listed as circle, cube, square prism, rectangular prism, triangular prism, sphere, and cylinder. Secondly, AR programs were investigated. As a result of this investigation, the Quiver app was chosen because it was convenient in terms of the content and access.

A purposive sampling method was used in the study while selecting the study group. In the purposive sampling method, a sample that is believed to provide the information needed by the researcher is selected based on the purpose of the research (Frankel, Wallen, & Hyun, 2012). While determining the study group, the following criteria were taken into consideration:

- Application classes begin in the second grade of primary school.
- Classes in different geographies (city, district, village) and with different socioeconomic levels should be considered.

In this context, the participants of the study comprised three primary school second-grade teachers and the students from these teachers' classrooms. The teachers worked in different regions of the country. Two of the teachers worked at schools located in rural areas, while the third teacher worked at an urban school. There were nineteen students in the first school, eight students in the second school, and eight students in the third school. The distribution of teachers and students is shown in Table 1.

Table 1. Distribution of Teachers and Students

Schools	Teachers	Students
School 1	T1	S1-S19
School 2	T2	S20-S27
School 3	T3	S28-S35

School 1

School 1 was located in a rural area. In this region, especially rural children may be disadvantaged than children living in urban areas. Children of families in this region are mostly seasonal agricultural workers. Therefore, socio-economic levels are slightly low. 19 students in School 1 participated in this study. The teacher of the participating class has been teaching in the setting for 3 years. The teacher stated that the academic success of the students in this school was average and the students' socioeconomic status was low. Some fathers were unemployed, and some mothers were housewives. The teacher taught the topic of geometric shapes using the AR application. While talking about geometric shapes in the introduction, the teacher received a file of the geometric shapes found in the Quiver program that he had received earlier. He distributed those files to the students. The students painted these black and white geometric shapes, coloring them in. After painting, the students saw the three-dimensional state of the geometric objects with the Quiver program installed on the smart phones. Because the students did not have their own smartphones, their families were contacted and the students used their families' phones on the day of the implementation. In order to observe the students' development in the lesson after the application, the post-test was applied. In the final part, semi-structured interviews were held with the students. After interviewing the teacher, the data collection part of the study was complete for School 1.

School 2

School 2 was located in another rural area. In this region, the socio-economic level of people may be lower than those living in urban areas. Children of families in this region are also seasonal agricultural workers. Eight students in School 2 participated in this study. The teacher of the participating class has been working in the setting for 4 years. He stated that the students' academic success was low. He also stated that the students were engaged in seasonal agricultural labor. Accordingly, the socioeconomic level of the students was also low. Since the school is in a village, the facilities are slightly more limited than those of schools in cities. Students do not always come to school as they go to help their families in the fields as summer approaches. For this reason, the teacher stated that they conduct lessons faster than schools in the city, to finish the subjects before the students leave. Before the application, a test consisting of visuals was carried out to monitor changes in the students' knowledge of geometric shapes. The teacher began the topic of geometric shapes. While talking about geometric shapes in the introduction, he received a file of the geometric shapes found in the Quiver program that he had received earlier. He distributed these files to the students. The students painted these black and white geometric shapes, coloring them in. After painting, the students saw the three-dimensional state of the geometric objects with the Quiver program installed on phones. In order to observe the students' development in the lesson, after the application, another test was administered to the students. In the final part, semi-structured interviews were held with the students. After interviewing the teacher, the data collection part of the study was complete for School 2.

School 3

School 3 was located in a large city. The teacher of the participating class has been working in the setting for 5 years. Nineteen students in School 3 participated in this study. It was stated by the teacher that the socioeconomic level of the school was high, and the students who participated in the application had high levels of academic success. The fathers of the students were engaged in commerce, while their mothers were housewives. Before the application, a test consisting of visuals was carried out to monitor the change in the students' knowledge of geometric shapes. The teacher introduced the topic of geometric shapes. While talking about geometric shapes in the introduction, he received a file of the geometric shapes found in the Quiver program that he had received earlier. He distributed these files to the students. The students painted these black and white geometric shapes, coloring them in. After painting, the students saw the three-dimensional state of the geometric objects with the Quiver program installed on phones. In order to observe the students' development in the lesson after the application, another test was administered to the students. In the final part, semi-structured interviews were held with the students. After interviewing the teacher, the data collection part of the study was complete for School 3.

Quiver Program

In this research, the Quiver program was the preferred AR application. In the Quiver program, users can paint by taking various shapes, animals, and other things from the library available at http://www.quivervision.com/. After the Quiver application is opened on a mobile device, the images appear in three dimensions after scanning the data matrix. The Quiver program was chosen because it is cost-effective, suitable for the students' ability, and easy to use on mobile devices, and it contains suitable content for the desired knowledge gains. In previous studies, it was stated that the Quiver program is suitable for elementary school students (Mota, Ruiz-Rube, Dodero, & Figueiredo, 2016; Panciroli, Macauda, & Russo, 2018). One previous study applied the Quiver program to investigate the effect of AR applications on student attitudes. Students in the sixth grade used the applications in the "Life Begins with Cells" unit of the science course. The study was experimentally designed with a pre-test and post-test. It was concluded that AR practices create positive developments in students' attitudes (Günel & Demir, 2018).

Augmented Reality Application (Quiver) in the Study

In this study, an AR application was chosen because AR allows students to view models better and embodies mathematics contents. Students can view abstract concepts in the visual presentations of objects while using an AR application. AR is easy to use and attractive for students (Hsu, Lin, & Yang, 2017), and the easiness and affordability of AR are among the reasons to use it in education.

AR application was used in the "Geometric Objects and Shapes" unit of elementary school second-grade mathematics lessons. The students in these three schools interacted with the Quiver App for three weeks. In order to measure students' awareness of geometric shapes before the application was carried out, illustrations made by some painters with geometric shapes and photos of some historical monuments were collected in a pool. Afterwards, these pictures and photographs were selected for use by obtaining the opinions of the participating second-grade teachers; after a discussion the researchers chose the appropriate ones. In order to increase the reliability of the research, geometric objects and shapes were applied one week before the pre-test application so that the students would not remember them. According to the Turkish Ministry of National Education (2020), the content made available from this unit for students should help them to:

a) Categorize geometric shapes according to the number of sides and corners.
b) Create structures using shape models, and draw the structures they create.
c) Recognize and distinguish cubes, square prisms, rectangular prisms, triangular prisms, cylinders, and spheres in the models.
d) Realize that geometrical features and shapes do not change when their direction, position, or size changes.

The terms related to this unit are stated as "circle, cube, square prism, rectangular prism, triangular prism, sphere, cylinder" (Ministry of Education, 2020). In this context, when teachers implement the "Geometric Objects and Shapes" unit, it is preferred to use content for these gains and terms from the Quiver application. The materials used are shown in Figure 1.

Figure 1. Materials used in the application

During the application, the teachers distributed these papers to the students and explained the geometric shapes and objects. Later, the students painted these papers in the colors of their choice. They used the Quiver application on mobile devices to see the three-dimensional versions of the shapes they painted. As a last step, the test of the knowledge of shapes was applied to the students. Visuals related to the student practices are shown in Figure 2.

Figure 2. Student's Practices

Data Analysis

In this study, a quasi-experimental study with pre-test and post-test without a control group was conducted. The knowledge test data was normally distributed as the skewness kurtosis coefficients were in the range of ±1.5 (Tabachnick & Fidell, 2013), so parametric tests were used in the analysis of the data. The results obtained from the pre- and post-test implementation of the questionnaire were analyzed via paired sample t-test. On the other hand, the data derived from the interviews and open-ended questionnaires were analyzed by using a content analysis method. After transcribing the qualitative data, the organization of codes including codes, categories, and themes was performed. The data were coded by each researcher, and then each version was reviewed together to see if the agreement between the coders was high enough. Qualitative findings were presented via pseudonyms such as S1 and S2 for students and T1 and T2 for teachers, as shown in Table 1.

FINDINGS

Second-Grade Students' Knowledge of Shapes Develop Through the Use of AR Applications in Mathematics Courses

The paired sample t-test was used to determine the differences between the pre-test and post-test results. The results of the paired sample t-test are given in Table 2.

Table. 2 Paired sample t-test results

	N	Mean	SD	Min	Max	t	p
Pre-test	35	7.54	3.21	4.00	25.00	-2.17	0.037
Post-test	35	8.91	5.07	6.00	30.00		

The results indicated that AR did increase the students' knowledge of shapes. The mean score for the pre-test was 7.54 (*SD* = 3.21) and the mean score for the post-test was 8.91 (*SD* = 5.08), showing that there is a significant difference between the pre-test and the post-test ($t(34)= -2.173$; $p < 0.05$).

The qualitative data collected in this study illustrated the participants' observations and views about the use of AR technologies. The data indicated that the students particularly found the integration of AR technologies very effective. Most students said that *they learned and had fun at the same time while using AR applications in their classes (i.e., S35; S24; S19; S15; S3)*. They stated that they actively participated in the learning processes, as well as taking responsibility for their own learning. The participants constantly repeated that they *learned better and were more motivated (e.g., S1; S5; S11; S20, S32)* while using the AR applications in learning geometrical shapes. Another essential finding that emerged from the interview data was the comparison between AR-integrated and usual mathematics classes. The students emphasized that the AR-integrated learning processes were more effective and meaningful. Some suggested that this was the result of *embodying abstract geometrical concepts via real-world illustrations (i.e., S12, S15, S21).*

In addition to the students, the teachers who implemented AR-integrated mathematics instruction highlighted the positive impacts of AR applications on their students' learning. They particularly emphasized the role of AR technologies for enriching students' abstract thinking. Moreover, the *students better understand the existence of geometrical shapes in daily life objects (T3)*, according to one of the teachers. The following excerpt shows how the teachers explained the potential of AR applications in geometry instruction:

You cannot explain, you cannot tell the child what the purpose of this triangle is if you begin with the geometric shapes topic directly, but when you introduce the topic with the app, the child can understand the purpose when you say there is a triangle or rectangle. Especially in this way, the mathematical science style becomes more effective in abstract lessons (T3).

Another teacher stated that the use of AR technologies can help students learn geometry concepts permanently, as well as having the ability to integrate these concepts in their daily lives. Finally, it was reported that the integration of AR technologies *enhanced students' visual memories (i.e., T1, T2, T3)*, thus positively affecting permanent learning.

Second-Grade Students' Learning of Shapes Changing With Different Contextual Factors

Since the data is normally distributed for each school, the researchers conducted a paired sample t-test between the pre-test and post-test mean scores of each school (Table 3).

Table 3. Pre-test and post-test results by school

		n	Mean	SD	Min.	Max.	t	p
School 1	Pre-test	19	6.21	2.72	0	12	0.81	0.43
	Post-test	19	5.63	3.33	0	12		
School 2	Pre-test	8	8.37	3.25	3	14	-1.98	0.88
	Post-test	8	9.87	2.03	7	13		
School 3	Pre-test	8	9.87	2.95	5	13	-7.67	0.00
	Post-test	8	15.75	2.96	11	19		

Table 3 shows that students' knowledge of shapes in School 3 increased significantly comparing the pre-test and post-test [$t(7)=-7.67$, $p<0.05$], while no significant difference was found between the pre-test and post-test mean scores of students' knowledge of shapes for School 2 [$t(_{7})=-1.98$, $p=0.88$], and for School 1 [$t(_{18})=0.81$, $p<0.05$].

The qualitative analysis also supported the findings above. The teachers working in the rural schools (School 1 and School 2) complained about the usability of the application in their classes due to disadvantages such as class size and lack of access to technologies. In addition, these teachers emphasized their students' lack of experience in using digital technologies. Hence, these disadvantages resulted in them not being able to take full advantage of the integration of AR technologies.

On the other hand, one of the teachers particularly highlighted a benefit of AR applications that was specific to his setting. Since the students in his school were transported from the villages around the school, an application that can be carried via a mobile device or a flash disk was an important advantage for teaching:

I work in a rural school. This is advantageous as it is an application that can be installed on a portable device for village schools and joined classrooms. It is more effective in central schools and places with high advantages (T1).

The teachers in rural schools also shared that their students usually struggled to understand mathematical and geometrical concepts because most of their students could not read. By using a visual medium in teaching those concepts, the students having difficulties in other subject areas were able to understand the content better via AR technologies.

In summary, the differences in the students' knowledge of shapes from urban and rural schools were detailed based on qualitative analysis. The contextual differences between the schools were portrayed by the participating teachers, as well as how those contextual differences between the three schools affected students' learning of geometrical concepts via AR applications.

DISCUSSION AND CONCLUSION

This study aimed to examine students' knowledge of shapes as well as the views of the students and their teachers about the use of AR applications in teaching and learning geometry in second-grade mathematics lessons. The quantitative findings indicated a significant difference between the mean pre-test and post-test scores for students' knowledge of shapes. This result shows that the AR application in the second-grade mathematics lessons positively affected the students' knowledge of shapes. Meanwhile, the qualitative findings revealed that both students and their teachers considered AR technologies as a facilitator for learning geometrical shapes.

Geometry was identified as one of the required mathematical skills in international reports such as the Programme for International Student Assessment (PISA) and the Trends in International Mathematics and Science Study (TIMSS), and geometry skills are of priority among mathematics educators and researchers (Lin, Chen, & Chang, 2015). The findings of this study showed that even though both teachers and students acknowledged the complexity of geometrical concepts, the students better understood the geometrical concepts. Hence, the results showed that AR-integrated mathematics instruction in the second grade positively affected students' knowledge, learning, and awareness of geometrical shapes. The literature (Kaufmann Steinbügl, Dünser, & Glück, 2005; Martín-Gutiérrez et al., 2010; Lin, Chen, & Chang, 2015) reveals similar results about the use of AR applications in mathematics lessons.

The findings of this study indicated positive outcomes, such as learning, motivation, and enjoyment, for the participating students from different regions. In addition to the test scores, the statements from both the teachers and their students showed that AR-integrated math instruction helped the students have rich and effective learning experiences. The literature also supports the claim that the use of AR technologies enhances students' active participation and motivation (Kerawalla et al., 2006; Özarslan, 2013; Sayımer & Küçüksaraç, 2015; Sayımer & Küçüksaraç, 2015), as well as their learning (Kaufmann & Schmalstieg, 2003; Küçük, Yılmaz, & Göktaş, 2014; Radu, 204). In addition, Garzón and Acevedo (2019) stated that AR has a medium effect on the learning gains of students. This study showed that, regardless of the socioeconomic context, both teachers and students found this particular technology quite helpful in the teaching and learning of mathematics and geometry concepts.

The data in this study were collected from both urban and rural settings in order to understand if there were particular advantages and disadvantages for each setting. Even though the quantitative findings of the study indicated that there was not a significant difference between the pre- and post-test results of the students in rural schools, the qualitative data showed that the use of AR technologies provided richer teaching and learning experiences for teachers and students in all three settings. To illustrate, because the AR application was a mobile technology, the teachers working in rural areas were able to integrate it into their classes easily in spite of the lack of classroom technologies. In addition, the mobile technology helped teachers use more student-centered pedagogies. Hence, students actively and collaboratively participated in the activities and took responsibility for their own learning. These findings are supported by the literature (Diegmann, Schmidt-Kraepelin, Eynden, & Basten, 2015; Dunleavy, Dede, & Mitchell, 2009; Kerawalla, Luckin, Selijefot, & Woolard, 2006), which argues that AR technologies provide more student-centered, interactive, and collaborative learning experiences for students.

Despite the positive outcomes stated above, this study also revealed some downsides of using AR applications in different settings. The teachers in the rural schools sometimes criticized the usability of the application in their classrooms. Some of those criticisms were their students' lack of access to digital technologies, as well as their lack of experiences in using these technologies. Based on his review of the literature, Schoepp (2015) listed problems with access as one of the most cited barriers to technology integration. Various studies also supported this claim (Keengwe, Onchwari, & Wachira, 2008). The lack of access and experience was a strong factor that results with students not being able to fully take advantage of the learning process, especially in the rural settings.

FUTURE RESEARCH DIRECTIONS

It has been observed that there are very few applications that have been developed commercially in the field of mathematics and geometry with AR and that offer educational benefits free of charge in application stores. The most frequently used applications are Arloon Geometry, GeoGebra Augmented Reality, and Cleverbooks Geometry. These applications offer users the opportunity to practice with 3D materials in a real environment for geometry and mathematics education.

This study indicated that the school located in the urban area showed more significant differences than the others in rural areas. Qualitative studies can be carried out to investigate the reasons behind the differences between those schools. A longer intervention with AR applications can help researchers understand the effects on students' learning and attitudes.

Jacobsen, Clifford, and Friesen (2002) stated that "when you begin to think differently about technology and learning and you have different spaces in which to learn and teach, you can design different approaches to learning" (p. 27). Different approaches to design AR technologies integrated learning processes can be useful to have a more comprehensive understanding of the learning gains on students.

REFERENCES

Ölçme & Başkanlığı. (2019). *2019 YKS Değerlendirme Raporu. 2019*. Academic Press.

Accascina, G., & Rogora, E. (2006). Using Cabri3d diagrams for teaching geometry. *The International Journal for Technology in Mathematics Education, 13*(1), 11–22.

Azuma, R., Baillot, Y., Behringer, R., Feiner, S., Julier, S., & Macintyre, B. (2001). Recent advances in augmented reality. *Computer and Graphics and Applications IEEE*, 34-47.

Azuma, R. T. (1997). A survey of augmented reality. *Presence (Cambridge, Mass.), 6*(4), 355–385. doi:10.1162/pres.1997.6.4.355

Billinghurst, M. (2002). Augmented reality in education. *New Horizons for Learning*, *12*(5), 1–5.

Byoung, G. A. (2001). Using calculators in mathematics education in korean elementary schools. *Journal of the Korea Society of Mathematical Education Series D: Research in Mathematical Education*, *5*(2), 107–118.

Christou, C., Jones, K., Pitta-Pantazi, D., Pittalis, M., Mousoulides, N., Matos, J. F., Sendova, E., Zachariades, T., & Boytchev, P. (2007). *Developing student spatial ability with 3D software applications.* Paper presented at the 5th Congress of the European Society for Research in Mathematics Education (CERME), Larnaca, Cyprus.

Clements, D. (1998). *Geometric and Spatial Thinking in Young Children.* Retrieved from https://files.eric.ed.gov/fulltext/ED436232.pdf

Clements, D. H. (1999). Concrete manipulatives, concrete ideas. *Contemporary Issues in Early Childhood*, *1*(1), 45–60. doi:10.2304/ciec.2000.1.1.7

Clements, D. H. (2004). Geometric and spatial thinking in early childhood education. *Engaging young children in mathematics: Standards for early childhood mathematics education*, 267-297.

Clements, D. H., Swaminathan, S., Hannibal, M. A. Z., & Sarama, J. (1999). Young Children's Concepts of Shape. *Journal for Research in Mathematics Education*, *30*(2), 192–212. doi:10.2307/749610

Creswell, J. W., & Plano Clark, V. L. (2010). *Designing and Conducting Mixed Methods Research.* Sage.

Di Serio, Á., Ibáñez, M. B., & Kloos, C. D. (2013). Impact of an augmented reality system on students' motivation for a visual art course. *Computers & Education*, *68*, 586–596. doi:10.1016/j.compedu.2012.03.002

Dunleavy, M., Dede, C., & Mitchell, R. (2009). Affordances and limitations of immersive participatory augmented reality simulations for teaching and learning. *Journal of Science Education and Technology*, *18*(1), 7–22. doi:10.100710956-008-9119-1

Dunleavy, M., Dede, C., & Mitchell, R. (2009). Affordances and Limitations of Immersive Participatory Augmented Reality Simulations for Teaching and Learning. *Journal of Science Education and Technology*, *18*(1), 7–22. doi:10.100710956-008-9119-1

Durak, A., & Karaoğlan-Yilmaz, F. G. (2019). Artırılmış gerçekliğin eğitsel uygulamaları üzerine ortaokul öğrencilerinin görüşleri. *Bolu Abant İzzet Baysal Üniversitesi Eğitim Fakültesi Dergisi*, *19*(2), 468–481. doi:10.17240/aibuefd.2019.19.46660-425148

Estapa, A., & Nadolny, L. (2015). The Effect of an Augmented Reality Enhanced Mathematics Lesson on Student Achievement and Motivation. *Journal of STEM Education*, *16*(3), 40–48.

Fonseca, D., Martí, N., Redondo, E., Navarro, I., & Sánchez, A. (2014). Relationship between student profile, tool use, participation, and academic performance with the use of Augmented Reality technology for visualized architecture models. *Computers in Human Behavior*, *31*, 434–445. doi:10.1016/j.chb.2013.03.006

Frankel, J. R., Wallen, N. E., & Hyun, H. H. (2012). *How to Design and Evaluate Research in Education* (8th ed.). McGraw-Hill.

Gall, M. D., Borg, W. R., & Gall, J. P. (1996). *Educational research: An introduction* (6th ed.). Longman.

Garzón, J., & Acevedo, J. (2019). Meta-analysis of the impact of Augmented Reality on students' learning gains. *Educational Research Review*, *27*, 244–260. doi:10.1016/j.edurev.2019.04.001

Gay, L. R., Mills, G. E., & Airasian, P. (2012). Educational Research. New Jersey: S4Carlisle Publishing Services.

Gecü-Parmaksız, Z. (2017). *Augmented reality activities for children: a comparative analysis on understanding geometric shapes and improving spatial skills* (Ph.D Thesis). Middle East Technical University Computer Education and Instructional Technology Department, Ankara.

Gopalan, V., Zulkifli, A. N., & Bakar, J. A. A. (2016). A study of students' motivation using the augmented reality science textbook. *Proceedings of AIP Conference*, 1761(1). 10.1063/1.4960880

Gün, E. (2014). *Artırılmış gerçeklik uygulamalarının öğrencilerin uzamsal yeteneklerine etkisi. Yüksek Lisans Tezi*. Gazi Üniversitesi Eğitim Bilimleri Enstitüsü, Bilgisayar ve Öğretim Teknolojileri Eğitimi Anabilim Dalı.

Hsu, Y., Lin, Y., & Yang, B. (2017). Impact of augmented reality lessons on students' STEM interest. *Research and Practice in Technology Enhanced Learning*, *12*(2). Advance online publication. doi:10.118641039-016-0039-z

Johnson, L., Adams Becker, S., Cummins, M., Estrada, V., Freeman, A., & Hall, C. (2016). *NMC Horizon Report: 2016 Higher Education Edition*. The New Media Consortium.

Kaarbo, J., & Beasley, R. K. (1999). A practical guide to the comparative case study method in political psychology. *Political Psychology*, *20*(2), 369–391. doi:10.1111/0162-895X.00149

Kara, A. (2018). *Artirilmiş gerçeklik uygulamalarinin eğitimde kullanilmasina yönelik arastirmlarin incelenmesi. Yüksek Lisans Tezi*. Ataturk Üniversitesi Eğitim Bilimleri Enstitüsü, Bilgisayar ve Öğretim Teknolojileri Eğitimi Anabilim Dalı.

Kaufmann, H., & Schmalstieg, D. (2003). Mathematics and geometry education with collaborative augmented reality. *Computers & Graphics*, *27*(3), 339–345. doi:10.1016/S0097-8493(03)00028-1

Kaufmann, H., Steinbügl, K., Dünser, A., & Glück, J. (2005). General training of spatial abilities by geometry education in augmented reality. *Annual Review of CyberTherapy and Telemedicine: A Decade of VR, 3*, 65-76.

Keengwe, J., Onchwari, G., & Wachira, P. (2008). Computer technology integration and student learning: Barriers and promise. *Journal of Science Education and Technology*, *17*(6), 560–565. doi:10.100710956-008-9123-5

Kerawalla, L., Luckin, R., Selijefot, S., & Woolard, A. (2006). Making it real: Exploring the potential of augmented reality for teaching primary school science. *Virtual Reality (Waltham Cross)*, *10*(3-4), 163–174. doi:10.100710055-006-0036-4

Klopfer, E., & Yoon, S. (2004). Developing games and simulations for today and tomorrow's tech savvy youth. *TechTrends*, *49*(3), 41–49.

Küçük, S., Yılmaz, R. M., & Göktaş, Y. (2014). Augmented reality for learning English: Achievement, attitude and cognitive load levels of students. *Education in Science*, 393–404.

Laboratory for Innovative Technology in Engineering Education (LITEE). (n.d.). Retrieved October 21, 2019 from https://www.learntechlib.org/p/151963/

Lai, Y.-S., & Hsu, J.-M. (2011). Development trend analysis of augmented reality system in educational applications. *2011 International Conference on Electrical and Control Engineering*, 6527-6531. 10.1109/ICECENG.2011.6056941

Lin, H. C. K., Chen, M. C., & Chang, C. K. (2015). Assessing the effectiveness of learning solid geometry by using an augmented reality-assisted learning system. *Interactive Learning Environments*, *23*(6), 799–810. doi:10.1080/10494820.2013.817435

Martín-Gutiérrez, J., Saorín, J. L., Contero, M., Alcañiz, M., Pérez-López, D. C., & Ortega, M. (2010). Design and validation of an augmented book for spatial abilities development in engineering students. *Computers & Graphics*, *34*(1), 77–91. doi:10.1016/j.cag.2009.11.003

Milgram, P., & Kishino, F. (1994). A Taxonomy Of Mixed Reality Visual Displays. *IEICE Transactions on Information and Systems*, *77*(12), 1–15.

Milli Eğitim Bakanlığı. (2018). *Matematik dersi öğretim programı*. Talim Terbiye Kurulu Başkanlığı.

Milli Eğitim Bakanlığı. (2019). *Ortaöğretim Kurumlarına İlişkin Merkezi Sınav Raporu*. T.C. Milli Eğitim Bakanlığı.

National Council of Teacher of Mathematics. (2008). *The role of technology in the teaching and learning of mathematics: A position of the National Council of Teachers of Mathematics*. Accessed at: http://www.nctm.org/uploadedFiles/About_NCTM/Position_Statements/Technology%20final.pdf

National Council Teacher of Mathematics. (2000). Principles and evaluation standards for school mathematics. Author.

NCTM. (2000). *Curriculum and Evaluation Standards for School Mathematics*. National Council of Teachers of Mathematics.

Özarslan, Y. (2013). Genişletilmiş Gerçeklik İle Zenginleştirilmiş Öğrenme Materyallerinin Öğrenen Başarısı Ve Memnuniyeti Üzerindeki Etkisi (Doktora Tezi). Eskişehir: Eskişehir Anadolu Üniversitesi.

Pomerantz, J. (2019). Teaching and learning with extended reality technology. *Information and technology transforming lives: connection, interaction, innovation*, 137-157. Retrieved from https://bib.irb.hr/datoteka/1033483.bobcatsss_proceedings4.pdf#page=137

Privitera, G. J., & Ahlgrim-Delzell, L. (2019). *Research Methods for Education*. Sage Edge.

Radu, I. (2014). Augmented reality in education: A meta-review and cross-media analysis. *Personal and Ubiquitous Computing*, *18*(6), 1533–1543. doi:10.100700779-013-0747-y

Royal Society and Joint Mathematical Council. (2001). *Teaching and Learning Geometry*. Royal Society/Joint Mathematical Council.

Sayımer, İ., & Küçüksaraç, B. (2015). Yeni teknolojilerin üniversite eğitimine katkısı: İletişim fakültesi öğrencilerinin artırılmış gerçeklik uygulamalarına ilişkin görüşleri. *International Journal of Human Sciences*, *12*(2), 1536–1554. doi:10.14687/ijhs.v12i2.3488

Schoepp, K. (2005). Barriers to technology integration in a technology-rich environment. *Learning and Teaching in Higher Education: Gulf Perspectives*, *2*(1), 1–24.

Somyürek, S. (2014). Öğretim sürecinde Z kuşağının dikkatini çekme: Artırılmış gerçeklik. *Eğitim Teknolojisi Kuram ve Uygulama*, *4*(1), 63–80.

Tabachnick, B. G., & Fidell, L. S. (2013). *Using Multivariate Statistics* (6th ed.). Allyn and Bacon.

Thornton, T., Ernst, J. V., & Clark, A. C. (2012). Augmented Reality as a Visual and Spatial Learning Tool in Technology Education. *Technology and Engineering Teacher*, *71*(8), 18–21.

Topper Website. (n.d.). Retrieved from https://www.toppr.com/guides/maths/basic-geometrical-ideas/basic-geometrical-shapes/

Toptaş, V. (2008). Geometri öğretiminde sınıfta yapılan etkinlikler ile öğretme-öğrenme sürecinin incelenmesi. *İlköğretim Online, 7*(1), 91-11.

Wang, X., Kim, M. J., Love, P. E. D., & Kang, S. C. (2013). Augmented Reality in built environment: Classification and implications for future research. *Automation in Construction*, *32*, 1–13. doi:10.1016/j.autcon.2012.11.021

Yin, C., Song, Y., Tabata, Y., Ogata, H., & Hwang, G.-J. (2013). Developing and implementing a framework of participatory simulation for mobile learning using scaffolding. *Journal of Educational Technology & Society*, *16*(3), 137–150.

Yin, R. (1994). *Case Study Research*. Sage.

Yuen, S., Yaoyuneyong, G., & Johnson, E. (2011). Augmented Reality: An Overview and Five Directions for AR in Education. *Journal of Educational Technology Development and Exchange*, *4*(1), 119–140. doi:10.18785/jetde.0401.10

ADDITIONAL READING

Chai, C. S., Ling Koh, J. H., Tsai, C. C., & Tan, L. (2011). Modeling primary school pre-service teachers' Technological Pedagogical Content Knowledge (TPACK) for meaningful learning with information and communication technology (ICT). *Computers & Education*, *57*(1), 1184–1193. doi:10.1016/j.compedu.2011.01.007

Clements, D. H., & Sarama, J. (2000). Young children's ideas about geometric shapes. *Teaching Children Mathematics*, *6*(8), 482–482.

Feiner, S., Macintyre, B., & Seligmann, D. (1993). Knowledge-based augmented reality. *Communications of the ACM*, *36*(7), 53–62. doi:10.1145/159544.159587

Johnston, C. J. (2012). Technology choices of pre-service elementary teachers while planning for mathematics instruction. *The International Journal for Technology in Mathematics Education*, *20*(4), 133–144.

Moyer, P. S., Bolyard, J. J., & Spikell, M. A. (2002). What are virtual manipulatives? *Teaching Children Mathematics*, *8*(6), 372.

National Council of Teachers of Mathematics. (2014). *Principles to actions: Ensuring mathematical success for all*. Author.

KEY TERMS AND DEFINITIONS

Augmented Reality: Technology where virtual objects blend with the real world, while real and virtual objects interact with each other.

Quiver Program: Is cost-effective, suitable for the students' ability, and easy to use on mobile devices, and it contains suitable content for the desired knowledge gains.

Technological Tools: Which can be used to increase the practice of the mathematics learning and teaching.

Chapter 12
Affordances and Pedagogical Implications of Augmented Reality (AR)-Integrated Language Learning

Babak Khoshnevisan
University of South Florida, USA

Sanghoon Park
https://orcid.org/0000-0001-9459-8880
University of South Florida, USA

ABSTRACT

Technologies have permeated the field of language education in recent decades. Language education has been informed by the technology-enhanced practices. Researchers have exhausted a variety of technologies and technological tools in the field of language education. Augmented reality (AR) is one of the emerging technologies that has been exploited in both education and language education. However, it is reported that educators' lack of knowledge and confidence in employing emerging technologies such as AR are limiting the use of these technologies in language education. To dive into the employed AR-related practices in language education, this chapter will (1) introduce the definition of AR, (2) discuss the underlying theories undergirding AR-integrated language learning, (3) present both the affordances and thorny issues accompanied with AR, and lastly, (4) share pedagogical implications of AR-integrated language learning to inform and usher the practices of language educators.

INTRODUCTION

Technology plays a vital role in our daily life from doing errands to heavy industrial works. In recent years, technology has been an indispensable part of our life. Technologies and technological devices have plagued almost every aspect of our life. Consistent with this mainstream, language educators and

DOI: 10.4018/978-1-7998-5043-4.ch012

researchers have conducted technology-related studies in the field of language/teacher education: literacy and augmented reality (Park & Khoshnevisan, 2019); augmented reality and teacher education (Khoshnevisan, 2019b); automatic writing evaluation (AWE) tools to enhance writing skills (Khoshnevisan, 2019f); animated pedagogical agents (Khoshnevisan, 2018a); augmented reality and language learning (Khoshnevisan & Le, 2018); audiotaped dialogue journals (Rashtchi & Khoshnevisan, 2008); AR-infused apps (Hadid, Mannion, Khoshnevisan, 2019); material development (Khoshnevisan, 2020) to name but a few. Aligned with this research backdrop, many researchers have widely examined the impact of technology on the participants' cognitive attainment and explored their perceptions about different types of technologies and technological tools (Trushell, Maitland, & Burrell, 2003; Specht, Ternier, & Greller, 2011; Yang, 2011; Smeets & Bus, 2012; Wojciechowski & Cellary, 2013; Di Serio, Ibáñez & Kloos, 2013; Wu, Chang, & Liang, 2013; Reinders & Lakarnchua, 2014; Küçük, Yılmaz, & Göktaş, 2014; Amer, 2014; Cheng & Tsai, 2016).

Khoshnevisan (2019b) portrays a rather comprehensive picture of the technologies being used in the field of language education. He takes an array of technologies into account to make a judicious inclusion for the incorporation of technologies in language education. Having chronologically considered different types of technologies, Khoshnevisan presents the results of technology-infused studies to showcase the conducive nature of technologies in education and its ramifications alike. The abundant pedagogical implications of technologies coupled with educators' lack of knowledge give rise to fewer practices interspersed with technologies (Khoshnevisan & Le, 2018).

Khoshnevisan (2019d) reported that the use of technology has widely been exploited to the extent that a myriad of foreign language education in the United States have harnessed an array of technologies to facilitate the process of language education. Geisler (2016) explains that many language schools such as Middlebury language schools integrated different technologies in their curriculum to develop blended language courses. Another example is how technology-mediated contexts became prominent in the language education domain in the United States. Alden (2016) posits that after World War Two, language education was extensively informed by technologies and technological tools. This technology education amounted to more cooperation and collaboration between teacher and language learners and among language learners, too.

On this account, we—researchers and language educators—are bound to enhance our understanding and create novel ways to employ technology in our Monday morning practice in classrooms. To achieve that, the present chapter aims to detail prior technology-infused studies in the pertinent literature. To gain an in-depth understanding about and deep insight into the promises that technology offers, language educators must focus on one type of technology. To achieve this, this chapter will center on augmented reality (AR) as an emerging technology. The impact of using AR technology in education has already been examined in different studies. However, the use of AR technology in the field of language education has yet to be investigated (Khoshnevisan & Le, 2018). The following sections, thus, will showcase AR and its role in language education.

DEFINITION OF AUGMENTED REALITY (AR)

There are plentiful definitions of AR in the pertinent field, however, the widely cited definition of AR is presented by Azuma (1997) emphasizing that AR is the seamless integration of the virtual objects and the real world. He explains that AR can superimpose a layer of digital information on the physical world around us. Azuma (1997) details three prominent aspects of AR—the combination of real and virtual worlds, real-time interaction, and finally 3D registration of virtual and real objects. He contends that the combination of these three factors makes AR a unique technological tool that can help designers to offer a unique learning experience to language learners. Cabero and Barroso (2016, p. 44) state that AR is "a technology which mixes real elements with other added virtual ones for the purpose of creating a new communicative scenography."

Di Serio et al. (2013) expound that AR has three prominent properties:

- combination of real and virtual objects within a virtual environment;
- mutual alignment between real and virtual objects; and
- interactive implementation in real time. (p. 587)

AR allows language learners see objects or other digital information superimposed on the physical environment. The definition of AR echoes the affordances that are offered by this emerging technology. As such, both language educators and learners can take advantage of this technology while learning a new language. To unlock the advantages of AR, in what follows, this chapter presents the two prominent types of AR that have been taken into account in AR-related studies.

TYPES OF AUGMENTED REALITY (AR)

Dunleavy and Dede (2014) identify two types of augmented reality (AR): (1) location-aware and (2) vision-based. In the location-aware AR, a digital layer is presented to users as they move in different physical areas by the use of Global Positioning System (GPS)-enabled devices such as smartphones. Another known type of AR is vision-based AR. In vision-based AR, in contrast, the digital layer is activated once users point the camera of their smart devices at an object, picture, or QR codes. The object works as a trigger to activate the digital layer.

Dunleavy and Dede (2014) detail the two types of AR within a scenario.

As the 7th grade life science student passes by an oak tree in her school playground, software leveraging GPS plays a video on her smartphone describing the various habitats and animals that are found near the tree (location-aware). At the end of the video, the student is prompted to point her phone's video camera at a placard at the base of the tree, which triggers a 3-dimensional model illustrating the anatomical structure of the oak (vision-based). (p. 735)

THEORIES SUPPORTING AR-INTEGRATED LANGUAGE LEARNING

According to Dunleavy and Dede (2014) There are two prominent theories that undergird augmented reality (AR): *Situated learning* theory and *Constructivist learning theory.* Whitehead's Aims of Education (Whitehead, 1932), and Dewey's Experience and Education (Dewey, 1938) interest in realistic learning give rise to reiterate on the role of context in learning. The mentioned perspectives have amounted to a philosophical foundation known as "learning by doing". Brown, Collins, and Duguid (1989) stress that if learning is embedded in the physical and social context within which it is used, meaningful learning will take place. In 1993, Brown and Duguid noted: "One of the most persistent educational questions following discussions of situated learning has been: How can these situated theories be operationalized?" (p. 10). As language teachers seek to reengage and motivate learners, surmount educational and cross-cultural issues, and provide learners with authentic learning, AR offers immersive and unique opportunity to establish an environment anchored in situated learning.

Brown, Collins, and Duguid (1989) proposed *situated learning theory*. This theory is built upon *sociocultural theory* (SCT) of Vygotsky (1978). *SCT* posits learning takes place in a certain context and that mutual interactions among the participants, objects, and cultural aspects within that context can enhance the learning process. AR has the potential to create a mixed-reality environment, which enables users to interact with other learners, figure out a problem, and apply what they learn to other situations. On this account, the quality of learning heavily relies on interactions among students in a learning community (Brown, Collins, & Duguid, 1989). *SCT* defines human learning as 'dynamic and social activity situated in physical, social context and distributed among persons, tools, and activities' (Vygotsky, 1978; Wertsch, 1991). Sociocultural perspective ultimately seeks "to explicate the relationship between human mental functioning, on the one hand, and the cultural, institutional, and historical situations in which this functioning occurs, on the other" (Wertsch, 1995, p. 3). *Sociocultural theory* explains human cognition is formed through engagement in social activities. *SCT* reiterates that it is the social relationships and the culturally constructed materials—signs and symbols referred to as semiotic artifacts—that mediate those relationships that create human forms of higher-level thinking. AR enables language learners to interact with other language learners in a socially and culturally diverse environment. This helps language learners negotiate abstract concepts with each other in a non-threatening atmosphere. Language learners can form virtual communities via AR. These communities facilitate negotiation of ideas and can ultimately learn both the language as well as the cultural elements.

Situated learning emanates from authentic learning. It also facilitates knowledge acquisition process and its transfer to the real-world practice (Herrington & Herrington, 2007; Lombardi, 2007a, 2007b). Aligned with authentic learning, context is key in *situated learning*. It is deemed that AR offers promises to provide the required context while learning a new language for language learners. Context is key in learning a new language. Often times than not, researchers in the field of language acquisition reiterated the significance of context in guessing the meaning of words and idioms used (Liontas, 1999; Khoshnevisan, 2019c). In Collins's (1991) words, *situated learning* is: "the notion of learning knowledge and skills in contexts that reflect the way the knowledge will be useful in real life" (p. 122). This definition aligns with the importance of context and real-life interaction. AR, in this sense, has promises to offer including providing a real-life setting via mixed-reality environments.

The following is an example of *situated learning* with fifth grade students using Past/Present. This is an immersive role-play simulation, which looks like a videogame (Dawley & Dede, 2014):

Louisa and James are 5th graders who are ready to begin their history unit on the industrial revolution. They sit together at a laptop, log into the simulation, and play as Anna Caruso, an immigrant textile mill worker during turn-of-the-century America. As Louisa and James work together to move Anna's avatar down the streets of Eureka Falls, they encounter her family members, the newspaper boy, co-workers in the factory, and other characters in the simulation. These characters provide important background information, help create a holistic storyline, and offer Louisa and James the ability to interact, analyze, and problem solve by choosing responses to options in the storyline. (p. 724)

In short, *situated learning* assumes that learning takes place in context and the quality of learning is contingent upon the interactions among the people, places, objects, processes, and culture in a specific context. In the process of language education, context facilitates the negotiation of meaning among interlocuters within a community. AR can supply language learners with the required context, so dialogues take place and learners negotiate ideas, guess, and ultimately learn within a learning community.

Wittrock (1974) posits that knowledge construction is equal to generative learning process. In this view, knowledge is constructed through individual observation and experimentation. In other words, knowledge is not normally constructed based upon verified facts and as a whole. Knowledge acquisition for learners and language learners is not the information provided or curriculum taught but rather emerges from the information landscape and collective encounters and relations that he establishes within a specific knowledge domain. If a learner seeks information in order to tackle an issue, the environments such as AR-integrated context can both engage language learners and supply learners with digital information to enhance his understanding.

Constructivism metaphorically posits that the knowledge acquisition process is equal to the construction of a building. *Constructivism* claims that human knowledge acquisition is formed through a process called active construction. Fox (2001) lists the main claims made by constructivism:

(1) Learning is an active process.
(2) Knowledge is constructed, rather than innate, or passively absorbed.
(3) Knowledge is invented not discovered.
(4a) All knowledge is personal and idiosyncratic.
(4b) All knowledge is socially constructed.
(5) Learning is essentially a process of making sense of the world.
(6) Effective learning requires meaningful, open-ended, challenging problems for the learner to solve. (p. 24)

Constructivism is an umbrella term that includes many other situated recognition, cognition, realistic learning environments, social negotiation (Driscoll, 2000). *Constructivist learning theory* assumes that individuals along with their prior knowledge and sociocultural background play a vital role in learning (Dunleavy & Dede, 2014; Vygotsky, 1978). In an AR environment, not only do language learners establish their personal version of the language based on their own experiences but also, they can interact with their partners (native or nonnative speakers) to negotiate the meaning (Dunleavy & Dede, 2014). AR then has the potential to afford educators with a unique tool to build new knowledge based on language learners' prior knowledge. Tackling cross-cultural issues is another significant aspect of learning a new language that can be realized through AR. AR can provide learners with a safe environment for cultural exchanges while language learners feel less threatened. AR makes a less threatening environment for practicing a new culture and becoming familiar with cultural aspects of a new language as the environment is less real.

POTENTIALS AND CHALLENGES OF AR-INTEGRATED LANGUAGE EDUCATION

Khoshnevisan (2019a) stresses that the technological tools employed in technology-infused studies invariably enhance learners' comprehension, increase their learning gains, and motivation level. To gain insight into the prior studies conducted in education and language education, in particular, we present the results of prior literature reviews conducted earlier. To date, three literature reviews have been conducted on augmented reality: Bacca, Baldiris, Fabregat, Graf, and Kinshuk (2014); Koutromanos, Sofos and Avraamidou (2015); and Akçayır and Akçayır (2017).

Bacca et al. (2014) conducted a systematic review about the use of AR in education. This review highlighted the use of AR technology in education and the AR-based applications of a wide range of subjects (e.g., science, language arts) from 2003 to 2013 in six journals. They retrieved a total number of 32 articles. The researchers identified three major trends: (1) marker-based AR is the most utilized type of AR; location-based AR is widely applied; (2) the major benefits of AR are cognitive attainment, motivation, interaction, and collaboration, and (3) mixed method is the most common research method in the studies. Bacca et al. (2014) put forth a short summary of the advantages and disadvantages of AR technology in this review:

- The main purpose of using AR has been for explaining a topic of interest as well as providing additional information. AR educational games and AR for lab experiments are also growing fields.
- The main advantages for AR are learning gains, motivation, interaction and collaboration.
- Limitations of AR are mainly: difficulties maintaining superimposed information, paying too much attention to virtual information and the consideration of AR as an intrusive technology.
- AR has been effective for: a better learning performance, learning motivation, student engagement and positive attitudes.
- Very few systems have considered the special needs of students in AR. Here there is a potential field for further research. (p. 146)

In another review study, Koutromanos et al. (2015) investigated the articles on AR mobile games in the field of education. This systematic review was carried out between 2000 and 2014 through two known databases: *ScienceDirect* and *ERIC*. The researchers examined 7 articles in the pertinent literature. The analyses of the review indicated that these studies supply us with strong evidence for the positive role of AR games in learning. These studies focused on natural sciences and took place in informal learning environments. Akçayır and Akçayır (2017) reviewed articles that focused on the advantages and limitations of AR in education. A total number of 68 research articles were retrieved from SSCI-indexed journals. They reported that AR research in education started in 2007, and dramatically grew from 2011. There is a wide range of participants (K-12, university, adult learner, technical school) in AR related studies. In the pool of 68 studies, only one study attended to the application of AR for students with special needs. Mobile AR, location-based AR, and computer AR were widely used. They asserted that AR offers educational potentials such as positive learning outcomes. Yet, it can be challenging owing to technical errors, cognitive overload, attention distractor, and insufficient teacher training in the field.

As explained, a growing body of the literature about AR has reported key features of AR such as its applications, affordances, effectiveness as well as limitations in different learning domains. Nonetheless, there was still a gap in the literature regarding a thorough investigation of the impact of AR on language education. Currently, Khoshnevisan and Le (2018) have addressed the issue and investigated the AR and QR codes related articles in the pertinent literature. This is considered as the solo literature review regarding the incorporation of emerging technologies such as AR and QR codes in language education. Khoshnevisan & Le (2018) scrutinized the studies on the use of AR technology in language education from 2007 to 2017. The articles were searched through education-related databases such as ProQuest and ERIC (Education Resources Information Center). A total number of 19 articles were retrieved from the literature. They reported that AR has numerous advantages in language education. There is a positive correlation between AR and both literacy and vocabulary learning. However, the impact of AR on other language skills has yet to be examined. There are a few pedagogical concerns (e.g., sustainability of the application in a big classroom in a long-term, and insufficient class time) that need to be addressed. One of the major drawbacks in AR studies is that language educators are predominantly unfamiliar with AR.

MOTIVATION

Motivation has been the topic of intense research in the field of language education. However, these studies did not attempt to investigate long-term engagement and motivation in learning, nor do they attend to the underlying challenges in increasing the learners' level of motivation. Furthermore, "the role of motivation in student accomplishment in authentic learning is another area of much interest that has not been fully explained" (Herrington, Reeves, & Oliver, 2014, p. 409). Dewy was the first researcher who reiterated that positive emotion amounts to deeper learning. Other researchers, consistent with Dewey's ideas, placed emphasis on the importance of positive emotion in learning (Schraw & Lehman, 2001).

In the context of language learning, AR technology has not been fully investigated. Nonetheless, it is evident that AR not only allows real-time interaction but also supplies learners with experiential learning, which augments learners' attention and motivation (Ibáñez, Di Serio, Villarán, & Kloos, 2014; Singhal, Bagga, Goyal, & Saxena, 2012). Regarding motivation and attitude in language education, researchers have conducted multiple studies to enhance language learning in an AR-infused environment (Cascales, Laguna, Pérez-López, Perona, & Contero, 2013; Cheng & Tsai, 2014). Khoshnevisan (2018a) contends that "multiple studies have been conducted to corroborate the theory that positive emotions have crucial effects on diverse cognitive processes such as communication process, information process, negotiation process, decision-making process, and problem-solving process" (p. 78). Dewey (1913) recognized interest in learning as a determining factor for academic success. In terms of motivation and attitude in language learning, different researchers have conducted studies to prompt language learning in an engaging and motivating environment (Cascales, Laguna, Pérez-López, Perona, & Contero, 2013; Cheng & Tsai, 2014).

In one study, Solak and Cakir (2015) conducted an empirical study to measure the motivation level of the participants who studied English with the AR-integrated material. The researchers also attempted to identify if there is a positive correlation between the students' cognitive attainment and their motivation level. To achieve this, 130 undergraduate students were recruited voluntarily in a Turkish University. They participated in a material motivation survey (IMMS) developed by Keller (2010). IMMS is based on the ARCS motivation model (Keller, 1987a, 1987b). This questionnaire indicated the extent to which the participants find the material motivational and interesting. The results of this study suggested that AR-integrated material has a positive impact on students' motivation level. In addition, it was identified that there is a positive significant correlation between the students' motivation level and their academic achievement regarding the incorporation of AR technology in learning vocabularies. They also found that AR increases the motivation level of the participants.

AR has positive impacts on the motivation, attention, and confidence of learners (Di Serio et al. 2013). AR is an appropriate tool to teach language and culture (Liu 2009). Accordingly, it seems that AR has promises to unleash the full potential of language learners. AR can not only motivate language learners to learn the subject matter but also enhances the learners' understanding through providing digital information that brings learners above and beyond the four corners of classrooms. To motivate learners while using AR, Talheimer (2004) asserts that instructional designers should augment text-based learning material by embedding interesting elements such as motivational stories, biographical details, clip arts, photographs, sounds, and video clips.

BOOK READING

Traditionally speaking, reading language books has been an effective way to learn a new language. As technologies advanced and matured, novel concepts such as electronic interactive books (Smeets & Bus, 2012; Trushell, Maitland, & Burrell, 2003) emerged in the germane literature. This is, however, worth mentioning that these technology-infused books cannot substitute traditional books. For one thing, Sellen and Harper (2003) reported that learners enjoy reading traditional books due to their tangibility. Learners, by and large, enjoy touching books and learning the content. AR-infused books have a lot to offer. In an AR book, a digital layer is superimposed to a book to create a unique experience of learning through contextualizing the content in a digital environment. This enables learners to interact with the book and with one another to learn the content of a book in a motivating way. The seamlessness between the real and virtual world that the learner's experience is a unique educational benefit (McKenzie & Darnell, 2004).

AR Games

Researchers have widely used AR-based games to examine how AR impacts on learning. In terms of language education, Barreira et al. (2012) conducted a study regarding the impact of AR games on the educational performance of children while learning words. To that end, the researchers developed an AR-based game known as MOW. MOW was primarily developed to teach elementary children words about endangered species in both Portuguese and English. This was implemented through their first visual encounter with the word and oral comprehension. The oral comprehension was followed by the recognition of written words. A variety of tasks in the game supported both oral comprehension and written aspects of learning words. MOW then supplied the children with matching tasks and provided them with visual and auditory cues to facilitate pronouncing and writing new words. Consistent with other studies regarding AR games (Juan, Llop, Abad, and Lluch, 2010; Juan, Toffetti, Abad and Cano, 2010), this AR game was developed using predefined markers.

Twenty-six children aged from 7 to 9 participated in this experiment. In this study, children in the experimental group played AR games and the children in the control group played real games. When compared, no significant difference was observed between the two groups (using AR-based games and real games). However, the researchers reported that the results of the questionnaires highlighted that 81% of the children, for some reason, preferred AR games to real games. The participants considered AR games easy to play. Positive pedagogical impacts of AR games on learning words were proved through this study. The results of this study suggest that children who play AR games have superior English learning progress. The results confirm that this game makes children correctly spell words by aligning the markers (representing each alphabet) in their positions.

A closer scrutiny of the AR studies reveals that researchers have extensively explored the affective and learning outcomes that AR offers. In one study, the researchers (Liu, Holden, & Zheng, 2016) created an AR mobile game, Guardians of the Mo'o (who is a gecko or Lizard Goddess in Hawaiian culture), which supply the learners in Mãnoa with a new engaging learning environment where they could interact with both virtual world (virtual drawings) and real world (trees and artworks on the campus). This game facilitated learners' language learning and enhanced their cultural understandings. Based on conversation analysis and multimodal analysis, Liu et al. explored that active learning took place through learner's collaborative negotiation and coordination among team gamers to solve the problems together.

AR and Vocabulary / Literacy Development

According to Khoshnevisan and Le (2018), there is prolific literature regarding the application of AR in enhancing vocabulary and literacy knowledge of learners. Ogata et al. (2011) argue that context plays an essential role in learning vocabulary since it makes a strong association between a word and the related objects in the real world. When it comes to learning vocabulary, context comes in a variety of forms. AR has the capability to provide us with a personalized learning system, which is a prevalent form of context used by multiple researchers (Yang, 2011). Other researchers have harnessed applications to improve student's vocabulary in physical contexts such as a library or a cafeteria.

Santos, Taketomi, Yamamoto, Rodrigo, Sandor, and Kato (2016) harnessed AR to improve the presentation of the instructional material to teach vocabulary. The researchers annotated real-world objects with sounds, texts, images, and animations. These types of visualizations were implemented through AR –3D registered onto the environment. The results of the study confirmed that various media have no effect on the learners' cognitive achievements. Additionally, (consistent with Fujimoto et al. 2012) the results show that the words associated with objects and places are remembered better. AR is once again proved to be motivating (consistent with Di Serio et al., 2013). Surprisingly, inconsistent with Di Serio et al. 2013, this study revealed that the students were slightly more confident to use non-AR.

Solak and Cakir (2015) conducted a study to determine the motivation level of the participants who studied English with the AR-infused material. In addition, this study sets out to identify if there is a correlation between the students' achievement and their motivation level. To this end, 130 undergraduate students from a Turkish university were recruited on a voluntary basis. They participated in a material motivation survey. The findings of this study indicated that AR-infused technology has a positive impact on encouraging students towards learning words. In addition, it was identified that there is a positive significant correlation between the students' motivation level and their academic achievement regarding the integration of AR technology in learning vocabularies. Solak and Cakir (2015) found that AR increases the motivation level of the participants. This finding was consistent with the Di Serio et al. 's findings in learning visual arts course. In this sense, Ibanez et al. (2014) report the same results. Mahadir and Phung (2013) found similar findings in that AR pop-up books contributed to the learning process.

Silva et al. (2013) harnessed ARBlocks to investigate its impact on the literacy skills of first graders. To evaluate this tool, the researchers employed a mixed methods inquiry (using two qualitative and one quantitative metrics). The results of this study suggested that this tool enhanced the literacy skills of the participants and increased their achievements. The results found no statistically significant difference in the role of genders. No other study has, to date, examined this factor in AR studies. Finally, there was a positive correlation between the motivation level and academic achievement. Multiple studies corroborated this last finding (Barreira et al., 2012; Ibanez et al., 2014; Lui et al., 2010; Mahadzir & Phung, 2013; Perez-Lopez & Contero, 2013; Silva et al., 2013; Tan & Lui, 2004).

AFFORDANCES AND LIMITATIONS

Augmented reality as the technology of future has potential challenges to safeguard against and potential opportunities to leverage. The results of AR-related studies substantiate that AR can help us concretize abstract concepts (Dori & Belcher, 2005), contribute to a deeper understanding of the concepts (Klopfer & Squire, 2008), visualize the concepts for better understanding (Kaufmann & Schmalstieg, 2003), boost engagement (Bujak et al., 2013), develop critical thinking and problem solving skills (Dunleavy, Dede & Mitchell, 2009), make learning an enjoyable process (Núñez et al., 2008), make learning more appealing and effective (Wojciechowski & Cellary, 2013), draw attention (Aziz et al., 2012), establish links with the real environment (Ternier et al., 2012), facilitate comprehension (Ivanova & Ivanov, 2011), and increase motivation level of learners (Di Serio et al., 2013).

When it comes to literacy, the AR literature indicates positive attitude of learners toward technology-infused material (Billinghurst, Kato, & Poupyrev, 2001; Clark & Dünser, 2012). The results of the AR-related studies suggest that improvements in students' gains in different areas including vocabulary (King, 2016); literacy (Cheng & Tsai, 2016), and language skills (Liu, 2009). Few studies confirmed that children benefit from AR-integrated books (Cheng and Tsai, 2014; Dünser & Hornecker, 2007; Hornecker & Dünser, 2009). Usefulness, ease of use, and satisfaction while utilizing technology-infused books have been reiterated in several AR-related studies (Billinghurst, Kato, & Poupyrev, 2001; Clark & Dunser, 2012).

Yang (2011) argued that language education requires constant exposure to authentic language so language learners can be familiar with not only the language but also with culture. Many studies have shown that contextualization is key when it comes to learning language items such as idiomatic phrases. For one thing, the figurative meaning of idiomatic phrases will be decoded only if the appropriate context is introduced for language learners (see Khoshnevisan, 2018b, 2019c). Another important aspect of context is the assimilation of learners with the target language and context. Context, if effectively and appropriately incorporated, can and should facilitate the language learning process. Yang reported that AR has the potential to provide language learners with the appropriate context in classrooms. It is also worth mentioning that AR-infused tools are useful, easy to use, and motivate language learners (Billinghurst, Kato, & Poupyrev, 2001; Clark & Dunser, 2012).

PEDAGOGICAL IMPLICATIONS AND FUTURE DIRECTIONS

As discussed earlier, AR books resemble printed books except that videos, audios, and pictures are superimposed on books. Educators can tailor the content of the books with AR and QR codes. For AR to be activated, educators may need pictures to trigger the virtual layer to be played upon the real-world pictures. However, QR codes do not require pictures or coding. QR codes, thus, are easier to be employed by educators and can be simply added to the printed books. Accordingly, AR and QR codes enrich the users' learning experiences and take the printed books to the next level.

Khoshnevisan and Le (2018, p. 66) explain that

AR studies in language education are predominantly concerned with either college students or K-12 with 43%. Other types of participants such as pre-K young learners include only 9% of the studies. Five percent of the selected studies did not specify their participants as they focused on the practical issues of AR.

Consistent with the findings of Akçayır & Akçayır (2017), a variety of learners have participated in AR-related studies. Among the pool of AR studies, K-12 language learners shape the majority of the participants. For one thing, these participants are generation Z and they are considered digital natives. The generation Z is already immersed in technology and technological tools. It is, thus, evident that these participants enjoy playing digital games, AR-based games, and the related technologies. The results of this review showed that Taiwanese, Portuguese, Turkish, and English were largely the first language of the participants in AR studies. The AR studies from 2007 included different types of studies including mixed-methods, qualitative, quantitative, and concept papers. It is then clear that language educators, aligned with the results of prior AR-related studies, can harness AR technology for language learners in K-12 because this age range is familiar with emerging technologies such as AR. The digital natives are in pursuit of technology-infused material as they are immersed with technology. It seems that language educators can accommodate their needs via AR books, AR games, and any other form of AR-infused material.

Khoshnevisan and Le (2018) also investigated the impact of AR on literacy development, vocabulary, AR games, and learners' attitude and cognitive load. They reported that AR has numerous advantages in language education. The results of this study suggest that there is a positive correlation between AR and both literacy and vocabulary learning. Having coded the AR-related articles, Khoshnevisan and Le (2018, p. 68) detailed the affordances that AR brings. They further mentioned that these affordances fall under two major classifications:

(1) affective outcomes and (2) learning outcomes. Affective outcomes focus on learner motivation and attitude toward AR integration into language classrooms whereas learning outcomes consist of a number of sub-categories such as cognition load, language performance and higher-order thinking skills (e.g., inquiry learning, creativity). Cultural understanding along with cooperative skills also plays a key role in efficient performance of language learners.

Language educators are highly recommended to use AR-infused material for reading and writing skills. Unfortunately, instructional designers and material developers have not extensively exploited AR. This is, however, not to say that language educators cannot develop AR-infused materials on their own (Khoshnevisan, 2020). The impact of AR on four language skills has yet to be examined. Researchers should study how best to integrate AR into all four language skills (listening, speaking, reading, and writing). Listening and speaking skills are under-researched and we are not fully aware of the results of the incorporation of AR into these skills. However, research findings have shown that AR has significant effect on language learners' motivation and learning gains. Another AR-related topic deserving more attention is AR games. Barreira et al. (2012) reported that children showed positive attitude toward AR games. Additionally, AR games culminate in the participants' cognitive attainment when it comes to spelling words. To date, only a handful of AR games have been introduced to the world of language education. However, knowing how to use these games in and out of the class can motivate language learners and offer them a unique way to learn a new language while playing games.

There are, however, a few pedagogical concerns (e.g., the sustainability of the application in a big classroom in a long-term, and insufficient class time) that need to be addressed. One of the major drawbacks of AR studies is that language educators are predominantly unfamiliar with AR. Khoshnevisan and Le (2018) report that "the common challenge is the complication to create and operate AR technology even for the teachers" (p. 70). To capture the difficulties of language education and to familiarize them with this technology, institutions need to hold more professional development sessions to educate teachers with the modus operandi of emerging technologies such as AR. Parallel to the professional development sessions, teacher education courses need to promote the use of technologies and technological tools. To build the trust in future educators, teacher education courses are bound to extensively invest time on current trends on technology and best practices, so language educators know how to integrate technology in their everyday lessons.

AR, for sure, is in its initiation form and many AR app developers are still seeking for more efficient forms of AR to engage and motivate learners. To date, multiple researchers have scrutinized the impact of vision-based and location-aware AR on students' cognitive attainment. However, future studies need to be conducted to juxtapose the two types of AR (vision-based and location-aware AR). Future studies are bound to develop AR- integrated material to investigate its impact on the language learning process. Prior studies have scrutinized and measured the impact of AR-related material and apps on literacy development and vocabulary learning (see Park & Khoshnevisan, 2019).

Another important strand of research is conducting more qualitative inquiries to become familiar with the perceptions of language educators, learners, and parents. One of the drawbacks of AR is educators' lack of confidence and knowledge to integrate it into their practice (Khoshnevisan & Le, 2018). Thus, more qualitative and mixed methods inquiries can be fruitful to examine the impact of AR and explore the experiences, attitude, and perceptions of all the main stakeholders such as learners, educators, and parents.

CONCLUSION

As discussed earlier in this chapter, AR offers promises that can unleash the full potential of language learners. The affordances that AR offer ranges from motivating language learners to facilitating the process of language education through concretizing abstract concepts in paper books (Dori & Belcher, 2005), providing context for guessing (see Khoshnevisan, 2018b, 2019c), visualizing the information (Barreira et al., 2012: Kaufmann & Schmalstieg, 2003), and building communities of learners to negotiate ideas like real environments (Ternier et al., 2012). These are prominent factors that serve as a catalyst to help students learn a second language. The promises of AR coupled with the permeation of this emerging technology in language education has prompted language educators and researchers to use it.

As we delineated in this chapter, there are different types of AR (location-aware and vision-based) that have been used in previous studies (Dunleavy & Dede, 2014). Different studies have employed either of these types of AR. However, a study that juxtaposes the two types of AR to investigate their impacts on language education and explore the perceptions and attitudes of language learners is missing in the literature. AR-infused books and flashcards are prominent technology-mediated material adopted in prior studies. The AR-infused books were used to develop language learners' literacy and enhance their vocabulary learning (Santos et al., 2016; Silva et al., 2013; Solak & Cakir, 2015). AR books motivate language learners and have the tangibility of printed books so they can increase the motivation level of language learners (Sellen & Harper, 2003). AR games are another significant line of research in AR studies. Barreira et al. (2012) reported that language learners showed positive attitude to these games. Additionally, AR games lead to higher cognitive attainment when learning a second language. There is only a few available AR games that language educators can use them. There is a rising trend in creating and using AR games, though. Hopefully, language educators will be equipped with more AR games in the years to come. Given the ubiquity of digital games for young learners, it is highly recommended that AR games are used in and out of classrooms.

Notwithstanding the affordances of AR, this chapter put forth the germane limitations in employing AR in language education. An underlying constraint of AR is related to the technological issues. AR is a novel technology and its systems are not fully developed so technical errors might arise when using this technology. Another important drawback is cognitive load, which may hinder learning. Language educators, if effectively trained to create or tailor AR material, are able to make the necessary changes to avoid cognitive load when learning a second language with the use of AR material. Above all, as put forth in this chapter, teacher education courses (for preservice teachers) and professional development sessions (for in-service teachers) can enhance the understanding of language teachers, expand their technology panorama, and encourage them to use emerging technologies such as AR in their practice to both motivate language learners and increase their learning gains. We hope that this chapter can usher future research endeavor of language educators, material designers, and app developers.

REFERENCES

Akçayır, M., & Akçayır, G. (2017). Advantages and challenges associated with augmented reality for education: A systematic review of the literature. *Educational Research Review*, *20*, 1–11. doi:10.1016/j.edurev.2016.11.002

Alden, G. (2016). The emergence of global language programs at Boston University – Bridging the cultural divide. In Foreign language education in America: Perspectives from K-12, university, government, and international learning (pp. 115–139). Palgrave Macmillan.

Amer, M. (2014). Language learner's usage of a mobile learning application for learning idioms and collocations. *CAILICO Journal*, *31*(3), 285–302. doi:10.11139/cj.31.3.285-302

Azuma, R. (1997). A survey of augmented reality. *Presence (Cambridge, Mass.)*, *6*(4), 355–385. doi:10.1162/pres.1997.6.4.355

Bacca, J., Baldiris, S., Fabregat, R., & Graf, S. (2014). Augmented reality trends in education: A systematic review of research and applications. *Journal of Educational Technology & Society*, *17*(4), 133.

Barreira, J., Bessa, M., Pereira, L. C., Adão, T., Peres, E., & Magalhães, L. (2012). MOW: Augmented Reality game to learn words in different languages: Case study: Learning English names of animals in elementary school. In *Proceedings of Information Systems and Technologies (CISTI), 2012 7th Iberian Conference on* (pp. 1-6). Madrid: IEEE.

Brown, J. S., Collins, A., & Duguid, P. (1989). Situated cognition and the culture of learning. *Educational Researcher*, *18*(1), 32–42. doi:10.3102/0013189X018001032

Brown, J. S., & Duguid, P. (1993). Stolen knowledge. *Educational Technology*, *33*(3), 10–15.

Cabero, J., & Barroso, J. (2016). The educational possibilities of Augmented Reality. *New Approaches in Educational Research*, *5*(1), 44–50.

Cascales, A. L. I., Pérez-López, D., Perona, P., & Contero, M. (2013). An experience on natural sciences augmented reality contents for preschoolers. In R. Shumaker (Ed.), *Virtual augmented and mixed reality: Systems and applications* (pp. 103–112). Springer.

Cheng, K., & Tsai, C. (2014). Children and parents' reading of an augmented reality picture book: Analyses of behavioral patterns and cognitive attainment. *Computers & Education*, *72*, 302–312. doi:10.1016/j.compedu.2013.12.003

Cheng, K. H., & Tsai, C. C. (2016). The interaction of child–parent shared reading with an augmented reality (AR) picture book and parents' conceptions of AR learning. *British Journal of Educational Technology*, *47*(1), 203–222. doi:10.1111/bjet.12228

Collins, A. (1991). Cognitive apprenticeship and instructional technology. In L. Idol & B. F. Jones (Eds.), *Educational values and cognitive instruction: Implications for reform* (pp. 121–138). Lawrence Erlbaum.

Dawley, L., & Dede, C. (2014). Situated learning in virtual worlds and immersive simulations. In J. M. Spector & ... (Eds.), *Handbook of Research on Educational Communications and Technology* (pp. 723–734). Springer. doi:10.1007/978-1-4614-3185-5_58

Dewey, J. (1913). *Interest and effort in education*. Riverside Press. doi:10.1037/14633-000

Dewey, J. (1938). *Experience and education*. Touchstone.

Di Serio, A., Ibáñez, M., & Kloos, C. (2013). Impact of an augmented reality system on students' motivation for a visual art course. *Computers & Education*, *68*, 586–596. doi:10.1016/j.compedu.2012.03.002

Dorogan, D. (2014). *How to use location-based chat and AR in dating and social*. Retrieved November 22, 2016, from https://quickblox.com/blog/how-to-use-location-based-chat-and-ar-in-dating-and-social/

Dunleavy, M., & Dede, C. (2014). Augmented reality teaching and learning. In *Handbook of Research on Educational Communications and Technology* (pp. 735–745). Springer. doi:10.1007/978-1-4614-3185-5_59

Fox, R. (2001). Constructivism examined. *Oxford Review of Education*, *27*(1), 23–35. doi:10.1080/03054980125310

Fujimoto, Y., Yamamoto, G., Kato, H., & Miyazaki, J. (2012). Relation between location of information displayed by augmented reality and user's memorization. In *Proceedings of Augmented Human International Conference* (pp. 71–78). New York: ACM. 10.1145/2160125.2160132

Geisler, M. (2016). 'Language Boot Camp': 100 years of Middlebury language schools. In Foreign language education in America: Perspectives from K-12, university, government, and international learning (pp. 151–168). Palgrave Macmillan.

Hadid, A., Mannion, P., & Khoshnevisan, B. (2019). Augmented reality to the rescue of language learners. *Florida Journal of Educational Research*, *57*(2), 81–89.

Herrington, A., & Herrington, J. (2007). What is an authentic learning environment? In L. A. Tomei (Ed.), *Online and distance learning: Concepts, methodologies, tools, and applications* (pp. 68–76). Information Science Reference.

Hornecker, E., & Dünser, A. (2009). Of pages and paddles: Children's expectations and mistaken interactions with physical-digital tools. *Interacting with Computers*, *21*(1–2), 95–107. doi:10.1016/j.intcom.2008.10.007

Ibáñez, M. B., Di Serio, Á., Villarán, D., & Kloos, C. D. (2014). Experimenting with electromagnetism using augmented reality: Impact on flow student experience and educational effectiveness. *Computers & Education*, *71*, 1–13. doi:10.1016/j.compedu.2013.09.004

Juan, C. M., Llop, E., Abad, F., & Lluch, J. (2010). Learning words using augmented reality. In *2010 IEEE 10th International Conference on advanced learning technologies* (pp. 422-426). IEEE. 10.1109/ICALT.2010.123

Juan, M. C., Toffetti, G., Abad, F., & Cano, J. (2010). Tangible cubes used as the user interface in an augmented reality game for edutainment, In *Proceedings of the IEEE International Conference on Advanced Learning Technologies Learning technologies in the Information society* (pp. 599-603) IEEE. 10.1109/ICALT.2010.170

Keller, J. (2010). *Motivational design for learning and performance*. Springer. doi:10.1007/978-1-4419-1250-3

Keller, J. M. (1987a). Development and use of the ARCS model of motivational design. *Journal of Instructional Development*, *10*(3), 2–10. doi:10.1007/BF02905780

Keller, J. M. (1987b). Strategies for stimulating the motivation to learn. *Performance and Instruction*, *26*(8), 1–7. doi:10.1002/pfi.4160260802

Khoshnevisan, B. (2018a). The Effect of Incorporating Animated Pedagogical Agents in Apps on L2 Idiom Acquisition and Retention. In W. B. James & C. Cobanoglu (Eds.), *Proceedings of the Global Conference on Education and Research (GLOCER) Conference* (Vol. 2, pp. 72–80). ANAHEI Publishing, LLC. https://scholarcommons.usf.edu/cgi/viewcontent.cgi?article=1017&context=anaheipublishing

Khoshnevisan, B. (2018b). *Idiom assessment: To go off the beaten path. In Proceedings of the Global Conference on Education and Research (GLOCER) Conference* (Vol. 2). ANAHEI Publishing, LLC. https://scholarcommons.usf.edu/cgi/viewcontent.cgi?article=1017&context=anaheipublishing

Khoshnevisan, B. (2019a). To integrate media and technology into language education: For and against. In W. B. James & C. Cobanoglu (Eds.), *Proceedings of the Global Conference on Education and Research (GLOCER) Conference* (Vol. 3, pp. 85–92). ANAHEI Publishing, LLC. https://scholarcommons.usf.edu/cgi/viewcontent.cgi?article=1021&context=anaheipublishing

Khoshnevisan, B. (2019b). Teacher education meets emerging technologies: Augmented Reality (AR). *TEIS Newsletter*. Retrieved fromhttp://newsmanager.commpartners.com/tesolteis/issues/2019-03-04/4.html

Khoshnevisan, B. (2019c). Spilling the beans on understanding English idioms using Multimodality: An idiom acquisition technique for Iranian language learners. *International Journal of Language. Translation and Intercultural Communication*, *8*, 128–143. doi:10.12681/ijltic.20281

Khoshnevisan, B. (2019d). Review of the book Foreign language education in America: Perspectives from K-12, university, government, and international learning, by S. Berbeco. *MEXTESOL Journal, 43*(3), 1-6. http://mextesol.net/journal/public/files/3551522e139e20a9515b08f099b4d600.pdf

Khoshnevisan, B. (2019e). The affordances and constraints of automatic writing evaluation (AWE) tools: A case for Grammarly. *ARTESOL EFL Journal*, *2*(2), 12–25.

Khoshnevisan, B. (2020). Materials development for the digital native generation: Teachers as materials developers. *MWIS Newsletter.* Retrieved from http://newsmanager.commpartners.com/tesolmwis/issues/2020-01-09/4.html

Khoshnevisan, B., & Le, N. (2018). Augmented Reality in Language Education: A Systematic Literature Review. In W. B. James & C. Cobanoglu (Eds.), *Proceedings of the Global Conference on Education and Research (GLOCER) Conference* (Vol. 2, pp. 57–71). ANAHEI Publishing, LLC. https://scholarcommons.usf.edu/cgi/viewcontent.cgi?article=1017&context=anaheipublishing

Koutromanous, G., Sofos, A., & Avraamidou, L. (2015). The use of augmented reality games in education: A review of the literature. *Educational Media International*, *52*(4), 253–271. doi:10.1080/09523987.2015.1125988

Küçük, S., Yılmaz, R. M., & Göktaş, Y. (2014). Augmented reality for learning English: Achievement, attitude and cognitive load levels of students. *Education in Science*, *39*(176), 393–404.

Liontas, J. I. (1999). *Developing a pragmatic methodology of idiomaticity: The comprehension and interpretation of SL vivid phrasal idioms during reading* (Unpublished doctoral dissertation). The University of Arizona, Tucson, AZ.

Liu, T., Tan, T., & Chu, Y. (2010). QR code and augmented reality-supported mobile English learning system. In *Mobile multimedia processing* (pp. 37–52). Springer. doi:10.1007/978-3-642-12349-8_3

Liu, T. Y. (2009). A context-aware ubiquitous learning environment for language listening and speaking. *Journal of Computer Assisted Learning*, *25*(6), 515–527. doi:10.1111/j.1365-2729.2009.00329.x

Liu, Y., Holden, D., & Zheng, D. (2016). Analyzing students' language learning experience in an augmented reality mobile game: An exploration of an emergent learning environment. *Social and Behavioral Sciences*, *228*, 369–374. doi:10.1016/j.sbspro.2016.07.055

Lombardi, M. M. (2007a). *Approaches that work: How authentic learning is transforming higher education.* ELI Report No. 5. Boulder, CO: EDUCAUSE Learning Initiative.

Lombardi, M. M. (2007b). *Authentic learning for the 21st century: An overview.* ELI Report No. 1. Boulder, CO: EDUCAUSE Learning Initiative.

Mahadzir, N. N. N., & Phung, L. F. (2013). The use of augmented reality pop-up book to increase motivation in English language learning for national primary school. *IOSR Journal of Research & Method in Education*, *1*(1), 26–38. doi:10.9790/7388-0112638

McKenzie, J., & Darnell, D. (2004). The eye Magic book. In *A report into augmented reality storytelling in the context of a children's workshop 2003*. New Zealand Centre for Children's Literature and Christchurch College of Education.

Ogata, H., Li, M., Hou, B., Uosaki, N., El-Bishouty, M. M., & Yano, Y. (2011). SCROLL: Supporting to share and reuse ubiquitous learning log in the context of language learning. *Research & Practice in Technology Enhanced Learning, 6*(2).

Park, S., & Khoshnevisan, B. (2019). Literacy meets augmented reality (AR): The use of AR in literacy. In W. B. James & C. Cobanoglu (Eds.), *Proceedings of the Global Conference on Education and Research (GLOCER) Conference* (Vol. 3, pp. 93–99). ANAHEI Publishing, LLC. https://scholarcommons.usf.edu/cgi/viewcontent.cgi?article=1021&context=anaheipublishing

Pérez-López, D., & Contero, M. (2013). Delivering educational multimedia contents through an augmented reality application: A case study on its impact on knowledge acquisition and retention. *The Turkish Online Journal of Educational Technology*, *12*(4).

Pilton, S. (2014). The augmented classroom. *Modern English Teacher*, *23*(3), 17–19.

Rashtchi, M., & Khoshnevisan, B. (2008). Audio-taped dialogue journal: A technique to improve speaking skill of Iranian EFL learners. *Journal of English Language Pedagogy and Practice*, *1*(3), 164–176.

Reinders, H., & Lakarnchua, O. (2014). Implementing mobile language learning with an augmented reality activity. *Modern English Teacher*, *23*(2), 42–46.

Santos, M., Lübke, A., Taketomi, T., Yamamoto, G., Rodrigo, M., Sandor, C., & Kato, H. (2016). Augmented reality as multimedia: The case for situated vocabulary learning. *Research & Practice in Technology Enhanced Learning*, *11*(1), 1. doi:10.118641039-016-0028-2 PMID:30613237

Schrawman, G., & Lehman, S. (2001). Situational interest; A review of the literature and directions for future research. *Educational Psychology Review*, *13*(1), 23–52. doi:10.1023/A:1009004801455

Sellen, A., & Harper, R. (2003). *The myth of the paperless office*. MIT Press.

Silva, M., Roberto, R., & Teichrieb, V. (2013). Evaluating an educational system based on projective augmented reality. In *Brazilian Symposium on Computers in Education* (Vol. 24, No. 1, p. 214). 10.5753/CBIE.SBIE.2013.214

Singhal, S., Bagga, S., Goyal, P., & Saxena, V. (2012). Augmented chemistry: Interactive education system. *International Journal of Computers and Applications*, *49*(15), 1–5. doi:10.5120/7700-1041

Smeets, D. J. H., & Bus, A. G. (2012). Interactive electronic storybooks for kindergartners to promote vocabulary growth. *Journal of Experimental Child Psychology*, *112*(1), 36–55. doi:10.1016/j.jecp.2011.12.003 PMID:22265347

Solak, E., & Cakir, R. (2015). Exploring the effect of materials designed with augmented reality on language learners' vocabulary learning. *The Journal of Educators Online*, *13*(2), 50–72. doi:10.9743/JEO.2015.2.5

Specht, M., Ternier, S., & Greller, W. (2011). Mobile augmented reality for learning: A case study. *Journal of the Research Center for Educational Technology*, *7*(1). www.rcetj.org/index.php/rcetj/article/view/151

Talheimer, W. (2004). *Bells, whistles, neon, and purple prose; When interesting words, sounds and visuals hurt learning and performance- A review of the seductive-augmentation research*. Work-Learning Research.

Tan, T. H., & Liu, T. Y. (2004). The mobile-based interactive learning environment (MOBILE) and a case study for assisting elementary school English learning. In *Proceedings of* the 2004 IEEE International Conference on Advanced Learning Technologies (pp. 530-534). IEEE.

Trushell, J., Maitland, A., & Burrell, C. (2003). Pupils' recall of an interactive storybook on CD-ROM. *Journal of Computer Assisted Learning*, *19*(1), 80–89. doi:10.1046/j.0266-4909.2002.00008.x

Vygotsky, L. (1978). Interaction between learning and development. *Readings on the Development of Children*, *23*(3), 34–41.

Wertsch, J. V. (1991). *Voices of the Mind: A Sociocultural Approach to Mediated Action*. Harvard University Press.

Wertsch, J. V. (1995). The need for action in sociocultural research. In J. V. Wertsch, P. del Río, & A. Álvarez (Eds.), *Sociocultural Studies of Mind* (pp. 56–74). Cambridge University Press. doi:10.1017/CBO9781139174299.004

Whitehead, A. N. (1932). *The aims of education and other essays*. Ernest Benn.

Wittrock, M. C. (1974). Learning as a generative process. *Educational Psychologist*, *19*(2), 87–95. doi:10.1080/00461527409529129

Wojciechowski, R., & Cellary, W. (2013). Evaluation of learners' attitude toward learning in ARIES augmented reality environments. *Computers & Education*, *68*, 570–585. doi:10.1016/j.compedu.2013.02.014

Wu, H., Lee, S., Chang, H., & Liang, J. (2013). Current status, opportunities and challenges of augmented reality in education. *Computers & Education*, *62*, 41–49. doi:10.1016/j.compedu.2012.10.024

Yang, Y. F. (2011). Engaging students in an online situated language learning environment. *Computer Assisted Language Learning*, *24*(2), 181–198. doi:10.1080/09588221.2010.538700

ADDITIONAL READING

Chen, C. H., Ho, C. H., & Lin, J. B. (2015). The development of an augmented reality game-based learning environment. *Procedia: Social and Behavioral Sciences, 174*, 216–220. doi:10.1016/j.sbspro.2015.01.649

Chen, N., Teng, D. C., Lee, C., & Kinshuk. (2011). Augmenting paper-based reading activity with direct access to digital materials and scaffolded questioning. *Computers & Education, 57*(2), 1705–1715. doi:10.1016/j.compedu.2011.03.013

Cheng, K. H. (2017). Reading an augmented reality book: An exploration of learners' cognitive load, motivation, and attitudes. *Australasian Journal of Educational Technology, 33*(4).

Chiang, T. H., Yang, S. J., & Hwang, G. (2014). Students' online interactive patterns in augmented reality-based inquiry activities. *Computers & Education, 78*, 97–108. doi:10.1016/j.compedu.2014.05.006

Hung, Y. H., Chen, C. H., & Huang, S. W. (2017). Applying augmented reality to enhance learning: A study of different teaching materials. *Journal of Computer Assisted Learning, 33*(3), 252–266. doi:10.1111/jcal.12173

Jonassen, D., Spector, M. J., Driscoll, M., Merrill, M. D., van Merrienboer, J., & Driscoll, M. P. (2008). *Handbook of research on educational communications and technology: a project of the association for educational communications and technology*. Routledge. doi:10.4324/9780203880869

Keller, J. M. (1987). Development and use of the ARCS model of instructional design. *Journal of instructional development, 10*(3), 2–10.

Vazquez, C. D., Nyati, A. A., Luh, A., Fu, M., Aikawa, T., & Maes, P. (2017). Serendipitous Language Learning in Mixed Reality. In *Proceedings of the 2017 CHI Conference Extended Abstracts on Human Factors in Computing Systems* (pp. 2172-2179). ACM. 10.1145/3027063.3053098

KEY TERMS AND DEFINITIONS

AR Books: AR books are printed books except that digital material is superimposed onto the pages to create a unique experience of learning in context with authentic material.

ARCS Model: Proposed by Keller (1987), ARCS model helps designers create effective instructional materials. ARCS stand for attention, relevance, confidence, and satisfaction. These factors contribute to motivation when designing a material.

Augmented Reality: AR is an emergent technology that enables us to amalgamate computer-generated items and the real world. AR helps us superimpose a layer of computer-generated information on real environments.

Constructivism: Constructivism posits individuals along with their prior knowledge and sociocultural background play an essential role in learning.

Location-Aware AR: Location-aware AR heavily relies on Global Positioning System (GPS) to accurately detect a user's location, so the related digital information is provided by different devices such as cell phones.

Situated Learning: According to situated learning, authentic context is key in quality education so learners can efficiently engage in the process of learning to undertake complex tasks. Educators then need to embed learners in different social communities to learn new concepts.

Sociocultural Theory: Sociocultural theory posits that learning occurs when humans are placed in different settings to perform different social activities. According to sociocultural theory, people need to negotiate meanings and interact with peers and tools to learn.

Chapter 13
Learning to Follow Directions in English Through a Virtual Reality Environment:
An Eye Tracking Study and Evaluation of Usability

Jorge Bacca-Acosta
Fundación Universitaria Konrad Lorenz, Colombia

Julian Tejada
Federal University of Sergipe, Brazil

Carlos Ospino-Ibañez
Fundación Universitaria Konrad Lorenz, Colombia

ABSTRACT

Learning how to give and follow directions in English is one of the key topics in regular English as a Foreign Language (EFL) courses. However, this topic is commonly taught in the classroom with pencil and paper exercises. In this chapter, a scaffolded virtual reality (VR) environment for learning the topic of following directions in English is introduced. An eye tracking study was conducted to determine how students perceive the scaffolds for completing the learning task, and an evaluation of acceptance and usability was conducted to identify the students' perceptions. The results show that scaffolds in the form of text and images are both effective for increasing the students' learning performance. The gaze frequency is higher for the textual scaffold, but the duration of gaze fixations is lower for the scaffolds in the form of images. The acceptance and usability of the VR environment were found to be positive.

INTRODUCTION

DOI: 10.4018/978-1-7998-5043-4.ch013

Learning how to give and follow directions in English as a Foreign Language (EFL) courses is necessary to develop skills so that students can understand how to get to another location by following instructions. This topic is taught in regular English classes and is a crucial topic in many curriculums (Taylor-Hamilton, 2004). In this topic, students learn the meaning of expressions such as "go straight", "turn left", "turn right", "cross the avenue", among others, and students develop skills to follow instructions to arrive at a particular place in a city. The possibility of transferring this knowledge to a real scenario could be facilitated if this topic were taught by doing practical exercises that can be as real as possible.

In EFL courses, there are situations where teachers do not have the proper resources to explain a topic other than in books and simple board exercises, and this can cause that many students lose the interest in learning this subject, making the teaching process more difficult. However, there are some positive experiences of integrating technology in language learning (Sabiri, 2020).

The authors of this chapter interviewed some EFL teachers in the Konrad Lorenz University in Colombia and teachers acknowledged that there should be more interactive ways to learn the topic of learning to follow directions in English by using mobile applications or other interactive technologies. Moreover, teachers are always looking for new ways to motivate the students and apply new technologies in the learning field (Jenkins, 2016). Furthermore, the interaction with computers and technological learning environments can be helpful to get a better understanding of a topic or subject (Martirosov & Kopecek, 2017).

From the interviews, the authors identified that most of the teachers are open to new technologies such as augmented reality, virtual reality or mobile applications that will help their students to be more interested in learning how to give and follow directions. According to the teachers, these technologies might even replace writing and board exercises and these technologies can be a proper support for the English class. The EFL teachers that participated in the interview argue that they explain the topic of giving and following directions using board exercises, photocopies and some practical exercises with objects from the classroom. However, according to the teachers, these exercises are not enough to capture the students' attention or increase their interest in the topic. In that regard, since technology is continually evolving and changing, a technological solution can help to improve the learning process of this topic.

Virtual Reality (VR) is an immersive technology used for the simulation of the real-world (N. Singh & Singh, 2017). According to Steuer (1992), the term "virtual reality" was coined in 1989 by Jaron Lanier and is defined as a medium that consists of a collection of technological hardware that includes computers, head-mounted displays (HMD) and sensors that provides a real-time animation that is controlled by the sensors, and the visualization is presented in stereoscopic displays. This term should not be confused with the term Augmented Reality (AR), which instead of creating a virtual environment to interact with as in VR, AR simulates artificial objects in real objects (Martirosov & Kopecek, 2017). Some studies show that VR environments allow improving learning, either in the simulation of activities in realistic contexts or just to improve certain skills of an individual (Al Awadhi et al., 2018; Martirosov & Kopecek, 2017) VR has multiple applications in many fields beyond education such as in the military field, medicine, marketing, entertainment among others (Singh & Singh, 2017; Jiang et al., 2017; Garcia-Cardona et al., 2017).

VR has also been applied to enhance the learning process of different languages (Lin & Lan, 2015) and there seems to be evidence of the effectiveness of VR for learning languages over traditional teaching methods. However, there are still some gaps in the literature on the use of VR for teaching English as a foreign language (Pinto et al., 2019; Radianti et al., 2020). One of those gaps is the lack of research on the effect of scaffolding mechanisms on the students' learning performance in immersive VR environments for EFL learning. Scaffolding is a strategy that can be used "to move learning forward in the zone of proximal development" (Shepard, 2005, p. 66). Studies that investigate the scaffolding instructional technique in VR have mainly focused on how VR is used as a scaffold (Mohamed & Badioze, 2011; Wang & Cheng, 2011; Singh, 2017) but there is a lack of research on how to design and develop scaffolds for immersive VR.

Moreover, most of the studies conducted to date around VR for second language acquisition have been conducted with non-immersive VR in environments such as Second Life, but there is an increasing interest in using immersive VR which implies the use of headsets for a complete immersion in a virtual world and more research is needed to identify the possibilities and restrictions of VR for language learning (Lan, 2020). To the best of our knowledge, there is a lack of research on the use of VR for teaching the topic of following directions in English.

Consequently, in this chapter, a VR learning environment for teaching the topic of following directions in English is introduced. An evaluation study using the eye tracking technique was also conducted to determine the effectiveness of some scaffolding mechanisms in VR for learning this topic. By investigating the effectiveness of the scaffolding mechanisms in the VR application through the eye tracking technique, it is possible to determine how students are using these scaffolds for their learning process and how the scaffolds affect the students' learning performance. The results of this study provide valuable insights for the design of future VR environments with scaffolds that effectively support the learning process in EFL courses. The eye tracking technique was adopted as a non-intrusive method to collect data about the gaze frequency, duration of gaze fixations and the time spent on some areas of interest in the VR environment.

The rest of this chapter is divided into the following sections: after the introduction, the related work section is presented. Then, the objectives of this study and research questions are presented. Then, the virtual reality environment for learning the topic of following directions in English is described. The evaluation study of the VR environment is then presented followed by the results and discussion. Finally, the advantages and drawbacks of VR for EFL, conclusions and future work are presented.

RELATED WORK

VR is a "technique for the simulation of real or virtual world by applying the theory of immersion into a virtual 3-D space in which stereoscopic vision, sense of hear, sense of touch and smell are very similar to that of real world" (Singh & Singh, 2017, p. 1). It is also defined as: as a kind of high technology simulation system assisted by computer technology (Lee, Shih, Chou, & Chen, 2017). VR is also defined as "a virtual simulated environment generated with [the] use of computer technology that creates a make-believe virtual world that is close to real life", (Chung, 2012, p. 2) or "a dynamic environment that is designed for users to have direct experience and communication, which acts as a new interface for users to interact with information, a medium that overlaps cyberspace, the real world, and the user" (Chung, 2012, p. 2). In the same vein, VR is also defined as a "computer system created by a computer to experience a virtual world. It acts on the users through the vision, hearing, smell, touch and so on, producing the immersive experience" (Ma, 2018, p. 2).

VR can be classified into three types: 1. Open virtual spaces such as Second life. 2. Multiplayer online games. 3. Synthetic immersive environments (Andujar & Buchner, 2019, p. 153). In that regard, the VR environment introduced in this chapter can be classified as an immersive synthetic environment.

VR has also been applied to the field of language learning with promising results. Wang et al. (2019) conducted a meta-analysis of studies in language learning and found that 3D virtual worlds have a moderated positive effect on linguistic gains and affective gains. From a systematic literature review of 398 journal articles, Shadiev and Yang (2020) found that most of the studies report an increase on the students learning outcomes and positive perceptions towards the use of technology (including VR) for language learning. Garcia, Laesker, Andujar, Kauer, and Nguyen (2019) introduced a VR experience created in Unity and deployed in Oculus Rift for learning about household items in the Spanish Language. Berns et al. (2013) developed a 3D virtual world for learning German language and found that games in a 3D virtual world help students to learn faster and easier. Moreover, according to Schwienhorst (2002), several researchers have concluded that VR can be used to create authentic language learning environments in terms of tools, space and speakers that are better than the physical classroom. Legault et al. (2019) developed two immersive VR environments for learning vocabulary in Mandarin language and found that the immersive VR environments were more effective for learning when compared to the traditional methods of vocabulary learning. Likewise, Xie et al. (2019) investigated how virtual reality might benefit the learning process of Chines as a second language. They found that VR provided an authentic context for learning that encouraged students to learn more about Chinese culture. Kaplan (2019) investigated the effect of stereoscopic 3D images on Polish vocabulary learning. As for the English language, there are also some learning experiences created with VR that are discussed in the next sub-section.

VR for Teaching and Learning English as a Foreign Language

Over the years, VR has also been used to teach different topics in the EFL curriculum. For instance, Chien et al. (2020) investigated the effect of 360° videos and peer assessment on the students' English speaking performance, motivation and critical thinking skills. The results showed that students who learnt with the 360° videos with peer assessment had a better learning performance than students who followed a traditional English speaking training. In the same vein, Chen & Hwang (2020) investigated the effect of both 360° videos in VR and cognitive styles on the students' learning performance in oral presentations in the context of a college course about tourism and restaurants. The results showed that students that were exposed to 360° videos in VR had a better learning performance in oral presentations compared to those who learnt with a conventional multimedia approach. Likewise, Adnan, Shak, Karim, Tahir, & Shah (2020) found that 360° videos in VR for learning English and other languages like Mandarin and Arabic are useful for fostering students' positive attitudes and increase the students' skills in the corresponding languages.

Apart from 360° videos in VR, Yeh et al. (2020) investigated how the use of VR might contribute to increase intercultural learning of college students in an EFL course. The results showed that students, as creators of VR content, increased their intercultural knowledge and communicated better in English. Peixoto et al. (2019) and Pinto et al. (2019) developed a VR learning environment to help students to practice listening in English in two contexts: an office for formal English conversations and a pub for informal conversations. The results showed that the VR environment creates an increased sense of presence and satisfaction, but the learning outcomes are similar to those obtained in a regular listening exercise without VR support. Jeong et al. (2018) developed a VR environment for practising conversations in English. The authors concluded that there were no significant differences in the learning outcomes of students who used the VR environment and those who used a computer-based environment. According to the systematic review by Wang & Zheng (2018), VR might improve language acquisition in adult learners and increase student motivation.

Lee et al. (2017) developed a VR environment for teaching English for tourism purposes. In particular, for teaching English in specific situations at an airport. Wang et al. (2017) developed a virtual environment called VILLAGE for teaching linking verbs, participles and action verbs and found that the virtual environment increases the sense of presence and immersion. Chen (2016) used a virtual island for learning languages in Second Life that is called VIRTLANTIS to investigate the affordances of virtual environments for learning English as a Second Language. The results of the study show that a combination of a 3D virtual environment and authentic tasks has a positive effect on the students' learning performance, motivation and engagement in English. Moreover, the students reported that the activities in the 3D virtual environment were not static as in traditional classrooms for learning English. Chen (2016) developed a VR environment that recreates a department store with six floors. From a study conducted with 448 university students in Taiwan, it was found that the VR environment was a potential facilitator of English linguistic knowledge of phonology, morphology, vocabulary and syntax. Lan (2015) introduced two VR learning environments developed in Second Life for learning English in two teaching contexts: ring toss and a restaurant. The results of a study conducted with 132 school students showed that the VR environments were useful for increasing the syntactic and conversation abilities in English. Moreover, Shih (2008) developed a VR environment to improve the students' communicative competence in English and found that students showed positive attitudes, increased motivation and a better interactive learning experience.

Notwithstanding the advances in research on VR for EFL learning and the wide variety of EFL topics that have been covered, there is still a need of more research to identify the benefits and drawbacks of immersive VR for language learning (Peixoto et al., 2019; Lan, 2020). Moreover, to the best of our knowledge, there is a lack of research on how immersive VR might help students to practice the topic of following directions in English. In that regard, this study attempts to fill that gap in the literature by introducing a VR application for that topic and conducting an evaluation study of eye tracking and usability.

OBJECTIVES OF THIS STUDY AND RESEARCH QUESTIONS

The primary purpose of this study is to provide insights into how students use some scaffolds to complete a learning task when students use an immersive VR environment designed for learning the topic of following directions in English. Another objective was to conduct an evaluation study on the usability and students' perceptions when using an immersive VR for learning the topic of following directions in English. In line with the gaps in the literature and the need of more research on the effect of scaffolding on the students' learning performance in immersive VR environments, the research questions addressed in this study are:

- **RQ1**: What is the impact of a scaffolded immersive VR environment for learning the topic of following directions in English?
- **RQ2**: What are the acceptance and self-reported usability of the immersive VR environment for learning how to follow directions in English?

To address RQ1, we applied the eye tracking technique as a non-intrusive method to collect data about the students' gaze behaviour when students use the scaffolds provided by the VR environment. Previous eye tracking studies in the field of language learning focused on spoken word recognition and 2D writing tasks (Michel & Smith, 2017). To the best of our knowledge, this is one of the first studies that use the eye tracking technique in VR to provide evidence about how students perceive and scan the VR environment for learning the topic of following directions in English. Eye tracking is useful for collecting evidence about some cognitive processes such as information processing that are difficult to observe using other methods such as self-reported questionnaires. To address RQ2, a questionnaire was used to collect information about the students' acceptance and usability.

A VR ENVIRONMENT FOR LEARNING ABOUT FOLLOWING DIRECTIONS IN ENGLISH

The VR learning environment was developed with the support of the EFL teachers for the purposes of this study. The VR learning environment simulates a small city in which the student can move in any direction. By using different assets, this scenario consists of elements found in a city, such as houses, building, trees, street roads, street lights, traffic signals, among others. The main objective was that the student feels as if he/she were in a real city (see Figure 1 and Figure 2). The VR application has four different levels with increased difficulty for each level. The VR environment was developed in Unity 5.6 with the SteamVR plugin (version 1.2.3) for the HTC Vive headset. Besides, the SMI eye tracker for the HTC Vive was used to record information about the eye movements of every student using the application. The eye tracking technique allowed the authors to collect data about how students scan the VR environment. This VR environment belongs to the category named "VR for Operation" and, in particular, to the sub-category "manipulation" according to the classification introduced by Lan (2020). This VR environment belongs to this category because it allows students to do a hands-on experience for learning the topic of following directions in English.

Levels for Practising the Topic

Each level has a different objective (as shown in Figure 3), but the main idea is to get to a specific place by following the instructions provided by the application. The application implements the scaffolding instructional technique to assist students during the learning process. According to Wood, Bruner, & Ross (1976), in the context of problem-solving, scaffolding is a process that enables a novice learner to solve a problem or carry out a task that is outside of their current skills or "beyond his unassisted efforts". In that regard, the VR environment provides some scaffolds (aids or cues) so that students can take advantage of them if they do not understand the instructions.

The objectives for each one of the levels are:

- **Level One:** A grey house.
- **Level Two:** City's park.
- **Level Three**: Hot dog car.
- **Level Four:** The tallest building in the city.

Figure 1. Screenshot of the students' perspective in the immersive VR learning environment for the topic of following directions in English

Figure 2. The city in which students are immersed to solve the learning task

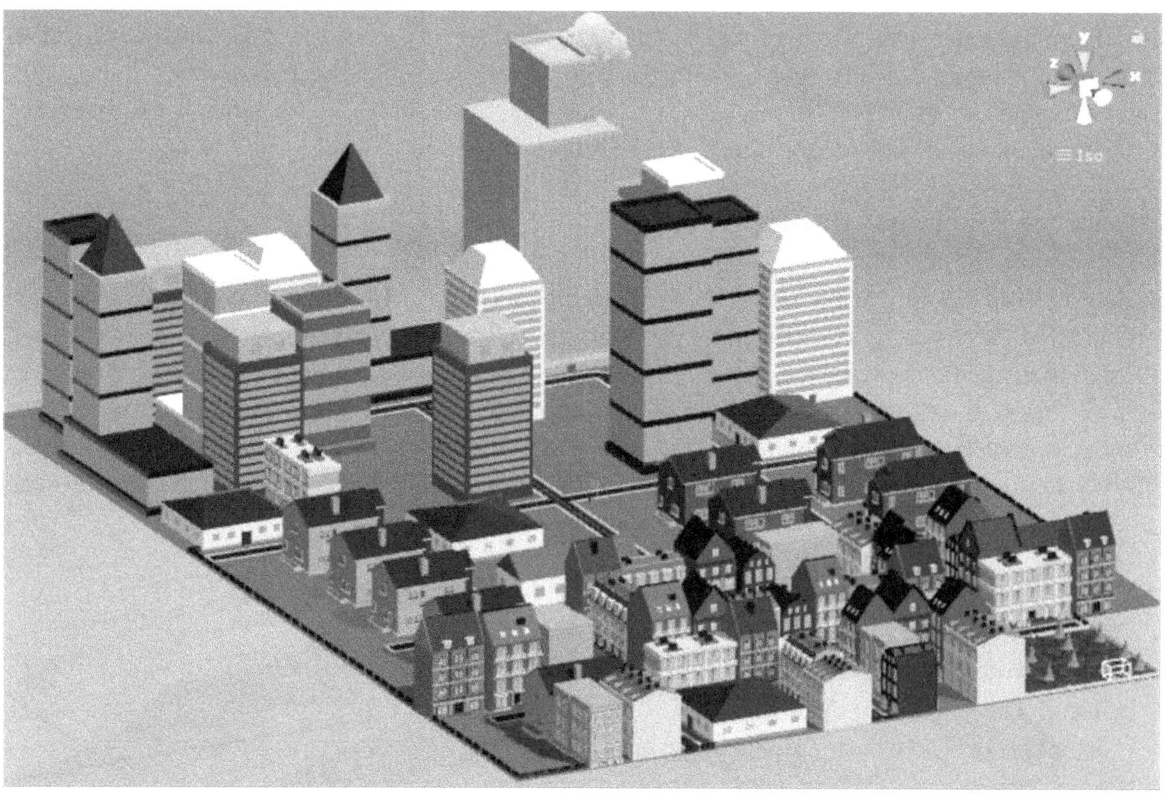

Figure 3. Practice levels, showcasing the objective of each of them

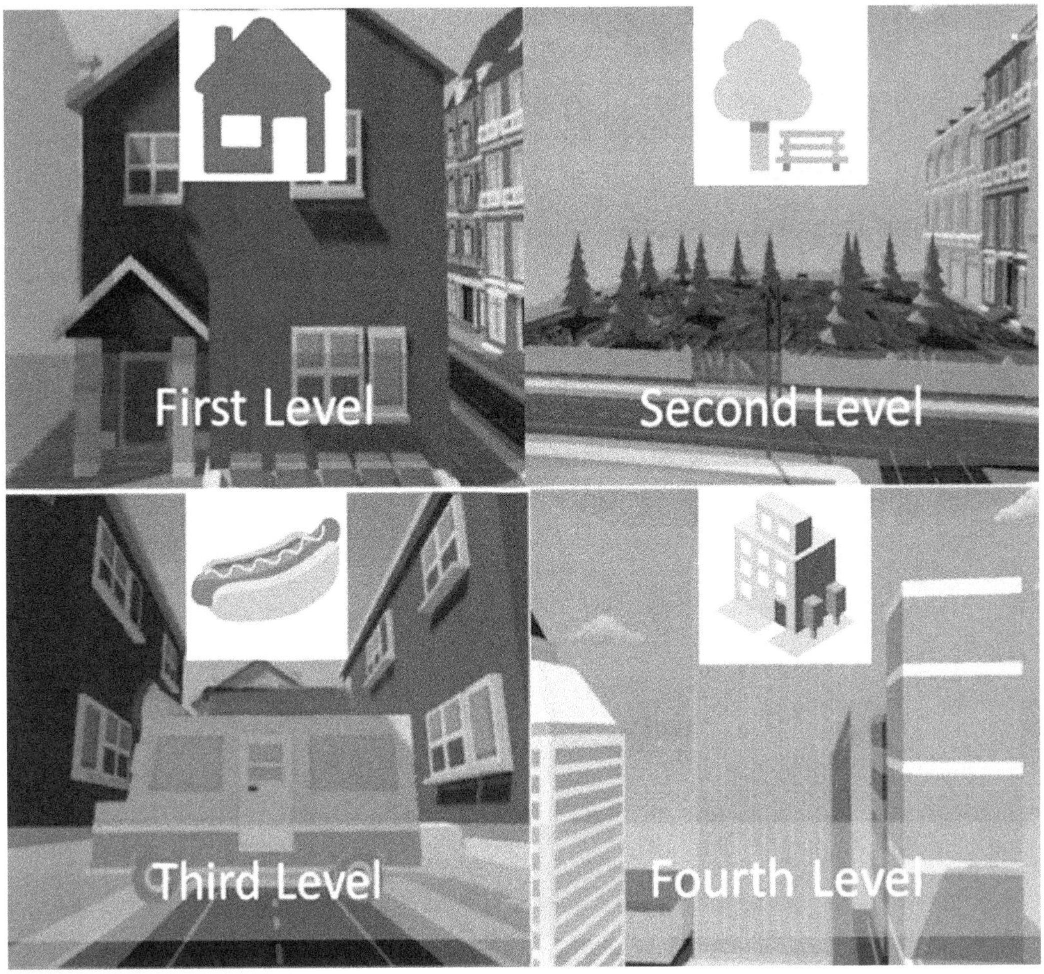

Mechanics

In this project, the authors used the HTC Vive controllers to give students the chance to interact and move around the scenario (considering the limitations of the room prepared for the VR experience).

- Listening to the instruction in English: Students first listen to the instruction in English. There are some buttons (see Figure 4) along the streets in the virtual city that allows the user to listen to the instructions they have to follow for each level to arrive at a particular place in the city. To activate the buttons, students touch them with the HTC Vive controller.

Figure 4. Buttons used to listen to the instruction and get help

- Getting Help (scaffolding aids): If students do not understand the instruction by listening to it. Two scaffolds assist students during the learning task:
    - Text Help: This scaffold shows the text of the instruction on the traffic signal. The user will be able to see this text for a short period (15 seconds). Figure 5 shows an example of this help from a user's perspective.

Figure 5. Text help (user's perspective)

- Visual Help: This scaffold provides a visual aid that indicates the correct direction according to the instruction (see Figure 6). This strategy will help students to make a connection between the instruction and the correct direction.

In line with the redundancy principle of the Cognitive Theory of Multimedia Learning (Mayer, 2009), in the VR application students first listen to the instruction, and after that, if they do not understand it, they can use the scaffolds to see the written text (using the Text Help) of the instruction in the traffic signal. In other words, students first listen to the instruction and then they can see the written text of the instruction. According to the redundancy principle, this reduces the extraneous cognitive load because auditory and visual channels are not competing for cognitive resources. Moreover, the signaling principle was also considered in the design and development of the VR environment because the traffic signals act as cues that capture the students' attention to the instruction they have to follow to arrive at a particular place in each level. The traffic signals direct the students' attention to the essential information, and this reduces the cognitive load as they focus their processing on the information provided by the traffic signal.

Figure 6. Visual scaffold (user's perspective)

The traffic signals in the learning activity were designed according to the spatial contiguity principle because the visual help (scaffold) appears next to the text help (scaffold) to reduce the cognitive resources that students need to create the correspondence between the text and images to understand the instruction.

It is important to note that the traffic signals are located in different positions in the city, and they provide the instructions for arriving at a particular place in the city, or they indicate if the current direction of the students is wrong. If the current direction is wrong students can change their direction to find the correct path.

Data Storage

To store data of interest every time the application is used by the students, this project makes use of data persistence, using the "PlayerPrefs" Unity property. This property storages and access data between game sessions (Unity Technologies, 2019). The data recorded is the total amount of time playing the application in every level, total time spent for each level and the total number of times that each scaffold was requested for each user. This information is shown in a panel of statistics that is displayed in the main menu of the VR application as shown in Figure 7. The purpose of this panel is that students can be aware of their performance in the application when they complete each level. The application also records all the information collected from the SMI eye tracker that is integrated into the VR headset. The information collected was analyzed after the experiment to collect evidence about how students perceived the VR environment.

Figure 7. The Panel of statistics in the main menu

EVALUATION STUDY

Methodology and Participants

This project follows the design-based research methodology (Wang & Hannafin, 2005), and in this chapter, the authors report the first evaluation of impact, acceptance and usability (using the eye tracking technique) of the system. The VR application was tested with 18 students (11 males and 7 females) from different university degrees (psychology, systems engineering, industrial engineering, mathematics and business administration) who are taking English courses in the university. The participants' age range was between 19 to 24 years old ($M = 20$; $SD = 1{,}6$).

Data Collection

For data collection the authors used the eye-tracking technique. Eye-tracking allows detecting temporal fluctuations in cognitive processes and perceptions that are difficult to detect using traditional self-reported measures (Alemdag & Cagiltay, 2018). In the field of language learning, eye tracking can be used to provide information about how students process the information in a second language (Michel & Smith, 2017).

For eye tracking, in this study, the authors used the *Tethered Eye Tracking VR HMD based on HTC Vive* provided by SensoMotoric Instruments (SMI). The eye tracker provides a Unity Application Programming Interface (API) for collecting data about the students' gaze position, orientation, pupil diameter, among others. The authors took advantage of Unity colliders in order to define areas of interest (AOI) to identify when the students' gaze collides with those areas of interest in order to measure the number of gaze fixations and saccades. This strategy has been used in VR in previous studies with eye tracking (Clay, König, & König, 2019). The colliders for the areas of interest were set up in the street signs, the black pedestals, houses, buildings and the area covered by the objective at the end of each level. The main areas of interest were: the text help (in the street sign), the visual scaffold (in the street sign) and the buttons that activate these scaffolds.

A survey with a Likert scale was also used to collect information about the students' acceptance and the usability of the system. The survey consists of 19 questions and is the result of adapting the following dimensions of the instruments introduced by Huang & Liao (2015) and Wild et al. (2017):

- **System Usability Scale (SUS)** (Brooke, 1996)**:** Questions 1 - 5. This dimension seeks to assess the usability of a system.
- **Ecological validity:** Questions 6 - 9. This dimension is defined as the degree in which the user perceives aspects of reality in a simulated environment.
- **Perceived ease of use:** Questions 10 - 12. It's defined as the degree to which the user perceives that the use of the system does not require a high amount of effort.
- **Engagement:** Questions 13 - 14. Level of attraction and attention caused by the application during its use.
- **Perceived usefulness:** Questions 15 - 17. It refers to the perception of technology as an element more useful than other previous technologies or resources.
- **Aesthetics:** Questions 18 - 19. Degree of visual attraction and entertainment perceived by the user.

Furthermore, the VR environment was used by two teachers from the Institute of Foreign languages from the University where this research was conducted, and a semi-structured interview was used to collect the teachers' perceptions about the VR environment.

Research Procedure

The research procedure was as follows:

1. Students from the English as a Foreign Language courses at the university were invited to participate in the research. Those who voluntarily decided to participate signed informed consent of participation in the research after the principal researcher explained the research objectives and the research procedure.
2. The researchers first explained how to use the application and then students used it for five minutes so that they get used to using the controllers and the headset.

3. The calibration process was conducted so that the tracker can accurately identify the students' eye movements. Five-point calibration was applied with the corresponding validation with a maximum of three repetitions. This process lasted for one minute. The eye tracking API provides an alert if the headset moves from the appropriate position and the eye tracker lose the eyes. Once the calibration is completed, students were allowed to use the application from the main menu where they can choose the level they would like to practice.
4. Students were required to use the first two levels at their own pace. This phase lasted between 15 to 20 minutes. During this time, the eye tracker recorded information about the students' gaze position in the VR environment and this information was dumped to a plain text file.
5. After using the application, students were required to answer the survey for collecting data about their perceptions on the acceptance of this VR environment.

Data Analysis

Data collected from the eye tracker was exported from Unity to CSV files that were processed after the experiment to obtain information about gaze frequency (number of times that students switch their gaze to the scaffolds in VR), duration of gaze fixations and the time to finish each task (i.e. the time spent to complete each instruction to arrive at a particular place). Since the authors defined some areas of interest in the VR environment using the Unity colliders (Clay et al., 2019), the authors identified the exact moment in which students' gaze was in any of the areas of interest. The areas of interest were mainly defined around the scaffolds (i.e. Text Help, visual help) and around the buttons that activate the scaffolds. To analyse the information collected from the eye tracker RStudio was used to conduct statistical tests. The results from this analysis is presented and discussed in the next section. Moreover, content analysis was used to extract information from the semi-structured interviews with teachers to identify their perceptions of the VR environment for the topic of following directions in English.

RESULTS AND DISCUSSION

The primary purpose of this study was to investigate the effectiveness of some scaffolding mechanisms in a VR application for learning the topic of following directions in English. This study provides insights into the effect of some scaffolds (Text Help and Visual Help) on the students' learning performance. This section presents the results and discussion to answer the two research questions addressed in this chapter.

RQ1: What is the impact of a scaffolded immersive VR environment for learning the topic of following directions in English?

As it was expected, the different scaffolding aids showed different patterns of use. The "Audio Help" (i.e. the button that triggers the instruction using audio) was the most used, in terms of gaze inputs (F (1.03,8.22) = 7.47, p = 0.02, $\eta^2 = 0.22$) and gaze duration ($F_{(1.10,8.82)}$=18.04, p = 0.002, $\eta^2 = 0.39$), followed by the text help (see Figure 8). Nevertheless, the results show that all of the instructions have the same level of difficulty, at least in terms of the way in which students visually explored the scaffolds to complete those instructions (see Figure 9). All of the instructions showed similar values of gaze inputs and gaze duration, regardless of the type of scaffold. This result might suggest that students did not find any difficulty with the instructions in level 1 and level 2 and the scaffolds were effective for helping students to complete the learning task in each level. Another interpretation of this result is that the scaffolds are useful for increasing the students' learning performance and might increase the students' learning outcomes. This result is in line with the findings in other studies that suggest a positive effect of scaffolding in immersive VR environments (Mohamed & Badioze, 2011; Wang & Cheng, 2011; Singh, 2017).

The results also show that there is a significant difference in the average frequency of gaze inputs between the Text Help and the Visual Help (see Figure 8). A possible explanation of this result might be that the latter was the last scaffold which provides clear information and avoid the need to look again (the scaffold that shows the image that represents the instruction). These results confirm the findings in previous studies in language learning regarding the positive effect of textual alternatives to increase listening comprehension (Mohsen, 2016). A practical implication of this result for the design of VR environments might be that the provision of a scaffold in the form of text as an alternative to audio could be as effective as providing an image as an alternative to the audio. However, the provision of both text and images seems to be positive for helping students to complete the learning task because some students need to use both the text and the visual help (image) to complete the learning task. However, in line with the redundancy principle of the cognitive theory of multimedia learning, showing text and images at the same time together with the audio of the instruction increases the students' cognitive load (Mayer, 2009). In the VR environment introduced in this chapter, the authors followed this principle to avoid an increase in the students' cognitive load and create more opportunities for learning.

As suggested by Mohsen (2016), it is also important to provide mechanisms so that students do not entirely depend on the scaffolds to complete the learning task. In that regard, faded scaffolding can be implemented to control this effect as well as adaptive and personalized mechanisms so that the scaffolds can be removed as students gain independence during the learning task. These results contribute to the body of research on the positive effect of scaffolding in VR environments. The results are in line with previous research that confirmed the positive effect of scaffolding on students' learning outcomes in VR learning environments (Dukes et al., 2013; Wang & Cheng, 2011).

However, in terms of the efficiency of scaffolds, the results might suggest that the Visual Help requires less time to get the information from the scaffold than the Text Help. In that regard, the visual help is a more efficient scaffold in terms of the amount of time needed to process the information. This result might be explained by the fact that visual cues are effective for directing the students' visual attention to important information (Alemdag & Cagiltay, 2018). Moreover, these cues can be helpful for reducing the students' cognitive load according to the signalling principle of the cognitive theory of multimedia learning (Mayer, 2009).

Figure 8. Average gaze frequency (A) from the number of gaze movements to the area of interest and time spent (B) in each type of scaffolding aids. The error bars represent standard errors of means and the marks significant differences between means (Tukey Test)

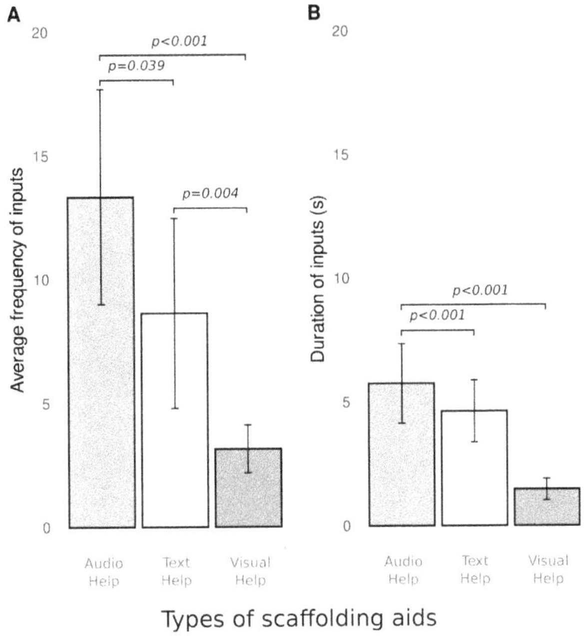

*Figure 9. Sections A, B and C show the average gaze frequency for the three scaffoldings aids: Audio help, Text help and Visual help, respectively. Sections D, E and F show the average gaze duration into the mentioned three scaffolding aids in the same order ((D) Audio help, (E) Text help and (F) Visual help). The error bars represent standard errors of means and the asterisk marks significant differences between means (Tukey Test at * p<0.01, ** p< 0.001)*

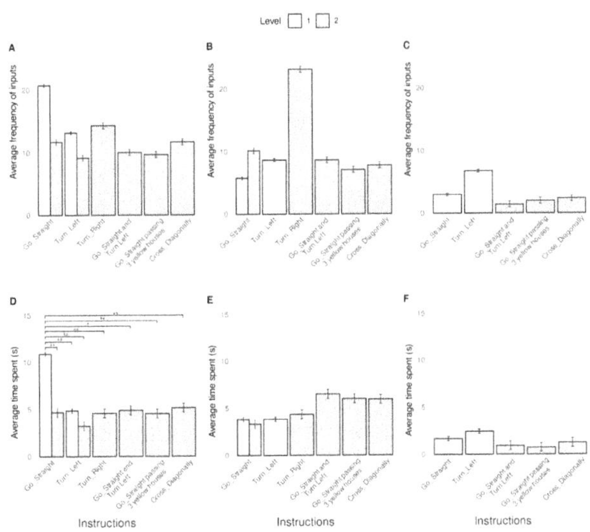

Figure 10. The average number of aids used in each instruction. The error bars represent standard errors of means and the marks represent significant differences between means with their respective p-value (Tukey Test)

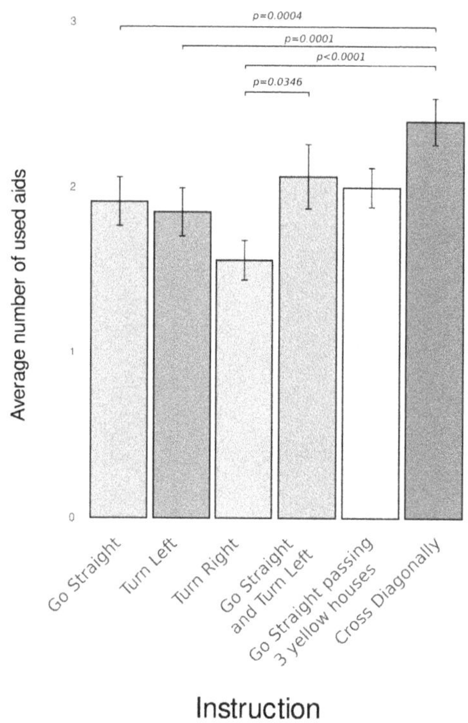

In terms of the number of scaffolds (aids) used, the authors found that students were able to understand most of the instructions listening to the audio or using the Text help (see Figure 10), with the exception of the instruction "*Cross diagonally*" ($F_{(5,\ 13.402)}$=6.9023, p<0.001, $\eta^2 = 0.24$). For this instruction, the Visual help (third aid) was frequently requested by the students (see Figure 10). The results show significant differences between the instruction "cross diagonally" and other instructions such as "Go straight", "Turn Left" and "Turn Right" in terms of the number of scaffolds (aids) used to complete the learning task. This result might suggest that the instruction "cross diagonally" was the most challenging instruction in the VR environment. The results show that students needed to use more scaffolds (Text Help and Visual Help) to understand this instruction when compared to the others. A practical implication of this result for the design of future VR environments for this topic might be to pay special attention to the inclusion of complicated instructions such as "Cross diagonally" or other instructions that involve the combination of single instructions such as "Go straight passing the three yellow houses to your right".

Finally, in terms of learning, it is possible to claim that the use of the virtual environment plus the scaffolding aids improved the students' performance. Students completed the learning task faster in the second session when compared to the first session ($t_{(17)} = 7.94$, $p < 0.001$, $d = 1.87$). This positive and significant result shows an increase in the students' performance from the first session to the second session. To interpret this result, it is also important to note that the number of instructions in the first session was smaller than the number of instructions in the second section. Moreover, there were instructions in the first session that appeared again in the second session. This result might suggest that students transferred the knowledge acquired in the first session to the second session. This result is in line with previous findings by Chen (2016), Yeh et al. (2020) and Shadiev and Yang (2020) in terms of the positive effect of immersive VR on the students' learning performance in EFL courses.

RQ2: What is the acceptance and self-reported usability of a VR application for learning how to follow directions in English?

Regarding the acceptance and self-reported usability, the median and mean of the score for the usability scale (SUS) and each one of its dimensions was above 4. For some scales (Engagement and Perceived Usefulness), almost all participants gave the maximum score on a scale from 1 to 5 (see Figure 11).

Figure 11. Box plots of the scores of the self-reported usability and acceptance of the VR learning environment

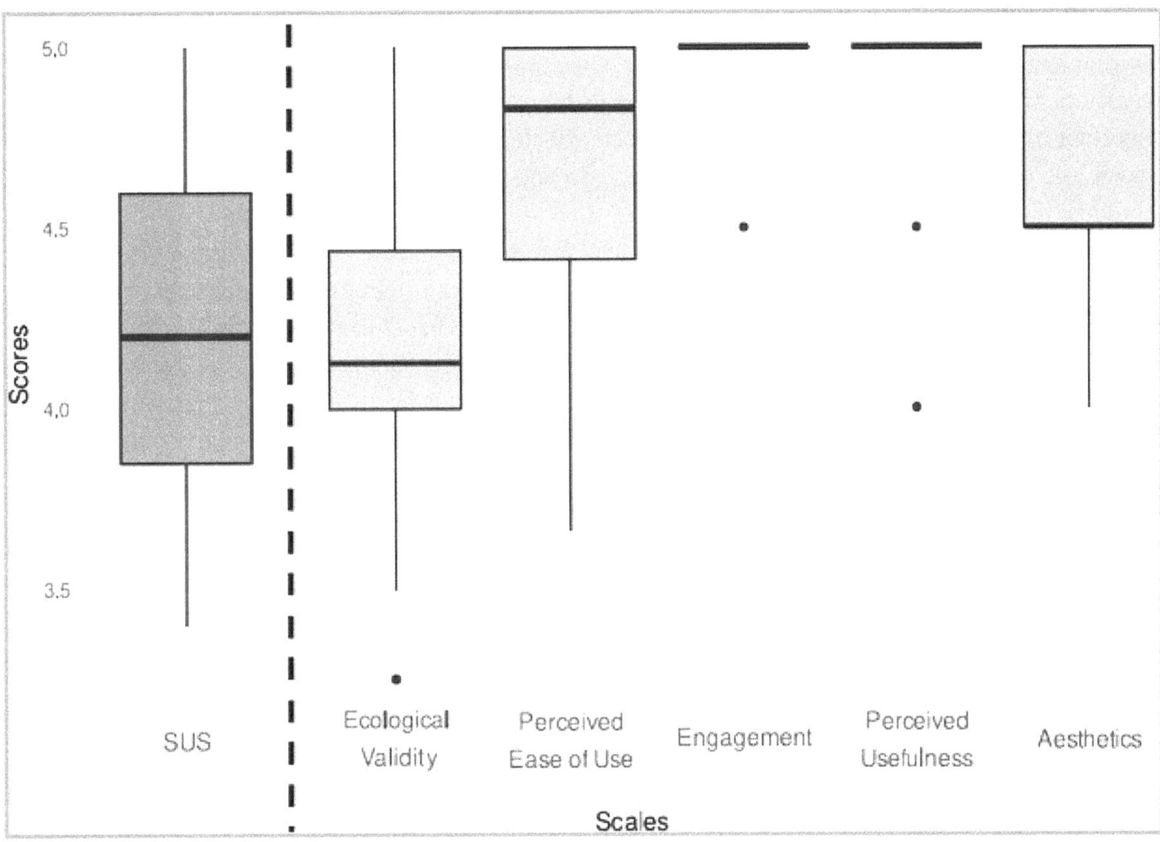

As shown in Figure 11, the students' perceptions toward the application were positive. Based on the results, it can be seen that the dimensions in the survey with better results were the dimensions of "Engagement" (*M*=4.98; *SD*=0.11) and "Perceived Usefulness" (*M* = 4.93; *SD* = 0.23). These results suggest that the application kept the attention of most of the users during their whole experience. Moreover, the results show that students perceived the application as useful for learning the topic of following directions in English.

Other dimensions with noticeable results were the dimensions of "Perceived Ease of Use" ($M = 4.68$; $SD = 0.41$) and the "Aesthetics" ($M = 4.65$; $SD = 0.37$), from which it can be inferred that the surveyed students found the system easy to use and were attracted by the aesthetics of the objects that form part of the virtual environment. This result might be explained by the quality of the 3D objects used to create the virtual city and also, the possibilities of interaction and mobility inside the application seem to support and improve the learning of this topic. Finally, the two dimensions with lower scores (but still high in a scale from 1 to 5) were the dimensions of the System Usability Scale that was considered to obtain a self-reported measure of usability ($M = 4.24$; $SD = 0.44$) and the Ecological Validity ($M = 4.19$; $SD = 0.48$). This result suggests that there are still some improvements that need to be done in the VR learning environment to increase its usability. In this study, the usability of the VR environment might have been affected by the previous experience of the students with VR. For most of the students, this was the first time they used a VR application.

As for ecological validity, the results might suggest that some improvements can be made to the VR environment. For instance, the VR environment does not have other people that can act as non-player characters or vehicles that make the city more realistic. Notwithstanding these promising results, it is important to note that the results might have been affected by the novelty of the technology effect or Hawthorne effect because this technology is new for most of the students. In that regard, the results should be interpreted with caution.

From the semi-structured interviews, the teachers pointed out that the use of VR might bring positive benefits for the learning process of the topic of following directions in English. The teachers highlighted the fact that this topic is traditionally taught by using pencil and paper exercises or basic exercises with objects in the classroom. However, the provision of an immersive environment for learning this topic was perceived as useful for meaningful learning. The teachers also provided some suggestions for the improvement of this tool. On the one hand, the teachers suggested that the learning environment might include non-player characters (other people) and vehicles in the city so that it can be more realistic. On the other hand, the teachers suggested adding objects that students need to carry to a particular location in the city and integrate other levels that include more complex expressions.

POTENTIAL BENEFITS AND DRAWBACKS OF VR FOR LEARNING THE TOPIC OF FOLLOWING DIRECTIONS IN ENGLISH

One of the potential benefits of the VR environment introduced in this chapter for learning the topic of following directions in English is that this VR environment simulates a real-world situation in which the student has to arrive at a particular location in the city and this simulated activity benefits their learning performance and alleviates the feeling of being in a traditional class as it has been recognized by previous research on VR for EFL learning (Chen, 2016). Unlike non-immersive VR environments such as the ones developed in Second Life, the VR environment introduced in this chapter was completely immersive. Consequently, students experienced a high level of interaction and a 360-degree scenario that provided a simulated environment that is closer to a real-world situation.

Another advantage of the immersive VR environment is the fact that the environment can provide just-in-time feedback because the system validates if students are following the instructions and provides appropriate feedback. Traditional strategies for learning this topic in the classroom such as pencil and paper exercises imply delayed feedback until the instructors check the decisions taken by the students and this might have a negative impact on the learning process.

The main drawback of using an immersive VR environment like the one introduced in this chapter for the topic of learning to follow directions in English is the high cost of the VR technology needed to deploy the experience in a large EFL class. Moreover, there is a need for a substantial amount of space if the experience is deployed for a large class. Another drawback is that it is difficult for teachers to add new content to the virtual experience if the teachers do not have skills in computer programming. These disadvantages have been recognized by other researchers in previous studies on the use of VR for EFL learning (Merchant, Goetz, Cifuentes, Keeney-Kennicutt, & Davis, 2014). The use of 360° videos, low-cost VR environments or non-immersive VR environments such as Second Life for EFL learning can be alternatives to tackle the issues discussed before of immersive VR environments until the technology becomes widely adopted in Universities and Schools.

CONCLUSIONS AND FUTURE WORK

The main contribution of this study is that it provides empirical evidence on how students use two scaffolds (Text Help and Visual Help) in a VR environment for learning the topic of following directions in English. Moreover, the results of our study have some practical and theoretical implications. For instance, the results can inform the design and development of future VR learning environments for EFL courses in this topic, and the results can be used to make decisions about how to tackle the main difficulties that students face when they are learning this topic.

Overall, the results show that the scaffolds (i.e. Text Help and Visual Help) in the immersive VR environment are effective for increasing the students' learning performance. The possibilities of spatial navigation in VR might benefit the learning process in the topic of following directions in EFL courses because the VR environment simulates situations that are closer to real-world situations. The immersive VR environment involved more than one sensorial modality, in particular, the vestibular, auditory and visual perception modalities. This multimodality provided by the VR has been found to improve learning (Ekstrand et al., 2018; Izard et al., 2018). Moreover, previous research has suggested that virtual environments are effective for improving spatial knowledge acquisition (Lokka & Çöltekin, 2020). In other words, VR can be useful for developing skills that involve spatial knowledge such as learning the topic of following directions in English.

The results showed that the use of scaffolds reflects the degree of difficulty between listening and reading when students are learning a foreign language. When the participants triggered the button that provided the audio of the instruction, they gazed for more time and looked at the help button with a high frequency, even when the virtual object that provided the Audio Help is smaller than the other scaffolds (the traffics signals for the Text and Visual help) in the VR environment. This behaviour might be related to the properties of the auditory stimuli, which has a fixed time that cannot be reduced, and probably, due to some difficulties when understanding the audio, the participants preferred to fix their gaze at the button while listening to the instruction in order to avoid distractions from the other objects in the VR environment. On the other hand, thc Visual Help was very clear for students as they did not need to look at it for long. As for the Text Help, this scaffold was gazed less than the Audio Help but more than the

Visual Help. This shows that the processing of the reading is faster than the listening for the same text, at least when learning a foreign language.

In general, the gaze pattern of exploration was similar for all the instructions. This means that the VR environment provided intuitive conditions in which it was easy to understand the different instructions. The only instruction that was gazed longer was "Go straight" because it was the most frequent instruction on both levels. Another measure that denotes the effects of the virtual environments is the average number of scaffolds used. For most of the cases, two aids were enough to solve any doubts that the participant had, and they did not have to use the Visual help for most of the instructions, with the exception of the instruction "Cross Diagonally". For that instruction, a significant number of participants asked for the third scaffold (i.e. the Visual help).

The students' acceptance and the perception of self-reported usability of the VR environment were also evaluated as factors that might affect the learning process both positively or negatively. The results show that the VR learning task was perceived as interesting and motivating and at the same time, visually appealing, with ecological validity and easy to use. This last aspect is essential because the interaction with the VR environment should be simple so as not to increase the cognitive load during the learning process.

Future research directions might include a comparative study between the VR environment with scaffolding and a VR environment without scaffolding to determine the effect of scaffolds on the students' learning outcomes. Moreover, future studies might consider the students' spatial abilities to determine the effect of different levels of spatial abilities when students are learning the topic of following directions in English. Further research can be conducted on the effect of personalized and adaptive scaffolding mechanisms to identify the most effective strategies to assist students during language learning tasks. Another future research direction might be to compare the effectiveness of the VR environment introduced in this chapter with respect to a non-immersive VR environment (that is a cheaper solution) to determine if there is any significant difference between the two VR approaches for this topic.

ACKNOWLEDGMENT

This research was supported by the Fundación Universitaria Konrad Lorenz (5INV7191). Our special thanks to the EFL teachers: Adriana Ahumada, Constanza Parra and Gloria Bello. Thanks to the head of the Institute of Foreign Languages Bibiana Martinez Piraquive for their constant support.

REFERENCES

Adnan, A., Shak, M., Karim, R., Tahir, M., & Shah, D. (2020). 360-degree videos, VR experiences and the application of education 4.0 technologies in Malaysia for exposure and immersion. *Advances in Science. Technology and Engineering Systems*, *5*(1), 373–381. doi:10.25046/aj050148

Al Awadhi, S., Al Habib, N., Al-Murad, D., Al deei, F., Al Houti, M., Beyrouthy, T., & Al-Kork, S. (2018). Interactive Virtual Reality Educational Application. *Advances in Science. Technology and Engineering Systems Journal*, *3*(4), 72–82. doi:10.25046/aj030409

Alemdag, E., & Cagiltay, K. (2018). A systematic review of eye tracking research on multimedia learning. *Computers & Education*, *125*, 413–428. doi:10.1016/j.compedu.2018.06.023

Andujar, A., & Buchner, J. (2019). The potential of 3D Virtual Reality (VR) for language learning: An overview. In I. Arnedillo, P. Isaias, P. Ravesteijn, & G. Ongena (Eds.), *15th International Conference on Mobile Learning (2019)*. Utrecht: IADIS. 10.33965/ml2019_201903R002

Berns, A., Gonzalez-Pardo, A., & Camacho, D. (2013). Game-like language learning in 3-D virtual environments. *Computers & Education*, *60*(1), 210–220. doi:10.1016/j.compedu.2012.07.001

Brooke, J. (1996). Usability Evaluation in Industry. Taylor & Francis.

Chen, J. (2016). The crossroads of English language learners, task-based instruction, and 3D multi-user virtual learning in Second Life. *Computers & Education*, *102*, 152–171. doi:10.1016/j.compedu.2016.08.004

Chen, M.-R. A., & Hwang, G.-J. (2020). Effects of experiencing authentic contexts on English speaking performances, anxiety and motivation of EFL students with different cognitive styles. *Interactive Learning Environments*, 1–21. Advance online publication. doi:10.1080/10494820.2020.1734626

Chen, Y. (2016). The Effects of Virtual Reality Learning Environment on Student Cognitive and Linguistic Development. *The Asia-Pacific Education Researcher*, *25*(4), 637–646. doi:10.100740299-016-0293-2

Chien, S.-Y., Hwang, G.-J., & Jong, M. (2020). Effects of peer assessment within the context of spherical video-based virtual reality on EFL students' English-Speaking performance and learning perceptions. *Computers & Education*, *146*, 103751. Advance online publication. doi:10.1016/j.compedu.2019.103751

Chung, L. Y. (2012). Incorporating 3D-virtual reality into language learning. *International Journal of Digital Content Technology and Its Applications*, *6*(6), 249–255. doi:10.4156/jdcta.vol6.issue6.29

Clay, V., König, P., & König, S. (2019). Eye Tracking in Virtual Reality. *Journal of Eye Movement Research*, *12*(1), 1–18. doi:10.16910/jemr.12.1.3

Dukes, L., Pence, T., Hodges, L., Meehan, N., & Johnson, A. (2013). SIDNIE: Scaffolded Interviews Developed by Nurses in Education. In *Proceedings of the 2013 international conference on Intelligent user interfaces - IUI '13*. Santa Monica: ACM Press. 10.1145/2449396.2449447

Ekstrand, C., Jamal, A., Nguyen, R., Kudryk, A., Mann, J., & Mendez, I. (2018). Immersive and interactive virtual reality to improve learning and retention of neuroanatomy in medical students: A randomized controlled study. *CMAJ Open*, *6*(1), E103–E109. Advance online publication. doi:10.9778/cmajo.20170110 PMID:29510979

Garcia, S., Laesker, D., Andujar, M., Kauer, R., & Nguyen, J. (2019). A virtual reality experience for learning languages. In *Conference on Human Factors in Computing Systems - Proceedings*, (pp. 1–4). Glasgow: ACM. 10.1145/3290607.3313253

Garcia-Cardona, S., Tian, F., & Prakoonwit, S. (2017). Tenochtitlan - An Interactive Virtual Reality Environment that Encourages Museum Exhibit Engagement. *Lecture Notes in Computer Science*, *10345*, 20–28. doi:10.1007/978-3-319-65849-0_3

Huang, T., & Liao, S. (2015). A model of acceptance of augmented-reality interactive technology : The moderating role of cognitive innovativeness. *Electronic Commerce Research*, *15*(2), 269–295. doi:10.100710660-014-9163-2

Izard, S., Juanes, J., García-Peñalvo, F., Gonçalvez, J., Ledesma, M., & Ruisoto, P. (2018). Virtual Reality as an Educational and Training Tool for Medicine. *Journal of Medical Systems*, *42*(3), 50. Advance online publication. doi:10.100710916-018-0900-2 PMID:29392522

Jenkins, J. (2016, September 7). *Virtual Reality in the classroom*. Retrieved from https://educationtechnologysolutions.com/2016/09/virtual-reality-classroom/

Jeong, J.-Y., Seo, S., Han, Y., Kim, S., & Jeong, H. (2018). Learning English Conversations in an Immersive Virtual Reality Environment. In Y.-T. Wu & et al. (Eds.), *Workshop Proceedings of the 26th International Conference on Computers in Education*. Metro Manila: Asia-Pacific Society for Computers in Education.

Jiang, Y., Guo, R., & Ma, F. (2017). Interactive Multimedia System for Chinese Traditional Costumes. In F. Tian, C. Gatzidis, A. El Rhalibi, W. Tang, & F. Charles (Eds.), *E-Learning and Games* (pp. 44–51). Springer International Publishing. doi:10.1007/978-3-319-65849-0_6

Kaplan, R. (2019). The Effect of Stereoscopic Three-Dimensional Images on Vocabulary Learning. *Contemporary Educational Technology*, *10*(4), 324–337. doi:10.30935/cet.634172

Lan, Y. (2020). Immersion, interaction, and experience-oriented learning: Bringing virtual reality into FL learning. *Language Learning & Technology*, *24*(1), 1–15. http://hdl.handle.net/10125/44704

Lan, Y. J. (2015). Contextual EFL learning in a 3D virtual environment. *Language, Learning and Technology*, *19*(2), 16–31. doi: 10125/44412

Lee, B. W., Shih, H. Y., Chou, Y. T., & Chen, Y. S. (2017). Educational Virtual Reality implementation on English for Tourism Purpose using knowledge-based engineering. In *Proceedings of the 2017 IEEE International Conference on Applied System Innovation: Applied System Innovation for Modern Technology, ICASI 2017*. Sapporo: Springer. 10.1109/ICASI.2017.7988550

Legault, J., Zhao, J., Chi, Y.-A., Chen, W., Klippel, A., & Li, P. (2019). Immersive Virtual Reality as an Effective Tool for Second Language Vocabulary Learning. *Languages*, *4*(1), 13. Advance online publication. doi:10.3390/languages4010013

Lin, T. J., & Lan, Y. J. (2015). Language learning in virtual reality environments: Past, present, and future. *Journal of Educational Technology & Society*, *18*(4), 486–497. https://drive.google.com/file/d/1NVe2QrgsqsqPKkW3_49Kxxu6MSI3ESf9/view

Lokka, I., & Çöltekin, A. (2020). Perspective switch and spatial knowledge acquisition: Effects of age, mental rotation ability and visuospatial memory capacity on route learning in virtual environments with different levels of realism. *Cartography and Geographic Information Science*, *47*(1), 14–27. doi:10.1080/15230406.2019.1595151

Ma, C. Y. (2018). Teaching application of computer virtual reality technology in international education of chinese language. *Kuram ve Uygulamada Egitim Bilimleri, 18*(6). Advance online publication. doi:10.12738/estp.2018.6.297

Martirosov, S., & Kopecek, P. (2017). Virtual Reality and its Influence on Traning and Education - Literature Review. In *Proceedings of the 28th International DAAAM Symposium 2017*. Zadar: DAAAM International. doi: 10.2507/28th.daaam.proceedings.100

Mayer, R. (2009). *Multimedia Learning* (2nd ed.). Cambridge University Press. doi:10.1017/CBO9780511811678

Merchant, Z., Goetz, E., Cifuentes, L., Keeney-Kennicutt, W., & Davis, T. (2014). Effectiveness of virtual reality-based instruction on students' learning outcomes in K-12 and higher education: A meta-analysis. *Computers & Education, 70*, 29–40. doi:10.1016/j.compedu.2013.07.033

Michel, M., & Smith, B. (2017). Eye-Tracking Research in Computer-Mediated Language Learning. In S. Thorne & S. May (Eds.), *Language, Education and Technology, Encyclopedia of Language and Education* (pp. 453–464). Springer International Publishing. doi:10.1007/978-3-319-02237-6_34

Mohamed, N., & Badioze, H. (2011). Scaffolding Poetry Lessons Using Desktop Virtual Reality. In Lecture Notes in Computer Science 7067. (pp. 231–241). doi:10.1007/978-3-642-25200-6_22

Mohsen, M. (2016). The use of help options in multimedia listening environments to aid language learning: A review. *British Journal of Educational Technology, 47*(6), 1232–1242. doi:10.1111/bjet.12305

Peixoto, B., Pinto, D., Krassmann, A., Melo, M., Cabral, L., & Bessa, M. (2019). *Using virtual reality tools for teaching foreign languages. Advances in Intelligent Systems and Computing 932*. Springer International Publishing. doi:10.1007/978-3-030-16187-3_56

Pinto, D., Peixoto, B., Krassmann, A., Melo, M., Cabral, L., & Bessa, M. (2019). *Virtual reality in education: Learning a foreign language. Advances in Intelligent Systems and Computing* (Vol. 932). Springer International Publishing. doi:10.1007/978-3-030-16187-3_57

Radianti, J., Majchrzak, T., Fromm, J., & Wohlgenannt, I. (2020). A systematic review of immersive virtual reality applications for higher education: Design elements, lessons learned, and research agenda. *Computers & Education, 147*, 103778. Advance online publication. doi:10.1016/j.compedu.2019.103778

Sabiri, K. (2020). ICT in EFL Teaching and Learning: A Systematic Literature Review. *Contemporary Educational Technology, 11*(2), 177–195. doi:10.30935/cet.665350

Schwienhorst, K. (2002). The State of VR: A Meta-Analysis of Virtual Reality Tools in Second Language Acquisition. *Computer Assisted Language Learning, 15*(3), 221–239. doi:10.1076/call.15.3.221.8186

Shadiev, R., & Yang, M. (2020). Review of Studies on Technology-Enhanced Language Learning and Teaching. *Sustainability, 12*(2), 524. Advance online publication. doi:10.3390u12020524

Shepard, L. A. (2005). Linking Formative Assessment to scaffolding. *Educational Leadership, 63*(3), 66–70. http://learnline.cdu.edu.au/commonunits/documents/Scaffolding%20and%20formative%20assessment.pdf

Shih, Y. (2008). A Collaborative Virtual Environment for Situated Language Learning Using VEC3D. *Eductional Technology & Society, 11*(1), 56–68. Retrieved from https://drive.google.com/file/d/1ymXnG_dDdRi6GKRyx9suTvBXoAA4s8Ae/view

Singh, G. (2017). Using virtual reality for scaffolding computer programming learning. In *Proceedings of the 23rd ACM Symposium on Virtual Reality Software and Technology - VRST '17.* New York: ACM Press. 10.1145/3139131.3141225

Singh, N., & Singh, S. (2017). Virtual reality: A brief survey. In *2017 International Conference on Information Communication and Embedded Systems, ICICES 2017.* Chennai: IEEE Xplore. doi:10.1109/ICICES.2017.8070720

Steuer, J. (1992). Defining Virtual Reality: Characteristics Determining Telepresence. *Journal of Communication, 42*(4), 73–94. doi:10.1111/j.1460-2466.1992.tb00812.x

Taylor-Hamilton, C. (2004). Giving directions as a speech behavior: A cross-cultural comparison of L1 and L2 strategies. In D. Boxer & A. Cohen (Eds.), *Studying speaking to inform Second Language Learning*. Multilingual Matters Ltd.

Unity Technologies. (2019). *PlayerPrefs*. Retrieved from https://docs.unity3d.com/ScriptReference/PlayerPrefs.html

Wang, C., Lan, Y.-J., Tseng, W.-T., Lin, Y.-T., & Gupta, K. (2019). On the effects of 3D virtual worlds in language learning – a meta-analysis. *Computer Assisted Language Learning*, 1–25. Advance online publication. doi:10.1080/09588221.2019.1598444

Wang, F., & Hannafin, M. J. (2005). Design-Based Research and Technology-Enhanced Learning Environments. *Educational Technology Research and Development, 53*(4), 5–23. doi:10.1007/BF02504682

Wang, L., & Zheng, C. (2018). A systematic literature review of virtual reality in adult foreign language education. In *Workshop Proceedings of the 26th International Conference on Computers in Education, ICCE 2018* (pp. 73–79). Metro Manila: Philippines: Asia-Pacific Society for Computers in Education.

Wang, S., & Cheng, Y. (2011). Designing a Situational 3D Virtual Learning Environment to Bridge Business Theory and Practice - The Role of Scaffolding. In R. Zhang, J. Cordeiro, X. Li, Z. Zhang, & J. Zhang (Eds.), *Proceedings of the 13th International Conference on Enterprise Information Systems* (pp. 313–315). Beijing, China: SciTePress - Science and and Technology Publications.

Wang, Y., Petrina, S., & Feng, F. (2017). VILLAGE—Virtual Immersive Language Learning and Gaming Environment: Immersion and presence. *British Journal of Educational Technology, 48*(2), 431–450. doi:10.1111/bjet.12388

Wild, F., Klemke, R., Lefrere, P., & Fominykh, M. (2017). Technology Acceptance of Augmented Reality and Wearable Technologies. In *Immersive Learning Research Network. iLRN 2017*. Springer. doi:10.1007/978-3-319-60633-0_11

Wood, D., Bruner, J. S., & Ross, G. (1976). The role of tutoring in problem solving. *Journal of Child Psychology and Psychiatry, and Allied Disciplines, 17*(2), 89–100. doi:10.1111/j.1469-7610.1976.tb00381.x PMID:932126

Xie, Y., Ryder, L., & Chen, Y. (2019). Using Interactive Virtual Reality Tools in an Advanced Chinese Language Class: A Case Study. *TechTrends*, *63*(3), 251–259. doi:10.100711528-019-00389-z

Yeh, H.-C., Tseng, S.-S., & Heng, L. (2020). Enhancing EFL students' intracultural learning through virtual reality. *Interactive Learning Environments*, 1–10. Advance online publication. doi:10.1080/10494820.2020.1734625

ADDITIONAL READING

Chien, S.-Y., Hwang, G.-J., & Jong, M. (2020). Effects of peer assessment within the context of spherical video-based virtual reality on EFL students' English-Speaking performance and learning perceptions. *Computers & Education*, *146*, 103751. Advance online publication. doi:10.1016/j.compedu.2019.103751

Jeong, J.-Y., Seo, S., Han, Y., Kim, S., & Jeong, H. (2018). Learning English Conversations in an Immersive Virtual Reality Environment. In Y.-T. Wu & et al. (Eds.), *Workshop Proceedings of the 26th International Conference on Computers in Education*. Kenting: Asia-Pacific Society for Computers in Education.

Lan, Y. (2020). Immersion, interaction, and experience-oriented learning: Bringing virtual reality into FL learning. *Language Learning & Technology*, *24*(1), 1–15. http://hdl.handle.net/10125/44704

Lin, T. J., & Lan, Y. J. (2015). Language learning in virtual reality environments: Past, present, and future. *Journal of Educational Technology & Society*, *18*(4), 486–497.

Peixoto, B., Pinto, D., Krassmann, A., Melo, M., Cabral, L., & Bessa, M. (2019). Using virtual reality tools for teaching foreign languages. In A. Rocha, H. Adeli, L. Reis, & S. Costanzo (Eds.), *Advances in Intelligent Systems and Computing. La Toja Island*. Springer International Publishing., doi:10.1007/978-3-030-16187-3_56

Pinto, D., Peixoto, B., Krassmann, A., Melo, M., Cabral, L., & Bessa, M. (2019). Virtual reality in education: Learning a foreign language. In A. Rocha, H. Adeli, L. Reis, & S. Costanzo (Eds.), *Advances in Intelligent Systems and Computing, La Toja Island*. Springer International Publishing., doi:10.1007/978-3-030-16187-3_57

Radianti, J., Majchrzak, T., Fromm, J., & Wohlgenannt, I. (2020). A systematic review of immersive virtual reality applications for higher education: Design elements, lessons learned, and research agenda. *Computers & Education*, *147*, 103778. Advance online publication. doi:10.1016/j.compedu.2019.103778

Shadiev, R., & Yang, M. (2020). Review of Studies on Technology-Enhanced Language Learning and Teaching. *Sustainability*, *12*(2), 524. Advance online publication. doi:10.3390u12020524

Wang, C., Lan, Y.-J., Tseng, W.-T., Lin, Y.-T., & Gupta, K. (2019). On the effects of 3D virtual worlds in language learning – a meta-analysis. *Computer Assisted Language Learning*, 1–25. doi:10.1080/09588221.2019.1598444

KEY TERMS AND DEFINITIONS

Acceptance: A measure that establishes if users perceive the system to be easy to use, useful, with aesthetics and engaging or not.

Eye Tracking: A technique that takes advantage of sensors to determine where the user is gazing at. The information is recorded and then processed to obtain information about gaze frequency and gaze duration over certain areas of interests.

Head-Mounted Display: A device that is worn on the head that contains a display for showing graphics and allows the users to experience virtual reality.

Scaffolding: An instructional technique that consists of a number of aids, cues or prompts to help students to complete a learning task.

Unity: A game engine that can be used to develop videogames, simulations or other interactive applications using the C# programming language or Javascript.

Usability: A measure that establishes how easy or difficult is to use a system from the perspective and perception of the user.

Virtual Reality: A technology that uses a head-mounted display (HMD) in which the user is immersed in a completely virtual environment. Everything the user sees is generated by computer.

Chapter 14
Virtual Reality Simulations in Science Education:
Learning Science by Writing

Richard Lamb
https://orcid.org/0000-0002-5730-9055
East Carolina University, USA

ABSTRACT

This study examines the role of virtual reality (VR) in the promotion of writing with greater complexity and lexical density. Using a combination of neuroimaging and traditional measures, the author characterizes differences in writing complexity and lexical density scores across four different pedagogical modalities: VR alone, VR followed by a textbook reading, textbook reading followed by VR, and textbook reading alone. Middle school students recruited from a rural middle school in the Mid-Atlantic Region of the United States responded to two prompts related to science content found in VR environments and a textbook. The authors hypothesized that exposure to a virtual environment prior to responding to the writing prompts would enhance both argumentative and summative writing products, when compared to participants who only had access to the textbook experiences. Participants who were exposed to the VR environment then had access to a textbook demonstrated significantly greater writing complexity and lexical density scores than those who had VR alone, or access to the text alone.

INTRODUCTION

Science education research has sought to understand and develop pedagogical approaches with supports that facilitate 21st Century skills such as critical thinking and written communication related to science (Chu et al., 2017). Of the myriad of options available to educators in the classroom, one of approaches that has been consistently in use in science education is the use of laboratories or activities illustrating specific learning points. However, with the specific illustration of a point there are limitations to the use of laboratories. The limitations arise particularly when the laboratories and activities do not allow individual student exploration or variations in the laboratory outcomes. Activities and laboratories without

DOI: 10.4018/978-1-7998-5043-4.ch014

exploration or variations in outcomes are considered rote hands-on activities. Researchers in fields such as neuroscience and learning sciences, have argued that it is necessary to focus less on rote laboratory outcomes and more on the creation of variable outcome experiences which then must be communicated and argued. The variability in outcomes allows students to collect evidence to substantiate claims. The writing to learn aspect occurs as students develop written arguments and analyze claims and evidence to construct scientific understanding and explanation. (Berland & Reiser, 2009; Abersek, 2017). Writing to learn promotes learning through student engagement with authentic contexts and the subsequent explanation of observed phenomena using precise disciplinary language and critique of ideas (Chen et al., 2013). Explanations through writing engage several cognitive systems related to long-term memory, working memory, subordinate functions within working memory such as critical thinking, and other superordinate cognitive systems such as executive function (Leinonen, Keune, Veermans, & Toikkanen, 2016). In short, writing to learn places written scientific communications in the role of a tool to facilitate learning of content within authentic contexts. With the apparent importance of writing to learn in science, the authors of this study are interest in understanding the relationship between aspects of modal presentation and the promotion of writing and critical thinking (Murphy, Rowe, Ramani, & Silverman, 2014).

Developing the practices of 21st Century Skills in written communication in science is a topic of intense research in science education, and adjacent fields such as literacy education, neuroscience, and cognitive science (Baram-Tsabari & Osborne, 2015). However, despite the decades of research on writing to learn in general and in science specifically, differing views regarding writing to learning arise from contrasting approaches of the role of writing. One paradigm suggests writing is a procedural activity (single channel cognitive process) which simply organizes existing knowledge and thinking without the production of new information (Hayes & Flowers, 1986). Other paradigms suggest that writing is an episodic, declarative, and procedural activity (multi-channel cognitive process) in which new knowledge is formulated (Galbraith, 2009). Evidence for each paradigm arises through identification of the cognitive systems which are used during the writing process. For example, evidence of critical thinking and novel information development would suggest the presence of a multi-channel cognitive process. While only the reorganization of existing materials would suggest a single-channel process. Writing to learn under a multi-channel approach suggests that scientific material is best learned via hands-on-experiences, it also is commonly argued that literacy in science derives from having an underlying comprehension of the *language* of science; i.e. the language first approach (Melby-Levag & Lervag, 2014). The *Language First Approach* advocates that writing is used to set up the opportunity to practice communicating (procedural) and explaining content (declarative) in the language of science. However, in developing the language of science it is necessary to activate prior knowledge for the language to interact with. Language first advocates suggest, that writing helps enhance students' conceptual processing and in the analyses of both prior knowledge and new information resulting in novel knowledge development (Chen, Park, & Hand, 2016). The presence of multi-channel processes would be an important consideration in science education contexts and would suggest that the greater the exposure to more authentic experiences would help to produce novel knowledge and promote deeper learning. Through the interactions of cognitive systems in working memory, language, science content, and prior knowledge it is possible to develop scientific language to describe observations of the world. Using scientific language to communicate through writing, students are more likely to engage in deep, meaningful, critical thinking, which results in learning (Townsend, 2015).

While there are many forms of writing the two dominant modes in science are argumentative writing i.e. writing to convince and summative writing i.e. writing to convey information. Current research in science education suggests that deeper conceptual understanding occur when students write to convince as opposed to writing to convey information (Chen et al., 2013). When analyzing a summary writing paragraph and an argumentative paragraph, argumentative writing is more complex and cognitively demanding. Researchers in science education suggest this occurs because argumentative writing is, writing designed to convince others about the validity of the idea and as a result must be more complex (Chen, Hand, & Park, 2016). The complexity and demand associated with scientific argumentative writing arises because the students use evidence and critique the validity of the evidence in relation to the claim and make a judgement as to its value (Manz, 2015). By comparison summative writing is descriptive with the goal of conveying information about a phenomenon for communicative purposes (Akaygun & Jones, 2014). As summative writing is descriptive, review of a summative paragraph would suggest that the writing is less complex, less demanding, and engages critical thinking and other cognitive systems to a lessor degree. However, when the two styles of writing are compared using neuroimaging examining cognitive demand, the results suggest the opposite; summative writing is more complex and argumentative writing is less-so (Torrance Van Waes, & Galbraith, 2007). Reconciliation of these findings would provide greater clarity as to the role of writing style in the science classroom and provide a deeper understanding of the types of experiences and supports needed for increased learning opportunities through writing. The success of writing to learn approaches in science continues to be investigated by studying both argumentative and summary writing styles through the products (i.e. student work) and processes (i.e. neuroimaging) of writing (Chen et al., 2013).

Purpose, Research Questions, and Hypotheses

Writing to persuade and to convey information along with the accompanying support tools in the classroom is a widely explored topic and continues to be researched (James, 2017; Kalman et al., 2008; Zambrano et al., 2020). However, despite the examination of specific support tools there has been little examination of support tools such as VR to promote writing. The purpose of this study is to explore the role textbooks and VR can play in promoting argumentative and summative writing. The study used four conditions to examine the effects of VR on writing: (1) VR alone, (2) VR followed by a textbook reading, (3) exposure to a textbook reading followed by VR, and (4) a textbook reading alone. It is hypothesized (Hypothesis 1) that students using VR alone and with a textbook, will illustrate increased measures of writing complexity and lexical density when compared to those students who only had access to the textbook. Secondly, (Hypothesis 2) argumentative writing will show greater cognitive demand as measured through hemodynamic response when compared to summary writing. One moderating variable which is not considered is, the quality of the VR and the text, as the researchers did not examine or compare the differences in quality between multiple VR experiences or textbooks.

Cognitive demand is the interaction of multiple task specific cognitive systems measured through the hemodynamic response of neural tissue (Lamb et al., 2019). Hemodynamic response is the response of neural tissue oxygen use during the completion of specific tasks related to the activation of specific areas of the brain (Aslin, Shukla, & Emberson, 2015). In addition to hemodynamic response, this response is also known as a blood oxygen level dependent signal (BOLD). By statistically coupling a BOLD signal to a time specific stimulus it is possible to ascertain specific cognitive states and their fluctuations (i.e. microstates) resulting from a task. This BOLD response is a proxy for cognitive demand (Hampshire & Sharp, 2015). To address these hypotheses, the authors will seek to answer the following research questions. Research Question 1, what combination/s of VR and textbook promote the greatest lexical density and complexity in summary and argumentative writing? Research Question 2, of summary and argumentative writing, which illustrates the greatest hemodynamic responses as a proxy for cognitive dynamics?

Scientific Argumentation

The analysis of claims and evidence during argument critique is a core science practice and an important 21st Century Skill (Chalkiadaki, 2018). The ability to critique and argue is a behavioral indicator of critical thinking (Lin, 2014). When children and adults are asked to create a high-quality scientific argument they often self-report that they find it difficult and extremely cognitively demanding. This suggests that at all levels (P-20) learners have difficulty with the application of critical thinking and would benefit from modes of instruction which assist development of critical thinking (Lodge, O'Connor, Shaw, & Burton, 2015). Critical thinking difficulties specifically related to science, may occur from; lack of content knowledge and how content knowledge and information fit together, lack of exposure to experiences, and difficulties with the integration of the practices and content of science. As the emphasis on experiences has increased in writing to learn practices researchers have begun to study the impact that technologies which promote experiential learning have on writing and underlying skills such as critical thinking. Several researchers have begun to examine not just the affordances of virtual and augmented realities in writing but how these technologies impact the cognitive actions associated with writing when using technologies such as VR (Huang et al., 2019; Zheng et al. 2019; Wang, 2017; Lamb & Etopio, 2019a; Lamb & Etopio, 2019b). Results of the work in this area state that the use of technologies as a support tool for writing, positively impacts educational outcomes and student learning opportunities. The recognition of technology support tools such as EVR may promote learning because of the multiple modes of presentation. By contrast in many classrooms, textbooks are used as support tools and as a potential way of developing prior knowledge for students to respond to writing prompts (Polikoff, 2015). In many cases, the textbook in the science classroom is the most predominant support tool for delivering content to students (Robinson, Fischer, Wiley, & Hilton III, 2014). Despite the constant presence of the textbook in the classroom, there is research which calls their usefulness into question (Mendez, Mendez, & Anguita, 2018).

Textbook Use in the Classroom

Early career science teachers are more likely to make use of textbooks when compared to their more senior counterparts. The reliance of textbooks may occur because they supply levels of organization and content knowledge around each unit and subject. While this may appear to be a positive attribute of textbooks, there are other attributes which may create a negative outcome when using a textbook. An important limitation to consider is the that teachers often become overly dependent on the organizational and assessment aspects of a textbook, instead of relying on their own understanding of the students in their charge (Grissett & Hoffman. 2019; Muwonge, Schiefele, Ssenyonga, & Kibedi, 2017). This can cause teachers and students to stop investigating outside authentic experiences to further learn and apply knowledge in science. Overreliance on textbooks can reduce the application of cognitive processes and 21st century skills that are reliant on open investigations. Textbooks tend to enforce the use of the "correct answer" approach, which reduces investigation and novel experience seeking (Muis, Trevors, Duffy, Ranellucci, & Foy, 2016). Under the correct answer thought process, students may incorrectly think they are learning content and application, when they only recalling low level facts or content. Textbooks also reduce individualized instruction and the teacher's ability to activate novel differentiated prior knowledge about content. This reduces the cognitive systems and 21st Century Skills engaged while learning. More inquiry and open-exploration tools may allow inferencing and greater activation of prior knowledge. Sources of experiences which supply flexible, individualized, open-ended, inquiry-based support scaffolds are garnering significant educational attention. Tools garnering this attention include; augmented reality, virtual reality, and other digital environments such as intelligent tutors and learning management systems. Experiences and opportunities afforded using these tools and VR environments could complement existing tools such as textbooks, promoting inquiry and open-exploration of ideas in the classroom.

Virtual Reality (VR) in the Science Classroom

Lower cost and greater accessibility to computers and underlying technology has increased the penetration of VR into the field of education and other related fields. VR use has been explored in areas related to trauma therapy, technical skills development, and entertainment (Baus & Bouchard, 2014). Research related to VR illustrates that it holds some promise in promoting educational experiences which may support learning (Martin-Gutierrez, Fabani, Benesova, Meneses, & Mora, 2015). VR may also promote understanding and conceptualization of abstract ideas by linking prior knowledge with novel experiences (Thorhill-Miller & Dupont, 2016).

Virtual reality is a system consisting of a computer and headset with user interfaces which create a 360-degree three-dimensional environment to supply the effect of immersion and interaction (Ihemedu-Steinke, Erbach, Halady, Meixner, & Weber, 2017). Ultimately, VR is a computer-generated simulation of a three-dimensional environment and or images including 360-degree videos (Freina & Ott, 2015; Lamb & Etopio, 2019). VR is thought to be useful in educational settings because it creates interactive, life-like, open-ended soft-failure environments with life like interactions for students to experience while still under the full control of the user. These interactions may increase motivation and provide the learner with novel new experiences through which they can build new knowledge.

Theoretical Framework

Given the role that experience-based interactions play in the learning process, it is important to make use of a theoretical frame which incorporates both characteristics. The authors suggest that embodied cognition readily provides an adequate framing for the results of this study. Embodied cognition suggests that complex cognitive functions (i.e. working memory, long-term memory, and critical thinking), and related outcomes such as learning, are addressed by a process of codetermination between the human and their surroundings (Semin & Smith, 2013). Core to this framework is that the observer constructs reality through interactions grounded in physical experiences (Nunez & Lakoff, 2013). Embodied cognition suggests that humans analyze and conceptualize novel information from the environment through interactions. Interactions between humans and the environment are individual, differentiated, contextual, and prompt cognitive tool use through interactions (Lamb, Hand, & Yoon, 2017). Importantly embodied cognition does not necessarily involve conscious processes during learning (Nunez et al.,1999). By virtue of interacting with the environment people learn novel information which they may not be aware of until it is activated, reorganized, and developed into novel knowledge during a task such as writing.

By engaging with a virtual environment, a student will be more likely to process information in working memory, encode that information into long-term memory, and combine it with prior knowledge to produce novel knowledge. Through individualization of the content and responses within and by the environment using artificial intelligence integration, it becomes possible to develop individualized educational approaches which facilitate independent student learning. As learning within the embodied cognition framework is unconsciously occurring it may be difficult to provide evidence through self-reports and specific learning products. The unconscious aspects of learning may only be available through analysis of the cognitive demand on the underlying cognitive systems.

Our perspective of embodied cognition for this specific context would suggest that, by experiencing almost identical physiological effects in VR as real-world experiences, learning is promoted. Embodied activities help to re-direct the analytical focus of research around learning from internal cognitive processes. This helps to broaden research around the cognitive aspects of learning to include more contextual factors and experiences, and their influence on cognition (Karoly, 1999). Embodied cognition allows us to consider both the biological and the experiential contexts of learning. Outcomes garnered from experiential learning support tools such as VR, combined with social factors, when analyzing the way students understand the world around them can provide a deeper and broader picture of the process and products associated with learning. As a mechanism of action to explain learning gains associated with embodied cognition, the author identifies the human motor system's influence on our cognitive processes (Guell, Gabrieli, & Schmahmann, 2017). The human motor system is an indelible part of human learning. The nature of this interaction is one of a feedback-cycle between writing (motor) and cognition, and cognition and writing, with one promoting the other. There are multiple styles of writing and major differences in levels of processing, complexity, and lexical density which may be evident in the writing style. Importantly, the information contained in each form of writing may change because of experiences (DeAnda, Poulin-Dubois, Zesiger, & Friend, 2016). Two forms of writing which are common in science are, argumentative and summary writing.

As a person learns, one of the markers is the encoding of information from working memory to long term memory. Manipulation of information in working memory critical thinking and encoding of information to long term memory would manifest as greater or more intense hemodynamic response (Oken, Chamine, & Wakeland, 2015). It is argued that exposure to a virtual environment with specific pedagogical approaches in mind, allows for the organization of *novel information* via working memory manipulations, and that the manipulated information will likely be encoded in conjunction with the grounded, physical experiences of VR (DeSutter & Stieff, 2017). In turn, the *novel information* exposure, will potentially provide greater context and reduce the cognitive resources needed, which may enhance writing complexity and lexical density. Since VR creates such an embodied experience, it may help facilitate deeper learning of subject matter when combined with other support tools in science.

Affordances of VR as a Support Tool for Embodied Learning and Cognition

Often learning paradigms require students to conceptualize specific abstract environments or situations which they have never personally experienced (Lamb et al., 2020). VR when used as a support tool for embodied activities allows students to experience environments they normally would not be able to experience. The experience may be visual, auditory, kinetic, olfactory, or a combination of these modes. An example of environments in science classes are, the inside of cells, the inside of an atom, or the deepest parts of the ocean. Examples of these environments may be found on Steam or in the Oculus store and are often available for little or no cost. Titles include Anthropocene VR, The Body VR, Universe Sandbox, Car Mechanic Simulator, and Mars Adventure. Importantly, VR offers the opportunity for students to interact within the environment in various ways.

Shian and Yunus (2016) have illustrated the that the use of audio clips in conjunction with textual materials promotes listening skills, language development and increases overall comprehension. While this is one example, the literature surrounding the inclusion of technological support tools such as video augmentation and other forms of assistive and augmentative technologies as supplements to the learning environment is large (Vo, Ledbetter, & Zuckerman, 2019; Mayer, 2019; Magana, Serrano, & Rebello, 2019). In addition to augmentation and assistance, the use of mediums such as social media platforms or collaborative mediums also promote learning and development of key skills in conjunction with traditional support tools such as a textbook (Gruzard, Paulin, & Haythornthwaite, 2016; Akgunduz & Akinogluy, 2016). Within VR and other platforms, the students can interact with each other and aspects of the environment in a digital VR soft-failure environment allowing students to learn from their explorations, mistakes, and failures (Lamb et al., 2018). Leanrin in these environments is partially due to interactions and critique of idea as students build new knowledge with the multiple modes of learning. A soft-failure environment is one in which, the person can make mistakes, explore, and test potential avenues, without consequence. This suggest that the supplementation of traditional support materials with technology support tools using multiple modalities and environments may illustrate enhanced effects in learning. Importantly, it is not simply the collaborative part of the technology only that seems to promote learning, it is the experiential part (Coker & Porter, 2017). In light of these findings, teachers may attempt to increase exposure to experiences using a variety of support tools, and novel environments to promote embodied experiences. Embodied experiences such as those offered by EVR are a recommend approach to the development of deep learning (Dede, Grotzer, Kamarainen, & Metcalf, 2017). Deep learning arises from psychological immersion within the digital context, manipulation of the information in working memory using subordinate functions such as working memory, and episodic encoding in long-term memory. The value of VR rests with the ability to create immersive, fluid, and authentic environments. When these three aspects are appropriately present the user's brain does not differentiate between the educational VR (EVR) environment and the real-world environment (Lamb & Etopio, 2020). The tying together of an on-demand experience in the classroom to textual materials allow the user to not only understand information from text in the abstract, but helps the student potentially build novel information contextually and experientially by making the experiences more concrete. In addition to cognitive development the student may develop added emotional skill such as empathy (Bailenson, 2018). As VR develops and is implemented in the classroom it may become a more significant tool for teachers.

While there are some aspects of VR which do not lend themselves to its adoption, affordability does not seem to be a major limitation. Virtual reality is increasingly becoming affordable for use in the classroom with the cost of some VR headsets costing less than the cost of a laptop computer or a tablet. Table 1 provides a table of current costs (2020) for off the shelf VR headsets and other technologies for comparison.

Table 1. Cost of Virtual Reality Headsets in US Dollars compared to other technologies.

Model	Stand Alone	Cost
Oculus Go	Yes	\$149 – \$199
Oculus Quest	Yes	\$299 – \$499
Oculus Rift S	No	\$399 – \$599
Google Carboard	Mobile Phone	\$1.99 – \$10.00
Samsung Gear	Mobile Phone	\$99 – \$129
Vive	No	\$499 – \$799
Laptop Computer	N/A	\$279 – \$2500
Samsung Tablet	N/A	\$199 – \$699
iPhone	N/A	\$449 – \$749

Argumentative Writing

Argumentative writing is a process through which critical thinking and goal-directed self-regulatory procedures are used to complete the task (Watson, Michalek, & Gable, 2016). As science teachers use argumentative writing to learn key content, there are sometimes challenges. These challenges arise due to a student's lack of exposure to the content of the writing and to the manner of the use of claims and evidence. For example, students may ignore evidence which refutes their claim. Ignoring evidence is antithetical to the goal of argumentative writing which, is to convince others that their scientific ideas are valid through claims and evidence (Osborne, Henderson, & MacPherson, 2016).

The ridged structure of argumentative writing involves the steps of formulating a claim, providing evidence, and interpreting the value of the evidence regarding a specific topic. When writing an argument out, students typically write out all of the information they know about a topic, then add complexity to the information throughout by connecting claims and evidence (Hemberger, Kuhn, Matos, & Shi, 2017; Shute, 2008). Missing linkages and evidence for claims reduces the writing complexity and lexical density.

Argumentative writing is useful within science because it pushes students to go beyond inquiry, and to critique and develop novel ideas about topics (Bell & Linn, 2000). Thus, argumentative writing increases discussion and critique of and with others building critical thinking skills, and constructing novel scientific knowledge (Duschl & Osborne, 2002). The internalized nature of argument development is often predicated on prior knowledge, novel recombination of information through integration of new experiences and making embodied experiences important for argument development. Due to synthesis involved in writing, increases in writing complexity and lexical density are indicative of learning novel information.

Summative Writing

Summative writing is considered basic because it is through to only convey low level information (measures through lexical density and complexity) about observations (Crossley, Allen, Snow, & McNamara, 2016). Summative writing is a default mode of writing and for the conveyance of prior knowledge on a topic. Summary writing makes use of low-level factual information and events in chronological order.

From a cognition perspective, environmental interactions and complex environmental events significantly require resources because students must identify salient components within long-term memory, translate them through working memory and critical thinking, and undergo a validity check. Upon the validation, the information can be produced and written. The added steps of information processing associated with validation are thought to increase BOLD signal intensity in summary writing. The examination of the BOLD signal intensity during writing allows observation of the process of writing, as opposed to the products of writing. Since the behavioral manifestation of embodied knowledge can be expressed through writing, examination of how technology supports affect the writing process and associated products is warranted.

METHODS

Participants

Fifty participants, 25 males and 25 females, were recruited from a rural middle school in the Mid-Atlantic region in the United States. Of the 50 participants, 20 were sixth graders, 20 were seventh graders, and 10 were eight graders. The mean age of the participants was 12.3 (*SD* =.4) years. All but four of the participants spoke English as their primary language. Participants were prescreened to ensure they were comfortable with neuroimaging equipment, were resilient to motion sickness, and had no previous seizures when exposed to flashing lights. In addition, achievement levels for reading and mathematics were on grade level, based upon evaluations using the Woodcock-Johnson Test of Achievement for sixth, seventh, and eighth graders. The researchers also pre-screened participants using the Wide Range Achievement Test Third Edition for memory and other variables related to their functional status. Additional screenings for neurological contraindications occurred through interviews and clinical history review as suggested in the *Compendium of Neuropsychological Tests* (Strauss, Sherman, & Spreen, 2006). The researchers did not eliminate any participants due to screening outcomes. A priori analysis of power suggested a .90 probability of observing a large effect with 12 participants per condition. Given the possibility of attrition it was decided to recruit a total of 50 participants which was 5% more students than required by the power analysis. Upon completion of the screening, participants were randomly placed into one of the conditions, and timed. Timing of the participants ensured time on task was not a factor within each condition. Upon completion of each modality condition, the participants were fitted with the fNIRS band and asked to respond to the prompts.

Materials and Measures

When the participants arrived at the Neurocognition Science Laboratory, they were escorted into a controlled setting with their parent and one of the four initial conditions was randomly selected for implementation. After completion of each of the conditions, an exit interview and observation of the participants was conducted to ensure there were no ill effects due to the VR or fNIRS.

Once comfortable, the participants spent a total of 20 minutes in their assigned condition. Thus, participants either: (a) engaged in the VR environment for 20 minutes; (b) engaged with the VR environment for 10 minutes and then used the textbook for an additional 10 minutes; (c) used the textbook for 10 minutes and then engaged with the VR environment for 10 minutes; (d) used the textbook for 20 minutes. Within the VR simulation participants could freely move around and explore the environment in a 4-meter by 3-meter square area.

Participants were then given instructions about the first prompt. The order of the prompts was counterbalanced across participants to prevent a practice effect. Each participant was given 10 minutes to complete each prompt. The participant was able to take a five-minute break between each prompt and prior to instruction on the second prompt. Total time for each participant was one hour.

The VR environment was experienced using a commercially available HTC Vive Virtual Reality headset with noise canceling headphones to reduce outside noise. No modification of the headset or computer was done to assist replicability of the study. The VR simulation was an Ocean Reef VR environment. The environment consisted of multiple sea creatures to include jellyfish and other species of fish within the Atlantic Ocean. Students were able to walk and touch the various animals and plants in the simulation using the handheld set of paddle controls. The VR environment was completely open without prompts of audio cueing.

The VR experience is of an Ocean Reef environment 50 meters deep in the Atlantic Ocean. The visuals of the VR system were naturally colored with bright colors for the fish and other organisms. This helped to keep interest and attention. Species in both the textbook and VR scenario were noted by the researcher to ensure attention and interest was equal between conditions. There were approximately ten different fish species, three coral species, and two jellyfish species represented. The total VR experience was a minimum of 10 minutes with all students completing the entire experience.

A chapter from the Earth Matters middle school ecology textbook was used. The pictures in the chapters consisted of color photos of plants and animals found in the Atlantic Ocean. Other figures consisted of colored diagrams depicting the relationship between various species within the environment. Text covered approximately 80% or more of most pages. Bold words in the text were considered important vocabulary words within the unit. Randomly selected sentences (10%), were typed into Microsoft Word 2016, to obtain the average Flesch Reading Ease (93.8), and Flesch-Kincaid Grade Level (5.2).

Writing Prompts

The first writing prompt asked the participants to write one letter to a fellow student at their grade level and explain the potential ways an ecosystem could be disturbed or damaged (Yoon, 2012). During the writing of the letters, the students were asked to discuss how removal, or the addition of variables may change the coral reef ecosystem.

A second prompt asked the participants to write one letter, again argumentative or summary depending on the first prompt, to a younger student about the marine ecosystem. The writer was to explain and describe, what an ecosystem is. This prompt promoted a summative style of writing by asking for a factual recall of information from the virtual environment.

Scoring of the Writing Samples

One score related to writing complexity and one score for lexical density was calculated for each paragraph. Writing complexity is content having interconnected parts with apparent complex thinking beyond facts (Gregg & Steinberg, 2016). Lexical density is the number of content words (i.e. nouns etc.) divided by the total number of words (Somasundaran, Riordan, Gyawalli, & Yoon, 2016). Writing complexity was scored based on, *The Complexity of Writing Rubric*, developed by Yoon in 2012 (Yoon, 2012; Hand, Villanueva, & Yoon, 2014).

Criteria for complexity consisted of having "A Single Line of Reasoning," single arguments, descriptions, and / or summaries without connection to underlying theoretical propositions received a "1". Reasoning is the linking of evidence to claims. Samples that showed "A Chain of Reasoning," describes a causal mechanism with and explanation. Chains of reasoning were scored with a "3". Writing that showed a "Reasoning Network," illustrated examples, and explained why and how a change in the ecosystem happened, were given a score of 5. Scores of 2 and 4 were used if the writing sample seemed to be between a 1, 3, or 5. Undergraduate research assistants calibrated by scoring five writing samples. Raters also examined how each separate clause supported the claims and arguments throughout the writing sample. Nineteen (38%) of the participants' writing samples had a Fleiss's Kappa equal to .97 (substantial agreement).

Lexical density in the writing samples was examined using the Lexical Density program (Analyze my Writing, https://www.analyzemywriting.com/). Lexical Density was calculated by measuring the percentage of words that give information (verbs, adverbs, nouns, and adjectives) then dividing by the total number of words. Ten percent of the writing samples were randomly selected and reviewed by raters. The raters compared their lexical density score with the scores from *Analyze my Writing*. Fleiss's Kappa was used to measure interrater reliability between the raters and *Analyze my Writing;* kappa was .93 (substantial agreement). Each participant received a total of four scores (2-Lexical Density, summary and argumentative and 2-Complexity, summary and argumentative).

fNIRS Measurements

Functional near infrared spectroscopy (fNIRS) is a non-invasive imaging technology, making use of light in the near infrared spectrum. Neuroimaging technologies such as functional near infrared spectroscopy (fNIRS) are well suited to examine cognitive demand measured through hemodynamic response in educationally relevant settings. For example, fNIRS measures have been shown to successfully quantify aspects of cognitive state and cognitive load to an 90% accuracy (Fishburn, Norr, Medvedev, & Vaidya, 2014; Uysal, 2016; Dan, Saha, Konar, Ralescu, & Nagar, 2016).

fNIRS used the following characteristics of infrared light and chromophores human tissue is transparent within the near infrared range 600 nm to 1000 nm. Light emitted in the NIRS range is absorbed by pigments known as chromophores such as hemoglobin. Light not absorbed by the hemoglobin or other chromophores is scattered. Light scattering is for more likely than absorption (Scholkmann, Kleiser, Metz, Zimmermann, Pavia, Wolf, & Wolf, 2014). Finally, fNIRS has excellent discrimination between large blood vessels and small vessels. This study specifically focused on signal detection at Optodes 1, 2, 3, and 4 and Optodes 13, 14, 15, and 16 because of their relation the cognitive variables of interest.

The fNIRS sensor pad consists of four infrared light sources and 16 detectors which can be position on the head to detect blood flow up to 10 mm below the scalp. The fixed source-detectors are spaced at 2.50 cm apart. Data acquisition and visualization occurred using COBI Studio software version 1.3.0.19. Data collection occurred in an A-B-A sequence; baseline (A, non-writing) and stimulus (B, writing conditions). During the A portion of the A-B-A sequence, the participant with the fNIRS band on their head was in a relaxed rest condition with their eyes closed; no limb motion was detected. A video camera was placed in a position to record the participant. This was intended to synchronize events and identify irregularities if present.

Signal processing and data preparation for statistical analysis occurred via fNIRS Soft Professional version and SPSS 24. Collected data consisted of fNIRS hemodynamic response data, video recording data, and the written responses from the participants. Additional synchronization beyond the video occurred using a MP150 data acquisition device. Data capture to a .01 second level occurred during the A condition allowing the researchers to account for preexisting states such as, excitement or anxiety. These states are emotional responses, are less transient, and stimulus dependent, when compared to cognitive states related to writing which are far more stable.

The stimulus response or BOLD signal for each participant was collected and converted to a block average. This means that, the hemodynamic readings for the stimulus represented a composite mean for the interaction of the student with the stimulus. This approach replicates a modified A-B-A (Baseline I, Stimulus, and Baseline II) single case design, often found in special education research. A-B-A data collections allowed each participant to act as an internal control condition during the study (Rispoli, Lang, Neely, Camargo, Hutchins, Davenport, & Goodwyn, 2013). The A-B-A design and the block average produces a time bound response average allowing isolation of the stimulus-response complex. Data collection and isolation via this method helps to reduce the chance that other variables, such as, affective response are causing the hemodynamic fluctuation.

Design and Procedure

The independent variable in this study is the exposure to a specific modality of information presentation: VR, VR followed by text, text followed by VR, and text only. The response variable used to measure the effects of the condition are writing lexical density and complexity and BOLD signal response. Analysis of this data occurred via a mixed model ANOVA (MX ANOVA). MX ANOVA allowed examination of differences between writing complexity and lexical density scores within the argumentative and summative writing prompts across the four exposure conditions. Post-hoc Tukey tests were used to determine which modality created differences from one another as the students engaged in different forms of writing. Comparisons using the MX ANOVA were also used to identify differing levels of hemodynamic response between Baseline I, Stimulus, and Baseline II.

Data Processing

Analysis of the data occured after the removal of the heart pulsations, respiration, and movement artifacts using a low pass filter of 0.14 Hz (Vitorio, Stuart, Rochester, Alcock, & Pantall, 2017). Using this cutoff for physiological noise such as, heartbeat, breathing cycle, and blood pressure, accounts for a loss of 17% of the fNIRS signal data across conditions. While a 17% data loss may suggest a lower measurement sensitivity associated fNIRS. When fNIRS is compared to fMRI, fNIRS signals are resistant to large movements, making it more useful in educational contexts. Hemodynamic values were standardized, with respect to Baseline I values. Standard scores were then time blocked and averaged across each subject.

Statistical Analysis of Hemodynamic Response

Statistical analysis was conducted on the standardized hemodynamic responses. These standardized hemodynamic responses were statistically tested for differences using a MX ANOVA and planned post-hoc comparisons by condition using SPSS version 24. In MX ANOVA the subjects serve as their own control making and are not subject to the limitations of repeated measures ANOVA. MX ANOVA is particularly useful for examining A-B-A within subject designs to allow simultaneous identification of optodes of interest and hemodynamic responses above Baseline I and II. In addition, MX ANOVA reduces error variance and increases the power of the test to detect differences, specifically between Baseline I, Stimulus, and Baseline II when completed in conjunction with multiple comparisons such as a Tukey-HSD post-hoc test.

Statistical Analysis of Writing Prompt Responses

Composite scores consisted of the lexical density score and complexity score added together. A Mixed Model ANOVA was used to assess differences across conditions on composite writing scores. Correlational analysis between writing scores and hemodynamic responses was done to show a relationship between the variables of interest. A significance level of .05 was used for tests and assumptions for each analysis were examined to ensure data compliance.

RESULTS

Increases in hemodynamic activity are associated with each of the writing tasks when compared to baseline I and II in optodes 13 and 14. Intense hemodynamic activations associated with critical thinking and retrieval of encoded long-term memory is associated with optodes 13 and 14 (Evans & Stanovich, 2013; Tai & Chau, 2009). In comparing argumentative and summary writing, summary writing showed a more intense hemodynamic response optode 13, $F(1,1199)=10.84$, $p<.001$ and optode 14, $F(1,1199)=8.21$, $p<.001$ when compared to argumentative writing.

The main effect of the learning condition is significantly different $F(3,77) = 9.76$, $p < .001$ in intensity of hemodynamic activation. Post-hoc comparisons using Tukey-HSD illustrates that the condition of VR and then text, produces greater writing complexity and lexical density when compared across conditions $t(38) = 2.98$, $p < .001$.

Correlational analysis between content outcomes and hemodynamic responses suggests a statistically significant relationship between individual scores on each writing task and composite hemodynamic response, $r(78)= .73$, $p < .001$, moderate. This suggests that as stimulus states are presented, there is a near simultaneous engagement of the hemodynamic response. This tightly binds the response to the stimulus. Table 2 provides an overview of the post hoc comparison for each condition and test.

Table 2. Results of comparisons between conditions.

Comparison 1	Comparison 2	Test Statistic	*p-value*	Effect	Interpretation	Significant
Baseline I	Summary Writing	3.21	<.001	.722	Medium	Yes
	Argumentative Writing	2.88	.002	.648	Medium	Yes
	Baseline II	.48	.36	No Effect	None	No
Baseline II	Summary Writing	3.16	.001	.711	Medium	Yes
	Argumentative Writing	2.71	.004	.609	Medium	Yes
VR	VR + Text	3.98	<.001	.895	Large	Yes
	Text + VR	2.74	.003	.616	Medium	Yes
	Text	1.27	.104	No Effect	None	No
VR + Text	Text + VR	2.88	.003	.648	Medium	Yes
	Text	3.45	<.001	.776	Medium	Yes
Text + VR	Text	2.17	.017	.488	Small	Yes
Summary Composite Scores	Argumentative Composite Scores	2.08	.020	.468	Small	Yes

Note. Effect sizes are considered as per Cohen, J. Statistical power analysis for the behavioral sciences. New York: Academic Press, 1969.

Results illustrate that using VR prior to text reading may increase levels of lexical density and complexity and seems to increase the intensity of hemodynamic response. fNIRS results indicate that there is greater hemodynamic response in the prefrontal cortex when participants are engaged in summary writing when compared to argumentative writing. These results seem to indicate that the ordering of the VR experience and the writing style significantly impact the levels of processing. These results were also consistent with a post activity interview. During the interview, the participants were asked "which type of writing made you think more?" Ninety three percent of the respondents said, the summary writing made them think more.

DISCUSSION

Writing in science, as in other disciplines, makes use of characteristics which are derived from student's prior knowledge and novel experiences. In answering Research Question 1 what combination/s of VR and textbook promote the greatest lexical density and complexity in summary and argumentative writing?; the combination of VR followed by text seem to produce the greater lexical density and complexity. This potentially points to basic aspects of how the understanding of the nature of the science discipline and inquiry influence factors such as critical thinking and memory. When translated into educationally relevant constructs critical thinking and memory are deeply identified with prior knowledge and the contextualization of experiences. These two constructs are key components in the construction and application of written scientific knowledge. VR seems to provide some additional supports through experiential learning. Tying VR experiences to textual information would seem to promote the interaction between long-term memory systems and working memory systems, essentially resulting in greater manipulation of content in working memory through critical thinking about facts and observation (declarative memory) with structured generation occurring during the sense making of the experience (procedural memory) in specific time-bound situations (episodic memory). The activations of the multi-channels of memory indicated by the intensity of activation when VR is present may suggest deeper learning potential when technology supports are present.

Research question 2, of summary and argumentative writing, which illustrates the greatest hemodynamic responses as a proxy for cognitive dynamics? Summary writing illustrates greater intensity of hemodynamic response. Greater hemodynamic responses or cognitive activity is present during the summary writing process within VR and textbook condition. This result is counter to existing research on writing to learn (Durst, 1987; Rahmi & Zhang, 2018; Taylor et al., 2019) but is consist with current neuroscience and cognitive science research related to writing (Bauml, Pastotter, & Hanslimayr, 2010; Janczyk et al., 2018) . In reconciling these differences an important consideration is the mode of measurement. Research illustrating that argumentative writing is more cognitively demand focuses on the writing itself examining word choice, linkages between words, and overall ideas. In contrast research illustrating that summary writing is more cognitively demand focuses the underlying on the processes of writing. Argumentative writing depends on external structures for organization and processing of information. External structures consist of the very format and nature of argumentative writing occurs because of a natural predefined means. The student presents their claim, evidence, and critique and attempts to persuade. The presence of the structure of argument predefined and does not necessitate the engagement of cognitive tools and may in many ways be automatic. Much of the organization, structure, and content is selected by the structure of written argument itself. Student may actually need to make use of fewer long-term memory based and process / manipulate less information which reduces learning (Arnold et al., 207). In contrast summary writing does not have a well-defined structure which increases cognitive demand, the student must engage in validity checking increasing demand, the student must recall from multiple long-term memory bases, and engage active components of working memory such as critical thinking. Importantly while all of these increase demand the cognitive work is hidden and not present in the writing itself as indicated by low lexical density and complexity scores. The workload associated with summary writing would only be visible during the actual production of the writing itself.

Based upon the idea that summary writing is more demanding during the process of writing and that the manipulation of content to engage cognitive tools sets is important, it follows that combinations of modal representation that change the what and how of engaged cognitive and potentially affective tools would be of interest. It would seem within summary writing the ordering of the combination of modality (VR and text) is useful in the development of underlying cognitive tools for writing to learn in science. It is even likely that the relative ratios of text, to picture, to sound etc. my play a role and should be considered for additional areas of research. VR then textbook versus textbook then VR suggest that how we stimulate specific interactions with the classroom, access of prior knowledge, working memory, and reasoning can create useful cognitive demand in summary writing which may increase the possibility of deep learning (Kirschner et al., 2018). A critical dimensions that need to be understood in terms of writing to learning is that summary and argumentative writing cannot be viewed as the reorganization of existing knowledge but is a combination of a series of interactions between environments such as VR, prior knowledge, memory, reasoning, and application of skills and procedures.

These findings have implications for the development of curriculum and materials related to writing to learning and how virtual experiences may support student development in scientific reasoning and associated cognitive tools. The primary value of student writing created due to priming using VR experiences and textual information is that there is the potential for deeper learning and incorporation of embodied experiences in science. This recommendation arises from suggestions by Jesson et al., 2018 to integrate classroom activities with 21st Century Skills such as written communication. Using a combination of measurements to examine both product and processes may allow the development of alternative evaluations which augment traditional evaluation through incorporation of hands-on aspects. Written communications would be a means to understand critical thinking and how well we have used development tools. Writing may not act only as evidence of student learning, application of knowledge, and engagement with science, but also represent the means through which students communicate their understanding and reasoning about an experience with multimodal representations.

IMPLICATIONS FOR PRACTICE

In linking the product (writing) with cognitive processes (hemodynamics), the mode of knowledge transmission and the student's confidence and comfort with writing frequently surface as issues, as they try to engage in summary and argumentative writing. The sequencing of different priming tasks i.e. VR and textbook, with contrasting contexts, purposes, and approaches can support writing complexity, lexical density, and underlying cognitive processing needed to achieve science reasoning. A critical feature of these series of tasks is that students are required to transform the modal experiences from one form to another through the act of writing and attend to multiple purposes. To address the conditions for success, the students' need to understand the nature and purposes of writing in science. The conditions are both, opportunities, and requirements, for developing reasoning skills related to 21st Century Skills and science practices. This study has identified areas for potential laboratory and classroom-based research on the role of writing in learning, to enhance critical thinking in science.

There is a need to identify which modes or combinations of modes are most effective in promoting aspects of writing, knowledge development, and cognitive processing that comprise the interdependent aspects of science writing. While more research is needed, this study clearly identifies VR and textbook use in combination with one another as an approach for greater promotion of writing, knowledge development, and cognition. There is a need to understand the effects of sequences of experiences and stimulation of specific cognition (processes) within and across writing (products). More research is needed to explore the effects of individual differences in relation to student writing, cognitive attributes, and beliefs about the effectiveness of support tools such as VR related to writing to learn in science.

LIMITATIONS

In considering the weaknesses in this study, as with most educational outcomes, the results of study outcomes depend almost entirely on the content and quality of the particular VR used, and the content and quality of the particular textbook used. For example, you are unlikely to find that VR alone outperforms a textbook if the VR experience is poorly constructed. Closely tied to this concern, examining one VR experience and one textbook does not allow for generalization to all textbooks and VR experiences. While physiological responses should be similar with similar stimuli, the patterns which have been identified may or may not be the same for other VR experiences combined with other textbooks.

The fNIRS sensor only has the ability to ascertain activations directly below the band and will not detect fluctuations in hemodynamics away from the band. In addition, there is not direct alignment between content effects and hemodynamic effects, i.e. only a moderate correlation indicating that other variables may moderate or mediate the observed effects. A second area of limitation when using the fNIRS is the high sensitivity to blood flow within the superficial or subcutaneous tissue of the scalp which is not an indicator of cognitive action (Kirlina, et al., 2012; Takahashi et al., 2011). Scalp tissue hemodynamics may illustrate a 10 to 20 times higher fluctuation than the changes in the cortical tissue. However, "extracranial and cerebral contributions to the fNIRS signal can be separated by means of regression during analysis" (Kirilina et al., 2012 p.79).

A final area of limitation, this study only examines life sciences content and does not consider additional aspects of critical thinking development occurring in other science courses or content. In addition to the measurement limitations, there are other limitations associated with aligning the VR content with curriculum standards and lesson objectives, as much of content in VR is not designed for educational purposes. Along these lines, one added obstacle to full realization of VR in the classroom is the ability of the school to obtain a sufficient number of headsets for each student. Though this is not a large obstacle, with proper planning it is possible to have groups of three to four students use one VR headset in group work.

CONCLUSION

The use of VR to promote writing in the science classroom provides a potential means to access and develop key underlying cognitive attributes, reasoning, and skills which are useful across the disciplines of science. These results also seem to suggest the presence of multi-channel cognitive systems lending support to Galbreath's 1999 model of writing to learn. Further research should be conducted to understand how additional cognitive resources are engaged and developed when integrating VR and textual information for classroom use in writing to learn. An understanding of how best to integrate VR, and which style of writing improves cognitive system engagement and may lead to more specific instructional practices for writing to learn in science. The findings from this work also support results found in other studies, such as Yamamoto and Nakakoji (2005), which suggest there are underlying cognitive attributes, such as critical thinking which, influence writing to learn in science classrooms.

REFERENCES

Aberšek, B. (Ed.). (2017). *Cognitive science in education and alternative teaching strategies*. Cambridge Scholars Publishing.

Akaygun, S., & Jones, L. L. (2014). Words or pictures: A comparison of written and pictorial explanations of physical and chemical equilibria. *International Journal of Science Education, 36*(5), 783–807. doi:10.1080/09500693.2013.828361

Akgunduz, D., & Akinoglu, O. (2016). The Effect of Blended Learning and Social Media-Supported Learning on the Students' Attitude and Self-Directed Learning Skills in Science Education. *Turkish Online Journal of Educational Technology-TOJET, 15*(2), 106–115.

Arnold, K. M., Umanath, S., Thio, K., Reilly, W. B., McDaniel, M. A., & Marsh, E. J. (2017). Understanding the cognitive processes involved in writing to learn. *Journal of Experimental Psychology. Applied, 23*(2), 115–127. doi:10.1037/xap0000119 PMID:28447809

Aslin, R. N., Shukla, M., & Emberson, L. L. (2015). Hemodynamic correlates of cognition in human infants. *Annual Review of Psychology, 66*(1), 349–379. doi:10.1146/annurev-psych-010213-115108 PMID:25251480

Baram-Tsabari, A., & Osborne, J. (2015). Bridging science education and science communication research. *Journal of Research in Science Teaching, 52*(2), 135–144. doi:10.1002/tea.21202

Baus, O., & Bouchard, S. (2014). Moving from virtual reality exposure-based therapy to augmented reality exposure-based therapy: A review. *Frontiers in Human Neuroscience, 8*, 112. doi:10.3389/fnhum.2014.00112 PMID:24624073

Bell, P., & Linn, M. C. (2000). Scientific arguments as learning artifacts: Designing for learning from the web with KIE. *International Journal of Science Education, 22*(8), 797–817. doi:10.1080/095006900412284

Berland, L. K., & Reiser, B. J. (2009). Making sense of argumentation and explanation. *Science Education, 93*(1), 26–55. doi:10.1002ce.20286

Chalkiadaki, A. (2018). A systematic literature review of 21st century skills and competencies in primary education. *International Journal of Instruction, 11*(3), 1–16. doi:10.12973/iji.2018.1131a

Chen, Y. C., Hand, B., & McDOWELL, L. E. A. H. (2013). The effects of writing-to-learn activities on elementary students' conceptual understanding: Learning about force and motion through writing to older peers. *Science Education, 97*(5), 745–771. doi:10.1002ce.21067

Chen, Y. C., Park, S., & Hand, B. (2016). Examining the use of talk and writing for students' development of scientific conceptual knowledge through constructing and critiquing arguments. *Cognition and Instruction, 34*(2), 100–147. doi:10.1080/07370008.2016.1145120

Chu, S. K. W., Reynolds, R. B., Tavares, N. J., Notari, M., & Lee, C. W. Y. (2017). *21st Century skills development through inquiry-based learning*. Singapore: Springer Singapore.

Coker, J. S., & Porter, D. J. (2017). Student motivations and perceptions across and within five forms of experiential learning. *The Journal of General Education, 65*(2), 138–156. doi:10.5325/jgeneeduc.65.2.0138

Crossley, S. A., Allen, L. K., Snow, E. L., & McNamara, D. S. (2016). Incorporating learning characteristics into automatic essay scoring models: What individual differences and linguistic features tell us about writing quality. *Journal of Educational Data Mining, 8*(2), 1–19.

D'esposito, M., & Postle, B. R. (2015). The cognitive neuroscience of working memory. *Annual Review of Psychology*, 66. PMID:25251486

Dan, M., Saha, A., Konar, A., Ralescu, A. L., & Nagar, A. K. (2016, July). A type-2 fuzzy approach towards cognitive load detection using fNIRS signals. In *2016 IEEE International Conference on Fuzzy Systems (FUZZ-IEEE)* (pp. 2508-2515). IEEE. 10.1109/FUZZ-IEEE.2016.7738009

DeAnda, S., Poulin-Dubois, D., Zesiger, P., & Friend, M. (2016). Lexical processing and organization in bilingual first language acquisition: Guiding future research. *Psychological Bulletin, 142*(6), 655–667. doi:10.1037/bul0000042 PMID:26866430

Dede, C., Grotzer, T. A., Kamarainen, A., & Metcalf, S. (2017). EcoXPT: Designing for deeper learning through experimentation in an immersive virtual ecosystem. *Journal of Educational Technology & Society, 20*(4), 166–178.

DeSutter, D., & Stieff, M. (2017). Teaching students to think spatially through embodied actions: Design principles for learning environments in science, technology, engineering, and mathematics. *Cognitive Research: Principles and Implications, 2*(1), 22. doi:10.118641235-016-0039-y PMID:28386586

Duschl, R. A., & Osborne, J. (2002). Supporting and promoting argumentation discourse in science education. *Studies in Science Education, 38*(1), 39–72. doi:10.1080/03057260208560187

Fishburn, F. A., Norr, M. E., Medvedev, A. V., & Vaidya, C. J. (2014). Sensitivity of fNIRS to cognitive state and load. *Frontiers in Human Neuroscience, 8*, 76. doi:10.3389/fnhum.2014.00076 PMID:24600374

Freina, L., & Ott, M. (2015, January). A literature review on immersive virtual reality in education: state of the art and perspectives. In *The International Scientific Conference eLearning and Software for Education (Vol. 1*, p. 133). "Carol I" National Defense University.

Galbraith, D. (2009). Cognitive models of writing. *German as a Foreign Language*, (2-3), 7-22.

Gregg, L. W., & Steinberg, E. R. (Eds.). (2016). *Cognitive processes in writing*. Routledge. doi:10.4324/9781315630274

Grissett, J. O., & Huffman, C. (2019). An open versus traditional psychology textbook: Student performance, perceptions, and use. *Psychology Learning & Teaching, 18*(1), 21–35. doi:10.1177/1475725718810181

Gruzd, A., Paulin, D., & Haythornthwaite, C. (2016). Analyzing social media and learning through content and social network analysis: A faceted methodological approach. *Journal of Learning Analytics, 3*(3), 46–71. doi:10.18608/jla.2016.33.4

Guell, X., Gabrieli, J. D., & Schmahmann, J. D. (2017). Embodied cognition and the cerebellum: Perspectives from the dysmetria of thought and the universal cerebellar transform theories. *Cortex*. PMID:28779872

Hampshire, A., & Sharp, D. J. (2015). Contrasting network and modular perspectives on inhibitory control. *Trends in Cognitive Sciences, 19*(8), 445–452. doi:10.1016/j.tics.2015.06.006 PMID:26160027

Hand, B., Villanueva, M. G., & Yoon, S. (2014). Moving from "fuzzi-ness" to canical knowledge: The role of writing in developing cognitive and representational resources. *Writing as Learning Activity, 17.*

Hayes, J. R., & Flower, L. S. (1986). Writing research and the writer. *The American Psychologist, 41*(10), 1106–1113. doi:10.1037/0003-066X.41.10.1106

Hemberger, L., Kuhn, D., Matos, F., & Shi, Y. (2017). A dialogic path to evidence-based argumentive writing. *Journal of the Learning Sciences, 26*(4), 575–607. doi:10.1080/10508406.2017.1336714

Huang, H. L., Hwang, G. J., & Chang, C. Y. (2019). Learning to be a writer: A spherical video-based virtual reality approach to supporting descriptive article writing in high school Chinese courses. *British Journal of Educational Technology*. Advance online publication. doi:10.1111/bjet.12893

Ihemedu-Steinke, Q. C., Erbach, R., Halady, P., Meixner, G., & Weber, M. (2017). Virtual reality driving simulator based on head-mounted displays. In *Automotive User Interfaces* (pp. 401–428). Springer. doi:10.1007/978-3-319-49448-7_15

James, M. A. (2017). A practical tool for evaluating the potential of ESOL textbooks to promote learning transfer. *TESOL Journal*, *8*(2), 385–408. doi:10.1002/tesj.279

Janczyk, M., Aßmann, M., & Grabowski, J. (2018). Oral Versus Written Recall of Long-Term Memory Items: Replicating and Extending the Writing Superiority Effect Across Knowledge Domains. *The American Journal of Psychology*, *131*(3), 263–272. doi:10.5406/amerjpsyc.131.3.0263

Jesson, R., McNaughton, S., Rosedale, N., Zhu, T., & Cockle, V. (2018). A mixed-methods study to identify effective practices in the teaching of writing in a digital learning environment in low income schools. *Computers & Education*, *119*, 14–30. doi:10.1016/j.compedu.2017.12.005

Kalman, C., Aulls, M. W., Rohar, S., & Godley, J. (2008). Students' perceptions of reflective writing as a tool for exploring an introductory textbook. *Journal of College Science Teaching*, *37*(4), 74.

Karoly, P. (1999). A goal system–self-regulatory perspective on personality, psychopathology, and change. *Review of General Psychology*, *3*(4), 264–291. doi:10.1037/1089-2680.3.4.264

Kirschner, P. A., Sweller, J., Kirschner, F., & Zambrano, J. (2018). From cognitive load theory to collaborative cognitive load theory. *International Journal of Computer-Supported Collaborative Learning*, *13*(2), 213–233. doi:10.100711412-018-9277-y PMID:30996713

Lamb, R., & Etopio, E. (2019b). Preservice Science Teacher Preparation Using Virtual Reality. In *Society for Information Technology & Teacher Education International Conference* (pp. 162-167). Association for the Advancement of Computing in Education (AACE).

Lamb, R., Etopio, E., Firestone, J. B., Zeder, J., & Hand, B. (2020). Realism, immersion, and interactivity. *Developing Science Literacy in the 21st Century*, 83.

Lamb, R., & Etopio, E. A. (n.d.). Virtual Reality: A Tool for Preservice Science Teachers to Put Theory into Practice. *Journal of Science Education and Technology*. Advance online publication. doi:10.100710956-020-09837-5

Lamb, R., Firestone, J., Schmitter-Edgecombe, M., & Hand, B. (2019). A computational model of student cognitive processes while solving a critical thinking problem in science. *The Journal of Educational Research*, *112*(2), 243–254. doi:10.1080/00220671.2018.1514357

Lamb, R., Hand, B., & Yoon, S. (2017). Examination of cognitive processing of science writing tasks. *Journal of Psychology and Brain Studies*, *1*(1), 1–5.

Lamb, R., Miller, D., Lamb, R., Akmal, T., & Hsiao, Y. J. (2018). Examination of the role of training and fidelity of implementation in the use of assistive communications for children with autism spectrum disorder: A meta-analysis of the Picture Exchange Communication System. *British Journal of Special Education*, *45*(4), 454–472. doi:10.1111/1467-8578.12243

Lamb, R. L., & Etopio, E. (2019a). Virtual Reality Simulations and Writing: A Neuroimaging Study in Science Education. *Journal of Science Education and Technology*, *28*(5), 542–552. doi:10.100710956-019-09785-9

Leinonen, T., Keune, A., Veermans, M., & Toikkanen, T. (2016). Mobile apps for reflection in learning: A design research in K-12 education. *British Journal of Educational Technology*, *47*(1), 184–202. doi:10.1111/bjet.12224

Lin, S. S. (2014). Science and non-science undergraduate students' critical thinking and argumentation performance in reading a science news report. *International Journal of Science and Mathematics Education*, *12*(5), 1023–1046. doi:10.100710763-013-9451-7

Lodge, J. M., O'Connor, E., Shaw, R., & Burton, L. (2015). Applying cognitive science to critical thinking among higher education students. In The Palgrave Handbook of Critical Thinking in Higher Education (pp. 391-407). Palgrave Macmillan.

Magana, A. J., Serrano, M. I., & Rebello, N. S. (2019). A sequenced multimodal learning approach to support students' development of conceptual learning. *Journal of Computer Assisted Learning*, *35*(4), 516–528. doi:10.1111/jcal.12356

Manz, E. (2015). Representing student argumentation as functionally emergent from scientific activity. *Review of Educational Research*, *85*(4), 553–590. doi:10.3102/0034654314558490

Martín-Gutiérrez, J., Fabiani, P., Benesova, W., Meneses, M. D., & Mora, C. E. (2015). Augmented reality to promote collaborative and autonomous learning in higher education. *Computers in Human Behavior*, *51*, 752–761. doi:10.1016/j.chb.2014.11.093

Mayer, R. E. (2019). Searching for the role of emotions in e-learning. *Learning and Instruction*, •••, 101213. doi:10.1016/j.learninstruc.2019.05.010

Melby-Lervåg, M., & Lervåg, A. (2014). Reading comprehension and its underlying components in second-language learners: A meta-analysis of studies comparing first-and second-language learners. *Psychological Bulletin*, *140*(2), 409–433. doi:10.1037/a0033890 PMID:23937316

Mendez, D., Mendez, M., & Anguita, J. (2018). Motivation of 14 Year-old Students using Tablets, compared to those using Textbooks and Workbooks. *International Journal of Interactive Mobile Technologies*, *12*(4), 86–96. doi:10.3991/ijim.v12i4.9203

Meritt, J., Gibson, D., Christensen, R., & Knezek, G. (2015). Teacher training using interactive technologies: Performance and assessment in second life and simschool. In *E-Learning systems, environments and approaches* (pp. 181–198). Springer. doi:10.1007/978-3-319-05825-2_13

Muis, K. R., Trevors, G., Duffy, M., Ranellucci, J., & Foy, M. J. (2016). Testing the TIDE: Examining the nature of students' epistemic beliefs using a multiple methods approach. *Journal of Experimental Education*, *84*(2), 264–288. doi:10.1080/00220973.2015.1048843

Murphy, P. K., Rowe, M. L., Ramani, G., & Silverman, R. (2014). Promoting critical-analytic thinking in children and adolescents at home and in school. *Educational Psychology Review*, *26*(4), 561–578. doi:10.100710648-014-9281-3

Mutlu-Bayraktar, D., Cosgun, V., & Altan, T. (2019). Cognitive load in multimedia learning environments: A systematic review. *Computers & Education*, *141*, 103618. doi:10.1016/j.compedu.2019.103618

Muwonge, C. M., Schiefele, U., Ssenyonga, J., & Kibedi, H. (2017). Self-regulated learning among teacher education students: Motivational beliefs influence on the use of metacognition. *Journal of Psychology in Africa*, *27*(6), 515–521. doi:10.1080/14330237.2017.1399973

Núñez, R. E., Edwards, L. D., & Matos, J. F. (1999). Embodied cognition as grounding for Osborne, J. F., Henderson, J. B., MacPherson, A., Szu, E., Wild, A., & Yao, S. Y. (2016). The development and validation of a learning progression for argumentation in science. *Journal of Research in Science Teaching*, *53*(6), 821–846.

Nunez, R. E., & Lakoff, G. (2013). The metaphorical structure of mathematics: Sketching out cognitive foundations for a mind-based mathematics. In *Mathematical reasoning* (pp. 29–98). Routledge.

Pelger, S., & Nilsson, P. (2018). Observed learning outcomes of integrated communication training in science education: Skills and subject matter understanding. *International Journal of Science Education. Part B*, *8*(2), 135–149.

Polikoff, M. S. (2015). How well aligned are textbooks to the common core standards in mathematics? *American Educational Research Journal*, *52*(6), 1185–1211. doi:10.3102/0002831215584435

Rahimi, M., & Zhang, L. J. (2018). Effects of task complexity and planning conditions on L2 argumentative writing production. *Discourse Processes*, *55*(8), 726–742. doi:10.1080/0163853X.2017.1336042

Robinson, T. J., Fischer, L., Wiley, D., & Hilton, J. III. (2014). The impact of open textbooks on secondary science learning outcomes. *Educational Researcher*, *43*(7), 341–351. doi:10.3102/0013189X14550275

Scholkmann, F., Kleiser, S., Metz, A. J., Zimmermann, R., Pavia, J. M., Wolf, U., & Wolf, M. (2014). A review on continuous wave functional near-infrared spectroscopy and imaging instrumentation and methodology. *NeuroImage*, *85*, 6–27. doi:10.1016/j.neuroimage.2013.05.004 PMID:23684868

Semin, G. R., & Smith, E. R. (2013). Socially situated cognition in perspective. *Social Cognition*, *31*(2), 125–146. doi:10.1521oco.2013.31.2.125

Shanahan, T., Fisher, D., & Frey, N. (2016). The challenge of challenging text. *On Developing Readers: Readings from Educational Leadership (EL Essentials)*, 100.

Shian, C. S., & Yunus, M. M. (2017). Audio clips in developing listening comprehension skills in Malaysian Primary ESL classrooms. *Proceedings of the ICECRS*, *1*(1). Advance online publication. doi:10.21070/picecrs.v1i1.511

Shute, V. J. (2008). Focus on formative feedback. *Review of Educational Research, 78*(1), 153–189. doi:10.3102/0034654307313795

Somasundaran, S., Riordan, B., Gyawali, B., & Yoon, S. Y. (2016). Evaluating Argumentative and Narrative Essays using Graphs. In *Proceedings of COLING 2016, the 26th International Conference on Computational Linguistics: Technical Papers* (pp. 1568-1578). Academic Press.

Sorden, S. D. (2012). The cognitive theory of multimedia learning. Handbook of Educational Theories, 1, 31.

Spence, K. K., & McDonald, M. A. (2015). Assessing vertical development in experiential learning curriculum. *Journal of Experiential Education, 38*(3), 296–312. doi:10.1177/1053825915571749

Taylor, K. S., Lawrence, J. F., Connor, C. M., & Snow, C. E. (2019). Cognitive and linguistic features of adolescent argumentative writing: Do connectives signal more complex reasoning? *Reading and Writing, 32*(4), 983–1007. doi:10.100711145-018-9898-6

Torrance, M., Van Waes, L., & Galbraith, D. (Eds.). (2007). *Writing and Cognition*. BRILL. doi:10.1163/9781849508223

Townsend, D. (2015). Who's using the language? Supporting middle school students with content area academic language. *Journal of Adolescent & Adult Literacy, 58*(5), 376–387. doi:10.1002/jaal.374

Uysal, M. P. (2016). Evaluation of learning environments for object-oriented programming: Measuring cognitive load with a novel measurement technique. *Interactive Learning Environments, 24*(7), 1590–1609. doi:10.1080/10494820.2015.1041400

Vitorio, R., Stuart, S., Rochester, L., Alcock, L., & Pantall, A. (2017). fnirs response during walking—Artefact or cortical activity? A systematic review. *Neuroscience and Biobehavioral Reviews, 83*, 160–172. doi:10.1016/j.neubiorev.2017.10.002 PMID:29017917

Vo, T., Ledbetter, C., & Zuckerman, M. (2019). Video delivery of toxicology educational content versus textbook for asynchronous learning, using acetaminophen overdose as a topic. *Clinical Toxicology, 57*(10), 842–846. doi:10.1080/15563650.2019.1574974 PMID:30806092

Wang, Y. H. (2017). Exploring the effectiveness of integrating augmented reality-based materials to support writing activities. *Computers & Education, 113*, 162–176. doi:10.1016/j.compedu.2017.04.013

Watson, S. M., Michalek, A. M., & Gable, R. A. (2016). Linking executive functions and written language intervention for students with language learning disorders. *International Journal of School and Cognitive Psychology, 3*(3). Advance online publication. doi:10.4172/2469-9837.1000178

Yoon, H. (2012). *Re-writing the writing script: Teachers and children translating curriculum in everyday practice* (Unpublished doctoral dissertation). University of Illinois at Urbana-Champaign.

Zambrano, J., Lee, G. A., Leal, C. C., & Thoman, D. B. (2020). Highlighting Prosocial Affordances of Science in Textbooks to Promote Science Interest. *CBE Life Sciences Education, 19*(3), ar24. doi:10.1187/cbe.19-09-0176 PMID:32559123

Zheng, W., Yi, X., & Shi, Y. (2019, July). Investigating the Interaction Experience with Augmented Reality Based Writing Tools. In *International Conference on Human-Computer Interaction* (pp. 461-466). Springer. 10.1007/978-3-030-23528-4_63

ADDITIONAL READING

Hand, B. (2017). Exploring the role of writing in science: A 25-year journey. *Literacy Learning: The Middle Years*, *25*(3), 16.

Khalil, N., & Osman, K. (2017). STEM-21CS module: Fostering 21st century skills through integrated STEM. *K-12 STEM Education, 3*(3), 225-233.

Parong, J., & Mayer, R. E. (2018). Learning science in immersive virtual reality. *Journal of Educational Psychology*, *110*(6), 785–797. doi:10.1037/edu0000241

Pelger, S., & Nilsson, P. (2016). Popular science writing to support students' learning of science and scientific literacy. *Research in Science Education*, *46*(3), 439–456. doi:10.100711165-015-9465-y

Pfeifer, M. D., Scholkmann, F., & Labruyère, R. (2018). Signal processing in functional near-infrared spectroscopy (fNIRS): Methodological differences lead to different statistical results. *Frontiers in Human Neuroscience*, *11*, 641. doi:10.3389/fnhum.2017.00641 PMID:29358912

Pinti, P., Tachtsidis, I., Hamilton, A., Hirsch, J., Aichelburg, C., Gilbert, S., & Burgess, P. W. (2020). The present and future use of functional near-infrared spectroscopy (fNIRS) for cognitive neuroscience. *Annals of the New York Academy of Sciences*, *1464*(1), 5–29. doi:10.1111/nyas.13948 PMID:30085354

Sengul, O., Enderle, P. J., & Schwartz, R. S. (2020). Science teachers' use of argumentation instructional model: Linking PCK of argumentation, epistemological beliefs, and practice. *International Journal of Science Education*, *42*(7), 1–19. doi:10.1080/09500693.2020.1748250

Shapiro, L., & Stolz, S. A. (2019). Embodied cognition and its significance for education. *Theory and Research in Education*, *17*(1), 19–39. doi:10.1177/1477878518822149

KEY TERMS AND DEFINITIONS

Argumentative Writing: Writing intended to persuade another person of your viewpoint.

Blood Oxygen Level Dependent Signal (BOLD): Signal alterations identified during fNIRS imaging that indicate increases or decreases in brain activity related to blood oxygen levels occurring during task completion.

Cognitive Demand: The interaction of multiple task specific cognitive systems measured through the hemodynamic response of neural tissue.

Embodied Cognition: Cognition is biased and deeply dependent on an independent agent's body state and external environment.

Functional Near Infrared Spectroscopy (fNIRS): A non-invasive neuroimaging technology, making use of light in the near infrared spectrum to obtain visualizations of blood flow throughout the brain.

Hemodynamic Response: Hemodynamic response is the response of neural tissue oxygen use during the completion of specific tasks and ties to specific areas of the brain.

Optode: An optical sensor that measures specific wavelengths of light reflected from a substance.

Summative Writing: Writing intended to convey information without interpretation, deductions, and opinions about an observation or experience.

Virtual Reality: Virtual reality is a system consisting of a computer and headset with user interfaces which create a 360-degree three-dimensional environment to supply the effect of immersion and interaction.

Chapter 15
COMPASS-AR:
Assessment of Teaching Competences Acquired With Augmented Didactic Itineraries

M. Esther Del-Moral
University of Oviedo, Spain

Lourdes Villalustre
University of Oviedo, Spain

María del Rosario Neira-Piñeiro
https://orcid.org/0000-0003-2355-4682
University of Oviedo, Spain

ABSTRACT

A description and psychometric validation is offered of the evaluation instrument COMPASS-Ar, conceived to check the level of competence achieved by future teachers—after participating in the ITINER-Ar Project (2018-19)—in the collaborative design of augmented didactic itineraries (ADIs) using augmented reality. This instrument—assessed by experts—consists of 30 items to measure the acquired didactic, digital, socio-collaborative, and creative competences involved in ADI development on the basis of an analytical rubric—created ad hoc and validated by means of the Delphi method—which specifies the requirements of each score through a (1-5) Likert-type scale. After evaluating a sample of 322 subjects, the assessment of reliability provided a Cronbach's alpha = .979. Construct validity was tested using factor analysis. Both the Kaiser-Meyer-Olkin test and Bartlett's sphericity test revealed that the instrument under study has a unidimensional nature. It can be concluded that this is a valid and reliable instrument.

DOI: 10.4018/978-1-7998-5043-4.ch015

INTRODUCTION

Twenty-first-century teacher training must focus on favoring the acquisition and development of teaching competencies suited to the needs of present-day society. The aim is to train would-be teachers not so much as experts in the utilization of Information and Communication Technologies (ICTs) but rather as individuals in charge of harmonizing their integration into the school curriculum seeking to help optimize the teaching-learning process (Del Moral & Villalustre, 2010; Petko, 2012). Logically, since they are framed within a technological and digital environment, the training of future teachers must be aimed at providing them with the ability to use emergent technological resources (Chen, Lim & Tan, 2010; Huang & Yang, 2016). Moreover, it is necessary to pay attention to the didactic-methodological approach to develop enriching ICT-mediated experiences (Del Moral & Villalustre, 2012; Erstad, Eickelmann & Eichhorn, 2015).

The ITINER-Ar Project (2018-19) arises in this context with the aim of boosting the design of training proposals able to activate the teaching competencies of would-be teachers linked to the utilization of technological resources and, especially, to the implementation of augmented reality (AR) in classrooms. More precisely, these interdisciplinary proposals promote the design of Augmented Didactic Itineraries (ADIs), i.e., enriched with AR, to favor learning inside and outside the classroom with the support of digital devices (Bower, Howe, McCredie, Robinson & Grover, 2014; Villalustre & Del Moral, 2016). The purpose is to create didactic routes meant to facilitate the journey of infant, primary and secondary education students through physical or virtual scenarios using AR (Neira-Piñeiro, Del Moral & Fombella, 2020; Villalustre, San Pedro & López, 2020).

The versatility of AR allows the creation of interactive and immersive learning environments, able to add multi-format content to real objects and to provide additional information, in order to facilitate content comprehension and assimilation, with the support of mobile devices (Akçayır & Akçayır, 2017; Del Moral & Villalustre, 2013). Thus, these new landscapes acquire an additional value using AR, as they give access to extra information, they add 3D elements and they increase interaction.

Recent research has pointed out the advantages of AR in several educational levels. Thus, regarding infant education, some studies have focused on the increase of motivation and the initial literacy acquisition (Masmuzidin & Aziz, 2018). Likewise, several works show the positive impact of AR in primary education, regarding students' attention, attitudes and motivation, as well as in the acquisition of knowledge and skills. In this stage, it is worth highlighting its great potential for science education, although it has also been applied in Social Sciences and linguistic matters (Fotaris, Pellas, Kazanidis & Smith, 2017). Besides, AR is used in secondary education for promoting scientific and linguistic learning, having also provided positive results in cognitive development (Buzko, Bonk & Tron, 2018; Estapa & Nadolny, 2015).

Most instructors consider that AR favors collaborative students' work, as well as the cooperation between teachers for creating game-based resources and activities. However, teachers are aware of their need for training, in order to design enriching proposals based on AR applications. Teachers also point out their lack of formulae and strategies to assess the knowledge acquired by their students with AR activities (Villalustre, Del Moral & Neira, 2019).

In a similar same way, Bacca, Baldiris, Fabregat and Graf (2014) point out some limitations of AR, such as technical problems, negative effects on students -who sometimes pay too much attention to the virtual contents-, and the fact that AR can be considered as an intrusive technology. Thus, the introduction of AR into school demands that teachers face the challenges linked to these emergent technologies.

These challenges are not only related to AR knowledge and use, but also to the acquisition of didactic, digital, creative and social competencies, so that its introduction into the classroom improves the teaching and learning process (Chicioreanu & Amza, 2015; Marques & Pombo, 2020).

The development of digital teaching competencies needs a comprehensive training that prepares teachers to employ emergent digital technologies from an educational perspective (Gudmundsdottir & Hatlevik, 2018; Marques & Pombo, 2020; Wang, Callaghan, Bernhardt, White & Peña-Rios, 2018). In this sense, the project ITINER-AR has systematized teacher training by means of the introduction and educational use of several AR resources and applications. This project focuses on the utilization of mobile devices in the classroom, in order to promote interdisciplinary curriculum contents. To do that, the opportunities offered by the usual didactic itineraries have been increased with AR resources -such as geolocation, interactive animations and/or 3D videos, sound recordings, QR codes, markers, etc.-, with the aim of creating significant learning.

Some innovative experiences supported on AR have had positive results both in university teaching and in teacher training contexts (Akçayır, Akçayır, Pektaş & Ocak, 2016; Crespo, Fernández, Gonzales, Esparza & León-Acurio, 2020; Delello, 2014; Ke & Hsu, 2015). Nevertheless, the need exists not only to specify and systematize the didactic strategies so that they can be extrapolated to other contexts but also to establish evaluation formulas for the identification of the competencies acquired by students. Therefore, the contribution made by ITINER-AR has focused on turning the design of Augmented Didactic Itineraries into a training project addressed to teachers. This implies the adoption of previously defined methodological patterns and, additionally, makes it possible to assess the teaching competencies activated through their preparation on a collaborative basis and with an interdisciplinary or globalizing approach.

This chapter consequently depicts the process of design and psychometric validation for the instrument COMPASS-AR (competencies Assessment with Augmented Reality), conceived to evaluate the level of competency acquired by future infant and primary education teachers from the collaborative design of Augmented Didactic Itineraries.

Firstly, the concept of Augmented Didactic Itinerary (ADI) and the methodology LBDADI (Learning based on the Design of Augmented Didactic Itineraries) are explained, as they are crucial for this study. Secondly, as the instrument COMPASS-AR was created as a part of the project ITINER-AR, it is necessary to provide information about the project itself. Thus, the chapter describes the stages of the project and the competencies developed through the methodology LBDADI.

Afterwards, the process of psychometric validation of the instrument is presented, followed by the discussion and conclusion. It is worth highlighting that this study analyzes the data related to the psychometric validation, to confirm the pertinence and appropriateness of the instrument COMPASS-AR.

AUGMENTED DIDACTIC ITINERARIES: A NEW DIDACTIC METHODOLOGY?

The term augmented itinerary started to take shape in the museum and tourism context with the intention of offering visitors an experience enriched with the support of computer applications by adding complementary information to artistic works (Brugnoli, Morabito, Bo & Murelli, 2007). It has gradually been adopted in the educational sphere to refer to AR-based didactic tours such as geolocated geological routes (Martínez-Graña, González-Delgado, Ramos & Gonzalo, 2018), or literary, historical, artistic or cultural itineraries (Panciroli, Macauda & Corazza, 2018). The Augmented Didactic Itinerary (ADI) can be defined as a tour of a real space that brings together different AR activators designed for an educational purpose. Augmented Reality expands the information coming from the physical route and seeks to foster learning. Thus, augmented itineraries have as their aim to generate contexts that favor immersive educational practices that are able to foster significant learning achievements amongst students at different educational levels.

The design of augmented itineraries demands that teachers update their knowledge to plan new didactic strategies which can integrate AR and favor students' multisensorial involvement, while simultaneously offering enriching and highly motivating experiences. That update requires the familiarization with digital and AR tools and applications, which provide added value to conventional classroom practices, to school visits or to field trips. Likewise, teachers need to select suitable resources to prepare activities that will add to the accomplishment of the targeted educational objectives. Teachers also need evaluation instruments to assess each student's progress, and to check whether the innovative experiences have proved successful or have simply become a game accepted to a greater or lesser extent. Teacher training must consequently revolve around the joint acquisition of didactic-methodological and digital competencies.

The ITINER-AR Project stems from an effort to find new approaches for Infant and Primary Education teacher training which advocate the adoption of active and participatory methodologies aimed at fostering the didactic exploitation of emergent technologies such as AR. More specifically, it helps consolidate the methodology of Learning Based on the Design of Augmented Didactic Itineraries (LBDADI). This project is characterized by its dual nature: a) *formative*, addressed to train teachers of different educational levels through ADI collaborative design, adopting a set of previously defined methodological patterns, and encouraging both collaborative and autonomous work (Martín-Gutiérrez, Fabiani, Benesova, Meneses & Mora, 2015); and b) *evaluative*, by making it possible to check the competencies activated in would-be teachers through the preparation of itineraries.

Learning Based on the Design of Augmented Didactic Itineraries

The ITINER-AR Project (2018-19) suggests turning the collaborative design of Augmented Didactic Itineraries (ADIs) into a training strategy meant to boost would-be teachers' competencies linked to AR implementation in classrooms. Besides, it can be considered that this project is attached to Project-Based Learning (PBL). This methodology is focused here on the design of Augmented Didactic Itineraries (ADI), adhered to some specific predetermined criteria.

It even would be possible to coin the expression Augmented Itineraries Design-Based Learning Methodology (LBDADI). LBDADI is a methodology based on the collaborative creation of Augmented Didactic Itineraries. The ADI creation provides a chance to learn, favoring the development of various key competencies for a teacher. Thus, the process of the collaborative ADI design offers an opportunity for preservice teachers professional training, focused on the creation of innovative resources based on AR.

The LBDADI didactic methodology shares some characteristics with Project-Based Learning PBL: first, it is a student-centered methodological approach oriented to favor a contextualized type of learning. Second, it prioritizes students' social interaction and collaborative work, so that the shared goals can be achieved more easily (Kokotsaki, Menzies & Wiggins, 2016). In this case, the actions of students are aimed at the preparation of an end product —the ADI— which has a number of very well defined characteristics and relies on the didactic use of AR. The LBDADI methodology materialized as follows in the ITINER-AR Project:

- Didactic training. The same as in PBL (Kokotsaki, Menzies & Wiggins, 2016), the scaffolding provided by the teacher becomes essential to facilitate the development of a task which in this case revolves around the design of a didactic resource with the support of a new technology. Hence our interest in equipping the key students for a correct planning and organization of their proposal.
- Technological training. They were likewise given technological training not only to handle digital tools and to become familiar with AR applications but also to explore their didactic possibilities before integrating them into their itineraries.
- Bet on collaborative work. The design and execution of proposals must reflect the involvement and cooperation of work team members. For that purpose, a choice was made to use the learning contract as a means to record the agreements, commitments, and responsibilities assumed between any teacher and their students, seeking to favor learning self-regulation (De Miguel, 2006). In this case, the learning contract included writing a weekly diary to check and assess both group progress and individual socio-collaborative skills.

Stages of the Project ITINER-AR

The ITINER-AR project included six stages (Figure 1):

Figure 1. Stages of ITINER-AR Project

Firstly, and before the implementation of the project, the objectives were defined, as well as the methodology ABDIDA. Besides, the instrument was designed and validated (stages I and II).

Secondly, (stage III), the task was explained and the future teachers received a document with the instructions for designing the ADI. Two examples of ADIs created by the instructors were shown to the students. Moreover, several sessions were devoted to technological training, so that the participants learnt to use several AR applications and programs for creating digital contents. In this way, they acquired the basic digital competencies required for the collaborative creation of the ADIs. Besides, the contents and resources needed for the development of the project were hosted on a website (https://gitecna.wixsite.com/proyectoitinerar). This site was also used to provide additional materials for the students interested in increasing their knowledge on AR.

Figure 2. Website of ITINER-AR Project

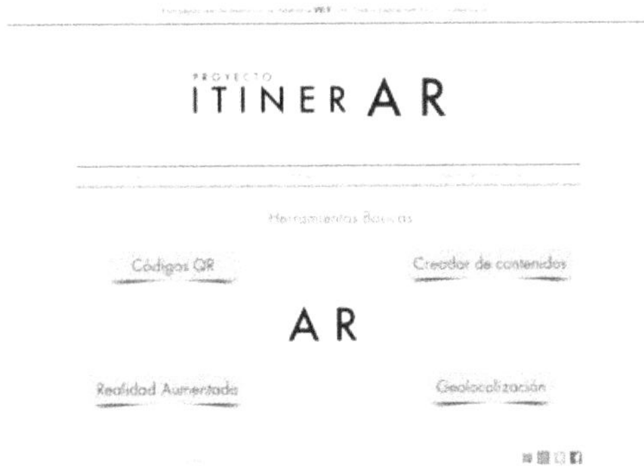

Later, (stage IV) the participants were organised in groups of 3 to 4 people. They were provided with a learning contract, which included a weekly detailed description of the group work. The members of each team reached an agreement regarding the contents and activities of their proposal. Subsequently, with the support of the instructors, the students selected digital resources and AR applications, which they included in their ADI. Thus, each team designed its ADI, created non-digital resources (lap books, models, etc.) and elaborated an educational guide made with the program Genially. Later, they presented their itineraries and delivered the learning contract.

Subsequently, (stage V), the university instructors assessed the work made by each student. In order to do that, they employed the instrument COMPASS-AR and the analytic rubric, using a Likert scale (1-5) (see Appendix 1 and 2). In this way, each participant received the corresponding score in each item. Afterwards, the numerical data coming from the students' assessment (Table 1) were statistically treated.

Finally (Stage VI), after the evaluation of the competency level acquired by the students, the results will be analyzed. As this stage is currently in progress, the results obtained will be presented in future works.

Teaching Competencies Involved in ADI Design

The evaluative nature intrinsic to the ITINER-AR Project entails the creation of a tool to check the extent to which the adoption of this methodology supported on the collaborative design of augmented didactic itineraries favors the acquisition and development of teaching competencies by future teachers. Hence the interest in identifying and defining those competencies which a priori seem to be more closely associated with the requested task (Figure 3):

Figure 3. Teaching competencies involved in the collaborative design of ADI

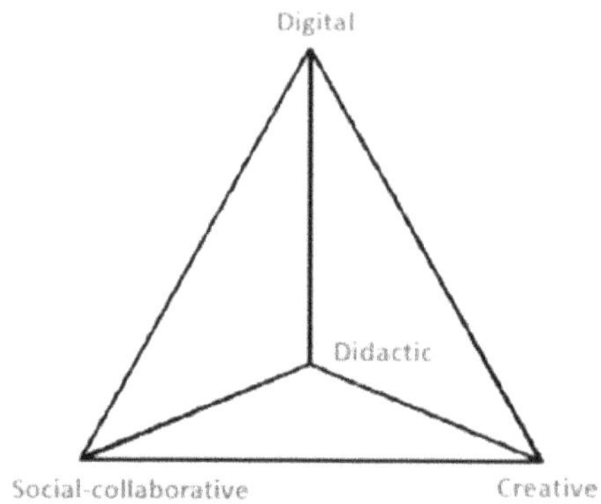

It is necessary to point out that the literature review did not provide a single assessment tool suitable for assessing the competencies level of the students participating in ITINER-AR. Therefore, it was necessary to create a tool specifically adapted for this purpose. In order to do that, several indicators were selected, taking into account previous studies on competencies assessment as well as the competencies involved in ITINER-AR project:

1) *Didactic competencies,* defined from 12 indicators related to:
    - The design of a coherent training proposal which affords a proper planning and organization (objectives, contents, and assessment criteria), and which addresses and applies curricular contents from an interdisciplinary or globalizing approach, by selecting the most suitable didactic resources, techniques and strategies that allow for the adaptation to a variety of contexts (Díaz-Mohedom & Vicente, 2014; Mynbayeva, Sadvakassova & Akshalova, 2017).
    - The preparation of a didactic guide which clearly explains the rationale for the proposal and its curricular context.
2) *Digital competencies,* associated with 6 indicators referred to the mastery, the use, and the application of technological tools or applications (Tondeur, Aesaert, Pynoo, van Braak, Fraeyman & Erstad, 2017; Yaman, Aydemir & Demirtaş, 2013) to ADI design. These competencies are inferred from the pertinence of the selected AR resources, the inclusion of diverse multimedia elements, their interactive capacity, the integration of our own developed resources, as well as the suitability of the technological implementations incorporated (GPS activators or coordinates,…).
3) *Socio-collaborative competencies*, defined from 6 indicators linked to the collaborative preparation (Forslund & Hammar, 2011) of ADIs. This implies assessing whether or not each subject has helped in favoring intergroup communication throughout the design process by generating and integrating a variety of ideas, and whether or not tasks have been planned and distributed beforehand to facilitate the assumption of individual responsibilities, as well as the collaboration and complementariness inside the group to solve the problems which arose during the execution of the task.
4) *Creative competencies,* considering 6 indicators associated with the skills inherent to the creative process and the elaboration of end products (Edwards, García, Sánchez, Quesada & Amara, 2015), ADIs this time. The creative competencies are verified from the esthetic quality and the harmonious combination of the resources included (balance, proportion, and correspondence between parts). They are inferred through the *flexibility* achieved (integration of different resources and/or applica-

tions, QR codes, geolocation, HP Reveal, images, markers, etc.), the *fluidity* reflected (diversity and functionality of a single resource), and the originality of each itinerary (its new, innovative, and exclusive nature), along with its versatility to consider various approaches when dealing with interdisciplinary contents.

METHOD: PSYCHOMETRIC VALIDATION OF THE INSTRUMENT COMPASS-AR

This study is framed within the ITINER-AR Project oriented to assess the competencies developed by future teachers from ADI design using the instrument COMPASS-AR, whose validation is provided in this work.

Procedure

The first construct drew on the contributions of several authors regarding different types of competencies: didactic (Díaz-Mohedom & Vicente, 2014; Mynbayeva, Sadvakassova & Akshalova, 2017), digital (Tondeur, Aesaert, Pynoo, van Braak, Fraeyman & Erstad, 2017; Yaman, Aydemir & Demirtaş, 2013) collaborative (Forslund & Hammar, 2011) and creative (Edwards, García, Sánchez, Quesada & Amara, 2015). An instrument which comprised 30 indicators with five answer options was designed to that end. In order to validate the contents, the instrument COMPASS-AR was examined by a panel of 3 experts —all of them university lecturers— coming from different areas within the fields of educational technology and education. A Likert-type scale with four answer options going from 1 (not suitable/intelligible at all) to 4 (highly suitable/relevant) served to determine the degree of intelligibility and pertinence per indicator. This process was carried out using the Delphi method (Clayton, 1997).

The instrument was applied with 322 university students. It was a non-probabilistic sample that included students enrolled in different subjects of the degrees in Infant and Primary Education Teacher Training —taught at the Faculty of Education at the University of Oviedo (Spain), during the 2018-19 academic year— in which the LBDADI methodology was used.

Thus, 48.2% of subjects belonged to the degree of Infant Education Teacher Training and the remaining 51.8% were enrolled in the degree of Primary Education Teacher Training. The distribution of all the students involved in the study was as follows: 22% of first-year students; 20% of second-year students; 17% of third-year students; and 41% of fourth-year students.

Psychometric validation took place using descriptive data analysis, factor analysis and correlations, with the aim of validating a unidimensional measuring instrument intended to assess the competencies acquired by would-be teachers through ADI collaborative design. It was carried out on the basis of the data obtained after evaluating the participating subjects, pursuant to the defined indicators and considering an analytical rubric where the requirements for each score are specified. This psychometric validation intends to confirm the pertinence and appropriateness of the instrument. The software used was SPSS v.6.

Instrument Design

The final instrument —validated through experts' judgment— considers 30 indicators associated with four teaching competencies involved in the ADI collaborative design process.

1) *Didactic*, defined from 12 indicators linked to teaching competencies:
   Didactic1. He/she justifies the pertinence of the itinerary.
   Didactic2. He/she properly locates the ADI in the curricular context.
   Didactic3. He/she properly plans and organizes the educational process.
   Didactic4. He/she specifies the assessment criteria in a coherent way.
   Didactic5. He/she provides an interdisciplinary and/or globalized approach.
   Didactic6. He/she presents the educational guide adequately.
   Didactic7. He/she includes specific contents in accordance with the educational proposal.
   Didactic8. He/she designs specific activities in accordance with the educational proposal.
   Didactic9. He/she selects adequate educational resources.
   Didactic10. He/she employs techniques and didactic strategies in accordance with the contents.
   Didactic11. He/she evidences the internal coherence of the educational proposal (objectives, contents, assessment...).
   Didactic12. He/she provides adaptability to the ADI, so that it can be implemented in several contexts.
2) *Digital*, comprising 6 indicators referred to competencies associated with the utilization and application of technological tools or applications for ADI design:
   Digital1. He/she shows the pertinence of the AR resources employed.
   Digital2. He/she masters several tools and techniques.
   Digital3. He/she provides interactivity to the elements included.
   Digital4. He/she designs and includes self-made resources (AR and /or geolocation applications).
   Digital5. He/she shows a proper use of technological resources (activators, GPS coordinates, etc).
   Digital6. He/she includes various multimedia resources.
3) *Socio-collaborative*, specified with 6 indicators involved in ADI collaborative creation:
   Social1. He/she favors the communication within the group through the ADI design process.
   Social2. He/she provides and integrates several ideas through the ADI design process.
   Social3. He/she gets involved in the organization and distribution of the tasks.
   Social4. He/she shows interest and takes responsibility.
   Social5. He/she collaborates and complements the group.
   Social6. He/she contributes to the resolution of the problems arisen.
4) *Creative*, considering 6 indicators related to the skills inherent to the creative process and the elaboration of end products:
   Creative1. He/she integrates various resources, providing flexibility to the ADI.
   Creative2. He/she explores the functionalities of the resources, fostering the fluidity of the ADI.
   Creative3. He/she shows originality (novelty, innovation and exclusivity).
   Creative4. He/she combines the resources with balance and proportion, searching for the correspondence and harmony between the parts.
   Creative5. He/she provides various formulae for addressing several topics.
   Creative6. He/she evidences the aesthetic quality of the physical support and the multimedia resources.

The measurement of indicators associated with each type of competency was performed by the university instructors by means of a Likert-type scale which places future teachers at the level of competency acquired when designing the ADI (1=very low; 2=low; 3=medium; 4=high; and 5=very high).

Table 1. Descriptive statistics

	X	SD	Principal component (*)	Difficulty index
Didactic1	3.93	1.031	.709	.58
Didactic2	4.02	1.024	.873	.60
Didactic3	3.82	1.046	.862	.56
Didactic4	345	1.170	.775	.49
Didactic5	3.71	1.190	.852	.54
Didactic6	3.87	1.069	.880	.57
Didactic7	3.70	1.127	.811	.54
Didactic8	3.70	1.149	.807	.54
Didactic9	3.70	1.009	.853	.54
Didactic10	3.62	.990	.805	.52
Didactic11	3.58	1.084	.745	.51
Didactic12	3.65	1.029	.782	.53
Digital1	3.64	1.007	.831	.52
Digital2	3.58	1.157	.808	.51
Digital3	3.32	1.056	.703	.46
Digital4	3.11	1.133	.624	.42
Digital5	3.42	1.075	.777	.48
Digital6	3.34	1.123	.781	.46
Social1	4.19	1.146	.756	.63
Social2	4.20	1.168	.763	.64
Social3	4.21	1.133	.774	.64
Social4	4.18	1.155	.763	.63
Social5	4.18	1.132	.747	.63
Social6	4.16	1.166	.760	.63
Creative1	3.38	1.000	.831	.47
Creative2	3.29	1.044	.825	.45
Creative3	3.27	1.087	.742	.45
Creative4	3.40	1.093	.821	.48
Creative5	3.52	1.149	.819	.50
Creative6	3.51	1.171	.787	.50

(*) Extraction Method: Principal Component Analysis.

This assessment is additionally determined by an ad-hoc designed analytical rubric previously validated through the Delphi method (see Appendix 1).

Table 2. Measures of adaptation of the variables to the factor analysis

Kaiser-Meyer-Olkin and Bartlett's Test		.949
Bartlett's Test of Sphericity	Approx. Chi-Square (χ2)	14436.799
	df	435
	Sig.	.000

Source: prepared by the authors

RESULTS

As can be seen in Table 1, the difficulty indices corresponding to all 30 items fluctuate between .42 and .64, since subjects' scores concentrate between 3 and 4. Every correlation exceeds .30. This suggests a good degree of item discrimination. Furthermore, Cronbach's alpha coefficient= .979 may be considered high. The Cronbach's alpha allows the evaluation of the reliability of a measure scale. The scores close to 1 indicate a higher internal consistency of the instrument. For this reason, the scores obtained using this tool reveal a satisfactory reliability level.

As can be seen in Table 1, the difficulty indices corresponding to all 30 items fluctuate between .42 and .64, since subjects' scores concentrate between 3 and 4. Every correlation exceeds .30. This suggests a good degree of item discrimination. Furthermore, Cronbach's alpha coefficient= .979 may be considered high. Expressed differently, the scores obtained using this tool reveal a satisfactory reliability level.

Likewise, the table 1 shows that the punctuations are satisfactory, as the values are higher than 3.10 in all the indicators. More specifically, the indicator 'He/she designs and includes self-made resources (AR and /or geolocation applications' (Digital4) has the lowest score (3.11). This can be due to the emerging use of programs for creating digital resources. For this reason, some of the students selected pre-designed resources obtained from the Internet (YouTube videos, online games, etc.). Inversely, the indicator 'He/she gets involved in the organization and distribution of the tasks' (Social3) has the highest score (4.21). The learning contract could have favored the well organization and distribution of the tasks within each team.

As regards didactic competencies, the highest score (4.02) is obtained in the indicator 'He/she properly locates the ADI in the curricular context' (Didactic2), and the lowest (3.45) in 'He/she specifies the assessment criteria in a coherent way' (Didactic4), followed by 'He/she evidences the internal coherence of the educational proposal -objectives, contents, assessment-' (Didactic11) (3.58). Referring to digital competencies, the highest score (3.64), is registered in the indicator 'He/she shows the pertinence of the AR resources employed' (Digital1) and the lowest (3.11) in 'He/she designs and includes self-made resources: AR and /or geolocation applications' (Digital4). Thus, although the creation of digital materials was relatively complex, the students were able to select other resources for their proposal.

Besides, social-collaborative competencies reveal the better results. The highest score (4.21) was obtained in the indicator 'He/she gets involved in the organization and distribution of the tasks' (Social3). The lowest (4.16) corresponds to 'He/she contributes to the resolution of the problems arisen' (Social6), although it is high if compared with other indicators. Overall, it is confirmed that the students satisfactorily developed their collaborative and communicative skills, accepting their responsibilities.

Table 3. Results of the initial extraction with the main axis method

Factor	Initial Eigenvalues			Extraction Sums of Squared Loadings			Sums of rotation of charges squared
	Total	% of Variance	% Cumulative	Total	% of Variance	% cumulative	Total
1	18.760	**62.533**	62.533	18.760	62.533	62.533	14.218
2	3.366	11.219	73.752	3.366	11.219	73.752	13.051
3	1.585	5.284	79.036	1.585	5.284	79.036	15.215
4	.776	2.587	81.623				
5	.734	2.446	84.069				
6	.617	2.056	86.125				
7	.534	1.780	87.905				
8	.468	1.561	89.466				
9	.368	1.228	90.694				
10	.315	1.052	91.745				
11	.288	.959	92.704				
12	.258	.860	93.564				
13	.242	.805	94.369				
14	.215	.718	95.087				
15	.197	.655	95.742				
16	.160	.533	96.275				
17	.146	.486	96.761				
18	.139	.462	97.223				
19	.111	.370	97.594				
20	.107	.355	97.949				
21	.094	.312	98.260				
22	.084	.281	98.542				
23	.081	.269	98.811				
24	.074	.246	99.057				
25	.065	.217	99.275				
26	.062	.207	99.482				
27	.049	.164	99.646				
28	.045	.151	99.797				
29	.038	.126	99.923				
30	.023	.077	100.000				

Source: prepared by the authors

Finally, regarding creative competency, the lowest indicator is 'He/she explores the functionalities of the resources, fostering the fluidity of the ADI' (Creative2), with 3.29. The highest is 'He/she provides various formulae for addressing several topics' (Creative5), with 3.52. In general, the scores obtained do not reach number 4 in any of the indicators.

Table 2 shows a high value for the KMO sampling adequacy measure (.949) —hence the possibility to factor this correlation matrix. These results permit to reject the null hypothesis at 99%, providing evidence that the correlation matrix does not correspond to an identity matrix. In conclusion, the correlation matrix can be factored.

Table 3 reports the eigenvalues extracted from the exploratory principal components analysis for each one of the factors, where it becomes visible that only three of them exceed 1.00. According to Burga (2006), an instrument supported on a set of items arguably has a unidimensional measure if the first factor accounts for 40% of variance (Carmines & Zeller, 1979), and around 20% of variance and ratio between the eigenvalues, using polychoric correlation matrices (Lord, 1980). Therefore, when it comes to COMPASS-AR, one can state that its measurement is essentially unidimensional, insofar as the proportion of variance accounted for by the first factor is 62.53% (>40%).

Nevertheless, it is worth highlighting that factors 2 (11.21%) and 3 (5.28%), both of them smaller than 20% (Lord, 1980), are neglected despite having eigenvalues above 1 because, according to Cattell's sedimentation graph (Figure 4), the first eigenvalue is far higher than the rest; and it offers sufficient evidence to opt for a unidimensional factorial solution.

Figure 4. Scree Plot for the 30 items

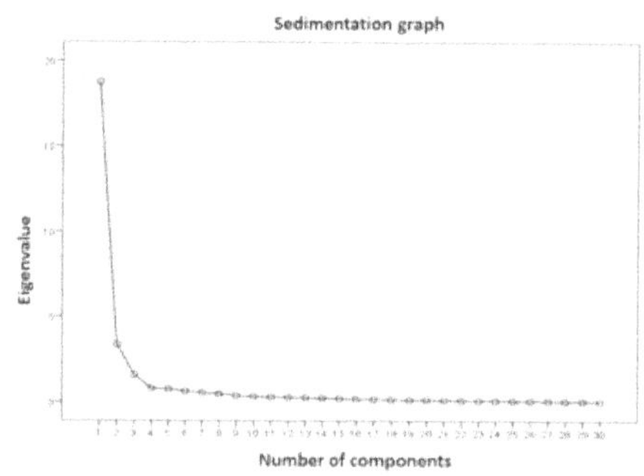

It is verified that there is a single dimension, which can be called 'competency level' reached by the students through the collaborative design of ADIs. This dimension is defined on the basis of the 30 indicators related to the various competencies, as indicated in the Appendix 1. Therefore, it can be stated that COMPASS-AR is a suitable instrument, from a psychometric point of view, to measure the variable called 'competency level' reached by the students through the collaborative design of ADIs.

DISCUSSION

The assessment of the instrument COMPASS-AR performed by three experts from different areas of knowledge was adequate. Thus, their judgment served to redefine some of the indicators supported on the rubrics created for that purpose.

Furthermore, as regards psychometric validation, the proportion of variance explained by the dominant factor accounts for 62.5% of total variance. This criterion suffices to defend the unidimensionality of this scale following the criteria developed by Carmines and Zeller (1979). Therefore, the first factor provides enough evidence to state that it is an essentially unidimensional scale.

In this way, the unidimensional instrument COMPASS-AR allows the assessment of the competency level acquired by future teachers. This competency level is understood as a single dimension based on the convergence of 30 indicators related to the didactic, digital, socio-collaborative and creative competencies involved in the task. The design of AR educational resources is a complex task, and, nevertheless necessary for teacher training. In that sense, university education needs to face the challenges generated by emergent technologies when they are integrated in the classroom (Chicioreanu & Amza, 2015; Marques & Pombo, 2020; Sáez-López, Cózar-Gutiérrez, González-Calero & Gómez Carrasco, 2020). For this reason, this tool, together with the rubric (Amelia, Rahman & Riyana, 2018), can be considered as a valuable formula for systematising the assessment and make it possible to introduce AR in teacher training.

Moreover, with regards the median scores reached by the participants, they are, overall, satisfactory, as the scores concentrate between 3 and 4. It is worth emphasizing the high scores in socio-collaborative competencies, which could have been favored due to the methodology employed. The scores related to didactic competencies are also good, as the students had a previous training on this field. However, the participants reached medium scores in digital and creative competencies. The elaboration of digital contents is a complex task, and requires specific skills. Although the students received basic training, the creation of AR resources was complicated for some of them. It was also verified that the presentation of examples could have strengthened their creativity.

CONCLUSION

One of the main contributions of this work is the tool COMPASS-AR, specially designed for assessing the competency level reached by future teachers through the design of Augmented Didactic Itineraries. This tool provides university teachers who develop their professional activity in the Education degrees with an evaluation formula linked to the methodology of Learning Based on the Design of Augmented Didactic Itineraries (LBDADI). This tool will allow them to check the level of activation for the different competencies in each subject.

Amongst the limitations would stand out that such a high alpha and the clearly unidimensional solution were estimated on an instrument which is an observation scale (an analytical type of assessment rubric) and which consequently starts from the consistency shown by the data and can have an evaluatory impact (a halo or similar effect).

This work additionally incorporates a new methodology —Learning Based on the Design of Augmented Didactic Itineraries— which turns out to be of special interest for teacher training. By relying on the collaborative design of augmented itineraries, the LBDADI methodology offers a chance for the development of digital competencies —especially those referred to AR utilization— as well as socio-collaborative, didactic, and creative ones in would-be teachers. The ITINER-AR Project thus provides a model which can be reproduced in analogous contexts.

On the basis of the median obtained, the competency level of the participants was very satisfactory. All of them exceeded the minimum required, with scores between the medium and the high level. This reveals the interest of future teachers by the design of ADIs. The activity was very motivating and enriching, as it presented new AR tools as well as an innovative methodology. The project as a hole provoked in the participants the desire for learning more about AR.

In conclusion, it can be stated that a good technological training is crucial for developing projects involving the creation of AR resources. This could require a larger number of face-to-face sessions to learn the use of programs and applications. Besides, it is necessary to search for formulae to foster creativity.

FUTURE RESEARCH DIRECTIONS

Finally, amongst future research lines stands out the examination of the data obtained with the ITINER-AR Project. Consequently, the verification of the consistency and validity corresponding to the instrument will be followed by an analysis of the data derived from the individual assessment of subjects seeking to identify their respective level of competency acquired after taking part in the project. Moreover, the future research lines will include the analysis of other issues linked to this project, such as the perceptions of instructors and students. Thus, the remaining data obtained from the implementation of ITINER-AR will be analyzed in future works. This will make it possible to check the extent to which the methodology of Learning based on the Design of Augmented Didactic Itineraries turns out to be effective in teacher training, and to provide suggestions for a better implementation of this kind of projects in teacher training.

ACKNOWLEDGMENT

This research was supported by the University of Oviedo (Spain) [project reference: PAPI-18-EMERG.22]

REFERENCES

Akçayır, M., & Akçayır, G. (2017). Advantages and challenges associated with augmented reality for education: A systematic review of the literature. *Educational Research Review*, *20*, 1–11. doi:10.1016/j.edurev.2016.11.002

Akçayır, M., Akçayır, G., Pektaş, H. M., & Ocak, M. A. (2016). Augmented reality in science laboratories: The effects of augmented reality on university students' laboratory skills and attitudes toward science laboratories. *Computers in Human Behavior*, *57*, 334–342. doi:10.1016/j.chb.2015.12.054

Amelia, D., Rahman, R., & Riyana, C. (2018, April). Development and Validation Instruments: Scoring Rubrics of Writing Synopsis and Scoring Sheets for Assessing Student's Writing Synopsis Ability. In *Proceeding of 2nd International Conference on Child-Friendly Education*, (pp. 323-327). Universitas Muhammadiyah Surakar, Indonesia.

Bacca, J., Baldiris, S., Fabregat, R., & Graf, S. (2014). Augmented reality trends in education: A systematic review of research and applications. *Journal of Educational Technology & Society*, *17*(4), 133–149.

Bower, M., Howe, C., McCredie, N., Robinson, A., & Grover, D. (2014). Augmented Reality in education–cases, places and potentials. *Educational Media International*, *51*(1), 1–15. doi:10.1080/09523987.2014.889400

Brugnoli, M. C., Morabito, F., Bo, G., & Murelli, E. (2007). "Augmented Itineraries": Mobile services differentiating what museum has to offer. *PsychNology Journal*, *4*(3), 311–335.

Burga, A. (2006). La unidimensionalidad de un instrumento de medición: Perspectiva factorial [The unidimensionality of a measuring instrument: factorial perspective]. *Revista de Psicología*, *24*(1), 53–80.

Buzko, V. L., Bonk, A. V., & Tron, V. V. (2018). Implementation of Gamification and Elements of Augmented Reality during the Binary Lessons in a Secondary School. In *Proceedings of the 1st International Workshop on Augmented Reality in Education*, (pp. 53-60). Kryvyi Rih.

Carmines, E., & Zeller, R. (1979). *Reliability and validity assessment*. Sage. doi:10.4135/9781412985642

Chen, W., Lim, C., & Tan, A. (2010). Pre-service teachers' ICT experiences and competencies: New generation of teachers in digital age. In B. Rachev & A. Smrikarov (Eds.), *Proceedings of the 18th International Conference on Computers in Education*, (pp. 631-638). Putrajaya, Malaysia: Asia-Pacific Society for Computers in Education.

Chicioreanu, T. D., & Amza, C. G. (2015). Are teachers ready for the augmented reality? In B. Pătrut, D. Andone, C. Holotescu, & G. Grosseck (Eds.), *International Conference Smart 2014, Social Media in Academia: Research and Teaching* (pp. 337–343). Medimond. Retrieved from https://bit.ly/31LVpW2

Clayton, J. (1997). Delphi: A technique to harness expert opinion for critical decision-marking tasks in education. *Education Psychology*, *17*(4), 373–386. doi:10.1080/0144341970170401

Crespo, M., Fernández, R., Gonzales, I., Esparza, K., & León-Acurio, J. (2020). The Augmented Reality in the Teaching-Learning Process of Children from 3 to 5 Years Old. In M. Botto-Tobar, J. León-Acurio, A. Díaz, & P. Montiel (Eds.), *Advances in Emerging Trends and Technologies. ICAETT 2019. Advances in Intelligent Systems and Computing* (pp. 207–218). Springer. doi:10.1007/978-3-030-32022-5_20

De Miguel, M. (Dir.). (2006). *Modalidades de enseñanza centradas en el desarrollo de competencias. Orientaciones para promover el cambio metodológico en el marco del EEES* [Teaching modalities focused on skills development. Guidelines to promote methodological change within the framework of the EHEA]. Oviedo: Universidad de Oviedo/MEC Retrieved from https://bit.ly/2NusykS

Del Moral, M.E., & Villalustre, L. (2010). Formación del profesor 2.0: desarrollo de competencias tecnológicas para la escuela 2.0 [Teacher training 2.0 development of technological skills for school 2.0]. *Magister: Revista miscelánea de investigación, 23*, 59-69.

Del Moral, M. E., & Villalustre, L. (2012). Didáctica universitaria en la era 2.0: competencias docentes en campus virtuales [University teaching in the era: virtual campus teaching competencies]. *RUSC. Revista de Universidad y Sociedad del Conocimiento*, *9*(1), 36–50. doi:10.7238/rusc.v9i1.1127

Del Moral, M. E., & Villalustre, L. (2013). Realidad aumentada: experimentando en el aula en 3D [Augmented reality: experimenting in the classroom in 3D]. In *R. Ron, A. Álvarez & P. Núñez (Coords.), Smartphones y tablets: ¿enseñan o distraen?* [Smartphones and tablets: do they teach or distract?] (pp. 107–124). ESIC Editorial.

Delello, J. A. (2014). Insights from pre-service teachers using science-based augmented reality. *Journal of Computers in Education*, *1*(4), 295–311. doi:10.100740692-014-0021-y

Díaz-Mohedo, M. T., & Vicente, A. (2014). Project based teaching as a didactic strategy for the learning and development of Basic competencys in future teachers. *Procedia: Social and Behavioral Sciences*, *141*, 232–236. doi:10.1016/j.sbspro.2014.05.040

Edwards, M., García, A., Sánchez, M., Quesada, H., & Amara, N. (2015). Disentangling competencys: Interrelationships on creativity, innovation and entrepreneurship. *Thinking Skills and Creativity*, *16*, 27–39. doi:10.1016/j.tsc.2014.11.006

Erstad, O., Eickelmann, B., & Eichhorn, K. (2015). Preparing teachers for schooling in the digital age: A meta-perspective on existing strategies and future challenges. *Education and Information Technologies*, *20*(4), 641–654. doi:10.100710639-015-9431-3

Estapa, A., & Nadolny, L. (2015). The Effect of an Augmented Reality Enhanced Mathematics Lesson on Student Achievement and Motivation. *Journal of STEM Education*, *16*(3), 40–48.

Forslund, K., & Hammar, E. (2011). Assessment of students' learning when working in groups. *Educational Research*, *53*(3), 331–345. doi:10.1080/00131881.2011.598661

Fotaris, P., Pellas, N., Kazanidis, I., & Smith, P. (2017). A systematic review of Augmented Reality Game-based applications in primary education. In *11th European Conference on Games Based Learning (ECGBL). Mini Track on Mixed Reality for Game-Based Learning proceedings*, (pp. 181-191). Graz, Austria: Academic Conferences and Publishing International Limited.

Gudmundsdottir, G. B., & Hatlevik, O. E. (2018). Newly qualified teachers' professional digital competency: Implications for teacher education. *European Journal of Teacher Education*, *41*(2), 214–231. doi:10.1080/02619768.2017.1416085

Huang, R., & Yang, J. (2016). Digital learners and digital teachers: challenges, changes, and competencies. In J. M. Spector, D. Ifenthaler, D. G. Sampson, & P. Isaias (Eds.), *Competencies in Teaching, Learning and Educational Leadership in the Digital Age (CELDA)* (pp. 47–56). Springer. doi:10.1007/978-3-319-30295-9_4

Ke, F., & Hsu, Y. C. (2015). Mobile augmented-reality artifact creation as a component of mobile computer-supported collaborative learning. *The Internet and Higher Education*, *26*, 33–41. doi:10.1016/j.iheduc.2015.04.003

Kokotsaki, D., Menzies, V., & Wiggins, A. (2016). Research Article. Project-based learning: A review of the literature. *Improving Schools*, *19*(3), 267–277. doi:10.1177/1365480216659733

Lord, F. M. (1980). *Applications of item response theory to practical testing problems*. L.E.A.

Marques, M. M., & Pombo, L. (2020). Game-Based Mobile Learning with Augmented Reality: Are Teachers Ready to Adopt It? In M. Rehm, J. Saldien, & S. Manca (Eds.), *Project and Design Literacy as Cornerstones of Smart Education. Smart Innovation, Systems and Technologies* (Vol. 158, pp. 207–218). Springer., doi:10.1007/978-981-13-9652-6_19

Martínez-Graña, A., González-Delgado, J. Á., Ramos, C., & Gonzalo, J. C. (2018). Augmented Reality and Valorizing the Mesozoic Geological Heritage (Burgos, Spain). *Sustainability*, *10*(12), 1–16. doi:10.3390u10124616

Masmuzidin, M. Z., & Aziz, N. A. A. (2018). The current trends of augmented reality in early childhood education. *The International Journal of Multimedia & Its Applications*, *10*(6), 47–58. doi:10.5121/ijma.2018.10605

Mynbayeva, A., Sadvakassova, Z., & Akshalova, B. (2017). Pedagogy of the Twenty-First Century: Innovative Teaching Methods. In O. Bernad & N. Llevot (Eds.), *New Pedagogical Challenges in the 21st Century-Contributions of Research in Education*. IntechOpen. doi:10.5772/intechopen.72341

Neira-Piñeiro, M. R., Del Moral, M. E., & Fombella, I. (2020). Stimulating Multiple Intelligences in Infant Education from an Augmented Didactic Itinerary. In R. Zheng (Ed.), *Examining Multiple Intelligences and Digital Technologies for Enhanced Learning Opportunities* (pp. 124–140). IGI Global. doi:10.4018/978-1-7998-0249-5.ch007

Panciroli, C., Macauda, A., & Corazza, L. (2018, July). Digital Cultural Heritage: From Educational Experience to the Artefact in Augmented Reality. In A. Luigini (Ed.), *Proceedings of the 1st International and Interdisciplinary Conference on Digital Environments for Education, Arts and Heritage*, (pp. 345-354). Cham: Springe.

Petko, D. (2012). Teachers' pedagogical beliefs and their use of digital media in classrooms: Sharpening the focus of the 'will, skill, tool' model and integrating teachers' constructivist orientations. *Computers & Education*, *58*(4), 1351–1359. doi:10.1016/j.compedu.2011.12.013

Sáez-López, J. M., Cózar-Gutiérrez, R., González-Calero, J. A., & Gómez-Carrasco, C. J. (2020). Augmented Reality in Higher Education: An Evaluation Program in Initial Teacher Training. *Education in Science*, *10*(2), 1–12. doi:10.3390/educsci10020026

Tondeur, J., Aesaert, K., Pynoo, B., van Braak, J., Fraeyman, N., & Erstad, O. (2017). Developing a validated instrument to measure preservice teachers' ICT competencies: Meeting the demands of the 21st century. *British Journal of Educational Technology*, *48*(2), 462–472. doi:10.1111/bjet.12380

Villalustre, L., & Del Moral, M. E. (2016). Itinerarios interactivos con geolocalización y realidad aumentada para un aprendizaje ubicuo en la formación inicial de docentes de educación infantil [Interactive itineraries with geolocation and augmented reality for ubiquitous learning in the initial training of early childhood teachers]. In *L. Villalustre & M.E. Del Moral (Coords.), Experiencias interactivas con realidad aumentada en las aulas* [Interactive experiences with augmented reality in the classroom] (pp. 81–100). Octaedro.

Villalustre, L., Del Moral, M.E., & Neira, M.R. (2019). Percepción docente sobre la Realidad Aumentada en la Enseñanza de Ciencias en Primaria. Análisis DAFO [Teachers' perception about Augmented Reality in Science Teaching in Primary Education]. *Revista Eureka sobre Enseñanza y Divulgación de las Ciencias, 16*(3), 3301. DOI: doi:10.25267/Rev_Eureka_ensen_divulg_cienc.2019.v16.i3.3301

Villalustre, L., San Pedro, B., & López, I. (2020). Geolocation for the Improvement of Spatial and Naturalist Intelligence in Primary Education. In R. Zheng (Ed.), *Examining Multiple Intelligences and Digital Technologies for Enhanced Learning Opportunities* (pp. 141–160). IGI Global. doi:10.4018/978-1-7998-0249-5.ch008

Wang, M., Callaghan, V., Bernhardt, J., White, K., & Peña-Rios, A. (2018). Augmented reality in education and training: Pedagogical approaches and illustrative case studies. *Journal of Ambient Intelligence and Humanized Computing*, *9*(5), 1391–1402. doi:10.100712652-017-0547-8

Yaman, H., Aydemir, Z. İ., & Demirtaş, T. (2013). The scale of preservice teachers' digital pedagogic competencies: Validity and reliability study. *The Online Journal of New Horizons in Education*, *3*(3), 26–35.

ADDITIONAL READING

Brugnoli, M. C., Morabito, F., Bo, G., & Murelli, E. (2007). "Augmented Itineraries": Mobile services differentiating what museum has to offer. *PsychNology Journal*, *4*(3), 311–335.

Burga, A. (2006). La unidimensionalidad de un instrumento de medición: Perspectiva factorial [The unidimensionality of a measuring instrument: factorial perspective]. *Revista de Psicología*, *24*(1), 53–80.

Díaz-Mohedo, M. T., & Vicente, A. (2014). Project based teaching as a didactic strategy for the learning and development of Basic competencys in future teachers. *Procedia: Social and Behavioral Sciences*, *141*, 232–236. doi:10.1016/j.sbspro.2014.05.040

Huang, R., & Yang, J. (2016). Digital learners and digital teachers: challenges, changes, and competencies. In J. M. Spector, D. Ifenthaler, D. G. Sampson, & P. Isaias (Eds.), *Competencies in Teaching, Learning and Educational Leadership in the Digital Age (CELDA)* (pp. 47–56). Springer. doi:10.1007/978-3-319-30295-9_4

Marques, M. M., & Pombo, L. (2020). Game-Based Mobile Learning with Augmented Reality: Are Teachers Ready to Adopt It? In M. Rehm, J. Saldien, & S. Manca (Eds.), *Project and Design Literacy as Cornerstones of Smart Education. Smart Innovation, Systems and Technologies* (Vol. 158). Springer., doi:10.1007/978-981-13-9652-6_19

Neira-Piñeiro, M. R., Del Moral, M. E., & Fombella, I. (2020). Stimulating Multiple Intelligences in Infant Education from an Augmented Didactic Itinerary. In R. Zheng (Ed.), *Examining Multiple Intelligences and Digital Technologies for Enhanced Learning Opportunities* (pp. 124–140). IGI Global., doi:10.4018/978-1-7998-0249-5.ch007

Tondeur, J., Aesaert, K., Pynoo, B., van Braak, J., Fraeyman, N., & Erstad, O. (2017). Developing a validated instrument to measure preservice teachers' ICT competencies: Meeting the demands of the 21st century. *British Journal of Educational Technology*, *48*(2), 462–472. doi:10.1111/bjet.12380

Villalustre, L., San Pedro, B., & López, I. (2020). Geolocation for the Improvement of Spatial and Naturalist Intelligence in Primary Education. In R. Zheng (Ed.), *Examining Multiple Intelligences and Digital Technologies for Enhanced Learning Opportunities* (pp. 141–160). IGI Global., doi:10.4018/978-1-7998-0249-5.ch008

KEY TERMS AND DEFINITIONS

Augmented Didactic Itineraries (ADIs): Tour of a real space that brings together different AR activators designed for an educational purpose. Augmented Reality expands the information coming from the physical route and seeks to foster learning.

Augmented Reality (AR): Technology based on the simultaneous combination of virtual information and physical information from the real world, in such a way that virtual contents are superimposed onto the perception of real elements. This technology offers users an enriched or augmented vision of the surrounding environment. A technological tool (computer or mobile device), a camera (which may be integrated into the device), an activator (which makes it possible to access the augmented contents when scanned), together with a specific software and an Internet connection, are required to implement it.

Creative Competencies: Set of knowledge, skills, and attitudes which enable someone to cope with challenges, to solve problems, and to generate elements (ideas, artistic products…) in a new, original way. This work examines the capacities which make it possible to design, elaborate, and combine the different elements shaping ADIs in an innovative manner.

Didactic Competencies: Set of knowledge, skills, and attitudes which enable someone to plan and implement—as a teacher—successful teaching-learning processes. This study considers the didactic competencies required to design augmented didactic itineraries.

Digital Competencies: Set of knowledge, skills, and attitudes which enable someone to effectively utilize digital technologies in different contexts. This work pays attention to the digital competencies referred to the selection, management, and creation of AR resources, as well as to their use for an educational purpose.

Learning Based on the Design of Augmented Didactic Itineraries (LBDADI): More broadly embedded into Problem-Based Learning (PBL), Learning based on the Design of Augmented Didactic Itineraries (LBDADI) is a methodology which relies on the collaborative creation of augmented didactic itineraries. The process through which ADIs are elaborated provides a chance to learn, favoring the development of various key competencies for a teacher.

Psychometric Validation: It refers to the ability for an instrument to significantly measure and quantify the feature for whose measurement this kind of validation was designed. A measuring instrument is thus valid inasmuch as empirical evidence legitimizes the interpretation of scores resulting from the test.

Socio-Collaborative Competencies: Set of knowledge, skills, and attitudes which enable someone to work collaboratively within a team. These competencies become essential and are particularly promoted with the LBDADI methodology.

APPENDIX

Compass-AR: Assessment of the Competencies Involved in the ADI Collaborative Design and Analytic Rubric to Assign the Score

Box 1. Didactic competencies

Please, indicate to what extent the pre-service teacher...		1 2 3 4 5
D1	justifies the pertinence of the itinerary.	
D2	properly locates the ADI in the curricular context.	
D3	properly plans and organises the educational process.	
D4	specifies the assessment criteria in a coherent way.	
D5	provides an interdisciplinary and/or globalised approach.	
D6	presents the educational guide adequately.	
D7	includes specific contents in accordance with the educational proposal.	
D8	designs specific activities in accordance with the educational proposal.	
D9	selects adequate educational resources.	
D10	employs techniques and didactic strategies in accordance with the contents.	
D11	evidences the internal coherence of the educational proposal (objectives, contents, assessment..).	
D12	provides adaptability to the ADI, so that it can be implemented in several contexts.	

Box 2. Digital competencies

Please, indicate to what extent the pre-service teacher:		1 2 3 4 5
DG1	shows the pertinence of the AR resources employed.	
DG2	masters several tools and techniques.	
DG3	provides interactivity to the elements included.	
DG4	designs and includes self-made resources (AR and /or geolocation applications).	
DG5	shows a proper use of technological resources (activators, GPS coordinates, etc.).	
DG6	includes various multimedia resources.	

Box 3. Social-collaborative competencies

Please, indicate to what extent the pre-service teacher:		1 2 3 4 5
S1	favors the communication within the group through the ADI design process.	
S2	provides and integrates several ideas through the ADI design process.	
S3	gets involved in the organization and distribution of the tasks.	
S4	shows interest and takes responsibility.	
S5	collaborates and complements the group.	
S6	contributes to the resolution of the problems arisen.	

Analytical Rubric: Score and Criteria

Box 4. Creative competencies

Please, indicate to what extent the pre-service teacher:		1 2 3 4 5
C1	integrates various resources, providing flexibility to the ADI.	
C2	explores the functionalities of the resources, fostering the fluidity of the ADI.	
C3	shows originality (novelty, innovation and exclusivity).	
C4	combines the resources with balance and proportion, searching for the correspondence and harmony between the parts.	
C5	provides various formulae for addressing several topics.	
C6	evidences the aesthetic quality of the physical support and the multimedia resources.	

(*) 1=very low, 2=low, 3=medium, 4=high, 5=very high

Table 4. Analytic rubric: scores and assessment criteria of the Didactic competencies (DC) developed with the ADI design. Made by the authors.

DC	1=very low	2=low	3=medium	4=high	5=very high
1.1	The pertinence of the itinerary is not justified.	Bad justified and not clear	Acceptable justification	Well justified.	Very well justified and argued.
1.2	Without references to the curricular context.	It is located in the curricular context but it does not properly follow the curriculum.	It is located in the curriculum.	It is quite properly located in the curriculum.	It is perfectly located in the curricular context.
1.3	Very incomplete, bad planned	Quite incomplete. The planning should be improved	Acceptable. It includes the basic elements, but it should be developed	Adequate, well planned, with the basic elements.	Excellent, very well planned. Entirely complete.
1.4	Without assessment criteria.	The assessment criteria are incoherent, inappropriate and wrongly expressed.	The assessment criteria are coherent, but with slight mistakes.	The assessment criteria are coherent and well expressed.	The assessment criteria are coherent perfectly expressed.
1.5	It addresses contents not included in the curriculum. There is not an interdisciplinary or globalised approach.	It only includes contents of one subjects of the curriculum.	It addresses and connects contents of 2 subjects of the curriculum	It addresses and connects contents of 3 subjects of the curriculum in an interdisciplinary way	It addresses and connects contents of all the subjects of the curriculum in an interdisciplinary way
1.6	Without a guide. The presentation is chaotic and the writing is of extremely poor quality	Bad organised and presented, with serious writing mistakes.	Organised and well-adjusted. The presentation and writing could be improved.	Well-adjusted and organised. Good presentation and writing.	Perfect organization, presentation and writing.
1.7	It does not include specific contents linked to the educational proposal.	Poor inclusion of specific contents linked to the educational proposal.	Acceptable inclusion of specific contents linked to the educational proposal.	Good inclusion of specific contents linked to the educational proposal.	Excellent inclusion of specific contents linked to the educational proposal.
1.8	Without activities in accordance with the educational proposal.	Poor design of activities in accordance with the educational proposal.	Acceptable design of activities in accordance with the educational proposal.	Good design of activities in accordance with the educational proposal.	Excellent design of activities in accordance with the educational proposal.
1.9	The selection of educational resources is inappropriate	The selection of educational resources is scarcely appropriate	The selection of educational resources is acceptable.	The selection of educational resources is quite appropriate.	Excellent selection of educational resources
1.10	Without techniques or strategies suitable for the proposal.	The techniques or strategies are inadequate for the proposal.	Some of the techniques or strategies are not suitable to the proposal.	Most of the techniques or strategies are suitable for the proposal.	All the techniques or strategies are suitable for the proposal.
1.11	Not coherent	With several internal incoherences	With a few minor internal incoherences.	Coherent.	Entirely coherent.
1.12	It cannot be adapted to several contexts.	Scarcely adapted and no explained.	Adaptable and explained.	Quite adaptable and well explained.	Totally adaptable and well explained.

Table 5. Analytic rubric: Scores and assessment criteria of the Digital competencies (DGC) developed with the IDA design. Made by the authors.

DGC	1=very low	2=low	3=medium	4=high	5=very high
2.1	The AR resources are not related to the content of the itinerary.	The AR resources are insufficient, inappropriate and / or irrelevant for the content.	There are sufficient AR resources. Most of them are adequate to the content.	There is enough variety and quantity of AR resources, adequate to the content.	There is a great variety and quantity of AR resources. They are entirely coherent.
2.2	No tools or techniques for creating AR resources are used.	Only QR code generators are used.	At least 2 tools have been used: a QR code generator and an AR marker generator, capable of transforming a picture into a marker.	GPS coordinates generators, QR codes generators and AR marker generators are used.	Several tools and techniques are used: GPS coordinates generators, QR code generators and AR generators capable of transforming a picture or an element of the physical environment into a marker.
2.3	It does not offer any kind of interactivity.	It offers low interactivity (less than 5 AR triggers)	It offers basic interactivity (5-8 AR triggers)	There is enough interactivity (9-12 AR triggers).	There is high interactivity (more than 12 AR triggers).
2.4	It does not include self-made resources.	It includes one self-made resource.	It includes 2 self-made resources. (videos, pictures or audios).	It includes 3 or 4 self-made resources. (videos, pictures or audios)	It includes 5 or more self-made resources.
2.5	The triggers have no content.	Only 2 triggers have content and work.	3 triggers have content and work.	Most triggers have content and work.	All the triggers have content and work.
2.6	There are no multimedia resources	There is only one type or resource (only pictures or only video)	There are 2 types of resources: video, pictures and /or audio.	There are 3 types of resources: video, pictures and audio.	There are various types of multimedia resources and even some 3D object.

Table 6. Analytic rubric: Scores and assessment criteria of Social-collaborative competencies (SC) developed with the IDA design. Made by the authors.

SC	1=very low	2=low	3=medium	4=high	5=very high
3.1	He/she does not communicate and interact with his/her teammates.	He/she has a low interaction and communication with his/ her teammates.	He/she ordinarily communicates and interacts with his/her teammates.	He/she shows a high level of communicatio, interaction and participation in discussions.	He /she stimulates the communication and interaction and promotes discussions.
3.2	He/she does not contribute with ideas.	He/she provides some idea, but does not consider the ideas or the others.	He/she provides accurate ideas, but does not integrate them with the ideas of the others.	He/she provides accurate ideas and integrates them with the ideas of the others.	He/she provides numerous and valuable ideas, and integrates them with the ideas of the others.
3.3	He/she does not get involved in the tasks organization and distribution.	He/she sporadically gets involved, provoking a tasks overlap.	He/she gets involved in the tasks organization and distribution, by consensus.	He/she actively gets involved in the tasks organization and accomplishes his/ her tasks with responsibility.	He/she perfectly gets involved in the tasks organization and equitable distribution.
3.4	He/she shows no interest in completing the tasks assigned.	He /she is scarcely motivated and shows little interest in the task He/she does not keep the working pace of the group.	He /she shows motivation and interest in the task but is too dependent on the group.	He /she is quite interested and motivated. He/she completes the tasks but does not meet the deadline.	He /she shows high motivation towards his /her individual task. He/she properly completes the task within the deadline.
3.5	He/she does not collaborates and complements the group. He/she is not capable of doing teamwork.	He/she scarcely collaborates and contributes to the group. He/she prefers individual work.	He/she collaborates with the others, but hardly provides personal ideas or suggestions.	He/she actively collaborates, providing interesting ideas or suggestions, but hardly provides personal ideas or suggestions	He/she actively collaborates and complements the group, providing valuable and original ideas.
3.6	He/she creates problems and/or makes it difficult to solve them.	He/she does not help to resolve the problems arisen.	He/she provides ideas to resolve the problems, but does not search for agreement.	He/she provides solutions and tries to mediate to reach an agreement.	He/she effectively solves problems and reaches agreements to move forward.

Table 7. Analytic rubric: scores and assessment criteria of the Creative competencies (CC) developed with the IDA design. Made by the authors.

CC	1=very low	2=low	3=medium	4=high	5=very high
4.1	Not flexible. It does not integrate varied resources.	Not very flexible. It integrates a poor variety of resources.	Somewhat flexible. It integrates varied resources.	Flexible. It integrates a good variety of resources.	Very flexible. It integrates a large variety of resources.
4.2	It does not explore the possibilities of the resources integrated.	It only explores one function of the resources integrated.	It only explores two functions of the resources integrated.	It explores several functions of the resources integrated.	It explores all the functions of the resources integrated.
4.3	Not original. Based on the replication of models. There is no development of own materials.	Scarcely original It replicates Internet models. It does not include self-made materials.	Somewhat original. It includes some self-made materials.	Original. Most of the material is own-produced.	Very original. Almost all the material is own-produced.
4.4	Without balance, proportion and correspondence between the parts.	Scarcely balanced, without proportion and correspondence between the parts.	Balanced and proportioned, but with little harmony between the parts.	Well-balanced, proportioned and with correspondence between the parts.	With the highest balance and proportion. Total harmony between the parts.
4.5	There are no various formulae for addressing several topics.	There is a single formula to address all the topics.	There are two formulae to address the topics.	There are more than 3 formulae to address the topics.	There is a great variety of formulae to address the topics.
4.6	The multimedia resources and the physical support have not aesthetic quality.	The multimedia resources and the physical support have little aesthetic quality.	The multimedia resources and the physical support have an acceptable aesthetic quality.	The multimedia resources and the physical support have enough aesthetic quality.	The multimedia resources and the physical support have high aesthetic quality.

Compilation of References

Aberšek, B. (Ed.). (2017). *Cognitive science in education and alternative teaching strategies*. Cambridge Scholars Publishing.

Accascina, G., & Rogora, E. (2006). Using Cabri3d diagrams for teaching geometry. *The International Journal for Technology in Mathematics Education, 13*(1), 11–22.

Achuthan, K., Francis, S. P., & Diwakar, S. (2017). Augmented reflective learning and knowledge retention perceived among students in classrooms involving virtual laboratories. *Education and Information Technologies, 22*(6), 2825–2855. doi:10.100710639-017-9626-x

Adler, J. L. (2001). Investigating the learning effects of route guidance and traffic advisories on route choice behavior. *Transportation Research Part C, Emerging Technologies, 9*(1), 1–14. doi:10.1016/S0968-090X(00)00002-4

Adnan, A., Shak, M., Karim, R., Tahir, M., & Shah, D. (2020). 360-degree videos, VR experiences and the application of education 4.0 technologies in Malaysia for exposure and immersion. *Advances in Science. Technology and Engineering Systems, 5*(1), 373–381. doi:10.25046/aj050148

Aebersold, M., Tschannen, D., & Bathish, M. (2012). Innovative Simulation Strategies in Education. *Nursing Research and Practice, 2012*, 1–7. doi:10.1155/2012/765212 PMID:22550573

Aebersold, M., Voepel-Lewis, T., Cherara, L., Weber, M., Khouri, C., Levine, R., & Tait, A. R. (2018). Interactive anatomy-augmented virtual simulation training. *Clinical Simulation in Nursing, 15*, 34–41. doi:10.1016/j.ecns.2017.09.008 PMID:29861797

Agrawal, A. J. (2018, February 15). *3 reasons augmented reality hasn't achieved widespread adoption*. Thenextweb. https://thenextweb.com/contributors/2018/02/16/3-reasons-augmented-reality-hasnt-achieved-widespread-adoption/

Agrawal, R., Knodler, M., Fisher, D. L., & Samuel, S. (2018). Virtual reality headset training: Can it be used to improve young drivers' latent hazard anticipation and mitigation skills. *Transportation Research Record: Journal of the Transportation Research Board, 2672*(33), 20–30. doi:10.1177/0361198118758311

Aguinas, H., Henle, C. A., & Beaty, J. C. Jr. (2001). Virtual reality technology: A new tool for personnel selection. *International Journal of Selection and Assessment, 9*(1-2), 70–83. doi:10.1111/1468-2389.00164

Akaygun, S., & Jones, L. L. (2014). Words or pictures: A comparison of written and pictorial explanations of physical and chemical equilibria. *International Journal of Science Education, 36*(5), 783–807. doi:10.1080/09500693.2013.828361

Akçayır, M., & Akçayır, G. (2017). Advantages and challenges associated with augmented reality for education: A systematic review of the literature. *Educational Research Review, 20*, 1–11. doi:10.1016/j.edurev.2016.11.002

Akçayır, M., Akçayır, G., Pektaş, H. M., & Ocak, M. A. (2016). Augmented reality in science laboratories: The effects of augmented reality on university students' laboratory skills and attitudes toward science laboratories. *Computers in Human Behavior*, *57*, 334–342. doi:10.1016/j.chb.2015.12.054

Aken, J. E. V. (2004). Management research based on the paradigm of the design sciences: The quest for field-tested and grounded technological rules. *Journal of Management Studies*, *41*(2), 219–246. doi:10.1111/j.1467-6486.2004.00430.x

Akgunduz, D., & Akinoglu, O. (2016). The Effect of Blended Learning and Social Media-Supported Learning on the Students' Attitude and Self-Directed Learning Skills in Science Education. *Turkish Online Journal of Educational Technology-TOJET*, *15*(2), 106–115.

Al Awadhi, S., Al Habib, N., Al-Murad, D., Al deei, F., Al Houti, M., Beyrouthy, T., & Al-Kork, S. (2018). Interactive Virtual Reality Educational Application. *Advances in Science. Technology and Engineering Systems Journal*, *3*(4), 72–82. doi:10.25046/aj030409

Alden, G. (2016). The emergence of global language programs at Boston University – Bridging the cultural divide. In Foreign language education in America: Perspectives from K-12, university, government, and international learning (pp. 115–139). Palgrave Macmillan.

Aldi, C., Crigler, A., Kates-McElrath, K., Long, B., Smith, H., Rehak, K., & Wilkinson, L. (2016). Examining the effects of video modeling and prompts to teach activities of daily living skills. *Behavior Analysis in Practice*, *9*(4), 384–388. doi:10.100740617-016-0127-y PMID:27920969

Alemdag, E., & Cagiltay, K. (2018). A systematic review of eye tracking research on multimedia learning. *Computers & Education*, *125*, 413–428. doi:10.1016/j.compedu.2018.06.023

Alexander, B., Ashford-Rowe, K., Barajas-Murphy, N., Dobbin, G., Knott, J., McCormack, M., Pomerantz, J., Seilhammer, R., & Weber, N. (2019). *EDUCAUSE Horizon report: 2019 higher education edition*. EDUCAUSE.

Alexander, T., Ripkens, A., Westhoven, M., Kleiber, M., & Pfendler, C. (2017). Virtual tele-cooperation: Applying AR and VR for cooperative tele-maintenance and advanced distance learning. In T. Andre (Ed.), *Advances in human factors in training, education, and learning sciences* (pp. 234–244). Springer International Publishing.

Alger, M. (2015). *Visual design methods for virtual reality*. Ravensbourne. http://aperturesciencellc.com/vr/VisualDesignMethodsforVR_MikeAlger.pdf

Alhalabi, W. (2016). Virtual reality systems enhance students' achievements in engineering education. *Behaviour & Information Technology*, *35*(11), 919–925. doi:10.1080/0144929X.2016.1212931

Alkhattabi, M. (2017). Augmented reality as E-learning tool in primary schools' education: Barriers to teachers' adoption. *International Journal of Emerging Technologies in Learning*, *12*(02), 91–100. doi:10.3991/ijet.v12i02.6158

Allen, K. D., Wallace, D. P., Renes, D., Bowen, S. L., & Burke, R. V. (2010). Use of video modeling to teach vocational skills to adolescents and young adults with autism spectrum disorders. *Education & Treatment of Children*, *33*(3), 339–349. doi:10.1353/etc.0.0101

Alqahtani, A. S., Daghestani, L. F., & Ibrahim, L. F. (2017). Environments and System Types of Virtual Reality Technology in STEM: A Survey. *International Journal of Advanced Computer Science and Applications*, *8*(6).

Alrehaili, E. A., & Osman, H. A. (2019). A virtual reality role-playing serious game for experiential learning. *Interactive Learning Environments*, 1–14. Advance online publication. doi:10.1080/10494820.2019.1703008

Althoff, T., White, R. W., & Horvitz, E. (2016). Influence of Pokémon Go on physical activity: Study and implications. *Journal of Medical Internet Research*, *18*(12), e315. doi:10.2196/jmir.6759 PMID:27923778

Alvarez-Marin, A., Castillo-Vergara, M., Pizarro-Guerrero, J., & Espinoza-Vera, E. (2017). Augmented Reality as a Support to the Formation of Industrial Engineers. *Formación Universitaria*, *10*(2), 31–42. doi:10.4067/S0718-50062017000200005

Amelia, D., Rahman, R., & Riyana, C. (2018, April). Development and Validation Instruments: Scoring Rubrics of Writing Synopsis and Scoring Sheets for Assessing Student's Writing Synopsis Ability. In *Proceeding of 2nd International Conference on Child-Friendly Education*, (pp. 323-327). Universitas Muhammadiyah Surakar, Indonesia.

Amer, M. (2014). Language learner's usage of a mobile learning application for learning idioms and collocations. *CAILICO Journal*, *31*(3), 285–302. doi:10.11139/cj.31.3.285-302

An, B., Matteo, F., Epstein, M., & Brown, D. (2018). Comparing the performance of an immersive virtual reality and traditional desktop cultural game. In *Proceedings of the 2nd International Conference on Computer-Human Interaction Research and Applications* (Vol. 1). CHIRA. 10.5220/0006922800540061

Andersen, K., Gaab, S. J., Sattarvand, J., & Harris, F. C. Jr. (2020). METS VR: Mining evacuation training simulator in virtual reality for underground mines. *Proceedings of the 17th International Conference on Information Technology: New Generations (ITNG 2020).*

Andersen, S. A. W., Konge, L., & Sørensen, M. S. (2018). The effect of distributed virtual reality simulation training on cognitive load during subsequent dissection training. *Medical Teacher*, *40*(7), 684–689. doi:10.1080/0142159X.2018.1465182 PMID:29730952

Anderson, M. (2019). *Mobile Technology and Home Broadband 2019*. Pew Research Center.

Andujar, A., & Buchner, J. (2019). The potential of 3D Virtual Reality (VR) for language learning: An overview. In I. Arnedillo, P. Isaias, P. Ravesteijn, & G. Ongena (Eds.), *15th International Conference on Mobile Learning (2019).* Utrecht: IADIS. 10.33965/ml2019_201903R002

Angulo, A., & de Velasco, G. V. (2014). Immersive simulation of architectural spatial experiences. *Proceedings of the XVII Conference of the Iberoamerican Society of Digital Graphics (SIGraDi).*

Anthes, C., García-Hernández, R. J., Wiedemann, M., & Kranzlmüller, D. (2016). *State of the art of virtual reality technology.* Paper presented at the 2016 IEEE Aerospace Conference. 10.1109/AERO.2016.7500674

Appelman, R. (2005). Designing experiential modes: A key focus for immersive learning environments. *TechTrends*, *49*(3), 64–74. doi:10.1007/BF02763648

Argaw, A. S., Haile, B. B., Ayalew, B. T., & Kuma, S. G. (2017). The effect of problem based learning (PBL) instruction on students' motivation and problem solving skills of physics. *Eurasia Journal of Mathematics. Science and Technology Education*, *13*(3), 857–871. doi:10.12973/eurasia.2017.00647a

Arnab, S., Lim, T., Carvalho, M. B., Bellotti, F., de Freitas, S., Louchart, S., Suttie, N., Berta, R., & De Gloria, A. (2015). Mapping learning and game mechanics for serious games analysis. *British Journal of Educational Technology*, *46*(2), 391–411. doi:10.1111/bjet.12113

Arnold, K. M., Umanath, S., Thio, K., Reilly, W. B., McDaniel, M. A., & Marsh, E. J. (2017). Understanding the cognitive processes involved in writing to learn. *Journal of Experimental Psychology. Applied*, *23*(2), 115–127. doi:10.1037/xap0000119 PMID:28447809

Arteaga, I. G., & Pino, C. W. (2018). *Augmented reality in educational settings. Atlante: Education and Development Notebooks.* Retrieved from https://www.eumed.net/rev/atlante/2018/09/realidad-aumentada-educativos.html

Arthur, C. (2013). *Google Glass: is it a threat to our privacy?* The Guardian. https://www.theguardian.com/technology/2013/mar/06/google-glass-threat-to-our-privacy

Aslin, R. N., Shukla, M., & Emberson, L. L. (2015). Hemodynamic correlates of cognition in human infants. *Annual Review of Psychology*, *66*(1), 349–379. doi:10.1146/annurev-psych-010213-115108 PMID:25251480

Augview Limited. (2016). *Augview | Augmented Reality Mobile GIS*. Author.

Ayers, J. W., Leas, E. C., Dredze, M., Allem, J. P., Grabowski, J. G., & Hill, L. (2016). Pokémon GO—A new distraction for drivers and pedestrians. *JAMA Internal Medicine*, *176*(12), 1865–1866. doi:10.1001/jamainternmed.2016.6274 PMID:27635638

Azuma, R., Baillot, Y., Behringer, R., Feiner, S., Julier, S., & Macintyre, B. (2001). Recent advances in augmented reality. *Computer and Graphics and Applications IEEE*, 34-47.

Azuma, R. T. (1997). A survey of augmented reality. *Presence (Cambridge, Mass.)*, *6*(4), 355–385. doi:10.1162/pres.1997.6.4.355

Azuma, R., Baillot, Y., Behringer, R., Feiner, S., Julier, S., & MacIntyre, B. (2001). Recent advances in augmented reality. *IEEE Computer Graphics and Applications*, *21*(6), 34–47. doi:10.1109/38.963459

Bacca, J., Baldiris, S., & Fabregat, R., & Kinshuk. (2019). Framework for designing motivational augmented reality applications in vocational education and training. *Australasian Journal of Educational Technology*, *35*(3).

Bacca, J., Baldiris, S., Fabregat, R., & Graf, S. (2014). Augmented reality trends in education: A systematic review of research and applications. *Journal of Educational Technology & Society*, *17*(4), 133–149.

Baddeley, A. (1992). Working memory. *Science*, *255*(5044), 556–559. doi:10.1126cience.1736359 PMID:1736359

Badilla Quintana, M. G., Vera Sagredo, A., & Lytras, M. D. (2017). Pre-service teachers' skills and perceptions about the use of virtual learning environments to improve teaching and learning. *Behaviour & Information Technology*, *36*(6), 575–588. doi:10.1080/0144929X.2016.1266388

Badilla, M., & Sandoval, A. M. (2015). Augmented reality as technology applied to higher education: A developing experience. *Innovaciones educativas, 17*(23), 41-49.

Bailenson, J. N. (2016). The trials and tribulations of narrative. *VR. MediaX.* Available at, https://vhil.stanford.edu/news/2016/the-trials-and-tribulations-of-narrative-in-vr-mediax/

Bamodu, O., & Ye, X. M. (2013). *Virtual reality and virtual reality system components*, Paper presented at the Advanced Materials Research. 10.2991/icsem.2013.192

Bandura, A. (1978). Social learning theory of aggression. *Journal of Communication*, *28*(3), 12–29. doi:10.1111/j.1460-2466.1978.tb01621.x PMID:690254

Bandura, A. (1997). The anatomy of stages of change. *American Journal of Health Promotion*, *12*(1), 8–10. doi:10.4278/0890-1171-12.1.8 PMID:10170438

Barab, S. (2006). *Design-Based Research: A Methodological Toolkit for the Learning Scientist*. Cambridge University Press.

Barab, S., & Squire, K. (2004). Design-based research: Putting a stake in the ground. *Journal of the Learning Sciences*, *13*(1), 1–14. doi:10.120715327809jls1301_1

Barak, M. (2007). Transition from traditional to ICT-enhanced learning environments in undergraduate chemistry courses. *Computers & Education*, *48*(1), 30–43. doi:10.1016/j.compedu.2004.11.004

Baram-Tsabari, A., & Osborne, J. (2015). Bridging science education and science communication research. *Journal of Research in Science Teaching*, *52*(2), 135–144. doi:10.1002/tea.21202

Baroudi, S., & Rodjan, M. (2019). Behind the scenes: Teachers' perspectives on factors affecting the implementation of inquiry-based science instruction. *Research in Science & Technological Education*, 1–22. doi:10.1080/02635143.2019.1651259

Barreira, J., Bessa, M., Pereira, L. C., Adão, T., Peres, E., & Magalhães, L. (2012). MOW: Augmented Reality game to learn words in different languages: Case study: Learning English names of animals in elementary school. In *Proceedings of Information Systems and Technologies (CISTI), 2012 7th Iberian Conference on* (pp. 1-6). Madrid: IEEE.

Baumeister, J., Ssin, S. Y., ElSayed, N. A., Dorrian, J., Webb, D. P., Walsh, J. A., Simon, T. M., Irlitti, A., Smith, R. T., Kohler, M., & Thomas, B. H. (2017). Cognitive cost of using augmented reality displays. *IEEE Transactions on Visualization and Computer Graphics*, *23*(11), 2378–2388. doi:10.1109/TVCG.2017.2735098 PMID:28809700

Baus, O., & Bouchard, S. (2014). Moving from virtual reality exposure-based therapy to augmented reality exposure-based therapy: A review. *Frontiers in Human Neuroscience*, *8*, 112. doi:10.3389/fnhum.2014.00112 PMID:24624073

Becker, S. A., Brown, M., Dahlstrom, E., Davis, A., DePaul, K., Diaz, V., & Pomerantz, J. (2018). *NMC horizon report: 2018 higher education edition*. EDUCAUSE.

Bellini, S., & Akullian, J. (2007). A meta-analysis of video modeling and video self-modeling interventions for children and adolescents with autism spectrum disorders. *Exceptional Children*, *73*(3), 264–287. doi:10.1177/001440290707300301

Bell, P., & Linn, M. C. (2000). Scientific arguments as learning artifacts: Designing for learning from the web with KIE. *International Journal of Science Education*, *22*(8), 797–817. doi:10.1080/095006900412284

Bengtsson, M. (2016). How to plan and perform a qualitative study using content analysis. *NursingPlus Open*, *2*, 8–14. doi:10.1016/j.npls.2016.01.001

Bennett, J. A., & Saunders, C. P. (2019). A virtual tour of the cell: Impact of virtual reality on student learning and engagement in the STEM classroom. *Journal of Microbiology & Biology Education*, *20*(2). Advance online publication. doi:10.1128/jmbe.v20i2.1658 PMID:31388392

Berg, B. L. (2001). *Qualitative research methods for the social sciences*. Pearson.

Berger, P., & Wolling, J. (2019). They need more than technology-equipped schools: Teachers' practice of fostering students' digital protective skills. *Media and Communication*, *7*(2), 137–147. doi:10.17645/mac.v7i2.1902

Berland, L. K., & Reiser, B. J. (2009). Making sense of argumentation and explanation. *Science Education*, *93*(1), 26–55. doi:10.1002ce.20286

Bernal, L., & Ballesteros-Ricaurte, J. (2017). Methodology for the construction of virtual learning objects supported in augmented reality. *Sophia*, *13*(1), 4–12. doi:10.18634ophiaj.13v.1i.209

Berns, A., Gonzalez-Pardo, A., & Camacho, D. (2013). Game-like language learning in 3-D virtual environments. *Computers & Education*, *60*(1), 210–220. doi:10.1016/j.compedu.2012.07.001

Berthoz, A. (1997). *Le sens du mouvement*. Odile Jacob.

Berthoz, A. (2003). *La décision*. Odile Jacob.

Bertrand, J., Bhargava, A., Madathil, K. C., Gramopadhye, A., & Babu, S. V. (2017a). The effects of presentation method and simulation fidelity on psychomotor education in a bimanual metrology training simulation. In *2017 IEEE Symposium on 3D User Interfaces, 3DUI 2017 — Proceedings* (pp. 59-68). 10.1109/3DUI.2017.7893318

Bharathi, A. K. B. G., & Tucker, C. S. (2015). *Investigating the impact of interactive immersive virtual reality environments in enhancing task performance in online engineering design activities*, Paper presented at the ASME 2015 International Design Engineering Technical Conferences and Computers and Information in Engineering Conference. 10.1115/DETC2015-47388

Bhargava, A., Bertrand, J. W., Gramopadhye, A. K., Madathil, K. C., & Babu, S. V. (2018). Evaluating multiple levels of an interaction fidelity continuum on performance and learning in near-field training simulations. *IEEE Transactions on Visualization and Computer Graphics*, *24*(4), 1418–1427. doi:10.1109/TVCG.2018.2794639 PMID:29543160

Billinghurst, M. (2002). Augmented reality in education. *New Horizons for Learning*, *12*(5), 1–5.

Billinghurst, M., Kato, H., & Poupyrev, I. (2001). The magicbook-moving seamlessly between reality and virtuality. *IEEE Computer Graphics and Applications*, *21*(3), 6–8.

Bitting, K. S., Teasdale, R., & Ryker, K. (2017). Applying the geoscience education research strength of evidence pyramid: Developing a rubric to characterize existing geoscience teaching assistant training studies. *Journal of Geoscience Education*, *65*(4), 519–530. doi:10.5408/16-228.1

Bjork, E. L., & Bjork, R. A. (2011). Making things hard on yourself, but in a good way: Creating desirable difficulties to enhance learning. In M. A. Gernsbacher, R. W. Pew, L. M. Hough, & J. R. Pomerantz (Eds.), *Psychology and the Real World: Essays Illustrating Fundamental Contributions to Society* (pp. 59–68). Worth Publishers.

Blas, D., Vázquez-Cano, E., Morales, M. B., & López, E. (2019). Use of augmented reality apps in University classrooms. *Campus Virtuales, 8*(1), 37-48. (www.revistacampusvirtuales.es)

Bloxham, J. (2013). *Augmented reality in education: teaching tool or passing trend?* The Guardian. https://www.theguardian.com/higher-education-network/blog/2013/feb/11/augmented-reality-teaching-tool-trend

Boling, E. (2010). The need for design cases: Disseminating design knowledge. *International Journal of Designs for Learning*, *1*(1), 1–8.

Bonsor, K., & Chandler, N. (2018). *How Augmented Reality Works.* Howstuffworks. https://computer.howstuffworks.com/augmented-reality.htm

Bortolaso, C., Bourdiol, J., & Graham, T. C. N. (2019). Enhancing communication and awareness in asymmetric games. *Joint International Conference on Entertainment Computing and Serious Games*, (pp. 250–262). Springer. 10.1007/978-3-030-34644-7_20

Bower, M. (2008). Affordance analysis - matching learning tasks with learning technologies. *Educational Media International*, *45*(1), 3–15. doi:10.1080/09523980701847115

Bower, M., Howe, C., McCredie, N., Robinson, A., & Grover, D. (2014). Augmented Reality in education–cases, places and potentials. *Educational Media International*, *51*(1), 1–15. doi:10.1080/09523987.2014.889400

Bowman, D. A., & McMahan, R. P. (2007). Virtual reality: How much immersion is enough? *Computer*, *40*(7), 36–43. doi:10.1109/MC.2007.257

Braun, V., & Clarke, V. (2006). Using thematic analysis in psychology. *Qualitative Research in Psychology*, *3*(2), 77–101. doi:10.1191/1478088706qp063oa

Bridges, S. A., Robinson, O. P., Stewart, E. W., Kwon, D., & Mutua, K. (2019). Augmented reality: Teaching daily living skills to adults with intellectual disabilities. *Journal of Special Education Technology*. Advance online publication. doi:10.1177/0162643419836411

Brooke, J. (1996). Usability Evaluation in Industry. Taylor & Francis.

Brown. (2020). *2020 EDUCAUSE Horizon report (Teaching and learning edition)*. EDUCAUSE.

Brown, J. S., Collins, A., & Duguid, P. (1989). Situated cognition and the culture of learning. *Educational Researcher*, *18*(1), 32–42. doi:10.3102/0013189X018001032

Brown, J. S., & Duguid, P. (1993). Stolen knowledge. *Educational Technology*, *33*(3), 10–15.

Brugnoli, M. C., Morabito, F., Bo, G., & Murelli, E. (2007). "Augmented Itineraries": Mobile services differentiating what museum has to offer. *PsychNology Journal*, *4*(3), 311–335.

Bucchiarone, A., Cicchetti, A., & Marconi, A. (2019). GDF: A gamification design framework powered by model-driven engineering. *Proceedings of the 2019 ACM/IEEE 22nd International Conference on Model Driven Engineering Languages and Systems Companion, MODELS-C 2019*, 753–758. 10.1109/MODELS-C.2019.00117

Buń, P., Górski, F., & Turkowska, K. (2018). Virtual Reality Training Application of Medical Procedure. In *Smart Technology* (pp. 49–58). Springer. doi:10.1007/978-3-319-73323-4_6

Burga, A. (2006). La unidimensionalidad de un instrumento de medición: Perspectiva factorial [The unidimensionality of a measuring instrument: factorial perspective]. *Revista de Psicología*, *24*(1), 53–80.

Burnham, S. (2007). Getting Year 7 to set their own questions about the Islamic Empire, 600-1600. *Teaching History*, *128*(September), 11–16.

Burton, C. E., Anderson, D. H., Prater, M. A., & Dyches, T. T. (2013). Video self-modeling on an iPad to teach functional math skills to adolescents with autism and intellectual disability. *Focus on Autism and Other Developmental Disabilities*, *28*(2), 67–77. doi:10.1177/1088357613478829

Bush, V. (1945). As we may think. *Atlantic Monthly*, *176*(1), 101–108.

Buttussi, F., & Chittaro, L. (2018). Effects of different types of virtual reality display on presence and learning in a safety training scenario. *IEEE Transactions on Visualization and Computer Graphics*, *24*(2), 1063–1076. doi:10.1109/TVCG.2017.2653117 PMID:28092563

Buzko, V. L., Bonk, A. V., & Tron, V. V. (2018). Implementation of Gamification and Elements of Augmented Reality during the Binary Lessons in a Secondary School. In *Proceedings of the 1st International Workshop on Augmented Reality in Education*, (pp. 53-60). Kryvyi Rih.

Byoung, G. A. (2001). Using calculators in mathematics education in korean elementary schools. *Journal of the Korea Society of Mathematical Education Series D: Research in Mathematical Education*, *5*(2), 107–118.

Cabero-Almenara, J., Vázquez-Cano, E., & López-Meneses, E. (2018). Use of Augmented Reality Technology as a Didactic Resource in University Teaching. *Formación Universitaria*, *11*(1), 25–34. doi:10.4067/S0718-50062018000100025

Cabero, J., & Barroso, J. (2016). The educational possibilities of Augmented Reality. *New Approaches in Educational Research*, *5*(1), 44–50.

Cabero, J., Barroso, J., & Llorente, C. (2019). Augmented reality in university education. REDU. *Revista de Docencia Universitaria*, *17*(1), 105–118. doi:10.4995/redu.2019.11256

Cai, S., Chiang, F.-K., Sun, Y., Lin, C., & Lee, J. J. (2017). Applications of augmented reality-based natural interactive learning in magnetic field instruction. *Interactive Learning Environments*, *25*(6), 778–791. doi:10.1080/10494820.2016.1181094

Carmigniani, J., & Furht, B. (2011). Augmented reality: An overview. In B. Furht (Ed.), *Handbook of augmented reality* (pp. 3–46). Springer. doi:10.1007/978-1-4614-0064-6_1

Carmigniani, J., Furht, B., Anisetti, M., Ceravolo, P., Damiani, E., & Ivkovic, M. (2011). Augmented reality technologies, systems and applications. *Multimedia Tools*, *51*(1), 341–377. doi:10.100711042-010-0660-6

Carmines, E., & Zeller, R. (1979). *Reliability and validity assessment*. Sage. doi:10.4135/9781412985642

Cascales, A. L. I., Pérez-López, D., Perona, P., & Contero, M. (2013). An experience on natural sciences augmented reality contents for preschoolers. In R. Shumaker (Ed.), *Virtual augmented and mixed reality: Systems and applications* (pp. 103–112). Springer.

Castaño-Calle, R., & González, F. (2019). Augmented and virtual reality: appraisals, perceptions and attitudes of university students and their application in the educational framework. *Instituto Politécnico de Braganca,* 1-19.

Castillo, J. L., Soberanes, A., Peña, A., & Martínez, M. (2016b). The industrial designer's learning process in the field of packaging. *Pistas Educativas, 122*(CITEC 2016), 86-99.

Castillo, J. L., Martínez, M., Soberanes, A., & Sánchez, J. M. (2016a). Definition of learning styles in university students according to neurolinguistic programming. *Docencia e Investigación Educativa*, *2*(3), 25–34.

Castro-Alonso, J. C., Paas, F., & Ginns, P. (2019). Embodied cognition, science education, and visuospatial processing. In J. C. Castro-Alonso (Ed.), *Visuospatial processing for education in health and natural sciences* (pp. 175–205). Springer. doi:10.1007/978-3-030-20969-8_7

Castro, M. V., Bissaco, M. A. S., Panccioni, B. M., Rodrigues, S. C. M., & Domingues, A. M. (2014). Effect of a virtual environment on the development of mathematical skills in children with dyscalculia. *PLoS One*, *9*(7), e103354. doi:10.1371/journal.pone.0103354 PMID:25068511

Catanzaro, M. (1988). Using qualitative analytical techniques. *Nursing research. Theory into Practice*, 437–456.

Caudell, T. P., & Mizell, D. W. (1992, January). Augmented reality: An application of heads-up display technology to manual manufacturing processes. In *Proceedings of the Twenty-Fifth Hawaii International Conference on System Sciences* (Vol. 2, pp. 659-669). 10.1109/HICSS.1992.183317

Cebrián, D. (2018). *Heading for Educational Mobile Applications*. Retrieved from https://corubric.com/index.php?r=publicrubric%2Fview&id=491

Cengizhan, S. (2007). Proje temelli ve bilgisayar destekli öğretim tasarimlarinin; bağimli, bağimsiz ve iş birlikli öğrenme stillerine sahip öğrencilerin akademik başarilarina ve öğrenme kaliciliğina etkisi. *Türk Eğitim Bilimleri Dergisi*, *5*(3), 377–403.

Chalkiadaki, A. (2018). A systematic literature review of 21st century skills and competencies in primary education. *International Journal of Instruction*, *11*(3), 1–16. doi:10.12973/iji.2018.1131a

Chang, C. W., Lee, J. H., Wang, C. Y., & Chen, G. D. (2010). Improving the authentic learning experience by integrating robots into the mixed-reality environment. *Computers & Education*, *55*(4), 1572–1578. doi:10.1016/j.compedu.2010.06.023

Chang, H. Y., Wu, H. K., & Hsu, Y. S. (2013). Integrating a mobile augmented reality activity to contextualize student learning of a socioscientific issue. *British Journal of Educational Technology*, *44*(3), 95–99. doi:10.1111/j.1467-8535.2012.01379.x

Chan, J. C., Leung, H., Tang, J. K., & Komura, T. (2010). A virtual reality dance training system using motion capture technology. *IEEE Transactions on Learning Technologies*, *4*(2), 187–195. doi:10.1109/TLT.2010.27

Chatzopoulos, D., Bermejo, C., Huang, Z., & Hui, P. (2017). Mobile augmented reality survey: From where we are to where we go. *IEEE Access: Practical Innovations, Open Solutions*, *5*, 6917–6950. doi:10.1109/ACCESS.2017.2698164

Che Hashim, N., Abd Majid, N. A., Arshad, H., & Khalid Obeidy, W. (2018). User Satisfaction for an Augmented Reality Application to Support Productive Vocabulary Using Speech Recognition. *Advances in Multimedia*, *2018*, 2018. doi:10.1155/2018/9753979

Chen, B. X. (2009). *If you're not seeing data, you're not seeing*. Wired Magazine. https://www.wired.com/2009/08/augmented-reality/

Chen, P., Liu, X., Cheng, W., & Huang, R. (2017). A review of using augmented reality in education from 2011 to 2016. In E. Popescu, Kinshuk, M. K. Khribi, R. Huang, M. Jemni, N.-S. Chen, & D. G. Sampson (Eds.), Innovations in smart learning (pp. 13–19). doi:10.1007/978-981-10-2419-1

Chen, W., Lim, C., & Tan, A. (2010). Pre-service teachers' ICT experiences and competencies: New generation of teachers in digital age. In B. Rachev & A. Smrikarov (Eds.), *Proceedings of the 18th International Conference on Computers in Education*, (pp. 631-638). Putrajaya, Malaysia: Asia-Pacific Society for Computers in Education.

Chen, C. H., Lee, I. J., & Lin, L. Y. (2015). Augmented reality-based self-facial modeling to promote the emotional expression and social skills of adolescents with autism spectrum disorders. *Research in Developmental Disabilities*, *36*, 396–403. doi:10.1016/j.ridd.2014.10.015 PMID:25462499

Chen, C. J. (2006). The design, development and evaluation of a virtual reality based learning environment. *Australasian Journal of Educational Technology*, *22*(1), 39–63. doi:10.14742/ajet.1306

Chen, C. J., Toh, S. C., & Fauzy, W. M. (2004). The theoretical framework for designing desktop virtual reality-based learning environments. *Journal of Interactive Learning Research*, *15*(2), 147.

Chen, C. J., Toh, S. C., & Ismail, W. M. F. W. (2005). Are learning styles relevant to virtual reality? *Journal of Research on Technology in Education*, *38*(2), 123–141. doi:10.1080/15391523.2005.10782453

Cheng, K. H. (2017). Reading an augmented reality book: An exploration of learner's cognitive load, motivation and attitudes. *Australasian Journal of Educational Technology*, *33*(4), 53–69.

Cheng, K. H. (2017). Reading an augmented reality book: An exploration of learners' cognitive load, motivation, and attitudes. *Australasian Journal of Educational Technology*, *33*(4).

Cheng, K. H., & Tsai, C. C. (2016). The interaction of child–parent shared reading with an augmented reality (AR) picture book and parents' conceptions of AR learning. *British Journal of Educational Technology*, *47*(1), 203–222. doi:10.1111/bjet.12228

Cheng, K.-H., & Tsai, C.-C. (2013). Affordances of augmented reality in science learning: Suggestions for future research. *Journal of Science Education and Technology*, *22*(4), 449–462. doi:10.100710956-012-9405-9

Cheng, K., & Tsai, C. (2014). Children and parents' reading of an augmented reality picture book: Analyses of behavioral patterns and cognitive attainment. *Computers & Education*, *72*, 302–312. doi:10.1016/j.compedu.2013.12.003

Cheng, Y., Huang, C.-L., & Yang, C.-S. (2015). Using a 3D immersive virtual environment system to enhance social understanding and social skills for children with autism spectrum disorders. *Focus on Autism and Other Developmental Disabilities*, *30*(4), 222–236. doi:10.1177/1088357615583473

Chen, J. (2016). The crossroads of English language learners, task-based instruction, and 3D multi-user virtual learning in Second Life. *Computers & Education*, *102*, 152–171. doi:10.1016/j.compedu.2016.08.004

Chen, M.-R. A., & Hwang, G.-J. (2020). Effects of experiencing authentic contexts on English speaking performances, anxiety and motivation of EFL students with different cognitive styles. *Interactive Learning Environments*, 1–21. Advance online publication. doi:10.1080/10494820.2020.1734626

Chen, X., Chen, Z., Li, Y., He, T., Hou, J., Liu, S., & He, Y. (2019). ImmerTai: Immersive motion learning in VR environments. *Journal of Visual Communication and Image Representation*, *58*, 416–427. doi:10.1016/j.jvcir.2018.11.039

Chen, Y. (2016). The Effects of Virtual Reality Learning Environment on Student Cognitive and Linguistic Development. *The Asia-Pacific Education Researcher*, *25*(4), 637–646. doi:10.100740299-016-0293-2

Chen, Y. C., Hand, B., & McDOWELL, L. E. A. H. (2013). The effects of writing-to-learn activities on elementary students' conceptual understanding: Learning about force and motion through writing to older peers. *Science Education*, *97*(5), 745–771. doi:10.1002ce.21067

Chen, Y. C., Park, S., & Hand, B. (2016). Examining the use of talk and writing for students' development of scientific conceptual knowledge through constructing and critiquing arguments. *Cognition and Instruction*, *34*(2), 100–147. doi: 10.1080/07370008.2016.1145120

Cheong, D. (2010). The effects of practice teaching sessions in second life on the change in pre-service teachers' teaching efficacy. *Computers & Education*, *55*(2), 868–880. doi:10.1016/j.compedu.2010.03.018

Chiang, T. H. C., Yang, S. J., & Hwang, G. J. (2014). An augmented reality-based mobile learning system to improve students' learning achievements and motivations in natural science inquiry activities. *Journal of Educational Technology & Society*, *17*(4), 352–365.

Chicioreanu, T. D., & Amza, C. G. (2015). Are teachers ready for the augmented reality? In B. Pătrut, D. Andone, C. Holotescu, & G. Grosseck (Eds.), *International Conference Smart 2014, Social Media in Academia: Research and Teaching* (pp. 337–343). Medimond. Retrieved from https://bit.ly/31LVpW2

Chien, S.-Y., Hwang, G.-J., & Jong, M. (2020). Effects of peer assessment within the context of spherical video-based virtual reality on EFL students' English-Speaking performance and learning perceptions. *Computers & Education*, *146*, 103751. Advance online publication. doi:10.1016/j.compedu.2019.103751

Cho, J. Y., & Lee, E. H. (2014). Reducing confusion about grounded theory and qualitative content analysis: Similarities and differences. *Qualitative Report*, *19*(32), 1.

Christou, C., Jones, K., Pitta-Pantazi, D., Pittalis, M., Mousoulides, N., Matos, J. F., Sendova, E., Zachariades, T., & Boytchev, P. (2007). *Developing student spatial ability with 3D software applications.* Paper presented at the 5th Congress of the European Society for Research in Mathematics Education (CERME), Larnaca, Cyprus.

Chu, S. K. W., Reynolds, R. B., Tavares, N. J., Notari, M., & Lee, C. W. Y. (2017). *21st Century skills development through inquiry-based learning.* Singapore: Springer Singapore.

Chuah, K. M., Chen, C. J., & Teh, C.-S. (2011). Designing a desktop virtual reality-based learning environment with emotional consideration. *Research and Practice in Technology Enhanced Learning*, *6*(1), 25–42.

Chu, H. C., Hwang, G. J., & Tsai, C. C. (2010). A knowledge engineering approach to developing mindtools for context-aware ubiquitous learning. *Computers & Education*, *54*(1), 289–297. doi:10.1016/j.compedu.2009.08.023

Chu, M., & Kita, S. (2011). The nature of gestures' beneficial role in spatial problem solving. *Journal of Experimental Psychology. General*, *140*(1), 102–116. doi:10.1037/a0021790 PMID:21299319

Chung, L. Y. (2012). Incorporating 3D-virtual reality into language learning. *International Journal of Digital Content Technology and Its Applications*, *6*(6), 249–255. doi:10.4156/jdcta.vol6.issue6.29

Cihak, D. F., Moore, E. J., Wright, R. E., McMahon, D. D., Gibbons, M. M., & Smith, C. (2016). Evaluating augmented reality to complete a chain task for elementary students with autism. *Journal of Special Education Technology*, *31*(2), 99–108. doi:10.1177/0162643416651724

Clark, R. C., & Mayer, R. E. (2016). *E-learning and the science of instruction: Proven guidelines for consumers and designers of multimedia learning*. John Wiley & Sons. doi:10.1002/9781119239086

Clark, R. W., Threeton, M. D., & Ewing, J. C. (2010). The Potential of Experiential Learning Models and Practices in Career and Technical Education and Career and Technical Teacher Education. *Journal of Career and Technical Education*, *25*(2), 46–62. doi:10.21061/jcte.v25i2.479

Clayton, J. (1997). Delphi: A technique to harness expert opinion for critical decision-marking tasks in education. *Education Psychology*, *17*(4), 373–386. doi:10.1080/0144341970170401

Clay, V., König, P., & König, S. (2019). Eye Tracking in Virtual Reality. *Journal of Eye Movement Research*, *12*(1), 1–18. doi:10.16910/jemr.12.1.3

Clements, D. (1998). *Geometric and Spatial Thinking in Young Children*. Retrieved from https://files.eric.ed.gov/fulltext/ED436232.pdf

Clements, D. H. (2004). Geometric and spatial thinking in early childhood education. *Engaging young children in mathematics: Standards for early childhood mathematics education*, 267-297.

Clements, D. H. (1999). Concrete manipulatives, concrete ideas. *Contemporary Issues in Early Childhood*, *1*(1), 45–60. doi:10.2304/ciec.2000.1.1.7

Clements, D. H., Swaminathan, S., Hannibal, M. A. Z., & Sarama, J. (1999). Young Children's Concepts of Shape. *Journal for Research in Mathematics Education*, *30*(2), 192–212. doi:10.2307/749610

Cochrane, T. D., Cook, S., Aiello, S., Christie, D., Sinfield, D., Steagall, M., & Aguayo, C. (2017). A DBR framework for designing mobile virtual reality learning environments. *Australasian Journal of Educational Technology*, *33*(6), 54–68. doi:10.14742/ajet.3613

Cohen, A. R., Lohani, S., Manjila, S., Natsupakpong, S., Brown, N., & Cavusoglu, M. C. (2013). Virtual reality simulation: Basic concepts and use in endoscopic neurosurgery training. *Child's Nervous System*, *29*(8), 1235–1244. doi:10.100700381-013-2139-z PMID:23702736

Cohen, J. (1960). A coefficient of agreement for nominal scales. *Educational and Psychological Measurement*, *20*(1), 37–46. doi:10.1177/001316446002000104

Coker, J. S., & Porter, D. J. (2017). Student motivations and perceptions across and within five forms of experiential learning. *The Journal of General Education*, *65*(2), 138–156. doi:10.5325/jgeneeduc.65.2.0138

Collins, A. (1991). Cognitive apprenticeship and instructional technology. In L. Idol & B. F. Jones (Eds.), *Educational values and cognitive instruction: Implications for reform* (pp. 121–138). Lawrence Erlbaum.

Corbett, B. A., & Abdullah, M. (2005). Video modeling: Why does it work for children with autism? *Journal of Early and Intensive Behavior Intervention: JEIBI*, *2*(1), 2–8. doi:10.1037/h0100294

Cotton, W. (2008). Supporting the use of learning objects in the K-12 environment: A design-based research project. *Emerging Technologies Conference 2008.*

Coulter, R., Saland, L., Caudell, T., Goldsmith, T. E., & Alverson, D. (2007). The effect of degree of immersion upon learning performance in virtual reality simulations for medical education. *InMedicine Meets Virtual Reality*, *15*, 155–160. PMID:17377256

Cowling, M., & Birt, J. (2018). Pedagogy before technology: A design-based research approach to enhancing skills development in paramedic science using mixed reality. *Information*, *9*(2), 29–44. doi:10.3390/info9020029

Cox, D. J., Brown, T., Ross, V., Moncrief, M., Schmitt, R., Gaffney, G., & Reeve, R. (2017). Can youth with autism spectrum disorder use virtual reality driving simulation training to evaluate and improve driving performance? An exploratory study. *Journal of Autism and Developmental Disorders*, *47*(8), 2544–2555. doi:10.100710803-017-3164-7 PMID:28540452

Craig, A. B. (2013). *Understanding augmented reality: Concepts and applications*. Morgan Kaufmann.

Crespo, M., Fernández, R., Gonzales, I., Esparza, K., & León-Acurio, J. (2020). The Augmented Reality in the Teaching-Learning Process of Children from 3 to 5 Years Old. In M. Botto-Tobar, J. León-Acurio, A. Díaz, & P. Montiel (Eds.), *Advances in Emerging Trends and Technologies. ICAETT 2019. Advances in Intelligent Systems and Computing* (pp. 207–218). Springer. doi:10.1007/978-3-030-32022-5_20

Creswell, J. W., & Plano Clark, V. L. (2010). *Designing and Conducting Mixed Methods Research*. Sage.

Crews, J. (2018). *Five ways teachers can use—and create—augmented reality experiences*. EdSurge. https://www.edsurge.com/news/2018-01-22-five-ways-teachers-can-use-and-create-augmented-reality-experiences

Cromby, J., Standen, P., Newman, J., & Tasker, H. (1996). Successful transfer to the real world of skills practiced in a virtual environment by student with severe learning disabilities. In P. M. Sharkey (Ed.), *Proceedings of the 1st European Conference on Disability, Virtual Reality and Associated Technologies* (pp. 305–313). Reading, UK: University of Reading.

Crossley, S. A., Allen, L. K., Snow, E. L., & McNamara, D. S. (2016). Incorporating learning characteristics into automatic essay scoring models: What individual differences and linguistic features tell us about writing quality. *Journal of Educational Data Mining*, *8*(2), 1–19.

Cruz, R., Soberanes, A., Martínez, M., & Juárez, C. (2012). Modeling the process of developing Computer Interactive Learning Environments (CILE): An aid to instructional design. In R. Juárez, H. Jadwiga, G. Ibargüengoitia, & A. Cárdenas (Eds.), *Tendencias en investigación e innovación en ingeniería de software: Un enfoque práctico* (1st ed., pp. 95–100). Universidad Autónoma de Baja California.

Cuban, L. (1986). *Teachers and machines: The classroom use of technology since 1920*. Teachers College Press.

Cubillo, J., Martín, S., Castro, M., & Colmenar, A. (2014). Autonomous digital resources through augmented reality. *RIED. Revista Iberoamericana de Educación a Distancia, 17*(2), 241-274. https://www.redalyc.org/articulo.oa?id=3314/331431248012

Cupitra-García, A., & Duque-Bedoya, E. (2018). Augmented teachers in the context of augmented reality: A reflection on its pedagogical use. *El Ágora USB*, *18*(1), 245–255. doi:10.21500/16578031.3178

D'esposito, M., & Postle, B. R. (2015). The cognitive neuroscience of working memory. *Annual Review of Psychology*, 66. PMID:25251486

Da Dalto, L., Steib, D., & Balet, O. (2008). CS WAVE: Learning welding motion in a virtual environment. *Proceedings of IIW Conference*, *52,* 167-172.

Da Dalto, L., Steib, D., Mellet-d'Huart, D., & Balet, O. (2007). *CS WAVE: Virtual reality for welder's training*. Welding in the World.

Dadwal, S. S., & Hassan, A. (2016). The augmented reality marketing: A merger of marketing and technology in tourism. In Mobile Computing and Wireless Networks: Concepts, Methodologies, Tools, and Applications (pp. 63-80). IGI Global. doi:10.4018/978-1-4666-8751-6.ch004

Dalgarno, B., Gregory, S., Reiners, T., & Knox, V. (2016). Practising teaching using virtual classroom role plays. *The Australian Journal of Teacher Education*, *41*(1), 126–154. doi:10.14221/ajte.2016v41n1.8

Dalgarno, B., & Lee, M. J. (2010). What are the learning affordances of 3-D virtual environments? *British Journal of Educational Technology*, *41*(1), 10–32. doi:10.1111/j.1467-8535.2009.01038.x

Dalim, C. S. C., Kolivand, H., Kadhim, H., Sunar, M. S., & Billinghurst, M. (2017). Factors influencing the acceptance of augmented reality in education: A review of the literature. *Journal of Computational Science*, *13*(11), 581–589. doi:10.3844/jcssp.2017.581.589

Dan, M., Saha, A., Konar, A., Ralescu, A. L., & Nagar, A. K. (2016, July). A type-2 fuzzy approach towards cognitive load detection using fNIRS signals. In *2016 IEEE International Conference on Fuzzy Systems (FUZZ-IEEE)* (pp. 2508-2515). IEEE. 10.1109/FUZZ-IEEE.2016.7738009

Dawley, L., & Dede, C. (2014). Situated learning in virtual worlds and immersive simulations. In J. M. Spector & ... (Eds.), *Handbook of Research on Educational Communications and Technology* (pp. 723–734). Springer. doi:10.1007/978-1-4614-3185-5_58

De Miguel, M. (Dir.). (2006). *Modalidades de enseñanza centradas en el desarrollo de competencias. Orientaciones para promover el cambio metodológico en el marco del EEES* [Teaching modalities focused on skills development. Guidelines to promote methodological change within the framework of the EHEA]. Oviedo: Universidad de Oviedo/MEC Retrieved from https://bit.ly/2NusykS

DeAnda, S., Poulin-Dubois, D., Zesiger, P., & Friend, M. (2016). Lexical processing and organization in bilingual first language acquisition: Guiding future research. *Psychological Bulletin*, *142*(6), 655–667. doi:10.1037/bul0000042 PMID:26866430

DeChenne, S. E., Enochs, L. G., & Needham, M. (2012). Science, Technology, Engineering, and Mathematics Graduate Teaching Assistants Teaching Self-Efficacy. *The Journal of Scholarship of Teaching and Learning*, *12*(4), 102–123.

Dede, C. (2009, January 02). Immersive interfaces for engagement and learning. *Science*, *323*(5910), 66–69. doi:10.1126cience.1167311 PMID:19119219

Dede, C., Grotzer, T. A., Kamarainen, A., & Metcalf, S. (2017). EcoXPT: Designing for deeper learning through experimentation in an immersive virtual ecosystem. *Journal of Educational Technology & Society*, *20*(4), 166–178.

Del Moral, M.E., & Villalustre, L. (2010). Formación del profesor 2.0: desarrollo de competencias tecnológicas para la escuela 2.0 [Teacher training 2.0 development of technological skills for school 2.0]. *Magister: Revista miscelánea de investigación, 23*, 59-69.

Del Moral, M. E., & Villalustre, L. (2012). Didáctica universitaria en la era 2.0: competencias docentes en campus virtuales [University teaching in the era: virtual campus teaching competencies]. *RUSC. Revista de Universidad y Sociedad del Conocimiento*, *9*(1), 36–50. doi:10.7238/rusc.v9i1.1127

Del Moral, M. E., & Villalustre, L. (2013). Realidad aumentada: experimentando en el aula en 3D [Augmented reality: experimenting in the classroom in 3D]. In *R. Ron, A. Álvarez & P. Núñez (Coords.), Smartphones y tablets: ¿enseñan o distraen?* [Smartphones and tablets: do they teach or distract?] (pp. 107–124). ESIC Editorial.

DeLay, R. (1996). Forming knowledge: Constructivist learning and experiential education. *Journal of Experiential Education, 19*(2), 76–81. doi:10.1177/105382599601900204

Delello, J. A. (2014). Insights from pre-service teachers using science-based augmented reality. *Journal of Computers in Education, 1*(4), 295–311. doi:10.100740692-014-0021-y

DeSutter, D., & Stieff, M. (2017). Teaching students to think spatially through embodied actions: Design principles for learning environments in science, technology, engineering, and mathematics. *Cognitive Research: Principles and Implications, 2*(1), 22. doi:10.118641235-016-0039-y PMID:28386586

Deterding, S., Dixon, D., Khaled, R., & Nacke, L. (2011). From game design elements to gamefulness: Defining gamification. *Proceedings of the 15th International Academic MindTrek Conference: Envisioning Future Media Environments*, 9–15. http://dl.acm.org/citation.cfm?id=2181040

Dewey, J. (1913). *Interest and effort in education*. Riverside Press. doi:10.1037/14633-000

Dewey, J. (1938). *Experience and education*. Touchstone.

Di Serio, Á., Ibáñez, M. B., & Kloos, C. D. (2013). Impact of an augmented reality system on students' motivation for a visual art course. *Computers & Education, 68*, 586–596. doi:10.1016/j.compedu.2012.03.002

Díaz-Campos, B. (2016). Augmented reality in education. *Revista Entorno*, (61), 47-53.

Díaz-Mohedo, M. T., & Vicente, A. (2014). Project based teaching as a didactic strategy for the learning and development of Basic competencys in future teachers. *Procedia: Social and Behavioral Sciences, 141*, 232–236. doi:10.1016/j.sbspro.2014.05.040

Dickey, M. D. (2002). 3D virtual worlds: an emerging technology for traditional and distance learning. Proceedings of Ohio Learning Network.

Didehbani, N., Allen, T., Kandalaft, M., Krawczyk, D., & Chapman, S. (2016). Virtual reality social cognition training for children with high functioning autism. *Computers in Human Behavior, 62*, 703–711. doi:10.1016/j.chb.2016.04.033

Dillenbourg, P. (1999). What do you mean by collaborative learning? In P. Dillenbourg (Ed.), Collaborative-learning: Cognitive and computational approaches (pp. 1–19). Academic Press.

Dixon, D. R., Miyake, C. J., Nohelty, K., Novack, M. N., & Granpeesheh, D. (2019). Evaluation of an immersive virtual reality safety training used to teach pedestrian skills to children with autism spectrum disorder. *Behavior Analysis in Practice*. Advance online publication. doi:10.100740617-019-00401-1

Dixon, D., Terton, U., & Greenaway, R. (2018). Reducing the split-attention effect in assembly based instruction by merging physical parts with holograms in mixed reality. *CSEDU 2018: Proceedings of the 10th International Conference on Computer Supported Education*, Vol. 1*: CSEDU*, 235–244. 10.5220/0006691202350244

Doak, D. G., Denyer, G. S., Gerrard, J. A., Mackay, J. P., & Allison, J. R. (2020). Peppy: A virtual reality environment for exploring the principles of polypeptide structure. *Protein Science, 29*(1), 157–168. doi:10.1002/pro.3752 PMID:31622516

Dodevska, Z. A., Mihić, M. M., & Manasijević, S. (2018). The role of augmented reality in defensive activities. In *Proceedings of the 8th International Scientific Conference on Defensive Technologies OTEH* (pp. 590-593). Academic Press.

Dörner, R., Broll, W., Grimm, P., & Jung, B. (2019). *Virtual und augmented reality (VR/AR): Grundlagen und Methoden der Virtuellen und Augmentierten Realität* (2nd ed.). Springer Vieweg. doi:10.1007/978-3-662-58861-1

Dorogan, D. (2014). *How to use location-based chat and AR in dating and social*. Retrieved November 22, 2016, from https://quickblox.com/blog/how-to-use-location-based-chat-and-ar-in-dating-and-social/

Downe-Wamboldt, B. (1992). Content analysis: Method, applications, and issues. *Health Care for Women International, 13*(3), 313–321. doi:10.1080/07399339209516006 PMID:1399871

Downs, F. S., & Fawcett, J. (1986). The relationship of theory and research. McGraw-Hill/Appleton & Lange.

Dukes, L., Pence, T., Hodges, L., Meehan, N., & Johnson, A. (2013). SIDNIE: Scaffolded Interviews Developed by Nurses in Education. In *Proceedings of the 2013 international conference on Intelligent user interfaces - IUI '13.* Santa Monica: ACM Press. 10.1145/2449396.2449447

Dunleavy, M. (2014). Design principles for augmented reality learning. *TechTrends, 58*(1), 28–34. doi:10.100711528-013-0717-2

Dunleavy, M., & Dede, C. (2014). Augmented reality teaching and learning. In J. Spector, M. Merrill, J. Elen, & M. Bishop (Eds.), *Handbook of research on educational communications and technology* (pp. 735–745). Springer. doi:10.1007/978-1-4614-3185-5_59

Dunleavy, M., Dede, C., & Mitchell, R. (2009). Affordances and limitations of immersive participatory augmented reality simulations for teaching and learning. *Journal of Science Education and Technology, 18*(1), 7–22. doi:10.100710956-008-9119-1

Durak, A., & Karaoğlan-Yilmaz, F. G. (2019). Artırılmış gerçekliğin eğitsel uygulamaları üzerine ortaokul öğrencilerinin görüşleri. *Bolu Abant İzzet Baysal Üniversitesi Eğitim Fakültesi Dergisi, 19*(2), 468–481. doi:10.17240/aibuefd.2019.19.46660-425148

Durlach, N., & Mavor, A. (Eds.). (1995). Virtual reality. scientific and technological challenges. Naval Training Systems Center.

Duschl, R. A., & Osborne, J. (2002). Supporting and promoting argumentation discourse in science education. *Studies in Science Education, 38*(1), 39–72. doi:10.1080/03057260208560187

Eckert, M., Volmerg, J. S., & Friedrich, C. M. (2019). Augmented reality in medicine: Systematic and bibliographic review. *JMIR mHealth and uHealth, 7*(4), e10967. doi:10.2196/10967 PMID:31025950

Edelson, D. C., Gordon, D. N., & Pea, R. D. (1999). Addressing the challenge of inquiry-based learning. *Journal of the Learning Sciences, 8*, 392–450. doi:10.120715327809jls0803&4_3

Edwards, M., García, A., Sánchez, M., Quesada, H., & Amara, N. (2015). Disentangling competencys: Interrelationships on creativity, innovation and entrepreneurship. *Thinking Skills and Creativity, 16*, 27–39. doi:10.1016/j.tsc.2014.11.006

Efstathiou, I., Kyza, E. A., & Georgiou, Y. (2018). An inquiry-based augmented reality mobile learning approach to fostering primary school students' historical reasoning in non-formal settings. *Interactive Learning Environments, 26*(1), 22–41. doi:10.1080/10494820.2016.1276076

Ekstrand, C., Jamal, A., Nguyen, R., Kudryk, A., Mann, J., & Mendez, I. (2018). Immersive and interactive virtual reality to improve learning and retention of neuroanatomy in medical students: A randomized controlled study. *CMAJ Open, 6*(1), E103–E109. Advance online publication. doi:10.9778/cmajo.20170110 PMID:29510979

El Araby, M. (2002). Possibilities and constraints of using virtual reality in urban design. *Proceedings of the 7Th International CORP Symposium.*

Eleftheria, C. A., Charikleia, P., Iason, C. G., Athanasios, T., & Dimitrios, T. (2013). An innovative augmented reality educational platform using gamification to enhance lifelong learning and cultural education. *IISA, 1–5.* Advance online publication. doi:10.1109/IISA.2013.6623724

Elmqaddem, N. (2019). Augmented Reality and Virtual Reality in Education. Myth or Reality? *International Journal of Emerging Technologies in Learning*, *14*(03), 234–242. doi:10.3991/ijet.v14i03.9289

Elo, S., & Kyngäs, H. (2008). The qualitative content analysis process. *Journal of Advanced Nursing*, *62*(1), 107–115. doi:10.1111/j.1365-2648.2007.04569.x PMID:18352969

Emiroğlu, B. G., & Kurt, A. A. (2017). Use of augmented reality in mobile devices for educational purposes. In G. Kurubacak & H. Altinpulluk (Eds.), *Mobile Technologies and Augmented Reality in Open Education* (pp. 95–117). doi:10.4018/978-1-5225-2110-5.ch005

English, D. L., Gounden, S., Dagher, R. E., Chan, S. F., Furlonger, B. E., Anderson, A., & Moore, D. W. (2017). Effects of video modeling with video feedback on vocational skills of adults with autism spectrum disorder. *Developmental Neurorehabilitation*, *20*(8), 511–524. doi:10.1080/17518423.2017.1282051 PMID:28632464

Erbas, C., & Demirer, V. (2019). The effects of augmented reality on students' academic achievement and motivation in a biology course. *Journal of Computer Assisted Learning*, *35*(3), 450–458. doi:10.1111/jcal.12350

Ermi, L., & Mäyrä, F. (2011). Fundamental Components of the Gameplay Experience: Analysing Immersion In S. Günzel, M. Liebe & D. Mersch (Eds.), *DIGAREC Keynote-Lectures 2009/10* (pp. 88-115) Potsdam: University Press. http://pub.ub.uni-potsdam.de/volltexte/2011/4983

Ermi, L., & Mäyrä, F. (2005). Fundamental components of the gameplay experience: Analysing immersion, *Worlds in play. International Perspectives on Digital Games Research*, *37*(2), 37–53.

Erstad, O., Eickelmann, B., & Eichhorn, K. (2015). Preparing teachers for schooling in the digital age: A meta-perspective on existing strategies and future challenges. *Education and Information Technologies*, *20*(4), 641–654. doi:10.100710639-015-9431-3

Escobedo, L., Tentori, M., Quintana, E., Favela, J., & Garcia-Rosas, D. (2014). Using augmented reality to help children with autism stay focused. *IEEE Pervasive Computing*, *13*(1), 38–46. doi:10.1109/MPRV.2014.19

Estapa, A., & Nadolny, L. (2015). The Effect of an Augmented Reality Enhanced Mathematics Lesson on Student Achievement and Motivation. *Journal of STEM Education*, *16*(3), 40–48.

Farra, S. L., Gneuhs, M., Hodgson, E., Kawosa, B., Miller, E. T., Simon, A., ... Hausfeld, J. (2019). Comparative cost of virtual reality training and live exercises for training hospital workers for evacuation. *CIN: Computers, Informatics. Nursing*, *37*(9), 446–454. PMID:31166203

Ferrer-Torregrosa, J., Torralba, J., Jimenez, M. A., García, S., & Barcia, J. M. (2015). ARBOOK: Development and assessment of a tool based on augmented reality for anatomy. *Journal of Science Education and Technology*, *24*(1), 119–124. doi:10.100710956-014-9526-4

Fidan, M., & Debbağ, M. (2019). Artırılmış ve sanal gerçeklik araçları. In 101 Araçla Web 2.0 (pp. 497-559). Ankara: Pegem Akademi Yayıncılık.

Fidan, M., & Tuncel, M. (2019). Integrating augmented reality into problem based learning: The effects on learning achievement and attitude in physics education. *Computers & Education*, *142*, 103635. Advance online publication. doi:10.1016/j.compedu.2019.103635

Fineman, B. (2018). *Securing your reality: Addressing security and privacy in virtual and augmented reality applications*. EDUCAUSE Review. https://er.educause.edu/articles/2018/5/securing-your-reality-addressing-security-and-privacy-in-virtual-and-augmented-reality-applications

Fiorella, L., & Mayer, R. E. (2016). Eight ways to promote generative learning. *Educational Psychology Review*, *28*(4), 717–741. doi:10.100710648-015-9348-9

Firestorm Viewer. (2019). *Firestorm* (Version 6.0.2). The Phoenix Firestorm Project, Inc. Retrieved March 30, 2020 from https://www.firestormviewer.org/

Fishburn, F. A., Norr, M. E., Medvedev, A. V., & Vaidya, C. J. (2014). Sensitivity of fNIRS to cognitive state and load. *Frontiers in Human Neuroscience*, *8*, 76. doi:10.3389/fnhum.2014.00076 PMID:24600374

FitzGerald, E., Ferguson, R., Adams, A., Gaved, M., Mor, Y., & Thomas, R. (2013). Augmented reality and mobile learning: The state of the art. *International Journal of Mobile and Blended Learning*, *5*(4), 43–58. doi:10.4018/ijmbl.2013100103

Folkestad, J., & O'shea, P. (2011). An analysis of engagement in a combination indoor/outdoor augmented reality educational game. *Journal of Science Education and Technology*, *7*(1), 30–37.

Fombona, J., Pascual-Sevillano, M. A., & González-Videgaray, M. C. (2017). M-learning y realidad aumentada: Revisión de literatura científica en el repositorio WoS. *Comunicar*, *25*(52), 63–72. doi:10.3916/C52-2017-06

Fonseca, D., Martí, N., Redondo, E., Navarro, I., & Sánchez, A. (2014). Relationship between student profile, tool use, participation, and academic performance with the use of Augmented Reality technology for visualized architecture models. *Computers in Human Behavior*, *31*, 434–445. doi:10.1016/j.chb.2013.03.006

Forkosh-Baruch, A., & Avidov-Ungar, O. (2019). ICT implementation in colleges of education: A framework for teacher educators. *Journal of Information Technology Education*, *18*, 207–229. doi:10.28945/4312

Forslund, K., & Hammar, E. (2011). Assessment of students' learning when working in groups. *Educational Research*, *53*(3), 331–345. doi:10.1080/00131881.2011.598661

Foster, A., Mishra, P., & Koehler, M. (2011). Digital game analysis: Using the Technological Pedagogical Content Knowledge framework to determine the affordances of a game for learning. In *Learning to Play: Exploring the Future of Education with Video Games*. Peter Lang Publications.

Fotaris, P., Pellas, N., Kazanidis, I., & Smith, P. (2017). A systematic review of Augmented Reality Game-based applications in primary education. In *11th European Conference on Games Based Learning (ECGBL). Mini Track on Mixed Reality for Game-Based Learning proceedings*, (pp. 181-191). Graz, Austria: Academic Conferences and Publishing International Limited.

Fotaris, P., Pellas, N., Kazanidis, I., & Smith, P. (2017). *A systematic review of augmented reality game-based applications in primary education*. Academic Conferences International Limited.

Fourtane, S. (2019). *Augmented reality: The future of education*. Interesting Engineering. https://interestingengineering.com/augmented-reality-the-future-of-education

Fowler, C. (2015). Virtual reality and learning: Where is the pedagogy? *British Journal of Educational Technology*, *46*(2), 412-422.

Fowler, C. (2015). Virtual reality and learning: Where is the pedagogy? *British Journal of Educational Technology*, *46*(2), 412–422. doi:10.1111/bjet.12135

Fox, J., Ahn, S. J., Janssen, J. H., Yeykelis, L., Segovia, K. Y., & Bailenson, J. N. (2015). Avatars versus agents: A meta-analysis quantifying the effect of agency on social influence. *Human-Computer Interaction*, *30*(5), 401–432. doi:10.1080/07370024.2014.921494

Fox, R. (2001). Constructivism examined. *Oxford Review of Education*, *27*(1), 23–35. doi:10.1080/03054980125310

Frankel, J. R., Wallen, N. E., & Hyun, H. H. (2012). *How to Design and Evaluate Research in Education* (8th ed.). McGraw-Hill.

Freina, L., & Ott, M. (2015). A literature review on immersive virtual reality in education: State of the art and perspectives. *The Role of Internet in Education – Change and Transformation*, (April), 199–205. doi:10.12753/2066-026X-13-131

Freina, L., & Ott, M. (2015, January). A literature review on immersive virtual reality in education: state of the art and perspectives. In *The International Scientific Conference eLearning and Software for Education (Vol. 1*, p. 133). "Carol I" National Defense University.

Freina, L., & Ott, M. A. (n.d.). *Literature review on immersive virtual reality in education: state of the art and perspectives*. Available from, https://progesis.itd.cnr.it/download/eLSE%202015%20Freina%20Ott%20Paper.pdf

Fujimoto, Y., Yamamoto, G., Kato, H., & Miyazaki, J. (2012). Relation between location of information displayed by augmented reality and user's memorization. In *Proceedings of Augmented Human International Conference* (pp. 71–78). New York: ACM. 10.1145/2160125.2160132

Galbraith, D. (2009). Cognitive models of writing. *German as a Foreign Language*, (2-3), 7-22.

Gall, M. D., Borg, W. R., & Gall, J. P. (1996). *Educational research: An introduction* (6th ed.). Longman.

Garcia-Cardona, S., Tian, F., & Prakoonwit, S. (2017). Tenochtitlan - An Interactive Virtual Reality Environment that Encourages Museum Exhibit Engagement. *Lecture Notes in Computer Science*, *10345*, 20–28. doi:10.1007/978-3-319-65849-0_3

Garcia, S., Laesker, D., Andujar, M., Kauer, R., & Nguyen, J. (2019). A virtual reality experience for learning languages. In *Conference on Human Factors in Computing Systems - Proceedings*, (pp. 1–4). Glasgow: ACM. 10.1145/3290607.3313253

Garzón, J., & Acevedo, J. (2019). Meta-analysis of the impact of Augmented Reality on students' learning gains. *Educational Research Review*, *27*(April), 244–260. doi:10.1016/j.edurev.2019.04.001

Garzón, J., Pavón, J., & Baldiris, S. (2019). Systematic review and meta-analysis of augmented reality in educational settings. *Virtual Reality (Waltham Cross)*, *23*(4), 447–459. doi:10.100710055-019-00379-9

Gay, L. R., Mills, G. E., & Airasian, P. (2012). Educational Research. New Jersey: S4Carlisle Publishing Services.

Gecü-Parmaksız, Z. (2017). *Augmented reality activities for children: a comparative analysis on understanding geometric shapes and improving spatial skills* (Ph.D Thesis). Middle East Technical University Computer Education and Instructional Technology Department, Ankara.

Geisler, M. (2016). 'Language Boot Camp': 100 years of Middlebury language schools. In Foreign language education in America: Perspectives from K-12, university, government, and international learning (pp. 151–168). Palgrave Macmillan.

Gibbs, S. (2014). *Google Glass review: useful – but overpriced and socially awkward*. The Guardian. https://www.theguardian.com/technology/2014/dec/03/google-glass-review-curiously-useful-overpriced-socially-awkward

Gillam, R., & Jacobson, J. (2015). *The Egyptian Oracle Project: Ancient ceremony in augmented reality*. Bloomsbury Publishing.

Goldin-Meadow, S., Cook, S. W., & Mitchell, Z. A. (2009). Gesturing gives children new ideas about math. *Psychological Science*, *20*(3), 267–272. doi:10.1111/j.1467-9280.2009.02297.x PMID:19222810

Goodwin, M. S., Wiltshire, T., & Fiore, S. M. (2015). *Applying research in the cognitive sciences to the design and delivery of instruction in virtual reality learning environments*, Paper presented at the International Conference on Virtual, Augmented and Mixed Reality. 10.1007/978-3-319-21067-4_29

Gopalan, V., Zulkifli, A. N., & Bakar, J. A. A. (2016). A study of students' motivation using the augmented reality science textbook. *Proceedings of AIP Conference*, 1761(1). 10.1063/1.4960880

Gouveia, C., Cook, C., Snyder, A., & Payne, S. (2017). "Nice to have" to "Can't do without": Aligning simulations and VR with current needs in the K-12 classroom. In B. K. Smith, M. Borge, E. Mercier, & K. Y. Lim (Eds.), *Making a difference: Prioritizing equity and access in CSCL, 12th International Conference on Computer Supported Collaborative Learning (CSCL) 2017, Volume 2* (pp. 723-724). Philadelphia, PA: International Society of the Learning Sciences.

Grabowski, A., & Jankowski, J. (2015). Virtual reality-based pilot training for underground coal miners. *Safety Science*, *72*, 310–314. doi:10.1016/j.ssci.2014.09.017

Graneheim, U. H., & Lundman, B. (2004). Qualitative content analysis in nursing research: Concepts, procedures and measures to achieve trustworthiness. *Nurse Education Today*, *24*(2), 105–112. doi:10.1016/j.nedt.2003.10.001 PMID:14769454

Gregg, L. W., & Steinberg, E. R. (Eds.). (2016). *Cognitive processes in writing*. Routledge. doi:10.4324/9781315630274

Gregor, S. (2002). Design theory in information systems. *AJIS. Australasian Journal of Information Systems*, *10*(1), 14–22.

Gregor, S., & Hevner, A. R. (2013). Positioning and presenting design science research for maximum impact. *Management Information Systems Quarterly*, *37*(2), 337–355. doi:10.25300/MISQ/2013/37.2.01

Grissett, J. O., & Huffman, C. (2019). An open versus traditional psychology textbook: Student performance, perceptions, and use. *Psychology Learning & Teaching*, *18*(1), 21–35. doi:10.1177/1475725718810181

Gruzd, A., Paulin, D., & Haythornthwaite, C. (2016). Analyzing social media and learning through content and social network analysis: A faceted methodological approach. *Journal of Learning Analytics*, *3*(3), 46–71. doi:10.18608/jla.2016.33.4

Guazzaroni, G. (2013). Emotional mapping of the archaeologist game. *Computers in Human Behavior*, *29*(2), 335–344. doi:10.1016/j.chb.2012.06.008

Gudmundsdottir, G. B., & Hatlevik, O. E. (2018). Newly qualified teachers' professional digital competency: Implications for teacher education. *European Journal of Teacher Education*, *41*(2), 214–231. doi:10.1080/02619768.2017.1416085

Guell, X., Gabrieli, J. D., & Schmahmann, J. D. (2017). Embodied cognition and the cerebellum: Perspectives from the dysmetria of thought and the universal cerebellar transform theories. *Cortex*. PMID:28779872

Gugenheimer, J., Stemasov, E., Frommel, J., & Rukzio, E. (2017). ShareVR: Enabling co-located experiences for virtual reality between HMD and non-HMD users. *Proceedings of the 2017 CHI Conference on Human Factors in Computing Systems*, 4021–4033. 10.1145/3025453.3025683

Gün, E. T., & Atasoy, B. (2017). The effects of augmented reality on elementary school students' spatial ability and academic achievement. *Egitim Ve Bilim, 42*(191).

Gün, E. (2014). *Artırılmış gerçeklik uygulamalarının öğrencilerin uzamsal yeteneklerine etkisi. Yüksek Lisans Tezi*. Gazi Üniversitesi Eğitim Bilimleri Enstitüsü, Bilgisayar ve Öğretim Teknolojileri Eğitimi Anabilim Dalı.

Hadid, A., Mannion, P., & Khoshnevisan, B. (2019). Augmented reality to the rescue of language learners. *Florida Journal of Educational Research*, *57*(2), 81–89.

Haj-Bolouri, A., Bernhardsson, L., Bernhardsson, P., & Svensson, L. (2016). An information systems design theory for adaptable e-learning. In *Proceedings of the 2016 49th Hawaii International Conference on System Sciences (HICSS)* (pp. 4414-4423). IEEE. 10.1109/HICSS.2016.550

Halarnkar, P., Shah, S., Shah, H., Shah, H., & Shah, A. (2012). A review on virtual reality. *International Journal of Computer Science Issues*, *9*(6), 325.

Hammady, R., Ma, M., & Temple, N. (2016). Augmented reality and gamification in heritage museums. In T. Marsh, M. Ma, M. F. Oliveira, J. Baalsrud Hauge, & S. Göbel (Eds.), *Serious Games: Second Joint International Conference, JCSG 2016* (pp. 181–187). Springer International Publishing. 10.1007/978-3-319-45841-0_17

Hampshire, A., & Sharp, D. J. (2015). Contrasting network and modular perspectives on inhibitory control. *Trends in Cognitive Sciences*, *19*(8), 445–452. doi:10.1016/j.tics.2015.06.006 PMID:26160027

Hand, B., Villanueva, M. G., & Yoon, S. (2014). Moving from "fuzzi-ness" to canical knowledge: The role of writing in developing cognitive and representational resources. *Writing as Learning Activity, 17.*

Hanson, K., & Shelton, B. E. (2008). Design and Development of Virtual Reality: Analysis of Challenges Faced by Educators. *Journal of Educational Technology & Society*, *11*(1), 118–131.

Harley, J. M., Poitras, E. G., Jarrell, A., Duffy, M. C., & Lajoie, S. P. (2016). Comparing virtual and location-based augmented reality mobile learning: Emotions and learning outcomes. *Educational Technology Research and Development*, *64*(3), 359–388. doi:10.100711423-015-9420-7

Hart, J. E., & Whalon, K. J. (2012). Using video self-modeling via iPads to increase academic responding of an adolescent with autism spectrum disorder and intellectual disability. *Education and Training in Autism and Developmental Disabilities*, 438–446.

Hayes, J. R., & Flower, L. S. (1986). Writing research and the writer. *The American Psychologist*, *41*(10), 1106–1113. doi:10.1037/0003-066X.41.10.1106

Hemberger, L., Kuhn, D., Matos, F., & Shi, Y. (2017). A dialogic path to evidence-based argumentive writing. *Journal of the Learning Sciences*, *26*(4), 575–607. doi:10.1080/10508406.2017.1336714

Hensen, B., Koren, I., & Klamma, R. (2019). Gamification support for learning in spatial computing environments. *Journal of Universal Computer Science*, *25*(12), 1644–1665.

Hermans, R., Tondeur, J., van Braak, J., & Valcke, M. (2008). The impact of primary school teachers' educational beliefs on the classroom use of computers. *Computers & Education*, *51*(4), 1499–1509. doi:10.1016/j.compedu.2008.02.001

Herrington, A., & Herrington, J. (2007). What is an authentic learning environment? In L. A. Tomei (Ed.), *Online and distance learning: Concepts, methodologies, tools, and applications* (pp. 68–76). Information Science Reference.

Herrington, J., Reeves, S. C., & Oliver, R. (2010). *A Practical Guide to Authentic e-learning*. Routledge.

Hevner, A. R., March, S. T., Park, J., & Ram, S. (2004). Design science in information systems research. *Management Information Systems Quarterly*, *28*(1), 75–105. doi:10.2307/25148625

Höffler, T. N. (2010). Spatial ability: Its influence on learning with visualizations—A meta-analytic review. *Educational Psychology Review*, *22*(3), 245–269. doi:10.100710648-010-9126-7

Höffler, T. N., & Leutner, D. (2007). Instructional animation versus static pictures: A meta-analysis. *Learning and Instruction*, *17*(6), 722–738. doi:10.1016/j.learninstruc.2007.09.013

Holopainen, J., Lähtevänoja, A., Mattila, O., Södervik, I., Pöyry, E., & Parvinen, P. (2020). Exploring the learning outcomes with various technologies - Proposing design principles for virtual reality learning environments. In *Proceedings of the 53rd Hawaii International Conference on System Sciences, Hawaii (UH).* 10.24251/HICSS.2020.004

Holz, S. (2018). *Education and Augmented Reality - Really?* Neo Blog. https://blog.neolms.com/education-augmented-reality-really/

Hornecker, E., & Dünser, A. (2009). Of pages and paddles: Children's expectations and mistaken interactions with physical-digital tools. *Interacting with Computers*, *21*(1–2), 95–107. doi:10.1016/j.intcom.2008.10.007

Hou, H. T. (2012). Analyzing the learning process of an online role-playing discussion activity. *Journal of Educational Technology & Society*, *15*(1), 211–222.

Howe, K. B., Suharlim, C., Ueda, P., Howe, D., Kawachi, I., & Rimm, E. B. (2016). Gotta catch'em all! Pokémon GO and physical activity among young adults: Difference in differences study. *BMJ (Clinical Research Ed.)*, 355. doi:10.1136/bmj.i6270 PMID:27965211

Hsiao, H. S., Chang, C. S., Lin, C. Y., & Wang, Y. Z. (2016). Weather observers: A manipulative augmented reality system for weather simulations at home, in the classroom, and at a museum. *Interactive Learning Environments*, *24*(1), 205–223. doi:10.1080/10494820.2013.834829

Hsieh, H. F., & Shannon, S. E. (2005). Three approaches to qualitative content analysis. *Qualitative Health Research*, *15*(9), 1277–1288. doi:10.1177/1049732305276687 PMID:16204405

Hsu, Y. S., Lin, Y. H., & Yang, B. (2017). Impact of augmented reality lessons on students' STEM interest. *Research and Practice in Technology Enhanced Learning*, *12*(1), 2. doi:10.118641039-016-0039-z PMID:30613251

Huang, H. L., Hwang, G. J., & Chang, C. Y. (2019). Learning to be a writer: A spherical video-based virtual reality approach to supporting descriptive article writing in high school Chinese courses. *British Journal of Educational Technology*. Advance online publication. doi:10.1111/bjet.12893

Huang, L. Y., & Yeh, Y. C. (2016). Mediated enactive experience versus perceived mastery experience: An enhancing mechanism versus a mediator of character attachment and internal political efficacy in serious games. *Computers in Human Behavior*, *55*, 1085–1096. doi:10.1016/j.chb.2015.10.029

Huang, R., & Yang, J. (2016). Digital learners and digital teachers: challenges, changes, and competencies. In J. M. Spector, D. Ifenthaler, D. G. Sampson, & P. Isaias (Eds.), *Competencies in Teaching, Learning and Educational Leadership in the Digital Age (CELDA)* (pp. 47–56). Springer. doi:10.1007/978-3-319-30295-9_4

Huang, T., & Liao, S. (2015). A model of acceptance of augmented-reality interactive technology : The moderating role of cognitive innovativeness. *Electronic Commerce Research*, *15*(2), 269–295. doi:10.100710660-014-9163-2

Hu-Au, E., & Lee, J. (2018). Virtual reality in education: A tool for learning in the experience age. *International Journal of Innovation in Education*, *4*. Advance online publication. doi:10.1504/IJIIE.2017.10012691

Humanante-Ramos, P. (2018). *The ICT competences of students entering university: An experience in the Faculty of Health Sciences of a Latin American university*. Educ Med. doi:10.1016/j.edumed.2018.02.002

Hume, A. C. (2012). Primary connections: Simulating the classroom in initial teacher education. *Research in Science Education*, *42*(3), 551–565. doi:10.100711165-011-9210-0

Hung, I.-C., Yang, X.-J., Fang, W.-C., Hwang, G.-J., & Chen, N.-S. (2014). A context-aware video prompt approach to improving students' in-field reflection levels. *Computers & Education*, *70*, 80–91. doi:10.1016/j.compedu.2013.08.007

Hu, R., Wu, Y. Y., & Shieh, C. J. (2016). Effects of Virtual Reality Integrated Creative Thinking Instruction on Students' Creative Thinking Abilities. *Eurasia Journal of Mathematics Science & Technology Education*, *12*(3), 477–486.

Hurley, D. (2017). *The future of language learning: Augmented reality vs virtual reality*. Pearson. https://www.pearsoned.com/future-language-learning-augmented-reality-vs-virtual-reality-pearson-blog/

Hussein, M., & Nätterdal, C. (2015). *The benefits of virtual reality in education-A Comparision Study* [Bachelor of Science Thesis, University of Gothenburg, Göteborg]. https://gupea.ub.gu.se/bitstream/2077/39977/1/gupea_2077_39977_1.pdf

Huttner, J., & Susanne, R. (2017). An immersive memory palace: Supporting the method of loci with virtual reality. *Proceedings of the 23th Americas Conference on Information Systems*, 1-10.

Hwang, G. J., Tsai, C. C., Chu, H. C., Kinshuk, K., & Chen, C.-Y. (2012). A context-aware ubiquitous learning approach to conducting scientific inquiry activities in a science park. *Australasian Journal of Educational Technology*, *28*(5), 931–947. doi:10.14742/ajet.825

Hwang, G. J., Wu, P. H., Zhuang, Y. Y., & Huang, Y. M. (2013). Effects of the inquiry-based mobile learning model on the cognitive load and learning achievement of students. *Interactive Learning Environments*, *21*(4), 338–354. doi:10.1080/10494820.2011.575789

Ibanez, M. B., & Delgado-Kloos, C. (2018). Augmented reality for STEM learning: A systematic review. *Computers & Education*, *123*, 109–123. doi:10.1016/j.compedu.2018.05.002

Ibáñez, M. B., Di Serio, Á., Villarán, D., & Kloos, C. D. (2014). Experimenting with electromagnetism using augmented reality: Impact on flow student experience and educational effectiveness. *Computers & Education*, *71*, 1–13. doi:10.1016/j.compedu.2013.09.004

Ibanez, M. B., Portillo, A. U., Cabada, R. Z., & Barron, M. L. (2020). Impact of augmented reality technology on academic achievement and motivation of students from public and private Mexican schools. A case study in a middle-school geometry course. *Computers & Education*, *145*, 103734. Advance online publication. doi:10.1016/j.compedu.2019.103734

Ihemedu-Steinke, Q. C., Erbach, R., Halady, P., Meixner, G., & Weber, M. (2017). Virtual reality driving simulator based on head-mounted displays. In *Automotive User Interfaces* (pp. 401–428). Springer. doi:10.1007/978-3-319-49448-7_15

Immerman, D. (2019). *Just-in-time: The revolutionary new way to learn.* PTC. https://www.ptc.com/en/product-lifecycle-report/just-in-time-revolutionary-new-way-to-learn

Izard, S., Juanes, J., García-Peñalvo, F., Gonçalvez, J., Ledesma, M., & Ruisoto, P. (2018). Virtual Reality as an Educational and Training Tool for Medicine. *Journal of Medical Systems*, *42*(3), 50. Advance online publication. doi:10.100710916-018-0900-2 PMID:29392522

Jacobson, J. (2017). Authenticity in immersive design for education. In D. Liu, C. Dede, R. Huang, & J. Richards (Eds.), *Virtual, Augmented, and Mixed Realities in Education* (pp. 35–54). Springer. doi:10.1007/978-981-10-5490-7_3

Jaeger, B. (2009, June). What educational activities fit virtual worlds: Towards a theoretical evaluation framework. In *2009 3rd IEEE International Conference on Digital Ecosystems and Technologies* (pp. 715-720). IEEE.

Jamaludin, A., San Chee, Y., & Ho, C. M. L. (2009). Fostering argumentative knowledge construction through enactive role play in Second Life. *Computers & Education*, *53*(2), 317–329. doi:10.1016/j.compedu.2009.02.009

Jambi, E., Gardner, M., & Callaghan, V. (2019, June). A Generalized Pedagogical Framework for Creating Mixed-Mode Role-Play in Multi-User Virtual Environments. In *International Conference on Immersive Learning* (pp. 158-171). Springer. 10.1007/978-3-030-23089-0_12

James, M. A. (2017). A practical tool for evaluating the potential of ESOL textbooks to promote learning transfer. *TESOL Journal*, *8*(2), 385–408. doi:10.1002/tesj.279

Janczyk, M., Aßmann, M., & Grabowski, J. (2018). Oral Versus Written Recall of Long-Term Memory Items: Replicating and Extending the Writing Superiority Effect Across Knowledge Domains. *The American Journal of Psychology*, *131*(3), 263–272. doi:10.5406/amerjpsyc.131.3.0263

Jen, C. C. (2007). Formative research on the instructional design process of virtual reality based learning environments. *ICT: Providing choices for learners and learning Proceedings ASCILITE Singapore 2007*, 149-156.

Jenkins, J. (2016, September 7). *Virtual Reality in the classroom.* Retrieved from https://educationtechnologysolutions.com/2016/09/virtual-reality-classroom/

Jeong, J.-Y., Seo, S., Han, Y., Kim, S., & Jeong, H. (2018). Learning English Conversations in an Immersive Virtual Reality Environment. In Y.-T. Wu & et al. (Eds.), *Workshop Proceedings of the 26th International Conference on Computers in Education.* Metro Manila: Asia-Pacific Society for Computers in Education.

Jesson, R., McNaughton, S., Rosedale, N., Zhu, T., & Cockle, V. (2018). A mixed-methods study to identify effective practices in the teaching of writing in a digital learning environment in low income schools. *Computers & Education, 119*, 14–30. doi:10.1016/j.compedu.2017.12.005

Jiang, Y., Guo, R., & Ma, F. (2017). Interactive Multimedia System for Chinese Traditional Costumes. In F. Tian, C. Gatzidis, A. El Rhalibi, W. Tang, & F. Charles (Eds.), *E-Learning and Games* (pp. 44–51). Springer International Publishing. doi:10.1007/978-3-319-65849-0_6

Johnson, E. A. (2010). *A study of the effects of immersion on short-term spatial memory* [Master of Science, Purdue University, Indiana]. https://docs.lib.purdue.edu/cgi/viewcontent.cgi?article=1030&context=techmasters

Johnson-Glenberg, M. C. (2019). The necessary nine. In Learning in a Digital World. Perspective on Interactive Technologies for Formal and Informal Education, Springer Singapore.

Johnson-Glenberg, M. C. (2018). Immersive VR and education: Embodied design principles that include gesture and hand controls. *Frontiers in Robotics and AI, 5*, 81. doi:10.3389/frobt.2018.00081

Johnson, L. F., Levine, A., Smith, R. S., & Haywood, K. (2010). Key emerging technologies for elementary and secondary education. *Education Digest, 76*(1), 36–40.

Johnson, L. F., Levine, A., Smith, R. S., & Haywood, K. (2010). Key emerging technologies for postsecondary education. *Education Digest, 76*(2), 34–38.

Johnson, L., Adams Becker, S., Cummins, M., Estrada, V., Freeman, A., & Hall, C. (2016). *NMC Horizon Report: 2016 Higher Education Edition.* The New Media Consortium.

Johnson, L., Adams, S., Estrada, V., & Freeman, A. (2014). *NMC Horizon Report: 2014.* The New Media Consortium.

Johnson, L., Becker, S. A., Cummins, M., Estrada, V., Freeman, A., & Hall, C. (2016). *NMC horizon report: 2016 higher education edition.* The New Media Consortium.

Johnson, L., Levine, A., Smith, R., & Stone, S. (2010). *The 2010 horizon report.* The New Media Consortium.

Johnson, L., Smith, R., Levine, A., & Haywood, K. (2010). *The 2010 Horizon report.* The New Media Consortium.

Johnson, L., Smith, R., Willis, H., Levine, A., & Haywood, K. (2011). *NMC horizon report* (2011 edition). The New Media Consortium.

Jonassen, D. H. (1999). *Computers as mindtools for schools, engaging critical thinking.* Prentice-Hall.

Jonassen, D. H., Carr, C., & Yueh, H. P. (1998). Computers as mindtools for engaging learners in critical thinking. *TechTrends, 43*(2), 24–32. doi:10.1007/BF02818172

Joseph, S. R., & Uther, M. (2009). Mobile devices for language learning: Multimedia approaches. *Research and Practice in Technology Enhanced Learning, 4*(01), 7–32. doi:10.1142/S179320680900060X

Josman, N., Ben-Chaim, H. M., Friedrich, S., & Weiss, P. L. (2008). Effectiveness of virtual reality for teaching street-crossing skills to children and adolescents with autism. *International Journal on Disability and Human Development: IJDHD*, *7*(1), 49–56. doi:10.1515/IJDHD.2008.7.1.49

Juan, C. M., Llop, E., Abad, F., & Lluch, J. (2010). Learning words using augmented reality. In *2010 IEEE 10th International Conference on advanced learning technologies* (pp. 422-426). IEEE. 10.1109/ICALT.2010.123

Juan, M. C., Toffetti, G., Abad, F., & Cano, J. (2010). Tangible cubes used as the user interface in an augmented reality game for edutainment, In *Proceedings of the IEEE International Conference on Advanced Learning Technologies Learning technologies in the Information society* (pp. 599-603) IEEE. 10.1109/ICALT.2010.170

Jung, J., & Ahn, Y. J. (2018). Effects of interface on procedural skill transfer in virtual training: Lifeboat launching operation study. *Computer Animation and Virtual Worlds*, *29*(3-4), e1812. doi:10.1002/cav.1812

Kaarbo, J., & Beasley, R. K. (1999). A practical guide to the comparative case study method in political psychology. *Political Psychology*, *20*(2), 369–391. doi:10.1111/0162-895X.00149

Kalman, C., Aulls, M. W., Rohar, S., & Godley, J. (2008). Students' perceptions of reflective writing as a tool for exploring an introductory textbook. *Journal of College Science Teaching*, *37*(4), 74.

Kamińska, D., Sapiński, T., Wiak, S., Tikk, T., Haamer, R. E., Avots, E., Helmi, A., Ozcinar, C., & Anbarjafari, G. (2019). Virtual reality and its applications in education: Survey. *Information*, *10*(10), 318. doi:10.3390/info10100318

Kandalaft, M. R., Didehbani, N., Krawczyk, D. C., Allen, T. T., & Chapman, S. B. (2013). Virtual reality social cognition training for young adults with high-functioning autism. *Journal of Autism and Developmental Disorders*, *43*(1), 34–44. doi:10.100710803-012-1544-6 PMID:22570145

Kaplan, R. (2019). The Effect of Stereoscopic Three-Dimensional Images on Vocabulary Learning. *Contemporary Educational Technology*, *10*(4), 324–337. doi:10.30935/cet.634172

Kara, A. (2018). *Artirilmiş gerçeklik uygulamalarinin eğitimde kullanilmasina yönelik arastirmlarin incelenmesi. Yüksek Lisans Tezi*. Ataturk Üniversitesi Eğitim Bilimleri Enstitüsü, Bilgisayar ve Öğretim Teknolojileri Eğitimi Anabilim Dalı.

Karagozlu, D., Kosarenko, N. N., Efimova, O. V., & Zubov, V. V. (2019). Identifying students' attitudes regarding augmented reality applications in science classes. *International Journal of Emerging Technologies in Learning*, *14*(22), 45–55. doi:10.3991/ijet.v14i22.11750

Karambakhsh, A., Kamel, A., Sheng, B., Li, P., Yang, P., & Feng, D. D. (2019). Deep gesture interaction for augmented anatomy learning. *International Journal of Information Management*, *45*, 328–336. doi:10.1016/j.ijinfomgt.2018.03.004

Karoly, P. (1999). A goal system–self-regulatory perspective on personality, psychopathology, and change. *Review of General Psychology*, *3*(4), 264–291. doi:10.1037/1089-2680.3.4.264

Kaufmann, H., Steinbügl, K., Dünser, A., & Glück, J. (2005). General training of spatial abilities by geometry education in augmented reality. *Annual Review of CyberTherapy and Telemedicine: A Decade of VR, 3*, 65-76.

Kaufmann, H., & Dünser, A. (2007). Summary of usability evaluations of an educational augmented reality application. In R. Shumaker (Ed.), *Proceedings of the 2nd international conference on Virtual reality* (pp. 660-669). Berlin: Springer. 10.1007/978-3-540-73335-5_71

Kaufmann, H., & Schmalstieg, D. (2003). Mathematics and geometry education with collaborative augmented reality. *Computers & Graphics*, *27*(3), 339–345. doi:10.1016/S0097-8493(03)00028-1

Ke, F., Yuan, X., Pachman, M., Dai, Z., Naglieri, R., & Xu, X. (2019). *Perspective Taking in Participatory Simulation-based Collaborative Learning*. Academic Press.

Keengwe, J., Onchwari, G., & Wachira, P. (2008). Computer technology integration and student learning: Barriers and promise. *Journal of Science Education and Technology*, *17*(6), 560–565. doi:10.100710956-008-9123-5

Ke, F., Dai, Z., Dai, C. P., Pachman, M., Chaulagain, R. S., & Yuan, X. (2020). Designing Virtual Agents for Simulation-Based Learning in Virtual Reality. In R. Zheng (Ed.), *Cognitive and Affective Perspectives on Immersive Technology in Education* (pp. 151–170). IGI Global. doi:10.4018/978-1-7998-3250-8.ch008

Ke, F., & Hsu, Y. C. (2015). Mobile augmented-reality artifact creation as a component of mobile computer-supported collaborative learning. *The Internet and Higher Education*, *26*, 33–41. doi:10.1016/j.iheduc.2015.04.003

Ke, F., & Im, T. (2013). Virtual-reality-based social interaction training for children with high-functioning autism. *The Journal of Educational Research*, *106*(6), 441–461. doi:10.1080/00220671.2013.832999

Ke, F., & Lee, S. (2016). Virtual reality based collaborative design by children with high-functioning autism: Design-based flexibility, identity, and norm construction. *Interactive Learning Environments*, *24*(7), 1511–1533. doi:10.1080/10494820.2015.1040421

Ke, F., Lee, S., & Xu, X. (2016). Teaching training in a mixed-reality integrated learning environment. *Computers in Human Behavior*, *62*, 212–220. doi:10.1016/j.chb.2016.03.094

Ke, F., Pachman, M., & Dai, Z. (2020). Investigating educational affordances of virtual reality for simulation-based teaching training with graduate teaching assistants. *Journal of Computing in Higher Education*, •••, 1–21. doi:10.100712528-020-09249-9

Kellems, R. O., Cacciatore, G., & Osborne, K. (2019). Using an augmented reality–based teaching strategy to teach mathematics to secondary students with disabilities. *Career Development and Transition for Exceptional Individuals*, *42*(4), 253–258. doi:10.1177/2165143418822800

Kellems, R. O., Eichelberger, C., Cacciatore, G., Jensen, M., Frazier, B., Simons, K., & Zaru, M. (2020). Using video-based instruction via augmented reality to teach mathematics to middle school students with learning disabilities. *Journal of Learning Disabilities*.

Kellems, R. O., Frandsen, K., Hansen, B., Gabrielsen, T., Clarke, B., Simons, K., & Clements, K. (2016). Teaching multi-step math skills to adults with disabilities via video prompting. *Research in Developmental Disabilities*, *58*, 31–44. doi:10.1016/j.ridd.2016.08.013 PubMed

Kellems, R. O., & Morningstar, M. E. (2012). Using video modeling delivered through iPods to teach vocational tasks to young adults with autism spectrum disorders. *Career Development and Transition for Exceptional Individuals*, *35*(3), 155–167. doi:10.1177/2165143412443082

Keller, J. (2010). *Motivational design for learning and performance*. Springer. doi:10.1007/978-1-4419-1250-3

Keller, J. M. (1987a). Development and use of the ARCS model of motivational design. *Journal of Instructional Development*, *10*(3), 2–10. doi:10.1007/BF02905780

Keller, J. M. (1987b). Strategies for stimulating the motivation to learn. *Performance and Instruction*, *26*(8), 1–7. doi:10.1002/pfi.4160260802

Kelley, K. R., Rivera, C. J., & Kellems, R. O. (2016). Effects of direct systematic instruction on Google glass orientation with individuals with intellectual disability. *Journal of Special Education Technology*, *31*(4), 207–216. doi:10.1177/0162643416673913

Keneman, M. (2016). Empowering the foreign language learner through critical literacies development. *Journal of Language and Literacy Education, 12*(2), 84–99.

Kerawalla, L., Luckin, R., Selijefot, S., & Woolard, A. (2006). Making it real: Exploring the potential of augmented reality for teaching primary school science. *Virtual Reality (Waltham Cross), 10*(3-4), 163–174. doi:10.100710055-006-0036-4

Khan, T., Johnston, K., & Ophoff, J. (2019). The impact of an augmented reality application on learning motivation of students. *Advances in Human-Computer Interaction, 2019*, 2019. doi:10.1155/2019/7208494

Khoshnevisan, B. (2019b). Teacher education meets emerging technologies: Augmented Reality (AR). *TEIS Newsletter*. Retrieved fromhttp://newsmanager.commpartners.com/tesolteis/issues/2019-03-04/4.html

Khoshnevisan, B. (2019d). Review of the book Foreign language education in America: Perspectives from K-12, university, government, and international learning, by S. Berbeco. *MEXTESOL Journal, 43*(3), 1-6. http://mextesol.net/journal/public/files/3551522e139e20a9515b08f099b4d600.pdf

Khoshnevisan, B. (2020). Materials development for the digital native generation: Teachers as materials developers. *MWIS Newsletter.* Retrieved from http://newsmanager.commpartners.com/tesolmwis/issues/2020-01-09/4.html

Khoshnevisan, B. (2018a). The Effect of Incorporating Animated Pedagogical Agents in Apps on L2 Idiom Acquisition and Retention. In W. B. James & C. Cobanoglu (Eds.), *Proceedings of the Global Conference on Education and Research (GLOCER) Conference* (Vol. 2, pp. 72–80). ANAHEI Publishing, LLC. https://scholarcommons.usf.edu/cgi/viewcontent.cgi?article=1017&context=anaheipublishing

Khoshnevisan, B. (2018b). *Idiom assessment: To go off the beaten path. In Proceedings of the Global Conference on Education and Research (GLOCER) Conference* (Vol. 2). ANAHEI Publishing, LLC. https://scholarcommons.usf.edu/cgi/viewcontent.cgi?article=1017&context=anaheipublishing

Khoshnevisan, B. (2019a). To integrate media and technology into language education: For and against. In W. B. James & C. Cobanoglu (Eds.), *Proceedings of the Global Conference on Education and Research (GLOCER) Conference* (Vol. 3, pp. 85–92). ANAHEI Publishing, LLC. https://scholarcommons.usf.edu/cgi/viewcontent.cgi?article=1021&context=anaheipublishing

Khoshnevisan, B. (2019c). Spilling the beans on understanding English idioms using Multimodality: An idiom acquisition technique for Iranian language learners. *International Journal of Language. Translation and Intercultural Communication, 8*, 128–143. doi:10.12681/ijltic.20281

Khoshnevisan, B. (2019e). The affordances and constraints of automatic writing evaluation (AWE) tools: A case for Grammarly. *ARTESOL EFL Journal, 2*(2), 12–25.

Khoshnevisan, B., & Le, N. (2018). Augmented Reality in Language Education: A Systematic Literature Review. In W. B. James & C. Cobanoglu (Eds.), *Proceedings of the Global Conference on Education and Research (GLOCER) Conference* (Vol. 2, pp. 57–71). ANAHEI Publishing, LLC. https://scholarcommons.usf.edu/cgi/viewcontent.cgi?article=1017&context=anaheipublishing

Kirkley, S. E., Tomblin, S., & Kirkley, J. (2005). *Instructional design authoring support for the development of serious games and mixed reality training*, Paper presented at the Interservice/Industry Training, Simulation and Education Conference (I/ITSEC).

Kirkley, S. E., & Kirkley, J. R. (2005). Creating next generation blended learning environments using mixed reality, video games and simulations. *TechTrends, 49*(3), 42–53. doi:10.1007/BF02763646

Kirschner, P. A., Sweller, J., Kirschner, F., & Zambrano, J. (2018). From cognitive load theory to collaborative cognitive load theory. *International Journal of Computer-Supported Collaborative Learning*, *13*(2), 213–233. doi:10.100711412-018-9277-y PMID:30996713

Kirschner, P., Sweller, J., & Clark, R. E. (2006). Why unguided learning does not work: An analysis of the failure of discovery learning, problem-based learning, experiential learning and inquiry-based learning. *Educational Psychologist*, *41*(2), 75–86. doi:10.120715326985ep4102_1

Kiryakova, G., Angelova, N., & Yordanova, L. (2018). The potential of augmented reality to transform education into smart education. *TEM Journal*, *7*(3), 556–565.

Klopfer, E., & Squire, K. (2008). Environmental Detectives—The development of an augmented reality platform for environmental simulations. *Educational Technology Research and Development*, *56*(2), 203–228. doi:10.100711423-007-9037-6

Klopfer, E., & Yoon, S. (2004). Developing games and simulations for today and tomorrow's tech savvy youth. *TechTrends*, *49*(3), 41–49.

Kokotsaki, D., Menzies, V., & Wiggins, A. (2016). Research Article. Project-based learning: A review of the literature. *Improving Schools*, *19*(3), 267–277. doi:10.1177/1365480216659733

Kolb, B. (1984). Functions of the frontal cortex of the rat: A comparative review. *Brain Research. Brain Research Reviews*, *8*(1), 65–98. doi:10.1016/0165-0173(84)90018-3 PMID:6440660

Kolb, D. A. (1984). *Experiential learning: Experience as the source of learning and development*. Prentice-Hall.

Kolb, D. A., & Fry, R. (1975). Toward an applied theory of experiential learning. In C. Cooper (Ed.), *Theories of group process*. Wiley.

Kong, X., Liu, Y., & An, M. (2018, July). Study on the Quality of Experience Evaluation Metrics for Astronaut Virtual Training System. In *International Conference on Virtual, Augmented and Mixed Reality* (pp. 416-426). Springer. 10.1007/978-3-319-91581-4_31

Kounavis, C. D., Kasimati, A. E., Zamani, E. D., & Giaglis, G. M. (2012). Enhancing the tourism experience through mobile augmented reality: Challenges and prospects. *International Journal of Engineering Business Management*, *4*(10), 1–6.

Koutromanos, G., & Avraamidou, L. (2014). The use of mobile games in formal and informal learning environments: A review of the literature. *Educational Media International*, *51*(1), 49–65. doi:10.1080/09523987.2014.889409

Koutromanos, G., Sofos, A., & Avraamidou, L. (2015). The use of augmented reality games in education: A review of the literature. *Educational Media International*, *52*(4), 253–271. doi:10.1080/09523987.2015.1125988

Krippendorff, K. (2004). *Content analysis: An introduction to its methodology* (2nd ed.). Sage.

Kroeker, K. L. (2010). Mainstreaming augmented reality. *Communications of the ACM*, *53*(7), 19–21. doi:10.1145/1785414.1785422

Krokos, E., Plaisant, C., & Varshney, A. (2019). Virtual memory palaces: Immersion aids recall. *Virtual Reality (Waltham Cross)*, *23*(1), 1–15. doi:10.100710055-018-0346-3

Krueger, M. W., Gionfriddo, T., & Hinrichsen, K. (1985, April). VIDEOPLACE—an artificial reality. In *Proceedings of the SIGCHI Conference on Human Factors in Computing Systems* (pp. 35-40). Academic Press.

Küçük, S., Kapakin, S., & Göktaş, Y. (2016). Learning anatomy via mobile augmented reality: Effects on achievement and cognitive load. *Anatomical Sciences Education*, *9*(5), 411–421. doi:10.1002/ase.1603 PMID:26950521

Küçük, S., Yılmaz, R. M., & Göktaş, Y. (2014). Augmented reality for learning English: Achievement, attitude and cognitive load levels of students. *Education in Science*, 393–404.

Küçük, S., Yılmaz, R., & Göktaş, Y. (2014). İngilizce öğreniminde artırılmış gerçeklik: Öğrencilerin başarı, tutum ve bilişsel yük düzeyleri. *Eğitim ve Bilim*, *39*(176), 393–404.

Kulik, A., Kunert, A., Beck, S., Reichel, R., Blach, R., Zink, A., & Fröhlich, B. (2011). C1x6: A stereoscopic six-user display for co-located collaboration in shared virtual environments. *ACM Transactions on Graphics, 30*(6), 188. doi:10.1145/2070781.2024222

Kunert, A., Weissker, T., Froehlich, B., & Kulik, A. (2019). Multi-window 3D interaction for collaborative virtual reality. *IEEE Transactions on Visualization and Computer Graphics, 1*. Advance online publication. doi:10.1109/TVCG.2019.2914677 PMID:31059449

Kwon, C. (2019). Verification of the possibility and effectiveness of experiential learning using HMD-based immersive VR technologies. *Virtual Reality (Waltham Cross)*, *23*(1), 101–118. doi:10.100710055-018-0364-1

Kye, B., & Kim, Y. (2008). Investigation of the relationships between media characteristics, presence, flow, and learning effects in augmented reality based learning augmented reality. *International Journal for Education Media and Technology*, *2*(1), 4–14.

Kyza, E. A., & Georgiou, Y. (2018). Scaffolding augmented reality inquiry learning: The design and investigation of the TraceReaders location-based, augmented reality platform. *Interactive Learning Environments*, 1–15.

Laboratory for Innovative Technology in Engineering Education (LITEE). (n.d.). Retrieved October 21, 2019 from https://www.learntechlib.org/p/151963/

Lagunes-Domínguez, A., Torres-Gastelú, C. A., Angulo-Armenta, J., & Martínez-Olea, M. Á. (2017). Exploration toward mobile learning in university students. *Formación Universitaria*, *10*(1), 101–108. doi:10.4067/S0718-50062017000100011

Lähtevänoja, A., Häkkinen, P., Vasalampi, K., Vesisenaho, M., & Holopainen, J. Learning outcomes in VR: Literature review. Manuscript in preparation.

Laine, T. (2018). Mobile educational augmented reality games: A systematic literature review and two case studies. *Computers*, *7*(1), 19. doi:10.3390/computers7010019

Lai, Y.-S., & Hsu, J.-M. (2011). Development trend analysis of augmented reality system in educational applications. *2011 International Conference on Electrical and Control Engineering*, 6527-6531. 10.1109/ICECENG.2011.6056941

Lamb, R., & Etopio, E. (2019b). Preservice Science Teacher Preparation Using Virtual Reality. In *Society for Information Technology & Teacher Education International Conference* (pp. 162-167). Association for the Advancement of Computing in Education (AACE).

Lamb, R., Etopio, E., Firestone, J. B., Zeder, J., & Hand, B. (2020). Realism, immersion, and interactivity. *Developing Science Literacy in the 21st Century*, 83.

Lamb, R. L., & Etopio, E. (2019a). Virtual Reality Simulations and Writing: A Neuroimaging Study in Science Education. *Journal of Science Education and Technology*, *28*(5), 542–552. doi:10.100710956-019-09785-9

Lamb, R., & Etopio, E. A. (n.d.). Virtual Reality: A Tool for Preservice Science Teachers to Put Theory into Practice. *Journal of Science Education and Technology*. Advance online publication. doi:10.100710956-020-09837-5

Lamb, R., Firestone, J., Schmitter-Edgecombe, M., & Hand, B. (2019). A computational model of student cognitive processes while solving a critical thinking problem in science. *The Journal of Educational Research*, *112*(2), 243–254. doi:10.1080/00220671.2018.1514357

Lamb, R., Hand, B., & Yoon, S. (2017). Examination of cognitive processing of science writing tasks. *Journal of Psychology and Brain Studies*, *1*(1), 1–5.

Lamb, R., Miller, D., Lamb, R., Akmal, T., & Hsiao, Y. J. (2018). Examination of the role of training and fidelity of implementation in the use of assistive communications for children with autism spectrum disorder: A meta-analysis of the Picture Exchange Communication System. *British Journal of Special Education*, *45*(4), 454–472. doi:10.1111/1467-8578.12243

Lan, Y. J. (2015). Contextual EFL learning in a 3D virtual environment. *Language, Learning and Technology*, *19*(2), 16–31. doi: 10125/44412

Landis, J. R., & Koch, G. G. (1977). The measurement of observer agreement for categorical data. *Biometrics*, *33*(1), 159–174. doi:10.2307/2529310 PMID:843571

Lane, C., & Rollnick, S. (2007). The use of simulated patients and role-play in communication skills training: A review of the literature to August 2005. *Patient Education and Counseling*, *67*(1), 13–20. doi:10.1016/j.pec.2007.02.011 PMID:17493780

Lan, Y. (2020). Immersion, interaction, and experience-oriented learning: Bringing virtual reality into FL learning. *Language Learning & Technology*, *24*(1), 1–15. http://hdl.handle.net/10125/44704

Laurillard, D. (2012). *Teaching as a design science: building pedagogical patterns for learning and technology*. Routledge.

Lave, J., & Wenger, E. (1991). *Situated learning: Legitimate peripheral participation*. Cambridge University Press. doi:10.1017/CBO9780511815355

LaViola, J. J. Jr, Kruijff, E., McMahan, R. P., Bowman, D. A., & Poupyrev, I. (2017). *3D user interfaces: Theory and practice*. Addison-Wesley.

Lecon, C., & Herkersdorf, M. (2014, August). Virtual Blended Learning virtual 3D worlds and their integration in teaching scenarios. In *2014 9th International Conference on Computer Science & Education* (pp. 153-158). IEEE.

Lee, B. W., Shih, H. Y., Chou, Y. T., & Chen, Y. S. (2017). Educational Virtual Reality implementation on English for Tourism Purpose using knowledge-based engineering. In *Proceedings of the 2017 IEEE International Conference on Applied System Innovation: Applied System Innovation for Modern Technology, ICASI 2017*. Sapporo: Springer. 10.1109/ICASI.2017.7988550

Legault, J., Zhao, J., Chi, Y.-A., Chen, W., Klippel, A., & Li, P. (2019). Immersive Virtual Reality as an Effective Tool for Second Language Vocabulary Learning. *Languages*, *4*(1), 13. Advance online publication. doi:10.3390/languages4010013

Leinonen, T., Keune, A., Veermans, M., & Toikkanen, T. (2016). Mobile apps for reflection in learning: A design research in K-12 education. *British Journal of Educational Technology*, *47*(1), 184–202. doi:10.1111/bjet.12224

Lele, A. (2013). Virtual reality and its military utility. *Journal of Ambient Intelligence and Humanized Computing*, *4*(1), 17–26. doi:10.100712652-011-0052-4

Lenay, C., Gapenne, O., Hanneton, S., Marque, C., & Genouëlle, C. (2004). Sensory substitution: limits and perspectives. In Touching for Knowing. John Benjamins Publishers. ff doi:10.1075/aicr.53.22lenff.ffhal-02434266f

León, A. P., Risco, E., & Alarcón, C. (2014). Learning strategies in higher education in a curricular competence model. *Revista de la Educación Superior*, *4*(172), 123–144.

León, F., Duque, E., & Escobar, P. (2018). Strategies for formulating quality questions mediated by augmented reality to strengthen scientific thinking. *Revista Mexicana de Investigación Educativa*, *23*(78), 791–815.

Leutner, D., & Schmeck, A. (2014). The generative drawing principle in multimedia learning. In R. Mayer (Ed.), *The Cambridge handbook of multimedia learning* (pp. 433–448). Cambridge University Press., doi:10.1017/CBO9781139547369.022

Levie, A. [levie]. (2016, July 10). *Experts 5 years ago: "Augmented reality will transform education, healthcare, construction, commerce..." Experts today: "Pokemon!!!"* [Tweet]. Twitter. https://twitter.com/levie/status/752197211602038784

Liang, S. (2016). Design principles of augmented reality focusing on the ageing population. In *Proceedings of the 30th International BCS Human Computer Interaction Conference: Fusion!* BCS Learning & Development Ltd. 10.14236/ewic/HCI2016.2

Liao, H., Inomata, T., Sakuma, I., & Dohi, T. (2010). 3-D augmented reality for MRI-guided surgery using integral videography autostereoscopic image overlay. *IEEE Transactions on Biomedical Engineering*, *57*(6), 1476–1486. doi:10.1109/TBME.2010.2040278 PMID:20172791

Liestol, G. (2011). *Learning through situated simulations: exploring mobile augmented reality*. ECAR.

Lindgren, R., & Johnson-Glenberg, M. (2013). Emboldened by embodiment: Six precepts for research on embodied learning and mixed reality. *Educational Researcher*, *42*(8), 445–452. doi:10.3102/0013189X13511661

Lin, H. C. K., Chen, M. C., & Chang, C. K. (2015). Assessing the effectiveness of learning solid geometry by using an augmented reality-assisted learning system. *Interactive Learning Environments*, *23*(6), 799–810. doi:10.1080/10494820.2013.817435

Lin, S. S. (2014). Science and non-science undergraduate students' critical thinking and argumentation performance in reading a science news report. *International Journal of Science and Mathematics Education*, *12*(5), 1023–1046. doi:10.100710763-013-9451-7

Lin, T. J., & Lan, Y. J. (2015). Language learning in virtual reality environments: Past, present, and future. *Journal of Educational Technology & Society*, *18*(4), 486–497. https://drive.google.com/file/d/1NVe2QrgsqsqPKkW3_49Kxxu6MSI3ESf9/view

Liontas, J. I. (1999). *Developing a pragmatic methodology of idiomaticity: The comprehension and interpretation of SL vivid phrasal idioms during reading* (Unpublished doctoral dissertation). The University of Arizona, Tucson, AZ.

Liou, H.-H., Yang, S. J. H., Chen, S. Y., & Tarng, W. (2017). The influences of the 2D image-based augmented reality and virtual reality on student learning. *Journal of Educational Technology & Society*, *20*(3), 110–121.

Liu, D., Dede, C., Huang, R., & Richards, J. (Eds.). (2017). *Virtual, Augmented, and Mixed Realities in Education*. Springer. doi:10.1007/978-981-10-5490-7

Liu, D., Jenkins, S. A., Sanderson, P. M., Fabian, P., & Russell, W. J. (2010). Monitoring with head-mounted displays in general anesthesia: A clinical evaluation in the operating room. *Society for Technology in Anesthesia*, *110*(4), 1032–1038. PMID:20357147

Liu, T. Y. (2009). A context-aware ubiquitous learning environment for language listening and speaking. *Journal of Computer Assisted Learning*, *25*(6), 515–527. doi:10.1111/j.1365-2729.2009.00329.x

Liu, T., Tan, T., & Chu, Y. (2010). QR code and augmented reality-supported mobile English learning system. In *Mobile multimedia processing* (pp. 37–52). Springer. doi:10.1007/978-3-642-12349-8_3

Liu, Y., Holden, D., & Zheng, D. (2016). Analyzing students' language learning experience in an augmented reality mobile game: An exploration of an emergent learning environment. *Social and Behavioral Sciences*, *228*, 369–374. doi:10.1016/j.sbspro.2016.07.055

Lodge, J. M., O'Connor, E., Shaw, R., & Burton, L. (2015). Applying cognitive science to critical thinking among higher education students. In The Palgrave Handbook of Critical Thinking in Higher Education (pp. 391-407). Palgrave Macmillan.

Lokka, I., & Çöltekin, A. (2020). Perspective switch and spatial knowledge acquisition: Effects of age, mental rotation ability and visuospatial memory capacity on route learning in virtual environments with different levels of realism. *Cartography and Geographic Information Science*, *47*(1), 14–27. doi:10.1080/15230406.2019.1595151

Lombardi, M. M. (2007a). *Approaches that work: How authentic learning is transforming higher education.* ELI Report No. 5. Boulder, CO: EDUCAUSE Learning Initiative.

Lombardi, M. M. (2007b). *Authentic learning for the 21st century: An overview.* ELI Report No. 1. Boulder, CO: EDUCAUSE Learning Initiative.

Looi, C. K. (1998). Interactive learning environments for promoting inquiry learning. *Journal of Educational Technology Systems*, *27*(1), 3–22. doi:10.2190/L4Q4-8QMM-QPJ3-B5LJ

Lord, F. M. (1980). *Applications of item response theory to practical testing problems*. L.E.A.

Lorenzo, G., Lledó, A., Arráez-Vera, G., & Lorenzo-Lledó, A. (2019). The application of immersive virtual reality for students with ASD: A review between 1990–2017. *Education and Information Technologies*, *24*(1), 127–151. doi:10.100710639-018-9766-7

Lorenzo, G., Pomares, J., & Lledó, A. (2013). Inclusion of immersive virtual learning environments and visual control systems to support the learning of students with Asperger syndrome. *Computers & Education*, *62*, 88–101. doi:10.1016/j.compedu.2012.10.028

Lotan, M., Yalon-Chamovitz, S., & Weiss, P. L. (2009). Improving physical fitness of individuals with intellectual and developmental disability through a virtual reality intervention program. *Research in Developmental Disabilities*, *30*(2), 229–239. doi:10.1016/j.ridd.2008.03.005 PMID:18479889

Lotan, M., Yalon-Chamovitz, S., & Weiss, P. L. (2010). Virtual reality as means to improve physical fitness of individuals at a severe level of intellectual and developmental disability. *Research in Developmental Disabilities*, *31*(4), 869–874. doi:10.1016/j.ridd.2010.01.010 PMID:20346616

Luft, J. A., Kurdziel, J. P., Roehrig, G. H., & Turner, J. (2004). Growing a garden without water: Graduate teaching assistants in introductory science laboratories at a doctoral/research university. *Journal of Research in Science Teaching*, *41*(3), 211–233. doi:10.1002/tea.20004

Lukosch, S., Billinghurst, M., Alem, L., & Kiyokawa, K. (2015). Collaboration in augmented reality. *Computer Supported Cooperative Work*, *24*(6), 515–525. doi:10.100710606-015-9239-0

Lv, Z., Feng, L., Li, H., & Feng, S. (2014). Hand-free motion interaction on google glass. In SIGGRAPH Asia 2014 Mobile Graphics and Interactive Applications (pp. 1-1). doi:10.1145/2669062.2669066

Lynch, T., & Ghergulescu, I. (2017). Review of virtual labs as the emerging technologies for teaching stem subjects. In *INTED2017 Proceedings of the 11th International Technology, Education and Development Conference* (pp. 6082-6091). 10.21125/inted.2017.1422

Ma, C. Y. (2018). Teaching application of computer virtual reality technology in international education of chinese language. *Kuram ve Uygulamada Egitim Bilimleri, 18*(6). Advance online publication. doi:10.12738/estp.2018.6.297

Macken, L., & Ginns, P. (2014). Pointing and tracing gestures may enhance anatomy and physiology learning. *Medical Teacher, 36*(7), 596–601. doi:10.3109/0142159X.2014.899684 PMID:24787529

Macpherson, K., Charlop, M. H., & Miltenberger, C. A. (2015). Using portable video modeling technology to increase the compliment behaviors of children with autism during athletic group play. *Journal of Autism and Developmental Disorders, 45*(12), 3836–3845. doi:10.100710803-014-2072-3 PMID:24573335

Magana, A. J., Serrano, M. I., & Rebello, N. S. (2019). A sequenced multimodal learning approach to support students' development of conceptual learning. *Journal of Computer Assisted Learning, 35*(4), 516–528. doi:10.1111/jcal.12356

Mahadzir, N. N. N., & Phung, L. F. (2013). The use of augmented reality pop-up book to increase motivation in English language learning for national primary school. *IOSR Journal of Research & Method in Education, 1*(1), 26–38. doi:10.9790/7388-0112638

Mahmoud, A. H. (2001). Can Virtual Reality Simulation Techniques Reshape the Future of Environmental Simulations. *Online Planning Journal.* http://www.casa.ucl.ac.uk/planning/articles4/vrsim.htm

Maier, H. W. (2002). Role playing: structures and educational objectives. *The International Child and Youth Care Network, 36.*

Ma, J. Y., & Choi, J. S. (2007). The Virtuality and Reality of Augmented Reality. *Journal of Multimedia, 2*(1), 32–37. doi:10.4304/jmm.2.1.32-37

Makransky, G., Terkildsen, T. S., & Mayer, R. E. (2019). Adding immersive virtual reality to a science lab simulation causes more presence but less learning. *Learning and Instruction, 60*, 225–236. doi:10.1016/j.learninstruc.2017.12.007

Malone, T. W. (1981). Toward a theory of intrinsically motivating instruction. *Cognitive Science, 5*(4), 333–369. doi:10.120715516709cog0504_2

Malone, T. W. (1982). Heuristics for designing enjoyable user interfaces: Lessons from computer games. *Proceedings of the 1982 Conference on Human Factors in Computing Systems*, 63–68. 10.1145/800049.801756

Manz, E. (2015). Representing student argumentation as functionally emergent from scientific activity. *Review of Educational Research, 85*(4), 553–590. doi:10.3102/0034654314558490

Maquilón, J. J., Mirete, A. B., & Avilés, M. (2017). Augmented Reality (AR). Resources and proposals for educational innovation. *Revista Electrónica Interuniversitaria de Formación del Profesorado, 20*(2), 183–203. doi:10.6018/reifop/20.2.290971

March, S. T., & Smith, G. F. (1995). Design and natural science research on information technology. *Decision Support Systems, 15*(4), 251–266. doi:10.1016/0167-9236(94)00041-2

Mark, K. P., Thadani, D. R., Calonge, D. S., Pun, C. F., & Chiu, P. P. (2011, October). In-service Teaching Assistant Training (InsTAT) for engineering and computer science graduate students in Hong Kong: A blended-learning approach. In 2011 Frontiers in Education Conference (FIE) (pp. F2E-1). IEEE.

Marques, M. M., & Pombo, L. (2020). Game-Based Mobile Learning with Augmented Reality: Are Teachers Ready to Adopt It? In M. Rehm, J. Saldien, & S. Manca (Eds.), *Project and Design Literacy as Cornerstones of Smart Education. Smart Innovation, Systems and Technologies* (Vol. 158, pp. 207–218). Springer., doi:10.1007/978-981-13-9652-6_19

Martínez, S., & Fernández, B. (2018, July). Objects of augmented reality: perceptions of pedagogy student. *Píxel-Bit. Revista de Medios y Educación*, (53), 207-220. doi:10.12795/pixelbit.2018.i53.14

Martínez, A., Martínez, J., & Navarro, F. (2018). *Virtual reality and augmented reality. Application development*. Ra-Ma.

Martínez-Graña, A., González-Delgado, J. Á., Ramos, C., & Gonzalo, J. C. (2018). Augmented Reality and Valorizing the Mesozoic Geological Heritage (Burgos, Spain). *Sustainability*, *10*(12), 1–16. doi:10.3390u10124616

Martín-Gutiérrez, J., Efrén Mora, C., Añorbe-Díaz, B., & González-Marrero, A. (2017). Virtual technologies trends in education. EURASIA J Math Sci and Tech, Ed, 13(2), 469-486.

Martín-Gutiérrez, J., Fabiani, P., Benesova, W., Meneses, M. D., & Mora, C. E. (2015). Augmented reality to promote collaborative and autonomous learning in higher education. *Computers in Human Behavior*, *51*, 752–761. doi:10.1016/j.chb.2014.11.093

Martín-Gutiérrez, J., Luís Saorín, J., Contero, M., Alcañiz, M., Pérez-López, D. C., & Ortega, M. (2010). Design and validation of an augmented book for spatial abilities development in engineering students. *Computers & Graphics*, *34*(1), 77–91. doi:10.1016/j.cag.2009.11.003

Martins, A., Fracchia, C. C., Allan, C., Parra, S., Baeza, N., Celeste, C., . . . Laurent, R. (2019). Development of computer tools and their applications in the educational field. In *XXI Workshop de Investigadores en Ciencias de la Computación* (WICC 2019). Universidad Nacional de San Juan.

Martirosov, S., & Kopecek, P. (2017). Virtual Reality and its Influence on Traning and Education - Literature Review. In *Proceedings of the 28th International DAAAM Symposium 2017*. Zadar: DAAAM International. doi: 10.2507/28th.daaam.proceedings.100

Masmuzidin, M. Z., & Aziz, N. A. A. (2018). The current trends of augmented reality in early childhood education. *The International Journal of Multimedia & Its Applications*, *10*(6), 47–58. doi:10.5121/ijma.2018.10605

Mast, S. M., Kleinlogel, E. P., Tur, B., & Bachmann, M. (2018). The future of interpersonal skills development: Immersive virtual reality training with virtual humans. *Human Resource Development Quarterly*, *29*(2), 125–141. doi:10.1002/hrdq.21307

Mata-López, W., & Tobón, S. (2019). Analysis of factors associated to the enrollment and demand of computing-related careers. *Social Sciences*, *8*(1), 1. doi:10.3390ocsci8010001

Matsutomo, S., Miyauchi, T., Noguchi, S., & Yamashita, H. (2012). Real-time visualization system of magnetic field utilizing augmented reality technology for education. *IEEE Transactions on Magnetics*, *48*(2), 531–534. doi:10.1109/TMAG.2011.2174208

Matuk, C. (2016). The learning affordances of augmented reality for museum exhibits on human health. *Museums & Social Issues*, *11*(1), 73–87. doi:10.1080/15596893.2016.1142815

Maturana, H. R. (1980). Biology of cognition. In H. R. Maturana & F. J. Varela (Eds.), *Autopoiesis and Cognition: The Realization of the Living* (pp. 5–58). Reidel Publishing. doi:10.1007/978-94-009-8947-4_1

Maturana, H. R., Mpodozis, J., & Letelier, J. C. (1995). Brain language and the origin of human mental functions. *Biological Research*, *28*, 15–26. www.informatik.umu.se/~rwhit/MatMpo&Let(1995).html PMID:8728817

Maturana, H. R., & Varela, F. J. (1987). *The tree of knowledge: The biological roots of human understanding*. New Science Library/Shambhala Publications.

Maturana, H., & Varela, F. (1980). *Autopoiesis and cognition: The realization of the living*. Reidel Publishing. doi:10.1007/978-94-009-8947-4

Mayer, R. E. (2014). Principles based on social cues in multimedia learning: Personalization, voice, image, and embodiment principles. In R. Mayer (Ed.), The Cambridge handbook of multimedia learning (16, pp. 345–370). Cambridge University Press.

Mayer, R. E. (2004). Should there be a three-strikes rule against pure discovery learning? *The American Psychologist, 59*(1), 14–19. doi:10.1037/0003-066X.59.1.14 PMID:14736316

Mayer, R. E. (2009). *Multimedia learning* (2nd ed.). Cambridge University Press. doi:10.1017/CBO9780511811678

Mayer, R. E. (2019). Searching for the role of emotions in e-learning. *Learning and Instruction*, •••, 101213. doi:10.1016/j.learninstruc.2019.05.010

Mayer, R. E., & Fiorella, L. (2014). 12 principles for reducing extraneous processing in multimedia learning: Coherence, signaling, redundancy, spatial contiguity, and temporal contiguity principles. In R. Mayer (Ed.), *The Cambridge handbook of multimedia learning* (p. 279). Cambridge University Press. doi:10.1017/CBO9781139547369.015

Mayer, R. E., & Moreno, R. (2003). Nine ways to reduce cognitive load in multimedia learning. *Journal of Educational Psychology, 38*(1), 43–52. doi:10.1207/S15326985EP3801_6

Mayes, J. T., & Fowler, C. J. (1999). Learning technology and usability: A framework for understanding courseware. *Interacting with Computers, 11*(5), 485–497. doi:10.1016/S0953-5438(98)00065-4

Mazuryk, T., & Gervautz, M. (n.d.). *Virtual reality - history, applications, technology and future*. http://citeseerx.ist.psu.edu/viewdoc/summary?doi=10.1.1.42.7849

McCartney, M. (2016). Margaret McCartney: game on for Pokémon GO. *BMJ: British Medical Journal (Online), 354*.

McKenzie, J., & Darnell, D. (2004). The eye Magic book. In *A report into augmented reality storytelling in the context of a children's workshop 2003*. New Zealand Centre for Children's Literature and Christchurch College of Education.

McMahon, D. D., Cihak, D. F., Wright, R. E., & Bell, S. M. (2016). Augmented reality for teaching science vocabulary to postsecondary education students with intellectual disabilities and autism. *Journal of Research on Technology in Education, 48*(1), 38–56. doi:10.1080/15391523.2015.1103149

McMahon, D., Cihak, D., & Wright, R. (2015). Augmented reality as a navigation tool to employment opportunities for postsecondary education students with intellectual disabilities and autism. *Journal of Research on Technology in Education, 47*(3), 157–172. doi:10.1080/15391523.2015.1047698

McVeigh-Schultz, J., Kolesnichenko, A., & Isbister, K. (2019). Shaping pro-social interaction in VR an emerging design framework. *Proceedings of the Conference on Human Factors in Computing Systems*, 1–12. 10.1145/3290605.3300794

Melby-Lervåg, M., & Lervåg, A. (2014). Reading comprehension and its underlying components in second-language learners: A meta-analysis of studies comparing first-and second-language learners. *Psychological Bulletin, 140*(2), 409–433. doi:10.1037/a0033890 PMID:23937316

Melero, J., Hernández-Leo, D., & Manatunga, K. (2015). Group-based mobile learning: Do group size and sharing mobile devices matter? *Computers in Human Behavior, 44*, 377–385. doi:10.1016/j.chb.2014.11.078

Mellet-d'Huart, D. (2004). *De l'intention à l'attention: contributions à une démarche de conception d'environnements virtuels pour apprendre à partir d'un modèle de l'(én)action* (Doctoral dissertation). Université du Maine, France.

Mellet-d'Huart, D. (2005). He/She-You-I formalism: a heuristic model of (en)action to make Decisions. *Modeling Natural Action Selection, Proceedings of an International Workshop Edinburgh.*

Mellet-d'Huart, D. (2006). A model of (en)action to approach embodiment: A cornerstone for the design of virtual environments for learning. *Virtual Reality (Waltham Cross)*, *10*(3-4), 253–269. doi:10.100710055-006-0038-2

Mellet-d'Huart, D. (2009). Virtual reality for training and lifelong learning - *Themes in Science and Technology Education, 2*(1).

Mendez, D., Mendez, M., & Anguita, J. (2018). Motivation of 14 Year-old Students using Tablets, compared to those using Textbooks and Workbooks. *International Journal of Interactive Mobile Technologies*, *12*(4), 86–96. doi:10.3991/ijim.v12i4.9203

Merchant, Z., Goetz, E. T., Cifuentes, L., Keeney-Kennicutt, W., & Davis, T. J. (2014). Effectiveness of virtual reality-based instruction on students' learning outcomes in K–12 and higher education: A meta-analysis. *Computers & Education*, *70*, 29–40. doi:10.1016/j.compedu.2013.07.033

Meritt, J., Gibson, D., Christensen, R., & Knezek, G. (2015). Teacher training using interactive technologies: Performance and assessment in second life and simschool. In *E-Learning systems, environments and approaches* (pp. 181–198). Springer. doi:10.1007/978-3-319-05825-2_13

Mesa-Gresa, P., Gil-Gómez, H., Lozano-Quilis, J.-A., & Gil-Gómez, J.-A. (2018). Effectiveness of virtual reality for children and adolescents with autism spectrum disorder: An evidence-based systematic review. *Sensors (Basel)*, *18*(8), 2486. doi:10.339018082486 PMID:30071588

Michel, M., & Smith, B. (2017). Eye-Tracking Research in Computer-Mediated Language Learning. In S. Thorne & S. May (Eds.), *Language, Education and Technology, Encyclopedia of Language and Education* (pp. 453–464). Springer International Publishing. doi:10.1007/978-3-319-02237-6_34

Miles, M. B., & Huberman, A. M. (1994). *Qualitative data analysis: An expanded sourcebook* (2nd ed.). SAGE Publications.

Milgram, P., Takemura, H., Utsumi, A., & Fumio, K. (1994). A class of displays on the reality-virtuality continuum. *SPIE Proceedings Volume 2351: Telemanipulator and Telepresence Technologies*, 282–292.

Milgram, P., & Kishino, F. (1994). A Taxonomy Of Mixed Reality Visual Displays. *IEICE Transactions on Information and Systems*, *77*(12), 1–15.

Milgram, P., & Kishino, F. (1994). A taxonomy of mixed reality visual displays. *IEICE Transactions on Information and Systems*, *77*(12), 1321–1329.

Miller, G. A. (1956). The magical number seven, plus or minus two: Some limits on our capacity for processing information. *Psychological Review*, *63*(2), 81–97. doi:10.1037/h0043158 PMID:13310704

Miller, H. L., & Bugnariu, N. L. (2016). Level of immersion in virtual environments impacts the ability to assess and teach social skills in autism spectrum disorder. *Cyberpsychology, Behavior, and Social Networking*, *19*(4), 246–256. doi:10.1089/cyber.2014.0682 PMID:26919157

Miller, M. R., Jun, H., Herrera, F., Villa, J. Y., Welch, G., & Bailenson, J. N. (2019). Social interaction in augmented reality. *PLoS One*, *14*(5), e0216290. doi:10.1371/journal.pone.0216290 PMID:31086381

Milli Eğitim Bakanlığı. (2018). *Matematik dersi öğretim programı*. Talim Terbiye Kurulu Başkanlığı.

Milli Eğitim Bakanlığı. (2019). *Ortaöğretim Kurumlarına İlişkin Merkezi Sınav Raporu*. T.C. Milli Eğitim Bakanlığı.

Mills, S., & Noyes, J. (1999). Virtual reality: An overview of user-related design issues revised paper for special issue on "Virtual reality: User Issues" in Interacting with Computers, May 1998. *Interacting with Computers*, *11*(4), 375–386. doi:10.1016/S0953-5438(98)00057-5

Mirliss, D. (2014). Preparing future teachers: Taking the Perspective of Diverse Learners through Virtual World Role-Play. *International Journal of Gaming and Computer-Mediated Simulations*, *6*(2), 15–29. doi:10.4018/ijgcms.2014040102

Mishra, P., & Koehler, M. J. (2006). Technological pedagogical content knowledge: A framework for teacher knowledge. *Teachers College Record*, *108*(6), 1017–1054. doi:10.1111/j.1467-9620.2006.00684.x

Mitchell, P., Parsons, S., & Leonard, A. (2007). Using virtual environments for teaching social understanding to 6 adolescents with autistic spectrum disorders. *Journal of Autism and Developmental Disorders*, *37*(3), 589–600. doi:10.100710803-006-0189-8 PMID:16900403

Mohamed, N., & Badioze, H. (2011). Scaffolding Poetry Lessons Using Desktop Virtual Reality. In Lecture Notes in Computer Science 7067. (pp. 231–241). doi:10.1007/978-3-642-25200-6_22

Mohsen, M. (2016). The use of help options in multimedia listening environments to aid language learning: A review. *British Journal of Educational Technology*, *47*(6), 1232–1242. doi:10.1111/bjet.12305

Molnar, G., & Szuts, Z. (2019). Augmented reality, games, art: Imersion and flow. In V. Geroimenko (Ed.), *Augmented reality games I: Understanding the Pokémon GO phenomenon*. Springer International Publishing., doi:10.1007/978-3-030-15616-9_5

Montes de Oca, N., & Machado, E. (2011). Teaching strategies and teaching-learning methods within Higher Education. *Humanidades Médicas*, *11*, 475–488.

Mørch, A. I., Hartley, M. D., & Caruso, V. (2015, July). Teaching interpersonal problem solving skills using roleplay in a 3D virtual world for special education: A case study in Second Life. In *2015 IEEE 15th International Conference on Advanced Learning Technologies* (pp. 464-468). IEEE.

Moreno, R. (2007). Optimising learning from animations by minimising cognitive load: Cognitive and affective consequences of signalling and segmentation methods. *Applied Cognitive Psychology: The Official Journal of the Society for Applied Research in Memory and Cognition*, *21*(6), 765–781. doi:10.1002/acp.1348

Mota, J. M., Ruiz-Rube, I., Dodero, J. M., & Arnedillo-Sánchez, I. (2018). Augmented reality mobile app development for all. *Computers & Electrical Engineering*, *65*, 250–260. doi:10.1016/j.compeleceng.2017.08.025

Mourtzis, D., Zogopoulos, V., & Vlachou, E. (2017). Augmented reality application to support remote maintenance as a service in the robotics industry. *Procedia CIRP*, *63*, 46–51. doi:10.1016/j.procir.2017.03.154

Muhanna, M. A. (2015). Virtual reality and the CAVE: Taxonomy, interaction challenges and research directions. *Journal of King Saud University-Computer and Information Sciences*, *27*(3), 344–361. doi:10.1016/j.jksuci.2014.03.023

Muir, T., Allen, J. M., Rayner, C. S., & Cleland, B. (2013). Preparing pre-service teachers for classroom practice in a virtual world: A pilot study using Second Life. *Journal of Interactive Media in Education*, *1*(3), 3. doi:10.5334/2013-03

Muis, K. R., Trevors, G., Duffy, M., Ranellucci, J., & Foy, M. J. (2016). Testing the TIDE: Examining the nature of students' epistemic beliefs using a multiple methods approach. *Journal of Experimental Education*, *84*(2), 264–288. doi:10.1080/00220973.2015.1048843

Mujber, T. S., Szecsi, T., & Hashmi, M. S. (2004). Virtual reality applications in manufacturing process simulation. *Journal of Materials Processing Technology*, *155*, 1834–1838. doi:10.1016/j.jmatprotec.2004.04.401

Müller-Plath, G. (2019). How does digital navigation on sailboats affect spatial abilities at sea? *TransNav. International Journal on Marine Navigation and Safety of Sea Transportation, 13*(2).

Mundy, M. A., Hernandez, J., & Green, M. (2019). Perceptions of the effects of augmented reality in the classroom. *Journal of Instructional Pedagogies*, 22.

Münzer, S., Zimmer, H. D., & Baus, J. (2012). Navigation assistance: A trade-off between wayfinding support and configural learning support. *Journal of Experimental Psychology. Applied, 18*(1), 18–37. doi:10.1037/a0026553 PMID:22141461

Murphy, P. K., Rowe, M. L., Ramani, G., & Silverman, R. (2014). Promoting critical-analytic thinking in children and adolescents at home and in school. *Educational Psychology Review, 26*(4), 561–578. doi:10.100710648-014-9281-3

Mutlu-Bayraktar, D., Cosgun, V., & Altan, T. (2019). Cognitive load in multimedia learning environments: A systematic review. *Computers & Education, 141*, 103618. doi:10.1016/j.compedu.2019.103618

Muwonge, C. M., Schiefele, U., Ssenyonga, J., & Kibedi, H. (2017). Self-regulated learning among teacher education students: Motivational beliefs influence on the use of metacognition. *Journal of Psychology in Africa, 27*(6), 515–521. doi:10.1080/14330237.2017.1399973

Mynbayeva, A., Sadvakassova, Z., & Akshalova, B. (2017). Pedagogy of the Twenty-First Century: Innovative Teaching Methods. In O. Bernad & N. Llevot (Eds.), *New Pedagogical Challenges in the 21st Century-Contributions of Research in Education*. IntechOpen. doi:10.5772/intechopen.72341

Naik, G., Chitre, C., Bhalla, M., & Rajan, J. (2020). Impact of use of technology on student learning outcomes: Evidence from a large-scale experiment in India. *World Development, 127*, 104736. doi:10.1016/j.worlddev.2019.104736

National Council of Teacher of Mathematics. (2008). *The role of technology in the teaching and learning of mathematics: A position of the National Council of Teachers of Mathematics*. Accessed at: http://www.nctm.org/uploadedFiles/About_NCTM/Position_Statements/Technology%20final.pdf

National Council Teacher of Mathematics. (2000). Principles and evaluation standards for school mathematics. Author.

NCTM. (2000). *Curriculum and Evaluation Standards for School Mathematics*. National Council of Teachers of Mathematics.

Neira-Piñeiro, M. R., Del Moral, M. E., & Fombella, I. (2020). Stimulating Multiple Intelligences in Infant Education from an Augmented Didactic Itinerary. In R. Zheng (Ed.), *Examining Multiple Intelligences and Digital Technologies for Enhanced Learning Opportunities* (pp. 124–140). IGI Global. doi:10.4018/978-1-7998-0249-5.ch007

Nestel, D., & Tierney, T. (2007). Role-play for medical students learning about communication: Guidelines for maximising benefits. *BMC Medical Education, 7*(1), 3. doi:10.1186/1472-6920-7-3 PMID:17335561

Newbutt, N., Sung, C., Kuo, H., & Leahy, M. J. (2016). The potential of virtual reality technologies to support people with an autism condition: A case study of acceptance, presence and negative effects. *Annual Review of Cybertherapy and Telemedicine, 14*, 149–154.

Nielsen, B. L., Brandt, H. & Swensen, H. (2016). Augmented Reality in science education–affordances for student learning. *Nordic Studies in Science Education, 12*(2), 157–174.

Nikopoulos, C. K., & Keenan, M. (2004). Effects of video modeling on social initiations by children with autism. *Journal of Applied Behavior Analysis, 37*(1), 93–96. doi:10.1901/jaba.2004.37-93 PMID:15154221

Nischelwitzer, A., Lenz, F. J., Searle, G., & Holzinger, A. (2007). Some aspects of the development of low-cost augmented reality learning environments as examples for future interfaces in technology enhanced learning. In *International Conference on Universal Access in Human-Computer Interaction* (pp. 728–737). Springer. 10.1007/978-3-540-73283-9_79

Núñez, R. E., Edwards, L. D., & Matos, J. F. (1999). Embodied cognition as grounding for Osborne, J. F., Henderson, J. B., MacPherson, A., Szu, E., Wild, A., & Yao, S. Y. (2016). The development and validation of a learning progression for argumentation in science. *Journal of Research in Science Teaching*, *53*(6), 821–846.

Nunez, R. E., & Lakoff, G. (2013). The metaphorical structure of mathematics: Sketching out cognitive foundations for a mind-based mathematics. In *Mathematical reasoning* (pp. 29–98). Routledge.

O'Connor, E. A. (2009). Instructional and design elements that support effective use of virtual worlds: What graduate student work reveals about Second Life. *Journal of Educational Technology Systems*, *38*(2), 213–234. doi:10.2190/ET.38.2.j

O'Shea, P., Dede, C., & Cherian, M. (2011). The results of formatively evaluating an augmented reality curriculum based on modified design principles. *International Journal of Gaming and Computer-Mediated Simulations*, *3*(2), 57–66. doi:10.4018/jgcms.2011040104

Oculus. (2020, April 10). *Oculus Quest homepage*. https://www.oculus.com/quest

Ogata, H., Li, M., Hou, B., Uosaki, N., El-Bishouty, M. M., & Yano, Y. (2011). SCROLL: Supporting to share and reuse ubiquitous learning log in the context of language learning. *Research & Practice in Technology Enhanced Learning*, *6*(2).

Ölçme & Başkanlığı. (2019). *2019 YKS Değerlendirme Raporu. 2019*. Academic Press.

Olmos-Raya, E., Ferreira-Cavalcanti, J., Contero, M., Castellanos-Baena, M. C., Chicci-Giglioli, I. A., & Alcañiz, M. (2018). Mobile virtual reality as an educational platform: A pilot study on the impact of immersion and positive emotion induction in the learning process. *Eurasia Journal of Mathematics, Science and Technology Education*, *14*(6), 2045–2057.

Ong, A. (2010). Contextualized interdisciplinary learning in mainstream schools using augmented reality-based technology: A dream or reality? *Educational Technology*, 23–27.

OpenSimulator. (2017). *OpenSim* (Version 0.9.0.0). Retrieved March 30, 2020 from http://opensimulator.org/

Osuagwu, O., Ihedigbo, C., & Ndigwe, C. (2015). Integrating Virtual Reality (VR) into traditional instructional design. *West African Journal of Industrial and Academic Research*, *15*(1), 68–77.

Ouellette, J. (2019). *Augmented reality changes how people interact and communicate, study finds*. Arstechnica. https://arstechnica.com/science/2019/05/augmented-reality-changes-how-people-interact-and-communicate-study-finds/

Ovtcharova, J., & Vieira, A. (1995). Virtual prototyping through feature processing. In *Virtual Prototyping* (pp. 78–90). Springer. doi:10.1007/978-0-387-34904-6_7

Özarslan, Y. (2013). Genişletilmiş Gerçeklik İle Zenginleştirilmiş Öğrenme Materyallerinin Öğrenen Başarısı Ve Memnuniyeti Üzerindeki Etkisi (Doktora Tezi). Eskişehir: Eskişehir Anadolu Üniversitesi.

Ozdemir, M., Sahin, Ç., Arcagok, S., & Demir, M. K. (2018). The effect of augmented reality applications in the learning process: A meta-analysis study. *Eurasian Journal of Educational Research*, *74*, 165–186. doi:10.14689/ejer.2018.74.9

Paivio, A. (1990). *Mental representations: A dual coding approach* (Vol. 9). Oxford University Press. doi:10.1093/acprof:oso/9780195066661.001.0001

Palmas, F., Labode, D., Plecher, D. A., & Klinker, G. (2019). Comparison of a gamified and non-gamified virtual reality training assembly task. *Proceedings of the 11th International Conference on Virtual Worlds and Games for Serious Applications (VS-Games)*, 1–8. 10.1109/VS-Games.2019.8864583

Panciroli, C., Macauda, A., & Corazza, L. (2018, July). Digital Cultural Heritage: From Educational Experience to the Artefact in Augmented Reality. In A. Luigini (Ed.), *Proceedings of the 1st International and Interdisciplinary Conference on Digital Environments for Education, Arts and Heritage*, (pp. 345-354). Cham: Springe.

Pangilinan, E., Lukas, S., & Mohan, V. (Eds.). (2019). *Creating augmented and virtual realities: Theory and practice for next-generation spatial computing*. O'Reilly Media, Inc.

Pantelidis, V. S. (1997). Virtual reality and engineering education. *Computer Applications in Engineering Education*, *5*(1), 3–12. doi:10.1002/(SICI)1099-0542(1997)5:1<3::AID-CAE1>3.0.CO;2-H

Papachristos, N. M., Vrellis, I., & Mikropoulos, T. A. (2017). A comparison between oculus rift and a low-cost smartphone VR headset: Immersive user experience and learning. In *Proceedings of the IEEE 17th International Conference on Advanced Learning Technologies, ICALT 2017* (pp. 477-481). 10.1109/ICALT.2017.145

Papagiannakis, G., Trahanias, P., Kenanidis, E., & Tsiridis, E. (2018). Psychomotor surgical training in virtual reality. In *The Adult Hip-Master Case Series and Techniques* (pp. 827–830). Springer. doi:10.1007/978-3-319-64177-5_41

Park, C. (2004). The graduate teaching assistant (GTA): Lessons from North American experience. *Teaching in Higher Education*, *9*(3), 349–361. doi:10.1080/1356251042000216660

Park, S., & Khoshnevisan, B. (2019). Literacy meets augmented reality (AR): The use of AR in literacy. In W. B. James & C. Cobanoglu (Eds.), *Proceedings of the Global Conference on Education and Research (GLOCER) Conference* (Vol. 3, pp. 93–99). ANAHEI Publishing, LLC. https://scholarcommons.usf.edu/cgi/viewcontent.cgi?article=1021&context=anaheipublishing

Parmar, D., Bertrand, J., Babu, S. V., Madathil, K., Zelaya, M., Wang, T., Wagner, J., Gramopadhye, A. K., & Frady, K. (2016). A comparative evaluation of viewing metaphors on psychophysical skills education in an interactive virtual environment. *Virtual Reality (Waltham Cross)*, *20*(3), 141–157. doi:10.100710055-016-0287-7

Parong, J., & Mayer, R. E. (2018). Learning science in immersive virtual reality. *Journal of Educational Psychology*, *110*(6), 785–797. doi:10.1037/edu0000241

Parsons, S., Leonard, A., & Mitchell, P. (2006). Virtual environments for social skills training: Comments from two adolescents with autistic spectrum disorder. *Computers & Education*, *47*(2), 186–206. doi:10.1016/j.compedu.2004.10.003

Parsons, S., Mitchell, P., & Leonard, A. (2004). The use and understanding of virtual environments by adolescents with autistic spectrum disorders. *Journal of Autism and Developmental Disorders*, *34*(4), 449–466. doi:10.1023/B:JADD.0000037421.98517.8d PMID:15449520

PBS Wisconsin Education. [PBSWisconsinEdu]. (2009, August 12). *What is the potential of augmented reality in education? Check out the video on Layar...* http://bit.ly/uEg5C [Tweet]. Twitter. https://twitter.com/PBSWisconsinEdu/status/3267430045

Peixoto, B., Pinto, D., Krassmann, A., Melo, M., Cabral, L., & Bessa, M. (2019). *Using virtual reality tools for teaching foreign languages. Advances in Intelligent Systems and Computing 932*. Springer International Publishing. doi:10.1007/978-3-030-16187-3_56

Pelger, S., & Nilsson, P. (2018). Observed learning outcomes of integrated communication training in science education: Skills and subject matter understanding. *International Journal of Science Education. Part B*, *8*(2), 135–149.

Pellas, N., Fotaris, P., Kazanidis, I., & Wells, D. (2019). Augmenting the learning experience in primary and secondary school education: A systematic review of recent trends in augmented reality game-based learning. *Virtual Reality (Waltham Cross)*, *23*(4), 329–346. doi:10.100710055-018-0347-2

Peng, W. (2008). The mediational role of identification in the relationship between experience mode and self-efficacy: Enactive role-play versus passive observation. *Cyberpsychology & Behavior*, *11*(6), 649–652. doi:10.1089/cpb.2007.0229 PMID:18954275

Pérez-López, D., & Contero, M. (2013). Delivering educational multimedia contents through an augmented reality application: A case study on its impact on knowledge acquisition and retention. *The Turkish Online Journal of Educational Technology*, *12*(4).

Pérez-López, D., & Contero, M. (2013). Delivering educational multimedia contents through an augmented reality application: A case study on its impact on knowledge acquisition and retention. *Turkish Online Journal of Educational Technology-TOJET*, *12*(4), 19–28.

Persico, D., & Pozzi, F. (2015). Informing learning design with learning analytics to improve teacher inquiry. *British Journal of Educational Technology*, *46*(2), 230–248. doi:10.1111/bjet.12207

Petko, D. (2012). Teachers' pedagogical beliefs and their use of digital media in classrooms: Sharpening the focus of the 'will, skill, tool' model and integrating teachers' constructivist orientations. *Computers & Education*, *58*(4), 1351–1359. doi:10.1016/j.compedu.2011.12.013

Phillips, R. (2001). Making history curious: Using initial stimulus material to promote enquiry, thinking and literacy. *Teaching History*, *105*, 19–24.

Pilton, S. (2014). The augmented classroom. *Modern English Teacher*, *23*(3), 17–19.

Pinto, D., Peixoto, B., Krassmann, A., Melo, M., Cabral, L., & Bessa, M. (2019). *Virtual reality in education: Learning a foreign language. Advances in Intelligent Systems and Computing* (Vol. 932). Springer International Publishing. doi:10.1007/978-3-030-16187-3_57

Plante, T. G., Cage, C., Clements, S., & Stover, A. (2006). Psychological benefits of exercise paired with virtual reality: Outdoor exercise energizes whereas indoor virtual exercise relaxes. *International Journal of Stress Management*, *13*(1), 108–117. doi:10.1037/1072-5245.13.1.108

Polikoff, M. S. (2015). How well aligned are textbooks to the common core standards in mathematics? *American Educational Research Journal*, *52*(6), 1185–1211. doi:10.3102/0002831215584435

Pomerantz, J. (2019). Teaching and learning with extended reality technology. *Information and technology transforming lives: connection, interaction, innovation*, 137-157. Retrieved from https://bib.irb.hr/datoteka/1033483.bobcatsss_proceedings4.pdf#page=137

Prendes, C. (2015). Augmented reality and education: Analysis of practical experiences. *Píxel-Bit. Revista de Medios y Educación*, *46*, 187–203.

Privitera, G. J., & Ahlgrim-Delzell, L. (2019). *Research Methods for Education*. Sage Edge.

Pugoy, R. A. D., Ramos, R. C., Figueroa, R. B., Rivera, M. H. C., Siritarungsri, B., Cheevakasemsook, A., Noimuenwai, P., & Kaewsarn, P. (2016). Augmented reality in nursing education: addressing the limitations of developing a learning material for nurses in the Philippines and Thailand. *Int J Open Distance e-Learning*. *2*(1), 11–24.

Quintana, C., Reiser, B. J., Davis, E. A., Krajcik, J., Fretz, E., Duncan, R. G., Kyza, E., Edelson, D., & Soloway, E. (2004). A scaffolding design framework for software to support science inquiry. *Journal of the Learning Sciences*, *13*(3), 337–386. doi:10.120715327809jls1303_4

Rabbi, I., & Ullah, S. (2013). A survey on augmented reality challenges and tracking. *Acta Graphica*, *24*(1-2), 29–46.

Radiantia, J., Majchrzak, T. A., Frommb, J., & Wohlgenanntc, I. (2020). A systematic review of immersive virtual reality applications for higher education: Design elements, lessons learned, and research agenda. *Computers & Education*, *147*(April), 103778. doi:10.1016/j.compedu.2019.103778

Radu, I. (2014). Augmented reality in education: A meta-review and cross-media analysis. *Personal and Ubiquitous Computing*, *18*(6), 1533–1543. doi:10.100700779-013-0747-y

Rahimi, M., & Zhang, L. J. (2018). Effects of task complexity and planning conditions on L2 argumentative writing production. *Discourse Processes*, *55*(8), 726–742. doi:10.1080/0163853X.2017.1336042

Rahn, A., & Kjaergaard, H. W. (2014). Augmented reality as a visualizing facilitator in nursing education. *Proceedings of the INTED*. 6560–8.

Ramasundaram, V., Grunwald, S., Mangeot, A., Comerford, N. B., & Bliss, C. (2005). Development of an environmental virtual field laboratory. *Computers & Education*, *45*(1), 21–34. doi:10.1016/j.compedu.2004.03.002

Rashtchi, M., & Khoshnevisan, B. (2008). Audio-taped dialogue journal: A technique to improve speaking skill of Iranian EFL learners. *Journal of English Language Pedagogy and Practice*, *1*(3), 164–176.

Ratan, R., & Ritterfeld, U. (2009). Classifying serious games. In U. Ritterfeld, M. Cody, & P. Vorderer (Eds.), *Serious games: Mechanisms and effects* (pp. 10–22). Routledge.

Rauschnabel, P. (2019). *Study: Augmented reality and privacy concerns*. Philipp Rauschnabel. http://www.philipprauschnabel.com/2019/02/research-on-augmented-reality-privacy/

Rauschnabel, P. A., He, J., & Ro, Y. K. (2018). Antecedents to the adoption of augmented reality smart glasses: A closer look at privacy risks. *Journal of Business Research*, *92*, 374–384. doi:10.1016/j.jbusres.2018.08.008

Rauschnabel, P. A., Rossmann, A., & tom Dieck, M. C. (2017). An adoption framework for mobile augmented reality games: The case of Pokémon Go. *Computers in Human Behavior*, *76*, 276–286. doi:10.1016/j.chb.2017.07.030

Reichelt, M., Kämmerer, F., Niegemann, H. M., & Zander, S. (2014). Talk to me personally: Personalization of language style in computer-based learning. *Computers in Human Behavior*, *35*, 199–210. doi:10.1016/j.chb.2014.03.005

Reinders, H., & Lakarnchua, O. (2014). Implementing mobile language learning with an augmented reality activity. *Modern English Teacher*, *23*(2), 42–46.

Reinhart, G., & Patron, C. (2003). Integrating augmented reality in the assembly domain-fundamentals, benefits and applications. *CIRP Annals*, *52*(1), 5–8. doi:10.1016/S0007-8506(07)60517-4

Richter, J., Scheiter, K., & Eitel, A. (2016). Signaling text-picture relations in multimedia learning: A comprehensive meta-analysis. *Educational Research Review*, *17*, 19–36. doi:10.1016/j.edurev.2015.12.003

Rideout, V., & Robb, M. B. (2019). *The Common Sense census: Media use by tweens and teens, 2019*. Common Sense Media.

Ritz, L. T., & Buss, A. R. (2016). A framework for aligning instructional design strategies with affordances of CAVE immersive virtual reality systems. *TechTrends*, *60*(6), 549–556. doi:10.100711528-016-0085-9

Riva, G., Mantovani, F., Capideville, C. S., Preziosa, A., Morganti, F., Villani, D., Gaggioli, A., Botella, C., & Alcañiz, M. (2007). Affective interactions using virtual reality: The link between presence and emotions. *Cyberpsychology & Behavior*, *10*(1), 45–56. doi:10.1089/cpb.2006.9993 PMID:17305448

Robinson, T. J., Fischer, L., Wiley, D., & Hilton, J. III. (2014). The impact of open textbooks on secondary science learning outcomes. *Educational Researcher*, *43*(7), 341–351. doi:10.3102/0013189X14550275

Roblyer, M. D., & Hughes, J. E. (2019). *Integrating educational technology into teaching: Transforming learning across disciplines* (8th ed.). Pearson.

Rochlen, L. R., Levine, R., & Tait, A. R. (2017). First-person point-of-view-augmented reality for central line insertion training: A usability and feasibility study. *Simulation in Healthcare*, *12*(1), 57–62. doi:10.1097/SIH.0000000000000185 PMID:27930431

Rogers, K., Röhlig, A., Weing, M., Gugenheimer, J., Könings, B., & Klepsch, M., … Weber, M. (2014). Piano: Faster piano learning with interactive projection. *Proceedings of the Ninth ACM International Conference on Interactive Tabletops and Surfaces*, 149–158.

Rogoff, B. (1998). *Cognition as a collaborative process. In* Handbook of Child Psychology (Vol. 2). John Wiley & Sons.

Rosenbaum, E., Klopfer, E., & Perry, J. (2007). On location learning: Authentic applied science with networked augmented realities. *Journal of Science Education and Technology*, *16*(1), 31–45. doi:10.100710956-006-9036-0

Rosenberg, L. B. (1993, September). Virtual fixtures: Perceptual tools for telerobotic manipulation. In *Proceedings of IEEE virtual reality annual international symposium* (pp. 76-82). IEEE. 10.1109/VRAIS.1993.380795

Royal Society and Joint Mathematical Council. (2001). *Teaching and Learning Geometry*. Royal Society/Joint Mathematical Council.

Roylance, W. (2017). *Augmented reality: A holistic approach to creativity*. Diplomatic Courier. https://www.diplomaticourier.com/posts/augmented-reality-holistic-approach-creativity

Roy, M., & Chi, M. T. H. (2005). The self-explanation principle in multimedia learning. In R. Mayer (Ed.), *The Cambridge handbook of multimedia learning* (pp. 271–286). doi:10.1017/CBO9780511816819.018

Rushin, J. W., De Saix, J., Lumsden, A., Streubel, D. P., Summers, G., & Bernson, C. (1997). Graduate Teaching Assistant Training: A Basis for Improvement of College Biology Teaching & Faculty Development? *The American Biology Teacher*, *59*(2), 86–90. doi:10.2307/4450255

Ryan, R. M., & Deci, E. (2000). Intrinsic and extrinsic motivations: Classic definitions and new directions. *Contemporary Educational Psychology*, *25*(1), 54–67. doi:10.1006/ceps.1999.1020 PMID:10620381

Ryan, R. M., & Deci, E. L. (2017). *Self-determination theory: Basic psychological needs in motivation, development, and wellness*. Guilford Publications. doi:10.1521/978.14625/28806

Sabiri, K. (2020). ICT in EFL Teaching and Learning: A Systematic Literature Review. *Contemporary Educational Technology*, *11*(2), 177–195. doi:10.30935/cet.665350

Sáez-López, J. M., Cózar-Gutiérrez, R., González-Calero, J. A., & Gómez-Carrasco, C. J. (2020). Augmented Reality in Higher Education: An Evaluation Program in Initial Teacher Training. *Education in Science*, *10*(2), 1–12. doi:10.3390/educsci10020026

Salmi, H., Kaasinen, A., & Kallunki, V. (2012). Toward an open learning environment via segmented reality (AR): Visualizing the invisible in science centres and schools for teacher education. *Social and Behavioral Sciences*, *45*, 284–295.

Salmi, H., Thuneberg, H., & Vainikainen, M. (2016). Making the invisible observable by augmented reality in informal science education context. *International Journal of Science Education. Part B*, *7*(3), 253–268.

Salomon, G. (2012). *Interaction of media, cognition, and learning: An exploration of how symbolic forms cultivate mental skills and affect knowledge acquisition*. Routledge. doi:10.4324/9780203052945

Sandoval, W. (2014). Conjecture mapping: An approach to systematic educational design research. *Journal of the Learning Sciences*, *23*(1), 18–36. doi:10.1080/10508406.2013.778204

Santos, B. S., Dias, P., Pimentel, A., Baggerman, J. W., Ferreira, C., Silva, S., & Madeira, J. (2009). Head-mounted display versus desktop for 3D navigation in virtual reality: A user study. *Multimedia Tools and Applications*, *41*(1), 161–181. doi:10.100711042-008-0223-2

Santos, M., Lübke, A., Taketomi, T., Yamamoto, G., Rodrigo, M., Sandor, C., & Kato, H. (2016). Augmented reality as multimedia: The case for situated vocabulary learning. *Research & Practice in Technology Enhanced Learning*, *11*(1), 1. doi:10.118641039-016-0028-2 PMID:30613237

Sathe, V., Gupta, P., Kaushik, K., Bhat, S., & Deshpande, S. (2017). Virtual reality websites (VR WEB). In *Proceedings of the 2017 International Conference of Electronics, Communication and Aerospace Technology (ICECA)* (Vol. 1, pp. 647-652). IEEE. 10.1109/ICECA.2017.8203619

Sayımer, İ., & Küçüksaraç, B. (2015). Yeni teknolojilerin üniversite eğitimine katkısı: İletişim fakültesi öğrencilerinin artırılmış gerçeklik uygulamalarına ilişkin görüşleri. *International Journal of Human Sciences*, *12*(2), 1536–1554. doi:10.14687/ijhs.v12i2.3488

Schild, J., Lerner, D., Misztal, S., & Luiz, T. (2018, May). EPICSAVE—Enhancing vocational training for paramedics with multi-user virtual reality. In *2018 IEEE 6th International Conference on Serious Games and Applications for Health (SeGAH)* (pp. 1-8). IEEE.

Schmalstieg, D., & Höllerer, T. (2016). *Augmented reality: Principles and practice*. Addison-Wesley Professional.

Schnotz, W., & Bannert, M. (2003). Construction and interference in learning from multiple representation. *Learning and Instruction*, *13*(2), 141–156. doi:10.1016/S0959-4752(02)00017-8

Schoepp, K. (2005). Barriers to technology integration in a technology-rich environment. *Learning and Teaching in Higher Education: Gulf Perspectives*, *2*(1), 1–24.

Scholkmann, F., Kleiser, S., Metz, A. J., Zimmermann, R., Pavia, J. M., Wolf, U., & Wolf, M. (2014). A review on continuous wave functional near-infrared spectroscopy and imaging instrumentation and methodology. *NeuroImage*, *85*, 6–27. doi:10.1016/j.neuroimage.2013.05.004 PMID:23684868

Schrawman, G., & Lehman, S. (2001). Situational interest; A review of the literature and directions for future research. *Educational Psychology Review*, *13*(1), 23–52. doi:10.1023/A:1009004801455

Schroeder, R. (2008). Defining Virtual Worlds and Virtual Environments. *Journal of Virtual Worlds Research*, *1*(1), 1–3. doi:10.4101/jvwr.v1i1.294

Schwienhorst, K. (2002). The State of VR: A Meta-Analysis of Virtual Reality Tools in Second Language Acquisition. *Computer Assisted Language Learning*, *15*(3), 221–239. doi:10.1076/call.15.3.221.8186

Scrivner, O., Madewell, J., Buckley, C., & Perez, N. (2016, December). Augmented reality digital technologies (ARDT) for foreign language teaching and learning. In 2016 future technologies conference (FTC) (pp. 395-398). IEEE.

Self, T., Scudder, R. R., Weheba, G., & Crumrine, D. (2007). A virtual approach to teaching safety skills to children with autism spectrum disorder. *Topics in Language Disorders*, *27*(3), 242–253. doi:10.1097/01.TLD.0000285358.33545.79

Sellen, A., & Harper, R. (2003). *The myth of the paperless office*. MIT Press.

Semin, G. R., & Smith, E. R. (2013). Socially situated cognition in perspective. *Social Cognition*, *31*(2), 125–146. doi:10.1521oco.2013.31.2.125

Seufert, T. (2003). Supporting coherence formation in learning from multiple representations. *Learning and Instruction*, *13*(2), 227–237. doi:10.1016/S0959-4752(02)00022-1

Shadiev, R., & Yang, M. (2020). Review of Studies on Technology-Enhanced Language Learning and Teaching. *Sustainability*, *12*(2), 524. Advance online publication. doi:10.3390u12020524

Shanahan, T., Fisher, D., & Frey, N. (2016). The challenge of challenging text. *On Developing Readers: Readings from Educational Leadership (EL Essentials)*, 100.

Shepard, L. A. (2005). Linking Formative Assessment to scaffolding. *Educational Leadership*, *63*(3), 66–70. http://learnline.cdu.edu.au/commonunits/documents/Scaffolding%20and%20formative%20assessment.pdf

Sherman, W. R., & Craig, A. B. (2018). *Understanding virtual reality: Interface, application, and design*. Morgan Kaufmann, Elsevier.

Shian, C. S., & Yunus, M. M. (2017). Audio clips in developing listening comprehension skills in Malaysian Primary ESL classrooms. *Proceedings of the ICECRS*, *1*(1). Advance online publication. doi:10.21070/picecrs.v1i1.511

Shih, Y. (2008). A Collaborative Virtual Environment for Situated Language Learning Using VEC3D. *Eductional Technology & Society*, *11*(1), 56–68. Retrieved from https://drive.google.com/file/d/1ymXnG_dDdRi6GKRyx9suT-vBXoAA4s8Ae/view

Shih, J. L., Chuang, C. W., & Hwang, G. J. (2010). An inquiry-based mobile learning approach to enhancing social science learning effectiveness. *Journal of Educational Technology & Society*, *13*(4), 50–62.

Shulman, L. S. (1986). Those who understand: Knowledge growth in teaching. *Educational Researcher*, *15*(2), 4–14. doi:10.3102/0013189X015002004

Shute, V. J. (2008). Focus on formative feedback. *Review of Educational Research*, *78*(1), 153–189. doi:10.3102/0034654307313795

Siltanen, S. (2012). Theory and applications of marker-based augmented reality. *VTT Science, 3*. Retrieved from http://www.vtt.fi/inf/pdf/science/2012/S3.pdf

Silva, M., Roberto, R., & Teichrieb, V. (2013). Evaluating an educational system based on projective augmented reality. In *Brazilian Symposium on Computers in Education* (Vol. 24, No. 1, p. 214). 10.5753/CBIE.SBIE.2013.214

Silver, M., & Oakes, P. (2001). Evaluation of a new computer intervention to teach people with autism or Asperger syndrome to recognize and predict emotions in others. *Autism*, *5*(3), 299–316. doi:10.1177/1362361301005003007 PMID:11708589

Sin, A. K., & Zaman, H. B. (2010). Live Solar System (LSS): Evaluation of an Augmented Reality book-based educational tool. In *International Symposium in Information Technology* (Vol. 1, pp. 1–6). IEEE. 10.1109/ITSIM.2010.5561320

Singh, N., & Singh, S. (2017). Virtual reality: A brief survey. In *2017 International Conference on Information Communication and Embedded Systems, ICICES 2017*. Chennai: IEEE Xplore. doi:10.1109/ICICES.2017.8070720

Singhal, S., Bagga, S., Goyal, P., & Saxena, V. (2012). Augmented chemistry: Interactive education system. *International Journal of Computers and Applications*, *49*(15), 1–5. doi:10.5120/7700-1041

Singh, G. (2017). Using virtual reality for scaffolding computer programming learning. In *Proceedings of the 23rd ACM Symposium on Virtual Reality Software and Technology - VRST '17*. New York: ACM Press. 10.1145/3139131.3141225

Slater, M. (2017). Implicit learning through embodiment in immersive virtual reality. In D. Liu, C. Dede, R. Huang, & J. Richards (Eds.), *Virtual, Augmented, and Mixed Realities in Education* (pp. 19–33). Springer. doi:10.1007/978-981-10-5490-7_2

Smeets, D. J. H., & Bus, A. G. (2012). Interactive electronic storybooks for kindergartners to promote vocabulary growth. *Journal of Experimental Child Psychology, 112*(1), 36–55. doi:10.1016/j.jecp.2011.12.003 PMID:22265347

Smith, M. J., Fleming, M. F., Wright, M. A., Losh, M., Humm, L. B., Olsen, D., & Bell, M. D. (2015). Brief report: Vocational outcomes for young adults with autism spectrum disorders at six months after virtual reality job interview training. *Journal of Autism and Developmental Disorders, 45*(10), 3364–3369. doi:10.100710803-015-2470-1 PMID:25986176

Smith, M. J., Ginger, E. J., Wright, K., Wright, M. A., Taylor, J. L., Humm, L. B., Olsen, D. E., Bell, M. D., & Fleming, M. F. (2014). Virtual reality job interview training in adults with autism spectrum disorder. *Journal of Autism and Developmental Disorders, 44*(10), 2450–2463. doi:10.100710803-014-2113-y PMID:24803366

Söbke, H. (2019). A case study of deep gamification in higher engineering education. In M. Gentile, M. Allegra, & H. Söbke (Hrsg.), *Proceedings of the Games and Learning Alliance, 7th International Conference*. 10.1007/978-3-030-11548-7_35

Söbke, H., Baalsrud Hauge, J., Stefan, I. A., & Stefan, A. (2019). Using a location-based AR game in environmental engineering. In E. van der Spek, S. Göbel, E. Y.-L. Do, E. Clua, & J. Baalsrud Hauge (Eds.), *Entertainment Computing and Serious Games: Joint International Conference on Entertainment Computing and Serious Games* (pp. 7–10). 10.1007/978-3-030-34644-7_47

Söbke, H., Baalsrud Hauge, J., & Stefan, I. A. (2017). Prime example ingress: Reframing the pervasive game design framework (PGDF). *International Journal of Serious Games, 4*(2), 39–58. doi:10.17083/ijsg.v4i2.182

Söbke, H., Zander, S., & Londong, J. (2018). Augmented Reality als Lernmedium: Potenziale und Implikationen. *Innteract, 3*. Advance online publication. doi:10.14464/awic.v3i0.282

Solak, E., & Cakir, R. (2015). Exploring the effect of materials designed with augmented reality on language learners' vocabulary learning. *The Journal of Educators Online, 13*(2), 50–72. doi:10.9743/JEO.2015.2.5

Soloway, E., Guzdial, M., & Hay, K. E. (1994). Learner-centered design: The challenge for HCI in the 21st century. *Interaction, 1*(2), 36–48. doi:10.1145/174809.174813

Soloway, E., & Wallace, R. (1997). Does the internet support student inquiry? *Don't ask. Communications of the ACM, 40*(5), 11–16. doi:10.1145/253769.253771

Somasundaran, S., Riordan, B., Gyawali, B., & Yoon, S. Y. (2016). Evaluating Argumentative and Narrative Essays using Graphs. In *Proceedings of COLING 2016, the 26th International Conference on Computational Linguistics: Technical Papers* (pp. 1568-1578). Academic Press.

Sommerauer, P., & Müller, O. (2014). Augmented reality in informal learning environments: A field experiment in a mathematics exhibition. *Computers & Education, 79*, 59–68. doi:10.1016/j.compedu.2014.07.013

Sommerauer, P., & Müller, O. (2018). Augmented reality for teaching and learning: A literature review on theoretical and empirical foundations. *26th European Conference on Information Systems: Beyond Digitization: Facets of Socio-Technical Change.*

Somyürek, S. (2014). Öğretim sürecinde Z kuşağının dikkatini çekme: Artırılmış gerçeklik. *Eğitim Teknolojisi Kuram ve Uygulama, 4*(1), 63–80.

Song, Y., & Looi, C. K. (2012). Linking teacher beliefs, practices and student inquiry-based learning in a CSCL environment: A tale of two teachers. *International Journal of Computer-Supported Collaborative Learning*, *7*(1), 129–159. doi:10.100711412-011-9133-9

Song, Y., & Wen, Y. (2018). Integrating various apps on BYOD (Bring Your Own Device) into seamless inquiry-based learning to enhance primary students' science learning. *Journal of Science Education and Technology*, *27*(2), 165–176. doi:10.100710956-017-9715-z

Sorden, S. D. (2012). The cognitive theory of multimedia learning. Handbook of Educational Theories, 1, 31.

Specht, M., Ternier, S., & Greller, W. (2011). Mobile augmented reality for learning: A case study. *Journal of the Research Center for Educational Technology*, *7*(1). www.rcetj.org/index.php/rcetj/article/view/151

Spence, K. K., & McDonald, M. A. (2015). Assessing vertical development in experiential learning curriculum. *Journal of Experiential Education*, *38*(3), 296–312. doi:10.1177/1053825915571749

Splitter, L. J. (1991). Critical thinking: What, why, when and how. *Educational Philosophy and Theory*, *23*(1), 89–109. doi:10.1111/j.1469-5812.1991.tb00178.x

Squire, K. D., & Jan, M. (2007). Mad City Mystery: Developing scientific argumentation skills with a place-based augmented reality game on handheld computers. *Journal of Science Education and Technology*, *16*(1), 5–29. doi:10.100710956-006-9037-z

Squire, K., & Klopfer, E. (2007). Augmented reality simulations on handheld computers. *Journal of the Learning Sciences*, *16*(3), 371–413. doi:10.1080/10508400701413435

Stepan, K., Zeiger, J., Hanchuk, S., Del Signore, A., Shrivastava, R., Govindaraj, S., & Iloreta, A. (2017). Immersive virtual reality as a teaching tool for neuroanatomy. *International Forum of Allergy & Rhinology*, *7*(10), 1006–1013. doi:10.1002/alr.21986 PMID:28719062

Steuer, J. (1992). Defining Virtual Reality: Characteristics Determining Telepresence. *Journal of Communication*, *42*(4), 73–94. doi:10.1111/j.1460-2466.1992.tb00812.x

Stewart, J., Gapenne, O., & Di Paolo, E. (Eds.). (2011). *Enaction: Towards a new paradigm for cognitive science*. MIT Press.

Stichter, J. P., Laffey, J., Galyen, K., & Herzog, M. (2013). iSocial: Delivering the social competence intervention for adolescents (SCI-A) in a 3D virtual learning environment for youth with high functioning autism. *Journal of Autism and Developmental Disorders*, *44*(2), 417–430. doi:10.100710803-013-1881-0 PMID:23812663

Strickland, D. C., McAllister, D., Coles, C. D., & Osborne, S. (2007). An evolution of virtual reality training designs for children with autism and fetal alcohol spectrum disorders. *Topics in Language Disorders*, *27*(3), 226–241. doi:10.1097/01.TLD.0000285357.95426.72 PMID:20072702

Suits, B. (2005). *The Grasshopper: Games, life and utopia*. Broadview Press Ltd.

Sutherland, I. E. (1968, December). A head-mounted three-dimensional display. In *Proceedings of the December 9-11, 1968, Fall Joint Computer Conference, Part I* (pp. 757-764). Academic Press.

Sweller, J., Ayres, P., & Kalyuga, S. (2011). *Cognitive load theory*. doi:10.1007/978-1-4419-8126-4

Sweller, J., Ayres, P. L., Kalyuga, S., & Chandler, P. (2003). The expertise reversal effect. *Educational Psychologist*, 23–31. doi:10.1207/S15326985EP3801_4

Sylaiou, S., Mania, K., Karoulis, A., & White, M. (2010). Exploring the relationship between presence and enjoyment in a virtual museum. *International Journal of Human-Computer Studies*, *68*(5), 243–253. doi:10.1016/j.ijhcs.2009.11.002

Tabachnick, B. G., & Fidell, L. S. (2013). *Using Multivariate Statistics* (6th ed.). Allyn and Bacon.

Taçgın, Z. (2017). *Ameliyathanede kullanılan cerrahi setlerin öğretimine yönelik bir sanal gerçeklik simülasyonunun geliştirilmesi ve değerlendirilmesi* [Development and evaluation of a virtual reality simulation to teach surgical sets used in the operating room] (473100) [Thesis of Doctoral, Marmara University, İstanbul]. http://dspace.marmara.edu.tr/handle/11424/39092

Tacgin, Z. (2018). Proposing an Instructional Design Model With Designing and Developing Sensory Immersive VRLE to Teach Concepts And Procedures. In Academic Studies in Educational Science. Montenegro: IVPE.

Tacgin, Z. (2019). From storyboard to practice: My virtual operating room. *Fusion Journal,* (16), 36-49. https://search.informit.com.au/fullText;dn=032943111810950;res=IELLCC

Taçgın, Z. (2020). The perceived effectiveness regarding Immersive Virtual Reality learning environments changes by the prior knowledge of learners. *Education and Information Technologies*, •••, 1–19.

Taçgın, Z. (2020a). The perceived effectiveness regarding Immersive Virtual Reality learning environments changes by the prior knowledge of learners. *Education and Information Technologies*, 1–19. doi:10.100710639-019-10088-0

Tacgin, Z. (2020b). *Virtual and Augmented Reality: An Educational Handbook.* Cambridge Scholar Press.

Taçgın, Z., Uluçay, N., & Özüağ, E. (2016). Designing and Developing an Augmented Reality Application: A Sample Of Chemistry Education. *Journal of Turkish Chemical Society: Chemical Education*, *1*(1), 147–164. https://www.cambridgescholars.com/virtual-and-augmented-reality

Takac, M., Collett, J., Blom, K. J., Conduit, R., Rehm, I., & De Foe, A. (2019). Public speaking anxiety decreases within repeated virtual reality training sessions. *PLoS One*, *14*(5), e0216288. doi:10.1371/journal.pone.0216288 PMID:31150399

Talheimer, W. (2004). *Bells, whistles, neon, and purple prose; When interesting words, sounds and visuals hurt learning and performance- A review of the seductive-augmentation research.* Work-Learning Research.

Tan, T. H., & Liu, T. Y. (2004). The mobile-based interactive learning environment (MOBILE) and a case study for assisting elementary school English learning. In *Proceedings of* the 2004 IEEE International Conference on Advanced Learning Technologies (pp. 530-534). IEEE.

Tan, J., & Gopinathan, S. (2000). Education reform in Singapore: Towards greater creativity and innovation? *National Institute for Research Advancement (NIRA). RE:view*, *7*(3), 5–10.

Tan, K. (2001). Assessment for learning in Singapore: Unpacking its meanings and identifying some areas for improvement. *Educational Research for Policy and Practice*, *10*(2), 91–103. doi:10.100710671-010-9096-z

Tarng, W., & Ou, K. L. (2012). A study of campus butterfly ecology learning system based on augmented reality and mobile learning. In *Proceedings of IEEE International Conference on Wireless, Mobile and Ubiquitous Technology in Education* (pp. 62–66). 10.1109/WMUTE.2012.17

Tatli, Z., & Ayas, A. (2011). Development process of virtual chemistry laboratory. In *International computer & instructional technologies symposium.* Fırat University.

Taylor, T. (2015, January 29). *Behind the NFL's yellow 1st down line, and what's next for sports TV.* Sports Illustrated. https://www.si.com/edge/2015/01/29/behind-nfl-yellow-first-down-line-sportsvision-technology

Taylor-Hamilton, C. (2004). Giving directions as a speech behavior: A cross-cultural comparison of L1 and L2 strategies. In D. Boxer & A. Cohen (Eds.), *Studying speaking to inform Second Language Learning*. Multilingual Matters Ltd.

Taylor, K. S., Lawrence, J. F., Connor, C. M., & Snow, C. E. (2019). Cognitive and linguistic features of adolescent argumentative writing: Do connectives signal more complex reasoning? *Reading and Writing*, *32*(4), 983–1007. doi:10.100711145-018-9898-6

Tecnológico de Monterrey. (2017). *Edu trends. Augmented Reality and Virtual Reality*, Monterrey: Tecnológico de Monterrey. Retrieved from https://observatorio.tec.mx/edu-trends-realidad-virtual-y-realidad-aumentada

Tekedere, H., & Göker, H. (2016). Examining the effectiveness of augmented reality applications in education: A meta-analysis. *International Journal of Environmental and Science Education*, *11*(16), 9469–9481.

Teranishi, S., & Yamagishi, Y. (2018). Educational effects of a virtual reality simulation system for constructing self-built PCs. *Journal of Educational Multimedia and Hypermedia*, *27*(3), 411–423.

Tetreault, A. S., & Lerman, D. C. (2010). Teaching social skills to children with autism using point-of-view video modeling. *Education & Treatment of Children*, *33*(3), 395–419. doi:10.1353/etc.0.0105

The Tech Expo. [TheTechExpo]. (2011, April 30). *The rise of augmented reality in #education* http://ow.ly/4Keq8 #AR *#augmentedreality*[Tweet]. Twitter. https://twitter.com/TheTechExpo/status/64262215791943680

Thornton, T., Ernst, J. V., & Clark, A. C. (2012). Augmented Reality as a Visual and Spatial Learning Tool in Technology Education. *Technology and Engineering Teacher*, *71*(8), 18–21.

Tixier, M., Lenay, C., Gapenne, O., & Aubert, D. (2013, February). From perceptual supplementation to the accessibility of digital spaces: The case of free exploration of city maps for blind persons. *IRBM*, *34*(1), 64–68. doi:10.1016/j.irbm.2012.12.005

Tondeur, J., Aesaert, K., Pynoo, B., van Braak, J., Fraeyman, N., & Erstad, O. (2017). Developing a validated instrument to measure preservice teachers' ICT competencies: Meeting the demands of the 21st century. *British Journal of Educational Technology*, *48*(2), 462–472. doi:10.1111/bjet.12380

Topper Website. (n.d.). Retrieved from https://www.toppr.com/guides/maths/basic-geometrical-ideas/basic-geometrical-shapes/

Toptaş, V. (2008). Geometri öğretiminde sınıfta yapılan etkinlikler ile öğretme-öğrenme sürecinin incelenmesi. *İlköğretim Online, 7*(1), 91-11.

Torrance, M., Van Waes, L., & Galbraith, D. (Eds.). (2007). *Writing and Cognition*. BRILL. doi:10.1163/9781849508223

Townsend, D. (2015). Who's using the language? Supporting middle school students with content area academic language. *Journal of Adolescent & Adult Literacy*, *58*(5), 376–387. doi:10.1002/jaal.374

Trushell, J., Maitland, A., & Burrell, C. (2003). Pupils' recall of an interactive storybook on CD-ROM. *Journal of Computer Assisted Learning*, *19*(1), 80–89. doi:10.1046/j.0266-4909.2002.00008.x

Tscholl, M., & Lindgren, R. (2014). Empowering digital interactions with real world conversation. *TechTrends*, *58*(1), 56–63. doi:10.100711528-013-0721-6

Turan, Z., Meral, E., & Sahin, I. F. (2018). The impact of mobile augmented reality in geography education: Achievements, cognitive loads and views of university students. *Journal of Geography in Higher Education*, *42*(3), 427–441. doi:10.1080/03098265.2018.1455174

Tzima, S., Styliaras, G., & Bassounas, A. (2019). Augmented reality applications in education: Teachers point of view. *Education in Science*, *9*(2), 99. doi:10.3390/educsci9020099

Unity Technologies. (2019). *PlayerPrefs*. Retrieved from https://docs.unity3d.com/ScriptReference/PlayerPrefs.html

Unreal Engine. (2020, April 10). *Pixel Streaming*. https://docs.unrealengine.com/en-US/Platforms/PixelStreaming/index.html

Uysal, M. P. (2016). Evaluation of learning environments for object-oriented programming: Measuring cognitive load with a novel measurement technique. *Interactive Learning Environments*, *24*(7), 1590–1609. doi:10.1080/10494820.2015.1041400

Vafa, S., Sappington, K., & Coombs-Richardson, R. (2018). Using augmented reality to increase interaction in online courses. *International Journal of Educational Technology and Learning*, *3*(2), 65–68. doi:10.20448/2003.32.65.68

Vainikainen, M.-P., Salmi, H., & Thuneberg, H. (2015). Situational interest and learning in a Science Centre Mathematics Exhibition. *Journal of Science Communication*, *14*(4), 1–19.

Vaismoradi, M., Turunen, H., & Bondas, T. (2013). Content analysis and thematic analysis: Implications for conducting a qualitative descriptive study. *Nursing & Health Sciences*, *15*(3), 398–405. doi:10.1111/nhs.12048 PMID:23480423

van Wyk, E., & De Villiers, M. R. (2014). Applying design-based research for developing virtual reality training in the South African mining industry. In *Proceedings of the Southern African Institute for Computer Scientist and Information Technologists Annual Conference 2014 on SAICSIT 2014 Empowered by Technology* (pp. 70-81). 10.1145/2664591.2664627

Varela, F. J. (1994). Autopoiesis and a biology of intentionality. In Autopoiesis and Perception. School of Electronic Engineering.

Varela, F. J., Thompson, E., & Rosch, E. (1991). *The embodied mind: Cognitive science and human experience*. MIT Press. doi:10.7551/mitpress/6730.001.0001

Venable, J. (2006.) The role of theory and theorising in design science research. In *Proceedings of the 1st International Conference on Design Science in Information Systems and Technology (DESRIST 2006)* (pp. 1-18). Academic Press.

Vergara, D., Rubio, M., & Lorenzo, M. (2017). On the design of virtual reality learning environments in engineering. *Multimodal Technologies and Interaction*, *1*(2), 11. doi:10.3390/mti1020011

Villagrasa, S., Fonseca, D., & Durán, J. (2014). Teaching case: Applying gamification techniques and virtual reality for learning building engineering 3D arts. *Proceedings of the Second International Conference on Technological Ecosystems for Enhancing Multiculturality*, 171–177. 10.1145/2669711.2669896

Villalustre, L., & Del Moral, M. (2018). Geolocation and Augmented Reality for Ubiquitous Learning in Initial Teacher Education. @tic. *Revista d'innovació educativa*, (21), 40-48.

Villalustre, L., Del Moral, M.E., & Neira, M.R. (2019). Percepción docente sobre la Realidad Aumentada en la Enseñanza de Ciencias en Primaria. Análisis DAFO [Teachers' perception about Augmented Reality in Science Teaching in Primary Education]. *Revista Eureka sobre Enseñanza y Divulgación de las Ciencias, 16*(3), 3301. Doi:10.25267/Rev_Eureka_ensen_divulg_cienc.2019.v16.i3.3301

Villalustre, L., & Del Moral, M. E. (2016). Itinerarios interactivos con geolocalización y realidad aumentada para un aprendizaje ubicuo en la formación inicial de docentes de educación infantil [Interactive itineraries with geolocation and augmented reality for ubiquitous learning in the initial training of early childhood teachers]. In *L. Villalustre & M.E. Del Moral (Coords.), Experiencias interactivas con realidad aumentada en las aulas* [Interactive experiences with augmented reality in the classroom] (pp. 81–100). Octaedro.

Villalustre, L., San Pedro, B., & López, I. (2020). Geolocation for the Improvement of Spatial and Naturalist Intelligence in Primary Education. In R. Zheng (Ed.), *Examining Multiple Intelligences and Digital Technologies for Enhanced Learning Opportunities* (pp. 141–160). IGI Global. doi:10.4018/978-1-7998-0249-5.ch008

Vincenzi, D. A., Valimont, B., Macchiarella, N., Opalenik, C., Gangadharan, S. N., & Majoros, A. E. (2003). The effectiveness of cognitive elaboration using augmented reality as a training and learning paradigm. *Proceedings of the Human Factors and Ergonomics Society Annual Meeting*, *47*(19), 2054–2058. doi:10.1177/154193120304701909

Visbal-Cadavid, D., Mendoza-Mendoza, A., & Díaz, S. (2017). Learning strategies in higher education. *Sophia*, *13*(2), 70–81. http://www.redalyc.org/pdf/4137/413751844008.pdf

Vitorio, R., Stuart, S., Rochester, L., Alcock, L., & Pantall, A. (2017). fnirs response during walking—Artefact or cortical activity? A systematic review. *Neuroscience and Biobehavioral Reviews*, *83*, 160–172. doi:10.1016/j.neubiorev.2017.10.002 PMID:29017917

Volkoff, O., & Strong, D. M. (2013). Critical realism and affordances: Theorizing IT-associated organizational change processes. *Management Information Systems Quarterly*, *37*(3), 819–834. doi:10.25300/MISQ/2013/37.3.07

vom Brocke, J., Winter, R., Hevner, A., & Maedche, A. (2019). Accumulation and evolution of design knowledge in design science research–A journey through time and space. *Journal of the Association for Information Systems*.

Vo, T., Ledbetter, C., & Zuckerman, M. (2019). Video delivery of toxicology educational content versus textbook for asynchronous learning, using acetaminophen overdose as a topic. *Clinical Toxicology*, *57*(10), 842–846. doi:10.1080/15563650.2019.1574974 PMID:30806092

Vygotsky, L. (1978). Interaction between learning and development. *Readings on the Development of Children*, *23*(3), 34–41.

Wade, J., Zhang, L., Bian, D., Fan, J., Swanson, A., Weitlauf, A., Sarkar, M., Warren, Z., & Sarkar, N. (2016). A gaze-contingent adaptive virtual reality driving environment for intervention in individuals with autism spectrum disorders. *ACM Transactions on Interactive Intelligent Systems*, *6*(1), 1–23. doi:10.1145/2892636

Walker, Z., Vasquez, E., & Wienke, W. (2016). The impact of simulated interviews for individuals with intellectual disability. *Journal of Educational Technology & Society*, *19*(1), 76–88.

Wallace, S., Parsons, S., & Bailey, A. (2017). Self-reported sense of presence and responses to social stimuli by adolescents with autism spectrum disorder in a collaborative virtual reality environment. *Journal of Intellectual & Developmental Disability*, *42*(2), 131–141. doi:10.3109/13668250.2016.1234032

Wallace, S., Parsons, S., Westbury, A., White, K., White, K., & Bailey, A. (2010). Sense of presence and atypical social judgments in immersive virtual environments: Responses of adolescents with Autism Spectrum Disorders. *Autism*, *14*(3), 199–213. doi:10.1177/1362361310363283 PMID:20484000

Wang, L., & Zheng, C. (2018). A systematic literature review of virtual reality in adult foreign language education. In *Workshop Proceedings of the 26th International Conference on Computers in Education, ICCE 2018* (pp. 73–79). Metro Manila: Philippines: Asia-Pacific Society for Computers in Education.

Wang, S., & Cheng, Y. (2011). Designing a Situational 3D Virtual Learning Environment to Bridge Business Theory and Practice - The Role of Scaffolding. In R. Zhang, J. Cordeiro, X. Li, Z. Zhang, & J. Zhang (Eds.), *Proceedings of the 13th International Conference on Enterprise Information Systems* (pp. 313–315). Beijing, China: SciTePress - Science and and Technology Publications.

Wang, C., Lan, Y.-J., Tseng, W.-T., Lin, Y.-T., & Gupta, K. (2019). On the effects of 3D virtual worlds in language learning – a meta-analysis. *Computer Assisted Language Learning*, 1–25. Advance online publication. doi:10.1080/09588221.2019.1598444

Wang, F., & Hannafin, M. J. (2005). Design-based research and technology-enhanced learning environments. *Educational Technology Research and Development*, *53*(4), 5–23. doi:10.1007/BF02504682

Wang, M., Callaghan, V., Bernhardt, J., White, K., & Peña-Rios, A. (2018). Augmented reality in education and training: Pedagogical approaches and illustrative case studies. *Journal of Ambient Intelligence and Humanized Computing*, *9*(5), 1391–1402. doi:10.100712652-017-0547-8

Wang, X., Kim, M. J., Love, P. E. D., & Kang, S. C. (2013). Augmented Reality in built environment: Classification and implications for future research. *Automation in Construction*, *32*, 1–13. doi:10.1016/j.autcon.2012.11.021

Wang, X., Ong, S., & Nee, A. (2016). A comprehensive survey of augmented reality assembly research. *Advances in Manufacturing*, *4*(1), 1–22. doi:10.100740436-015-0131-4

Wang, Y. H. (2017). Exploring the effectiveness of integrating augmented reality-based materials to support writing activities. *Computers & Education*, *113*, 162–176. doi:10.1016/j.compedu.2017.04.013

Wang, Y., Anne, A., & Ropp, T. (2016). Applying the technology acceptance model to understand aviation students' perceptions toward augmented reality maintenance training instruction. *International Journal of Aviation, Aeronautics, and Aerospace*, *3*(4), 1–13. doi:10.15394/ijaaa.2016.1144

Wang, Y., Petrina, S., & Feng, F. (2017). VILLAGE—Virtual Immersive Language Learning and Gaming Environment: Immersion and presence. *British Journal of Educational Technology*, *48*(2), 431–450. doi:10.1111/bjet.12388

Watson, S. M., Michalek, A. M., & Gable, R. A. (2016). Linking executive functions and written language intervention for students with language learning disorders. *International Journal of School and Cognitive Psychology*, *3*(3). Advance online publication. doi:10.4172/2469-9837.1000178

Webel, S., Bockholt, U., Engelke, T., Gavish, N., Olbrich, M., & Preusche, C. (2013). An augmented reality training platform for assembly and maintenance skills. *Robotics and Autonomous Systems*, *61*(4), 398–403. doi:10.1016/j.robot.2012.09.013

Wei, X., Weng, D., Liu, Y., & Wang, Y. (2015). Teaching based on augmented reality for a technical creative design course. *Computers & Education*, *81*, 221–234. doi:10.1016/j.compedu.2014.10.017

Wen, Y. (2018). Chinese character composition game with the augment paper. *Journal of Educational Technology & Society*, *21*(3), 132–145.

Wen, Y. (2019). An Augmented Paper Game with Socio-Cognitive Support. *IEEE Transactions on Learning Technologies*. Advance online publication. doi:10.1109/TLT.2019.2924216

Wen, Y., & Looi, C. K. (2019). Review of augmented reality in education: Situated learning with digital and non-digital resources. In *Learning on a Digital World: Perspective on Interactive Technologies for Formal and Informal Education* (pp. 179–193). Springer. doi:10.1007/978-981-13-8265-9_9

Wertsch, J. V. (1991). *Voices of the Mind: A Sociocultural Approach to Mediated Action*. Harvard University Press.

Wertsch, J. V. (1995). The need for action in sociocultural research. In J. V. Wertsch, P. del Río, & A. Álvarez (Eds.), *Sociocultural Studies of Mind* (pp. 56–74). Cambridge University Press. doi:10.1017/CBO9781139174299.004

Whitehead, A. N. (1932). *The aims of education and other essays*. Ernest Benn.

Wild, F., Klemke, R., Lefrere, P., & Fominykh, M. (2017). Technology Acceptance of Augmented Reality and Wearable Technologies. In *Immersive Learning Research Network. iLRN 2017*. Springer. doi:10.1007/978-3-319-60633-0_11

Wiley, J., Sanchez, C. A., & Jaeger, A. J. (2014). The individual differences in working memory capacity principle in multimedia learning. In R. E. Mayer (Ed.), *Cambridge handbooks in psychology. The Cambridge handbook of multimedia learning* (pp. 598–619). Cambridge University Press., doi:10.1017/CBO9781139547369.029

Williams, A. S. [AdamScottWillia]. (2018, November 10). *A great look at the pro's & cons of AR in the classroom! #eci833 #education #edtech Augmented reality in education* [Tweet]. Twitter. https://twitter.com/AdamScottWillia/status/1061138121096654848

Wilson, M. (2002). Six views of embodied cognition. *Psychonomic Bulletin & Review*, *9*(4), 625–636. doi:10.3758/BF03196322 PMID:12613670

Wingfield, N., & Isaac, M. (2016). *Pokémon Go brings augmented reality to a mass audience*. The New York Times. https://www.nytimes.com/2016/07/12/technology/pokemon-go-brings-augmented-reality-to-a-mass-audience.html

Winn, W. (2002). Learning in artificial environments: Embodiment embeddedness and dynamic adaptation. *Techniques Instruction Cognition and Learning.*, *1*, 2002.

Winn, W. (2003, November-December). Beyond constructivism: A return to Science-based research and practice. *Educational Technology*, *43*(6), 5–14.

Wittrock, M. C. (1974). Learning as a generative process. *Educational Psychologist*, *19*(2), 87–95. doi:10.1080/00461527409529129

Wojciechowski, R., & Cellary, W. (2013). Evaluation of learners' attitude toward learning in ARIES augmented reality environments. *Computers & Education*, *68*, 570–585. doi:10.1016/j.compedu.2013.02.014

Wong, C., Odom, S. L., Hume, K. A., Cox, A. W., Fettig, A., Kucharczyk, S., Brock, M. E., Plavnick, J. B., Fleury, V. P., & Schultz, T. R. (2015). Evidence-based practices for children, youth, and young adults with autism spectrum disorder: A comprehensive review. *Journal of Autism and Developmental Disorders*, *45*(7), 1951–1966. doi:10.100710803-014-2351-z PMID:25578338

Wood, D., Bruner, J. S., & Ross, G. (1976). The role of tutoring in problem solving. *Journal of Child Psychology and Psychiatry, and Allied Disciplines*, *17*(2), 89–100. doi:10.1111/j.1469-7610.1976.tb00381.x PMID:932126

Wu, H. K., Lee, S. W. Y., Chang, H. Y., & Liang, J. C. (2013). Current status, opportunities and challenges of augmented reality in education. *Computers & Education*, *62*, 41–49. doi:10.1016/j.compedu.2012.10.024

Wüller, H., Behrens, J., Garthaus, M., Marquard, S., & Remmers, H. (2019). A scoping review of augmented reality in nursing. *BMC Nursing*, *18*(1), 19. doi:10.118612912-019-0342-2 PMID:31123428

Wu, P.-H., Hwang, G.-J., Yang, M.-L., & Chen, C.-H. (2018). Impacts of integrating the repertory grid into an augmented reality-based learning design on students' learning achievements, cognitive load and degree of satisfaction. *Interactive Learning Environments*, *26*(2), 221–234. doi:10.1080/10494820.2017.1294608

Xie, Y., Zhang, Y., & Cai, Y. (2019). Virtual reality engine disassembly simulation with natural hand-based interaction. In Y. Cai, W. van Joolingen & Z. Walker (Eds.), VR, Simulations and Serious Games for Education (pp. 121–128). Springer. doi:10.1007/978-981-13-2844-2_11

Xie, Y., Ryder, L., & Chen, Y. (2019). Using Interactive Virtual Reality Tools in an Advanced Chinese Language Class: A Case Study. *TechTrends*, *63*(3), 251–259. doi:10.100711528-019-00389-z

Yaman, H., Aydemir, Z. İ., & Demirtaş, T. (2013). The scale of preservice teachers' digital pedagogic competencies: Validity and reliability study. *The Online Journal of New Horizons in Education*, *3*(3), 26–35.

Yang, Y. D., Allen, T., Abdullahi, S. M., Pelphrey, K. A., Volkmar, F. R., & Chapman, S. B. (2017). Brain responses to biological motion predict treatment outcome in young adults with autism receiving virtual reality social cognition training: Preliminary findings. *Behaviour Research and Therapy*, *93*, 55–66. doi:10.1016/j.brat.2017.03.014 PMID:28384509

Yang, Y. F. (2011). Engaging students in an online situated language learning environment. *Computer Assisted Language Learning*, *24*(2), 181–198. doi:10.1080/09588221.2010.538700

Yeh, H.-C., Tseng, S.-S., & Heng, L. (2020). Enhancing EFL students' intracultural learning through virtual reality. *Interactive Learning Environments*, 1–10. Advance online publication. doi:10.1080/10494820.2020.1734625

Yıldırım, A., & Şimşek, H. (2016). *Sosyal bilimlerde nitel araştırma yöntemleri (10. baskı)*. Seçkin Yayıncılık.

Yilmaz, R. M., & Goktas, Y. (2017). Using augmented reality technology in storytelling activities: Examining elementary students' narrative skill and creativity. *Virtual Reality (Waltham Cross)*, *21*(2), 75–89. doi:10.100710055-016-0300-1

Yilmaz, Z. A., & Batdi, V. (2016). A meta-analytic and thematic comparative analysis of the ıntegration of augmented reality applications into education. *Education in Science*, *41*(188), 273–289.

Yin, C., Song, Y., Tabata, Y., Ogata, H., & Hwang, G.-J. (2013). Developing and implementing a framework of participatory simulation for mobile learning using scaffolding. *Journal of Educational Technology & Society*, *16*(3), 137–150.

Yin, R. (1994). *Case Study Research*. Sage.

Yin, R. K. (1994). *Case study research design and methods* (2nd ed.). Sage Publications.

Yoon, H. (2012). *Re-writing the writing script: Teachers and children translating curriculum in everyday practice* (Unpublished doctoral dissertation). University of Illinois at Urbana-Champaign.

Yoon, S. A., & Wang, J. (2014). Making the invisible visible in science museums through augmented reality devices. *TechTrends*, *58*(1), 49–55. doi:10.100711528-013-0720-7

Yoon, S., Anderson, E., Koehler-Yom, J., Evans, C., Park, M., Sheldon, J., Schoenfeld, I., Wendel, D., Scheintaub, H., & Klopfer, E. (2016). Teaching about complex systems is not simple matter: Building effective professional development for computer-supported complex systems instruction. *Instructional Science*, *45*(1), 99–121. doi:10.100711251-016-9388-7

Yoon, S., Anderson, E., Lin, J., & Elinich, K. (2017). How augmented reality enables conceptual understanding of challenging science content. *Journal of Educational Technology & Society*, *20*(1), 156–168.

Yoshinaga, T. (2017). Introduction to next-generation AR devices: Overview and case study of Microsoft HoloLens and Google Tango. *Journal of the Visualization Society of Japan*.

Yuan, S. N. V., & Ip, H. H. S. (2018). Using virtual reality to train emotional and social skills in children with autism spectrum disorder. *London Journal of Primary Care*, *10*(4), 110–112. doi:10.1080/17571472.2018.1483000 PMID:30083244

Yuen, S., Yaoyuneyong, G., & Johnson, E. (2011). Augmented Reality: An Overview and Five Directions for AR in Education. *Journal of Educational Technology Development and Exchange*, *4*(1), 119–140. doi:10.18785/jetde.0401.10

Zambrano, J., Lee, G. A., Leal, C. C., & Thoman, D. B. (2020). Highlighting Prosocial Affordances of Science in Textbooks to Promote Science Interest. *CBE Life Sciences Education*, *19*(3), ar24. doi:10.1187/cbe.19-09-0176 PMID:32559123

Zander, S., Montag, M., Wetzel, S., & Bertel, S. (2020). A gender issue? How touch-based interactions with dynamic spatial objects support performance and motivation of secondary school students. *Computers & Education*, *143*, 103677. doi:10.1016/j.compedu.2019.103677

Zarraonandia, T., Aedo, I., Díaz, P., & Montero Montes, A. (2014). Augmented presentations: Supporting the communication in presentations by means of augmented reality. *International Journal of Human-Computer Interaction*, *30*(10), 829–838. doi:10.1080/10447318.2014.927283

Zender, R., Weise, M., von der Heyde, M., & Söbke, H. (2018). Lehren und Lernen mit VR und AR: Was wird erwartet? Was funktioniert? In D. Schiffner (Ed.), *DeLFI Workshops 2018 Proceedings der Pre-Conference-Workshops der 16. E-Learning Fachtagung Informatik co-located with 16th e-Learning Conference of the German Computer Society (DeLFI 2018)*. Academic Press.

Zheng, W., Yi, X., & Shi, Y. (2019, July). Investigating the Interaction Experience with Augmented Reality Based Writing Tools. In *International Conference on Human-Computer Interaction* (pp. 461-466). Springer. 10.1007/978-3-030-23528-4_63

Zhu, E., Hadadgar, A., Masiello, I., & Zary, N. (2014). Augmented reality in healthcare education: An integrative review. *Journal of Life and Environmental Sciences*, *2*, e469. doi:10.7717/peerj.469 PMID:25071992

Zichermann, G. (2011). *A long engagement and a shotgun wedding: Why engagement is the power metric of the decade.* Presentation at Gamification Summit, San Francisco. http://goo.gl/jlaO0

Zinchenko, Y. P., Khoroshikh, P. P., Sergievich, A. A., Smirnov, A. S., Tumyalis, A. V., Kovalev, A. I., Gutnikov, S. A., & Golokhvast, K. S. (2020). Virtual reality is more efficient in learning human heart anatomy especially for subjects with low baseline knowledge. *New Ideas in Psychology*, *59*, 100786. doi:10.1016/j.newideapsych.2020.100786

Zirzow, N. K. (2015). Signing avatars: Using virtual reality to support students with hearing loss. *Rural Special Education Quarterly*, *34*(3), 33–36. doi:10.1177/875687051503400307

Zuber-Skerritt, O. (1992). *Professional Development in Higher Education: A Theoretical Framework for Action Research.* UK Kogan Page.

Zünd, F., Ryffel, M., Magnenat, S., Marra, A., Nitti, M., Kapadia, M., Noris, G., Mitchell, K., Gross, M., & Sumner, R. W. (2015). Augmented creativity: Bridging the real and virtual worlds to enhance creative play. In SIGGRAPH Asia 2015 Mobile Graphics and Interactive Applications (pp. 1-7). Academic Press.

About the Contributors

Gokce Akcayir is a SSHRC postdoctoral fellow at the University of Alberta. She joined the Educational Technology, Knowledge, Language and Learning Analytics (EdTeKLA) research group in 2018. She was a visiting researcher at the Faculty of Science and Technology in Athabasca University. She received both of her masters and Ph.D. degrees in Educational Technology. Her research interests include augmented reality and social networking sites in education, flipped classrooms and computer science education.

Carrie Demmans Epp joined the University of Alberta as an assistant professor in 2018. She teaches courses on HCI and the use of AI in educational applications. Carrie completed her postdoctoral research at the Learning Research and Development Center of the University of Pittsburgh. Before moving to Pittsburgh, Carrie held Weston and Walter C. Sumner Memorial Fellowships. She was also a visiting researcher with the Open Learner Models at Birmingham group (UK) and the Graduate School of Language, Communication, and Culture at Kwansei Gakuin University in Japan. She earned her PhD from the University of Toronto, where she developed an adaptive mobile-assisted language-learning tool and explored its use. While earning her MSc at the University of Saskatchewan, Carrie integrated her undergraduate studies in Russian and Computer Science by building an adaptive pronunciation tutor that supported student motivation.

* * *

Ahmet Akçay is an assistant professor at Eskisehir Osmangazi University. He teaches elementary mathematics education. His interests are in technology integration, mathematics education, teacher preperation, and STEM education.

Jorge Bacca-Acosta is an Associate Professor at Fundación Universitaria Konrad Lorenz in Bogotá. Jorge Bacca holds a Ph.D in Technology from the University of Girona (Spain) and a master's degree in industrial informatics from the same university. His areas of interest are the use of augmented reality and virtual reality in education, motivation for learning, engagement and mobile-based assessment systems.

Briella Baer Chen is currently a doctoral student studying special education at the University of Maryland, College Park.

Mehmet Bozan, in 2015, completed his undergraduate education as a primary school teacher at Kırıkkale University. In 2018, he completed his postgraduate education at Eskisehir Osmangazi University, department of primary school teaching. He is a PhD student at Hacettepe University Primary Education Department since 2018. He taught Turkish to Syrian refugees for about two years. He is still a research assistant at İstanbul Aydın University. He has studies on STEM education and teaching Turkish to foreigners.

Chih-Pu Dai is a doctoral student of the Department of Educational Psychology and Learning Systems at Florida State University. His research interests include immersive learning in virtual reality environments and game-based learning environments.

Zhaihuan Dai is a doctoral student of the Educational Psychology and Learning Systems Department at Florida State University's College of Education. Her current research areas include technology enhanced learning, teaching training, and problem-based learning.

Barney Dalgarno is Executive Dean of the Faculty of Education at the University of Canberra. Professor Dalgarno's research interests include the educational and social impact of digital technologies, the learning affordances of virtual, mixed and augmented realities, and the future of universities and schools in the age of digital disruption. He has had international influence through over 100 presentations and publications, award winning online learning innovations and editorship of educational technology journals and conference proceedings.

M. Esther del Moral Pérez is a Professor of Educational Technology. Department of Education Sciences University of Oviedo (Spain).

Mustafa Fidan has received his doctoral degree (PhD) in curriculum and instruction department of Bolu Abant Izzet Baysal University. He has studied as a researcher in Bartin University, Turkey, since 2011. His research interests include augmented reality, flipped learning, video-based learning, e-learning, distance education, problem-based learning, mind maps, social networks, curriculum evaluation.

Aroutis Foster is an Associate Professor of Learning Technologies in the School of Education at Drexel University in Philadelphia, PA. He is also the Associate Dean of Academic Affairs and Graduate Studies. He leads the Games and Learning in Interactive Digital Environments (GLIDE) Lab and is the founder of the Drexel Learning Games Network. He teaches and conducts research on the theoretical and practical applications of designed environments such as games and interactive digital environments to advance our understanding of learners' knowledge, identity, and motivation in different settings including schools, workplaces, informal, and online environments. His broad research interests focus on the design of technology, computer-based learning environments, automated and personalized learning, technology integration, identity exploration, motivation, cognition, and learning. His research aims to explore the learning process including motivation to learn and learners' identity change using immersive digital technologies, such as games. He is a Phi Beta Kappa Member, a Mellon Mays Fellow, and the recipient of a Spencer Research Training Grant, and a NSF CAREER award.

Päivi Häkkinen is a Professor of educational technology at the Finnish Institute for Educational Research, University of Jyväskylä. Her research focuses on technology-enhanced learning, computer-supported collaborative learning and the progression of twenty-first-century skills (i.e., skills for problem solving and collaboration).

Jani Holopainen is coordinating and managing a multidisciplinary research group Mixed Reality Hub at the University of Helsinki. His research concentrates on cutting-edge technologies and innovative system designs. Theoretically, the intersection of information systems, management and pedagogics is the focal point.

Engin Karahan works as an assistant professor at Eskisehir Osmangazi University. He earned his MA and PhD degrees in the field of STEM Education at the University of Minnesota. His research interests include STEM education, socioscientific issues, and student/teacher agency.

Fengfeng Ke is a professor of educational psychology and learning systems at Florida State University. Her main research interests include simulation and game-based learning, computer-supported collaborative learning, and inclusive design of e-learning.

Ryan Kellems is an Associate Professor in the Counseling Psychology and Special Education department at Brigham Young University. Prior to coming to BYU Dr. Kellems was on the faculty at the University of Oregon where he worked with the National Post-School Outcomes Center. His primary research interests are video modeling, transition for students with disabilities, post-school outcomes of students with disabilities, assistive technology, and working with young adults with autism in community-based vocational settings. One of Dr. Kellems areas of expertise is using the latest technology to assist students with disabilities as they transition to life after school. Prior to completing his doctoral degree Dr. Kellems was a high school teacher where he worked in both rural and urban settings as a special education and Social Studies teacher. Dr. Kellems is currently conducting studies exploring the use of Augmented Reality and Live Animation to teach different skills (social, academic and independent living) to individuals with disabilities such as autism, LD and ID. Dr. Kellems also conducts professional development across the country related to implementing video modeling in academic and community-based settings.

Babak Khoshnevisan is a PhD candidate in the Technology in Education and Second Language Acquisition (TESLA) Program at the University of South Florida (USF). He is a teacher educator of ESOL courses at USF. He is also an instructor at INTO USF, teaching EAP and academic English course. His research interests include teacher education, idiomaticity, AR, virtual reality, and computer-assisted language learning.

Richard Lamb joined the Department of Special Education, Foundations, and Research Methods at East Carolina University as an associate professor. He is currently the director of the East Carolina University Neurocognition Science Laboratory. He earned his Ph.D. in 2013 from George Mason University, College of Education and Human Development in science education and educational measurement. Lamb previously served as an assistant professor at Washington State University, where he taught in the elementary education program and courses on advanced quantitative methods such as multilevel modeling and structural equation modeling. His research interests focus on the identification and measurement of cognitive processes engaged while using technology in the learning of science and other fields. The tools Lamb uses to complete his research are interdisciplinary and drawn from multiple fields to include neuropsychology, neuroscience, educational measurement, and computer science. He has published over 70 articles and over 100 professional research presentations on topics related to the use of technology for learning and therapy. Lamb has been awarded multiple times for his research to include the 2016 NARST Early Career Researcher Award, the 2018 AERA Best Paper Award SIG-IT, and the 2020 John C. Park National Technology Leadership Initiative Award.

Daniel Mellet-d'Huart, PhD., had been a pioneer in supporting and developing the use of virtual reality in the context of AFPA, a large vocational training organisation in France. He had been an associated researcher in CERV (Centre Européen de Réalité VIrtuelle) in France.

Jared Morris is an Assistant Professor in the Department of Counseling Psychology and Special Education at Brigham Young University. He received his PhD in special education with a minor in educational psychology at The Pennsylvania State University. He also received a graduate certificate in applied behavior analysis from Penn State. He completed a master's degree in special education from The University of Utah and a bachelor's degree in English from Brigham Young University. Jared taught students with disabilities in a variety of settings for 5 years. His research interests focus on incorporating technology and instructional practices to increase student's academic outcomes.

María del Rosario Neira-Piñeiro is a lecturer at the Faculty of Educacion of the University of Oviedo (Spain). She is a member of the research group TEcn@: Technology and Learning. Her research interests are: children's literature and literary education, cinema and ICT in education, digital storytelling, augmented reality and teacher training.

Carlos Ospino-Ibañez is a systems engineer from the Fundacion Universitaria Konrad Lorenz. He has extensive experience in the development of VR applications in Unity. His areas of interest are VR in education, big data and database management systems.

Mariya Pachman is an educational researcher specialized in learning and new technologies. Her background is in instructional design, multimedia learning and Cognitive Load Theory. She has worked with various population groups in secondary and higher education settings throughout Australia and the USA. As a post-doctoral fellow at FSU Mariya was exploring the affordances of a Mixed-Reality-Integrated Learning Environment (MILE) in enhancing teaching competencies in STEM disciplines.

Sanghoon Park is an associate professor in the Instructional Technology program at the University of South Florida. His research focuses on the design and development of augmented reality-based mobile learning, 3D printing integration in the classroom, interactive multimedia, learning motivation, and online learning experience analysis.

Mark Petrovich Jr. is a third-year doctoral candidate in the Education PhD program with a concentration in STEM education. He is a research assistant within Drexel University's School of Education as well as a member of the Games and Learning in Interactive Digital Environments (GLIDE) lab. His research interests include educational technology, informal learning, maker-centered learning, motivation, and identity exploration. Mark earned a BS/MS in Digital Media from Drexel University in 2012. His current research examines teaching and learning within informal contexts using immersive technologies such as augmented and virtual reality.

Anabelem Soberanes-Martín graduated in Administrative Computer Systems, Teacher in Education, master's in computer science course, Doctor in Educational Sciences has the Desirable Profile Recognition (PRODEP), member of the National System of Researchers (SNI-I), Certified as Distance Activity Coordinator (San Diego Global Knowledge University), Certified as Instructor of face to face Courses (CONOCER), works in the Centro Universitario UAEM Valle de Chalco of the Universidad Autónoma del Estado de México. She has held the positions of Licentiate Coordinator, Academic Sub-Director, and Academic Faculty Leader. She is currently a full-time professor, teaching in the bachelor's degrees in Computer Engineering, Administrative Informatics, in the master's and Doctorate degrees in Computer Science.

Heinrich Söbke holds a research position at the Bauhaus-Institute for Infrastructure Solutions (b.is) at the Bauhaus-Universität Weimar, Germany. Focusing his research on applied educational technology in engineering education, he designs and validates learning scenarios using digital learning instruments, primarily from the fields of serious games, gamification and mixed reality.

Zeynep Tacgin has worked in the education technologies field for more than 10 years. She is a post-doctoral researcher at Charles Sturt University and a Lecturer at Marmara University. She graduated at the top of one's class from Computer Education and Instruction Technologies program at Marmara University in 2012. She received master degree in Education Administration and Supervision program in 2013. She received Ph.D. degree in Computer Education and Instruction Technologies program in 2017. Her Ph.D. thesis was about immersive virtual reality learning environments. She has been working on AR/VR/MR technology usage in education for 5 years. Also she designs and develops virtual environments for educational purposes. She has the interest to merge MR technologies and distance education. Her fields of interest are educational, wearable technologies, innovative learning environments, technology integration to education, education management, and policies, distance education, augmented reality, virtual reality, simulations, instructional design, and material development.

Julian Tejada is a graduate in Psychology (2002) from National University of Colombia and PhD in Psychobiology from University of São Paulo (2010). Nowadays He is Professor of Federal University of Sergipe, Visiting Professor of Fundación Universitaria Konrad Lorenz in Bogotá and Collaborator Member of Pós-Graduação em Ciências Fisiológicas of the Federal University of Sergipe. He has worked with computational neuroscience and experimental psychology to characterize animal and human behavior in different areas from social psychology up to marketing.

Yun Wen is an Assistant Professor in the Learning Sciences and Assessment Academic Group at the National Institute of Education (NIE), Nanyang Technological University (NTU Singapore). Her research interests include Computer-supported Collaborative Learning, Computer-assisted Language Learning, Learning Design, and Learning Analytics. She works on investigating how people learn through interaction and conversations in multimodal environments, and how to use technology (e.g., representational tools, augmented reality, etc.) to spark and support collaborative learning.

Alex Wheatley is a former special education teacher and current school psychology student. He received his MEd in special education from the University of Idaho. He went on to do post graduate work in assistive technology. Alex has research interests in assistive technology, video modeling, and innovative therapeutic strategies in school-based counseling.

Mario Wolf is a research associate at the Bauhaus-Institute for Infrastructure Solutions (b.is) with a specialization in Urban Water Management at Bauhaus-Universität Weimar, Germany. His research aims to strengthen the link between urban planning as well as urban design and the realization of innovative approaches of waste water infrastructure. In his current research project he focuses on the potential of Mixed Reality applications in educational settings teaching waste water management.

Longkai Wu is currently a Research Scientist and faculty member at the Office of Education Research, National Institute of Education, Singapore. He holds a Doctor of Philosophy in the area of Learning Sciences and Technologies at Nanyang Technological University (NTU), Singapore. His research is on the development of sustainable frameworks to translate and scale education innovations into classroom practices in Singapore school system. He has worked closely with local primary and secondary schools, as well as Ministry of Education, to formulate the nexus among research innovations, scaled practices and education policies. Over the years, he has also been involved in international collaboration with Hong Kong, Taiwan, US, Finland and UK universities on classroom and school improvement. He is an International Committee Member for SysTech Value Network, a scaling initiative supported by Tekes, the Funding Agency for Technology and Innovation, Finland. He is also program committee member for international conferences organized by IEEE Technical Committee on Learning Technology, International AI & Education Society, Asia-Pacific Society of Computers in Education, and Global Chinese Society on Computers in Education.

Gulnoza Yakubova is an Assistant Professor of Special Education at the University of Maryland, College Park. Her research focuses on using technology-based interventions to teach students with Autism Spectrum Disorders (ASD) the skills they need to have a successful life after school. Most of her research activities involve examining video-based instructional strategies, mobile technology, virtual and augmented reality in teachings vocational and mathematics skills to students with ASD and enhancing their independence in school and community settings.

Vanesa Yepes-Serna studied media design in Bogota and Weimar. As part of her research on Instructional Design, she evaluates multimedia design principles for instructional environments. In the context of her dissertation, she develops design guidelines for user interfaces of MR-based educational tools.

Xin Yuan is a full Professor in the Department of Computer Science at Florida State University. He obtained his B.S. and M.S degrees in Computer Science from Shanghai Jiaotong University in 1989 and 1992, respectively. He earned his Ph.D degree in Computer Science from the University of Pittsburgh in 1998. His research interests include high performance computing, cloud computing, parallel and distributed systems, and interconnection networks. He has published more than 100 papers in leading journals and conferences. The STAR-MPI software package that he and his students developed has been incorporated in the MPI stack of the IBM Blue Gene/P system. Dr. Yuan currently serves as an associate editor for the IEEE transactions on Cloud Computing, and has served as the Program Chairs and vice-Chairs for several international conferences and workshops such as IEEE IPDPS, the International Conference on Parallel Processing (ICPP) and the IEEE International Conference on High Performance Computing (HiPC), and as Program Committee Members for many international conferences and workshops. He is a senior member of ACM and IEEE.

Steffi Zander studied educational science in Erfurt, Germany, and earned her doctorate in Saarbrücken on motivational learning conditions in Cognitive Load Theory. From 2013, to 2019, she has held a professorship for Instructional Design - Didactics of Media Learning Environments at Bauhaus-Universität Weimar. Since 2019 she is professor for General Psychology at the University of Applied Sciences Magdeburg-Stendal. Her current research interests include emotion and motivation in AR-supported learning processes.

Index

E

F

G

H

I

K

L

M

V

W

www.ingramcontent.com/pod-product-compliance
Lightning Source LLC
LaVergne TN
LVHW081250011026
849162LV00006BA/1322
* 9 7 8 1 7 9 9 8 5 0 4 3 4 *